D0861398

Batsford Chess Library

New Ideas in the Nimzo-Indian Defence
TONY KOSTEN

An Owl Book
Henry Holt and Company
New York

To my parents

Henry Holt and Company, Inc.
Publishers since 1866
115 West 18th Street
New York, New York 10011

Henry Holt® is a registered
trademark of Henry Holt and Company, Inc.

Copyright © 1994 by Tony Kosten
All rights reserved.

First published in the United States in 1994 by
Henry Holt and Company, Inc.
Originally published in Great Britain in 1994 by
B. T. Batsford Ltd.

Library of Congress Catalog Card Number: 93-80832

ISBN 0-8050-3286-X (An Owl Book: pbk.)

First American Edition—1994

Printed in the United Kingdom
All first editions are printed on acid-free paper.∞

10 9 8 7 6 5 4 3 2 1

Adviser: R. D. Keene, GM, OBE
Technical Editor: Graham Burgess

Contents

Symbols

++	Double check
#	Checkmate
± (∓)	Slight advantage to White (Black)
± (∓)	Clear advantage to White (Black)
+− (−+)	Winning advantage to White (Black)
=	Level position
!	Good move
?	Bad move
!!	Outstanding move
??	Blunder
!?	Interesting move
?!	Dubious move
Ch	Championship
Wch	World Championship
Z	Zonal
IZ	Interzonal
C	Candidates
OL	Olympiad
corr.	Postal game

When Nimzowitsch introduced his defence in the 1920's, his idea was that Black would fight for control of the centre (in particular the square e4) with pieces rather than pawns. His concept, the Nimzo-Indian Defence, rapidly became one of Black's most popular defences and established a reputation for offering a wide range of strategically rich possibilities to both sides. In particular, Black is often prepared to give up the bishop pair to saddle White with doubled pawns, or even simply to obtain easy development.

During the 1970's and early 1980's Black was so successful, in particular with Hübner's variation, that White players came to avoid 3 ♘c3 and the Queen's Indian Defence was the obvious benefactor. I remember reading, in the first edition of *BCO*, Jon Tisdall suggesting that the Queen's Indian Defence was 'not likely to decrease in popularity until White decides to bypass it and face up to the Nimzo'.

Well, gradually during the 80's, White began to do just that — at first with Rubinstein's variation, and then with the 4 ♘f3 and 5 g3 line pioneered by World Champion Garry Kasparov. More recently, in the last few years in fact, 4 ♛c2 and 4 f3 have enjoyed an enormous boom at all levels.

It is no longer possible to play the 'Nimzo' guided by general principles alone, as I discovered to my cost some years back when I was severely mauled three times on the Black side of the 4 f3 variation, and even amateur players will find that older books on the Nimzo-Indian are insufficient protection when faced with players armed with more sophisticated, modern knowledge. Chess theory has changed a great deal recently, and the time therefore seems right for a re-assessment of this opening.

Interestingly, whereas 4 e3 used to dominate in tournament practice, and a vast body of theory had built up around it, nowadays it is 4 ♛c2 which is in the ascendancy. I have decided to arrange this book to reflect this fact and the reader will find that the book is divided into three sections, the first dealing with 4 ♛c2, the second with 4 e3 and the third with 4 f3 and other fourth moves. I hope that this will facilitate the reader's orientation.

The reader will also notice that where a variation has a name I have included it, although these labels are quite personal and may not correspond exactly with those of other writers.

The book is geared to the last four or five years but I have naturally put more emphasis on the latest games; the title of the book is, after all, '*New Ideas ...*'. I must admit I found choosing the material quite difficult; of the many thousands of games that I considered, a surprisingly high number were significant from a theoretical point of view. So many, in fact, that it would be possible to write a book on each individual chapter!

The format of the book mirrors that of the others in this series; that is, each chapter commences with a summary of its contents and contains a number of complete games with comment and analysis which represent the most important lines, lesser variations being covered in the notes.

♘d4 ♗b7 Marinelli-Palac, Vinkovci 1989, is uninspiring) 6...c5 7 a3!? (7 e3 would transpose to the main game, whereas 7 dxc5 ♘a6 8 a3 ♗xc3+ 9 ♕xc3 ♘xc5 10 ♗xf6 ♕xf6 11 ♕xf6 gxf6 12 b4 ♘a4 13 e3 b6 14 ♘f3 ♗a6 15 ♘d2 ♗b7 16 ♗d3 ♖ac8 = 17 ♖c1 d5 18 ♔e2 dxc4 19 ♘xc4 ♖fd8 20 ♖hd1 ♗a6 21 ♖d2?? b5 0-1 was the brevity Kožul-Kasparov, Belgrade 1989) 7...♗xc3+ 8 bxc3 cxd4 9 cxd4 ♕a5+ 10 ♕d2 ♕xd2+ 11 ♔xd2 g5 12 ♗g3 ♘c6 13 e3 ♘a5 14 ♖b1 b6 15 ♗d3 ♗a6 16 c5 ♗xd3 17 ♔xd3 was equal in Nikčević-Farago, Rome 1990.

　　4) 5...d6 6 e3 and now it seems the time has come for the ...e6-e5 thrust, since Black's other choices, whilst solid, are all a little passive:

⇨ 6...♘bd7 7 ♗d3 h6 8 ♗h4 e5 9 ♘e2 exd4 10 exd4 d5 11 c5 c6 12 0-0 ♗a5 13 ♗g3 ♖e8 14 ♖ab1 ♘f8 15 b4 ♗c7 16 ♕d2 ♗g4 ± J.Horvath-Kosten, Budapest 1989.

⇨ 6...h6 7 ♗h4 b6 (7...e5 8 ♘e2 ♖e8?! 9 0-0-0! ♗xc3 10 ♘xc3 ♘bd7 11 dxe5 ♖xe5? 12 e4 b6? 13 f4 was very good for White in Lautier-Lau, Polanica Zdroj 1991) 8 ♘e2 c5 9 0-0-0 cxd4 10 ♘xd4 ♗xc3 11 ♕xc3 ♘bd7 12 ♕a3 ♘c5 13 f3 ♗b7 14 e4 ♕e7 15 ♔b1 with a palpable White advantage; Tunik-Moldobaev, Belgorod 1989.

⇨ 6...e5 7 ♘e2 exd4 8 ♘xd4 ♘bd7 9 ♗d3 h6 10 ♗h4 ♘c5 11 0-0 ♘xd3 12 ♕xd3 ♗xc3 13 ♕xc3 ♗d7 14 f3 ♖e8 15 ♖fe1 ♖e5 16 e4 ♖h5 17 ♗g3 (opposite-colour bishops notwithstanding, White has an advantage based on his extra space) 17...♘h7 18 ♖ad1 ♕f6 19 ♘e2 ♗c6 20 ♕d2

b6 21 b4 ♕d8 22 b5 ♗b7 23 e5 ♕c8 24 e6! fxe6 25 ♘f4 ♖f5 26 ♘xe6 ♘f8 27 ♘d4 ♖f7 28 ♖e3 a6 29 a4 axb5 30 axb5 ♕d7 31 ♖de1 d5 32 cxd5 ♗xd5 33 ♕b4 ♕d8 34 h3 ♕f6 35 ♖e5 ♖d8 36 ♖f5 ♕g6 37 ♖xf7 ♗xf7 38 ♗xc7 ♖d5? 39 ♘c6 1-0 Vladimirov-Makarychev, Moscow 1990.

6 e3

⇨ 6 d5!? (offering a novel pawn sacrifice, but Black prefers to avoid unnecessary risks and equalizes in a simple manner) 6...d6 7 ♘f3 h6 8 ♗h4 g5 9 ♗g3 ♗xc3+ 10 bxc3 e5 (Black has adopted a set-up similar to that of a Leningrad) 11 ♘d2 ♘h5 12 f3 ♘xg3 13 hxg3 ♔g7 = 14 g4 f5 15 gxf5 ♗xf5 16 e4 ♗g6 17 ♖b1 b6 18 g3 g4 19 ♖h4 gxf3 20 ♔f2 ♘d7 21 ♗h3 ♖f4 22 ♖g4 ♖xg4 23 ♗xg4 ♘f6 24 ♗xf3 ♕d7 25 ♖h1 ♖f8 26 ♔g2 ♘h7 27 ♗d1 ♘g5 28 ♕d3 ♕c8 29 ♗e2 ♖f6 30 ♗d1 ♗e8 31 ♗e2 ♗d7 32 ♖h4 ♕a6 33 ♕c2 ♕c8 34 ♕d3 ½-½ Lautier-Andersson, Biel 1991.

6...h6 7 ♗h4 cxd4 8 exd4 ♘c6

This seems the most accurate, although 8...d5 is possible: 9 cxd5 exd5 10 ♗d3 ♘c6 11 ♘e2 ♗e7 12 a3 ♗e6?! (12...♕b6! 13 ♖d1 ♔h8 would pose White the question of how he was intending to defend the d-pawn, 14 ♗xf6 ♗xf6 15 ♘xd5 ♕a5+ being favourable to Black) 13 f3 ♖c8 14 0-0 a6 15 ♗f2 ♗d6 16 g4 ♕d7?! 17 ♖ad1 ♘a5 18 ♗g3! ± ♘c4 19 ♗xc4 ♖xc4 20 ♗xd6 ♕xd6 21 ♕d2 ♖fc8 22 ♕f4 ♕b6 23 ♖d2 ♘e8 24 ♕e5 f6? 25 ♘xd5! winning; Stohl-Ligterink, Tilburg 1992.

9 ♘f3

⇨ 9 ♖d1?! (this fails to control e5 and Black reacts accordingly) 9...e5!? 10 dxe5?! ♘xe5 11 ♗d3 ♘xd3+ 12 ♕xd3 (12 ♖xd3 g5 13 ♗g3 d5 ∓) 12...♗xc3+ 13 ♕xc3 ♘e4! 14 ♗xd8 ♘xc3 15 bxc3 ♖xd8 16 ♖d4 b6 (Black is better, but the wily old fox Korchnoi is at his best when under the cosh) 17 ♘f3 ♗a6 18 ♔d1 ♖ac8 19 ♘d2 d5! 20 ♖xd5 (if 20 cxd5 ♖xc3 with the idea of ...♖d3 is strong) 20...♗xc4 21 ♖xd8+ ♖xd8 22 a3 ♗b3+! 23 ♔e2 ♗c2 24 ♘f3 ♗e4 25 ♖e1 ♔f8?! 26 g3! ♗xf3+ 27 ♔xf3 ♖c8 28 ♖c1 ♖c4 29 ♔e3 ♖a4 30 ♖a1 ♔e7 31 ♔d3 ♔d6 32 ♔c2 ♔c6 33 f3! ♖a5 34 a4 g5 35 ♔b3 ♖f5 36 ♖f1 ♔c5 37 ♖f2 a6 38 ♖f1 ♖d5 39 ♔c2 ♖f5 40 ♔d3 ♔c6 41 ♔c4 ♖c5+ 42 ♔b3 ♖e5?! 43 g4! f5 44 f4 gxf4 ½-½ Korchnoi-van der Wiel, Wijk aan Zee 1990.

9...♗e7 10 ♖d1 d5 11 a3 b6 12 ♗d3

After this natural move White soon gets into difficulties. Alternatively he can try:

⇨ 12 cxd5 (this seems to lead, almost by force, to a draw; 12 ♘e5!? ♗b7 13 ♕d2 ♖c8 14 ♗e2 dxc4 15 ♘xc4 a6 16 ♘e3 b5 also led to equality in Van Manen-Steiner, Dr.Blass mem 1990) 12...♘xd5 13 ♗b5 ♗b7 14 ♘xd5 ♗xh4 15 ♗xc6 ♗xc6 16 ♕xc6 exd5 17 0-0 ♗f6 18 ♖fe1 ♖c8 19 ♕a4 ♖c7 20 ♖c1 ♕d6 21 g3 h5 22 h4 g6 23 ♔g2 ♔g7 24 ♖xc7 ♕xc7 25 ♘e5 ♖c8 26 ♖e3 ♕b7 27 ♕b3 ♖c1 28 ♕d3 ½-½ Finegold-Schmittdiel, Dortmund 1990.

12...♗b7!

12...dxc4 13 ♗xc4 ♘d5 14 ♗g3 ♘xc3 15 ♕xc3 ♘a5 16 ♗e2 ♗b7 Van Manen-Kramer, Dr.Blass mem 1990, is also fine.

13 ♗xf6?!

13 0-0 is probably not so bad, e.g. 13...dxc4 14 ♗xc4 ♘a5 15 ♗a2 ♖c8!? (there is nothing wrong with the obvious 15...♗xf3 16 gxf3, although instead of 16...♘d5? unnecessarily giving up a pawn, 17 ♗xd5 exd5 18 ♗xe7 ♕xe7 19 ♕f5 ♖fe8 20 ♘xd5 ± Finegold-Ashley, Groningen 1990, Black should not have had too many problems after 16...♘h5 for instance) 16 ♕e2 ♖e8 17 ♘e5 ♘d5 18 ♕h5 ♖f8 19 ♗xd5 ♗xd5 20 ♗xe7 ♕xe7 21 ♘xd5 exd5, as in Finegold-Martens, Wijk aan Zee 1991.

13...♗xf6 14 cxd5 exd5 15 0-0 ♖e8 16 h3 ♖c8 17 ♕a4 a6! 18 ♗b1 g6 19 ♖fe1 ♕d6 20 ♖xe8+ ♖xe8 21 ♔f1 ♔g7

21...b5!

22 ♕c2? ♘a5 23 ♖e1 ♖xe1+ 24 ♔xe1 ♘c4 25 ♗a2 b5

Black's dark-squared bishop, pressing on d4, gives him the edge.

26 a4 ♕b6 27 axb5 axb5

28 ♕d3 ♕a5 29 ♗xc4 dxc4 30 ♕d2 b4 31 ♘d1 ♗a6 32 ♕e3 ♕d5 33 ♕d2 ♕b5 34 ♕e2 ♕a5 35 ♕e3 ♗b5 36 ♘e5 h5 37 g3 ♕a1 38 ♕d2 ♗xe5 39 dxe5 ♗a4 0-1

Game 2

Vladimirov-Wells
Hastings 1990

1 d4 ♘f6 2 c4 e6 3 ♘c3 ♗b4 4 ♕c2 0-0 5 ♗g5 c5 6 e3 h6 7 ♗h4 b6!?

This is a very playable alternative to 7...cxd4, as in game 1.

8 dxc5

White must take care, for after 8 ♘f3 ♗b7 9 ♗e2 ♗e4! 10 ♕b3 ♘c6 11 0-0 ♘a5 12 ♗xf6 gxf6 13 ♕d1 ♗xc3 14 bxc3 ♗xf3 and 15...♖c8, Black wins a pawn, as once occurred in a game of Suba's.

8...♗xc5 9 ♘f3 ♗b7 10 ♗e2 ♗e7 11 0-0 a6 12 ♖fd1 ♕c7 13 ♖ac1 d6 14 ♕d2 ♖d8 15 b4 ♘bd7 16 ♗g3 ♘f8 17 ♘d4 ♖ac8 18 b5!? ♘g6! 19 bxa6 ♗xa6 20 ♘db5 ♕b8 21 ♘xd6 ♗xd6

21...e5 22 c5 ♗xe2 23 ♕xe2 ♖xc5 is equal, according to Vladimirov, but it is hard to see why 22 ♘xc8 ♖xd2 23 ♘xe7+ ♘xe7 24 ♖xd2 should not be advantageous for White.

22 ♗xd6 ♕a7 23 ♘b5 ♗xb5 24 cxb5 ♖xc1 25 ♕xc1 ♕xa2 26 ♗f3 ♕b3 27 ♕c7 ♖d7 28 ♕xb6 ♘e4 29 ♕b8+ ♔h7 30 ♖f1?!

30 h3 was a better chance, but 30...♕c2! 31 ♖f1 (31 ♔h2 ♖xd6! 32 ♖xd6 ♘h4! wins for Black) ♘d2 32 ♖a1 ♘xf3+ 33 gxf3 ♘h4 is still

good for Black.

30...♘xd6?

30...♘d2! 31 ♖e1 ♘xf3+ 32 gxf3 ♘h4 wins for Black.

31 ♗c6! ♘h4 32 ♗xd7 ♘e4 33 ♕f4 ♘d2 34 ♖c1 1-0 (time)

Game 3

Beliavsky-Yusupov
Linares 1992

1 d4 ♘f6 2 c4 e6 3 ♘c3 ♗b4 4 ♕c2 0-0 5 ♘f3 d6 6 ♗d2

⇨ 6 ♗g5 is the normal move and will be very similar to the material analysed in game 1, e.g. 6...♘bd7 7 e3 h6 (if 7...e5 then 8 0-0-0!? is a strong possibility: 8...♗xc3 9 ♕xc3 ♕e7 10 ♘d2 ♖e8 11 ♕c2 e4 12 ♗e2 c6 13 g4 d5 14 ♗f4 dxc4 15 ♘xc4 when d6 appears weak, Greenfeld-Gausel, Oslo 1992) 8 ♗h4 b6 9 0-0-0 ♗xc3 10 ♕xc3 ♗b7 11 ♗d3 a6 12 ♕c2 ♕b8 13 e4 c5 14 d5 e5 15 ♖dg1 ♘h7 16 g4 with a powerful attack coming; Timoshchenko-Sturua, Moscow Alekhine mem 1992.

⇨ 6 e4!? (ambitious) 6...e5 7 ♗d3
(7 d5?! ♗xc3+ 8 bxc3 ♘a6 9 ♘d2
♘h5 10 ♘b3 f5 ∓ Hulak-Short, Wijk
aan Zee 1987) 7...♖e8 8 d5 a5 9 0-0
♘a6 10 ♗d2 ♗g4 11 ♘e1 ♘c5 12 f3
with the better prospects for White,
although he later lost; Dragomaret-
sky-Savon, Moscow 1991.

**6...c5 7 a3 ♗xc3!? 8 ♗xc3 cxd4 9
♘xd4 e5 10 ♘f5!? ♕c7 11 ♖d1
♖d8 12 e3?! d5 ∓ 13 f4?!**

White embarks on a dangerous
adventure rather than allow his
queen's bishop to be exchanged off
after 13 cxd5 ♘xd5 14 ♗e2 ♘xc3 ∓.

**13...♘c6 14 fxe5 ♘xe5 15 ♗e2
♗e6 16 0-0 dxc4 17 ♘h6+ ♔h8**

Black has a solid pawn more and a
better position.

**18 ♗d4 ♘fd7 19 ♘f5 f6 20 ♖f4
♘g6 21 ♖f3 ♘de5 22 ♖h3 ♖d5 23
♖f1 ♕d7 24 ♖h5 ♔g8 25 ♘h4? ♗f7
26 ♘f5 b5 27 ♕c3 ♖d8 28 g4 ♘e7!**

29 ♘xg7

Desperation in a lost position.

**29...♔xg7 30 g5 ♗xh5 31 gxf6+
♔g8 32 ♗xh5 ♘7g6 33 ♗xe5 ♖xe5
34 f7+ ♔f8 35 ♗xg6 ♕g4+ 36 ♔h1
♕h3 37 ♗d3 cxd3 38 ♕b4+ ♖e7 0-1**

Game 4

Remlinger-Schmittdiel
Gausdal 1991

**1 d4 ♘f6 2 c4 e6 3 ♘c3 ♗b4 4 ♕c2
0-0 5 a3 ♗xc3+ 6 ♕xc3 a5!?**

Alternatively, 6...♘e4!? (this deserves to be played more often) 7
♕c2 f5 8 ♗f4?! (this is probably not
very good as the bishop will become
a target when Black prepares the
...e5 push; 8 ♘f3 d6 9 g3 c5 10
♗g2 ♕a5+ 11 ♗d2 ♘xd2 12 ♕xd2
♕xd2+ 13 ♔xd2 ♘c6 14 ♔c3 ½-½
was Grünberg-Kharitonov, Moscow
1989, but 8 e3 is probably better,
continuing with ♗d3, ♘e2 and f3)
8...d6 9 f3 ♘f6 10 ♘h3 ♕e7 11 e4?
fxe4 12 fxe4 e5 13 dxe5 dxe5 14 ♗g5
♘c6 15 c5 ♘d4 16 ♕c3 h6 17 ♗xf6
♖xf6 18 ♗c4+ ♔h8 19 ♘f2 ♕xc5 ∓
Touzane-Kholmov, Sochi 1990.

7 b3

It is not clear that this move is entirely necessary; other possibilities:

1) 7 ♗g5! can be met by:
⇨ 7...d6 8 f3 h6 9 ♗h4 ♕e7 10 e4 e5
11 ♘e2 ♖e8 12 ♕c2 ♘bd7 13 ♖d1
c6 14 ♘c3 ♘f8 15 d5 ♘g6 16 ♗f2
cxd5 17 cxd5 ± ♗d7 18 a4 ♖ec8 19
h4!? (White's play is very provocative, but I feel he would be better off
developing his king's bishop and
castling kingside) 19...♘e8 20 h5
♘f8 21 ♗h4 f6 22 ♗d3 ♘c7 23 ♕b3
♗e8 24 ♗f2 ♘a6 25 ♗b5 ♘c5 26
♕a3 ♘fd7 27 g4 ♘b6 28 ♗xe8
♕xe8 29 ♘b5? ♘c4! (Oops!) 30
♕a2 ♘xa4 31 ♕xa4 ♖xb2 32 ♕b3
♘xd1 ∓ Mohr-Schmittdiel, Bundesliga 1992.

⇨ 7...a4 8 e3 b6 9 ♗d3 d6 10 ♘e2 ♗b7 11 0-0 ♘bd7 12 ♕c2 h6 13 ♗h4 ♖a5?! (this doesn't make a lot of sense) 14 f3 ♕e7 15 ♗e1 ♖aa8 16 ♘c3 e5 17 ♗f5 g6 18 ♗h3 ♘h7 19 ♗xd7 ♕xd7 20 dxe5 dxe5 21 ♖d1 ♕e6 22 ♘d5 ♖fc8 23 e4 ♘f6 24 ♗c3 with an enduring advantage, in view of the dark-squared weaknesses on the kingside; Kir.Georgiev-Kurajica, Burgas 1992.

2) 7 g3 d6 8 ♗g2 a4 9 ♘f3 ♘c6 10 0-0 h6 11 ♗f4?! ♕e7 12 ♖ad1 ♖e8 13 d5 ♘a5 14 dxe6?! ♗xe6 (revealing the point of his moves ...a5 and ...a4 — the white c-pawn is weak!) 15 ♘d4 ♗xc4 16 ♗xb7 ♘xb7 17 ♕xc4 ♘c5 18 ♖fe1 ♕d7 19 ♕c2 ♕h3 ∓ Gretarsson-Schmittdiel, Gausdal 1992.

7...b6

7...b5?! is surely far too provocative. C.Horvath-Schmittdiel, Budapest 1990 continued: 8 cxb5 c6 9 e3 ♗b7 10 f3 cxb5 11 ♗xb5 ♕b6 12 ♕d3 e5!? 13 dxe5 ♘g4 14 ♕e2 ♘xe5 15 ♘h3 ♗a6 16 ♗xa6 ♘xa6 17 ♖b1 ♘c5 18 0-0 ♘c6 19 ♕c2. White has to suffer a little inconvenience, but will certainly win.

8 ♗g5 ♗b7 9 f3 h6 10 ♗h4 d5 11 e3 ♘bd7 12 cxd5 exd5 13 ♗d3 ♕e7 14 ♗f2 c5

This is very similar to the main line considered in the next chapter and should be fine for Black.

15 ♘e2 ♖fc8 16 0-0 cxd4 17 ♕xd4 ♘c5 18 ♗f5 ♖c6

18...♘xb3 19 ♕xb6 ♘xa1 20 ♗xc8 ±.

19 ♖fb1 g6 20 ♗h3 ♗c8 21 ♗xc8 ♖axc8 22 ♕d2 ♘e6 23 ♖c1 ♖xc1+ 24 ♖xc1 ♖xc1+ 25 ♕xc1 ♘d7 26

♘c3 ♕c5 27 ♕b2 ♕d6 28 b4 axb4 29 axb4

29...♕e5?!

The isolated d-pawn is a nuisance, but Black should be fine. As it is, he manages to put his queen off-side and nearly loses.

30 ♕d2 ♘f6 31 ♗g3 ♕g5 32 ♘b5 ♕f5 33 h3 h5 34 ♔h2 g5 35 ♘d6 ♕b1 36 ♕c3 d4 37 ♕c8+ ♘f8 38 ♕c4 ♘e6

White has a winning position, but he gradually loses the thread of the game and eventually allows Black to escape with a draw. 39 ♗e5! ♘d7 40 ♗xd4 appears simplest, winning the pawn without weakening White's pawn structure.

39 exd4 h4 40 ♗e5 ♘d7 41 ♕c8+ ♘ef8 42 ♕e8 ♕g6 43 ♘e4 ♕f5 44 ♗d6 ♔g7 45 ♕e7 ♘h7 46 ♘c3 ♘hf6 47 ♕e2 ♕e6 48 ♕xe6 fxe6 49 g4?! hxg3+ 50 ♔xg3 ♔g6 51 ♘e4 ♔f5 52 ♘c3 ♘h5+ 53 ♔f2 e5 54 ♗xe5 ♘xe5 55 dxe5 ♘f4 56 b5?! ♘xh3+ 57 ♔g3 ♘f4 58 ♘e4 ♘e2+ 59 ♔h3 ♘d4 60 ♘d6+ ♔xe5 61 ♘c4+ ♔f4 62 ♔g2 ♘xb5 63 ♘xb6 ½-½

Game 5 C/M L

Gelfand-Adams
Palma 1989

1 d4 ♘f6 2 c4 e6 3 ♘c3 ♗b4 4 ♕c2 0-0 5 a3 ♗xc3+ 6 ♕xc3 b5!? 7 cxb5 ♘d5!?

A new and original interpretation of this position. 7...c6 is almost invariably played here: 8 bxc6 (alternatives are discussed in game 6) 8...♘xc6 and now:

1) 9 e3 a5!? (9...♗b7 10 b4 ♖c8 11 ♕b2 e5 12 dxe5 ♘g4 13 ♘f3 ♖e8 14 ♗e2 ♘cxe5 15 ♘xe5 ♘xe5 16 0-0 ♖c6 17 f3 ♕c7 18 ♗d2 ♖c2 19 ♕d4 ♘c6 20 ♕d3 ♘e5 21 ♕d4 ♘c6 ½-½ Wegner-Vonthron, Bundesliga 1991) 10 ♗d3 ♘b4! (a nice trick, and the point of Black's preceding play—obviously 11 axb4? axb4 wins the rook on a1) 11 ♘e2 ♘xd3+ 12 ♕xd3 ♗a6 13 ♕d1 ♕b6 14 0-0 ♗c4 15 f3 ♖fc8 16 ♖f2 ♗b3 17 ♕e1 ♖c2 with good play, Brenninkmeijer-van der Wiel, Dutch Ch 1990.

2) 9 ♘f3 ♗b7 10 b4 (giving the queen a safe haven on b2) 10...♖c8 11 ♕b2 ♘e4 12 e3 ♘e7 13 ♗d2 ♘xd2 14 ♕xd2 ♕c7 15 ♗d3 ♕c3? 16 ♕xc3 ♖xc3 17 ♔d2 ♖fc8 18 ♖hc1 ♖xc1 19 ♖xc1 ♖xc1 20 ♔xc1 and a solid pawn to the good, White went on to win in Flear-Bellón Lopez, Palma 1991.

3) 9 b4!? ♗a6! (a strong new idea forcing White to forego kingside castling) 10 ♗g5 and now:
⇨ 10...♖c8 11 ♕b2 ♕b6 12 ♗xf6 gxf6 13 ♘f3 d5 14 ♕d2 ♘e7 15 e3 ♗xf1 16 ♔xf1 ♕b5+ 17 ♕e2 ♕a4

18 ♕d1 ♕b5+ 19 ♔g1 (he should probably take the draw here) 19...♖c3 20 g3 ♖fc8 21 ♔g2 ♘f5 22 ♖e1 ♖c2 23 ♘g1 ♘d6 24 ♖e2 ♖2c3 25 ♖b2 ♘e4 26 ♘e2 ♖d3 27 ♕e1 ♕a4 28 ♕b1 ♖d2 29 ♖xd2 ♘xd2 30 ♕d3 ♖c2 ∓ 31 ♖d1 ♘c4 32 ♘f4?? (32 ♖e1 was forced but Black should be able to recapture his sacrificed pawn and keep the initiative quite easily) 32...♘b2 0-1 Wiedenkeller-Lundin, Swedish Ch 1991.
⇨ 10...h6 11 ♗xf6 ♕xf6 12 ♘f3 ♖ac8 13 ♕b2 ♖c7! 14 e3 ♗xf1 15 ♔xf1 ♖fc8 16 ♔e2! ♘a5 17 ♖hc1 ♘c4 18 ♕c3 e5! 19 ♕d3 d6 20 ♘d2 ♘xd2 21 ♕xd2 ♖xc1 22 ♖xc1 ♖xc1 23 ♕xc1 exd4 24 exd4 ♕xd4 25 ♕c8+ (I am sure that White was very happy to take a perpetual here) 25...♔h7 26 ♕f5+ ♔g8 ½-½ Polugaevsky-Dzindzichashvili, Reykjavik 1990.

8 ♕c2 f5 9 ♘f3 c6 10 a4 ♗b7 11 e3 cxb5 12 ♗xb5 ♖f6 13 0-0 ♖g6 14 ♗e2 ♘c6 15 ♗d2 ♕f6 16 ♖fc1 ♖f8 17 ♕b3 ♗a8 18 ♕a3

18...♕f7
Black starts going backwards, for

although all his pieces seem aggressively placed, White's position has no weaknesses.

19 b4 ♕e8 20 b5 ♘ce7 21 ♘e5 ♘c3 22 ♗f1 ♘e2+

This looks dangerous but, in fact, White defends easily.

23 ♗xe2 ♖xg2+ 24 ♔f1 ♖xh2 25 ♗f3 ♘g6 26 ♕d6 f4 27 e4 ♘xe5 28 ♕xe5 ♖h3 29 ♗b4 ♖f6 30 ♕c7 ♔f7 31 ♕c8 ♕xc8 32 ♖xc8 1-0

Game 6 CML

Mohr-Christiansen
Germany 1989

1 d4 ♘f6 2 c4 e6 3 ♘c3 ♗b4 4 ♕c2 0-0 5 a3 ♗xc3+ 6 ♕xc3 b5 7 cxb5 c6 8 f3?!

This seems to be a luxury White can ill afford. 8 ♗g5 may be White's most solid move: 8...cxb5 9 e3 ♗b7 10 ♘f3 and now:

⇨ 10...a6 11 ♗e2 d6 (11...h6 12 ♗h4?! g5! 13 ♗g3 ♘e4 14 ♕c2 f5 15 ♗xb8 ♖xb8 16 0-0 ♖c8 17 ♕d1 ♕a5 with at least equality, Karason-Tisdall, Gausdal 1991) 12 ♗xf6 gxf6 13 0-0 ♘d7 14 a4 bxa4 15 ♖xa4 ♘b6 16 ♖a5 with an edge for White; Djukić-Dizdar, Zeleznicar-Bosna 1989.

⇨ 10...h6 11 ♗xf6 (11 ♗h4! a6 12 ♗d3 ±) 11...♕xf6 12 ♖c1 (or 12 ♕c7 ♗xf3 13 gxf3 ♘c6 14 ♕xd7 ♕xf3 15 ♖g1 ♖ad8 16 ♕c7 ♖c8 17 ♕g3 ♕f6 18 ♗xb5 ♖fd8 when White must be better but went on to lose in Djukić-Kengis, Pula 1990) 12...♘a6 13 ♗xb5 ♖ac8 14 ♕d2 ♕g6 15 ♗e2 ♖xc1+ 16 ♕xc1 ♖c8

17 ♕d1 ♕xg2 18 ♖g1 ♕h3 19 ♖g3 ♕f5 20 ♘e5 ♕c2 21 ♕xc2 ♖xc2 22 ♘d3 d6 23 ♔d1 ♖c8 24 ♔d2 ♘c7 ½-½ Olafsson-Seirawan, Reykjavik 1990.

8...♘d5 9 ♕d2 f5 10 ♘h3 cxb5 11 e3 ♘c6 12 ♗xb5 ♘a5 13 ♕d3 ♖b8 14 b4 ♖xb5!

15 bxa5?

15 ♕xb5 ♘b3 16 ♖b1 ♕h4+ 17 ♘f2 ♘xc1 18 ♖xc1 ♘xe3 is less clear, but nevertheless rather unpleasant for White.

15...♗a6 ∓ 16 ♗d2 ♖b6! 17 ♕c2 ♖c6 18 ♕d1 ♕h4+ 19 ♘f2 ♕g5 20 g3 ♘xe3 21 ♘h3 ♕h6 22 ♕b3 ♘g2+ 0-1

Game 7 CML

Marin-Psakhis
Tallinn 1989

1 d4 ♘f6 2 c4 e6 3 ♘c3 ♗b4 4 ♕c2 0-0 5 a3 ♗xc3+ 6 ♕xc3 d6 7 g3

This stops Black from fianchettoing his queen's bishop. The other possibilities are:

⇨ 7 ♘f3 ♘bd7 8 g3 b6 9 ♗g2 ♗b7 10 0-0 ♕e7 11 b4! c5 12 ♗b2 cxd4 13 ♕xd4 ♖fc8 14 ♖fd1 ♘e8 15 e4 ♖c7 16 ♘d2 ♖ac8 17 ♖ac1 ♕f6 18 ♕xf6 ♘exf6 19 f3 ± Kasparov-Andersson, Skellefteå 1989.

⇨ 7 f3 ♘bd7?! (I think that either 7...d5, or 7...e5!? 8 dxe5 dxe5 9 ♕xe5 ♘c6 ∞ should be played here) 8 e4 e5 9 ♗e3 exd4 10 ♗xd4 a6 11 ♘h3 ♕e7 12 ♗e2 ♖e8 13 ♘f4 c5 14 ♗f2 b5 15 cxb5 d5 16 0-0-0 axb5 17 ♗xb5 d4 18 ♕c2 when Black has insufficient compensation for his pawn; Kramnik-Vehi Bach, Groningen 1991.

⇨ 7 ♗g5 ♘bd7 8 f3 (8 e3 b6 transposes to a variation considered next chapter) 8...d5 9 e3 ♖e8 10 ♘h3 (possibly 10 cxd5!? is more accurate: 10...exd5 11 ♗h4 ♕e7 12 ♗f2 c5 13 ♘e2 b6 14 ♘g3 cxd4 15 ♕xd4 ♘c5 16 ♖d1 ♗d7 17 b4 ♘e6 18 ♕b2 ♗a4 19 ♖d2 ♖ac8 20 ♗e2 ♕d7 21 0-0 ♖c7 22 ♘f5 ♖ec8 23 ♕e5? when 23 ♗a6! would have consolidated White's advantage; Seirawan-Sax, Wijk aan Zee 1992) 10...h6 11 ♗h4 c6 12 ♘f2 (12 cxd5 exd5 13 ♗f2 c5 14 ♘f4 cxd4 15 ♕xd4 ♕a5 16 b4 ♕b6 led to a draw in Kasparov-Sax, Reykjavik 1988) 12...e5! 13 dxe5 ♘xe5 14 ♖d1 ♕e7 15 cxd5 cxd5 16 ♗b5 ♗d7 17 ♗xf6 ♕xf6 18 ♗xd7 ♘xd7 19 ♕xf6 (White should be a little better in this endgame but a draw is the likely outcome) 19...♘xf6 20 ♔d2 ♖ac8 21 ♖c1 ♔f8 22 ♘d3 ♔e7 23 g4 ♔d6 24 h4 ♘d7 25 h5 ♖c6 26 ♘b4 ♖xc1 27 ♖xc1 ♘e5 28 ♔e2 a5 29 ♘d3 ♘c4 ½-½ Hjartarson-Psakhis, Moscow 1990.

7...e5 8 ♘f3

Though natural, this move allows to Black to grab the initiative with a series of accurate moves. 8 dxe5 may be White's best choice; at least, I've always had problems against it!: 8...dxe5 9 ♗g2! (9 ♕xe5?! ♘c6 10 ♕c3 ♘e4 11 ♕c2 ♘d4!) 9...♖e8 10 ♘f3 e4?! (unwisely opening the a1-h8 diagonal) 11 ♘d4 c5 12 ♘c2 ♗g4 13 h3 ♗h5 14 b4 ♘bd7 15 g4 ♗g6 16 ♗b2 ± Arlandi-Kosten, Imperia 1992.

8...exd4 9 ♘xd4 d5! 10 ♗g5 c5 11 ♘b3 d4 12 ♕f3 ♘bd7 13 ♗xf6 ♘xf6!

Sacrificing a pawn for a strong initiative.

14 ♘xc5 ♗g4 15 ♕f4 ♖e8 16 0-0-0!? ♕b6 17 ♘d3 ♕c6 18 f3 ♕xc4+ 19 ♔b1 ♗e6 20 ♘b4 a5 21 ♖xd4 ♕b5 22 e4?

22 e3 is necessary.

22...♕c5 23 ♘c2 ♗b3 24 ♖d2 ♖ac8 25 ♗d3 ♖ed8 26 ♖c1

26...♖xd3!

Forcing the gain of two pieces and a rook for the queen, which is enough to win.

27 ♖xd3 ♕xc2+! 28 ♖xc2 ♗xc2+
29 ♔a1 ♗xd3 30 ♕d2 ♗c4! 31 b3
♗xb3 32 ♕xa5 ♘d7! 33 ♕f5 ♗e6
34 ♕b5 ♘c5 35 ♔b2 ♖c6 36 ♔a1
    36 a4 is met by 36...♗b6! ∓.
    **36...h6 37 h4 h5 38 e5 ♘b3+ 39
♔b2 ♖c2+! 40 ♔b1 ♖c1+ 41 ♔b2
♖c2+ 42 ♔b1 ♘d4 0-1**

Game 8

Bareev-Bischoff
Novi Sad OL 1990

**1 d4 ♘f6 2 c4 e6 3 ♘c3 ♗b4 4 ♕c2
0-0 5 a3 ♗xc3+ 6 ♕xc3 ♕e8 7 f3**
⇨ 7 ♕c2!? is an interesting idea:
7...d6 8 ♗g5 ♘fd7 9 e4 e5 10 d5 a5
11 ♖d1 a4 12 ♗e3 ♖a5 13 ♘e2 ♘c5
14 ♘g3 c6 15 ♗xc5 dxc5 16 ♗e2
♕e7 17 0-0 ± Kharlov-Ward, Gausdal 1992.
⇨ 7 g3 d6 8 ♘f3 a5!? (this is much
more challenging than the 8...b6 9
♗g2 ♗b7 10 0-0 ♘bd7 11 b4 ♘e4
12 ♕c2 f5 13 ♘g5 ♕g6 14 ♘h3 e5
15 f3 ♘ef6 16 ♘g5 ♖ae8 17 d5 c6 18
♗h3! ± of Korchnoi-Lerner, Lugano
1989) 9 b3 (it may be possible to ig-
nore the positional threat of ...a4, although 9 ♗g2!? a4 10 0-0 ♘c6 11
♗f4 ♘a5 12 ♘d2 ♕e7 13 e4 ♘h5 14
♗e3 e5 15 dxe5 dxe5 16 b4 axb3
was just equal in Chabanon-Storing,
Gifhorn 1992) 9...a4!? (attempting
to win the queenside light-squares)
10 b4 b5! 11 c5 (11 cxb5 ♖a7 12
♕c2 ♗b7 13 ♗g5 ♗e4 14 ♕b2 ♘d5
led to an unclear position in Kolev-
Pavlović, Vrnjačka Banja 1990)
11...♗b7 12 ♗g2 ♗d5 13 0-0 ♘c6
14 ♗b2 (White must be careful

here, for instance: 14 ♖e1?! ♘e7 15
♕d3?! ♗e4 16 ♕d1 dxc5! ∓ 17 dxc5
♖d8 18 ♗d2 ♘c6 19 ♖a2 ♕d7 20
♕a1 ♗d5 21 ♖b2 ♘e4 22 ♗c1 e5 23
♘d2 ♘g5 24 e4 ♗e6 25 ♘f3 ♘xf3+
26 ♗xf3 ♘d4 with a quick win in
sight; Medančić-Kosten, Amantea
1992) 14... ♘e7 15 ♖fe1 (15 ♘d2)
15...♘e4 16 ♕c2 f5 17 ♘d2 ♘xd2
18 ♕xd2 ♗xg2 19 ♔xg2 ♘d5 (Kasparov has suggested 19...d5 with the
idea of playing ...♘g6, and ...f4, and
this does indeed look promising for
Black) 20 ♕d3 ♖f6 21 ♖ac1 f4! 22
♖h1! ♕f7 23 f3 ♘e3+ 24 ♔f2 ♘c4
25 ♕c3 ♖f8 26 ♖cg1 ♔h8?
(26...e5!) 27 ♗c1 e5 28 dxe5 dxe5
29 ♕d3 ♕e7 30 ♕e4 ♖d8 31 ♖d1
♖xd1 32 ♖xd1 g5 33 ♖g1 ♖g6 34
♖d1 ♖f6 35 ♔g2 c6 36 h4! ♖g6 37
g4 ♔g8 38 ♕f5 ♖e6 39 hxg5 ♕e8 40
♕e4 ♔g7 41 ♕f5 ♕f7 42 ♖d8 ♖e8
43 ♖d1 ♖e7 44 ♔h3 ♖e6 45 ♖d3
♕e7 46 ♗d2 ♘b2 47 ♖d6 ♖xd6 48
cxd6 ♕xd6 49 ♗c3 ♘c4 50 ♕xf4
♔g8 51 ♕f5 ♕d1 52 g6 hxg6 53
♕xg6+ ♔f8 54 ♕f6+ ♔g8 55 ♗xe5
♕h1+ 56 ♔g3 ♕e1+ 57 ♔f4 1-0
M.Gurevich-Adams, Palma 1989.

    7...d6 8 ♗g5
8 e4 e5 9 d5 (9 ♗e3 ♘c6 10 ♘e2
a5 11 d5 ♘e7 12 h4 a4 13 h5 ♘d7 14
g4 b6 15 ♘g3 ♘c5 = Gulko-Adams,
Hastings 1989) 9...♘bd7 10 ♘e2 a5
11 g4 a4 12 g5 (12 ♘g3 first would
seem more sensible; perhaps White
had overlooked that the knight on h5
can be defended) 12...♘h5 13 ♘g3
f6 14 gxf6 ♖xf6 ∞ Tesić-Sher, Pula
1990.
    **8...♘bd7 9 e3 e5 10 0-0-0 b6 11
♗d3 ♗b7 12 ♗f5 e4! 13 ♔b1! h6
14 ♗h4 g6 15 ♗h3 b5!? 16 d5! g5?**

It would be better to avoid this weakening of the kingside, as he pays dearly for it later on. Instead 16...♕e5! 17 ♕xe5 dxe5 18 c5 g5 19 c6 gxh4 20 cxb7 ♖ab8 21 fxe4 ♖xb7 22 ♘f3 is unclear.

17 ♗g3 bxc4 18 ♗xd7 ♘xd7 19 h4! ± f6 20 hxg5 hxg5 21 ♘e2 exf3 22 gxf3 ♕g6+ 23 e4 ♘b6 24 ♗f2 ♖ae8

(see next diagram)

25 ♘f4! gxf4

Black was bound to lose material anyway, after 25...♕f7 26 ♘e6.

26 ♖dg1 ♕xg1+ 27 ♖xg1+ ♔f7

28 ♖g4 ♔e7 29 ♖xf4 f5 30 ♕g7+ ♔d8 31 ♖h4 1-0

2

Since 1988 the 4 ♕c2 variation has undergone a renaissance, and from being considered a minor variation which allows Black an easy game, it has become White's principal weapon.

In the many thousands of games that have been played in this time the theory of the line with 4...0-0 has been fine-tuned to a considerable extent. Following 5 a3 ♗xc3+ 6 ♕xc3 b6 White's most popular choice is the pin 7 ♗g5, and 7 ♘f3 also has its adherents, but in game 9 we will look at his other possibilities, none of which, it has to be said, offer White too much.

The following two games discuss 7 ♘f3. In game 10 White fianchettoes his king's bishop, which is a solid choice, and in the game he gradually accumulated some advantage, but then let Karpov's counterattack get out of control. Game 11 covers 8 e3 when White can then decide whether to play b3 (or b4) and ♗b2, or simply continue his kingside development. In all cases Black will continue with a sort of Dutch formation, ...♘e4 and ...f5, when the slightest slip by White can be disastrous, as is amply demonstrated by I.Sokolov-van der Wiel.

In the game I.Sokolov-Luther, White popularized an idea of Ljubojević's that can be considered a sort of hybrid of 7 ♘f3 and 7 ♗g5. Instead of playing (after 7 ♗g5) f3 and e4, he played 8 ♘f3-d2 and then f3, reasoning that the knight might be more useful on d2 than, say, h3. In game 13 Kharlov added a new twist:

13 ♖g1 and g4 with the intention of opening the g-file. Game 14 impressed me a great deal when I first saw it; the players give an excellent lesson in strategy, although the white bishops always seem to hold the whip hand.

In recent years some players have experimented with a quick ...c5. This is dealt with in games 15 to 19. The rationale behind it is that should White play 8 dxc5 then, after 8...bxc5, Black may be able to profit from not playing ...♗b7. For instance, if White decides to castle long, then Black can immediately use the b-file, by ...♘c6 and ...♖b8, as in Scherbakov-Savon, whilst Chabanon-Dorfman is a good example of what can happen to White if he is imprecise.

Nevertheless, White almost invariably does reply with dxc5 since although this gives Black a majority of central pawns, it seems that White's pressure down the d-file is more important; besides, if White decides not to take on c5, then Black's quick development offers good play, as in game 15.

To my mind, White's play in game 16 represents his best set-up; from move 18 onwards Smagin just gets driven backwards, whereas Black's purposeful play in game 17 would repay closer study. However he later blunders; perhaps it was the Hastings air?

In fact, taken as a whole, I would say that ♗d3 and ♘e2 seems to be White's most successful formation throughout this entire chapter.

White can often damage Black's

kingside pawn structure by capturing twice on f6 but these endings seem fine for Black as is shown by game 18 and the sub-game Kumaran-Dorfman.

Another attempt to disrupt the smooth development of the white forces is 7...♗a6, when after, say, 8 e3 d5 9 cxd5?! ♗xf1 10 ♔xf1 is rather awkward for White, who must forego castling. This was briefly popular, but game 20 shows that the chances rest with White.

The rest of this chapter covers Black's 'normal' continuation, the natural 7...♗b7.

The system with 8 e3 and 9 f3 is dealt with in games 21 to 24 and is showing signs of an increase in popularity for White. Previously White had answered Black's ...♖c8 with Karpov's ♕d2 but this doesn't appear to give Black too many problems any more. Psakhis' important new move 19...♖c6! will spell the end of 16 b3 whereas 16 cxd5 leads to at most a draw. Two new ideas have recently emerged: Sokolov's 12 ♕b3 (game 21) and Sorokin's 13 b4 (game 22).

The Ukrainian IM Lëgky has been successful with a speciality of his involving ...e5, and this idea is well worth considering. Black has a 100% success rate in the material considered in game 24.

Games 25 to 27 cover 8 ♘h3. I do not believe that this is the right square for the knight; Black does very well with both ...c5 (game 26) and ...d5 (game 27).

White's most logical try is 8 f3, intending to construct a full centre.

The combination of ...♗b7 and ...c5 has much in common with the material considered in games 15 to 19 but seems, if anything, even worse for Black as he suffers mightily in games 28 to 31.

8...d6 which is dealt with in game 32 has fallen out of favour this last two or three years.

Black's most solid possibility after 8 f3 is 8...h6 9 ♗h4 d5 whence he stops the formation of a large white centre, e4 being impossible. Grandmaster Ivan Farago, who plays this for both White and Black, told me recently that he considered it to be completely equal. At first White tried 10 cxd5, but it was soon discovered that Black had plenty of opportunities for counterplay along the e-file following 10...exd5, the e3 square being particularly vulnerable. Since 1989 it has been rarely seen.

Attention then turned to 10 e3 and after 10...♘bd7, 11 cxd5 when 11...exd5 is too passive, Timman losing badly to Kasparov in game 33; but here 11...♘xd5 is possible as in game 34 when the endgame is fine for Black despite White's two bishops.

So if White cannot get the advantage from capturing on d5, what about simple development? Unfortunately, as game 35 shows, White cannot play 11 ♗d3 — Farago finds the perfect counter. So that leaves 11 ♘h3 and on 11...c5 12 cxd5, but apart from 12...♘xd5 (game 36) and 12...exd5, there is also Timoshenko's strong 12...cxd4! which seems to give immediate equality.

Game 9

Garcia Palermo-Lautier
Manila OL 1992

1 d4 ♘f6 2 c4 e6 3 ♘c3 ♗b4 4 ♕c2 0-0 5 a3 ♗xc3+ 6 ♕xc3 b6 7 b3!?
⇨ 7 ♕g3? (White was in a flippant mood when he played this!) 7...♘e4 8 ♕e5 f5 9 d5 d6 10 ♕d4 e5 11 ♕e3 a5 12 f3 ♕h4+ 13 g3 ♘xg3 14 ♕f2 f4 15 e3 ♘f5 16 exf4 exf4 17 ♕xh4 ♘xh4 ∓ Chabanon-Feller, Torcy 1991; however the game was later drawn.
⇨ 7 f3 d5 8 ♗g5 ♗a6?! (8...♗b7 would transpose to 7 ♗g5 lines) 9 cxd5 exd5 10 ♖c1 c5?! (10...c6 avoids losing a pawn, but Black probably didn't like the thought of having to retreat his bishop to b7 later should he wish to develop his queen's knight) 11 dxc5 d4 12 ♕d2 bxc5 13 ♖xc5 ♖e8 14 e4 with some advantage; Luce-Cavendish, London 1990.
⇨ 7 b4 ♗b7 8 ♗b2 a5 9 f3 c5 10 dxc5 axb4 11 axb4 ♖xa1+ 12 ♗xa1 bxc5 13 b5 d5 14 e3 ♘bd7 15 ♔f2 e5! (Black has used his lead in development to construct a mobile centre) 16 ♘h3 d4 17 exd4 cxd4 18 ♕b4 ♕b6 19 ♗d3 e4? (a very tempting continuation, but faulty, 19...♘c5 was very strong; once Black has White's queenside pawns firmly blockaded he can set about unleashing his powerful centre) 20 fxe4 ♗xe4 21 ♖d1 ♘g4+ 22 ♔g1 ♗xg2 23 ♘f2 ♘xf2 24 ♗xd4! ♕h6 25 ♗xf2 ♗a8 26 ♕d2 ♕h5 27 ♗g3 ♕f3 28 ♕e2 ♕h1+ 29 ♔f2 ♕g2+ 30

♔e1 ♕g1+ 31 ♔d2 ♕b6 32 ♔c2 ♘f6 33 ♖a1 ♖e8? (but Black was in trouble anyway, his attack having fizzled out, and the c and b-pawns, supported by the two bishops, getting ready to roll) 34 ♕xe8+ 1-0 Nadera-Johansen, Manila OL 1992.
⇨ 7 e3 ♗b7 8 b3 d6 9 f3 ♘bd7 10 ♗d3 e5 11 ♗f5 ♖e8 12 ♘e2 e4! 13 f4 d5 (Black has decided to put his pawns and pieces on light squares) 14 c5? (this is a bit too acquiescent) 14...♗a6 15 a4 ♘f8 16 ♗a3 ♘g4! 17 g3 ♘h6 18 ♗h3 ♘e6 19 ♖c1 ♕f6 20 ♕d2 ♕g6 21 ♗g2 ♘f5 22 0-0 h5 (this resembles a pure 'Nimzowitschian' blockade, and just like Nimzowitsch Black manages to turn it into a decisive attack) 23 ♖f2 h4! 24 gxh4 ♕g4 25 cxb6 cxb6 26 ♔h1 ♕xh4 27 ♘c3 ♘exd4! 28 ♕e1 ♘f3 29 ♗xf3 exf3 30 ♖xf3 ♕xe1+ 31 ♖xe1 d4 0-1 Arlandi-Greenfeld, Haifa 1989.

7...♗b7 8 ♗b2 ♘e4 9 ♕c2 f5 10 ♘h3 d6 11 f3 ♘g5 12 ♘f2 ♘d7 13 h4?!
13 e3 is more sensible.
13...♘f7 14 e3 c5! ∓ 15 ♖h3?! cxd4 16 exd4 ♖c8 17 g4? d5!

White has too many weaknesses, and his position soon disintegrates.
18 ♗d3
18 gxf5 exf5 19 ♕xf5 fails to 19...♕e8+ and ...♘fe5.
18...♘d6 19 ♕e2 ♖e8 20 ♔f1 ♖c7! 21 ♗c1 e5! 22 gxf5 dxc4 23 bxc4 exd4 24 ♗g5 ♕c8 25 ♕b2 ♘c5 26 ♕xd4 ♘xf5 27 ♗xf5 ♕xf5 28 ♖g3 ♘b3 0-1

Game 10

Korchnoi-Karpov
Biel 1992

1 d4 ♘f6 2 c4 e6 3 ♘c3 ♗b4 4 ♕c2 0-0 5 a3 ♗xc3+ 6 ♕xc3 b6 7 ♘f3 ♗b7 8 g3 d6 9 ♗g2 ♘bd7 10 0-0 a5?!

10...♕e7 might be better: 11 b4 a5 12 ♗b2 axb4 13 axb4 ♖xa1 14 ♖xa1 ♖a8 15 ♖xa8+ ♗xa8 (Black plays overtly for the draw, knowing that his solid position will be difficult to crack) 16 ♗h3 ♕f8 17 ♘d2 c5 18 ♗a3 ♕b8 19 dxc5 dxc5 20 bxc5 ♘xc5 21 ♕d4 ♕c7 22 ♗b2 h6 = Lautier-Psakhis, Halkidiki 1992.

11 b3 ♕e7 12 ♗b2 ♖fe8 13 ♖fe1 ♗e4?! 14 ♗f1! c5 15 ♘d2 cxd4 16 ♕xd4 e5 17 ♕c3 ♖ac8!

Black has to concede another bishop for knight exchange, as the variation 17...♗c6 18 e4 ♘c5 19 f3 ♖ab8 20 a4 is clearly better for White.

18 ♘xe4 ♘xe4 19 ♕e3 ♘ef6 20 ♖ac1 ♕e6 21 ♖ed1 d5 22 cxd5 ♘xd5 23 ♕d3 ♘5f6 24 b4 axb4

With bishops against knights on an open board White must be a lot better.

25 axb4 h5 26 ♗g2 h4 27 e4 hxg3 28 hxg3 ♖xc1 29 ♗xc1 ♖a8 30 ♗e3 ♖a2 31 ♕c3 ♔h7 32 ♖d2 ♖a8 33 ♕c1 ♖a4 34 ♕c3 ♕g4 35 ♖d6 b5 36 ♕e1 ♘f8 37 f3 ♕c8 38 ♗f1 ♖a3 39 ♖d3 ♖a2 40 ♖d2 ♖a3 41 ♗xb5 ♘e6 42 ♗f1 g5 43 ♖d3! ± ♖a4 44 g4 ♕b8 45 ♖b3 ♘d4 46 ♗xd4 exd4 47 e5 ♘d7 48 f4 ♕b6!

Finding counterplay in a difficult position.

49 ♗d3+ ♔g8 50 f5 ♖a2 51 e6?
A bad blunder. White seems to be much better, but his king is badly exposed. Probably he should resign himself to a draw after 51 ♕b1 ♖d2! 52 ♕e1 ♖a2.

51...♕d6! 52 ♗e2 ♘e5 53 ♕c1 ♖xe2 54 ♕xg5+ ♔f8 55 ♕h6+ ♔e8! 56 ♖a3? ♖e1+ 0-1

Game 11

I.Sokolov-van der Wiel
Wijk aan Zee 1993

1 d4 e6 2 c4 ♘f6 3 ♘c3 ♗b4 4 ♕c2 0-0 5 a3 ♗xc3+ 6 ♕xc3 b6 7 ♘f3

♗b7 8 e3 d6 9 ♗e2

One of several alternatives:

1) 9 b4 ♘e4 10 ♕c2 and now:

⇨ 10...♘d7 11 ♗b2 f5 12 ♗d3 ♘df6 13 0-0 ♕e8 14 ♘e1 ♘g4 15 ♕e2 ♘gf6 16 f3 ♘g5 17 d5? ♕h5 18 ♘c2 exd5 19 ♗xf5 ♖ae8 20 ♖ad1 ♘e6 21 ♗xe6+ (naturally, White would prefer not having to concede his light-squared bishop, but if 21 ♗d3 ♘f4 and it will be exchanged just the same) 21...♖xe6 22 cxd5 ♘xd5 23 ♕c4 ♔h8 24 e4 ♘f4 25 ♖d2 ♖h6 (Black suddenly has a winning attack) 26 g4 ♘h3+ 27 ♔h1 ♕g5 28 ♖fd1 ♖xf3 0-1 Ree-Goldin, Palma 1989.

⇨ 10...a5 11 b5 ♘d7 12 ♗b2 f5 13 ♗e2 ♕e7 14 0-0 ♖ae8 15 d5 (15 ♘d2?! ♕g5! 16 f4 ♕e7 17 ♗f3 ♘df6 18 ♖fe1 ♗a8 {18...h6!? ∓ contemplating ...♔h7 and ...g5} 19 ♘xe4 ♘xe4 {19...♗xe4!} 20 a4 ♕h4 21 g3 ♕h6 22 ♕e2 ♖d8 23 ♖ed1 was fairly equal in Kožul-Khalifman, Wijk aan Zee 1991) 15...e5 = 16 ♘e1 ♗c8 17 ♗d3 ♘dc5 18 f4 exf4 19 exf4 ♘f6 20 ♗d4 ♘xd3 21 ♘xd3 ♕e2 22 ♕xe2 ♖xe2 23 ♗xf6 ♖xf6 24 ♖f2? (24 ♖fe1!? =) 24...♖e4 25 ♖c2 ♖d4! ∓ Kožul-Bareev, Ljubljana Vidmar mem 1991.

2) 9 b3 ♘bd7 10 ♗b2 ♘e4 11 ♕c2 f5 12 ♗d3 ♕e8 (12...♘g5 13 d5 ♘c5 14 b4 ♘xd3+ 15 ♕xd3 e5 16 ♘d2 f4? 17 exf4 ♖xf4 18 h4 ♘f7 19 g3 ♖f6 20 ♘e4 ♖f5 21 ♗c1 ♕d7 22 g4 {trapping Black's unfortunate rook} 22...♖f4 23 ♗xf4 exf4 24 ♘g5 ♖e8+ 25 ♔d2 1-0 Ree-Douven, Amsterdam 1989) 13 0-0 ♕h5 14 d5!? (a standard sacrifice in this variation; in return for the pawn White opens the a1-h8 diagonal and the c-file, and also obtains the d4 square for his knight) 14...exd5 15 ♘d4 ♘e5 16 ♗e2 ♕g6 17 f3 ♘c5 18 cxd5 ♗xd5 19 ♖ad1 ♔h8 20 b4 ♘cd7 21 ♔h1 (and not 21 ♕xc7?? ♖fc8) 21...c6 22 b5 ♘c5 23 ♕b1 ♖ad8 24 ♗a1 cxb5 25 ♗xb5 ♗c4 26 ♘e2 ♗xb5 27 ♕xb5 ♕f7 28 ♘f4 ♘c4 29 ♘d5 ♘xa3 30 ♕e2 b5 31 ♕b2 b4 32 ♘xb4 ♘c4 33 ♕c3 ♘a4 34 ♕d4 ∞ Bareev-Timman, Tilburg 1991.

9...♘bd7 10 0-0 ♘e4 11 ♕c2

11 ♕d3 f5 12 ♘d2?! ♕h4 13 f3 ♘g5 14 g3 ♕h3 15 b4 ♘f6 16 d5 exd5 17 ♗b2 dxc4 18 ♕xc4+ ♗d5 19 ♕d3 (White cannot very well consider 19 ♕xc7 as 19...♖ac8-c2 is awkward) 19...c6 20 ♗xf6 ♖xf6 21 b5 ♖h6 22 ♖f2 ♕h5 23 bxc6 ♗xc6 24 ♔f1 ♕f7 25 ♖c1 ♗b7 26 ♘b3 ♖f8 27 ♘d4 ♘e4! 28 ♖g2 (28 fxe4? loses to 28...fxe4 29 ♖xf7 ♖xf7+) 28...♗d5 29 ♔g1 ♘g5 30 ♗d1 ♘e6 31 ♘xe6 ♕xe6 32 ♖d2 ♗a8 33 ♗b3 d5 34 ♗xd5 led to a draw in Kožul-Yusupov, Novi Sad OL 1990.

11...f5 12 b4

⇨ 12 ♘e1 is less ambitious: 12...♕h4! 13 f3 ♘g5 14 f4 (it seems strange to concede the important e4 square, but Karpov just about manages to get away with it) 14...♘e4 15 ♘f3 ♕h6 16 ♗d3 ♘df6 17 ♕e2 ♘g4 18 ♕e1?! (18 b4) 18...♖ae8 b4 e5 20 fxe5 dxe5 21 h3 ♘ef2!? 22 ♗e2 ♗xf3 23 ♗xf3 e4 (possibly 23...♘d3 was best here) 24 ♗d1! ♘xd1 25 ♕xd1 ♘xe3 26 ♕e2 f4 27 ♗xe3 fxe3 28 ♖xf8+ ♖xf8 29 ♖e1 ♖d8 30 d5 c6 31 dxc6 ♕xc6 32

♕xe3 ♕xc4 33 ♕xe4 (after all the excitement, a drawn rook and pawn ending results) ½-½ Karpov-Yusupov, London Ct 1989.

12...♕f6!?

An aggressive new plan; 12...♖f6 intending ...♖g6 is also good. Others:

⇨ 12...a5 13 ♗b2 ♘g5 14 d5 ♘xf3+ 15 ♗xf3 e5 16 ♗e2 ♕e7 17 f3 g6 (not fearing the weak dark squares around his king) 18 ♗d3 ♘f6 19 ♖ae1 axb4 20 axb4 b5! (in this position the d5-pawn impedes Black's bishop, and the e5-pawn White's. Both players set about undermining their respective obstacles) 21 f4! bxc4 22 ♗xc4 ♗xd5 23 fxe5 dxe5 24 ♗xd5+ ♘xd5 25 e4 fxe4 26 ♕xe4 c6 27 b5? (a mistake; this being a quick game White no doubt overlooked that he could not take on e5 later as f1 is *en prise*) 27...♕c5+ 28 ♔h1 ♕xb5 ∓ I.Sokolov-Anand, Brussels Swift (rapid) 1992.

⇨ 12...♘df6 (the usual, rather mundane approach) 13 d5 e5 14 ♘e1 a5 15 f3 ♘g5 16 ♖b1 axb4 17 axb4 ♗c8 (attempting to find a more productive diagonal) 18 ♗b2 ♕e8 19 ♔h1 ♘h5 20 f4 exf4 21 exf4 ♘e4 22 ♔g1 ♗d7 23 ♕d1 ♘hf6 with equality; I.Sokolov-Khalifman, Manila OL 1992.

13 ♗b2 ♕h6 14 d5! ♖ae8!? 15 ♕a4! ♖e7 16 ♘d4

16 ♕xa7?! is a mistake, as 16...♘dc5! 17 bxc5 ♘xc5 traps the queen.

16...e5 17 ♘e6

It is odd that this superbly-placed knight will be the source of White's coming problems.

17...♖f6 18 f4 ♖g6 19 ♕xa7?!

19 ♗f3! is best.

19...♖xg2+!

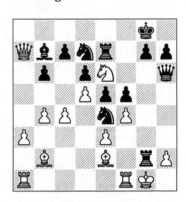

20 ♔xg2 ♖xe6 21 ♖f3?

21 dxe6 ♕g6+ 22 ♔h3 is best; Black has no more than a draw by perpetual.

21...♖g6+ 22 ♖g3 ♘xg3 23 hxg3 exf4 24 g4 fxg4 25 exf4 ♕h3+ 26 ♔f2 g3+ 27 ♔e3 g2+ 28 ♔d2 g1♕ 29 ♖xg1 ♖xg1 30 ♕xb7 ♕g3! 31 ♗d3 ♕e1+ 32 ♔c2 ♖g2+ 33 ♔b3 ♕d1+ 0-1

Game 12

I.Sokolov-Luther
Ålborg Politiken Cup 1991

1 d4 e6 2 c4 ♘f6 3 ♘c3 ♗b4 4 ♕c2 0-0 5 a3 ♗xc3+ 6 ♕xc3 b6 7 ♘f3 ♗b7 8 ♗g5 d6 9 ♘d2!? ♘bd7 10 f3 h6

Black can also defer this move: 10...c5 11 e4 ♖e8 12 ♗e2 (12 ♗e3!? ♖c8 13 ♗e2 d5 14 e5 ♘xe5?! {a neat tactic, but at the end of it White has a considerable space advantage

and the d6 square} 15 dxe5 d4 16
♕b3 dxe3 17 ♕xe3 ♘d7 18 0-0-0
♕c7 19 f4 ± Flear-Breyther, Bern
1992) 12...♘d5!? 13 cxd5 ♕xg5 14
dxe6 ♕xg2!? (risky, but playable) 15
0-0-0 ♕xe2?! 16 exd7 ♖ed8 17 dxc5
♖xd7 18 ♘c4 ♕f2 19 ♖xd6 ♖c7 20
♖hd1 h5 21 cxb6 axb6 22 ♔b1
♕xh2? (22...b5!) 23 ♕d4! ± ♖ac8
24 ♘xb6 ♕c2+ 25 ♔a2 ♗a6 26 ♖g1
winning quickly for White; Flear-
Levitt, Hastings 1991/2.

11 ♗h4 e5

Or 11...c5 12 e4 (12 dxc5 bxc5 13
e3 a5 14 ♗d3 a4 15 0-0 ♕b6 16
♖ad1 ♗c6 17 ♘b1 ♖ab8 18 ♖d2 ∞
Draško-Dzevlan, Yugoslav Ch 1991)
and:

⇨ 12...♖e8 13 ♗f2 ♖c8 14 dxc5
bxc5 15 ♗d3 d5 16 cxd5 (it might be
better to allow ...d4; as played White
loses a pawn) 16...exd5 17 0-0 dxe4
18 fxe4 ♗xe4 19 ♘xe4 ♘xe4 20
♗xe4 ♖xe4 with a full pawn more
although the game was later drawn;
Korchnoi-Ljubojević, Tilburg 1989.

⇨ 12...♖c8 13 dxc5 ♘xc5 14 ♕d4
e5 15 ♕g1 (a sad necessity; 15 ♕c3
allows 15...♘fxe4, and 15 ♕e3
♘g4) 15...♗e6 16 0-0-0 ♕e7 17
♔b1 ♖c7 18 ♗f2 ♖fc8 19 ♗e3 b5!
20 cxb5 d5 21 ♘b3 dxe4 22 ♘a5
♗a8 23 fxe4 ♘xe4 24 ♔a1 ♖c3!
and the threat of ...♖xa3+ forced
White to jettison material in Dydy-
shko-Ionov, St. Petersburg 1992.

**12 e4 exd4 13 ♕xd4 c5 14 ♕f2
b5!? 15 cxb5 d5 16 0-0-0 c4**

It would appear that Black, needing a win for a GM norm, is developing a dangerous initiative on the
queenside, but with a few accurate
moves White crushes it.

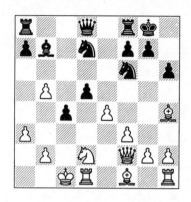

**17 ♘b1! ♕a5 18 ♘c3 dxe4 19
fxe4 a6**

19...♗xe4!? 20 ♖xd7 ♘xd7 21
♘xe4 ♕xb5 would have offered
more counterchances.

**20 bxa6 ♖xa6 21 ♕d4! ♖c8 22
♗xf6 ♘xf6 23 e5 ♘h7 24 ♗xc4
♖ac6**

25 ♕d5! ± ♕a7

If 25...♕c7, White can force a
winning liquidation by 26 ♕xf7+!
♕xf7 27 ♗xf7+ ♔xf7 28 ♖d7+ followed by ♖xb7.

**26 ♕xf7+ ♔h8 27 ♖d7 ♕e3+ 28
♔b1 ♕xe5 29 ♖e7 ♕g5 30 ♖e8+
1-0**

Game 13

Kharlov-Wedberg
Haninge 1992

**1 d4 ♘f6 2 c4 e6 3 ♘c3 ♗b4 4 ♕c2
0-0 5 a3 ♗xc3+ 6 ♕xc3 b6 7 ♗g5
♗b7 8 ♘f3 h6 9 ♗h4**

9 ♗f4?! d6 10 h3 ♘bd7 11 e3
♘e4 12 ♕c2 f5 is pleasant for Black;
From-Wedberg, Copenhagen 1991.

9...d6 10 ♘d2 c5

10...♘bd7 11 e3 c5 12 dxc5 ♘xc5
13 b4 ♘cd7 14 f3 ♖e8 15 ♕b2 ♘e5
16 ♗e2 ♘g6 17 ♗g3 e5 18 0-0 d5 19
♖fd1 ♕e7 20 cxd5 ♘xd5 21 ♗f2
White has an edge but little ambition
and the game was soon drawn; Lutz-
Karpov, Baden-Baden 1992.

11 dxc5

It is correct to take immediately
on c5, rather than allow 11 f3 cxd4!
12 ♕xd4 e5 13 ♕d3 ♕e7 14 ♖d1
♖d8 15 e4 ♘bd7 16 b4 a5 17 ♗f2
axb4 18 axb4 ♖a4 19 ♖b1 b5! ∓ with
Black enjoying some initiative, although White is, as ever, solid;
Crouch-Kosten, Hastings 1991.

11...bxc5 12 e3 ♘bd7 13 ♖g1!

An original divergence from the
normal f3 or ♗d3. White decides to
lever open the g-file.

13...d5 14 g4 ♘e4

It is understandable that Black
should wish to exchange queens, but
White has the advantage in the
endgame, too.

**15 ♗xd8 ♘xc3 16 ♗a5 ♘a4 17
cxd5 exd5 18 ♗b5 ♘ab6 19 g5!**
**hxg5 20 ♖xg5 f6 21 ♖g3 ♘e5 22
f4?!**

22 b3 preserves a small advantage.

22...♘ec4

This simplification makes a draw
the likely result.

**23 ♘xc4 ♘xc4 24 ♗xc4 dxc4 25
0-0-0 ♖f7 26 h4 ♗e4 27 h5 ♔h7 28
♗c3 ♔h6 29 ♖f1 ♗f5 30 e4**

White presses boldly for a win.

**30...♗xe4 31 f5 ♗d3 32 ♖f4 ♖e8
33 ♖g6+ ♔xh5!**

33...♔h7 34 h6 is very dangerous.

**34 ♖g1 ♖e4 35 ♖h1+ ♔g5 36 ♖f2
♖e2 37 ♗d2+ ♔g4 38 ♖g1+ ♔h5 39
♖h1+ ♔g4 40 ♖g1+ ♔h5 41 ♖h1+**
½-½

Game 14

I.Sokolov-Beliavsky
Belgrade 1991

**1 d4 ♘f6 2 c4 e6 3 ♘c3 ♗b4 4 ♕c2
0-0 5 a3 ♗xc3+ 6 ♕xc3 b6 7 ♘f3
♗b7 8 ♗g5 c5 9 e3 d6 10 dxc5 bxc5
11 ♘d2 a5 12 ♗d3 ♘bd7 13 0-0 a4**

Fixing b2 and b3, and aiming to
infiltrate on the b-file.

14 ♖ad1 ♖a6 15 ♕c2 ♕a8 16 f3
h6?

16...♖b8 17 ♘b1 ♖b6 18 ♘c3 ♗c6 is unclear.

17 ♗h4 ♖b6 18 ♘b1!

The king's knight comes to replace the queen's knight on c3! This is the knight's best square, from where it will eye the a4-pawn and also the squares b5 and d5.

18...♖b8 19 ♗g3! e5

A common idea for Black; the pawn on e5 reduces the scope of White's queen's bishop.

20 ♘c3 ♗c6 21 ♖f2 ♖8b7 22 ♗f5 ♕b8 23 ♖dd2

23...♖b3

In many ways this is fairly typical of the ♕c2 variation; Black seems to have done all the right things, but he is still worse!

24 ♕d1 ♘e8 25 ♕c1 g6 26 ♗d3 ♘f8 27 ♗b1 ♘e6 28 ♗a2 ♖3b6 29 ♘d5 ♗xd5 30 cxd5 ♘6g7 31 ♖fe2 ♕d8 32 ♖c2 ♘f6 33 ♗e1

Now it's the bishop's turn to go to c3, pointing at f6 and g7.

33...♕e8 34 ♗c3?

Imprecise; 34 ♗c4 ♖a7 35 e4! ±.

34...♘f5! 35 ♗c4 ♖a7 36 ♕e1 h5 37 g3 ♖b8 38 ♖g2 ♕d8 39 ♖cd2

♘h7 40 ♕e2 ♖e7 41 ♔h1 ♕f8 42 ♖d1 ♕h6 43 ♖e1 h4! 44 g4 h3 45 ♖f2 ♘h4 46 ♕c2 ♘g2 47 ♖ee2 ♖a7?

Black misses his chance: 47...♘xe3! 48 ♕d2 ♕f4! 49 ♗a2 ♘g2 ∓.

48 f4! exf4 49 exf4 ♕h4 50 g5 ♖aa8 51 f5! ♘xg5

52 fxg6 f6 53 ♗xf6 ♖e8 54 ♕f5 ♘e3 55 ♖xe3! ♖xe3 56 ♗xg5 ♕e4+ 57 ♕xe4 ♖xe4 58 ♗f1 ♖g4 59 ♗f6

Two bishops should be too much for a rook.

59...♖e8 60 ♗c3 c4 1-0

Game 15 – *Chess Master*

Karpov-Ljubojević
Reykjavik 1991

1 d4 ♘f6 2 c4 e6 3 ♘c3 ♗b4 4 ♕c2 0-0 5 a3 ♗xc3+ 6 ♕xc3 b6 7 ♗g5 ♗b7 8 f3 c5 9 e3!? cxd4 10 ♕xd4 ♘c6 11 ♕d6 ♘e4 12 ♗xd8 ♘xd6 13 ♗h4 ♗a6 14 b3

It is one of the strange properties of the 4 ♕c2 variation that even with no development for White, and all of Black's pieces in play, White still has a good position!

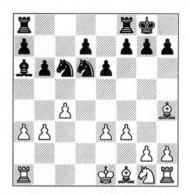

14...♘f5 15 ♗f2 ♘a5 16 ♖b1 d5 17 cxd5 ♗xf1 18 ♔xf1 exd5 19 g4! ♘e7! 20 ♘e2 ♖ac8 21 ♖b2

21 ♔g2 ♖c2 22 ♘d4 maintains a small advantage.

21...f5! 22 ♔g2

22 g5 f4! ∓.

22...fxg4 23 fxg4 h5! 24 gxh5 ♖f5 25 h6

According to Karpov, this was White's last chance to keep an edge by 25 ♖d1 or 25 ♖c1. From now on Karpov gets outplayed.

25...♖g5+! 26 ♗g3 ♘f5 27 ♔f2 ♘xh6 28 ♘d4 ♘g4+ 29 ♔e2 ♘f6 30 ♔f3 ♘c6 31 ♘e6 ♖f5+ 32 ♔g2 ♖e8 33 ♘d4 ♘xd4 34 exd4 ♖e3 35 ♖e1 ♖d3 36 ♖e5! ♖ff3 37 ♖e7 a5 38 b4?!

38 ♗e5!.

38...♘h5! 39 bxa5 ♘xg3 40 hxg3 ♖xg3+ 41 ♔h2 bxa5 42 ♖d7 ♖g5 43 ♖g2 ♖xg2+ 44 ♔xg2 ♖xd4 45 ♔f3 ♖d3+ 46 ♔e2 ♖xa3 47 ♖xd5 ♔h7 48 ♔f2 ♔h6 49 ♖c5 g5 50 ♔g2 ♔h5 51 ♖d5 ♔h4 0-1

Game 16

Foisor-Smagin
Nîmes 1991

1 d4 ♘f6 2 c4 e6 3 ♘c3 ♗b4 4 ♕c2 0-0 5 a3 ♗xc3+ 6 ♕xc3 b6 7 ♗g5 c5 8 dxc5 bxc5 9 e3

⇨ 9 ♘f3 ♘c6 10 e3 h6 (10...♖b8 11 ♗d3 ♕b6 12 ♗xf6 gxf6 13 0-0-0 ♔g7 14 g4 ♕b3 effectively forces play into an endgame which looks fairly equal, but was won by Black in Yrjölä-Lobron, Manila OL 1992) 11 ♗h4 g5 12 ♗g3 ♘e4 13 ♕c2 f5 14 0-0-0 ♕f6 15 ♗d3 (15 ♗c7?! {hardly an improvement, as it seems to lose a piece!} 15...♖f7 16 h3 d6 17 ♗xd6 e5 18 ♘xe5 ♘xe5 19 ♗xe5 ♕xe5 20 ♖d8+ ♔g7 21 ♖d5 ♕e7. I imagine White should lose this, but somehow he managed to scrape a draw in Obukhov-Savon, Moscow 1991) 15...♘xg3 (not fearing the open h-file; if necessary Black can always defend h6 with ...♔g7 and ...♖h8) 16 hxg3 ♖b8 17 ♕h5 g4!? 18 ♘d2! ♘e5 19 ♗e2 ♗b7 20 f3! gxf3 21 gxf3 ♗c6! (not 21...♕f7? 22 f4! ±) 22 ♕c3?! ♔g7! 23 g4 ♘g6 24 ♕xf6+ ♖xf6 25 f4 ♘e7! 26 g5 hxg5 27 ♖xg5+ ♖g6 28 ♖xg6+ ♔xg6 29 ♘f3 ♔f6 30 ♘e5 ♖b3 31 ♖d3 ♖xd3 32 ♘xd3 d6 33 b4 cxb4 34 axb4 ♗e4 35 ♘f2 e5 36 fxe5+ ♔xe5 37 ♔d2 d5 38 c5 d4 39 b5 dxe3+ 40 ♔xe3 ♘d5+ 41 ♔d2 ♔d4 ½-½ Kir.Georgiev-Smagin, Dortmund 1991.

9...d6

⇨ 9...♗b7 is similar to material considered later: 10 ♘f3 h6 11 ♗xf6 (if

11 ♗h4 g5 12 ♗g3 ♘e4 is unclear,
but playing the ending gives Black
no particular problems) 11...♕xf6
12 ♕xf6 gxf6 13 0-0-0 ♖d8 14 ♗e2
♔f8 15 ♔c2 ♔e7 16 b4 a5! ∓ 17 b5
d6 18 ♗d3 f5! 19 ♖he1 ♖g8 20 ♘h4
♘d7 21 ♗xf5!? ♗xg2?! (there was
no objection to taking the piece:
21...exf5 22 ♘xf5+ ♔d8 23 ♘xd6
♗xg2 24 ♘xf7+ ♔c7 ∓) 22 ♖g1
♗b7 23 ♗d3 ♖g5! 24 ♗e2 ♖ag8 25
♖g3 ♘f6 26 ♘f3 ♖f5 27 ♖f1 ♗xf3
28 ♖xf3 ♖xf3 29 ♗xf3 ♘d7 30 ♔c3
♘b6 (Black has achieved the ideal
endgame: White's queenside is sure
to fall) 31 h3 ♖g5 32 h4 ♖g6 33 h5
♖g5 34 ♗e2 ♖g2 35 ♗d3 ♔f6 36
♗e4 ♖h2 37 ♖g1 ♖xf2 38 ♖g8 ♖a2
39 ♗d3 ♖xa3+ 40 ♔c2 d5 41 cxd5
c4 42 ♗f1 0-1 Kumaran-Dorfman,
Metz 1992.

10 ♗d3 ♘bd7 11 ♘e2

White's development in this game
looks to me like the most accurate.

**11...♗b7 12 0-0 a5 13 ♕c2 h6 14
♗h4 a4 15 ♘c3**

Just as in I.Sokolov-Beliavsky,
but here the knight takes a shorter
route to c3.

**15...♕b6 16 ♖fd1 ♖fb8 17 ♗f1
♕c6 18 ♗g3 ♘e8**

18...e5!? has its points.

**19 ♖d2 ♘b6 20 f3 ♖c8 21 e4
♗a6 22 ♘d1 ♖cb8 23 ♘e3 ♘c8 24
e5! ♖b3 25 ♖e1 f6 26 exf6 ♘xf6 27
♗h4 ♘d7 28 ♘g4 ♘f8 29 ♖de2
♕d7?**

(see next diagram)

30 ♖xe6!

It is hardly surprising that there
should be a forced win for White
considering how poorly placed the
black pieces are.

30...♘xe6 31 ♕g6 ♔f8 32 ♘xh6!
Opening up the king.

**32...gxh6 33 ♖xe6 ♖a7 34 ♖f6+
♕f7 35 ♕xh6+ ♔g8 36 ♖xf7 ♖xf7
37 ♗f6 ♖fb7 38 ♗d3 ♖xd3 39
♕g6+ ♔f8 40 ♕xd3 ♔e8 41 ♕f5
1-0**

Game 17

Bareev-Polugaevsky
Hastings 1993

**1 d4 ♘f6 2 c4 e6 3 ♘c3 ♗b4 4 ♕c2
0-0 5 a3 ♗xc3+ 6 ♕xc3 b6 7 ♗g5
h6 8 ♗h4 c5 9 dxc5 bxc5 10 e3 d6**

10...a5?! 11 ♗d3 d6 12 ♘e2
♘bd7 13 ♖d1 ♗b7 14 0-0 d5 15
cxd5 ♘xd5? (a flawed combination)
16 ♗h7+ ♔h8 (16...♔xh7? 17
♕d3+ is all over) 17 ♖xd5 ♕xh4 18
♖xd7 ♗c8 (if Black did not have this
resource he would lose a whole
piece) 19 ♖c7 ♔xh7 20 ♖xc5 ±
Flear-Garcia Padron, Fuerteventura
1992.

**11 ♗d3 ♘bd7 12 ♘e2 ♗b7 13
0-0 ♘e5 = 14 ♗b1 ♘g6 15 ♗g3 e5
16 b4 ♕c7 17 f3 ♘d7 18 ♗d3 ♘e7**

19 ♝h4 ♖fe8 20 ♖fc1?

20 ♕c2 was worth considering, stopping Black's next, or 20 ♖fd1 =.

20...e4!

Only a temporary sacrifice as the white pawn on e4 is not likely to survive for too long.

21 fxe4 ♘g6 22 ♝g3 ♘f6 23 ♖d1 ♖ad8?!

23...♘e5! ∓.

24 ♘f4! ♘xf4 25 ♝xf4 ♘xe4 26 ♕e1! ♖e6 27 ♖a2! ♖de8 28 h3 ♝a8 29 ♝xe4! ♝xe4 30 bxc5 ♕xc5 31 ♕b4 ♕c6!?

Offering a pawn for the attack, but 31...g5 32 ♕xc5 dxc5 33 ♝d6 ♖c8 = wasn't bad either.

32 ♖xd6 ♖xd6 33 ♝xd6 ♖e6 34 ♝g3!

34 c5?! ♖g6 35 g3 ♕d5!.

34...♖g6 35 ♔h2 h5

35...♖xg3?? 36 ♕b8+.

36 h4 ♕e6 37 ♖d2! ♔h7 38 ♖d6 ♕g4 39 ♖xg6 ♕e2?

Probably a time-trouble miscalculation; 39...♕xg6 should draw.

40 ♖xg7+! ♔xg7 41 ♝e5+ ♔h7??

41...♔g6 might still hold.

42 ♕b2

Is this what Black had missed?

42...♕e1

42...♕xc4 43 ♕b8 ♕e2 44 ♕h8+ ♔g6 45 ♕g7+ ♔f5 46 ♕f6+ ♔g4 47 ♕g5#.

43 ♝g3 ♕f1 44 c5 ♝c6

44...f6 loses to 45 c6 ♝xc6 46 ♕c2+.

45 ♕c2+ ♔g8 46 e4 ♕f6 47 ♕d1 ♕e6 48 ♕xh5 ♕xe4 49 ♕g5+ ♔h7 50 ♝e5 ♕g6 51 ♕xg6+ fxg6 52 g4

Two extra pawns more than two files apart is a simple technical win even with opposite-colour bishops.

52...♔g8 53 h5 gxh5 54 gxh5 ♝f3 55 h6 ♝e4 56 ♔g3 ♔f7 57 ♔f4 ♝h7 58 c6 ♔e6 59 c7 1-0

Game 18

Olafsson-Ehlvest
New York 1992

1 d4 ♘f6 2 c4 e6 3 ♘c3 ♝b4 4 ♕c2 0-0 5 a3 ♝xc3+ 6 ♕xc3 b6 7 ♝g5 h6 8 ♝h4 c5 9 dxc5 bxc5 10 ♘f3 ♘c6 11 ♝xf6

I believe that White will soon give up playing these endings, as although he has damaged Black's kingside structure, in revenge Black has a solid pawn phalanx in the centre and can operate on the b- and g-files.

11...♕xf6 12 ♕xf6 gxf6 13 0-0-0?!

13 ♘d2! is more promising.

13...f5 14 e3 ♖d8 = 15 ♝e2 ♔f8 16 ♖hg1 ♝b7 17 g4 ♘e7 18 g5?!

Normally a typical Black objective in this endgame would be to exchange his two weakling a- and h-pawns, so it is mistaken of White to do Black's work for him. The passed h-pawn is more of a weakness than a threat, needing constant defence.

18...hxg5 19 ♖xg5 ♘g8! 20 h4 ♘f6 21 ♘e5 d6 22 ♘d3 ♘e4 23 ♖gg1 ♔e7

This is the ideal spot for the king, both protecting, and being protected by, the pawn centre.

24 f3 ♘f6 25 ♘f4 e5 26 ♘d3 ♖h8 27 ♖h1 ♘h5 28 ♖dg1 ♖ag8 29 ♖xg8 ♖xg8 30 ♗d1 ♖g3

Forcing White onto the defensive.

31 ♘e1 ♖g7 32 ♔c2 f4! ∓

33 e4 ♘g3 34 ♖g1 ♖h7 35 ♘g2 f5 36 exf5 ♘xf5 37 ♔d3 ♖g7 38 h5 ♖g3 39 b4 ♔f6 40 bxc5 dxc5 41 ♗e2? e4+ 0-1

Game 19

Scherbakov-Savon
Cheliabinsk 1991

1 d4 ♘f6 2 c4 e6 3 ♘c3 ♗b4 4 ♕c2 0-0 5 a3 ♗xc3+ 6 ♕xc3 b6 7 ♗g5 h6 8 ♗h4 c5 9 dxc5 bxc5 10 f3 ♘c6

10...♗b7 would transpose into a position considered later.

11 0-0-0

⇨ 11 e3 ♖b8 12 ♗g3?! (worried about ...♘e4 tricks, but it wastes time; 12 0-0-0 is possible) 12...e5 13 ♖d1 ♕b6 14 ♖d2 ♖d8 15 e4 d6 16 ♗d3 ♘h5 17 ♗h4 g5! (Black plays with a lot of energy) 18 ♗f2 ♘f4 19 ♗e3 ♕a5! 20 ♗xf4 ♕xc3 21 bxc3 exf4 22 g3 ♘e5 23 gxf4 gxf4 24 ♔f2 ♖b2 25 ♔e2 ♖b3 0-1 Chabanon-Dorfman, Cannes 1992.

11...♖b8 12 ♗g3?!

12 e3 is better.

12...e5! 13 ♗xe5?! ♘xe5 14 ♕xe5 ♗a6 15 e4 ♕a5 16 ♘e2!

Hoping to 'buy off' Black with the c-pawn, e.g 16...♗xc4 17 ♘c3 ♗xf1 18 ♖hxf1 when White has completed his development and can look forward to a promising middle-game.

16...♖b3! 17 ♘d4! ♖xa3!

Essentially forced; 17...♖b6 18 ♘f5 would be an admission of defeat.

18 bxa3 ♕c3+ 19 ♔b1 cxd4

20 ♕d6!

Both 20 ♖xd4 d5! and 20 c5 ♕b3+ 21 ♔c1 ♖b8 22 ♕xd4 ♕a2 win for Black.

20...♕b3+ 21 ♔c1 ♕c3+ ½-½

Game 20

Bareev-Farago
Rome 1990

1 d4 e6 2 c4 ♘f6 3 ♘c3 ♗b4 4 ♕c2 0-0 5 a3 ♗xc3+ 6 ♕xc3 b6 7 ♗g5 ♗a6 8 e3

⇨ 8 ♖c1 h6 9 ♕f3!? ♘c6 10 ♗xf6 ♕xf6 11 ♕xf6 gxf6 12 e3 ♘e7 13 ♘f3 c5 14 ♗e2 cxd4 15 ♘xd4 ♖ac8 16 ♔d2 ♖c7 17 f4 ♖fc8 18 b3 = Lerner-Rozentalis, Lvov Z 1990.

⇨ 8 ♘f3 c5 9 dxc5 bxc5 10 e3 ♘c6?! 11 ♗d3 ♕a5 (Farago likes to play endings, but his opponent has other ideas!) 12 ♗xf6 gxf6 13 b4! cxb4 14 ♕xf6 bxa3+?! (14...b3!?) 15 ♔e2 ♕c5 16 ♖hc1 ♕e7 (Black insists) 17 ♕xe7 ♘xe7 18 ♖xa3 ♗b7 19 ♖b1 ♗xf3+ (19...♗c6 20 ♘e5 ±) 20 gxf3 ♘c6 21 ♗e4 ♖ab8 22 ♖b5! ♖b6 23 f4 ♖fb8 24 ♗xc6 dxc6 25 ♖g5+ ♔f8 26 ♖xa7 ♖b2+ 27 ♔f3 ♖c2 28 ♖c5 ♖b4 29 f5! (the black king finds itself in a mating net) 29... ♖bxc4 30 f6 ♔e8 31 ♖g5 1-0 L.Hansen-Farago, Tåstrup 1990.

8...d5

Alternatively:

⇨ 8...h6 9 ♗h4 c5 (9...d6 can be met by 10 ♗d3 ♘bd7 11 ♘e2 c5 12 b4 cxd4 13 exd4 ♖c8 = Flear-Rozentalis, Chiasso 1991, or 10 ♘f3 ♘bd7 11 ♗d3 c5 12 0-0 cxd4 13 exd4 ♖c8 ½-½ Yrjölä-Olafsson, Espoo Z 1989) 10 dxc5 bxc5 11 ♗d3! ♗b7

(perhaps the bishop didn't achieve a great deal on a6 if it has to return to b7 so soon) 12 f3 d6 13 ♘h3 ♘bd7 14 ♘f2 ♕b6 15 0-0 a5 16 ♖ad1 ♖fe8 17 ♗b1 with a clear advantage; Yrjölä-Pinter, Haifa 1989.

⇨ 8...c6!? 9 ♗d3 h6 10 ♗h4 d6 11 ♘f3 ♘bd7 12 0-0 ♖e8 13 ♘d2 ♖c8 14 ♕c2 d5 15 ♕a4 ♘b8 16 ♕b3 dxc4 17 ♗xc4 b5 18 ♗d3 ♘bd7 19 ♖fd1 ♕b6 20 ♗xf6 ♘xf6 21 ♘e4 ♖cd8 22 ♘xf6+ gxf6 23 ♖ac1 and again White has a clear edge, but was content with a draw soon after in Neidhardt-Pinter, France 1991.

9 ♘f3 ♘bd7 10 cxd5 ♗xf1 11 ♖xf1 exd5 12 ♘e5! ♘xe5

12...c5 13 ♘xd7 ♕xd7 14 ♗xf6 gxf6 15 dxc5 ♖ac8 16 ♕xf6 ±.

13 dxe5 ♘e4 14 ♗xd8 ♘xc3 15 ♗xc7 ♘b5 16 ♗d6 ♘xd6 17 exd6 ♖fd8 18 ♔e2! ♖xd6 19 ♖fd1 ♖ad8 20 ♖ac1 ♔f8 21 ♖c7 ♖6d7?

The ending is very difficult for Black, because of the weakness of d5 and d4, but Bareev demonstrates fine technique to haul in the full point.

22 ♖dc1 ♔e7 23 ♔d3 ♖xc7 24 ♖xc7+ ♖d7 25 ♖c8 h5?

25...a5 puts up more resistance, but in such an unpleasant situation it is easy for Black to lose patience.

26 b4! ♔e6 27 ♔d4

(see next diagram)

27...f6 28 h4 ♔f5 29 f3 ♔g6 30 a4 ♔f7 31 a5 ♔e6 32 a6! ♔d6 33 b5 ♔e6 34 g3 g6 35 ♖e8+! ♔d6 36 ♖f8 ♔e6 37 ♖c8 ♔d6 38 ♖c6+ ♔e7 39 g4 ♔f7 40 gxh5 gxh5 41 ♖c8 ♔e6 42 ♖e8+ ♔d6 43 ♖h8 ♖c7 44 ♖d8+ ♔e6 45 ♖xd5 f5 46 e4 fxe4 47 fxe4 ♖h7 48 ♖d8 ♖c7 49 ♖e8+ ♔f6 50

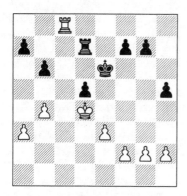

e5+ ♔f7 51 ♖h8 ♖c5 52 ♖xh5 ♔e6
53 ♖h6+ ♔e7 54 ♔e4! ♖xb5 55 ♔f5
1-0

Game 21

I.Sokolov-Kir.Georgiev
Burgas 1992

1 d4 ♘f6 2 c4 e6 3 ♘c3 ♗b4 4 ♕c2
0-0 5 a3 ♗xc3+ 6 ♕xc3 b6 7 ♗g5
♗b7 8 e3 d6 9 f3 ♘bd7 10 ♗d3 c5
11 ♘e2 ♖c8 12 ♕b3!?

Previously, Karpov's move had
been played and Black was fine: 12
♕d2 ♖e8 13 0-0 ♗a6 14 ♖ac1 ♘e4!
(this is the move that White should
try to prevent) 15 ♗xe4 ♕xg5 = 16
f4 ♕e7 17 ♗d3 g6 18 b4 ♘f6 19 e4
cxd4 20 ♘xd4 e5 21 ♘b5 ♗xb5
with equality; Toth-Razuvaev, Dortmund 1992.

12...h6 13 ♗h4 d5

13...cxd4 14 exd4 d5 (14...e5!?)
15 0-0 dxc4 16 ♗xc4 ♘b8!? 17 ♕d3
♗d5 18 ♗xd5 ♕xd5 19 ♗xf6 gxf6
20 ♘c3 ♕c4 21 ♕e3 ♔g7 22 ♖ad1
♘d7 23 ♔h1 f5 24 d5 ♖fe8 25 dxe6
♖xe6 26 ♕f2 ♘e5 occurred in

Zsu.Polgar-Ioseliani, Monaco (3)
1993, when by playing 27 ♘e2 followed by ♖d4 and ♘f4 White would
have secured a large advantage, due
to Black's feeble kingside pawns.

**14 cxd5 ♗xd5 15 ♕d1 cxd4 16
♘xd4 ♗c4 17 0-0 a6?! 18 ♖c1 b5?!
19 ♗xc4 ♖xc4 20 ♖xc4 bxc4 21
♕a4 ± ♕b6 22 ♕xc4 ♕xb2 23
♕xa6 ♘d5 24 ♗f2 ♘c5**

25 ♕d6?!

This is stronger than 25 ♕c4 ♕xa3
26 e4, when instead of 26...♘e3? 27
♘b5! ♘xc4 28 ♘xa3 ♘xa3 29
♗xc5 ♖a8 29 ♖a1 winning, John
Nunn suggests 26...♘c3! 27 ♘c2
♕b3 and Black hangs on.

**25...♘d3! 26 ♘xe6 fxe6 27
♕xe6+ ♔h8 28 ♕xd5 ♘xf2 29
♕c5?**

Nunn points out that 29 ♕e6!
leads to an easy win, for instance
29...♘d3 30 ♕d6 or 29...♖d8 30
♖xf2 ♖d1+ 31 ♖f1 when there is no
perpetual check.

29...♘h3+ 30 ♔h1

White didn't want to risk 30 gxh3
♖f6!.

30...♘f2+ 31 ♔g1 ♘h3+ ½-½

Game 22

Sorokin-Atalik
Cheliabinsk 1991

1 d4 ♘f6 2 c4 e6 3 ♘c3 ♗b4 4 ♕c2
0-0 5 a3 ♗xc3+ 6 ♕xc3 b6 7 ♗g5
♗b7 8 e3 d6 9 f3 h6 10 ♗h4 ♘bd7
11 ♗d3

⇨ 11 0-0-0?! d5! 12 c5 ♗c6 13 cxb6
cxb6 14 ♔b1 ♖c8 15 ♖c1 ♗b7?
(15...a5!?) 16 ♕e1 ♖xc1+ 17 ♕xc1
♕a8 18 ♗d3 a5 19 ♕f1! ± Gelfand-
Anand, Munich 1991.

11...c5 12 ♘e2 ♖c8
⇨ 12...cxd4 13 exd4 ♖c8 14 ♕d2
♗a6 15 ♖c1 d5 16 cxd5 ♗xd3 17
♖xc8 ♕xc8 18 ♕xd3 ♘xd5 19 0-0
♕b7 20 ♖c1 is fine for Black who
controls d5; Dokuchaev-Magerra-
mov, Moscow 1991.

13 b4!?
⇨ 13 ♕d2 is an important possibility: 13...cxd4 14 exd4 ♗a6 15 ♖c1
d5 16 b3?! (or 16 cxd5 ♗xd3 17
dxe6 {17 ♖xc8 ♕xc8 18 dxe6 ♕c4
19 exd7 ♘xd7 20 ♘c1 ♖e8+ 21 ♔d1
♗c2+ 22 ♕xc2 ♕xd4+ 23 ♘d3
♕xh4 24 ♔c1 ♘c5 25 ♘xc5 ♖c8 26
♔b1 ♖xc5 27 ♕d3 ♕e7 ½-½
Molenbroek-Weins, EU Ch 1990}
17...♗xe2 18 ♖xc8 ♕xc8 19 exd7
♕xd7 20 ♔xe2 ♘d5?! {Black has
the two better choices: 20...g5 21
♗g3 ♖e8+ 22 ♔d1 ♕f5 23 ♖e1
♕b1+ 24 ♕c1 ♕d3+ 25 ♕d2 ♕b1+
½-½ Lima-van der Wiel, Manila OL
1992, and 20...♖e8+ 21 ♔f2 ♘e4+!
also leading to equality; Flear-Sum-
mermatter, Chiasso 1991} 21 ♖e1
♖c8 22 ♔f1 ♕f5 23 ♖e5 ♕b1+ 24
♗e1 ♖c2 25 ♖e8+ ♔h7 26 ♕d3+ g6

27 ♕b3 1-0 since Black loses his
knight; Baburin-Schlosser, Budapest 1991) 16...dxc4 17 bxc4 e5 18
0-0 exd4 19 ♘g3 ♖c6! (a strong novelty providing lateral defence for the
f6 knight; previously 19...♘c5 20
♘h5 ♘fe4 had been played in P.Nik-
olić-Short, Tilburg 1988, and was
unclear) 20 ♘f5 ♘c5 21 ♗b1 d3! 22
♕c3 ♗c8! 23 ♘d4 ♖d6 24 ♘b5 ♖d7
25 ♗f2 ♘h5! 26 g3 ♕g5 27 ♖ce1
♗b7 (Black assumes the ascendancy; in particular his d-pawn is
strong) 28 ♖e5 ♕g6 29 ♕d2 ♘e6 30
♖e3 ♖fd8 (30...♘g5! 31 ♗e1 ♕f5
was more effective) 31 ♘c3! ♘g5
32 ♗e1 ♘f4 33 h4! ♘ge6 34 ♔h2
♘h5 35 ♗f2 ♘c5 36 ♖fe1 ♘f6 37
g4! h5! 38 g5 ♘h7 39 ♗a2! ♕f5 40
♘d5 ♘f8 41 ♖e5 ♕xf3 42 ♗xc5
bxc5 43 ♖1e3 ♗xd5 (Black can afford to give up his queen, as the re-
maining white pieces will find it
difficult to restrain the d-pawn) 44
♖xf3 ♗xf3 45 ♔g3 ♘g6 46 ♖xc5
♗a8 47 ♖d5 ♗xd5 48 cxd5 ♖xd5!
49 ♗xd5 ♖xd5 50 ♔f2 ♘xh4 51
♕e1 ♖f5+ 52 ♔g3 ♘g6 53 ♕e8+
♔h7 54 ♕d8 h4+ 55 ♔g4 ♖f4+ 56
♔h3 ♖f3+ 57 ♔h2 ♘f4 58 ♕d7
♖f2+ 59 ♔g1 ♖g2+ 60 ♔f1 ♖xg5 61
♔e1 h3 0-1 Lautier-Psakhis, Baden-
Baden 1992.

**13...d5 14 dxc5 bxc5 15 b5 ♘b6?
16 ♗xf6 ♕xf6 17 ♕xf6 gxf6 18
cxd5 ♗xd5**
White enjoys the better pawn
structure and the possibility of creating an outside passed pawn.
**19 ♘c3 ♗c4 20 ♗xc4 ♘xc4 21
♔e2 ♖fd8 22 ♖hd1 f5 23 a4 ♔f8 24
♖ac1 ♘a5 25 ♖xd8+ ♖xd8 26 ♘b1**
The knight is heading for c4 to

exchange Black's knight and un-
block White's pawns.

**26...♖d5 27 ♘d2 f4?! 28 exf4
♖d4 29 ♘e4 ♖xa4 30 ♖xc5 ♘b3 31
♖c8+ ♔g7 32 ♔e3 ♘d4 33 ♘d6
♖b4 34 ♖c7 ♘xb5 35 ♖xf7+ ♔g6
36 ♖e7**

Black is completely lost.

**36...♖b3+ 37 ♔f2 ♘d4 38 ♖xa7
♖b2+ 39 ♔e3 ♘c2+?**

39...♘c6 is more stubborn.

**40 ♔d2 ♘b4+ 41 ♔c3 ♖b1 42 g3
♘d5+ 43 ♔d4 ♘f6 44 ♘c4 ♖d1+
45 ♔e3 ♘d5+ 46 ♔e2 ♖h1 47 ♘e5+
♔h5 48 ♘g4 ♔g6 49 ♔f2 ♖b1 50
♘e5+ ♔h5 51 ♔g2 ♖b2+ 52 ♔h3
♘xf4+**

A last-ditch stalemate attempt.

53 gxf4 ♖b7

54 ♘c6 1-0

Game 23

Kir.Georgiev-Razuvaev
Burgas 1992

**1 d4 ♘f6 2 c4 e6 3 ♘c3 ♗b4 4 ♕c2
0-0 5 a3 ♗xc3+ 6 ♕xc3 b6 7 ♗g5**

♗b7 8 e3 d6 9 f3 ♘bd7 10 ♘h3 h6

10...c5 11 dxc5 bxc5 12 ♗d3 ♕b6
13 0-0 d5 14 ♕c2 h6 15 ♗h4 a5 16
cxd5 ♗xd5 17 ♗f2 e5 18 ♗f5 e4!
(this is similar to Bareev-Polugaev-
sky; Black will recapture the e4-
pawn sooner or later with pressure
on e3) 19 ♗xd7 ♘xd7 20 ♘f4 ♗b7
21 fxe4 ♖ae8 22 ♘d5 ♕g6 23 ♖ad1
♖xe4 = Petursson-Yusupov, Novi
Sad OL 1990.

11 ♗h4 c5

⇨ I would prefer to preface this
move with 11...♖c8, in order to be
able to recapture with the rook, e.g.
12 ♗d3 c5 13 0-0 cxd4 14 ♕xd4
♕e7 15 ♗e2 e5!? (this d6 and e5 set-
up complements the black minor
pieces and limits White's dark-
squared bishop) 16 ♕d2 g5 17 ♗g3
♘c5 18 ♖ad1 ♖fd8 19 e4 ♘e6 20
♗f2 ♘h5 21 ♖fe1 ♔h7 22 ♗f1 ♖d7
23 ♗e3 ♖g8 24 ♘f2 ♘hf4 25 ♘g4!
♖dd8 26 ♗f2 h5 27 ♘e3 ♘d4 (the
black knights have taken up menacing posts) 28 ♔h1 h4 29 ♘d5 ♗xd5
30 exd5? (30 cxd5! h3 31 g3 ♘xf3
32 ♕c3 ♘xe1 33 gxf4 g4 34 ♖xe1
exf4 35 ♗xh3!) 30...♘f5 31 ♗d3
♕f6 32 ♗e4 ♔h8 33 ♕c2 ♘h6 34
♗e3 g4 35 ♕d2 ♖g5 36 fxg4? (36
♗xf4 ♕xf4 37 ♕xf4 exf4 38 ♗b1
h3!) 36...♘xg4 37 ♗xf4 ♕xf4 38
♕xf4 exf4 39 ♖d2 ♖e8 40 ♖de2 (the
ending is losing immediately for tactical reasons) 40...h3! 41 gxh3 f3 42
hxg4 (42 ♗xf3? ♘f2+ 43 ♖xf2
♖xe1 mates) 42...fxe2 43 ♗f5 ♖e5!
44 b4 ♖g8 45 c5 bxc5 46 bxc5 ♖xd5
47 ♖xe2 dxc5 48 ♖e7 ♖d2 49 ♔g1
♖b8 0-1 Petursson-Salov, Manila IZ
1990.

12 dxc5

⇨ 12 0-0-0?! (too risky here) 12...♖c8 13 ♔b1 d5 14 cxd5 ♘xd5 15 ♕e1 ♕c7 16 ♖c1 ♕c6 17 e4 ♘c7 18 dxc5 bxc5 19 ♗f2 ♗a6 20 ♗xa6 ♕xa6 21 ♘f4 ♖b8 22 ♕c3 ♕a4 23 ♗e1 ♖b3 24 ♕a5 ♕c6 25 ♖c2 ♖fb8 26 ♗g3 ♕b7 27 ♕d2 ♘e5 0-1 Yrjölä-Kir.Georgiev, Komotini 1992 (28...♘c4 is unstoppable).

12...bxc5 13 ♗e2 a5 14 0-0 d5 15 ♖fd1 ♕b6 16 ♖d2 ♗c6! 17 ♗f2 ♖fb8! 18 ♗d1! e5?!

18...a4!?.

19 cxd5 ♗xd5 20 ♗a4 ♕e6! 21 ♖ad1! ♘b6! 22 ♗c2

22...♗xf3 23 gxf3 ♕xh3

Black has managed to expose the white king, but White defends accurately.

24 ♕xe5! ♖e8 25 ♕xc5! ♘bd5 26 e4 ♖ac8 27 ♕d4 ♘f4 28 ♗g3 ♘6h5 29 e5! ♘e6 30 ♕f2 ♘hf4 31 ♗a4 ♕f5 32 ♔h1 ♖f8 33 ♕e3 ♖c5! 34 ♖e1 ♖b8 35 ♗d7! ♘d5? 36 ♗xe6?

Time-trouble; White could have won by 36 ♕f2!.

36...♘xe3 37 ♗xf5 ♘xf5 38 e6 ♘xg3+ 39 hxg3 fxe6 40 ♖xe6 ♖cb5

41 ♖ee2 ♖8b7 42 ♔g2 ♔f7 43 f4 h5?!

Black should have reasonable drawing chances after 43...a4.

44 ♔h3 g5? 45 a4 ♖f5 46 fxg5 ♖xg5 47 ♖e3! ± ♖c5 48 b3 ♔f6 49 ♖f2+ ♔g5 50 ♖fe2 ♖f5 51 ♖c2 ♖b6 52 ♖c8 ♖d6 53 ♖ec3 ♖dd5 54 ♖g8+ ♔h6 55 ♖c6+ ♔h7 56 ♖b8 ♖f7 57 ♖cb6 ♖fd7 58 ♖8b7 ♖xb7 59 ♖xb7+ ♔g6 60 ♖b6+ 1-0

Game 24

Greenfeld-Milov
Israel 1993

1 d4 ♘f6 2 c4 e6 3 ♘c3 ♗b4 4 ♕c2 0-0 5 a3 ♗xc3+ 6 ♕xc3 b6 7 ♗g5 ♗b7 8 e3 d6 9 f3 ♘bd7 10 ♗d3 h6 11 ♗h4 e5!? 12 0-0-0!?

⇨ 12 ♗f5?! exd4 13 exd4 ♖e8+ 14 ♔d2 (14 ♘e2 ♘d5! 15 ♗xd8 ♘xc3 16 bxc3 ♖axd8 17 ♔d2 ♘b8! 18 ♘f4 c5 19 ♖he1 ♖xe1 20 ♖xe1 ♔f8 21 ♗e4 ♗a6 22 ♔d3? d5! ∓ worked out well for Black in Ilinčić-Lëgky, Novy Bečej 1991) 14...c5! 15 ♗xd7 ♕xd7 16 d5 b5! 17 b3 (17 ♗xf6 gxf6 18 b3 bxc4 19 bxc4 ♗a6 gives Black good counterplay but may have been worth trying) 17...bxc4 18 bxc4 ♕f5 19 ♗xf6 ♕f4+! 20 ♔d1 ♖e3 21 ♘e2 ♖xc3 22 ♘xf4 gxf6 23 ♖c1 ♖xa3 24 ♖e1 ♔f8 25 ♔d2 ♗a6?! 26 ♘h5 ♖a4 27 ♘xf6 ♖xc4 28 ♖xc4 ♗xc4 29 ♖e4! ♗b5 30 ♖g4 ♗e8 31 ♘h7+ ♔e7 32 ♖e4+ ♔d8 33 ♘f6 ♗d7 34 ♖h4 ♗f5! 35 ♖xh6 ♔e7 36 ♘e4 ♗g6 37 ♖h4 ♖b8 38 ♘f2 ♖b2+ 39 ♔e3 a5 40 ♖a4 ♖b5 41 ♘e4 ♖b3+ 42 ♔d2 ♖b2+ 43 ♔e3

♗xe4 44 fxe4! ♔f6! 45 ♖xa5? (45 ♔f4!! holds the draw) 45...♔e5 46 ♖a7 ♖b3+ 47 ♔f2 ♔xe4 48 ♖xf7 ♖b2+ 49 ♔g3 c4 50 ♖c7 ♔d3 51 h4 c3 52 h5 c2 53 h6 ♖b1 54 ♔f4 c1♕+ 55 ♖xc1 ♖xc1 56 g4 ♖f1+ 57 ♔g5 ♔e4 58 ♔g6 ♖g1 0-1 Flear-Lëgky, Le Touquet 1991.

12...e4 13 ♗c2

13 fxe4? would concede the e4-square: 13...♕e8 ∓.

13...♕e7 14 f4 b5!

Opening up the queenside and gaining use of the d5-square.

15 cxb5 ♕e6 16 ♗xf6 ♘xf6 17 ♘e2 ♘d5 18 ♕b3 a6 19 f5!? ♕xf5 20 ♘g3 ♕g5?!

20...♕e6!?.

21 ♗xe4 ♖ab8 22 ♖he1 ♘f6?! 23 ♗d3 ♗c6 24 ♘f5! ♗xb5 25 h4 ♕g4 26 ♖f1 ♗xd3 27 ♕xd3 ♘e4 = 28 ♔b1?

28 ♕c2 was the only move, as now Black has the time to mount a decisive attack.

28...♖b5! 29 ♘e7+ ♔h8 30 ♖c1 ♖b3!

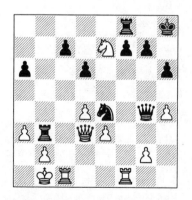

31 ♕c2 ♖fb8 32 ♖xf7 ♕e6 33 ♖cf1 ♖xb2+ 34 ♕xb2 ♘d2+ 35

♔c1 ♖xb2 36 d5 ♕e4 37 ♔xb2 ♘xf1 38 h5 ♘xe3 39 ♘g6+ ♔h7 40 ♖f8 ♕c2+ 41 ♔a1 ♕d1+ 0-1

Game 25

Kharlov-Smagin
Poliot-Petrosian 1991

1 d4 ♘f6 2 c4 e6 3 ♘c3 ♗b4 4 ♕c2 0-0 5 a3 ♗xc3+ 6 ♕xc3 b6 7 ♗g5 ♗b7 8 ♘h3 h6

⇨ 8...d6 9 f3 ♘bd7 10 e4 c5 11 ♗e2!? h6 12 ♗e3 (it seems unusual to retreat the bishop here, but of course 12 ♗h4 allows the 12...♘xe4! tactic) 12...♖c8 (12...d5!? 13 cxd5 exd5 14 e5 ♘e8 15 0-0 ±) 13 0-0 ♗a6 (again, Black cannot free his position with 13...d5?! due to 14 cxd5 exd5 15 e5 ♘e8 16 f4 ♘c7 17 f5 ♖e8 18 ♗f4 cxd4 19 ♕xd4 ♕e7 20 ♖ae1 ♘xe5 21 ♗h5 ♘b5 22 ♕e3 ♕h4 23 ♕g3 ±) 14 ♖fe1! ♖e8 (14...d5? 15 cxd5 ♗xe2 16 dxe6 ±) 15 ♗f1 ♕c7 16 ♖ad1 ♕b8? (16...cxd4 17 ♕xd4 e5 18 ♕xd6 ♗xc4 19 ♗xc4 ♕xc4 20 ♘f2 ±) 17 ♘f2 cxd4 18 ♕xd4 ♘e5 19 b3 ♖ed8 20 ♕b2! ♖d7? (20...♘e8 is better, the d7-square will be required by one of the knights later) 21 ♗d4 b5 (Black intends to offer the exchange for a pawn and a durable position, but Lautier finds a much stronger line) 22 c5! ♖xc5 23 f4! ♘g6 24 ♗xf6 gxf6 25 ♘g4 ± ♖dc7 26 ♘xf6+ ♔f8 27 ♖xd6 ♕c8 28 ♖ed1 ♔e7 29 ♕d4 e5 30 fxe5 ♘xe5 31 b4 1-0 Lautier-Piket, Lyon Z 1990.

9 ♗h4 d6

Alternatively:

⇨ 9...♖e8 10 e3 ♕e7 11 f3 d5 12 ♗d3! ♘bd7 13 cxd5! exd5 14 0-0! c5 (he cannot play 14...♕xe3+ because 15 ♗f2 ♕e7 16 ♕xc7 is very good for White) 15 ♖fe1 ♖ac8 16 ♘f2! cxd4 17 ♕xd4 ♘e5?! 18 ♗b5 ♘c6? 19 ♗xc6 ♖xc6 20 ♘g4! ± ♖c4 21 ♗xf6 ♕e6 22 ♕d2 and now Black tried 22...♖xg4 since 22...gxf6 23 ♘xh6+ was unappetizing, but White was winning anyway; Chernin-Brunner, Dortmund 1990.

⇨ 9...g5 (rather loosening) 10 ♗g3 ♘e4 11 ♕c2 f5 12 f3 ♘xg3 13 hxg3 ♕f6 14 ♘f2 ♘c6 15 e3 ♔g7 16 ♗e2 ♘e7 17 0-0-0 ± Olafsson-Arnason, Espoo Z 1989.

10 f3 ♘bd7

⇨ 10...a5!? 11 e4 c5 12 d5 ♘bd7 13 ♕c2 ♘e5 14 ♗e2 ♘g6 15 ♗f2 e5 16 ♗e3 ♗c8 17 ♘f2 ♘f4 18 ♗f1 a4 19 g4 ♘h7 20 ♗xf4 exf4 21 ♘d3 ♖e8 22 h4 b5 with unclear play; Miles-Cebalo, Palma 1989.

11 ♘f2!?

⇨ 11 e4 (11 e3 c5 12 dxc5 bxc5 13 ♗e2 a5 14 b3 ♖e8!? 15 0-0 ♕b6 16 ♖fd1 e5! ∓ Steingrimsson-Arnason, Icelandic Ch 1990) 11...c5 12 dxc5 bxc5 13 ♗d3 d5 14 exd5 exd5 15 0-0-0 d4 16 ♕c2 ♕b6 17 ♖he1 ♖fe8 18 ♖xe8+ ♖xe8 19 ♖e1 ♖xe1+ 20 ♗xe1 ♘e5 21 ♗f1 ♕d6 22 ♘f2 ±. White has the better prospects because of the bishop pair and the possibility of the undermining move b4; Gelfand-Browne, Dortmund 1990.

11...♕e8 12 e3?!

12 e4!.

12...♘h7! 13 ♗e2 f5 14 ♘d3 c5 15 ♖g1 e5?! 16 dxe5 dxe5?! 17 ♗g3! ± e4 18 ♘e5 ♘df6 19 0-0-0

♕e6 20 f4 ♖fd8 21 ♗h4 g5?

22 g4!

Thus justifying his 15th move.

22...♖xd1+ 23 ♗xd1 ♖d8

Obviously not 23...gxh4?? 24 gxf5+ winning the queen.

24 gxf5 ♕xf5 25 fxg5 hxg5 26 ♗e2 ♖e8 27 ♗xg5 ♘xg5 28 h4 ♘fh7 29 ♘g4! ♖e6 30 hxg5 ♘xg5

With his king wide open Black can hardly hope to defend.

31 ♖h1 ♔f8 32 ♖h5 ♕g6 33 ♕h8+ ♔e7 34 ♘e5 ♕f5? 35 ♕g7+ 1-0

Game 26

Hauchard-Shirov
Santiago 1990

1 d4 ♘f6 2 c4 e6 3 ♘c3 ♗b4 4 ♕c2 0-0 5 a3 ♗xc3+ 6 ♕xc3 b6 7 ♗g5 ♗b7 8 ♘h3 h6 9 ♗h4 c5 10 dxc5 bxc5 11 f3

⇨ 11 e3?! (a mistake, which lands White in all sorts of trouble) 11...g5! 12 ♗g3 ♘e4 ∓ 13 ♕c2 ♕a5+ 14 ♔e2 f5?! (14...d5 has its points) 15

f3 ♘xg3+ 16 hxg3 ♘c6 17 ♘f2 ♘e5
18 ♘d3 ♘xd3 19 ♕xd3 ♖f6 ½-½
Topalov-Luther, Altensteig 1990.

11...♘c6 12 ♗f2?!

It's understandable that White
should miss Black's strong reply.

**12...d5! 13 ♗xc5 d4 14 ♕d2 ♖e8
15 e4 e5 16 ♘f2 ♕c7! 17 b4 ♘d8!**

The white bishop is stuck on c5
and must await its fate.

18 ♘d3?

18 ♗e2 ∓.

18...♘e6 19 ♗e2 ♗xe4!

Typical of Shirov's dynamism; he
clears the path for his centre in the
most radical manner.

**20 fxe4 ♘xe4 21 ♕c2 ♘4xc5! 22
♘xc5 ♘xc5 23 bxc5 e4 24 0-0 ♖ad8
25 ♖ad1! ♕xc5**

26 ♔h1 d3 27 ♗xd3

White returns the piece but
Black's advantage remains.

27...exd3 28 ♕c3

Not 28 ♖xd3? ♕f5!!.

**28...♖e3 ∓ 29 h3 ♕c6 30 ♔g1
♖e2 31 ♖f3 ♖c2! 32 ♕a5 ♖d6 33
♕f5 ♖g6! 34 g4 ♖f6! 35 ♕xd3
♕xf3 36 ♕xc2 ♕g3+ 37 ♔g2 ♕e3+
38 ♔h1 ♖f2 0-1**

Game 27

Flear-Hellers
San Bernardino 1990

1 d4 ♘f6 2 c4 e6 3 ♘c3 ♗b4 4 ♕c2
0-0 5 a3 ♗xc3+ 6 ♕xc3 b6 7 ♗g5
♗b7 8 ♘h3 h6 9 ♗h4 d5 10 cxd5
exd5 11 e3 c5

11...♘bd7 12 ♗d3 c5 13 f3 ♕e7
14 ♗f5 g5 15 ♗g3 ♖fe8 16 ♔f2
cxd4 17 ♕xd4 ♘c5 18 ♖ad1 ♖ad8!?
(18...♗c8 was also fine in Gulko-
Yusupov, Hastings 1989: 19 ♗b1
♗d7 20 b4 ♘e6 21 ♕d2?! ♘g7! 22
♖he1 ♗f5 ∓) 19 ♖he1 ♗c8 20 ♗b1
♘e6 with good chances; Karpman-
Kushch, Simferopol 1990.

12 dxc5

If instead 12 ♗xf6!? ♕xf6 13
dxc5 then not the 13...d4?! 14 ♕xd4
♕xd4 15 exd4 ♖e8+ 16 ♔d2 ♖d8 17
♔c3 ± of Glek-Langeweg, Kusa-
dasi 1990, but 13...♕e7! 14 ♗e2 (14
cxb6? is too greedy: 14...♘c6 15
♗e2 d4 ∓) 14...bxc5 15 0-0 d4 =.

12...d4!?

⇨ 12...g5!? is also playable: 13 ♗g3
d4 14 ♕xd4 ♕xd4 15 exd4 ♖e8+ 16
♗e5 ♘bd7 17 0-0-0 ♘xe5 18 dxe5
♖xe5 19 cxb6 ♗e4 20 b4 axb6 21
♔b2 ♖c8 (21...g4 might be even better: 22 ♘g1 ♖c8 23 ♖d2 ♗f5 24
♗a6 ♖a8 25 ♗b7 ♖a7 26 ♗c6 ♖e1
27 ♖e2 ♖b1+ 28 ♔a2 ♖xb4 29 ♖b2
♖c4 30 ♖xb6 ♖c2+ 31 ♔b3 ♖c1
{White is all tied up} 32 ♔a2 ♗e4
33 ♗xe4 ♘xe4 0-1 Schwartzmann-
Levin, Groningen 1991) 22 ♗a6
♖c2+ 23 ♔b3 ♖c7 24 ♖he1 b5 25
♖c1?! ♗xg2? (going for complications that turn out badly; 25...♖xc1

26 ♖xc1 ♗xg2 ∓) 26 ♖xe5 ♖xc1 27 ♘xg5 (perhaps Black had over-looked this) 27...♖b1+ 28 ♔c2 ♖h1 29 ♖f5 ♘e4 30 ♘xf7 ♔g7 31 f3 ♘f6 32 ♘d6 ♖xh2 33 ♔b3 h5 34 ♗xb5 h4 35 ♖g5+ ♔f8 36 ♖g6 ♘h5 37 ♘f5 ♗xf3 38 ♗c4 1-0 (the black king is caught in a mating net) Stohl-Psakhis, Amsterdam 1990.

13 ♕xd4?!

In the light of what follows, it may be better to try 13 ♗xf6 dxc3! 14 ♗xd8 cxb2 15 ♖b1 ♖xd8 16 ♖xb2 ♘d7! 17 cxb6 axb6 = as in Vaiser-Lobron, Paris 1990.

13...♕xd4 14 exd4 ♖e8+ 15 ♔d2 g5 16 ♗g3 ♘c6 17 ♗b5?!

⇨ 17 ♖d1 ♘xd4 18 ♔c1 ♘b3+ 19 ♔b1 ♗e4+ 20 ♔a2 ♘xc5 21 f3 ♗c2 ½-½ although both sides can con-sider continuing; Østenstad-Hmadi, Novi Sad OL 1990.

17...♖ed8! 18 ♗xc6 ♗xc6 19 f3 ♖xd4+ 20 ♔e3 bxc5

Black has recovered his sacrificed material but retains a strong attack.

21 ♖hd1 ♖e8+ 22 ♔f2 ♗a4! 23 ♖xd4 cxd4 24 ♖e1 ♖c8 25 ♗e5? ♖c2+ 26 ♔g1 d3 0-1

Black wins material after 27 ♗xf6 d2 28 ♖f1 ♖c1 29 ♘f2 ♗b5 30 ♖d1 ♗e2.

Game 28

Ivanov-Kishnev
Berlin 1992

1 d4 ♘f6 2 c4 e6 3 ♘c3 ♗b4 4 ♕c2 0-0 5 a3 ♗xc3+ 6 ♕xc3 b6 7 ♗g5 h6 8 ♗h4 c5 9 dxc5 bxc5 10 e3 ♗b7 11 f3 d6?!

An inaccuracy, as this pawn will need defending. The following se-quence leaves Black in trouble.

12 0-0-0 a5 13 ♗xf6! gxf6 14 ♘h3

Aiming for h5.

14...♖a6 15 ♘f4 ♘d7 16 ♘h5 ♖e8 17 ♗d3 ♔f8 18 ♗c2 a4 19 ♖d2

Renewing the attack on d6.

19...♔e7 20 ♖hd1 ♕c7 21 e4 ± ♖g8? 22 f4 ♖b8 23 ♕g3 ♗c8 24 e5!

With all his pieces on perfect squares, it would be surprising if White had no way to break through.

24...fxe5 25 ♕h4+ ♔f8

26 ♖xd6! ♖xd6 27 ♖xd6 exf4

27...♕xd6? allows 28 ♕d8#.

28 ♘xf4! ♖b6

28...♕xd6 again walks into mate: 29 ♕d8+ ♔g7 30 ♘h5#.

29 ♕xh6+ ♔e7 30 ♖xe6+! fxe6 31 ♘g6+ ♔f6 32 ♕h8+ ♔f7 33 ♕h7+ 1-0

Game 29

Ljubojević-Speelman
Linares 1992

1 d4 ♘f6 2 c4 e6 3 ♘c3 ♗b4 4 ♕c2
0-0 5 a3 ♗xc3+ 6 ♕xc3 b6 7 ♗g5 c5
8 dxc5 bxc5 9 e3 ♗b7 10 f3 a5
⇨ 10...h6 11 ♗h4 ♘c6 (this didn't
work out any better for Speelman)
12 0-0-0 ♖c8 13 ♗xf6 gxf6 14 ♔b1
± d5?! 15 cxd5 exd5 16 ♕xc5
(Black's position is a shambles)
16...♘e5 17 ♕d4 ♕c7 18 ♘h3
♕c2+ 19 ♔a1 ♘c6 20 ♕g4+ ♕g6
21 ♕d7! ± ♘a5 22 ♗d3 ♘b3+ 23
♔b1! ♖c1+ 24 ♔a2 ♖xd1 25
♖xd1! ♘c5 26 ♕xb7 ♘xd3 27 ♕b5
1-0 Hjartarson-Speelman, Reykjavik 1991.

    11 ♗d3
⇨ 11 ♘h3 d6 12 ♖d1 (12 ♗e2 ♘bd7
13 0-0 h6 14 ♗h4 ♖a6 15 b3 ♕a8 16
♖fd1 ♖c8 17 ♗g3 ♘e8 18 ♘f2 ♖b6
19 ♖d2 ± Chernin-Cebalo, Palma
1989) 12...♖a6 13 ♗e2 ♘bd7 14 0-0
a4 15 ♘f2 ♗a8 16 ♖d2 ♕e7 17 e4
♖b8 18 ♘d1 (yet another road to c3
for the king's knight) 18...h6 19 ♗h4
♖b3 20 ♕c1 ♘e5 21 ♘c3 ♗c6 22
♖fd1 ♖ab6? (a blunder) 23 ♖xd6
♖xb2 24 ♗g3 ♘fd7 25 f4 (all
Black's pieces start dropping after
this move) 25...♖xe2 26 fxe5 ♖bb2
27 ♘xe2 ♖xe2 28 ♖xc6 ♘xe5 29
♗xe5 ♕h4 30 ♖c8+ ♔h7 31 ♕f4
♖e1+ 32 ♖xe1 ♕xe1+ 33 ♕f1 1-0
Farago-Röder, Budapest 1990.

    **11...d6 12 ♘e2 ♘bd7 13 ♕c2 h6
14 ♗f4!? d5 15 ♗g3 ♘b6 16 ♖d1
♕e7 17 0-0 dxc4?! 18 ♗xc4 ♘xc4
19 ♕xc4 ♗a6**
The bishop gains an active diagonal, but at a price: the c-pawn is weak.
    **20 ♕c2 ♘d5 21 ♔f2! ♕g5!? 22
♕d2 f5 23 ♖fe1 ♖fd8 24 ♕c1 ♕f6**
The black position looks very
menacing at present.

    **25 ♔g1! ♖ac8 26 e4! fxe4 27 fxe4
♘e7 28 ♗d6**
The bishop takes root on d6.
    **28...♘g6 29 ♘g3 ♖d7 30 e5 ♕f4
31 ♕c2 ♕g5 32 ♘e4 ♕f5 33 ♕f2
♘xe5?**
33...♘f4 was better; with the opposite-colour bishops, any advantage for White must be minimal.
    34 ♕xf5 exf5 35 ♘xc5
Wins the exchange and the game.
    **35...♖xd6 36 ♖xd6 ♖xc5 37
♖xa6 ♘d3 38 ♖b1 ♖b5 39 ♖d6 ♖b3
40 ♖d5 a4 41 ♖xf5 ♘xb2 42 ♖f4
♘d3 43 ♖xb3 axb3 44 ♖f5! 1-0**

Game 30

Lautier-Spraggett
Manila OL 1992

1 d4 ♘f6 2 c4 e6 3 ♘c3 ♗b4 4 ♕c2
0-0 5 a3 ♗xc3+ 6 ♕xc3 b6 7 ♗g5
♗b7 8 f3 h6 9 ♗h4 c5 10 dxc5 bxc5
11 e3
⇨ 11 ♘h3 ♘c6 (11...d6 12 0-0-0 e5
13 ♕d2 ♘e4 14 ♕e1 ♘f6 15 ♕d2
♘e4 16 ♗xd8 ♘xd2 17 ♗e7 ♖e8 18
♖xd2 ♖xe7 19 ♖xd6 with advantage,

although White later went on to lose a rook versus two pawns endgame in Piskov-Karpman, Minsk 1990) 12 0-0-0 e5! (12...♘e4 13 ♕e1 g5 14 ♗f2 ♘xf2 15 ♘xf2 ♘e5 16 ♕c3 ♕f6 17 e3 ♔g7 18 h4 ♖fd8 19 ♔b1?! ♘xf3! ∓ 20 ♕xf6+ ♔xf6 21 gxf3 ♗xf3, the rook and two pawns outweighing the two pieces in this ending; Sherbakov-Tunik, Anapa 1991) 13 e3 ♖b8 14 ♗d3? ♗a6 15 ♘f2 g5? 16 ♗g3 ♕b6 17 ♘e4 ± ♘xe4 18 ♗xe4 ♘d4! (a reasonable practical try in a terrible position) 19 exd4 cxd4 20 c5! ♕e6 21 ♕c2 ♖fc8 22 ♖he1 d6 23 ♗f5? ♕a2 24 ♗xc8 ♖xc8 (what chance has Black, a whole rook down?) 25 c6 ♗b5 26 c7 d3 27 ♕c3 ♖xc7! 28 ♕xc7 ♕a1+ 29 ♔d2 ♕xb2+ 30 ♔e3 ½-½ since 30...♕d4+ gives a perpetual; Gulko-Ivanov, USA Ch 1989.

11...a5 12 ♗d3 d6 13 ♘e2 ♘bd7 14 0-0 ♕b6 15 ♖ad1 ♖fe8?!

15...d5 16 ♗f2 ♗a6 ±.

16 ♖d2! ±

Preparing to line up on the d-file.

16...d5 17 ♗f2 ♗a6?! 18 ♖fd1 ♖ac8 19 ♘f4 ♗b7 20 ♗b1

Lautier's play is very logical; he brings even more pressure to bear on d5.

20...♕a6 21 ♗a2! ♘b6 22 ♗h4!

Black's position is stretched to breaking point.

(see next diagram)

22...d4 23 exd4 cxd4

23...g5 is met by 24 dxc5.

24 ♖xd4 ♘a4

24...e5 25 ♖d6 exf4 26 ♗xf6 gxf6 27 c5! ±.

25 ♕c2 e5 26 ♖d6 ♖c6 27 ♖xc6 ♕xc6 28 ♗xf6 exf4 29 ♗d4

The game is effectively over.

29...♖d8 30 ♗b1 g6 31 b3 ♘c5 32 ♗b2 ♕e8 33 ♖xd8 ♕xd8 34 b4 axb4 35 axb4 ♘e6 36 ♕c3 f6 37 ♗xg6 ♕d1+ 38 ♔f2 ♘g5 39 ♕d3 1-0

Game 31

Dorfman-Korchnoi
Polanica Zdroj 1992

1 d4 ♘f6 2 c4 e6 3 ♘c3 ♗b4 4 ♕c2 0-0 5 a3 ♗xc3+ 6 ♕xc3 b6 7 ♗g5 ♗b7 8 e3 d6 9 f3 c5?!

As we have seen in some of the other games, the d6 pawn can make a good target for White if he can open the d-file, but 9...♘bd7 didn't fare too well either in Karpov-Andersson, Haninge 1990: 10 ♘h3 c5 11 dxc5 bxc5 12 ♗e2 a5 13 ♖d1 h6 14 ♗f4!? d5 15 0-0 ♕b6 16 ♗g3 ♗a6 17 ♖f2 ♖a7 18 cxd5 ♘xd5 19 ♕c1 ♗xe2 20 ♖xe2 ♕b5 21 ♖c2 ♖b7 22 ♘f2 ♘5f6 23 e4 ♖c8 24 ♖d3 ♘b6 25 b3! ♖d7 26 ♖dc3 ±.

10 dxc5 bxc5 11 ♖d1 ♘c6 12 ♘h3! ♖b8 13 ♗e2 ♗a8 14 0-0 h6

15 ♗h4 ♖e8 16 ♘f2 g5 17 ♗g3 e5 18 ♖d2 ♕e7 19 ♗d3 ♕e6 20 ♖fd1 ♖b6 21 ♗b1 ♘e7 22 b4

Black has to decide whether to allow b5, or after 22...cxb4 23 axb4, the possibility of the c5 thrust undermining e5 and opening the d-file.

22...♖c8 23 b5 ♘e8 24 e4 h5 25 h4?!

25 h3 ± was more circumspect.

25...gxh4 26 ♗xh4 ♘g6 27 ♗g3 ♖b7 28 ♖f1

Freeing the d1 square for the knight, whereupon it will go to e3 controlling d5 and f5.

28...f6 29 ♘d1 ♖g7 30 ♘e3 ♘e7 31 ♔f2? ♗b7 32 ♖h1 ♕f7 33 a4 ♖d8 34 ♕a5? ♖a8 35 ♗h2 ♗c8 36 ♘f5 ♘xf5 37 exf5 ♗b7 38 ♕c3 ♖g5 39 ♔f1 a6 40 ♗c2 axb5 41 cxb5 c4! 42 a5

Things have started getting messy; the white queenside looks menacing, but so does the black centre.

42...♘c7 43 a6 ♗d5 44 ♕a5! c3 45 ♖xd5 ♕xd5 46 ♕xc7 ♕d2 47 ♕c4+ ♔h8 48 ♕e2

48...♖xg2! 49 ♕xg2

49 ♕xd2? ♖xd2 leaves White's rook and queen's bishop shut out of the game.

49...♕c1+ 50 ♔f2 ♕xc2+ 51 ♔f1 ♕c1+ 52 ♔f2 ½-½

Game 32 *CML*

Beliavsky-Timman
Lucerne 1989

1 d4 ♘f6 2 c4 e6 3 ♘c3 ♗b4 4 ♕c2 0-0 5 a3 ♗xc3+ 6 ♕xc3 b6 7 ♗g5 ♗b7 8 f3 d6 9 e4 c5

⇨ 9...e5!? 10 dxe5 dxe5 11 ♖d1 ♕e7 12 ♘e2 ♘c6 13 ♘g3 ♘d4! 14 ♗d3 ♕e6 15 0-0 ♘d7 16 ♘f5 f6 17 c5! ♘xc5?! 18 ♗c4+ ♔h8 19 ♗e3 ♕e8 20 ♘xd4 exd4 21 ♖xd4 f5? 22 exf5 ♖xf5? 23 ♖g4 1-0 L.Hansen-Steinbacher, Ostend 1991.

10 d5 ♘bd7 11 ♘h3 h6

⇨ 11...♖e8 12 dxe6 fxe6 13 0-0-0 ♕c7 14 ♕d2 d5 15 cxd5 exd5 16 ♗b5 d4 17 ♗f4 ♘e5 18 ♗xe8 ♖xe8 19 ♔b1 ♘fd7 20 ♘f2 ♘c6 21 ♘d3 ♘c4 22 ♕c2 ♗a6 23 ♕b3 ♔h8 24 ♖c1 ♘a5 25 ♕c2 ½-½ Mohr-Weber, Bundesliga 1991.

⇨ 11...exd5 12 cxd5 ♖e8 13 0-0-0 c4 14 ♔b1 b5 15 g4 (the game has quickly developed into a race between opposite wings, with White tripping up!) 15...a5 16 ♗f4 ♘e5 17 ♗e2 ♗a6 18 g5 ♘fd7 19 ♗d2 ♘c5 20 ♘f2 b4 21 ♕e3 c3 0-1 Videki-Arkhipov, Kecskemet 1990.

12 ♗f4 ♖e8!?

Probably 12...exd5 is better. After 13 cxd5 ♖e8!? 14 0-0-0 ♘e5:

⇨ 15 g4 ♗c8 16 ♔b1? ♘xf3! 17 ♕xf3 ♗xg4 18 ♕b3 (18 ♕d3 ♖xe4 ∓)

18...♗xd1 19 ♕xd1 ♘xe4 20 ♗b5 ♕f6 21 ♗xe8 ♖xe8 22 ♕g4 ♕g6 23 ♕xg6 fxg6 with advantage to Black as the pawns are worth much more than the piece in this ending; Hjartarson-Timman, Belgrade 1989.

⇨ 15 ♘f2 a6 16 ♗d2 b5 17 ♕a5 (an unusual method of blockading the black queenside) 17...♕e7 18 ♔b1 ♖eb8 19 ♖e1 ♗c8 20 ♘d1 ♗d7 21 ♔a1 b4 22 axb4 and now, instead of 22...c4? when the b-file remained permanently blocked, 22...cxb4 23 ♗xb4 would have been unclear in Agdestein-Short, Belgrade 1989.

13 dxe6

13 ♗e2 ♘f8 14 ♕d2 ♘g6 15 ♗g3 e5 is unclear.

13...fxe6 14 ♗xd6 e5

At first sight it seems that the bishop is trapped, and must surely perish.

15 0-0-0 ♖e6 16 ♗e2 ♕c8

16...♘e8? 17 ♗xe5 ♖xe5 18 ♖xd7 ±.

17 ♖d3! ♘e8 18 ♖hd1 ♕c6 19 b4!

19...cxb4
Although White has had to go

through contortions to save his bishop, it demonstrates fine judgement for at the end he has the advantage. Beliavsky analysed instead 19...♘xd6 20 b5 ♕c7 21 ♕d2 ♘xe4 22 ♖xd7 ♘xd2 23 ♖xc7 ♘b3+ 24 ♔b2 ♘d4 25 ♗d3 e4 26 ♘f4 ♖ee8 27 ♖xb7 exd3 28 ♖xd3 g5 29 ♘d5 ♖e2+ 30 ♔c1 ♖xg2 31 ♖e3 as good for White.

20 ♗xb4 ♘df6 21 ♕b3 a5 22 ♗c3 ♗a6 23 ♖3d2 ♖c8 24 ♔b1 ♔h7?!

24...♗xc4!? 25 ♗xc4 ♕xc4 26 ♕xc4 ♖xc4 27 ♗b2 is only a little better for White.

25 ♗b2 ♘d6 26 c5 ♘b5 27 cxb6 ♕xb6 28 ♔a1 a4 29 ♕b4 ♖b8 30 f4 ♕c7 31 fxe5 ♖xe5 32 ♖c1 ♕e7 33 ♕xe7 ♖xe7 34 e5 ♘d7 35 e6 ♘f8 36 ♘f4 g5 37 ♘d5 ♖xe6 38 ♘f6+ ♔g6 39 ♗h5+ 1-0

Game 33

Kasparov-Timman
Linares 1993

1 d4 ♘f6 2 c4 e6 3 ♘c3 ♗b4 4 ♕c2 0-0 5 a3 ♗xc3+ 6 ♕xc3 b6 7 ♗g5 ♗b7 8 f3 d5

There is no advantage in deferring ...h6 like this; normally 8...h6 9 ♗h4 d5 10 e3 will transpose, whilst 10 cxd5 exd5 11 e3 (winning a pawn by 11 ♗xf6 ♕xf6 12 ♕xc7 is considered a little doubtful: 12...♗a6 13 ♕e5 ♕g6 {13...♕xe5!? 14 dxe5 ♘d7?! 15 f4 ♖ac8 16 ♘f3 ♘c5 17 ♘d4 ♘e6 18 e3 ± Prudnikova-Kakhiani, Azov wom IZ 1990, but 13...♕c6 is also good} 14 ♕e3 ♘c6

15 b4 ♖fe8 16 ♕d2 ♖ac8 17 ♘h3 ♕f6 18 ♖d1 ♘e7 19 ♘f2?! ♘f5 20 e4 ♗xf1 21 ♔xf1 dxe4 22 ♘xe4 ♖xe4 23 fxe4 ♖c2! ∓ Kelečević-Abramović, Banja Vrucica 1990) 11...♖e8 12 ♘h3 is *passé*:

⇨ 12...♕e7! (forcing White onto the defensive, and the reason 10 cxd5 has been forsaken) 13 ♗f2 c5 14 ♗b5 ♗c6 (14...♖c8 15 0-0 cxd4 16 ♕xd4 ♖c5 17 ♗a4 ½-½ Seirawan-Rohde, USA Ch 1989) 15 ♗e2 (15 ♗d3 cxd4 16 ♕xd4 ♗d7! 17 0-0 ♗xh3 ∓ Shneider-Brodsky, Kherson 1989) 15...♗d7 16 0-0 (16 ♘f4? g5! ∓ Alterman-Ulybin, Santiago 1990) 16...♗xh3 17 gxh3 ♘bd7 18 ♔h1 ♘h5 19 ♖g1 ♘df6 20 dxc5?! bxc5 21 ♖ae1 ♖ab8! 22 ♗h4 ♕e5! with a crushing advantage; Gulko-Chandler, Hastings 1990.

⇨ 12...c5 13 ♗b5 ♗c6 14 a4 (after 14 ♗e2 g5 15 ♗f2 cxd4 16 ♕xd4 ♗d7 17 0-0 ♘c6 18 ♕d2 ♘e5 19 ♖fe1 ♗xh3 20 gxh3 ♕d7 21 ♔g2 ♖ad8 22 ♖ad1 ♕f5 23 ♕d4 ♘h5 White's bishop pair compensated for his shattered pawn formation in Rodriguez-Polugaevsky, Palma 1989) 14...a6 15 ♗e2 ♘bd7 16 0-0 ♕e7 = 17 ♖a3?! (this is an unwieldy square for a rook; 17 ♗f2 is preferable) 17...c4! 18 ♗e1 b5 19 a5 ♘b8! 20 ♘f2 ♗d7 21 ♗d2 ♘c6 22 b4! ♗f5 and the passed c-pawn offered Black good long term prospects in Lalić-Psakhis, Palma 1989.

⇨ 12...♘bd7 is worse: 13 ♗e2 ♘e4? (13...c5 14 0-0 ♕e7 15 ♗f2 ♖ac8 16 ♖fe1 cxd4 17 ♕xd4 ♘c5 18 ♖ad1 ♘e6 19 ♕d2 ♘c5 20 ♗b5 ♖ed8 21 ♘f4 g5?! 22 b4! ± Beliavsky-Vaganian, Odessa 1989) 14 ♗xd8

♘xc3 15 ♗xc7 ♖xe3 (15...♘xe2 16 ♔xe2 leaves White a pawn up) 16 bxc3 ♗a6 17 ♘f4 ♖ae8 (17...g5 18 ♔d2 gxf4 19 ♗xa6 wins) 18 ♔f2 ♖xe2+ (Black has to offer the exchange as 18...♗xe2? 19 ♖fe1 wins) 19 ♘xe2 ♖xe2+ 20 ♔g3 ± Beliavsky-Greenfeld, Haifa 1989.

9 e3 ♘bd7 10 cxd5 exd5 11 ♗d3 ♖e8 12 ♘e2 h6

Black decides to play ...h6 after all, seeing that the tactic 12...c5 13 0-0 ♘e4? loses to 14 fxe4 ♕xg5 15 ♗b5 cxd4 16 ♕c7!.

13 ♗h4 c5

Not 13...♖xe3? because of 14 ♗xf6 ♘xf6 15 ♗h7+ picking up the exchange.

14 0-0 ♖c8 15 ♕d2 ♕e7 16 ♗f2 ♗c6 17 ♘c3 ♘f8?! 18 ♖fe1 ♘e6 19 ♗h4 ♘g5 20 ♗f5 ♗d7 21 ♗c2 ♗c6

There is very little that Black can undertake here without seriously compromising his position.

22 ♖ad1 ♕e6 23 ♕f2 ♖cd8 24 h3 ♘gh7 25 dxc5 bxc5 26 e4!

26...dxe4 27 ♖xd8 ♖xd8 28 ♕xc5 ♘g5 29 ♗xg5 hxg5 30 ♕xg5 ♕c4 31 fxe4 ♕d4+ 32 ♕e3 ♕xe3+

33 ♖xe3 ♖d2 34 ♖e2 ♖xe2 35 ♘xe2 ♘xe4 36 ♗xe4 ♗xe4 37 ♔f2

White has won a pawn and should have every chance to win.

37...♔f8 38 g3 ♔e7 39 ♔e3 ♗c6 40 h4 ♗d7 41 ♔f4 ♔d6 42 g4 f6 43 h5 ♔e7 44 ♘d4 ♔f7 45 b4 ♗a4 46 ♘f5 g6 47 ♘d6+ ♔g7 48 ♘c8 a6 49 ♘d6 ♗d1?

Black should at least try 49...gxh5.

50 ♘e8+ ♔f7 51 ♘xf6! ♔xf6 52 g5+ ♔f7 53 h6 1-0

Black's king is tied to the h6 pawn so that White can stroll his king to a5, queen his b-pawn and then return to win the king and pawn ending.

Game 34

M.Gurevich-Karpov
Linares 1991

1 d4 ♘f6 2 c4 e6 3 ♘c3 ♗b4 4 ♕c2 0-0 5 a3 ♗xc3+ 6 ♕xc3 b6 7 ♗g5 ♗b7 8 f3 h6 9 ♗h4 d5 10 e3 ♘bd7 ⇨ 10...♗a6!? (a recent idea of Chandler's) 11 ♖c1! ♘bd7 12 cxd5 ♗xf1 13 ♔xf1 exd5 14 ♕xc7 ♖c8 15 ♕xc8 ♕xc8 16 ♖xc8 ♖xc8 17 ♘e2 ♖c2 18 b4 ♖a2 19 ♔f2 ♖xa3 20 ♖c1 ♖b3 21 ♖c8+ ♔h7 22 ♗xf6 ♘xf6 23 ♖c7 a6 (23...♔g8 24 ♖a7 g6 25 g4 ±) 24 ♖xf7! ♖xb4 25 ♖a7 a5 26 g4 ♖b2 27 h4 ♘e8 28 ♔e1 ♖b1+ 29 ♔f2 ♖b2 30 ♔e1 ♖b1+ 31 ♔f2? (short of time, White agrees to repeat, but 31 ♔d2! would have maintained his advantage) ½-½ Chekhov-Chandler, Bundesliga 1992.

11 cxd5 ♘xd5! 12 ♗xd8 ♘xc3 13 ♗h4

⇨ 13 ♗xc7 ♘d5 14 ♗d6 ♘xe3 15 ♔f2 ♘c2 16 ♖d1 ♖fc8 17 ♗b5 ♘f6 18 ♘e2 a6 (18...♘d5 19 ♖d3 a6 20 ♗a4 a5 21 ♘c3 ♖d8 22 ♘xd5 ♖xd6 23 ♘c7 ♖c8 24 ♘b5 ♖dd8 25 ♖hd1 ½-½ Klarenbeek-van der Wiel, Dutch Ch 1992) 19 ♗a4 (19 ♗d3 ♘d5 20 g4 ♖c6! 21 ♗f4 ♘xf4 22 ♘xf4 ♘xd4 23 ♗e4 e5 gave Black good play in Ulybin-Rodriguez, Bayamo 1991) 19...b5 20 ♗b3 ♗d5 21 ♗xd5 ♖xd5 (this ensures that the knight on c2 will be able to escape) 22 ♖d3 ♖c6 23 ♗c5 e5 24 b4 ♘xd4 25 ♘xd4 exd4 26 ♖xd4 ♘b6 27 ♗xb6 ♖xb6 28 ♖c1 ♖e8 29 ♖d3 ½-½ Salov-Karpov, Skellefteå 1989.

13...♘d5 14 ♗f2 f5!?

This pawn will become a weakness needing defence later; 14...c5 15 e4 ♘e7 = is safer; M.Gurevich-Polugaevsky, New York 1989.

15 ♗c4! ♖ac8 16 ♘e2 c5 17 ♗b5 ♖f7

17...♖fd8 18 ♖d1 a6 19 ♗d3 b5 20 0-0 c4 21 ♗c2 a5 22 e4 fxe4 23 fxe4 ♘5f6 24 ♗e1 ♗xe4 25 ♗xe4 ♘xe4 26 ♗xa5 was more or less equal in Draško-Kir.Georgiev, Yugoslavia 1991.

18 0-0 a6 19 ♗d3 b5 20 ♖ac1 c4 21 ♗c2 e5 22 dxe5 ♘xe5

Black's centrally placed knights and queenside majority impress, but White's two bishops are also to be reckoned with.

23 ♖fd1 ♖e8 24 ♘c3 ♘xc3 25 bxc3 g5! 26 ♖d6!? g4 27 fxg4 ♘xg4 28 ♖g6+!? ♔f8 29 ♗g3 ♖xe3 30 ♖d1!

Attempting to weave a mating net.

30...♖f6 31 ♖xf6+ ♘xf6 32 ♗xf5

♗e4 33 ♖d6 ♘e8 34 ♗xe4 ♖xg3 35 ♖xh6 ♖xc3 36 ♖xa6

White has emerged from the complications with a pawn more.

36...♔e7 37 h4 ♘f6 38 ♗f5 ♖b3 39 ♖e6+ ♔f7 40 ♖b6 ♔e7 41 ♖e6+ ♔f7 42 ♖e5! ♔f8 43 ♔h2 c3! 44 ♔g1??

44 g3 ♘h5 45 ♗c2 ♖b2 46 ♖xh5 ♖xc2 47 ♔h3 wins.

44...♖xa3 45 ♖xb5

45...♘g4! 46 ♗xg4

46 ♖b1 ♘e3 47 ♗g6 c2 =.

46...♖a1+ 47 ♔h2 c2 ½-½

White will have to give up his rook for the c-pawn leaving bishop and two pawns against rook, which is a straightforward draw.

Game 35

Graf-Farago
Garmisch-Partenkirchen 1991

1 d4 ♘f6 2 c4 e6 3 ♘c3 ♗b4 4 ♕c2 0-0 5 a3 ♗xc3+ 6 ♕xc3 b6 7 ♗g5 ♗b7 8 f3 h6 9 ♗h4

⇨ 9 ♗f4!? is less troublesome for

Black: 9...d5 10 c5 ♘h5 11 ♘h3 bxc5 12 ♕xc5 ♘xf4 13 ♘xf4 ♘d7 14 ♕c3 ♖c8 15 ♘d3 c5! (a neat equalizing idea) 16 dxc5 ♕h4+ 17 g3 ♕c4 18 ♖c1 ♘xc5 19 ♕xc4 dxc4 20 ♘xc5 ♖xc5 = Ilinčić-Farago, Aosta 1990.

9...d5 10 e3 ♘bd7 11 ♗d3?!

11...dxc4

⇨ 11...♖c8 looks to be effective as well: 12 ♘e2 c5 13 cxd5 cxd4! 14 ♕xd4 e5 15 ♕b4 g5 16 ♗f2 ♘xd5 17 ♕d2 ♘c5 18 ♗c2 ♕f6 19 b4?! (this is really courting disaster, but if 19 0-0, then 19...♖fd8 is awkward to meet) 19...e4 20 ♘d4 exf3! (with the white king trapped in the centre this type of sacrifice cries out to be played) 21 gxf3 ♘e6 22 ♕d3 ♖xc2! 23 ♘xc2 ♕xf3 24 ♖g1 ♘df4 25 ♕f1 ♖d8 26 ♖g3 ♕e4 27 ♖d1 0-1 because 27...♕xc2 28 ♖xd8+ ♘xd8 29 exf4 ♕c1+ 30 ♔e2 ♗a6+ wins White's queen; Obukhov-Brodsky, Moscow 1991.

12 ♗xc4 ♖c8! 13 ♘e2 c5 14 0-0

14 dxc5 ♖xc5 ∓.

14...cxd4! 15 ♕xd4 e5! 16 ♕d3 ♕e7! ∓ 17 ♗xf6 ♘xf6 18 ♕b3

White is unable to stop Black's next move, as 18 e4?? ♕c5+ picks up the bishop.

18...e4! 19 f4 ♘g4! 20 ♖ac1

This allows a nice combination, but 20 h3 ♘xe3! 21 ♗xf7+ ♕xf7 22 ♕xe3 ♖c2 is also good for Black.

20...♖xc4! 21 ♕xc4

21 ♖xc4 ♗d5 22 ♖fc1 ♗xc4 23 ♖xc4? ♕h4 is extremely painful.

21...♕h4 22 h3 ♘xe3 23 ♕c7 ♘xf1 24 ♕xb7 ♘d2 25 ♕d7 e3

25...♘f3+! 26 gxf3 exf3 is perhaps even clearer.

26 ♖c8? ♘f3+! 27 gxf3 ♕e1+

Picking up White's kingside with check.

28 ♔h2 ♕xe2+ 29 ♔g1 ♕f2+ 30 ♔h1 ♕xf3+ 31 ♔g1 ♕f2+ 32 ♔h1 ♕f1+ 33 ♔h2 ♕xf4+ 0-1

Game 36

Khenkin-Ulybin
Minsk 1990

1 d4 e6 2 c4 ♘f6 3 ♘c3 ♗b4 4 ♕c2 0-0 5 a3 ♗xc3+ 6 ♕xc3 b6 7 ♗g5

♗b7 8 f3 h6 9 ♗h4 d5 10 e3 ♘bd7 11 ♘h3 c5

⇨ 11...♖e8 12 ♘f2 c5 13 cxd5 g5 14 ♗g3 ♘xd5 15 ♕d2 cxd4 16 ♕xd4 e5 17 ♕d2 ♘c5 18 ♗c4 b5 19 ♗a2 ♘f4?! (tempting, but it turns out badly) 20 0-0-0 ♕xd2+ 21 ♖xd2 ♖ac8 22 ♔b1 ♘xg2 23 ♘g4 ♗xf3 24 ♘f6+ ♔g7 25 ♖f1 ♘e4 (if 25...g4 then 26 ♘xe8+ ♖xe8 27 ♗xf7 is possible) 26 ♘xe8+ ♖xe8 27 ♖d7 (now Black is in big trouble) 27...g4 28 ♗xf7 ♖f8 29 ♖xf3! gxf3 30 ♗d5+ ♔f6 31 ♗xe4 ♔e6 32 ♖d3 f2 33 ♗xg2 f1♕+ 34 ♗xf1 ♖xf1+ 35 ♔a2 ♖f3 36 ♖c3 ♔d5 37 e4+ ♔xe4 38 ♖xf3 ♔xf3 39 ♗xe5 1-0 Granda Zuniga-Korchnoi, Las Palmas 1991.

12 cxd5 ♘xd5!?

⇨ 12...cxd4! (an improvement on the older 12...exd5 whereupon 13 ♗b5 ♘e4 14 ♗xd8 ♘xc3 15 bxc3 ♖fxd8 16 a4 ♖ac8 17 ♔d2 ♘b8 18 a5 a6 19 ♗d3 b5 20 ♘f4 ♖c7 21 g4 ♘c6 22 ♖hc1 ♘e7 23 h4 ♘c8 24 ♖g1 g6 25 dxc5 ♖xc5 26 g5 h5 27 ♗xg6! secured a White advantage in Goldin-Ruban, Sochi 1989 since 27...fxg6? 28 ♘e6 wins the exchange) 13 ♕xd4 e5 14 ♕d2 ♗xd5 15 ♘f2 (or 15 ♗b5 ♗e6 16 0-0 ♘c5 17 ♕e2 a6 18 ♖ad1 ♕c8 19 ♗c4 b5 20 ♗xe6 ♕xe6 21 ♘f2 ♖ac8 = Iashvili-Shipov, Belgrade 1992) 15...♗e6! 16 ♗b5 (16 ♗e2 ♘e4! 17 ♗xd8 ♘xd2 18 ♗e7 ♖fe8 ∓) 16...♘c5 17 ♕e2?! (it's probably better to play 17 ♕xd8 ♖fxd8 18 b4 a6! =) 17...a6 18 ♗c4 (18 ♖d1 ♕e7 19 ♗c4 b5 20 ♗xe6 ♕xe6 is also slightly better for Black) 18...♗xc4 19 ♕xc4 ♕d5 20 ♕xd5 ♘xd5 21

♔e2 f6! ∓ (this keeps the white bishop out of play) 22 ♖ad1 ♖fd8 23 ♘d3 ♘b3 24 ♘c1 ♘a5 25 ♖d3 ♘e7 26 ♖hd1 ♖xd3 27 ♘xd3 ♖c8 28 ♖c1 ♖xc1 29 ♘xc1 ♘c4 ½-½ Kramnik-Timoshenko, USSR 1991.

13 ♝xd8 ♘xc3 14 ♝e7

14 bxc3 ♖fxd8 =.

14...♖fe8 15 ♝h4 ♘d5 16 ♝b5 g5!

Not 16...♘xe3? 17 ♔f2! (17 ♝xd7 ♘xg2+ 18 ♔f2 ♘xh4 19 ♝xe8 ♖xe8) 17...♘f5 18 ♝xd7 ♘xh4 19 ♝xe8 ♖xe8 20 dxc5 with a clear plus for White.

17 ♝xd7

17 ♝f2 ♖ed8 18 e4 ♘5f6 19 0-0-0 ♖ac8 20 dxc5 ♘xc5 21 ♖xd8+ ♖xd8 22 ♝xc5 ♖c8 23 b4 bxc5 24 ♔d2 cxb4 25 axb4. Now the position is quite equal, although Black indulged in the winning attempt 25...♘xe4+!? 26 fxe4 ♝xe4 27 ♘f2 ♝xg2 in Shabalov-Ulybin, Minsk 1990.

17...♖ed8 18 ♝f2 ♖xd7 19 dxc5

19 e4 g4! 20 exd5 gxh3 21 dxe6 ♖e8 22 0-0 ♖xe6.

19...bxc5 20 ♖c1 ♝a6!

Offering a pawn to confine the white king.

21 e4

21 ♖xc5 ♖ad8 22 ♖c1 ♘b6.

21...♘b6 22 ♝xc5 ♘a4 23 ♘f2 ♘xb2 24 ♝b4 f5 25 h4 g4 26 fxg4 fxe4 27 ♖h3 ♖f7 28 ♖c2 ♘d3+ 29 ♘xd3 exd3 30 ♖c6 ♖f1+ 31 ♔xf1

It seems that White must allow the pawn to queen since after 31 ♔d2 ♖f2+ 32 ♔d1 ♝b5 33 ♖xe6 ♖c8, the menace of 34...♝a4+ decides.

31...d2+

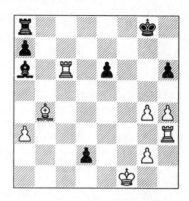

32 ♖xa6 d1♕+ 33 ♔f2 ♕c2+ 34 ♔g1 ♕c4 35 ♖a5 ♖d8 36 ♖f3 ♕xg4 37 ♔h2! ♕xh4+ 38 ♖h3 ♕d4 39 ♝c5 ♕f4+?

I feel that Black should be better here although there are still a few tricks to be negotiated, e.g. 39...♕e5+! 40 ♖g3+ ♔h8 41 ♝e7 ♖d5 42 ♖xa7 ♕f4! 43 ♖a8+ ♔h7 44 ♖a7 ♕b8 with some winning chances.

40 ♖g3+ ♔h8 41 ♝e3! ♕d6?

Black might still draw after 41...♕f7.

42 ♖h5 ♖d7 43 ♝xh6 1-0

Black drops his queen after 43...♖h7 44 ♝g7+ ♔g8 45 ♝e5+.

3 This active reply leads to a more open, tactical, game and has been responsible for some of the most exciting games played with 4 ♕c2. Black also retains the prospect of holding on to his dark-squared bishop, a possibility denied him in most other lines. In one respect it is perhaps even more important than 4...0-0 because after 4...0-0 5 ♘f3 (or 5 ♗g5) 5...c5 6 dxc5 Black finds himself playing a line from this chapter anyway. Therefore anyone who intends playing 4...0-0 must also be prepared to play a defence involving 4...c5.

After 4...c5 White should reply 5 dxc5 when 5...♘a6, which for a long time was considered somewhat inferior, has been stealing all the limelight recently.

6 e3 (game 37) is not too exciting, so the attention of the chess world has been firmly fixed on 6 a3 ♗xc3+ 7 ♕xc3 ♘xc5 when White has two choices: he can either chase the knight with 8 b4, or prepare b4 with 8 f3. Two games of de Firmian's from Manila brought both moves to prominence, and have led to an interesting sequel.

Firstly, in game 38, following 8 b4 ♘ce4, White plays the slightly inferior 9 ♕b2. Although this should be a little better for White, the manner of White's demise has dissuaded players from following in his footsteps.

Next, in game 39, White plays the stronger 9 ♕d4 and on 9...d5 10 c5 Black prepares to evacuate his knight with 10...h6.

In game 40 de Firmian was not content to play so passively and, instead, offered a dangerous piece sacrifice. Ivanchuk, however, with a series of accurate moves, apparently refuted it. That would have been that, if it had not have been for Timman who, armed with some new analysis, subsequently introduced the important innovation 18...♕e5! and won a fine game against Gurevich (game 41).

And the saga continues, with improvements coming thick and fast. It is still far from clear if the sacrifice is sound or not, but one thing is clear: the last word remains to be written.

It seems that White may do best to avoid the complications of 10 c5 and play the quieter 10 cxd5 as in game 44 with chances of a small edge.

Christiansen recently introduced a further possibility for Black, 8...♘a4!?, which is shown in game 45 although it did not fare too well against White's accurate play.

White's other possibility, 8 f3, is examined in games 46 and 47. The other outstanding novelty of de Firmian's at Manila (game 46) featured an improvement over an old game of Rubinstein's. In a very complicated struggle Black managed to keep the initiative and won in fine style. Unfortunately, White can spoil much of Black's fun by playing ♗g5 on move ten.

Game 48 deals with the old move 6...♕a5!? which has come out of mothballs recently, Flear's 12 ♗d4 appears to guarantee White a pleasant advantage in the resulting endgame.

In game 49 we consider 5...♞c6, and in games 50 to 52 the odd-looking move 5...♕c7.

This stops White from playing 6 ♗f4 and prepares counterplay down the c-file. Often, Black adopts a sort of Hedgehog formation; game 51 is a good example of Black's possibilities here. If White is looking for a refutation then 7 b4 ♗e7 8 ♞b5 must be the way, and this certainly looked very convincing in game 52. The ball is firmly in Black's court.

Another move that looks a bit dodgy at the moment is 5...♗xc5. Nowadays this move is played with the intention of continuing with 6...♕b6, and after 7 e3 ♕c7. This apparent waste of a move is justified by the locking in of White's queen's bishop. However, in games 53 and 54 White puts his bishop on b2 and Black finds himself subjected to a violent attack quite soon after the opening, which tends to cast doubt upon the validity of the idea.

And so we arrive at Black's most reputable continuation, 5...0-0, whereby he continues his development and keeps his options open. White's two main options are 6 a3 and 6 ♞f3; other moves are included in the notes to game 55.

Firstly we consider 6 a3 which is covered in games 55 to 57. In game 56 a new move of Arkell's is dealt a crushing blow by White's carefree sacrificial play.

Marshall's manoeuvre 6...♗xc5 7 ♞f3 ♞c6 8 ♗g5 ♞d4 9 ♞xd4 ♗xd4 10 e3 ♕a5 11 exd4 ♕xg5 12 ♕d2 ♕xd2+ leads almost by force to an endgame where White's chances are better; he has more space and an active king. The one bright spot for Black, though, is Ljubojević's idea of 16...♞h5 and 17...f5, looking for kingside counterplay, which is considered in game 57.

The final games in this chapter deal with the principal line 6 ♞f3 ♞a6 7 g3 (7 ♗g5 and 7 ♗d2 are discussed in game 58) 7...♞xc5.

8 ♗d2 should not give Black too many problems (game 59) so that White's attention has focused on 8 ♗g2 when Black's best choice would seem to be 8...♞ce4; lesser alternatives are dealt with in game 60. White probably does best to avoid doubled pawns here by 9 ♗d2 although Black may be just fine after the 11...d4 of Korchnoi-Greenfeld, or one of the variations discussed in game 61. The move 9 0-0, which is much in vogue, needs some repairs after the defeat White suffered at the hands of Karpov (15...♞e8!) in game 62.

Game 37

P.Nikolić-Gelfand
Sarajevo Ct (6) 1991

1 d4 ♞f6 2 c4 e6 3 ♞c3 ♗b4 4 ♕c2 c5 5 dxc5

This is almost invariably played, although 5 ♞f3 is legal: 5...0-0 6 a3 ♗xc3+ 7 bxc3 (7 ♕xc3?! cxd4 8 ♕xd4 ♞c6 9 ♕h4 d5 10 cxd5 ♕xd5 11 ♗g5 ♞d7 12 e4 ♕b3 13 ♖b1 ♕c2 14 ♞d2 ♞c5 15 b4 f6! 16 bxc5 fxg5 17 ♕xg5 ♖d8 18 ♖d1 h6 19 ♕e3 ♞e5 20 ♗e2 ♞d3+ and White

was already in big trouble in Yak-
ovich-Karpov, Moscow Tal mem
(active) 1992) 7...d5 8 e3 b6 9 ♗b2
♗a6 10 cxd5 ♗xf1 11 ♔xf1 ♕xd5
12 c4 ♕c6 13 ♘e5 ♕c7 14 dxc5
♕xc5 15 ♗d4 ♕c7 16 ♕b2 ♘e4 17
♕c2 ♘d6 18 c5 ♖c8 19 ♖c1 bxc5 20
♗a1 f6 21 ♘d3 ♘d7 22 ♘f4 ♘f8 23
g4 with vague attacking chances to
compensate for his pawn less; Dydy-
shko-Lerner, St. Petersburg 1992.

5...♘a6 6 e3

⇨ 6 e4? ♘xc5 7 f3 d5 8 cxd5 exd5 9
a3 ♗xc3+ 10 ♕xc3 ♘e6 11 e5 d4 12
♕b4 ♘d5 13 ♕b5+ ♕d7 14 ♘h3
0-0 15 f4 ♕d8 16 ♗d2 a6 17 ♕e2
♖e8 18 0-0-0 ♘c5 19 ♕h5 g6 20
♕h6 ♗f5 21 ♗c4 ♕c7 22 ♗c3
(White is lost, for example 22 ♗xd5
♘b3#) 22...♘xc3 23 ♖xd4 ♘e2+ 24
♔d1 ♖xd4 25 ♘g5 ♗c2+ 26 ♔e1
♖xe5+ 0-1 Nguyen-Grünfeld, Manila OL 1992.

**6...♘xc5 7 ♗d2 0-0 8 ♘f3 b6 9
♗e2 ♗a6 10 0-0 d5 11 cxd5 ♗xc3?!
12 ♗xc3 ♘xd5 13 ♗xa6 ♘xa6 14
♗d4 ♕d7?! 15 ♘g5 f5 16 ♘f3
♘ab4 17 ♕e2 ♘c6 18 ♖ad1 ♖ac8
19 ♖fe1 ♘xd4 20 ♖xd4 ♕c6 21 h3
♘f6 22 ♖ed1 ♕c2?!**

22...♖fe8!? ±.

**23 ♖4d2 ♕c4 24 ♕xc4 ♖xc4 25
♘e5**

White has a distinct edge due to
the well-placed knight on e5 and
control of the d-file.

**25...♖c7 26 ♖d6 ♖e8 27 ♖c6! ±
♖xc6 28 ♘xc6 ♔f7 29 ♖d6 ♖c8 30
♘xa7 ♖c1+ 31 ♔h2 ♘e4 32 ♖d7+
♔f6 33 f3 ♘c5 34 ♖d2 ♖e1 35 ♘c8
b5 36 ♘d6 b4 37 ♖d4?!**

37 ♘c4 is preferable.

37...♖xe3 38 ♖xb4 ♖e2 39 a4

♘d3 40 ♖b7 ♘f4

As Black can do little to directly
stop White's queenside pawns from
queening, his only chance for counterplay is to generate threats around
the white king.

**41 a5 ♔xg2+ 42 ♔h1 ♖d2 43
♘e8+? ♔g5 44 ♔g1 ♔h4 45 ♔f1?**

45 ♖xg7 ♖xb2 46 a6 is unclear.

**45...♔g3 46 ♔e1 ♖d8 47 ♘c7
♘g2+ 48 ♔e2 ♘f4+ 49 ♔e1 ♖d3 50
a6 ♘g2+ 51 ♔e2 ♘f4+ 52 ♔e1
♔xf3 53 ♖b3**

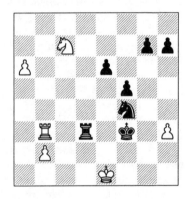

**53...♘g2+ 54 ♔f1 ♘e3+ 55 ♔g1
♖xb3!! 56 a7 ♖d3 57 a8♕+ ♔g3**

White has to return his new queen
immediately to stop mate.

**58 ♕a1 ♖d1+ 59 ♕xd1 ♘xd1 60
♘xe6 g6 61 b4 f4! 62 ♘c5 ♘c3 63
♘d3 g5 64 ♘f2 h5 65 ♔f1 ♔h2 0-1**

Game 38

Greenfeld-Mokry
Haifa 1989

1 d4 ♘f6 2 c4 e6 3 ♘c3 ♗b4 4 ♕c2
c5 5 dxc5 ♘a6 6 a3 ♗xc3+ 7 ♕xc3

♘xc5 8 b4 ♘ce4 9 ♕b2 d5 10 c5 h6

10...d4!? is probably too loosening: 11 e3! e5 (11...♘g4!? 12 ♗b5+ ♔f8 13 ♘h3 dxe3 14 f3 ♘ef2 15 ♘xf2 exf2+ 16 ♔e2 a6 17 ♗a4 ♘f6 18 ♗g5 ♗d7? {a terrible blunder that loses a piece} 19 ♗xf6 gxf6 20 ♖hd1 +− Hoeksema-Grosar, Groningen 1991) 12 ♗b5+ ♗d7 13 ♗xd7+ ♕xd7 14 ♘f3 ♘g4 15 0-0 0-0-0 16 exd4?! (16 h3! h5 17 exd4 exd4 18 ♗f4 ±) 16...exd4 17 ♗d2 ♖he8! (Black's pieces have taken up active posts but there is a risk that his king may become exposed when the white queenside advances) 18 ♖ac1 ♘e5 19 ♘xe5 ♖xe5 20 ♗f4 ♖d5 21 b5 ♕f5 22 b6 a6 (22...♕xf4? 23 bxa7 ♔c7 24 ♕b6+ ♔d7 25 ♕xb7+ and 26 a8♕ ±) 23 ♗c7 ♖e8 24 c6 d3 25 ♗g3 ♘c5 (Black must block the c-file) 26 ♖fe1 ♖xe1+ 27 ♖xe1 ♘e6! ∓ 28 h3 d2 29 ♖d1 ♕e4 30 f3?! ♕d4+ 31 ♕xd4 ♘xd4 32 cxb7+ ♔xb7 33 ♔f2 ♘b5 34 ♗f4 ♘xa3 35 ♖xd2 ♖xd2+ 36 ♗xd2 ♘c4 37 ♗c3 f6 38 g4 ♘xb6 and after all the excitement, Black has a winning ending; Remlinger-Chekhov, Gausdal 1991.

11 ♘h3?

11 f3 first is better. After 11...♘g5:

⇨ 12 ♗f4 ♘h5 13 ♗d6 f5 14 e3 ± ♘f7 15 ♗b5+ ♗d7 16 ♗xd7+ ♕xd7 17 ♗e5 0-0 18 ♘e2 ♕b5 19 ♗d4 ♖ae8 20 f4 ♘d8 21 a4 ♕d7 22 b5 ♘f6 23 0-0. White's queenside pawns and strong bishop give him a plus; Lputian-Zaichik, Moscow 1989.

⇨ 12 ♕e5 ♘gh7 13 ♗b2 0-0 14 e3 ♘e8 15 ♗d3 ♗d7 16 ♘e2 b6 17 ♖c1

bxc5 18 ♖xc5 ♘hf6 19 0-0 ♗a4 20 ♖a5 ♘d7 21 ♕g3 ♘b6 22 ♘d4 ♕d6 23 ♖c1 ♗d7 24 f4 g6 25 e4 dxe4 26 ♗xe4 ♘d5 27 ♘f5! exf5 28 ♗xd5 ♖c8 29 ♖xc8 ♗xc8 30 ♗e5. White's pieces have taken up powerful positions, and he went on to win in the game Kharlov-Tunik, Budapest 1992.

11...d4 12 f3

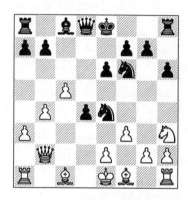

12...e5!! 13 fxe4 ♗xh3 14 gxh3 ♘xe4 15 ♗g2 ♕h4+ 16 ♔d1 ♘c3+! 17 ♔c2 ♕h5! 18 e4

White has to block the b1-h7 diagonal; 18 ♖e1? ♕g6+ wins on the spot.

18...♕g6 19 ♖g1 ♘xe4 20 ♗xe4 ♕xe4+

For the piece sacrificed, Black has severely compromised the white king and has picked up several pawns to boot.

21 ♔d1 0-0-0 22 ♕b3?

A serious error because the queen has to return next move; 22 ♕e2 was the only chance, and then 22...♕d5 is unclear.

22...d3 23 ♕b2 ♕f3+ 24 ♔e1 ♖d4 25 ♖g4 f5! 0-1

Game 39

M.Gurevich-Korchnoi
Wijk aan Zee 1990

1 d4 ♘f6 2 c4 e6 3 ♘c3 ♗b4 4 ♕c2 c5 5 dxc5 ♘a6 6 a3 ♗xc3+ 7 ♕xc3 ♘xc5 8 b4 ♘ce4 9 ♕d4 d5 10 c5 h6 11 ♘h3!?

The most ambitious, attempting to stop the e4 knight's escape. Instead, with 11 f3 ♘g5 12 h4 ♘gh7 13 g4 0-0 14 g5 ♘h5 15 ♗b2 b6! 16 gxh6 f6 17 ♕g4 ♕e8 18 hxg7 ♘xg7 19 cxb6 e5 20 ♕g2 White is trying to attack without developing any pieces; Hjartarson-Timman, Reykjavik 1991.

11...0-0 12 f3 e5!? 13 ♕xe5 ♖e8 14 ♕d4 ♗xh3 15 gxh3 ♘g5

It is difficult to believe that Black really has enough compensation for the pawn and bishop pair, but judging by his readiness to return most of his gains, Gurevich at least was convinced.

16 ♗xg5 hxg5 17 ♖g1 ♘h5!
This is better than 17...♘d7 18

♖d1 (18 f4! ♘f8 19 fxg5 is clearly better for White) 18...♘e5 19 ♔f2 ♕f6 20 h4 g4 21 ♖g3 ♖ad8? 22 f4 ♕f5 23 h3 ♔f8 24 e3?! (24 ♗g2!) 24...♘c6 25 hxg4 ♕h7! 26 ♕d3 ♕xh4 27 ♔f3 ♖e4 28 ♖h3 which gave rise to a very wild position in Petursson-Korchnoi, Wijk aan Zee 1990.

18 h4! gxh4 19 ♖d1 ♕f6?!
19...a5! is more accurate: 20 ♕xd5 ♕f6! 21 ♕xh5 ♕c3+ 22 ♔f2 ♕e3+ with the further point that 23 ♔g2? may be met by the reply 23...♖e5 ∓.

20 ♖g4! ♖e5!
20...♕xf3 21 ♖d3 ♕f5 22 ♗h3.

21 f4!? ♖e4 22 ♕xf6 ♘xf6 23 ♖xh4 ♖ae8?
23...a5! 24 ♗g2 ♖c4 25 ♗xd5 ♘xd5 26 ♖xd5 g6! would have led to equality.

24 ♖h3! a5 25 ♖b3 ± ♖xf4 26 ♗g2?!
26 bxa5 maintains White's advantage.

26...♖g4 27 ♗f3 a4! 28 ♖bd3 ♖h4 29 ♗xd5 ♘xd5 30 ♖xd5 ♖xh2 31 ♖1d2 ♖e3 32 ♖5d3! ♖e5
32...♖hxe2+ would produce a comical situation, but loses after the continuation 33 ♖xe2 ♖xd3 34 ♖e7 ♖xa3 35 ♖xb7.

33 ♖c2 g5 34 b5 ♖h1+ 35 ♔d2 ♖h2 36 ♔e1 ♖h1+ 37 ♔d2 ♖h2 38 ♖e3 ♖d5+ 39 ♔e1 ♔g7 40 c6 bxc6 41 bxc6 ♖h8 42 ♖e4! ♖a5 43 ♖d4 ♖c8 44 c7 ♔f6?
44...♖a7 45 ♖d7 is just slightly better for White.

45 ♖d8 ♖aa8 46 ♖cd2! ± ♔f5 47 ♔f2 ♔g4 48 ♖2d4+ ♔h5 49 ♔f3 ♔g6 50 ♔e4 1-0

Game 40

Ivanchuk-de Firmian
Manila IZ 1990

1 d4 ♘f6 2 c4 e6 3 ♘c3 ♗b4 4 ♕c2
c5 5 dxc5 ♘a6 6 a3 ♗xc3+ 7 ♕xc3
♘xc5 8 b4 ♘ce4 9 ♕d4 d5 10 c5

Threatening to win the e4 knight.
Instead after 10 f3 ♘d6 11 c5 ♘f5 12
♕e5 ♘d7 13 ♕b2 0-0 14 ♘h3 e5 15
e4 dxe4 16 fxe4 ♘d4 17 ♗e3 ♘xc5
(a bit desperate, but otherwise White
has a large strategic plus) 18 bxc5
♗xh3 19 ♗xd4 exd4 20 gxh3 ♕h4+
21 ♔d1 d3 22 ♖g1 g6 23 ♗xd3 ♖fd8
24 ♖g3 ♕xe4 25 ♔c2 ♕d5 26 ♖f1
♕xc5+ 27 ♔b1 ♖d6 28 ♗c2 ♖d2 29
♖c3 ♕e7 30 ♖cf3 ♖f8 31 ♕c3 ♖d7
32 ♗b3 White had successfully rear-
ranged his pieces and went on to win
in Šahović-Marić, Yugoslav Ch
1991.

**10...b6!? 11 f3 bxc5 12 bxc5
♕a5+**

⇨ Perhaps 12...0-0 is playable as
well: 13 fxe4 ♘xe4 14 ♘f3 ♖b8!
(better than the original 14...f6?! 15
g3 e5 16 ♕e3 ± Gavrikov-Tolnai,
Budapest 1988) 15 e3 f6 16 ♗e2 e5
17 ♕d1 ♕a5+ 18 ♗d2 ♕xc5 19 0-0
♖b2! 20 ♔h1 ♘xd2 (20...♗e6!?) 21
♘xd2 ♗e6! (not 21...♕xe3? 22
♘c4!! dxc4 23 ♗xc4+ ♔h8 24 ♕d6!
♖e8 25 ♖xf6! producing a winning
attack from nowhere) 22 ♕e1 ♕xe3
23 ♗g4 ♕b6 24 ♗xe6+ ♕xe6 ∓ 25
♖c1 ♕g4 26 ♖f2 ½-½ Vilela-Le-
bredo, Havana 1991.

13 ♕b4 ♕c7

Forced; 13...♕xb4+? 14 axb4
♘c3 15 ♗b2 ♘b5 16 e4 ♗d7 17

♗xf6 gxf6 18 exd5 exd5 19 ♗xb5
♗xb5 20 ♘e2 ♔d7 21 ♘d4 ± Anas-
tasian-Ipek, Manila OL 1992.

**14 fxe4 ♖b8 15 ♕a4+ ♗d7 16
c6!?**

16...0-0!

If 16...♗xc6 17 ♗f4! is the point
of White's play.

17 ♗d2 ♗xc6 18 ♕a5 ♖b6

18...♕xa5 19 ♗xa5 ♘xe4 20
♗b4! ±.

**19 e3 ♖fb8 20 ♖c1 ♘xe4 21 ♘f3
♕e7?**

21...♘xd2 22 ♕xd2 ♕e7 23 ♗d3
with just an edge for White.

22 ♗b4 ±

Obstructing the b-file and rendering Black's doubled rooks redun-
dant.

**22...♕b7 23 ♗d3 ♗b5 24 ♗xe4
dxe4 25 ♘d4 ♗d3 26 ♔f2 f6 27
♖he1 h6 28 ♔g1**

White finally manages to castle
by hand.

**28...♕f7 29 ♘c6 ♖a8 30 ♘e7+
♔h7 31 ♘c8 ♖b5 32 ♕c7 ♕h5 33
♖c5 ♖xc5 34 ♗xc5 a5 35 ♗f8 ♕g5
36 ♕b7 ♖a6 37 ♘d6 ♕g6 38 ♘e8!
♔g8 39 ♘c7 1-0**

Game 41

M.Gurevich-Timman
Linares 1991

1 d4 ♘f6 2 c4 e6 3 ♘c3 ♗b4 4 ♕c2 c5 5 dxc5 ♘a6 6 a3 ♗xc3+ 7 ♕xc3 ♘xc5 8 b4 ♘ce4 9 ♕d4 d5 10 c5 b6 11 f3 bxc5 12 bxc5 ♕a5+ 13 ♕b4 ♕c7 14 fxe4 ♖b8 15 ♕a4+ ♗d7 16 c6 0-0 17 ♗d2 ♗xc6 18 ♕a5 ♕e5!?

Since 18...♖b6 and the doubling of rooks achieved little in the last game.

19 ♖c1 ♘xe4 20 ♘f3 ♕b2! 21 e3 ♗b5 22 ♕b4 ♗xf1 23 ♕xb2 ♖xb2 24 ♖xf1

Normally it would be considered an achievement to reach an endgame when material up, but here White still has considerable problems to negotiate.

24...♖fb8 25 ♗c3?!

25 g4 is better.

25...♖xg2 26 ♗e5 ♖a8 ∓ 27 ♖g1?

Presumably the point of White's play, but he has overlooked a tactical point.

27...♘d2! 28 ♖xg2 ♘xf3+ 29 ♔f1 ♘xe5 30 ♖c7 ♘c4 31 ♖e2 ♘xa3 32 ♖a2 ♘b5 33 ♖b7 ♘d6 34 ♖axa7 ♖f8

With all the pawns on one side of the board, the knight is a particularly effective piece, making this a fairly trivial win.

35 ♖d7 ♘e4 36 ♔e2 ♘f6 37 ♖dc7 g6 38 ♔f3 g5 39 ♖e7 h5 40 ♖ab7 ♘g4 41 h3 ♘e5+ 42 ♔g3 ♘g6 43 ♖ec7 ♔g7 44 e4 dxe4 45 ♖b4 h4+ 46 ♔h2 ♖a8 47 ♖xe4 ♘f4 48 ♖e5 ♔g6 49 ♖c3 f5 50 ♖f3 ♔f6 51 ♖b5 ♖a4 52 ♖b8 g4 53 hxg4 fxg4 54 ♖f8+ ♔e5 55 ♖f1 g3+ 56 ♔g1 h3 57 ♖e1+ ♖e4 58 ♖a1 ♘e2+ 59 ♔h1 g2+ 60 ♔h2 ♖g4 61 ♔xh3 ♖g3+ 0-1

Game 42

Shirov-Lautier
Biel 1991

1 d4 ♘f6 2 c4 e6 3 ♘c3 ♗b4 4 ♕c2 c5 5 dxc5 ♘a6 6 a3 ♗xc3+ 7 ♕xc3 ♘xc5 8 b4 ♘ce4 9 ♕d4 d5 10 c5 b6 11 f3 bxc5 12 bxc5 ♕a5+ 13 ♕b4 ♕c7 14 fxe4 ♖b8 15 ♕a4+ ♗d7 16 c6 0-0 17 ♗d2 ♗xc6 18 ♕a5 ♕e5 19 ♗c3!?

White's turn to reinforce the theory.

19...♕xe4

At the time of writing 19...♕f4!? is the last word in this position:

⇨ 20 ♘h3 ♕h4+ 21 g3 ♕xe4 22 ♘f2 ♖b1+ 23 ♔d2 ♕g6 24 ♖xb1 ♕xb1 25 ♕b4 ♕f5 26 ♗xf6 ♕xf6 27 ♘g4 ♕g5+ 28 ♕f4 ♕e7 29 ♕b4 ♕g5+ 30 ♕f4 ♕e7 31 ♕b4 ½-½ Nadera-Antonio, Cebu 1992.

⇨ 20 ♗xf6 ♕xf6 21 e5!? ♕xe5 22 ♖c1 ♕f4! 23 ♕d2 ♕d6 24 ♘f3 ♖fc8 25 ♕d4?! (25 ♔e3!?) 25...♕xa3 26 ♖a1 ♕d6 27 ♖xa7 ♖b4! 28 ♕d2 ♗a4! ∓ (surrounding the rook on a7) 29 e3 ♕b6 30 ♔f2 ♖b2 31 ♖xa4 ♖xd2+ 32 ♘xd2 ♕b2 33 ♖d4 ♖c2 34 ♔e1 ♖a1+ 35 ♔e2 ♕a2! 36 g3 e5 37 ♖d3 ♕a6! 38 ♔d1 ♖c5? (38...♖a2 39 ♖xd5 ♖a1+ 40 ♔c2 ♕a2+ finishes the game immediately) 39 ♖b3 ♕a4 40 ♔e2 ♕g4+ 41 ♔f2 h5 42 ♗d3 e4 43 ♗b1 ♕h3 (with the threat of ...♖c6-f6) 0-1 Kiss-Stoica, Romania 1991.

20 ♗xf6 gxf6 21 ♘f3 d4! 22 ♕d2 e5 23 h4?!

23...♕g6?
Missing 23...♖b3! 24 ♖h3 ♖e3! ∓.
24 ♔f2 ♔h8 25 h5! ♕g7 26 ♖c1 ♖b6 27 g4! e4? 28 ♕xd4
Returning the piece for a positional advantage.
28...exf3 29 h6! ♕g6 30 exf3 ♗b7 31 ♗d3 ♕g5 32 ♖b1 ♖xb1 33 ♗xb1 ♕e5 34 ♕xe5?
34 ♕d3 is better.
34...fxe5 35 ♗f5 ♗c8 36 ♖c1 ♗xf5 37 gxf5

Black's difficulties arise from his king, trapped on the back rank by the h6 pawn.
37...♖b8 38 ♖c7 ♔g8 39 ♔e3! ♔f8 40 f6! ♔e8 41 ♖e7+ ♔f8 42 ♖xa7 ♔e8 43 ♔e4 ♖b1 44 a4 ♖h1 45 a5 ♖xh6 46 ♔xe5 ♖h1 47 a6 1-0

Game 43

Forintos-Aseev
Sestola 1991

1 d4 ♘f6 2 c4 e6 3 ♘c3 ♗b4 4 ♕c2 c5 5 dxc5 ♘a6 6 a3 ♗xc3+ 7 ♕xc3 ♘xc5 8 b4 ♘ce4 9 ♕d4 d5 10 c5 b6 11 f3 bxc5 12 bxc5 ♕a5+ 13 ♕b4 ♕c7 14 fxe4 ♖b8 15 ♕a4+ ♗d7 16 ♕c2!?

An additional possibility for White.
16...♘xe4
⇨ Improving on the original game in this line which continued 16...0-0?! 17 exd5 ♕e5 18 ♖a2 ♖fc8 19 ♘f3 ♕xd5 20 e4! ± (developing *à tempo*) 20...♘xe4 21 ♗c4 ♕xc5 22 ♕xe4 ♗b5 23 ♗e3 ♕xc4 24 ♕xc4 ♗xc4 25 ♖c2 ♖b1+ 26 ♗c1 ♗a6 (Black's two extra pawns are scant compensation for the piece) 27 ♖xc8+ ♗xc8 28 ♔d2 ♗b7 29 ♖e1 ♗d5 30 ♖e3 h6 31 g3 ♔h7 32 ♘d4 ♖b6 33 ♘e2 ♖b6 34 ♖c3 ♗b7 35 ♖c5 ♖d7 36 ♗b2 f6 37 ♘f4 ♗a2+ 38 ♔e2 e5 39 ♘d3 ♗d5 40 ♗c1 ♗e4 41 ♘b4 ♗b7 42 ♖a5 1-0 Savchenko-Gezalian, Balassagyarmat 1990.
17 ♘f3 ♗b5 18 ♗e3 0-0 19 ♖c1 ♖fb8 20 c6 ♖b2 21 ♕a4 ♖b1 22 ♕c2
White is unlikely to fall for 22

cxd7?? ♕c3+ 23 ♔d1 ♘f2+ (or, of course, 23...♖c1+ first) 24 ♗xf2 ♖c1#.

22...♖1b2 23 ♕a4 ♖b1 24 ♕c2 ♕a5+

Black decides that he can play for the win, probably on the grounds that White's kingside will take quite some unravelling.

25 ♗d2 ♘xd2 26 ♘xd2 ♖xc1+ 27 ♕xc1 ♖c8 28 ♕b2 ♖xc6 29 ♕b4 ♕c7 30 g3 a5 31 ♕h4?!

The queen does little to help the defence here.

31...e5 32 e3 ♖f6

33 ♗e2 ♕c1+ 34 ♗d1 ♕c3 35 ♗e2 ♕c1+ 36 ♗d1 ♕xa3 37 e4 ♕e3+ 38 ♗e2 ♗b5 39 ♕g4 h5 40 ♕xh5 ♖f2 0-1

Game 44

Hort-de Firmian
Biel 1990

1 d4 ♘f6 2 c4 e6 3 ♘c3 ♗b4 4 ♕c2 c5 5 dxc5 ♘a6 6 a3 ♗xc3+ 7 ♕xc3 ♘xc5 8 b4 ♘ce4 9 ♕d4 d5 10 cxd5!?

This is less ambitious than 10 c5, but assures White a small advantage and avoids the complications of de Firmian's piece sacrifice.

10...exd5

⇨ 10...0-0!? might be the best move: 11 ♘f3 a5! (weakening White's queenside, and better than 11...♕xd5 12 ♗b2 b6 13 e3 ♗b7 14 ♕xd5 ♗xd5 15 ♗d3 ♖fd8 16 ♘e5 ♖ac8 17 f3 ♘d6 18 ♔e2 ± Finegold-Vanheste, Groningen 1991) 12 b5 ♕xd5 13 ♕xd5 ♘xd5 14 e3 ♗d7 15 ♘e5 ♗e8 16 f3 ♘c5 17 a4 ♘c3 18 ♗c4 ♘3xa4 19 ♗a3 f6 20 ♘d3 ♘xd3+ 21 ♗xd3 ♖f7 22 ♗c4 ♗d7 23 ♔f2 ♘b6 24 ♗a2 ♘d5 25 ♖hd1 ♗xb5 26 e4 ♘c7 27 ♗d6 ♗c6 when Black should have some winning chances despite White's active bishops; Bönsch-Tischbierek, Hannover 1991.
⇨ 10...♕xd5 11 ♗b2 0-0 12 f3 ♘d6 13 ♖d1 ♕xd4 14 ♖xd4 ♘f5 15 ♖d3 b6 16 e4 ♘e7 17 ♖d6 ♘g6 18 h4 h5 19 g3 ♗b7 20 ♖h2! (White chooses an unusual, but effective, way of developing his kingside) 20...♖fd8 21 ♖hd2 ♖xd6 22 ♖xd6 ♘e8 23 ♖d2 ♖c8 24 ♗b5 ♘c7 25 ♗a4 f6 26 ♘e2 e5 27 ♗b3+ ♔h7 28 ♔f2 ♘f8 29 ♔e3 (White has a clear advantage) 29...♘ce6 30 f4 exf4+ 31 gxf4 ♗a6 32 f5 ♘d8 33 ♘f4 ♘c6 34 ♘e6 ♘e5 35 ♗xe5 fxe5 36 ♘g5+ ♔h8 37 ♔f2 ♖c3 38 b5 ♖xb3 39 ♖d8 ♔g8 40 bxa6 ♖xa3 41 ♘e6 ♖xa6 42 ♖xf8+ 1-0 Scherbakov-Hlavnicka, Pardubice 1992.

11 ♗b2 0-0 12 e3 ♘d6 13 ♘f3 ♗f5 14 ♗e2 ♗e4 15 0-0 ±

In my opinion this is not a favourable IQP position for Black because he has no method of impeding

b3 a4 23 ♗xa4 ♘xb2

4 ♖xe5! ♕xe5 25 ♗d4 ♕f5+ 26
...b2

To all intents and purposes the
...me is over.

...26...♖fd8 27 ♗c3 ♖xd1 28 ♕xd1
...e5 29 ♕d3 h5 30 ♗c2 g6 31 f4
...f8 32 a4 ♖c8 33 f5 gxf5 34 ♕g3+
...f8 35 ♕g7+ ♔e8 36 ♕h8+ 1-0

Game 48

.Flear-Franco
Palma 1991

1 d4 ♘f6 2 c4 e6 3 ♘c3 ♗b4 4 ♕c2
...c5 5 dxc5 ♘a6 6 a3 ♕a5!? 7 ♗d2
♘xc5 8 ♖c1!?

By relieving the pin White
obliges Black to capture on c3.

Alternatively:

⇨ 8 ♘f3 d6 (8...♗xc3!? 9 ♗xc3
♕a4 10 ♕xa4?! ♘xa4 11 ♗xf6 gxf6
12 0-0-0 ♘c5 13 ♘d2 a5 14 g3 a4 15
♗g2 f5 16 ♔c2 ♔e7 and Black is already looking to take the advantage;
A.Marić – Akhmylovskaya-Donaldson, Novi Sad OL wom 1990) 9 ♘b5

♗xd2+ 10 ♘xd2 ♕b6 11 b4 ♘cd7
12 ♖d1 (12 ♕d3 ♗e7 13 ♘f3 a6 14
♘c3 a5 is fine) 12...a6 13 ♘c3
♕c6!? 14 e4 0-0 15 ♗e2 b6 16 0-0
♗b7 17 ♕d3 ♖fd8 18 ♖fe1 ♖ac8 19
♕e3 ♕c7 20 f4 ♘f8 21 ♘a4 ♘8d7
22 ♘b2 ♕b8 23 ♘d3 b5 24 cxb5
axb5 25 ♘f2 ♗c6 with a very promising 'Hedgehog' type position for
Black; M.Gurevich-Korchnoi, Amsterdam 1991.

⇨ 8 f3 ♗xc3 (hardly forced) 9 ♗xc3
♕a4 10 ♕xa4 ♘xa4 11 ♗d4 d6 12
0-0-0 ♔e7 13 b3 ♘c5 14 ♔b2 e5 15
♗f2 a6 16 e4 ♗e6 17 ♘e2 b5 18
♘c3 bxc4 19 ♗xc5 dxc5 20 ♗xc4
♖hd8 21 ♗xe6 fxe6 22 ♘a4 ♘d7 23
♖d3 with advantage to White because of Black's weak pawns; Obukhov-Tunik, Krasnodar 1991.

⇨ 8 b3!? 0-0 9 ♘f3? d6 10 ♖a2
♗xc3 11 ♗xc3 ♕d8! 12 e3 e5 13
b4? ♘ce4! ∓ 14 ♗a1 ♗e6 15 ♗d3
♖c8! (Black is relying on this tactic;
if 16 ♗xe4? then 16...♖xc4 ∓) 16 a4
a5 17 b5 ♘c5 and Black has the edge
(solid centre and a good square on
c5); Yudasin-Korchnoi, Pamplona
1991.

**8...♗xc3 9 ♗xc3 ♕a4 10 b4
♕xc2 11 ♖xc2 ♘a4!**

Again, this funny knight move to
the edge of the board, but it does
have an influence here; the alternative, 11...♘ce4?!, certainly does not
impress after 12 ♗a1! d5 13 c5 h6 14
♘f3 ♘g5 15 h4!? ♘gh7 16 e3.

12 ♗d4!

⇨ Stronger than 12 ♗xf6!? (12 ♗e5
♔e7! 13 ♖d2 ♘e8! 14 e4 d6 15 ♗g3
b6) 12...gxf6 13 e4 a5! 14 ♗d3
♖g8?! (14...d6 15 f4! ♔e7 16 ♔f2
♗d7 17 ♘f3 axb4 18 axb4 ♘b6 =)

White's pressure along the a1-h8 diagonal.

**15...♘c4 16 ♗c3! a6 17 ♘d2
♘xd2 18 ♕xd2 ♖e8 19 ♖fd1 h6 20
♖ac1 ♘h7 21 ♕d4! ±**

21...♘f6

If 21...f6? then 22 ♗c4! wins the
d-pawn, 22...dxc4? 23 ♕xc4+ being
impossible.

**22 ♗b2 ♖c8 23 ♖xc8?! ♕xc8 24
♖c1 ♕e6 25 h3 ♖c8 26 ♖c5 ♖xc5 27
♕xc5**

Even after the exchange of rooks
White's advantage persists.

**27...♘e8! 28 ♗d4 ♘d6 29 ♕c7
b5 30 ♗g4 ♗f5 31 ♗h5 ♘c4?! 32
♕d8+ ♔h7 33 ♕f8 f6 34 ♗f7 ♕c8
35 ♕e7 ♕d7 36 ♕xd7 ♗xd7 37
♗xd5 ♘xa3 38 ♗b7 ♘c4 39 ♗xa6
♗c6 40 f3 ♔g6 41 ♔f2 ♔f7 42 h4
♘d6 43 ♗c5! ♗b7**

If 43...♔e6 44 e4 ±, but White
will win anyway.

**44 ♗xb7 ♘xb7 45 h5! f5 46
♗b6! ♘d6 47 ♔e2 g6 48 hxg6+
♔xg6 49 ♔d3 ♘c4 50 ♗c7 h5 51
♔d4 ♘f6 52 ♗f4 ♔e6 53 ♗c5 ♘a3
54 ♗g3 ♘c4 55 ♗f2 ♘d6 56 ♔c6!
♔e7 57 ♗h4+ ♔e6 58 ♗g5! 1-0**

Game 45

M.Gurevich-Christiansen
Munich 1992

1 d4 ♘f6 2 c4 e6 3 ♘c3 ♗b4 4 ♕c2
c5 5 dxc5 ♘a6 6 a3 ♗xc3+ 7 ♕xc3
♘xc5 8 b4 ♘a4!?

Ignoring Lasker's advice, for he
has an interesting idea in mind.

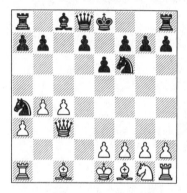

9 ♕c2 b5 10 cxb5 ♘b6

Black has a central majority and a
certain amount of activity for his
pawn.

**11 ♘f3 ♗b7 12 e3 ♖c8 13 ♕d1
♘e4 14 ♗b2 0-0 15 ♗e2 ♘c4 16
♗d4 d6 17 0-0 e5 18 ♖c1!**

Better than 18 ♗xa7 ♖a8 when
there is the likelihood that Black will
recover one or more pawns.

**18...♘b6 19 ♗xb6 axb6 20 ♕b3
♕f6 21 ♕b2! h5?!**

This weakness will take on
greater import later.

**22 ♘d2 ♖xc1 23 ♕xc1 ♖c8 24
♘xe4 ♕g6 25 ♕d1! ♗xe4 26 ♗f3
♗xf3 27 ♕xf3 ♕d3 28 ♕b7! ♖c3 29
♕xb6 ♖xa3 30 h3 ♖b3 31 ♕c6 ♔h7**

32 ♕f3 ♕g6 33 ♖d1 ♖xb4

Despite regaining his pawn, Black finds that he is worse.

34 ♕e2 ♔g8 35 ♔h2 ♕e6 36 ♖d2! ± e4 37 ♕xh5 f5 38 ♕g5 ♕e5+ 39 g3 ♖xb5 40 ♕d8+ ♔f7 41 ♕d7+ ♔g8 42 ♖xd6

It's not the extra pawn so much as Black's exposed king that decides this position.

42...♔h7 43 ♔g2 ♖a5 44 ♖e6! ♕b8 45 ♕f7 ♖e5 46 ♖g6 1-0

Game 46 CML

Miles-de Firmian
Manila IZ 1990

1 d4 ♘f6 2 c4 e6 3 ♘c3 ♗b4 4 ♕c2 c5 5 dxc5 ♘a6 6 a3 ♗xc3+ 7 ♕xc3 ♘xc5 8 f3 d5 9 cxd5 b6!?

This pawn offer is the natural consequence of 8...d5.

⇨ 9...♕xd5 leads to a clear advantage for White after 10 e4 ♕h5 11 ♘h3 ♘cd7 12 ♗e3 0-0 13 ♗e2 e5 14 ♘f2 ♕g6 15 0-0; Bern-Kristiansen, Gjøvik 1991.

10 b4

The best move may be 10 ♗g5 (10 e4?! exd5 11 ♗b5+ ♗d7 12 ♕e5+ ♔f8 13 ♕d6+ ♕e7 14 ♕xe7+ ♔xe7 15 ♗xd7 ♘xd7 is already better for Black owing to his advanced development; Elbilia-Boudre, Paris 1991), with the following possibilities:

⇨ 10...exd5 11 e3 (11 ♖d1 0-0 12 ♗xf6 gxf6 13 b4 ♘e6 14 ♕c6!? ♗d7 15 ♕xd5 ♗a4 16 ♕xd8 ♖fxd8 17 ♖xd8+ ♖xd8 18 e3 ♖d1+ 19 ♔f2 ♖a1 with reasonable chances for

Black; Grotnes-Ernst, Gausdal 1992) 11...0-0 12 ♘e2 ♗b7 13 ♗xf6 gxf6 14 ♘d4 ♖e8 15 ♗b5 ♖e5 16 0-0 ♖c8 17 ♕d2 a6 18 ♗d3 ♔f8 19 f4 ♘e4 20 ♕e2 ♖ee8 21 ♕g4+ ♔h8 22 ♘f5 ♖c6 23 ♖ac1 ♕g8 24 ♕xg8+ with a good ending for White; Baburin-Tunik, Budapest 1992.

⇨ 10...0-0 11 ♗xf6 gxf6 12 e3 (can White 'take the bull by the horns' by 12 b4 ♘a6 13 dxe6, say?) 12...exd5 13 ♘e2 ♖e8 14 ♘d4 ♕e7 15 ♗b5! (after 15 ♔f2?! ♘a4 16 ♕b3 ♘c5 17 ♕c3 ♘a4 18 ♕b3 ♘c5 ½-½ the white queen is obliged to remain on the third rank defending e3; Kramnik-Garcia, Groningen 1991) 15...♕xe3+ 16 ♕xe3 ♖xe3+ 17 ♔f2 ♖e5 18 b4 ♘b7 19 ♗c6 a5 20 ♖hb1 ♖a7 21 ♘b5 ♖a6 22 ♘c7 ♖a7 23 ♘b5 ♖a6 24 ♘c7 ♖a7 25 ♘xd5 ♘d8 26 ♘xb6 ♘xc6 27 ♘xc8 ± Luther-Nagatz, Bad Lauterberg 1991.

10...♘a4 11 ♕b3 b5 12 e4 a6 13 ♘e2 0-0 14 ♗g5 h6 15 ♗h4 exd5 16 e5 ♖e8!

A curious situation has arisen where, because the white kingside

development is retarded, Black can afford to sacrifice a piece. To be fair, though, the alternative 16...g5 17 ♗f2 is good for White.

17 f4!?

17 exf6? d4 18 ♖d1 ♗e6 19 ♕b1 ♗c4 gives Black a raging attack.

17...g5 18 ♗f2 ♘e4 19 ♗d4 ♗e6 20 ♕f3 ♖c8 21 f5 ♗d7 22 ♘g3?

22 e6!? ♗xe6 23 fxe6 ♖xe6 24 g3! ♘ac3 25 ♗h3 ♘d2 is unclear.

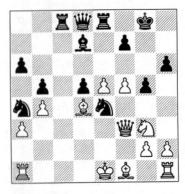

22...♖xe5!!

An absolutely amazing move.

23 ♗e2

If 23 ♗xe5 ♕e8 leaves White in all sorts of trouble.

23...♕e8 24 ♘h5 ♖xf5 25 ♕e3 ♖c3!

Black just doesn't let up.

26 ♗xc3 ♘axc3 27 ♗g4 d4! 28 ♕xd4 ♘c5+ 29 ♔d2 ♘b3+ 30 ♔xc3 ♘xd4 31 ♗xf5 ♕e3+ 32 ♗d3 ♗f5 33 ♖ad1 ♘e2+ 34 ♔c2 ♕e5 35 ♔d2

If 35 ♗xf5 ♕c3+ 36 ♔b1 ♕b3+ 37 ♔a1 ♕xa3+ 38 ♔b1 ♕b4+ 39 ♔a1 ♕a3+ 40 ♔b1 ♘c3+ 41 ♔c2 ♘xd1 42 ♖xd1 ♕c5+ and Black wins.

35...♕b2+ ♕d4# (0-1)

A poetic ga...

Ga...

I.Sokolov-M...
Ålborg Politik...

1 d4 ♘f6 2 c4 e6... c5 5 dxc5 ♘a6 6 ♘xc5 8 f3 a5

⇨ It is difficult to... sions from the 8...♕b3 ♗d7 11 e4 0-0... ♖c1 ♖fc8 ½-½ of... Krumbach 1991, al... say that White is a li... end.

9 e4 d6 10 ♗e3 b6

10...♕c7 11 ♖d1 ♕b6? (a strange decis... was forced) 13 ♕xd... ♖xd6 ± Ilinčić-Goved... jelovac 1991.

11 ♘e2 0-0 12 ♕c2

Making room for the...

12...d5

Worried about the p... White playing 0-0-0 an... with strong pressure on d6...

13 0-0-0 ♗b7 14 ♘c3... ♔b1 ♕e7 16 e5 ♘fd7 17 cx... 18 ♘xd5 ♗xd5 19 ♖xd5... ♗b5! ±

As a direct result of... eighth move, the b5 square is...

20...♕e6 21 ♖hd1 ♘cd3

Black tries to whip up some... plications, as well he might,... the long run White's two bishop... too powerful.

15 ♘e2 (this is easy to understand:
15...♖xg2 seems impossible because
after 16 ♘g3 the rook is trapped, but
Korchnoi has seen further; 15 f4! d6
16 ♔f2 ± is better) 15...♖xg2!! 16
♘g3 axb4 17 axb4 (17 ♗f1? b3!)
17...♘c5 18 ♗f1 ♘d3+! 19 ♗xd3
♖xg3 20 hxg3 ♖a1+ 21 ♔d2 ♖xh1
22 ♖a2 d6! 23 ♖a8 ♔d7! (23...♔d8?
24 e5! dxe5 25 ♗e4 ±) 24 ♗c2 ♖f1
½-½ Seirawan-Korchnoi, Novi Sad
OL 1990.

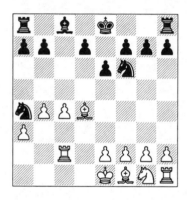

12...b6 13 e3

⇨ 13 f3 d6 14 e4 e5 15 ♗e3 ♗e6 16
♗d3 ♔e7 17 ♘e2 ♖hc8 18 ♔d2
♖c7 19 ♖hc1 ♖ac8 20 ♘g3 g6 21
♗g5 (White should probably not
give up his bishop pair so readily)
21...♖h8! 22 ♘f1 h6 23 ♗xf6+
♔xf6 24 ♘e3 ♗b7 25 ♘d5+ ♔g7 26
♖a2 a6 27 ♗c2 ♗d7 28 ♗b3 ♖c8 29
♖ac2 is slightly better for White;
G.Flear-García Ilundain, Oviedo (active) 1992.

13...♔e7

13...d6 14 f4 a5 15 ♘f3 ♗a6 16
♗e2!? ♔e7 17 0-0 ♖hc8 18 ♖fc1 ±
Flear-Arkell, Dublin 1991.

14 ♗d3 ♗a6 15 ♘e2 ♖hc8 16 0-0

♖c7 17 ♖fc1 ♖ac8 18 e4 d6 19 f4! ±
♘d7 20 ♔f2 ♔f8 21 e5 dxe5 22 fxe5
f6 23 exf6 gxf6 24 g4!

Fixing the target on f6.

24...♔f7 25 ♘g3 ♘f8 26 ♔e3!
♖d7 27 ♗a1! ♖cd8 28 ♗e2 ♘g6 29
♖f1 e5 30 ♘h5! ♖d4!

A good attempted diversion.

31 ♖xf6+ ♔e7

32 ♗xd4?!

32 ♖c1 would avoid the coming
complications.

32...exd4+ 33 ♔f2 d3 34 ♖d2!
♘c3! 35 ♗xd3! ♘e5! 36 ♖e2! ♘xe2
37 ♗xe2 ♗xc4 38 ♖f5 ♘d3+ 39
♔e3 b5 40 ♘f4 ♘xf4 41 ♖xf4 ♗xe2
42 ♔xe2 ♖d6 43 ♖f5 a6 44 ♔f2
♖d2+ 45 ♔g3 ♖a2 46 ♖f3 ♔e6 47
g5 ♔e5 48 h4 ♔e4 49 ♔g4 ♖g2+ 50
♖g3 ♖c2 51 ♔h5 ♔f4 52 ♖d3 ♖c6
53 ♖d7 1-0

Game 49

Petursson-Xu Jun
Novi Sad OL 1990

1 d4 ♘f6 2 c4 e6 3 ♘c3 ♗b4 4 ♕c2

c5 5 dxc5 ♘c6 6 ♘f3 ♗xc5 7 ♗g5 ♕a5

⇨ 7...♘d4 is similar to the variation 5...0-0 6 a3 ♗xc5 7 ♘f3 ♘c6 8 ♗g5 ♘d4, e.g. 8 ♘xd4 ♗xd4 9 e3 ♕a5 10 exd4 ♕xg5 11 ♕d2 ♕xd2+ 12 ♔xd2 b6 13 b4 ♗b7 14 f3 ♔e7 15 ♗d3 ♖hc8 16 a4 a5 17 ♖hb1 ♗a6 18 bxa5 bxa5 19 c5 ♗xd3 20 ♔xd3 ♘e8 21 ♖b7 ± Marin-Skembris, Kavala Balkaniad 1990.

8 ♖d1

⇨ 8 e3 ♗b4 (8...♘g4!? 9 ♗f4 ♗b4 10 h3 ♘ge5 11 ♘xe5 ♘xe5 12 ♖c1 f6 13 a3 ♗e7 14 ♗e2 0-0 15 0-0 a6 16 ♖fd1 ♕c7 17 ♘a4 b6 18 c5 bxc5 19 ♘xc5 ♖a7 20 b4 d6 21 ♘b3 ♕xc2 22 ♖xc2 ♗d7 23 ♖dc1 ± Azmaiparashvili-Marjanović, Moscow 1989) 9 ♗d3 ♘e5 10 ♘xe5 ♕xe5 11 ♗f4 ♗xc3+ 12 ♕xc3 ♕xc3+ 13 bxc3 b6 14 c5 bxc5 15 ♗d6 ♗b7 16 f3 ♘d5 17 ♔d2 ♖c8 18 ♖hb1 ♘b6 19 a4 c4 20 ♗c2 ♖a8 21 ♗c5 ♗c6 22 a5 ♘c8 23 ♗a4 ♘e7 24 a6 d6 25 ♗xa7 with approximate equality; Yrjölä-Petursson, Espoo Z 1989.

⇨ 8 a3!? ♘d4 9 ♘xd4 ♗xd4 10 ♗d2 ♕b6 11 e3 ♗e5! 12 f4! ♗xc3 13 ♕xc3 d6 14 ♕d4? (better 14 ♕d3! ±) 14...♕xd4 15 exd4 b6 16 ♗e2 ♗b7 17 ♗f3 (an odd looking move, but 17 ♖g1 is very passive) 17...♗xf3 18 gxf3 ♔d7 19 ♔e2 is fairly equal; Seirawan-Hübner, Novi Sad OL 1990.

8...♘g4 9 e3 ♗b4 10 ♗e2 ♘ge5 11 ♗f4 ♗xc3+

⇨ 11...♘xf3+ 12 gxf3 e5 13 ♗g3 d6 14 f4 ♗e6 15 ♖g1 0-0-0 16 f5 ♗d7 17 ♗h4 ♖dg8 18 ♗f3 f6! 19 ♗d5 g5 20 fxg6 ♖xg6 21 ♖xg6 hxg6 22

♗xf6 ♖xh2 led to interesting play in Savchenko-Romanishin, Kherson 1989.

12 bxc3 ♘xf3+ 13 gxf3 e5!? 14 ♗g3

I find it amusing that White plays 4 ♕c2 in order to avoid having doubled pawns, and a few moves later acquires two such complexes!

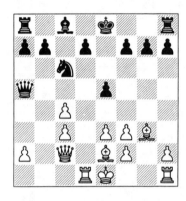

14...0-0 15 ♖d5?!

Missing a chance to undermine Black's centre: 15 f4! ♕c7 16 ♕e4 d6 17 c5! dxc5 18 fxe5 ♗e6 19 f4 with a clear plus for White.

15...♕c7 16 f4 d6 17 ♕d2

Again 17 c5! dxc5 18 fxe5 ♘e7 19 ♖d2 ±, although this is less effective now than at move 15.

17...♗e6! 18 ♖xd6 ♘a5 19 c5! ♕xc5 20 fxe5 ♖ac8 21 0-0 ♘c4 22 ♗xc4 ♕xc4 23 f4 ♕xc3 24 f5 ♕xd2 25 ♖xd2 ♗c4

The opposite-coloured bishops make the draw a very likely outcome.

26 ♖f4 b5 27 ♖fd4 a5 28 ♖d7 a4 29 ♗h4! b4 30 ♗e7 ♖fe8 31 ♗xb4 ♖xe5 32 ♖c7 ♖ce8 33 e4 f6 34 a3 ♗b3 35 ♖d4 h5 ½-½

Game 50

Chernin-Portisch
Moscow 1990

1 d4 ♘f6 2 c4 e6 3 ♘c3 ♗b4 4 ♕c2 c5 5 dxc5 ♕c7

An idea that is familiar to players of the Paulsen Sicilian.

6 ♘f3

Apart from this and the main move 6 a3, which is considered in the subsequent games, White has:

⇨ 6 e4?! 0-0 7 ♗d3 ♘c6 8 ♘f3 ♘g4 (8...♗xc5 9 0-0 ♘g4 10 g3 d6 is a better continuation, intending to play 11...♘ge5 and if 12 ♘xe5 then 12...dxe5 with a good grip on the centre) 9 h3 ♘ge5 10 ♗e3 ♘xf3+ 11 gxf3 ♕a5 12 f4 f6?! 13 0-0-0 ♗xc5 14 e5 f5 15 ♗e2 d6 16 exd6 ♖d8 17 ♗xc5 ♕xc5 18 ♕d2 ♕xf2 19 ♖hf1 ♕c5 20 ♘a4 ♕b4 21 ♕xb4 ♘xb4 22 a3 ± ♘a6 23 b4 ♗d7 24 ♘b2 ♖ac8 25 ♗f3 ♗c6 26 ♗xc6 bxc6 27 c5 and the protected passed d-pawn guarantees the win; Beliavsky-Oll, Odessa 1989.

⇨ 6 ♗g5 ♗xc5 7 ♘f3 ♗e7 8 e4 d6 9 0-0-0 a6 10 ♗e2 ♘bd7 11 ♘d4 0-0 12 f4 ♖e8 13 ♘f3 b6 14 ♔b1 h6 15 e5 (initiating wild complications) 15...dxe5 16 fxe5 hxg5 17 exf6 ♗xf6 18 ♘e4 g4 19 ♘fg5 ♗xg5 20 ♘xg5 ♘f6 21 ♗xg4 e5 22 ♗h5 g6 23 ♖hf1 ♘xh5 24 ♖xf7 ♕c6 25 ♖df1 ♗f5 26 ♖7xf5 gxf5 27 ♕xf5 ♖e7 28 ♘f7 ♕g7 29 ♘xe5 ♕xg2 0-1 Vera-Yudasin, Leningrad 1989.

6...♗xc5 7 ♗g5

⇨ 7 g3 ♗e7 8 ♘b5 ♕c6 9 ♗f4 d6 10 ♖d1 e5 11 ♗g5 ♘bd7 12 ♗g2 a6 13

♘h4 ♕b6 14 ♗e3 ♘c5 15 ♘c3 0-0 16 0-0 g6 17 ♘f3 with only the slightest of advantages; Karpman-Neverovsky, Smolensk 1991.

7...a6 8 ♗xf6!?

⇨ 8 e3 is sounder, for example 8...♗e7 9 ♗e2 d6 10 0-0 and now:

1) 10...♘bd7 11 a4 b6 12 ♘d4 0-0 13 a5 bxa5 14 ♘b3 (White's plan is similar to that in Lerner-Yudasin) 14...a4 15 ♘xa4 ♖b8 16 ♖fc1 ♗b7 17 ♘d4 h6 18 ♗h4 ♖fc8 19 ♕d1 ♗a8 20 ♕e1 e5 21 ♘f3 g5 22 ♗g3 ♘e4 23 ♘d2 ♘ec5 24 ♘xc5 ♘xc5 25 ♖cb1 ♖b4 Lautier-Csom, Cannes 1989. Black is already better; he has pressure on the b-file and White's g3 bishop is out of play.

2) 10...♗b7 11 ♖fd1 d6 12 ♖d2 ♘bd7 13 ♖ad1 0-0-0?! (very risky; White's queenside attack comes very quickly) 14 b4 h6 15 ♗f4 e5 16 ♗g3 g5 17 a4 ♖dg8 18 a5 bxa5 19 c5! g4 20 cxd6 ♗xd6 21 ♖xd6 gxf3 22 ♗xa6 ♗xa6 23 ♖xa6 axb4 24 ♖a8+ ♘b8 25 ♕f5+ 1-0 Finegold-Gelfand, Amsterdam 1989, due to the twin possibilities 25...♘d7 26 ♖xd7! and 25...♔b7 26 ♖a7+!.

8...gxf6 9 g3!? b5!

⇨ 9...♗e7 10 b3 b5! 11 ♗g2 bxc4 12 bxc4 ♘c6 13 0-0 ♘a5 14 ♘d2 ♗b7 15 ♗xb7 ♘xb7 16 ♖ab1 ♖c8 17 ♘ce4 ♘a5 18 ♕b2 ♕e5 19 ♕b6 ♘xc4 20 ♘xc4 ♕xe4 21 ♘d6+ ♗xd6 22 ♕xd6 ♕e5 23 ♕a3 d6 24 ♕a4+ ♔f8 25 ♖b7 with just enough play to balance his pawn minus; Baburin-Atlas, Leukerbad 1992.

10 ♗g2

Obviously 10 cxb5? axb5 11 ♘xb5?? loses to 11...♗xf2+.

10...♗b7 11 0-0! bxc4 12 ♘a4

White has correctly calculated that he will be able to regain his pawn.

**12...♗e7 13 b3 d5 14 bxc4 ♘d7!
15 ♖ab1 ♖c8 16 ♘d2 ♗a8! 17 ♕d1
dxc4 18 ♗xa8 ♖xa8 19 ♘xc4!**

This tactic is the point of White's play.

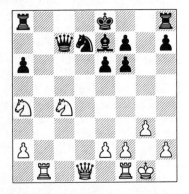

**19...♕xc4 20 ♕xd7+ ♔xd7 21
♘b6+ ♔c6 22 ♘xc4 ♖hb8 = 23
♘a5+ ♔d7 24 ♖fd1+ ♔e8 25 ♘c6
♖xb1 26 ♖xb1 ♗d6 27 e3 ♔d7 28
♘a5 ♖c8 29 ♖b6 ♖c1+ 30 ♔g2 ♖c2
31 ♖xa6 ♖xa2 ½-½**

Game 51

Lerner-Yudasin
Lvov Z 1990

**1 d4 ♘f6 2 c4 e6 3 ♘c3 ♗b4 4 ♕c2
c5 5 dxc5 ♕c7 6 a3 ♗xc5 7 ♘f3 a6
8 ♗g5**

This bishop might be more usefully employed on the a1-h8 diagonal: 8 e3 ♗e7 9 b4 d6 10 ♗b2 b6 11 ♗e2 ♗b7 12 0-0 ♘bd7 13 ♖ac1 ♖c8 14 ♖fd1 0-0 15 ♘d2 ♕b8 16 ♘ce4

♕a8 17 ♗f3 b5 18 ♘xf6+ ♘xf6 19 ♗xb7 ♕xb7 20 ♕d3 ♖fd8 21 ♘b3 bxc4 22 ♖xc4 ♖xc4 23 ♘a5 ♕e4 24 ♕xc4 ♕xc4 25 ♘xc4 although this is completely equal; Anastasian-Petrosian, Erevan 1989.

**8...♗e7 9 e3 d6 10 ♗e2 ♘bd7 11
0-0**

⇨ 11 0-0-0!? (rather daring) 11...b6 12 ♘d2 ♗b7 13 ♖hg1 ♖c8 14 g4 d5 15 ♗f4 e5 16 ♗g3 dxc4 17 ♘xc4 b5 18 g5 bxc4 19 gxf6 ♗xf6 20 ♕a4 ♕c6 21 ♕b4 ♗e7 22 ♕a5 ♗d8 (an unusual perpetual attack on the queen) 23 ♕b4 ♗e7 24 ♕a5 ½-½ Xu Jun-Petrosian, Shenzhen 1992.

11...b6 12 ♘d4

The start of an interesting, but ultimately unsuccessful, strategy that involves putting this knight on a5. Personally, I prefer to double rooks on the d-file.

12...♗b7 13 a4!?

⇨ 13 ♖ac1 ♖c8 14 f4 (White plans f5, forcing ...e5 and weakening the d5 square) 14...♕b8 15 f5 e5 16 ♘b3 ♕a8 17 ♖f2 h6 18 ♗h4 d5! 19 cxd5 ♘xd5 20 ♗xe7 ♔xe7! and the king is quite safe here, so Black can count on some advantage, which he converted in Petursson-Csom, San Bernardino 1992.

**13...0-0 14 a5 bxa5 15 ♘b3 ♖ab8
16 ♘xa5 ♗a8 17 ♖fb1 ♖b4! 18 e4
♖fb8 19 ♖a2 ♘c5 20 ♗f3 ♘cd7 21
♗d2 ♘e5 22 ♗e2 ♗d8 23 h3 ♕a7
24 ♗e3 ♗b6**

Achieving the exchange of his less active bishop.

**25 ♗xb6 ♕xb6 26 b3 ♘fd7 27
♖a3 ♘c5 ∓**

The black pieces have found their optimum positions.

**28 ♔h1 h6 29 f3 ♘c6 30 ♘xc6
♗xc6 31 ♗d1 ♗a4!**

Bringing additional pressure to
bear on b3 and obliging White to exchange into a bad bishop versus
good knight situation.

**32 ♘xa4 ♘xa4 33 ♕d2 ♘c5 34
♗c2 ♕c7 35 ♖d1 ♖4b6 36 ♕c3 e5!
37 ♖d5 ♘e6 38 ♖da5 ♘c5 39 ♔h2
♔h7 40 ♕d2 g6 41 ♖a2 ♔g7 42
♖5a3 ♕e7 43 ♕f2 ♕g5**

Notice that all the black pieces are
on dark squares; a good recipe to follow if your opponent has a light-
squared bishop!

44 ♖a1 ♘xb3 45 ♗xb3 ♖xb3

So that 46 ♖xa6 ♖b1 47 ♖xd6
♕f4+ 48 g3 ♕c1 wins for Black.

**46 ♖xb3 ♖xb3 47 h4 ♕f4+ 48
♕g3 ♕xg3+ 49 ♔xg3 ♖b6**

The rook and pawn ending
doesn't present Black with any particular problems.

**50 ♖a5 ♖c6 51 ♔f2 h5 52 ♖a4
♔f6 53 g4 ♔e6 54 ♔g3 ♖b6 55 ♖a5
♔d7 56 gxh5 gxh5 57 ♖a3 ♔c7 58
♖a5 ♔b7 59 ♖a3 ♖c6 60 ♖a4 ♔b6
61 ♖b4+ ♔c5 62 ♖b7 f6! 63 ♖h7 a5
64 ♖xh5 a4 65 ♖h8 ♖a6 66 h5 a3 67
h6 a2 68 ♖c8+ ♔d4 0-1**

Game 52

Dorfman-Tal
Barcelona 1992

**1 d4 ♘f6 2 c4 e6 3 ♘c3 ♗b4 4 ♕c2
c5 5 dxc5 ♕c7 6 a3 ♗xc5 7 b4 ♗e7
8 ♘b5!**

⇨ 8 e4 is another sharp possibility:
8...a6 9 f4 d6 10 ♗d3 ♘bd7 11 ♘f3
♘b6!? 12 ♕e2 d5!? (meeting White's
aggressive set up with a central
thrust) 13 exd5 ♘bxd5 14 ♘xd5
exd5 15 c5? (15 0-0! ±) 15...b6 ∓
(Black cannot afford to hang around)
16 ♗e3 ♘e4 17 ♗d4?! bxc5 18
♗xg7 ♖g8 19 ♗e5 ♕b6 20 ♖b1 ♗f5
21 bxc5 ♕a5+! 22 ♔f1 ♕xa3 23
♗c2 ♕xc5 24 ♖b2 ♕a3 25 ♕d1 ♖d8
26 ♖b7 ♖c8! 27 ♘d4 ♗g4 28 ♕e1
♖xc2 29 ♘xc2 ♕d3+ 30 ♔g1 ♗c5+
31 ♘d4 ♗xd4+ 32 ♗xd4 ♕xd4+
winning material; Chekhov-Petro-
sian, Moscow 1991.

8...♕c6 9 ♘f3 d6 10 ♘fd4 ♕d7

Recently A.Petrosian has preferred 10...♕b6!?:

⇨ 11 ♗e3?! (too obvious; after
Black moves his queen, the bishop
will obstruct White's development)
11...♕d8 12 ♘b3 a6 13 ♘c3 b6 14
f3 ♘bd7 15 ♗f2 ♗b7 16 e4 ♖c8 17
♗d4 ♘e5 18 ♘a4 ♘fd7 19 ♕f2
♗h4 20 g3 ♗f6 ∓ van Riemsdijk-
Petrosian, Groningen 1990.

⇨ 11 ♘b3 a6 12 ♘5d4 ♘c6 13 ♗b2
♗d7 14 e3 ♖c8 15 ♗e2 ♘e5 16 ♘d2
0-0 = Scherbakov-Petrosian, Armenia 1991.

⇨ 11 e3! ♘bd7 12 ♗e2 a6 13 ♘c3
♕c7 14 0-0 b6 15 f4 ♗b7 16 ♗b2
♖c8 17 ♖ac1 ♕b8 18 ♗d3 0-0 19

♕e2 g6 20 e4 (White's pieces have found their most harmonious squares) 20...b5?! (attempting to drum up counterplay, but White is well placed to meet this) 21 cxb5 e5 22 ♘c6 ♗xc6 23 bxc6 ♕b6+ 24 ♔h1 ♖xc6 25 ♗xa6 exf4 26 ♗b5 ♖c7 27 ♗xd7 ♖xd7 28 ♖xf4 (the menace of ♖xf6 and ♘d5 gains the d5 square) 28...♘h5 29 ♖ff1 ♗g5 30 ♘d5 ♕d8 31 ♖c4 ± f6 32 a4 ♖df7 33 a5 ♖e8 34 ♕d3 ♕d7 35 ♖c7 ♕g4 36 ♖xf7 ♔xf7 37 a6 ♗h4 38 ♕f3 ♕c8 39 ♗xf6 1-0 Baburin-Petrosian, Budapest 1991.

11 ♗b2 b6?! 12 ♖d1 ♗b7 13 ♘f3! d5

Else ♗xf6 is a problem.

14 e4! 0-0 15 e5 ♘h5

Not a move that Black wants to play, as the knight is out on a limb, but if instead 15...♘e8 it is not easy to see how Black continues his development.

16 cxd5 ♗xd5 17 ♘c3 ± ♕c7

18 ♖xd5! exd5 19 ♕f5 ♖d8

Hoping to get his d-pawn going; 19...g6 20 ♘xd5 ♕d8 21 ♕e4 ♘d7 22 ♗b5 is hopeless for Black.

20 ♕xh5 d4 21 ♘d1 d3 22 e6! White continues his attack anyway.

22...fxe6 23 ♕g4 ♗f8 24 ♕xe6+ ♔h8 25 ♘e5 1-0

Game 53 *C M L*

Kožul-Ionescu
Berga 1991

1 d4 ♘f6 2 c4 e6 3 ♘c3 ♗b4 4 ♕c2 c5 5 dxc5 ♗xc5 6 ♘f3 ♕b6

⇨ 6...a6!? 7 ♗f4 ♘c6 8 ♖d1 b5!? (a violent attempt to grab the initiative that is typical of Anastasian's style) 9 cxb5 axb5 10 e3 ♕a5 11 ♗xb5 ♘b4 12 ♕b3 ♘bd5!? 13 a4 ♘e4 14 ♗e5?! (14 ♖xd5!? is tempting) 14...♘dxc3 15 bxc3 0-0 16 0-0 d6 17 ♗d4 ♗xd4 18 cxd4 ♘c3 19 ♖c1 ♘xb5 20 axb5 ♖b8 21 ♖c6 ♖xb5 22 ♕c2 ♕d8 23 ♖b1!? ♖b7! 24 h3 h6 25 ♔h2 ♕d7 26 ♖c1 ♖b8 27 ♖c7 ♕b5 28 ♕c6 ♕xc6 29 ♖1xc6 ♖d8 30 ♖e7!? and although Black still has a little work to do, this should be drawn; M.Gurevich-Anastasian, Moscow Alekhine mem 1992.

7 e3 ♕c7

⇨ 7...a6 8 ♗e2 ♗e7 9 b3 ♕c7 10 ♗b2 d6 11 g4!? h6 12 ♖g1 b6 13 h4 ♘c6? 14 g5 hxg5 15 hxg5 ♘d7 16 ♘d5 exd5 17 cxd5 ± Bykhovsky-Xu Jun, Beijing 1991.

8 b3 b6

⇨ 8...a6 9 ♗b2 ♘c6 (9...b6 10 ♗d3 ♗b7 11 ♘e4 ♗e7 12 0-0!? d6 13 ♘xf6+ ♗xf6 14 ♗xf6 gxf6 15 ♗e4 d5 16 ♗d3! with a slight advantage for White; Yakovich-M.Gurevich, Moscow 1992) 10 ♗e2 b6 11 0-0

♗b7 12 ♖ad1 ♖c8?! 13 ♘g5! ♘b4
14 ♕b1 ♗e7 15 ♖d2 h5 (not 15...0-0
because 16 a3 ♘c6 17 ♘d5! exd5 18
♗xf6 wins, but 15...h6 was playable) 16 ♘f3! ♘g4 17 e4 ♘c6 18
♘a4 ♗g5 19 ♖dd1 ♗f6 20 h3 ♘ce5
21 ♘xe5 ♗xe5 22 ♗xe5 ♘xe5 23
♕b2 ♗xe4 24 ♘xb6 ♖b8 25 c5
♕xc5 26 ♘a4 ♕c7? 27 ♖c1 ♘c6 28
♘c5 ♕f4 29 ♕xg7 ♔e7 30 ♕c3
♖hg8 31 g3 ♕f5 32 ♘xe4 ♕xe4 33
♗f3 ♕f5 34 ♗xc6 ± and Black's
king in the centre finally told against
him in Dreev-Romanishin, Lvov Z
1990.
   **9 ♗b2 ♗b7 10 ♖d1 ♗e7 11 ♗d3
♘a6 12 ♘b5 ♕c6 13 ♕d2!? ♘c5**
   I think that 13...♗b4!? 14 ♗c3
♗xc3 is a better bet.
   **14 0-0 a6 15 ♘bd4 ♕c7 16 ♗b1
0-0 17 ♘e2! ♖fd8 18 ♘g3 d6? 19
♘g5!**
   Starting a decisive attack.
   19...h6 20 f4

   **20...♖ac8 21 ♕c2 ♘cd7 22 ♘h5
hxg5 23 ♗xf6 ♘xf6 24 ♘xf6+
♗xf6 25 fxg5 ♗xg5 26 ♕h7+ ♔f8
27 ♗g6 ♗xe3+**
   Unfortunately for Black 27...♗f6

loses to the beautiful 28 ♕h8+ ♔e7
29 ♕xg7!! ♗xg7 30 ♖xf7+ ♔e8 31
♖xc7+ ♔f8 32 ♖xb7 ±.
   **28 ♔h1 d5 29 ♖xf7+ ♕xf7 30
♗xf7 ♔xf7 31 ♖f1+ ♔e7 32 ♕xg7+
♔d6 33 ♕g3+! 1-0**

Game 54

Scherbakov-M.Gurevich
Helsinki 1992

**1 d4 ♘f6 2 c4 e6 3 ♘c3 ♗b4 4 ♕c2
c5 5 dxc5 ♗xc5 6 ♘f3 ♕b6 7 e3
♕c7 8 a3**

   Apart from this and 8 b3 (considered in the previous game) there are:
   ⇨ 8 ♗d3!? b6 9 ♘b5 ♕d8 10 ♗d2
a6 11 ♘bd4 ♗b7 12 0-0 ♗e7 13
♗c3 d6 14 ♘g5 ♕c8 15 f4 (again,
this seems to be a favourite plan of
Petursson) 15...h6 16 ♘gxe6!? fxe6
17 ♗g6+ ♔f8 18 e4 ♕xc4 19 e5 (regaining the piece) 19...♘c6 20 exf6
♘xd4! (20...♗xf6?! 21 ♘xc6 ±) 21
fxe7+ ♔xe7 22 ♕f2 ♘e2+ 23 ♔h1
♘xc3 24 bxc3 ♖hf8 25 ♕xb6 ♕c6
26 ♕g1 when Black was clearly better; Petursson-Schüssler, Espoo Z
1989.
   ⇨ 8 ♗e2 a6 9 0-0 ♗e7 10 b3 b6 11
♗b2 ♗b7 12 ♖ac1 d6 13 ♘d4 ♘bd7
14 ♗f3 0-0 15 ♕e2 ♖fc8 16 ♖fd1
♘e5 17 ♗xb7 ♕xb7 18 f4 ♘c6 19
♘f3 ♖ab8 20 ♘g5 h6 21 ♘ge4 ♘e8
22 ♘g3 b5 23 cxb5 axb5 24 f5 ♗f6 ∓
Kakageldiev-M.Gurevich, Manila
OL 1992.
   ⇨ 8 ♗d2 0-0 9 ♗d3 ♘c6 10 a3 b6 11
g4!? (intending 0-0-0 followed by
a sharp kingside attack, although
Black's counterchances are not to be

underestimated) 11...g6 12 g5 ♘h5 13 ♘e4 ♗b7 14 0-0-0 ♘e7 15 ♗c3 ♖ac8 16 ♘e5 ♖fd8 17 ♗e2 ♗xe4 18 ♕xe4 d5 19 ♕c2 ♗d6 20 ♘g4 ♔f8 21 ♔b1 dxc4 22 ♘h6 ∞ Lerner-A.Sokolov, Odessa 1989.

8...a6 9 ♗d3 ♗e7 10 0-0 d6 11 b4 b6 12 ♗b2 ♗b7 13 ♕e2 ♘bd7 14 h3! 0-0 15 e4 ♖fd8 16 ♖ac1 ♖ac8 17 ♕e3 ♕b8 18 ♘e2

Preparing to add its presence to the kingside, much as in Kožul-Ionescu above.

18...a5?! 19 ♖fd1 axb4 20 axb4 ♗f8?!

Better is 20...♗c6.

21 ♘g3 ♗c6 22 e5!

Scherbakov is in his element in such positions.

22...dxe5 23 ♘xe5 ♗a4 24 ♖e1 ♗xb4 25 ♘xd7 ♘xd7 26 ♘h5

26...♗f8??

⇨ 26...e5 was the best chance, but even then 27 c5!! ♗xe1 28 ♕g5 ♔f8 29 ♕xg7+ would give White a ferocious attack.

27 ♗xg7! ± ♗xg7 28 ♕g5 ♔f8 29 ♖xe6! ♕e5

Hopeless, of course.

30 ♖xe5 ♗xe5 31 ♖e1 ♖e8 32 ♕h6+ ♔e7 33 f4 1-0

Game 55

Petursson-Gulko
New York 1991

1 d4 ♘f6 2 c4 e6 3 ♘c3 ♗b4 4 ♕c2 c5 5 dxc5 0-0 6 a3

This and 6 ♘f3 are White's main ideas, but there are others:

⇨ 6 e3 ♗xc5 7 ♘f3 d5 8 a3 ♗e7 9 ♗e2 dxc4 10 ♗xc4 a6 11 ♗d3 b5 12 e4 ♘bd7 13 e5 ♘c5 14 ♗e2 ♘d5 15 ♘xd5 ♕xd5 and Black has good chances for equality; P.Nikolić-de Firmian, Lugano 1989.

⇨ 6 ♗g5 ♘a6 7 e4? ♗xc3+! ∓ 8 bxc3 e5 9 f3 ♘xc5 10 ♘h3 d6 11 ♘f2 ♗e6? (11...h6) 12 ♕d1! = ♖c8 13 ♘e3 h6 14 ♗h4 ♘cd7 15 ♗e2 and White gradually began to assume the ascendancy in Bareev-Romanishin, Lvov Z 1990.

⇨ 6 ♗f4 (an old idea of Donner's) 6...♗xc5 7 ♘f3 ♘c6 8 a3 ♘h5 9 ♗g3 f5 10 e4!? g6 11 0-0-0! b6 12 ♕d2! a5!? 13 ♗h4 ♗e7 14 ♗xe7 ♕xe7 15 e5 g5! 16 ♕e3 ♖b8 17 ♘d4 ♗b7 18 ♘db5 ♘f4 19 h4 ♘g6 20 hxg5 ♘cxe5 21 ♕d2 ♗c6 22 ♘d6 ♘f7 23 ♘xf7 ♖xf7 24 f4 ♕c5 25 ♔b1 ♖e8 26 ♖h6? (26 ♖h2!? e5 27 g3 ±) 26...e5 27 fxe5 ♖xe5 28 ♗d3? ♕e3! 29 ♕xe3 ♖xe3 30 ♘d5 ♗xd5 31 cxd5 ♖g3 32 d6 ♘e5?! (Black would have the advantage after 32...♔g7! 33 ♗c2 ♖xg5; as it is he now finds himself with difficult problems to solve) 33 ♗c2 f4? (33...♖xg5 =) 34 ♗e4 ♔f8 35 ♗d5

♖g7 36 ♖f6+ 1-0 Gelfand-Andersson, Tilburg 1990.

6...♗xc5 7 ♘f3

7 b4 ♗e7 8 ♗b2 d6 9 ♘f3 ♘bd7 10 e4 b6 11 ♗e2 ♗b7 12 0-0 a6 13 ♖fd1 ♕c7 14 ♖ac1 ♖ac8 with a fairly typical 'Hedgehog' type position; Granda-Vladimirov, Tilburg (active) 1992.

7...b6

⇨ 7...♗e7!? worked out well for Black in Hauchard-Tiviakov, Oakham 1992: 8 ♗f4 b6 9 e4 ♗b7 10 ♗d3 d6 11 ♖d1 ♘bd7 12 ♕e2 a6 13 0-0 ♕c7 14 ♗b1 ♖ac8 15 ♗a2 ♘e5 16 ♘d2 ♖fe8 17 h3 ♘fd7 18 ♗h2 ♗f6 19 ♔h1 ♘c5 20 ♘db1 ♗c6 21 f4 ♘g6 22 b4 ♘a4 23 ♘xa4 ♗xa4 24 ♖c1 ♕b8 25 ♘c3 ♗c6 and he went on to win.

8 ♗g5

⇨ 8 ♗f4 ♗b7 9 ♖d1 ♘c6 10 e4 ♘g4 11 ♗g3 f6 12 ♘b5 ♘ge5 13 ♗e2 (an improvement on 13 ♘xe5 fxe5 14 b4 a6 15 ♘c3 ♗e7 16 ♕b2 ♖f7 ½-½ Kramnik-Serper, USSR 1991) 13...♖c8 14 0-0 ♘xf3+ 15 ♗xf3 e5 (trying to mask the weakness on d6) 16 ♗g4 ♘d4 17 ♘xd4 ♗xd4 18

♖xd4! (freeing the g3-bishop's diagonal) 18...exd4 19 ♖d1 ♕e8 20 f3 g6 21 ♖xd4 ♗c6 22 ♗d6 f5? (desperately trying to break out of the bind, but it would have been better to hang on to the exchange and await events) 23 ♗xf8 fxg4 24 ♗d6 gxf3 25 gxf3 ± ♕f7 26 ♕d3 a6 27 ♗b4 ♖e8 28 ♕e3 ♖e6 29 ♗c3 g5 30 ♖d2 h6 31 ♕d4 (once the queen and bishop achieve this formation, the writing is on the wall for Black) 31...♔h7 32 h4 ♖e8 33 hxg5 ♖g8 34 ♖h2 ♖xg5+ 35 ♔f2 ♖g8 36 ♕e5 ♕g6 37 ♕e7+ 1-0 Lautier-Wahls, Baden-Baden 1992.

8...♗b7 9 e4

Alternatively:

⇨ 9 ♖d1 ♗e7 10 e3 ♘c6 11 ♗e2 d6 12 ♖d2 ♕b8 13 0-0 h6 14 ♗h4 ♖d8 15 ♖fd1 (this doubling of rooks on the half-open d-file is simple but effective) 15...♘a5 16 b4 ♘c6 17 ♗g3 ♘h5 18 ♘g5 hxg5 19 ♗xh5 ♘e5 20 ♗xe5 dxe5 21 ♖xd8+ ♗xd8 22 ♖d7 ♗c6 23 ♗xf7+! (Black must have thought that this was impossible) 23...♔f8 24 ♗h5! ♖xd7 25 ♕g6 ♔g8 26 ♕f7+ ♔h8 27 ♗f3 ♗e7 28 ♗xa8 ♕e8 29 ♕xe8+ with a winning advantage; Korchnoi-Tiviakov, Tilburg 1992.

⇨ 9 e3 h6 10 ♗h4 ♗e7 11 ♗e2 d5 (11...♘c6 12 0-0 ♖c8 13 ♖fd1 ♘h5 14 ♗xe7 ♕xe7 15 b4 ♘f6 16 ♖d2 ♖fd8 17 ♖ad1 d6 18 h3 a6 19 ♕b3 ♕c7 20 ♖c2 ♘e7 21 ♘a4 ♘g6 22 ♖dc1 ½-½ Psakhis-Serper, Amsterdam 1990) 12 ♗xf6 ♗xf6 13 cxd5 ♗xc3+ 14 ♕xc3 ♗xd5 15 0-0 ♘d7 16 b4 ♖c8 17 ♕d4 ♕c7 18 ♗a6 ♗b7 19 ♗xb7 ♕xb7 20 ♖fd1 ♖c7 = Marin-Rechlis, Novi Sad OL 1990.

9...♗e7 10 ♖d1 ♘c6 11 ♗e2 a6?! 12 0-0 ♕c7?!

Allowing a standard 'sacrifice'; 12...♖c8!? is better.

13 ♘d5! exd5 14 cxd5 ♖ac8 15 dxc6 dxc6 16 e5 ♘d5 17 ♕e4! ±

Although White has not won any material as such, the position is very advantageous for him because the black kingside will be difficult to defend.

17...♖fe8 18 ♗c4 ♗f8 19 ♖fe1 h6 20 ♗c1 ♖cd8 21 ♘d4! c5 22 ♘f5 ♘f6? 23 ♘xh6+!

This combination wins a pawn.

23...gxh6 24 ♕g6+ ♔h8 25 ♕xf6+ ♗g7 26 ♕xf7 ♕xf7 27 ♗xf7 ♖xd1 28 ♖xd1 ♖xe5 29 ♖d8+ ♔h7 30 ♗g8+ ♔g6 31 ♖d6+ ♗f6 32 ♗d2 ♖e8 33 ♗c3 ♖xg8 34 ♖xf6+ ♔h5 35 f3 1-0

The black king is in a mating net to add to his other problems.

Game 56

Crouch-K.Arkell
Isle of Man 1992

1 d4 ♘f6 2 c4 e6 3 ♘c3 ♗b4 4 ♕c2 c5 5 dxc5 0-0 6 a3 ♗xc5 7 ♘f3 ♕b6!?

New, but very similar to material already examined.

⇨ 7...b6?! 8 ♗g5 ♗b7 9 e4! h6 10 ♗h4 ♗e7 11 ♗e2 ♘h5?! (since Seirawan manages to show up the deficiencies of this strategy, it might be better to play 11...d6, i.e. 12 0-0 ♘bd7 13 ♘d4 ♖c8 14 ♖fd1 a6 15 a4 ♘e5 16 b3 ♕c7 17 ♗g3 ♘g6 18 ♖ac1 ♕c5 19 ♕b1 a5 20 ♔h1 h5 21 h3 h4 22 ♗h2 ♕g5 23 ♘f3 ♕h6 unclear; Petursson-Rechlis, Manila IZ 1990) 12 ♗xe7 ♕xe7 13 ♕d2! (eyeing the d6 square) 13...♖d8 14 ♖d1 ♘f6 (14...♘c6 15 0-0 d6 16 ♕e3 ♘f6 17 ♘d4 ♖c8 18 ♖d2 ♘a5 19 ♘db5 ♘xc4 20 ♗xc4 ♖xc4 21 ♘xd6 with an edge to White; Yrjölä-Franco, Novi Sad OL 1990) 15 e5 ♘e8 16 ♘b5 ± (Black is in a bind) 16...♘c6 17 0-0 ♖ac8 18 ♕f4 ♗a6! 19 ♖d2?! f6?! 20 exf6! (better than 20 ♘d6?! ♘xd6 21 exd6 ♕f7 22 b4 ♗b7 23 ♗d3; Yrjölä-Kveinys, Lithuania 1992) 20...♕xf6 21 ♕xf6 gxf6 22 ♖fd1 ♗xb5 23 cxb5 ♘b8 24 ♘d4 ♔f7?! (24...♘g7) 25 ♗h5+ ♔e7 26 ♗xe8 ♖xe8 27 f4! ♖c5 28 ♔f2 h5? 29 ♔g3 ♖g8+ 30 ♔h3 ♗f7 31 g3 ♖gc8 32 a4 ♖d5! 33 ♔h4 ♔g6 34 f5+? (White slips up; 34 h3! ♖c4 35 b3 ♖c3 36 f5+ would have kept him well on top) 34...♔f7 35 b3 ♖g8 36 fxe6+? dxe6 37 ♘c6 ♘xc6 38 ♖xd5 exd5 39 bxc6 ♔e6 40 c7? ♖c8 41 ♖c1 ♔f5 42 ♖f1+ ♔g6 43 ♖d1 ♖xc7 44 ♖xd5 ♖c3 45 ♖b5 ♖d3 46 ♖xh5 ♖xb3 47 ♖b5 ♖a3 48 ♖b4 a5 49 ♖g4+ ♔h6 50 ♖f4 ♔g6 51 ♖g4+ ½-½ Seirawan-Kveinys, Manila OL 1992.

8 e3 ♗e7 9 b3 a6 10 ♗b2 ♕c7

An alternative is 10...d6.

11 ♘g5! g6

Too weakening; 11...♖e8 is better.

12 h4 d6 13 h5 e5 14 ♘xh7!!

An intuitive sacrifice, it being impossible to calculate to the very end.

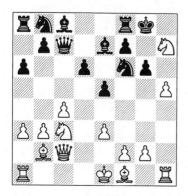

14...♔xh7 15 hxg6+ ♔g7 16 ♘d5 ♘xd5 17 ♖h7+ ♔f6 18 gxf7!

White shows an admirable disregard for material values.

18...♗d8 19 ♕e4!! ♘b6?!

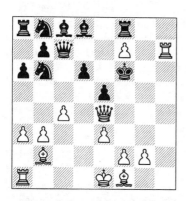

20 ♗xe5+! dxe5 21 ♕h4+ ♔e6 22 ♕g4+ ♔e7 23 ♕g5+ ♔d7 24 ♖d1+ ♕d6 25 ♖xd6+ ♔xd6 26

♖h6+ ♗e6 27 ♕f5 ♘6d7 28 ♕xe6+ ♔c7 29 g3 a5 30 c5 ♔c8 31 ♖g6 ♖a6! 32 ♗xa6 ♘xa6

Finally reaching a sensible material balance, but White's f- and g-pawns will win.

33 ♖g8 ♘c7 34 ♕f5 ♗e7 35 b4 axb4 36 axb4 ♘d5? 37 ♕e6 1-0

Game 57

Salov-Ljubojević
Reykjavik 1991

1 d4 ♘f6 2 c4 e6 3 ♘c3 ♗b4 4 ♕c2 c5 5 dxc5 0-0 6 a3 ♗xc5 7 ♘f3 ♘c6 8 ♗g5

⇨ 8 ♗f4 ♗e7 9 ♖d1 ♕a5 10 e4 ♖d8 11 ♗e2 d5 (seems to be a good method of equalizing) 12 exd5 exd5 13 0-0 dxc4 14 ♗xc4 ♕f5 15 ♖xd8+ ♗xd8 16 ♕d2 ♗e6 17 ♗d3 ♕a5 18 ♕c2 h6 19 ♘b5 ♘d5 20 ♗d6 ♗e7 21 ♗xe7 ♘dxe7 ½-½ Chekhov-Unzicker, Bundesliga 1992.

8...♘d4

This leads to a rather dull ending (especially from Black's viewpoint).

9 ♘xd4 ♗xd4 10 e3 ♕a5 11 exd4 ♕xg5 12 ♕d2 ♕xd2+ 13 ♔xd2 b6

Or 13...d6 14 ♗d3 ♗d7 15 b4 e5 16 ♘e4 ♘xe4+ 17 ♗xe4 ♖ac8 18 ♖hc1 b6 19 dxe5 dxe5 20 c5 ♖fd8 21 ♔e3 bxc5 22 ♖xc5 f5 23 ♗d5+ ♔f8 24 ♖ac1 ♔e7 25 ♗b7 ♖xc5 26 ♖xc5 when White's tiny advantage is insufficient to trouble Black unduly; Lautier-Korchnoi, Biel 1992.

14 ♗d3 ♗a6

The other option is 14...♗b7 15 f3 and now:

⇨ 15...d6 16 b4 ♖fd8 17 ♖hb1 ♗c6 18 ♘d1 g6 19 ♘e3 ± ♔f8 20 ♖b2 h5 21 h4 ♔e7 22 ♖e1 ♔f8 23 ♖a1 ♔e7 24 ♖e1 ♔f8 25 ♘d1 ♗d7 26 ♘c3 ♖dc8 27 ♖eb1 ♗c6 28 ♖a1 ♔e7 29 ♖e1 ♔f8 30 ♖bb1 ♗d7 31 ♖ec1 ♖ab8 32 ♖b2 ♖a8 33 ♘d1 ♖c7 34 ♘e3 ♔e7 35 ♖bc2 ♖ac8 36 ♖c3 ♗e8 37 ♗e2 ♗d7 38 c5 (finally!) 38...dxc5 39 dxc5 bxc5 40 ♖xc5 ♖xc5 41 ♖xc5 ♖xc5 42 bxc5 with just enough advantage to win; Salov-Andersson, Reykjavik 1991.

⇨ 15...♖fc8 16 b4 ♗a6 (16...d6 17 ♖hc1 ♔f8 18 ♘d1 g5 19 ♘e3 h5 20 ♖f1 ♔e7 21 h4 gxh4 22 ♖h1 a5 23 b5 ♖g8 24 ♖xh4 ± Kumaran-K.Arkell, British Ch 1992) 17 c5 ♗xd3 18 ♔xd3 (the white king starts to become very active) 18...bxc5 19 dxc5 d6 20 cxd6 ♘e8 21 ♘e4 ♖d8 22 ♖hd1 f5 (22...♘d6 23 ♘xd6 ♖xd6+ 24 ♔c4 ♖c6+ 25 ♔b5 ±) 23 ♘c5 ♖xd6+ 24 ♔c4 ♔f7? (24...♖ad8 25 ♖xd6 ♖xd6 26 ♖a2 ±) 25 ♖xd6 ♘xd6+ 26 ♔b3 g5 27 ♖d1 ♖d8 28 a4 ♘b7 29 ♖d7+! ♖xd7 30 ♘xd7 ♔e7 31 ♘e5 a6 32 ♔c4 f4 33 ♔d4 h5 34 a5 ♘d6 35 ♔c5 ♘f5 36 b5 1-0 Bareev-Rajković, Germany 1991.

15 ♖hc1 ♖ac8 16 ♘d1 ♘h5!?

This plan of Ljubojević's looks like Black's only chance of activity at the moment.

17 g3 f5

Now White must beware ...f4 when Black will have counterplay on the f-file.

(see next diagram)

18 a4 ♗b7 19 a5 ♘f6 20 b4 d6 21 axb6 axb6 22 ♖a7 ♖f7 23 f4 ♗e4 24 ♖a6 ♖b7 25 ♗e2 ♗c6 26 ♘c3 ♘e4+ 27 ♘xe4 ♗xe4 28 ♖c3 ♔f7 29 ♔e3

h6 30 h4 ♔f6 31 h5 ♗c6 32 ♖ca3 d5 33 c5 bxc5 34 bxc5 ♗b5! 35 ♖a7 ♖xa7 36 ♖xa7 ♗xe2 37 ♔xe2 ♖b8! = 38 ♔d2 ♖b4 39 ♔c3 ♖c4+ 40 ♔d3 ♖c1 41 ♔d2 ♖c4 42 ♔d3 ♖c1 43 ♖d7 ♖g1 44 c6 ♖c1 45 c7 ½-½

Game 58

I.Sokolov-Ribli
Manila OL 1992

1 d4 ♘f6 2 c4 e6 3 ♘c3 ♗b4 4 ♕c2 0-0 5 ♘f3 c5 6 dxc5 ♘a6 7 ♗g5!?

⇨ The rest of this chapter deals with White's main move 7 g3, but apart from this and 7 ♗g5, 7 ♗d2 is also possible: 7...♘xc5 8 e3 b6 9 ♗e2 ♗b7 10 0-0 ♖c8!? 11 ♘b5!? ♗xd2 12 ♘xd2 a6 13 ♘d6 ♖c6 14 ♘xb7 ♘xb7 15 b4 a5! 16 a3 d5 17 ♕b2 dxc4 18 ♘xc4 ♕c7 19 bxa5! ♘xa5 20 ♘xa5 ♖c2! 21 ♖fc1! ♖xb2! (21...♕xh2+ 22 ♔xh2 ♖xb2 23 ♘c4 ♖xe2 24 ♔g3! traps the rook!) 22 ♖xc7 ♖xe2 23 ♘c6 g5 24 ♘d4 ♖b2 25 ♖ac1 ♘d5 ½-½ Timoshchenko-Chandler, London 1991.

7...♘xc5 8 ♘d2 h6

⇨ 8...♕a5 looks like a good move: 9 ♗xf6 gxf6 10 ♘db1 (this seems like an absurd length to go to, to defend c3) 10...♘a4 11 e3 b6 12 ♗e2 ♗b7 13 0-0 ♗xc3 14 ♘xc3 ♘xc3 15 bxc3 ♕g5 = Timoshchenko-Davies, London 1992.

9 ♗h4 d5 10 cxd5 g5 11 ♗g3 exd5 12 a3 ♗xc3 13 ♕xc3 b6 14 e3 ♖e8! 15 ♗e5 ♘fe4 16 ♘xe4 ♘xe4 17 ♕d4 ♕e7 18 ♗g3 h5?!

Black had to find 18...♘c5! 19 ♗b5! ♘b3 20 ♕a4 ♘xa1 21 ♗xe8 ♗f5 22 0-0 ♕xe8 =.

19 ♗b5 ± ♗d7 20 ♗xd7 ♕xd7 21 f3 ♘c5

Black's position is full of weaknesses.

22 ♖d1 ♖ad8?! 23 h4?! ♕e7?! 24 hxg5 ± ♕xg5 25 ♔f2 ♕g6 26 ♗h4! ♘b3 27 ♕d3! ♖c8 28 ♕xg6+ fxg6 29 ♖xd5 ♖c2+ 30 ♔g3 ♖xe3 31 ♖d8+ ♔f7 32 ♖d7+ ♔e8

Confined to the back rank, the black king will soon find itself the victim of mating threats.

33 ♖hd1 ♘c5 34 ♖xa7 ♘d3 35 ♗f6! h4+ 36 ♗xh4 ♖ee2 37 ♖xd3 ♖xg2+ 38 ♔h3 ♖h2+ 39 ♔g4 1-0

Game 59

M.Gurevich-Ehlvest
France 1992

1 d4 ♘f6 2 c4 e6 3 ♘c3 ♗b4 4 ♕c2 0-0 5 ♘f3 c5 6 dxc5 ♘a6 7 g3 ♘xc5 8 ♗d2 d5

Alternatively: 8...b6 9 ♗g2 ♗b7 10 0-0 and now:

⇨ 10...♖c8 11 ♖fd1 ♕e7 12 ♗f4 d5 13 cxd5 exd5 14 ♘b5 ♘ce4 15 ♕b3 ♗c5 16 ♘bd4 ♘g4 17 ♖f1 ♕f6 18 ♖ad1? g5! (White suddenly finds himself in big trouble) 19 ♗c1 ♘gxf2! 20 ♖xf2 ♗xd4 (and not 20...♘xf2? 21 ♔xf2 g4 22 ♗g5) 21 e3 ♘xf2 22 ♔xf2 ♗c5 23 ♔g1 ♖cd8 24 ♘d4 ♗a6 25 ♕c2 ♖c8 26 ♕a4 ♗xd4 27 exd4 ♗e2 28 ♖e1 ♖c4 29 ♕a3 ♖c2 30 ♕e3 ♗b5 31 ♕xg5+ ♕xg5 32 ♗xg5 ♖e8 winning easily; M.Gurevich-Ivanov, Moscow Tal mem (active) 1992.

⇨ 10...♘ce4!? 11 ♘xe4 ♗xe4 12 ♕a4 ♗xd2 13 ♘xd2 ♗xg2 14 ♔xg2 (following wholesale exchanges the position has become completely equal) 14...♕c7!? 15 ♕a3!? ♖fc8 16 ♖ac1 h6 17 ♖fd1 ♕e5 18 ♘f3 ♕e4 19 ♕d3 ♕xd3 20 exd3 ♖c7 21 ♘d4 ♔f8 22 ♖c3 d5 23 ♘b5 ♖b7! 24 ♖a3?! ♖d7! and Black may even have a slight plus; M.Gurevich-Kir.Georgiev, Manila OL 1992.

9 cxd5 exd5 10 a3 ♗xc3 11 ♗xc3 ♘fe4!?

⇨ 11...♘ce4!? 12 ♗d4 ♗g4 13 ♗g2 ♖c8 14 ♕a4 a6 15 0-0 ♗xf3 16 exf3 (driving the knight from e4) 16...♘c5 17 ♕d1 ♘e6 18 ♗e5 ♘d7 19 ♗d6 ♖e8 20 f4 ♕b6 21 ♗b4 ♘f6

22 f5 ♘d4 23 ♖b1 ♘e2+ 24 ♔h1 ♖e5 25 ♗f3 ♖ce8 26 ♕d3 ♘d4 27 ♗g2 ♘e2 (it is understandable that Black is not happy with a draw by repetition, but 27...♘xf5!? might have been a better way of proceeding; at least I cannot find a flaw, e.g. 28 f4 ♕e3! 29 ♖d1? ♘xg3+ winning) 28 ♗f3 h5 29 ♖bd1 h4 30 ♖d2 hxg3 31 ♖xe2 ♖xe2 32 ♗xe2 gxf2 with complications that eventually went White's way; Dydyshko-Serper, USSR 1991.

12 b4 ♘e6 13 ♗g2 ♕c7 14 ♖c1 ♗d7 15 ♘e5! ♗a4 16 ♕b2 ♖ac8 17 ♗xe4

White decides to part with his light-squared bishop in order to preserve its dark-squared counterpart, aiming for an attack on g7.

17...dxe4 18 0-0 ♕b6 19 ♘g4 ♖c6 20 ♘e3 ♕b5 21 ♗e5 ♖xc1 22 ♖xc1 f6 23 ♗d6 ♖d8?

Better is 23...♖e8, though an interesting reply is then 24 g4!?.

24 ♗e7 ± ♖e8

25 ♗xf6! gxf6 26 ♘g4 f5?
Allowing immediate mate, but 26...♖f8 27 ♘xf6+ ♔f7 28 ♘xh7

♖e8 29 ♕f6+ ♔g8 30 ♕g6+ ♔h8 31 ♘f6 also loses.

27 ♘h6+ ♔f8 28 ♕f6# (1-0)

Game 60

Timman-Korchnoi
Brussels 1991

1 d4 ♘f6 2 c4 e6 3 ♘c3 ♗b4 4 ♕c2 0-0 5 ♘f3 c5 6 dxc5 ♘a6 7 g3 ♘xc5 8 ♗g2 ♘ce4

⇨ 8...b6 9 0-0 ♗b7 10 ♗f4!? ♘ce4 11 ♘xe4 ♗xe4 12 ♕a4 ♗e7 13 ♖fd1 ♕c8 14 ♘e5 ♗xg2 15 ♔xg2 ♖d8 16 ♗g5 a6! (both 16...h6? 17 ♗xf6 ♗xf6 18 ♘xd7 ♗xb2 19 ♖ab1 ♗a3 20 ♖b3 ♗e7 and 16...♕c7 17 ♘xd7! ♖xd7 18 ♖xd7 ♘xd7 19 ♗xe7 are good for White) 17 ♗xf6 (17 ♘xd7? b5!) 17...b5 (17...gxf6 18 ♖xd7 fxe5 19 ♖xe7 ♔f8 20 ♕a3 ±) 18 cxb5 ♗xf6 19 ♘f3 ♗xb2 20 ♖ab1 axb5 21 ♕xb5 ♗f6 22 a4 ♕c2 23 a5 ♕a2 24 ♘e5 ♗xe5 25 ♕xe5 (at this point the game seems to have fizzled out) 25...♖xa5?? (25...♕xa5 26 ♕xa5 ♖xa5 27 ♖xd7 ♖f8 =) 26 ♖xd7?? (missing 26 ♖b8! ♖a8 27 ♖a1, winning on the spot) 26...♖f8 27 ♖b2 ♖xe5 ½-½ Crouch-Speelman, Hastings 1993.

⇨ 8...♘fe4!? 9 0-0 ♗xc3 10 bxc3 d6! 11 ♘d4 f5 12 ♘b3 ♗d7 13 ♘xc5 ♘xc5 14 ♗f4 e5 15 ♗e3 e4 16 f3 ♕c7! 17 ♕d2 ♗c6 18 ♖ad1 ♖ad8 19 ♗f4 ♕b6?! (better is 19...♕f7! 20 ♗xd6 ♗a4 21 ♗xc5 ♖xd2 22 ♖xd2 ♖e8 23 fxe4 ♕xc4 24 ♗d4 with unclear play) 20 ♔h1 ♖d7 21 ♗xd6 ♕d8 22 ♕d4 ♘e6 23 ♕e5 ♖e8 24 fxe4 ♘g5 25 ♕xf5 ♘xe4 26 ♗e5!

g6 27 ♖xd7 gxf5 28 ♖xd8 ♖xd8 29 ♗d4 ♖f8 30 ♔g1 h5 31 ♗h3 ♗d7 32 ♖f4 ♖f7 33 ♗g2 ♗c6 34 ♖h4 ♖h7 35 ♗f3 ♗e8 36 ♗xa7 ♔g7 37 ♗d4+ ♔g6 38 ♖xe4 1-0 M.Gurevich-Beliavsky, Reggio Emilia 1992.

9 ♗d2 ♘xd2 10 ♘xd2 d5 11 0-0 ♗d7

⇨ 11...d4!? is worth trying: 12 ♘ce4 e5 13 c5 ♗f5 14 ♘xf6+ ♕xf6 15 ♗e4 ♗h3 16 ♖fc1 (obviously 16 ♗xh7+? ♔h8 loses material to the dual threats of ...♗xf1 and ...g6) 16...♖ac8 17 ♗xb7 ♖c7 18 ♗f3 ♗xc5 19 ♘e4 ♕b6 20 ♗g2 ♗f5 21 g4 ♗g6 22 h4 ♖fc8 23 ♕b3 ♕xb3 ½-½ Korchnoi-Greenfeld, Beer-Sheva 1992.

12 cxd5 exd5 13 a3 ♗xc3 14 ♕xc3 ♕b6 15 ♕b3 ♗b5 16 ♖fe1 ♕a6 17 e3 ♖ac8 18 ♖ec1?!

A better move is 18 ♖ac1.

18...♖c6! = 19 ♕b4 ♖fc8 20 ♖xc6 ♕xc6 21 ♖e1 ♕c5 22 ♕xc5 ♖xc5 23 ♘f3 ♔f8?! 24 ♘d4 ♗a4 25 ♗f1 g6 26 f3 ± ♗d7 27 ♔f2 ♘e8 28 ♖d1 ♔e7 29 ♖d2 ♗a4 30 ♗e2

30...♘c7 31 ♗d3 ♘e6 32 b3 ♗d7 33 ♘e2 ♖c7 34 ♗b1 ♗c6

Black has placed his pieces on the best defensive squares controlling d5 and d4, but, with the better bishop and the d4 square, White can improve at his leisure.

35 b4 ♖d7 36 ♗a2 a6 37 ♗b3 ♖d8 38 ♖d1 ♖d7 39 g4 ♖d8 40 h4 h6 41 ♖d2?! f5! 42 ♔g3 ♔f6 43 ♖d1 fxg4 44 fxg4? g5! = 45 ♖f1+ ♔e7 46 ♘d4 ♘xd4 47 exd4 ♖f8 48 ♖xf8 ½-½

Game 61

Korchnoi-Timman
Tilburg 1991

1 d4 ♘f6 2 c4 e6 3 ♘c3 ♗b4 4 ♕c2 0-0 5 ♘f3 c5 6 dxc5 ♘a6 7 g3 ♘xc5 8 ♗g2 ♘ce4 9 ♗d2 ♘xd2 10 ♘xd2 a6

Interesting is 10...♖b8 11 0-0 b6 12 ♘de4 ♘xe4 13 ♗xe4 and now:

⇨ 13...f5!? 14 ♗g2 ♗b7 15 ♗xb7 ♖xb7 16 a3 ♗e7 17 ♖ad1 ♕c8 18 ♕d3 a6 19 ♖d2 ♖c7 20 ♘a4 ♕b7 21 b4 b5 22 ♘b2 bxc4 23 ♘xc4 ♕b5 24 ♘d6 ♕xd3 25 ♖xd3 looks fairly equal; Korchnoi-Gelfand, Tilburg (active) 1992.

⇨ 13...h6 14 ♖ad1 a6 15 a3 ♗e7 16 ♖d2 ♕c7 17 ♕d3 ♖d8 18 ♖fd1 d6 19 e3 ♗d7 20 a4 ♖bc8 21 b3 ♗e8 22 ♘e2 b5! (a temporary pawn sacrifice to permit ...d5, scotching White's d-file pressure) 23 axb5 axb5 24 cxb5 d5 25 ♗g2 ♕b6 26 ♘d4 ♗f6 27 ♗f1 ♖b8 28 e4 ♗xd4 29 ♕xd4 ♗xb5 30 ♗c4 ♕xd4 31 ♖xd4 ♗c6 32 exd5 exd5 33 ♗xd5 ½-½ M.Gurevich-Sax, Moscow 1990.

11 0-0 ♕c7 12 ♘ce4

Or 12 ♖fc1 ♖b8 (better than
12...♗e7 13 ♘a4 d6 14 c5 d5 15 b4 ±
♖b8 16 ♖ab1 ♖d8 17 ♘b3 ♗d7 18
♘b6 ♗c6 19 a4 with a useful queenside initiative; Bönsch-Lobron, Hannover 1991) and now:

⇨ 13 ♘ce4 ♘xe4 14 ♗xe4 h6 15 a3
♗e7 16 c5 b6 17 cxb6 ♕xb6 18
♘c4 ♕b3 19 ♗h7+ (a useful trick
pushing the black king further from
the centre at no cost) 19...♔h8 20
♕xb3 ♖xb3 21 ♗c2 ♖b8 22 b4 g5
23 ♗d3 ♔g7 24 ♖a2 ♗b7 25 ♘a5
♖fc8 26 ♖ac2 ♖xc2 27 ♖xc2 ♗c8 28
e3 ♗d8 = Illescas-Salov, Linares
1992.

⇨ 13 a3 ♗e7 14 ♘a4 b6 15 b4 a5!
(immediately contesting White's
queenside build up) 16 b5?! ♗b7 17
♕d3 ♖fc8 18 ♖c3 ♗xg2 19 ♔xg2
♕b7+ 20 ♕f3?! d5! 21 cxd5 ♘xd5
22 ♖c4 ♗g5 23 ♖xc8+ ♕xc8 24
♘e4 ♗e7 25 ♕b3 ♕c7 26 ♖d1 ♖c8
(taking command of the c-file) 27
♖d3 ♕c4 28 ♘d2 ♕xb3 29 ♖xb3 f5
∓ (ensuring that the knight can remain on d5) 30 ♘b1 ♗f6 31 ♘d2
♖c2 32 ♖d3 ♗e7?! (32...♗f7 ∓) 33
♘f3 ♗f6 (33...♖xe2 allows 34 ♘d4
♖e1 35 ♘xe6 =) 34 ♖d2 ♖c1?! 35
♘d4 ♗xd4 36 ♖xd4 ♖b1 37 f3!
♖xb5 38 e4 fxe4 39 fxe4 ♘e3+ 40
♔f2 ♖b3 41 h3 ♘c2 42 ♖d6 ♘xa3
43 ♘xb6 (White has managed to
generate enough play to make a
draw) 43...♔f7 44 ♖c6 ♖b2+ 45
♔f3 ♖c2 46 ♖d6 ♘b5 47 ♖d7+
♔f6 48 ♖b7 ♘d6 49 ♖a7 ♖a2 50
♘d7+ ♔g5 51 h4+ ♔h5 52 ♘c5
♔g6 ½-½ Bönsch-Ivanchuk, Terrassa 1991.

**12...♘xe4 13 ♘xe4 f5 14 ♕b3
♗e7 15 ♘c3 ♖b8 16 ♖ad1?**

White should play 16 ♖fd1.
16...♗f6 17 ♖d3 b5! ∓ **18 cxb5
axb5 19 ♘xb5 ♕e5 20 a4 ♕xe2**

A pleasant operation for Black,
swapping his queenside for White's
centre.

**21 ♖b1 f4 22 ♗f3 ♕e5 23 g4 ♖d8
24 ♕d1 d5 25 ♘d4 ♕d6 26 b4
♗xd4?**

This bishop is too strong to give
up; 26...♗d7 27 b5 ♖dc8 ∓.

**27 ♖xd4 ♗b7 28 b5 e5 29 ♖d2
♕e6 30 ♗e4!**

Ingenious! 30 ♖b4 is met by
30...♕e7! and 31...e4 ∓.

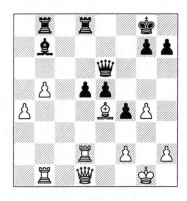

**30...d4 31 ♗xb7 ♖xb7 32 a5 e4
33 a6 e3 34 fxe3 ♕xe3+?**

Dividing his pawns; 34...fxe3 ±.

**35 ♖f2 ♖b6 36 ♖b3 ♕e4 37 ♕f3
♕xf3 38 ♖fxf3 g5 39 ♖fd3 ♔f7 40
♖b4 ♔e6 41 ♔f2 ♖db8 42 ♖dxd4
♖xb5 43 ♖xb5 ♖xb5 44 ♖a4 ♖b8
45 ♔f3**

The a-pawn supported by the rook
wins.

**45...♖a8 46 a7 ♔f6 47 ♔e4 ♔g6
48 h4 h6 49 hxg5 hxg5 50 ♖a5! ±
♔h6 51 ♖a1 ♔g6 52 ♔d5 f3 53 ♔c6
♔f6 54 ♖a5 1-0**

Game 62

Hertneck-Karpov
Baden-Baden 1992

1 d4 ♘f6 2 c4 e6 3 ♘c3 ♗b4 4 ♕c2 0-0 5 ♘f3 c5 6 dxc5 ♘a6 7 g3 ♘xc5 8 ♗g2 ♘ce4 9 0-0 ♘xc3

⇨ 9...♗xc3 10 bxc3 ♕a5 11 ♘d4! d5! 12 cxd5 exd5 13 c4 ♖e8 14 cxd5 ♕xd5 15 ♗b2 ♗d7 16 f3 ♖ac8 17 ♕d3 ♘c5 18 ♕d2 ♘a4 19 e4 ♕d6 20 ♖ad1 ♘xb2 21 ♕xb2 ♖c4 22 ♖fe1? (22 ♘b3) 22...♗a4 ∓ 23 ♘b3 ♕b6+ 24 ♔h1 ♖b4 25 ♖d2 ♘d7! 26 ♕a1 ♘e5 27 ♘d4 ♖d8? (this allows an unusual drawing tactic; 27...g6! would have kept the advantage) 28 ♘f5! ♖xd2 29 ♕xe5 ♕f6 (and not 29...f6?? 30 ♕e7) 30 ♕c5 ♕b6 (30...♖b5? 31 ♕c4! ♖a5 32 ♕b4 ±) 31 ♕e5 ½-½ Vera-Adla, Havana Capablanca mem 1992.

10 bxc3 ♗e7 11 e4!?

⇨ 11 ♗f4 d6 12 c5!? (causing some disarray in the black camp at the cost of a pawn) 12... dxc5 13 c4 ♘d7 14 ♖ab1 ♕e8 15 ♗c7 ♗d8 16 ♗d6 ♗e7 17 ♗c7 ♗d8 18 ♗d6 ½-½ Crouch-Polugaevsky, Hastings 1992/93.

11...d6 12 e5 dxe5 13 ♘xe5 ♕c7 14 ♕e2 ♗d6

⇨ 14...♘d7 15 ♗f4 ♘xe5 16 ♗xe5 ♗d6 17 ♗xd6 ♕xd6 18 ♖ab1 ♖b8 19 ♖fd1 ♕c7 20 ♕e3 b6 21 c5 ♗d7 22 cxb6 axb6 23 ♕d4 ♗c6 24 ♕d6 ♕xd6 25 ♖xd6 ♗xg2 26 ♔xg2 was equal and dull in Bareev-Korchnoi, Tilburg 1991.

⇨ 14...♘e8!? 15 ♖d1 f6 16 ♘g4 ♘d6 17 ♗a3 ♖e8 18 c5 ♘f5 19 ♖d2 ♖f8? 20 ♕c4 ♖b8? 21 ♖e1 ♔h8 22 ♖xe6! h5! (22...♗xe6 23 ♕xe6 g6 24 ♖d7 ♕c8 25 ♗e4 is winning) 23 ♗e4 ♘d6? 24 ♕d5 ♘xe4 25 ♕xh5+ ♔g8 26 ♘h6+ with a crushing attack; Hertneck-Wahls, Bundesliga 1992.

15 ♗f4 ♘e8!?

This seems to be strongest:

⇨ 15...g5? fails completely to 16 ♘g4 ♘xg4 17 ♗xd6 ±.

⇨ 15...♘d7?! is possibly a mistake: 16 ♘xd7 ♗xd7 17 ♗xd6 ♕xd6 18 ♗xb7 ♖ab8 19 ♖fd1 (19 ♖ab1 ♗c6! 20 ♖fd1 ♕c5 21 ♗xc6 ♖xb1 22 ♖xb1 ♕xc6 23 ♕e5 ♕xc4 24 ♖b8 g6 = Lobron-Rechlis, Bern Z 1990) 19...♕c7 20 ♗e4 ♗c8! 21 ♖d4 (it is not White's extra pawn—which is isolated and doubled—so much as his space advantage that counts here) 21...e5 22 ♖d5 f5 23 ♗g2 e4 24 ♖ad1 ♗e6 25 ♖5d4 ♖bc8 26 ♗f1 ♕f7 27 ♕e3! h6 28 ♖d6 ♗xc4?! (allowing White's rook on to the seventh rank) 29 ♖d7 ♕f6 30 ♖1d6 ♕e5? 31 ♗xc4+ ♖xc4 32 ♕xa7! ♖fc8 33 ♖e7! 1-0 M.Gurevich-Petursson, Reggio Emilia 1990. 34 ♖dd7 is coming.

16 ♖ab1 f6 17 ♘d3 ♕xc4 18 ♗xd6 ♘xd6 19 ♖b4 ♕c7 20 ♘f4 ♖e8

Black has gained a pawn for insufficient compensation.

21 ♖d1 a5 22 ♖bd4 ♖a6 23 ♕h5 ♖f8 24 g4 a4! 25 c4 ♘f7 26 h4

White tries hard to generate some play for his pawn, but Karpov doesn't give him a chance.

26...♖a5 27 g5 ♖f5 28 ♘h3 g6 29 ♕e2 fxg5 30 h5 ♔g7 31 ♗e4 ♖f6 32 ♕g4 gxh5 33 ♕xh5 ♖h6 34 ♕g4 ♖h4 35 ♕g2 e5 36 ♖4d3 g4 37 f4 exf4 38 ♖d5 ♕b6+ 39 c5 ♕f6 0-1

4

Many years ago 4...d5 was considered the perfect reply to 4 ♕c2, mainly because of a game Keres-Botvinnik from 1941, which resulted in a crushing win for Black. More recently Kasparov improved significantly on Keres' play and the pendulum swung the other way. However, following Fischer's successful adoption of 4...d5 against Spassky in their return match, it would not be in the least surprising if there is an upsurge of interest in this line. There are plenty of variations that offer Black lots of tactical play.

White has two major possibilities, 5 cxd5 and 5 a3.

After 5 cxd5 the plan of Alekhine's, 5...♕xd5, has been adopted recently by Romanishin, with some new ideas. However, after seeing his game against I.Sokolov (game 63) there are unlikely to be many players willing to follow his lead. Often, White gets the two bishops on an open board, although as Gulko-Smyslov shows, Black does retain certain counterchances.

Following 5...exd5 6 ♗g5 Black should play 6...h6 when, instead of the dull 7 ♗xf6, the sharp 7 ♗h4 has been pioneered by the World Champion, Kasparov. Game 65 shows some of his impressive efforts.

So Black players were forced to return to the drawing board and, instead of 11...♕f6, 11...♕a5 was the result. At the moment Black seems to be OK here providing he plays Fischer's 14...♕xc5! (game 67), although the interesting 12...♘xd2

featured in game 66 certainly merits more attention.

The other main line starts 5 a3 and typically leads to variations where Black sacrifices pawns to open the position and take advantage of his lead in development. In game 68, after 6...♘e4 7 ♕c2 c5 8 dxc5 ♘c6, Gurevich decided to take the bull by the horns and played 9 cxd5. This leads to wild complications which are thought to be advantageous for White, although in this case Gurevich avoided the theoretical 16 ♖d1, and found an original path. Perhaps he feared an improvement.

In game 69, instead of 7...c5, Kotronias tries 7...e5 and finds a bright new method of conducting the black pieces. Unfortunately, he then proceeds to mar his conception with a pathetic blunder.

Game 63

I.Sokolov-Romanishin
Barcelona 1992

1 d4 ♘f6 2 c4 e6 3 ♘c3 ♗b4 4 ♕c2 d5 5 cxd5 ♕xd5 6 ♘f3 0-0

A major alternative is 6...c5 7 ♗d2 ♗xc3 8 ♗xc3 and now:

1) 8...♘c6 with a further division: ⇨ 9 dxc5 ♕xc5 10 ♖c1 ♗d7 11 e3 ♖c8 12 ♗e2 ♘d5 13 ♕b1 ♘xc3 14 ♖xc3 ♕e7 15 0-0 0-0 16 ♖fc1 (although he has conceded his dark-squared bishop, White is still a little better) 16...♘b4 17 ♖c7 ♖xc7 18 ♖xc7 ♖c8 19 ♖xb7 ♕d6 20 ♕d1 ♘d5 21 g3 ♗c6 22 ♖xa7 ± (in a normal game Black could resign, but

this being quick chess he ploughs on) 22...♕b8 23 ♕d4 ♘f6 24 ♖a3 ♗d5 25 ♖c3 ♖d8 26 ♖d3 ♕a8 27 a3 ♖d7 28 ♕f4 h6 29 ♘e1 ♖b7 30 ♕d4 ♕b8 31 b4 e5 32 ♕b2 ♖b6 33 ♖c3 ♖d6 34 ♖c1 ♖d8 35 b5 g5 36 ♗f3 ♘e4 37 ♖d1 f5 38 b6 ♗b7 39 ♖xd8+ ♕xd8 40 a4?? g4 41 ♗g2? ♕d1 ∓ Gulko-Smyslov, Tilburg (active) 1992.

⇨ 9 ♖d1 b6 10 e3 ♗b7 11 dxc5 ♕xc5 12 ♗d3 0-0 13 a3 ♖ac8 14 0-0 ± ♕h5 15 ♕e2 ♘d5 16 ♗d2 ♘e5 17 ♘d4 ♕xe2 18 ♗xe2 ♘c4 19 ♗c1 a6 20 e4 ♘f6 21 f3 (setting up a solid wall of pawns to hinder the bishop on b7) 21...h6 22 b3 ♘a5 23 ♗e3 b5 24 ♗d2 ♘c6 25 ♘xc6 ♖xc6 26 ♗b4 ♖fc8 27 ♖d2 ♖c2 28 ♖fd1 ♖xd2 29 ♖xd2 ♗c6 30 ♖c2 (I don't agree with this, allowing the exchange of rooks, though it is true that the natural 30 ♔f2?! meets with 30...♗xe4!) 30...♗d7 31 ♖xc8+ ♗xc8 32 ♔f2 and although White retains an advantage Smyslov managed to hold the draw in Gulko-Smyslov, Tilburg 1992.

2) 8...b6!? 9 dxc5!? ♕xc5 10 b4 ♕c7 11 ♕b2 ♕e7 12 e4 0-0 13 ♗d3 ♗b7 14 0-0 ♖d8 15 ♕e2 ♘bd7 16 a3 ♖ac8 17 ♖ac1 ♘f8 18 e5 (a rather two-sided decision, hoping for a kingside attack but closing the a1-h8 diagonal and conceding the d5 square) 18...♘d5 19 ♗d2 h6 20 h4 ♘c7!? 21 ♗e4 ♗xe4 22 ♕xe4 ♕d7 23 ♕g4 ♔h8 24 ♕h5 ♕e8! 25 ♖c4 ♘d5 26 ♖fc1 ♖xc4 27 ♖xc4 b5! 28 ♖c5 a6 29 ♘g5 ♘d7! 30 ♘xf7+ ♔g8 31 ♖xd5 exd5 32 e6 ♘f8 33 e7 ♕xe7 34 ♘xd8 ♕xd8 ∓ 35 ♕g4 ♕d7 36 ♕d4 ♕f5 37 ♕c3 ♕g4 38

♕d3! ♕c4?! (38...d4 ∓) 39 ♕f5 d4 40 g4 d3 41 h5 ½-½ Beliavsky-Lerner, Odessa 1989.

7 ♗d2

⇨ 7 e3 c5 8 ♗d2 ♕h5! 9 ♗e2 cxd4 10 ♘xd4 ♕g6 11 0-0 e5 12 ♗d3 ♕h5 13 ♘de2 ♘c6 14 a3 ♗xc3 15 ♗xc3 ♗e6 16 ♘g3 ♕h4 17 ♘f5 ♕h5 18 ♘g3 ♕h4 19 ♘f5 ½-½ I.Sokolov-Romanishin, Groningen 1991.

7...♗xc3 8 ♗xc3 b6

Otherwise there is 8...♗d7!? 9 ♘d2! ♘c6 10 e4 ♕g5 11 g3 ♖ad8 12 ♗d3 ♕h6 13 f4 ♘g4 14 ♗e2 e5 15 dxe5 ♘e3 16 ♕d3 ♘g2+ 17 ♔f2 ♗g4 18 ♕c2 ♗h3 19 ♖hg1 ♘xe5 20 ♖xg2 ♕b6+ 21 ♔f1 ♘d7 22 ♘c4 ♕c6 23 ♘e3 ♘f6 24 ♗f3 ♖fe8 25 ♘d5 ♕c4+ 26 ♔g1 ♘xd5 27 exd5 ♗xg2 28 ♔xg2 winning; Mohr-Romanishin, Bad Lauterberg 1991.

9 ♘d2! ±

Better than:

⇨ 9 e3 a5 10 ♗d2 ♗a6 11 ♗xa6 ♘xa6 12 0-0 c5 13 dxc5 ♘xc5 14 ♗c3 ♘fe4 (fairly equal) 15 ♖fd1 ♕b7 16 ♗d4 ♖fc8 17 ♖ac1 ♕a6 18 ♘e5 f6 19 ♘c4 b5 20 ♗xc5 ♖xc5 21 ♕xe4 ♖ac8 22 g3 ♕c6?? (falling for an evil trick; simply 22...♖xc4 was quite satisfactory) 23 ♘d6! 1-0 Flear-Nikčević, Rome 1990. After 23...♕xe4, 24 ♖xc5! threatens mate on c8, and 23...♖xc1 24 ♕xe6+ is Philidor's legacy.

9...♗b7 10 f3 ♕g5 11 e4 ♘c6 12 ♘b3 a5 13 ♕f2 ♖fd8

13...♘h5 14 g4! ♘f4 15 h4 ♕e7 16 ♕h2 ±.

14 ♖d1 a4 15 ♘c1 a3! 16 b3 e5!? 17 h4 ♕g6 18 d5 ♘d4 19 ♗xd4 exd4 20 ♗d3! ±

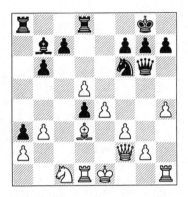

20...♘d7 21 0-0 ♘c5 22 ♘e2!
♕f6 23 ♖fe1 c6 24 ♘xd4 ♘xd3 25
♖xd3 cxd5 26 e5

The white kingside pawns are
well supported and free to advance,
whilst the black bishop is restricted
by the pawn on d5 and is no help
against White's powerful knight.

26...♕g6 27 ♖de3 b5 28 f4 ♕b6
29 ♖g3 g6 30 h5 ♔h8 31 hxg6 fxg6
32 e6 ♖ac8 33 ♕e3 ♕c7 34 ♘xb5
1-0

Game 64

Agdestein-Piket
Tilburg 1989

1 d4 ♘f6 2 c4 e6 3 ♘c3 ♗b4 4 ♕c2
d5 5 cxd5
⇨ 5 ♘f3!? (thought to be a mistake
on account of Black's reply) 5...dxc4
6 a3 ♗e7?! (6...♗xc3+ 7 ♕xc3 b5 is
worthy of consideration) 7 e4 ♘c6 8
e5 ♘d5 9 ♗xc4 ♘b6 10 ♗e2 0-0 11
♗e3 f5 12 exf6 ♗xf6 13 ♗d3 h6 14
0-0 ♔h8 15 ♖ad1 ♗d7 16 ♕d2 ♕e7
17 ♗b1 ♕f7 18 ♕c2 ♕g8 19 ♘e5
♗e8 20 ♕c1 ♘xe5 21 dxe5 ♗xe5 22

♗xh6! ♕f7 23 ♖d3 gxh6 24 ♕xh6+
♔g8 25 f4! ♗xf4 26 ♖xf4 1-0 I.Sok-
olov-Nikčević, Nikšić 1991.
⇨ 5 ♗g5 dxc4 6 e3 c5 7 dxc5 ♘bd7
8 c6 bxc6 9 ♗xc4 ♕a5 10 ♗xf6
♘xf6 11 ♘e2 0-0 12 0-0 ♗e7 13
♖ac1 ♗b7 14 ♘d4 ♖ab8 15 ♗e2
♗a8 16 b3 ♗a3 ½-½ Beliavsky-
Korchnoi, Amsterdam 1989.

5...exd5 6 ♗g5 c5!?

Any move apart from this and
6...h6 allows White to play a favourable version of the QGD exchange.

7 a3?!

The best move, 7 dxc5, is covered
in the following games, while 7 ♘f3
0-0 would transpose into M.Gure-
vich-Rodriguez, Barcelona 1992,
which continued: 8 e3 cxd4 9 ♘xd4
♘c6 10 ♘xc6 bxc6 11 ♗e2 h6 12
♗h4 g5 13 ♗g3 ♘e4 (the black position is active but his kingside is
loose) 14 0-0 ♘xg3 15 hxg3 ♕f6 16
♗d3 ♖d8 17 ♘a4 ♗d7 18 b3 ♗e8
19 ♕e2 ♗a3 (stopping White from
continuing ♖c1 and ♘c5, fixing the
black c-pawn) 20 ♖ad1 ♖ac8 21 ♖d2
c5 22 ♗b5 ♗xb5 23 ♕xb5 c4 24
♖e2? (certainly not 24 bxc4?? ♖b8
25 ♕a5 ♗b4 ∓, but 24 ♕a5 is unclear) 24...♖b8 25 ♕a5 cxb3 26 axb3
d4 27 exd4 ♕xd4 28 ♕f5? (28 ♖e3
=) 28...♖xb3 ∓ 29 ♖e4 ♕d7 30 ♕f6
♗f8 31 ♔h2 ♖b5 32 ♖fe1 ♖f5 33
♕b2 ♕d2 34 ♖1e2 ♕xb2 35 ♘xb2
♗c5 with a relatively straightforward win.

**7...♗xc3+ 8 ♕xc3 c4 9 g3 ♘c6
10 ♗g2 ♗e6 11 ♘h3 h6 12 ♗xf6
♕xf6 13 ♘f4 ♕xd4! 14 ♕xd4
♘xd4 15 ♖d1 ♘b3! 16 ♘xd5?**

Better was 16 ♗xd5 ♗xd5 17
♖xd5; now the queenside majority

and knight on b3 give Black the edge.

16...0-0-0 17 f4 b5?

17...♖d7! and doubling rooks was very strong.

18 a4 a6 19 axb5 axb5 20 ♔f2 ♗xd5 21 ♗xd5 f6 22 e4 ♔c7 23 ♔f3 ♔b6 24 ♔g4 ♔c5 25 ♔h5 ♘d4 26 b4+ cxb3 27 ♖d3 b2 28 ♖b1 f5 29 ♖c3+ ♔b6 30 ♖xb2 fxe4 31 ♗xe4 ♖he8 32 ♗g6? ♖e6 33 f5 ♖e5 34 g4 ♘e2 35 ♖f3 ♖d4! ∓ 36 ♗f7 ♘f4+ 37 ♔h4 ♘d3?

37...♖ee4 ∓.

38 ♖d2?

38 ♖b3.

38...♘e1 39 ♖df2 ♖d2??

The last few moves bear all the hallmarks of a time-scramble, but even so it is surprising that Black didn't play 39...♘xf3+ 40 ♖xf3 ♖d6 ∓.

40 ♖f4! ± ♘g2+ 41 ♔g3 ♘xf4 42 ♖xd2 ♘e2+ 43 ♔f3 ♖e7 44 ♗e6 ♘c3 45 ♔f4?

45 h4!.

45...b4 46 h4 ♘a4 47 ♖d6+ ♔c7! = 48 ♔e5 b3 49 ♖d4 b2 50 ♖b4 ♘c5

Indirectly defending the b-pawn.

51 ♔d4 ♘xe6+ ½-½

Game 65

Kasparov-Spassky
Linares 1990

1 d4 ♘f6 2 c4 e6 3 ♘c3 ♗b4 4 ♕c2 d5 5 cxd5 exd5 6 ♗g5 h6 7 ♗h4!?

⇨ 7 ♗xf6 is solid and a little better for White. It is without risk, but not nearly as interesting: 7...♕xf6 8 a3 (not 8 e3?! 0-0 9 ♘f3 ♗f5! = Petran-Ravia, Ajka 1992) 8...♗xc3+ 9 ♕xc3 c6 10 e3 0-0 11 ♘f3 ♖e8 12 ♗e2 ♘d7 13 0-0 ♘f8 14 b4 g5?! 15 b5 (the minority attack) 15...♘g6 16 bxc6 bxc6 17 ♖fc1 ± Eslon-Andarias, Javea 1992.

7...c5

Black may instead chase the bishop immediately: 7...g5 8 ♗g3 ♘e4 9 e3 and now:

1) 9...h5!? is interesting: 10 ♗d3!? (sharper than 10 f3 ♘xg3 11 hxg3 ♕d6 12 g4 h4 13 a3 ± Sakaev-Orlov, USSR 1990) 10...h4 11 ♗e5 f6 12 ♗xe4 dxe4 13 d5! ♔f7 14 ♕xe4 ♕e7 15 ♕c4 ♘a6 16 ♗d4 c5 17 dxc6+ ♗e6 18 ♕e2 ♖ad8 19 ♘f3 g4 20 ♘d2 bxc6 21 ♘de4 ♖h6 22 ♕xa6 ♖xd4 23 exd4 ♗xc3+ 24 bxc3 ♗f5 25 f3 gxf3 26 gxf3 ♗xe4 27 ♕e2! ♗xf3 28 ♕xe7+ ♔xe7 29 ♖g1 and White went on to win; Seirawan-Al Hadhrani, Novi Sad OL 1990.

2) 9...c6?! 10 ♗d3 ♘xg3 11 hxg3 ♗e6 12 a3! ♗f8 (12...♗d6 13 0-0-0 ♘d7 14 ♘f3 ♕e7 15 e4! dxe4 16 ♗xe4) 13 f4! gxf4 14 gxf4 ♗g4 15

♗f5! ♗xf5?! (15...♖g8! 16 ♘f3 ♘d7 17 0-0-0 ♕a5!?) 16 ♕xf5 ♘d7 17 e4 ♕f6?! 18 ♕xf6 ♘xf6 19 e5 ♘d7 20 ♘ge2 ♘b6 21 b3 ♖g8 22 ♔f2 ♔d7 23 ♘g3 (White has the better pawn structure — f7 and h6 will give Black problems) 23...♖c8 24 ♔f3! c5 25 dxc5 ♖xc5 26 ♘ce2 ♖c6 27 ♖hc1! ♖xc1 28 ♖xc1 ♗xa3 29 ♖a1 ♗c5 30 ♘f5!? (30 ♖xa7 ♘c4 31 ♖a2! ♘e3 32 ♖a5 ♗b6 33 ♖b5 ± was simpler) 30...♖a8 31 ♘xh6 ♔e6 32 g4 a5 33 ♖c1! ♘d7 34 ♘c3 ♖a6 35 ♖e1! d4 36 f5+ ♔e7 37 ♘d5+ ♔f8 38 e6 fxe6 39 fxe6 ♘b8 40 ♘f5 ♘c6 41 g5 1-0 Kasparov-P.Nikolić, Belgrade 1989.

8 dxc5 ♘c6

Probably best, but there is also:

1) 8...0-0?! 9 e3 ♘bd7 10 ♗d3 ♕a5 11 ♘e2 ♗xc3+ 12 ♕xc3 ♕xc3+ 13 ♘xc3 ♘xc5 14 ♗c2 g5 15 ♗g3 ♗e6 16 f3! ± a6 17 h4 ♖fc8 18 hxg5 hxg5 (it is not just the isolated queen's pawn and White's two bishops that make this position so difficult for Black, but also his weakened kingside) 19 0-0-0 ♘cd7 20 ♔b1 ♔g7 21 ♗b3 ♖c5 22 e4 dxe4 23 ♗xe6 fxe6 24 ♘xe4 ♖a5 25 ♖he1 ♘f8 26 ♘d6 b6 27 ♗f2 ♘d5 28 ♗d4+ ♔g6 29 ♘c4 1-0 Kasparov-Korchnoi, Tilburg 1989. The resignation might seem a little premature, but on 29...♖b5, 30 ♘e5+ is very hard to meet.

2) 8...g5!? 9 ♗g3 ♘e4 10 e3 and now:

2a) 10...♕f6?! 11 ♗b5+ ♗d7 12 ♗xd7+ ♘xd7 13 ♘e2 ♗xc3+ 14 bxc3 0-0 15 ♖d1 ♕e6 16 h4 g4 17 ♗d6?! (this is a faulty conception) 17...♘xd6 18 cxd6 ♕xd6 19 e4

♖ae8 20 ♖xd5 ♕e6 21 ♖d4 ♘c5 22 0-0 (White must return the pawn for if 22 ♘g3 f5) 22...♘xe4 23 ♘f4 ♕f5 24 ♘d5 ♖e5 25 c4 ♖fe8 26 f3 gxf3 27 ♖xf3 ♕g6 28 h5? ♕c6 29 ♕d3 ♕c5 30 ♕e3 (what else?) 30...♘g5 31 ♕f4 ♘xf3+ winning; Goldin-Lautier, Palma 1989.

2b) 10...♕a5!? was Nigel Short's new idea for his match against Garry Kasparov. Black chooses to step up the pressure on c3 by the fastest possible means while preventing White developing quickly with ♗b5+, at the cost of allowing White to use the e5 square. Complex tactics result:

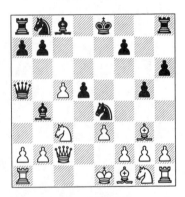

⇨ 11 ♗e5 0-0 12 ♗d3 ♘c6 13 ♗xe4 ♘xe5 14 ♗xd5 (Kasparov felt that White's position after 14 ♗h7+ ♔g7 15 ♗d3 d4 16 exd4 ♘xd3+ 17 ♕xd3 ♖e8+ 18 ♘e2 b6 intending ....♗a6 would have been "most uncomfortable") 14...♗g4! 15 ♘f3 ♗xf3 16 ♗xf3 (16 gxf3? ♖ac8! is unpleasant for White) 16...♘xf3+ 17 gxf3 ♖ac8 18 0-0 ½-½ Kasparov-Short, London *Times* Wch (5) 1993.

⇨ 11 ♘e2 ♗f5 12 ♗e5 was Kasparov's new approach in Game 9. Short mentioned the possibility 12...♗g6 13 ♗xh8 ♘xc3 14 ♕xc3 ♗xc3 15 ♗xc3 ♕xc5 16 h4 with good compensation; the alternative 12...♘xc3 is met by 13 ♕xf5 ♘e4+ 14 ♘c3 ♘xc3 15 ♕c8+ ♔e7 16 ♗d6+ ♔f6 17 ♕xh8+ ♔f5 18 ♗d3+ ♘e4+ 19 ♔e2 winning (Crouch). The game continued 12...0-0 (a much criticised move) 13 ♘d4 and now 13...♗g6? 14 ♘b3 ♘xc3 15 ♗xc3 ♗xc2 16 ♘xa5 ♗xc3+ 17 bxc3 b6 18 ♔d2 left White with a large advantage; Kasparov-Short, London *Times* Wch (7) 1993. Instead Crouch suggests that 13...♖e8 is promising for Black, e.g. 14 ♘xf5 ♖xe5 15 ♘xh6+ ♔g7 16 ♘g4 ♖e6!; 14 ♘b3 ♕a4! 15 0-0-0 ♘xc3 16 ♕xf5 ♘xa2+ 17 ♔c2 ♘c6 or 14 ♗xb8! ♘xc3! 15 ♘xf5 ♘e4+ 16 ♔d1 ♖axb8 with a very unclear position.

9 e3 g5 10 ♗g3 ♘e4 11 ♘f3 ♕f6?! 12 ♗b5!

⇨ 12 ♖c1?! ♗f5 13 ♗d3 h5 14 h4?! (14 ♘d2 ∞) 14...g4 15 ♘g5 ♘xc3?! (15...♘xg3 16 fxg3 ♗xd3 17 ♕xd3 0-0-0 18 ♖f1 ♘e5! 19 ♕d4 ♕e7! ∓) 16 bxc3 ♕xc3+! 17 ♕xc3 ♗xd3 (the position looks completely random) 18 ♗d6! ♗f5 19 f3 ♗xc3+ 20 ♖xc3 f6 21 fxg4 ♗xg4 22 ♘f3 ♗xf3! 23 gxf3 ♔d7 24 ♖b3 b6 = 25 ♔f2 ♔e6 26 ♖g1 ♖hg8 27 ♖xg8 ♖xg8 28 ♖b5 ♖c8 29 ♗f4 bxc5 30 ♖xc5 ♘e7 31 ♖xc8 ♘xc8 ½-½ Gelfand-Balashov, Odessa 1989.

12...♘xc3 13 ♗xc6+ bxc6?

13...♕xc6 14 bxc3 ♗xc5 15 0-0 ±.

14 a3! g4! 15 ♗e5!

(see next diagram)

15...♘e4+ 16 axb4 ♕f5 17 ♗xh8 gxf3 18 ♖g1!

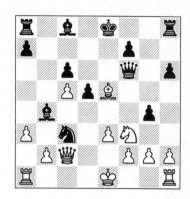

18 gxf3?! ♕xf3 19 ♖g1 ♗g4 ∓.

18...♕g4?

Even after the superior 18...fxg2! 19 ♕e2! (but not 19 ♖xg2?! ♕f3 20 ♖g8+ ♔e7 when Black has sufficient compensation) ♘g5 20 f4! ♘e4 21 ♖xg2 White has a clear advantage.

19 ♕d1! ± ♘g5 20 ♕d4! ♘e4 21 ♕e5+ ♗e6 22 ♕f4

White's strange queen manoeuvres have netted the f-pawn.

22...♕g6 23 ♕xf3 f6 24 ♕f4 ♔f7 25 f3 ♘g5 26 ♔d2! ♕f5 27 h4 ♕xf4 28 exf4 ♘h7 29 g4 1-0

After 29...♖xh8 30 ♖xa7+ Black's cause is hopeless.

Game 66

Draško-Maksimović
Yugoslavia 1991

1 d4 ♘f6 2 c4 e6 3 ♘c3 ♗b4 4 ♕c2 d5 5 cxd5 exd5 6 ♗g5 h6 7 ♗h4 c5 8 dxc5 ♘c6 9 e3 g5 10 ♗g3 ♘e4 11 ♘f3 ♕a5! 12 ♘d2! ♗xd2!?

This is a playable alternative to 12...♘xc3, the main move, but there is also 12....♗xc3!? 13 bxc3 ♕xc3 14 ♕xc3 ♘xc3 15 f3 ♗f5 16 ♔f2 0-0 17 h4 ♖fe8 18 hxg5 hxg5 19 ♘b3 ♔g7 20 ♔g1? (it is true that White has some problems moving his pieces, but this just loses a pawn; 20 ♘d4 is OK) 20...♖xe3 21 ♗f2 ♘e2+ 22 ♗xe2 ♖xe2 23 ♘d4 ♘xd4 24 ♗xd4+ ♔g6 25 g4 ♗d3 26 ♖h2 ♖ae8 27 ♖d1 ♗c4 28 ♖d2 and White eventually managed to hold the draw in Korchnoi-Portisch, Amsterdam 1990.

13 ♕xd2 ♗e6 14 ♖c1?! d4! 15 exd4 0-0-0 16 a3

16...♘xd4! 17 axb4 ♕xb4 18 ♗d6?!

Perhaps 18 ♘b1! was the best chance, when Nunn indicates the attractive line 18...♗g4! 19 ♗d3 ♖he8+ 20 ♔f1 ♕xd2 22 ♘xd2 ♘e2 and a likely equality.

18...♘b3 19 ♕c2 ♖he8 20 ♗d3 ♘xc1 21 ♕xc1 ♗c4+ 22 ♔d2 b6!

Not falling for the geometrical trick 22...♗xd3 23 ♔xd3 ♕xc5? 24 ♘b5.

23 ♗f5+ ♔b7 24 ♖e1 ♕xc5 25 ♗e4+ ♖xe4 26 ♘xe4 ♕d4+ 0-1

Game 67

Spassky-Fischer
Sveti Stefan m(10) 1992

1 d4 ♘f6 2 c4 e6 3 ♘c3 ♗b4 4 ♕c2 d5 5 cxd5 exd5 6 ♗g5 h6 7 ♗h4 c5 8 dxc5 ♘c6 9 e3 g5 10 ♗g3 ♕a5! 11 ♘f3 ♘e4 12 ♘d2 ♘xc3 13 bxc3 ♗xc3 14 ♖b1! ♕xc5!

Fischer's improvement on 14...a6?! 15 ♗d6! (defending the c-pawn, when Black will have no compensation for his weaknesses) 15...♗e5 16 ♗xe5 ♘xe5 17 ♗e2 0-0 18 0-0 ♕c7 19 ♖b6 ♘c6 20 ♘f3 ♖e8 21 ♖fb1 ♕e7 22 ♗d3 ♕f6 23 ♘d4 ♘xd4 24 exd4 ♕xd4 25 ♖xh6 ± Glek-Yuferov, Moscow 1989.

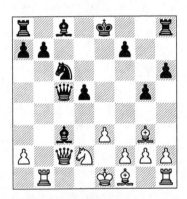

15 ♖b5 ♕a3! 16 ♖b3 ♗xd2+ 17 ♕xd2 ♕a5 18 ♗b5?

18 ♕xa5 ♘xa5 19 ♖b5 ♘c6 20 ♖xd5 ♗e6 21 ♖d2 =.

18...♕xd2+ 19 ♔xd2 ♗d7 20 ♗xc6 ♗xc6 21 h4

The opposite-colour bishops and Black's tatty pawn structure give White good chances of drawing in spite of the minus pawn.

21...♔e7 22 ♗e5 f6 23 ♗d4 g4 24 ♖c1 ♔e6 25 ♖b4 h5 26 ♖c3 ♖hc8 27 a4! b6 28 ♔c2 ♗e8! 29 ♔b2 ♖xc3 30 ♗xc3 ♖c8 31 e4?!

31 ♖f4! f5 32 ♖b4!.

31...♗c6 32 exd5+ ♗xd5 33 g3 ♗c4 34 ♗d4 ♔d5 35 ♗e3 ♖c7 36 ♔c3 f5 37 ♔b2 ♔e6 38 ♔c3 ♗d5+ 39 ♔b2 ♗e4 40 a5 bxa5 41 ♖b5 a4 42 ♖c5 ♖b7+ 43 ♔a3 a6 44 ♔xa4 ♗d5 45 ♔a5 ♔e5 46 ♔xa6 ♖b3 47 ♖c7 ♔e4 48 ♖h7

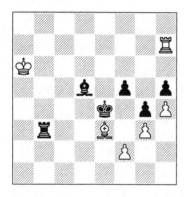

48...♖xe3!?

The only winning try, and the point of Black's preceding play. Whilst the white king is far away he gives up the exchange to create two passed pawns; however, the white rook can capture on h5 and his h-pawn will give him the necessary counterplay.

49 fxe3 ♔xe3 50 ♖xh5 ♗e4 51 ♖h8 ♔f3 52 ♖e8 ♔xg3 53 h5 ♗d3+ 54 ♔b6 f4 55 ♔c5 f3 56 ♔d4 ♗f5!

56...f2? would lose: 57 ♖f8 f1♕ 58 ♖xf1 ♗xf1 59 h6 and White wins.

57 ♖f8 ♔f4 58 h6 g3

58...f2 59 h7 f1♕ 60 h8♕ ♕a1+ 61 ♔c5 ♕xh8 62 ♖xh8 g3 63 ♖h1.

59 h7 g2 60 h8♕ g1♕+ 61 ♔c4 ♕c1+ 62 ♔b3 ♕c2+ 63 ♔b4 ♕e4+ 64 ♔c3 ♕c6+ 65 ♔b3 ♕d5+ 66 ♔c3 ♕c5+ 67 ♔b2 ♕b4+ 68 ♔a2 ½-½

There is no escape from the checks.

Game 68

M.Gurevich-Franzoni
Lucerne 1989

1 d4 ♘f6 2 c4 e6 3 ♘c3 ♗b4 4 ♕c2 d5 5 a3 ♗xc3+

⇨ 5...♗e7?! seems rather pointless: 6 cxd5 exd5 7 ♗g5 c6 8 e3 ♘bd7 9 ♗d3 ♘h5 10 ♗xe7 ♕xe7 11 ♘ge2 ♘df6 12 0-0 0-0 13 b4 ± Petursson-Østenstad, Espoo Z 1989.

6 ♕xc3 ♘e4 7 ♕c2 c5 8 dxc5 ♘c6 9 cxd5

⇨ 9 e3?! ♕a5+ 10 ♗d2 ♘xd2 11 ♕xd2 ♕xc5 (11...dxc4 =) 12 b4 ♕e7! 13 ♘f3 0-0 14 b5 ♕f6 15 ♖d1 ♘e7 16 c5! (White's queenside pawns promise good long-term chances) 16...a6 17 a4 axb5 18 axb5 ♖a1 19 ♖c1?! ♖xc1+ 20 ♕xc1 ♗d7 (20...e5!?) 21 ♗d3 e5 22 ♗e2 ♖c8 23 0-0 ♘g6 24 ♕a3! d4 25 ♕a7! dxe3 26 c6! ± (winning a piece) 26...exf2+ 27 ♖xf2 ♗xc6 28 bxc6 ♕xc6 29 ♗f1! h6 30 ♗d3! ♖d8 31 ♕e3 ♘c3 32 ♖d2 ♖f8 33 ♖c2 ♕a1+ 34 ♖c1 ♕a3 35 ♔f2 ♕e7 36 ♗xg6 fxg6 37 ♖c4 g5 38 ♖e4 ♕d7 39 h3 ♔h8 40 ♔g3 ♕d6 41 ♕c3 ♖f4 42 ♖xe5 ♖f8 43 ♕c5 ♕f6 44 ♖e4 b6 45 ♕e5 ♕f7 46 ♔h2 ♕b7 47 ♖c4 ♕f7

48 ♖c7 ♕f4+ 49 ♕xf4 ♖xf4 50 ♖d7 ♖b4 51 ♘d4 ♔h7 52 ♘f5 ♔g6 53 ♘xg7 ♖e4 54 g4 ♔f6 55 ♘f5 h5 56 ♘g3 1-0 M.Gurevich-Portisch, Reggio Emilia 1990.

9...exd5 10 ♘f3 ♗f5!? 11 b4 0-0 12 ♗b2 b6 13 b5 bxc5 14 bxc6 ♕a5+

Played automatically, but the new idea 14...♖b8! looks better, when M.Gurevich-A.Sokolov, Clichy 1993, continued 15 ♘d2 (15 ♗e5!? is more to the point) 15...d4 16 ♘xe4 ♗xe4 17 ♕d2 ♕b6 18 ♗c1 c4 with good compensation for the piece.

15 ♘d2 ♖ab8 16 c7!?

Trying to gain time by deflecting Black's queen; 16 ♖d1 is the theoretical move.

16...♖b3!? 17 ♗e5!

17 ♖d1? c4 18 f3 ♘xd2 19 ♕xd2 c3 allows Black to muddy the waters.

17...c4

17...f6 18 f3! ♘xd2 19 ♕xd2 ♕xd2+ 20 ♔xd2 fxe5 21 e4! ±.

18 f3 ♘xd2?

18...♘g3! 19 ♕xb3 cxb3 20 hxg3 was far from clear.

19 ♕xd2 c3 20 ♕g5! c2+ 21 ♔f2 ♕c5+ 22 e3 ♗g6 23 ♗a6!

Finally developing his kingside.

23...f6 24 ♕f4! fxe5 25 ♕xf8+! ♔xf8 26 c8♕+ ♕xc8 27 ♗xc8 d4 28 e4 1-0

Game 69

Atalik-Kotronias
Mangalia 1992

1 d4 ♘f6 2 c4 e6 3 ♘c3 ♗b4 4 ♕c2 d5 5 a3 ♗xc3+ 6 ♕xc3 ♘e4 7 ♕c2 e5

⇨ 7...♘c6 8 ♘f3 a5!? 9 e3 ♗d7 10 ♗d3 ♘d6 11 b3 a4 12 cxd5 exd5 13 bxa4 ♘e7 14 0-0 ♗xa4 15 ♕b1 c6 16 ♗d2 ♗b5 17 ♗xb5 ♘xb5 with a perfectly reasonable position for Black; Gaprindashvili-Gurgenidze, Tbilisi 1991.

8 e3 exd4 9 cxd5 ♕xd5 10 ♘f3 ♘d6

More combative than 10...♕c6?! 11 ♘xd4! ♕xc2 12 ♘xc2 ♘c6 13 b4 ♗e6 14 ♗b2 0-0 15 ♖c1 ♘d6 and instead of 16 b5? with equality (Kasparov-P.Nikolić, Barcelona 1989), 16 f3 keeps an edge.

11 ♘xd4 ♗d7! 12 f3 ♘c6 13 ♘xc6 ♗xc6 14 ♗e2 f5! 15 a4! 0-0-0 16 b4 ♕e6 17 ♖a3 ♔b8 18 ♖c3 ♗d5! 19 b5?!

Better is 19 0-0.

19...g5 20 0-0 g4 21 e4 gxf3 22 exd5 ♕xe2 23 ♖fxf3 ♕xc2 24 ♖xc2 ♖he8 25 ♗f4?! ♖e4 26 ♗xd6 cxd6 27 ♖xf5 ♖xa4 28 ♖b2! ♖d7??

An unusual blunder; 28...♖c4 gives Black the better endgame.

29 ♖f8+ 1-0

In view of 29...♔c7 30 b6+ axb6 31 ♖c2+ ♖c4 32 ♖xc4#.

5

This little-played system shows no signs of improving its standing as yet. White normally gains a pleasant advantage without any problems.

Following 5 ♞f3 (5 e3 is not the most accurate move here as it does little to stop Black's projected ...e5; nevertheless it is playable and should allow White a slight edge—see the notes to game 70) 5...d6, White's most popular plan is to play ♗d2 and then a3, recapturing on c3 with the bishop; but there is a nuance he can try. It is first to play 6 ♗g5 and on 6...h6 only then return to d2. The idea is that Black weakens his kingside with ...h6. Of course, he might find the adverse to be true and the bolt-hole on h7 might prove useful later on; I suppose it is very much a question of taste. Game 70 illustrates this idea in action, whereas the immediate 6 ♗d2 is covered in game 71.

6 a3 is also more than satisfactory for White, and in game 72 he finds an improvement that seems to refute a hitherto satisfactory variation for Black.

Game 70

Miles-Benjamin
USA Ch 1989

1 d4 ♞f6 2 c4 e6 3 ♞c3 ♗b4 4 ♛c2 ♞c6 5 ♞f3

Instead 5 e3 e5 can be met in two ways:

➩ 6 dxe5!? ♞xe5 7 ♞f3!? ♞xf3+ 8 gxf3 b6 9 ♗d2 ♗b7 10 ♗e2 ♛e7 11 0-0-0 ♗xc3 12 ♗xc3 0-0-0 (obviously Black's king is safer here than on the kingside) 13 ♛f5 ♛e6 14 ♛xe6 fxe6 15 ♖hg1 ♖hg8 16 ♖g3 ♖df8 17 ♖dg1 g6 18 ♖h3 ♖f7 19 ♔d2 ♖gf8 20 ♔e1 ♖e7 21 ♗xf6 ♖xf6 22 f4 = Seirawan-Makarychev, Moscow 1990.

➩ 6 d5 ♞e7 7 ♞e2 c6!? 8 a3 ♗xc3+ 9 ♞xc3 d6 10 dxc6?! (trying to save time but 10 e4 ± is better) 10...bxc6 11 ♗e2 0-0 12 0-0 d5 13 cxd5 cxd5 (Black's centre is very mobile) 14 ♖d1 ♗f5 15 ♛a4 a5! 16 ♗d2 ♛b6 17 b4 d4 18 exd4 exd4 19 ♞a2 axb4 20 ♛xb4 ♛a7 21 ♗g5 ♞ed5 22 ♛xd4 ♛xd4 23 ♖xd4 ♖xa3 24 ♖dd1 ♗c2 (24...♖fa8 25 ♗f3! ♖xa2 26 ♖xa2 ♖xa2 27 ♗xf6!) 25 ♖dc1 ♗b3 26 ♗xf6 gxf6 27 ♞b4! (a saving resource in an apparently desperate position) 27...♖xa1 28 ♖xa1 ♞xb4 29 ♖b1 ♖e8 30 ♗f1 ♗c2 31 ♖xb4 ♖e1 32 ♖d4 ♖d1 ½-½ G.Flear-Motwani, Dundee 1991.

5...d6 6 ♗g5!? h6 7 ♗d2!

➩ Not 7 ♗h4? g5 8 ♗g3 g4 9 d5!? (9 ♞h4 ♞xd4 10 ♛d3 e5 ∓) 9...exd5 10 cxd5 ♞xd5 11 ♗h4 ♛d7 12 ♖d1 ♛e6 13 e4 ♗xc3+ 14 bxc3 gxf3 15 ♖xd5 fxg2 16 ♗xg2 ♛g4 17 ♗g3 ♗e6 18 ♖b5 0-0-0 when White had negligible compensation for his pawn; Buddensieg-Unzicker, Moscow 1991.

7...♛e7

Here Black has a choice of continuations, but they all have essentially the same aim; to play ...e5:

➩ 7...0-0 8 g3!? (8 e3 ♖e8 9 ♗e2 a5 10 0-0 e5 11 d5 ♞e7 12 e4 ♗g4 13 a3 ♗xc3 14 ♗xc3 ♞d7 15 ♞e1

♗xe2 16 ♕xe2 ♘g6 17 g3 ♕g5 18
♔h1 f5 19 f3 fxe4 20 fxe4 ♖f8 21
♘d3 Amura-Gonzalez, Havana Capablanca mem 1992, seems quite
equal, Black's pawn chain present-
ing a solid wall against White's
dark-squared bishop; 8 a3! might
be the most accurate) 8...e5 9 dxe5
dxe5 10 a3 ♗e7 11 ♗g2 ♗e6 12 b3
e4!? 13 ♘g1 (a bit awkward but 13
♘xe4 ♗f5 14 ♘h5 ♘d4 is even
worse) 13...♗c5 14 b4? (for better or
for worse White had to try 14 e3
♘e5 15 ♘xe4 ♘d3+ 16 ♔f1 ∞)
14...♗xf2+! 15 ♔xf2 e3+ 16 ♔e1
(16 ♗xe3 ♘g4+ and 16 ♔xe3?
♕d4+ 17 ♔f3 ♗g4# were certainly
no better) 16...♗f5 (16...exd2+ 17
♕xd2 ♕xd2+ 18 ♔xd2 ♗xc4 is
simpler) 17 ♕c1 exd2+ 18 ♕xd2
♕xd2+ 19 ♔xd2 ♖ad8+ winning
quickly; Dzevlan-Ostojić, Yugoslav
Ch 1991.
⇨ 7...e5 8 d5?! (8 a3 ♗xc3 9 ♗xc3
♕e7 10 d5 ♘b8 11 e4 ± M.Gure-
vich-Benjamin, New York 1989)
8...♗xc3 9 ♗xc3 ♘e7 10 e4 ♘h5 11
♘d2 f5 12 0-0-0 0-0 13 c5 fxe4 14
♘xe4 ♗f5 15 f3 ♘f6 16 ♘xf6+
♖xf6 17 ♕b3 b6 18 c6 ½-½ Bagi-
rov-Unzicker, Daugavpils 1990.

8 a3

⇨ 8 e3 e5 9 d5 ♗xc3 10 ♗xc3 ♘b8
11 ♗e2 0-0 12 h3 c6 13 dxc6! ♘xc6
(13...bxc6? is impossible here because of 14 c5!) 14 0-0 ± ♗e6 15
♖fd1 b6 16 b4 ♕c7 17 ♖ac1 ♖ac8 18
a3 a5 19 c5 bxc5 20 bxc5 dxc5 21
♗b5 ♘d7 22 ♗xc6 ♕xc6 23 ♘xe5
♘xe5 24 ♗xe5 ♖fe8 25 ♖d6 ♕b7 26
♗c3 left White with slightly the better prospects in Finegold-Sosonko,
Amsterdam 1989.

**8...♗xc3 9 ♗xc3 0-0 10 e3 e5 11
d5!**

Better than 11 dxe5 dxe5 12 ♗e2
♗g4 13 0-0 ♗h5 14 b4 e4 15 ♗xf6
gxf6 16 ♘d4 ♘xd4 17 exd4 ♗g6, although White has an edge even here;
Brglez-Holzhäuer, Eger 1992.

**11...♘b8 12 ♘d2! ♘bd7 13 ♗e2
e4?**

I know that it can be tempting to
make this advance, but it is better
to maintain the c7/d6/e5 pawn chain
to stifle White's queen's bishop, and
play for ...f5; now this bishop becomes very powerful on c3.

**14 0-0 ♔h8 15 ♗d4 ♘e5 16 ♗d1
♗d7 17 ♕c3 ♗f5 18 ♗c2**

Miles has a good feel for placing
his pieces on their best squares.

**18...♗g6?! 19 ♗xe5!? dxe5 20
♕b4 ♕d6 21 f3 exf3 22 ♗xg6 fxg6**

22...fxg2 23 ♖xf6 ♕xf6 24 ♗e4
with a clear plus for White.

**23 ♖xf3 a5 24 ♕xd6 cxd6 25
♖af1 ± ♔g8 26 a4**

It appears strange to shut the
queenside like this but White has
seen that he will be able to convert
his extra queenside pawn later anyway.

**26...♖ac8 27 h4 ♖cd8 28 b3 b6
29 ♖1f2 ♘g4 30 ♖f1 ♖xf3 31 ♖xf3
♘f6 32 ♔f1 ♘d7 33 ♔e2 ♘c5 34
♔d1 ♘d3 35 ♖f1 ♖d7 36 ♔c2
♘c5 37 ♔c3 ♘a6 38 g4! ♖d8 39 g5
h5**

Now that White has devalued
Black's extra kingside pawn, his superiority emanates from the fact that
he alone has the possibility of creating a passed pawn.

**40 ♖f3 ♖f8? 41 ♖xf8+ ♔xf8 42
c5!**

42...bxc5

Both 42...♘xc5 and 42...dxc5 lose to 43 ♔c4.

43 ♘c4 ♔e7 44 ♘xa5 ♘c7 45 ♔c4 ♔d7 46 ♘c6 ♘a6 47 e4 ♘c7 48 a5 1-0

Game 71

M.Gurevich-Timman
Rotterdam 1990

1 d4 ♘f6 2 c4 e6 3 ♘c3 ♗b4 4 ♕c2 ♘c6 5 ♘f3 d6

⇨ 5...d5 is similar to material covered in the previous chapter, e.g. 6 a3 (6 ♗g5 h6 7 ♗xf6 ♕xf6 8 e3 0-0 9 a3 ♗xc3+ 10 ♕xc3 ♖e8 ± Krüger-Rotshtein, Berlin 1992) 6...♗xc3+ 7 ♕xc3 0-0 8 ♗g5 h6 9 ♗xf6 ♕xf6 10 e3 b6!? 11 cxd5 exd5 12 ♗e2 ♗b7 13 0-0 ♖fc8 14 b4 ♘d8 15 ♖fc1 c6 16 a4 ± Lalić-Inkiov, Haifa 1989.

6 ♗d2 0-0

⇨ 6...e5 7 a3 (7 dxe5 dxe5 8 0-0-0 is also feasible) 7...♗xc3 8 ♗xc3 exd4 9 ♘xd4 0-0 10 ♘xc6 bxc6 11 g3 c5 12 ♗g2 ♖b8 13 b4 ± ♘d7 14 ♗e4 h6 15 0-0 ♗b7 16 ♗h7+ ♔h8 17 ♗f5

♕e7 18 ♖ad1 f6 19 ♖fe1 ♖fe8 20 ♕c1 ♖ed8 21 ♕f4 ♕f7 22 ♗d3 ♕e6 23 f3 ♗c6 24 ♖b1 ♖e8 25 ♗f5 ♕e3+ 26 ♕xe3 ♖xe3 27 ♗d2 ♖e7 28 ♔f2 ♖a8 29 ♗xd7 ♖xd7 30 bxc5 d5 31 cxd5 ♖xd5 32 ♗f4 with some drawing chances for Black because of the opposite-colour bishops; Hübner-Unzicker, Bundesliga 1991.

7 a3 ♗xc3 8 ♗xc3 ♕e7

⇨ 8...a6?! (I can't quite make out the point behind this) 9 e4 (9 e3 must be good) 9...e5! (forced, as Black has no time for preparation, i.e. 9...♕e7 10 e5! dxe5 11 dxe5 ♘d7 12 ♗d3 ±) 10 dxe5 dxe5 11 ♘xe5 ♘d4! (White may have underestimated this) 12 ♕d3 c5 13 ♗xd4 cxd4 14 0-0-0 b5! 15 ♕xd4 ♕c7 16 c5 ♗b7! 17 ♗d3 ♖ad8 18 ♕c3 ♗xe4 19 f4 ♘d5 20 ♕d4 ♗xg2 21 ♖hg1 f6 22 ♖xg2 fxe5 23 ♕e4! (naturally, it is very tempting to press on with the attack when one has an open g-file) 23...♕xc5+ 24 ♔b1 ♘f6 25 ♕f5!? ♕c6? (25...♕d5! 26 ♕g5 g6 27 fxe5 ♘e4 28 ♕g4 ♕xe5 ∞) 26 ♖dg1 ± e4 27 ♖xg7+ ♔h8 28 ♕g5! ♖d7 29 ♕h6 ♕c5 30 ♗xe4 ♖ff7

31 ♕xh7+! 1-0, Kramnik-Rashk-
ovsky, USSR Ch. 1991.

9 g3!? e5 10 d5 ♘d8?!

A favourite move of Timman's.
Sometimes the knight can go to f7 to
support a kingside pawn advance; in
this example, unfortunately, it remains on d8 for the rest of the game!

11 ♗g2 ♗g4?

Better is 11...♘h5.

**12 ♘h4! c6 13 0-0 cxd5 14 cxd5
♕d7 15 f4! ±**

This is the move White wants to
play in such positions; if he can re-
move the e5-pawn the future of the
bishop on c3 is assured.

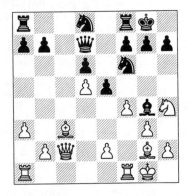

**15...♕b5 16 e4 ♗e2 17 ♖fe1 ♗d3
18 ♕d2 ♖e8 19 ♔h1 g6 20 a4!**

White plans to incarcerate the
black bishop.

**20...♕a6 21 b3! ♖c8 22 ♗f3!
♘d7 23 ♖ad1 ♘c5 24 fxe5 b5 25
♗d4 bxa4 26 ♗xc5 1-0**

Game 72

Baburin-Becker
Berlin 1991

**1 d4 ♘f6 2 c4 e6 3 ♘c3 ♗b4 4 ♕c2
♘c6 5 ♘f3 d6 6 a3 ♗xc3+ 7 ♕xc3
0-0**

⇨ 7...♕e7 8 g3 e5 9 d5 ♘b8 10 ♗g2
0-0 11 0-0 h6 12 b4!? b5 13 cxb5 a6
14 ♘d2!? (White ignores the offered
pawns but aims instead for long term
positional gains; the weaknesses on
c6 and c7 won't run away) 14...axb5
15 ♗b2 ♗b7 16 ♕d3 ♘bd7 17 ♖ac1
♘b6 18 e4 ♖fd8 19 f4 ♘e8!? 20
♗h3 ♗a6 21 ♖f2 ♘c4 22 ♘xc4
bxc4 23 ♕c3 ♗b5 24 ♗f1 ♘f6 25
♖e1 c6 26 ♗xc4 ♗xc4 27 ♕xc4 ±
M.Gurevich-Rozentalis, Groningen
1992.

⇨ 7...♘e4!? 8 ♕c2 f5 9 e3 0-0 10
♗d3 d5 11 b3 a5 12 ♗b2 ♕e7 (I prefer 12...♗d7 and ...♘e7 here) 13 g3
♗d7 14 ♘h4 a4 15 b4 ♘xb4?! 16
axb4 ♕xb4+ 17 ♔f1 a3 when Black
does not have enough compensation
for the piece; Akhsharumova-Po-
drazhanskaya, Novi Sad OL 1990.

⇨ 7...a5 8 b3 0-0 9 e3 ♕e7 10 ♗b2
♖e8 11 ♗e2 e5 12 d5 ♘b8 13 0-0
♗g4 14 ♖ae1 c6 15 dxc6 ♘xc6 16
♕c2 ♖ac8 17 e4 ♘d7 18 h3 ♗e6 19
♕d1 ♘c5 20 ♗d3? a4! 21 b4 ♘xd3
22 ♕xd3 ♘d4! (winning the c-pawn;
23 ♘xd4? ♗xc4) 23 ♘d2 ♘b3 24
♖e3 ♘xd2 25 ♕xd2 ♗xc4 ∓ Dou-
ven-Rashkovsky, Alma-Ata 1989.

8 b4

⇨ 8 e3 a5 9 b3 e5 10 dxe5 dxe5 11
♗b2 ♖e8 12 ♕c2 ♗g4 13 ♗e2 ♗h5
14 ♖d1 ♕e7 15 0-0 ♖ad8 16 c5 h6
17 h3 ♖b8 18 ♖fe1 ♗g6 19 ♕c4
♘e4 20 ♖d5 ♘f6 21 ♖dd1 ♘e4 22
b4 axb4 23 axb4 b5 24 cxb6 ♖xb6 25
b5 ♘d6 26 ♕a4 e4 27 ♘d4 ♘e5 28
♗a3 ♕g5 29 ♕c2?! (careless)
29...♘f3+! 30 ♔h1 ♘xe1 31 ♖xe1

♘xb5?! ½-½ King-Speelman, New
York 1990. Fortunately for White he
had good compensation for the exchange, but even so 31...♕e7 is perfectly reasonable. After 31...♘xb5?!
32 ♗xb5 ♖xb5 33 ♘xb5 ♕xb5 34
♕xc7 the game is a dead draw.

**8...e5 9 dxe5 ♘e4 10 ♕e3 f5 11
♗b2 ♕e7 12 exd6 ♕xd6 13 ♖c1
♗e6 14 g3 ♖ad8 15 ♗h3!**

A big improvement on 15 ♗g2.

15...♗xc4

15...♔h8 16 0-0 f4 17 ♕xe4
♗xh3 18 ♖fe1 is also favourable to
White.

16 ♗xf5

(see next diagram)

16...♘f6

16...♖xf5 is no better: 17 ♕xe4
♗e6 18 0-0 ♖d5 19 ♖fe1 ±.

17 ♕c3 b5

17...♗a6? 18 b5 ♗xb5 19 ♕b3+
♘d5 20 ♗xh7+.

**18 0-0 ♘e7 19 ♗d3 ♗xd3 20
♖fd1 ± ♕e6 21 ♖xd3 ♕xe2?**

Losing the queen.

22 ♕b3+ ♘fd5 23 ♖e1 1-0

6

4...b6 is a popular move that can lead to a wide variety of different types of position. At first we will consider the straightforward 5 ♘f3, when Black can play in 'Dutch' style by putting his knight on e4, following up with ...f5. The bishop on b7 can, after all, become a very dangerous attacking piece pointed at White's king. In game 73 White plays ♕c2 to lend support to c3, and in game 74 he tries to make do without. Normally White's plan involves playing his king's knight to e1 or d2 and then playing f3 in order to eject the e4 knight, but in game 74 White plays 9 d5!? instead, initiating wild complications and a sharp attack.

Black does dispose of alternative strategies, for instance he can capture on c3 with his knight and also on f3; however, in game 75 he soon finds himself in a passive position.

Black's other important possibility is to castle and play ...c5 (if Black decides to play 7...d5 immediately this will transpose into material considered in the following chapter), and then, later, ...d5. This often leads to IQP positions similar to the modern attacking 'classic', game 76.

More often than not, White will prefer 5 ♘e2, avoiding the dreaded doubled pawns. Should Black continue 5...♘e4 stepping up the pressure on c3, then White has a choice between 6 ♕c2 (game 77), 6 ♗d2 (giving up the bishop pair, but gaining a space advantage—see game 78) and 6 f3 (game 79), accepting doubled pawns.

6 f3 seems the weakest of the sixth moves, although it takes very accurate play from Black to show just why.

Simply continuing development with 5...♗b7 cannot be bad, and after 6 a3 Black must decide whether to take on c3 or retreat, both of which are covered in game 80.

Games 81 to 83 deal with 5...♗a6, a favourite of Fischer's, when the pressure on c4 forces White to modify his plans. In games 81 and 82 White reacts with 6 ♘g3, allowing Black, if he so wishes, to take on c3. In the first of these the players reach an endgame that appears to be perfectly satisfactory for Black, although he soon goes wrong, whilst in game 82 White's sharp eighth move provokes unfathomable complications. Despite looking at the game several times, I still haven't a clue what's going on!

In game 83, an attacking 'evergreen', White plays 6 a3 and consents to losing his castling rights—a decision he quickly regrets.

Game 73

Hernandez-Arnason
Palma 1989

1 d4 ♘f6 2 ♘f3 e6 3 c4 b6 4 ♘c3 ♗b4 5 e3 ♘e4

This gives White less options than 5...♗b7.

6 ♕c2 ♗b7 7 ♗d3 f5 8 0-0 ♗xc3 9 bxc3 0-0 10 ♘e1

The alternative knight retreat 10 ♘d2 has the same motive, i.e. chasing the active knight from e4: 10...♕h4 11 f3 ♘xd2 12 ♗xd2 ♘c6 13 ♖ab1 d6 14 e4 fxe4 15 ♗xe4 ♘a5 16 ♗xb7 ♘xb7 17 ♖be1 ♖ae8 18 ♕a4 ♘a5 (the e6 weakness is less important than that on c4) 19 f4 ♕h5 20 ♖f3 e5 21 dxe5 dxe5 ∓ Sokolov-Hansen, Novi Sad OL 1990.

10...♕h4!?

⇨ 10...♘c6 11 f3 ♘d6 12 ♗a3 ♖f6 13 ♕e2 ♗a6 14 ♘c2 ♘a5 (Black applies the maximum pressure to c4) 15 c5 ♗xd3 16 ♕xd3 ♘dc4 17 ♗b4 d5 18 cxd6 cxd6 19 ♗xa5 ♘xa5 20 c4 ♖c8 21 ♘a3 ♖f7 22 ♖ac1 ♖fc7 23 d5 ♕d7 24 ♘b5 ♖xc4 25 ♖xc4 ♘xc4 26 ♘d4 exd5 27 ♘xf5 ♖c5 and Black's extra pawn finally told in Olesen-Wedberg, Gausdal 1991.

11 f3 ♘g5 12 ♕f2

12 c5! is more ambitious.

12...♕xf2+

12...♕h5 is less logical. Hoffman-Wedberg, Novi Sad OL 1990 continued: 13 ♗e2 ♕g6 14 ♕g3 d6 15 ♘d3 ♘d7 16 h4 ♘f7 17 ♕xg6 hxg6 18 ♘f4 ♖fe8 19 ♘xg6 c5 20 ♗d2 ±.

13 ♖xf2 d6 14 c5!? dxc5 15 dxc5 ♘d7! 16 e4!

16 cxb6 axb6 would grant Black a slight edge, but by hitting g5 White starts a tactical *mêlée*.

16...fxe4 17 ♗b5

17...c6 18 ♗c4 ♘f7 19 ♗e3 ♖fe8 20 fxe4 ♘fe5 21 ♗b3 bxc5! 22 ♖d1

Although Black has an extra pawn and the e5 square for his knight, the bishop pair and d-file grant White sufficient counterchances.

22...♘f6 23 ♗xc5 ♘xe4 24 ♖e2 ♘xc5 25 ♖xe5 ♘xb3 26 axb3 ♔f7 27 ♘d3 ♖ad8 28 ♖f1+ ♔g8 29 ♘c5 ♗c8 30 ♖a1 ♖e7 31 b4 ♖d2 32 ♖ae1 ♖d5 33 ♖5e3 a5 34 ♘xe6 axb4 35 cxb4 ♖xe6 36 ♖xe6 ½-½

Game 74

Rechlis-Brunner
Bern Z 1990

1 d4 ♘f6 2 c4 e6 3 ♘c3 ♗b4 4 e3 b6 5 ♗d3 ♗b7 6 ♘f3

Here White can try an interesting pawn sacrifice: 6 ♘e2 ♗xg2 (it might be more sensible to avoid this capture in favour of 6...0-0, or 6...c5 whereupon Urday-Izeta, Candás 1992, continued 7 a3 &xc3+ 8 ♘xc3 cxd4 9 exd4 d5 10 cxd5 ♘xd5 11 ♕g4 ♘f6 12 ♕h4 ♘c6 13 &e3 0-0 14 0-0-0 ♘e7 15 &g5 ♘g6 16 &xg6 fxg6 17 f3 ♕d7 which looks fairly equal) 7 ♖g1 and now:

⇨ 7...&f3 8 ♖xg7 ♘e4 9 ♕c2 ♘xc3 (9...♕h4!?) 10 bxc3 &d6 11 e4 ♕f6 12 ♖g5 &xe2 13 ♕xe2 &f4 14 &xf4 ♕xf4 15 ♕h5 ♘c6 16 ♔e2 0-0-0 17 ♖ag1 with some advantage to White who controls the only open file, and can threaten the h- and f-pawns; Barsov-Mandekić, Pula 1990.

⇨ 7...&e4 8 a3 &xc3+ 9 ♘xc3 &xd3 10 ♕xd3 0-0 11 e4 ♘e8 12 &d2 ♘c6 13 0-0-0 e5 14 dxe5 ♘xe5 15 ♕e2 f6 16 f4 ♘f7 17 ♘d5 c6 18 ♘e3 ♘fd6 19 ♕d3 ♘f7 20 &c3 d6 21 ♘f5 (White has certainly built up a dangerous attacking position) 21...♔h8 22 ♘xg7! ♘xg7 23 ♖xg7! ♔xg7 24 ♕g3+ ♔h8 25 ♖g1 (threatening 26 ♕g7#, and if 25...♖g8? 26 ♕xg8+ wins) 25...♘g5 26 fxg5 ♕e8 27 ♕f4 ♕f7 28 ♕f5 ♕g6 29 ♕e6 ♖ae8 30 &xf6+ ♖xf6 31 ♕xf6+ ♔g8 32 ♕xg6+ hxg6 33 ♖g4 (after the complications, mostly forced, White reaches an ending a pawn to the good, but Black's drawing chances are considerable) 33...♖f8 34 ♔c2 ♖f3 35 ♖g3 ♖xg3 36 hxg3 ♔f7 37 ♔d3 ♔e7 38 ♔e3 ♔d7 39 ♔d3 ♔e7 40 ♔e3 ♔d7 41 b4 ♔e6 42 ♔d4 c5+ 43 bxc5 bxc5+ ½-½ Verdikhanov-Poluliakhov, Moscow 1991.

6...♘e4 7 0-0 &xc3

Should Black play 7...f5 first, then 8 ♘e2 is playable. The normal move is then 8...&d6; instead:

⇨ In Lautier-Adams, Wijk aan Zee 1991, there followed: 8...&e7 9 b3 0-0 10 &b2 &f6 11 ♕c2 c5 12 ♖ad1 ♕e7 13 ♘g3 ♘xg3 14 hxg3 ♘c6 15 ♕e2 g6 16 &b1 d6 17 e4 ♖ad8 18 d5 ♘b8 (probably better than 18...exd5 19 &xf6 ♖xf6 20 cxd5 ♘b4 21 ♖fe1 fxe4 22 &xe4 when the knight on b4 has no good squares) 19 exf5 exf5 20 ♕xe7 &xe7 21 ♖fe1 (here White has a fine position) 21...♔f7 22 ♖e2 ♖fe8 23 ♖de1 ♘d7 24 &c1 &f6 25 &f4 ♖xe2 26 ♖xe2 &e7 27 ♔f1 b5! 28 &g5 ♖e8 29 cxb5 &xd5 30 &xe7 ♖xe7 31 ♘g5+ ♔f6 32 ♖xe7 ♔xe7 33 ♘xh7 c4 34 &c2 ♘c5 35 b4 ♘e6 (trapping the knight) 36 ♔e1 &xg2 37 ♔d2 d5 38 f4 d4 39 ♘g5 c3+ 40 ♔e2 ♘xg5 41 fxg5 &d5 0-1.

⇨ 8...0-0 was explored in Ibragimov-Sisniega, São Paulo 1991: 9 ♘g3?! &d6 10 ♕c2 &xg3 11 hxg3 ♖f6! 12 b3 ♘c6?! (12...♖h6! 13 ♘d2 d5 would have led to interesting play) 13 &a3 ♘e7 14 d5! exd5 15 cxd5 &xd5 16 &xe7! ♕xe7 17 ♕xc7 ♘c5 18 &e2 a5 19 ♖fd1 &f7 20 ♘e5! &e8? 21 &f3 ♕d8 22 ♕xd8 ♖xd8 23 ♘c6 1-0.

8 bxc3 f5 9 d5!?

The traditional move in this position is 9 ♘e1: 9...0-0 10 f3. It is a curiosity of this line that despite being attacked and not defended the c3 pawn is rarely open to capture. Now:

⇨ 10...♘g5 11 ♖b1!? (surprisingly enough, preparing a kingside attack; 11 ♘c2 d6 12 ♖e1 ♘d7 13 e4 f4 14 h4 ♘f7 15 &xf4 ♕xh4 16 ♕d2 ½-½ Marin-Inkiov, Haifa 1989) 11...d6 12 ♖b2 ♘d7 13 ♖bf2 e5 14 c5 dxc5 15 h4 e4 16 ♕b3+ ♔h8 17 &b1 c4

18 ♕xc4 ♘f7 19 ♗a3 ♘d6 20 ♗xd6 cxd6 21 fxe4 is better for White; Portisch-Inkiov, Cannes 1992.

⇨ 10...♘d6 11 ♗a3 c5!? (offering a pawn for the c5 square and play along the c-file) 12 dxc5 bxc5 13 ♗xc5 ♕c7 14 ♗a3 ♘a6 15 ♗e2 ♘c5 16 ♕d4 ♖fc8 17 ♘d3 ♘ce4? (flashy, but not good) 18 fxe4 ♘xc4 19 exf5! (19 ♗c1? e5 traps the queen. Unfortunately for Black, White simply returns the piece for a winning attack) 19...♘xa3 20 f6 gxf6 21 ♕xf6 ♕xc3 22 ♘e5 ♕xe3+ 23 ♖f2 ♖f8 24 ♘f7 ♖xf7 25 ♕xf7+ ♔h8 26 ♕f6+ ♔g8 27 ♗h5 1-0 Lukacs-Lendvai, Kecskemet 1991.

9...♘c5 10 ♗a3 ♘ba6 11 ♖e1 0-0 12 e4 fxe4 13 ♗xe4 ♖f4!? 14 ♗c2 ♖xc4 15 ♘e5 ♖xc3?

A bit too greedy; 15...♖h4 would have avoided what follows.

16 ♗xh7+!

Here White is obliged to play for the attack.

16...♔xh7 17 ♕h5+ ♔g8 18 ♗b2 ♕f6

Black is in serious trouble, i.e. 18...♘a4 19 ♗xc3 ♘xc3 20 ♕f7+

♔h8 21 ♖e3, or 18...♖c2 19 ♕f7+ ♔h7 20 ♖e3 with a clear advantage for White in both cases.

19 ♗xc3 ♗xd5 20 ♘g6 ♕xc3 21 ♘e7+ ♔f8 22 ♘xd5 g6

If 22...exd5, then 23 ♕h8+ ♔f7 24 ♕xa8 wins.

23 ♕xg6 ♕g7

23...exd5 24 ♕f5+ ♔g8 25 ♕xd5+ ♔h8 26 ♕xa8+ wins material.

24 ♘f4 ♕xg6 25 ♘xg6+ ♔g7 26 ♘e5

Black has done well to escape to an endgame; now it is a question of whose pawns get going first.

26...♘b4 27 ♖e2 d6 28 a3! ♘d5 29 ♘c6 a6 30 ♖f1 ♖f8 31 g3 ♘c3 32 ♖e3 ♘d5 33 ♖e2 ♘c3 34 ♖ee1 e5 35 ♔g2 ♔f6 36 ♖e3 ♘d5 37 ♖f3+ ♔g7 38 ♖xf8 ♔xf8 39 h4 a5 40 ♔h3 ♘c3 41 h5 ♔g7 42 f4 e4 43 ♘d4 ♘d3 44 f5 ♘e5 45 g4 e3 46 f6+ ♔f8 47 g5 e2 48 ♖e1 c5 49 ♘xe2 ♘e4 50 g6 ♘xf6 51 ♘g3 c4 52 ♖f1 ♔g7 53 ♘f5+ ♔g8 54 ♔h4 c3 55 ♘d4 ♘e4 56 ♘e6 ♘d7 57 h6 c2 58 ♖g1 ♘ef6 59 ♖c1 ♘c5 60 ♖xc2 1-0

Game 75

Lin Weiguo-Miles
Beijing 1991

1 d4 e6 2 c4 ♗b4+ 3 ♘c3 b6 4 e3 ♗b7 5 ♘f3 ♘f6 6 ♗d3 ♘e4

Black can also occupy the e4 square with the bishop: 6...0-0 7 0-0 ♗xc3 8 bxc3 ♗e4 9 ♗e2 c5 10 ♘d2 ♗b7 11 a4 ♘c6 12 ♘b3 d6 13 f3 ♕c7 14 e4 h6 15 ♗e3 e5 16 a5 ♖ad8 17 ♕d2 ♘e7 18 ♖fb1 ♘d7 19 ♕b2 f5 20 ♘d2 ♖b8 (a game of cat and mouse, with Black trying to provoke White into direct action and White trying to avoid committing himself to moves like d5) 21 axb6 axb6 22 ♗d1 fxe4 23 fxe4 ♗c8 24 d5 ♘f6 25 h3 ♘g6 26 ♖a3 ♘h4 27 ♘f3 ♘xf3+ 28 ♗xf3 ♕f7 29 ♕f2 (there is no time for 29 ♖b3 because 29...♕g6 attacks e4 and h3) 29...♕g6 30 ♕h4 ♘xd5 31 ♗h5 ♕f6 32 ♕xf6 ♘xf6 33 ♗g6 ♗b7 34 ♗f5 ♗xe4. A lot of players would have resigned White's position here, but the young French grandmaster showed a lot of fighting spirit and somehow made a draw in Lautier-Andersson, Biel 1990.

7 ♕c2 f5 8 0-0 ♘xc3 9 bxc3 ♗xf3

This series of exchanges is thought to be a little dubious, but I am certain that Tony Miles had something prepared.

10 gxf3 ♗d6

⇨ 10...♕g5+ doesn't work out too well either: 11 ♔h1 ♗d6 12 f4 ♕h6 13 ♖g1 0-0 14 ♗b2 ♘c6 15 ♖g3 ♖f7 16 ♖ag1 ♔h8 17 ♗f1 ♘a5 18 ♖h3

♕f6 19 c5 ♗f8 20 c4 ± Gligorić-Blagojević, Yugoslav Ch 1991.

11 f4!?

11 e4 has been suggested.

11...♕h4 12 ♕e2 0-0 13 ♔h1 ♖f6 14 ♖g1 ♖h6 15 ♖g2 ♕h3 16 ♗d2 ♔h8 17 ♖ag1 ♘c6 18 f3 ♖g8 19 ♖g5 ♗e7 20 ♗e1!

Showing who is the real master of the kingside. If now 20...♗xg5?, 21 fxg5 ♖g6 22 f4 corners the rook, and soon after the black queen.

20...♖f6 21 e4 ♖f7 22 ♖5g3 ♕h6 23 ♗d2 ♗h4 24 ♖3g2 ♘e7 25 ♗e3 ♘g6 26 ♕d2 ♕h5 27 ♗e2 ♖b8 28 ♖b1 ♖ff8 29 ♖b3 ♗e7 30 ♖g3 ♕h4 31 ♖g1 ♕f6 32 ♖f1 ♕f7 33 a4 ♕g8 34 ♖b5 ♖f7 35 ♖a1 ♕f8 36 e5 ♕c8 37 a5

Black's position is solid, but it is White who has all the play.

37...♖f8 38 ♖ab1 ♖a8 39 ♖5b3 ♕e8 40 c5 bxc5 41 dxc5 ♗h4 42 ♖b7 ♘e7 43 c4 ♕c8 44 a6 ♘c6 45 ♗d1 ♖f7 46 ♗a4 h6 47 ♖g1 ♗e7 48 ♖d1 ♗f8 49 ♖g1 ♔h7 50 ♕g2 ♖e7 51 ♕g6+ ♔g8 52 ♖gb1 ♖f7 53 ♗f2 ♗e7 54 ♖d1 ♗f8 55 ♗xc6 dxc6 56 ♖d6!!

Superbly imaginative.

56...♗xd6 57 cxd6 ♕e8 58 ♗xa7 ♕c8 59 ♔g2 c5 60 ♔g3 h5 61 h4 ♕e8 62 ♖xc7 ♖d8 63 ♕xf7+ ♕xf7 64 ♖xf7 ♔xf7 65 ♗xc5 ♖a8 66 d7 1-0

Game 76 CHL

Yusupov-Ivanchuk
Brussels Ct(8) 1991

1 d4 ♘f6 2 c4 e6 3 ♘c3 ♗b4 4 e3 b6 5 ♗d3 ♗b7 6 ♘f3

Of late the move 6 f3 has been quite popular in this position, but as yet the results seem to favour Black. After 6...c5, White's reply depends on how he wishes to recapture on c3:

1) 7 ♘e2 0-0 and now:

⇨ 8 a3 ♗xc3+ 9 ♘xc3 d5 10 dxc5 bxc5 11 0-0 ♘c6 12 cxd5 exd5 13 e4 d4 14 ♘a4 ♘d7 15 ♗f4 ♕e7 16 ♖c1 ♖fc8 17 ♖f2 ♘d8 18 ♗g3 ♘e6 19 ♗c4 ± Maiztegui-Franco, Pamplona 1991.

⇨ 8 0-0 cxd4 9 exd4 d5 10 ♗g5 ♗e7 (alternatively, 10...dxc4 11 ♗xc4 ♗e7 12 ♕d3 ♘c6 13 a3 ♖c8 14 ♖ad1 ♘d5 15 ♗xd5 ♗xg5 16 ♗a2 ♘e7 17 ♖fe1 ♘d5 18 ♘xd5 ♗xd5 19 ♗xd5 ♕xd5 20 ♘c3 ♕b3 = Vera-Brynell, Leningrad 1989) 11 f4 dxc4 12 ♗xc4 ♘g4 13 ♕d2 ♘d7 14 ♘g3 h6 15 ♗xe7 ♕xe7 16 h3 ♘gf6 17 ♖ae1 ♕d6 18 ♕f2 ♖ad8 19 ♖d1 g6 20 ♗d3 ♖fe8 21 ♘b5 ♕b8 22 f5 exf5 23 ♗xf5 ♖e7 24 ♘c3 ♖f8 25 d5 ♖e5 26 ♗xd7 ♘xd7 27 ♕f4 ♔h7 28 ♘ge4 f5! fighting off the attack and going on to win; Gamundi-Gligorić, Palma 1989.

2) 7 a3 ♗xc3+ 8 bxc3 ♘c6 9 ♘e2

d6 10 0-0 ♕c7 11 e4 0-0-0 12 ♗e3 e5 13 a4 ♖hg8 14 ♔h1 g5 15 ♘c1 ♖g6 16 ♖b1 ♘d7 17 ♘b3 a5! (putting paid to White's a5 lever) 18 ♖f2 ♖dg8 19 ♖fb2 ♗a6 20 ♗f1 ♘d8 21 ♘d2 h5 22 ♘b3 ♗b7 23 ♘a1 ♗c6 24 ♖d2 ♔b8 25 ♕b3 ♔a7 26 ♘c2 g4 27 ♘a3 (and in this interesting position, faced with the threat of d5 and ♘b5+, instead of 27...♕b8! ∞ Black played the vulgar ...) 27...cxd4? 28 cxd4 exd4 29 ♗xd4 ♘c5 30 ♗xc5 dxc5 31 f4 ♖f6 32 f5 h4 33 ♖bd1 ♕e7 34 ♘b5+ ♔a6 35 ♘d6 ♘b7 36 e5 ♕xe5 37 ♖b1 b5 38 axb5+ ♔a7 39 bxc6 ♘xd6 40 ♕b6+ 1-0 Høi-Østenstad, Gausdal 1991.

6...0-0

Black can also consider the immediate 6...c5: 7 0-0 cxd4 8 exd4 0-0 9 ♖e1 (9 ♗g5!? ♗xc3 10 bxc3 d6 11 a4 ♘bd7 12 ♘d2 ♕c7 13 a5! ♖ac8 14 ♕b3 d5 15 axb6 axb6 16 c5! bxc5 17 ♖a7 ♖b8 18 ♖b1 c4 with unclear complications in Rotshtein-Kosten, Metz 1992) 9...♖e8 10 ♕e2 ♗e7 11 ♗f4 d6 12 ♘g5 ♘c6 13 d5 ♘d4 14 ♕d1 e5 15 ♗e3 g6 16 ♗xd4 exd4 17 ♘b5 ♘xd5 18 cxd5 ♗xg5 19 ♖xe8+ ♕xe8 20 ♘c7 ♕e5 21 ♘xa8 ± although Black achieved a draw in Gligorić-Cvetković, Yugoslav Ch 1990.

7 0-0 c5

⇨ 7...♗xc3 8 bxc3 c5 9 a4! d6 10 ♘d2 ♘c6 11 ♘b3 ♖c8 12 a5 ♕c7 13 f3 bxa5 14 e4 ♗a8?! 15 ♖f2! ♖b8 16 d5 exd5 17 exd5 ♘e5 18 ♗f1 ♖b6 19 ♘xa5 ♗b7 20 ♗g5 ♘fd7?! (allowing the white f-pawn to march to f6, but White would have a clear advantage even after 20...♘ed7) 21 f4 ♘g6 22 f5 ♘ge5 23 f6 g6 24 ♘b3

♖a6 25 ♖f4 ♖xa1 26 ♕xa1 ♗c8 27
♕e1 ♕b6 28 ♘d2 ♖e8 29 ♕h4 ±
Gligorić-Romanishin, Erevan 1989.

8 ♗d2

⇨ 8 ♘a4 has a good reputation, Vil-
leneuve-Spassky, French Ch 1990
continuing: 8...cxd4 9 exd4 (9 a3
♗e7 10 exd4 d5 11 c5 bxc5 12 ♘xc5
♗xc5 13 dxc5 ♕c7 14 ♗g5 ♘e4 15
♖c1 ♘c6 16 b4 ♘xg5 17 ♘xg5 h6
18 ♗h7+ ♔h8 19 ♗b1 g6 20 ♘f3
♗a6 21 ♕d2 ♔h7 with some edge to
White; Speelman-El Assiouti, London Lloyds Bank 1992) 9...♗e7 10
♖e1 d6 11 ♘c3!? ♘bd7 12 ♗g5 ♖e8
13 ♖c1 ♖c8 14 ♘d2 d5 15 b3 ♘b8
16 cxd5 ♘xd5 17 ♗xe7 ♖xe7 18
♘xd5 ♗xd5 =.

**8...cxd4 9 exd4 d5 10 cxd5 ♘xd5
11 ♖c1!?**

⇨ Although this move is new in this
particular position, it is of course
very typical in this sort of schema:
11 ♕e2 ♘d7!? 12 ♖ac1 ♘7f6 13
♘e5 ♖c8 14 ♖fd1 ♕e7 15 ♗a6 ♖fd8
16 h3 ♗d6 17 ♗g5 ♘xc3 18 bxc3
♗xa6 19 ♕xa6 h6 20 ♗xf6 ♕xf6 21
♕xa7 ♗xe5 22 dxe5 ♖xd1+ 23
♖xd1 ♕xe5 ½-½ King-Crawley,
British Ch 1989.

11...♘c6 12 ♖e1 ♖c8 13 ♖e4!?

Initiating a relatively crude attacking plan, but it was an important
part of Yusupov's match preparation
to put his opponent under exactly
this sort of pressure. (*Editor's note*:
see Dvoretsky's *Secrets of Chess
Tactics*, pp.167-173, for a full dis-
cussion of the psychology behind
this plan.)

**13...♘ce7 14 ♘xd5 ♘xd5 15
♖h4 g6 16 ♖xc8 ♕xc8 17 ♘g5 ♗e7
18 ♕g4 ♗a6 19 ♕h3 h5**

20 ♖xh5!

Guaranteeing at least a draw,
should Black find the best defence.

**20...gxh5 21 ♗h7+ ♔g7 22
♕xh5 ♘f6?**

It appears that 22...♗b4! was correct, whereupon 23 ♘xf7! ♖xf7 24
♕h6+ ♔h8 25 ♗f5+ ♔g8 26 ♗xe6
♕c2 27 ♗xf7+ is equal.

**23 ♘xe6+! fxe6 24 ♕h6+ ♔h8
25 ♗f5+ ♔g8 26 ♕g5+ ♔h8 27
♕h4+ ♔g8 28 ♕g5+ ♔h8 29 ♕h4+
♔g8 30 ♕g3+ ♔h8 31 ♕h3+ ♔g7
32 ♕g3+ ♔h8 33 ♕h3+ ♔g7 34
♗xe6 ♕xe6 35 ♕xe6 ♗d8? 36 g4!
♖e8 37 ♕f5 ♗c4 38 g5 1-0**

Game 77 CML

I.Sokolov-Korchnoi
Novi Sad OL 1990

**1 d4 ♘f6 2 c4 e6 3 ♘c3 ♗b4 4 e3 b6
5 ♘e2 ♘e4 6 ♕c2 ♗b7 7 a3**

⇨ 7 f3 ♘xc3 8 bxc3!? (8 ♘xc3)
8...♗e7 9 ♘g3 h5 10 ♗d3 h4 11
♘e4 ♘c6 12 0-0 ♘a5 13 ♘f2 c5 14
e4 cxd4 15 cxd4 ♖c8 16 ♕e2 ♗a6
17 c5 ♗xd3 18 ♘xd3 bxc5 19 dxc5

♘b7 20 ♗e3 ♘xc5 21 ♖ac1 d6 and Black managed to convert his pawn plus in Kadimova-Kuzmin, Moscow 1991.

7...♗xc3+ 8 ♘xc3 ♘xc3

The alternative is 8...f5:

⇨ 9 d5 ♘xc3 10 ♕xc3 ♕e7 11 dxe6 dxe6 12 b3 ♘d7 13 ♗b2 e5! equalized in I.Sokolov-Cu.Hansen, Groningen 1991, and following 14 0-0-0 0-0-0 15 b4 ♖he8 16 f3 ♕h4 17 ♕e1?! ♕h6 18 ♔b1 g5 19 ♕f2 e4 20 ♗e2 f4 21 fxe4 ♗xe4+ 22 ♔a1 fxe3 23 ♕g3 ♕g6! 24 ♖he1 h5 25 ♖d4 g4 26 ♗f1 ♕f7! Black even held a clear advantage.

⇨ 9 b3 0-0 10 ♗b2 d6 11 0-0-0!? ♕e7 12 f3 ♘xc3 13 ♕xc3 ♘d7 14 ♗d3 e5 15 dxe5 ♘xe5 16 ♗c2 ♖ae8 17 h4 a5 18 ♖d4 ♘c6 19 ♖f4 ♕xe3+ 20 ♕xe3 ♖xe3 21 ♖xf5 ♖xf5 22 ♗xf5 ♘e7 (22...♖xb3 23 ♖e1 ♘e5 24 ♗c2 ♖xb2 25 ♔xb2 ♘xc4+ is probably to White's advantage) 23 ♗c2 ♖e2 24 ♖g1 d5 25 ♔d1 ♖e6 26 ♖e1 ♖xe1+ 27 ♔xe1 dxc4 28 bxc4 = Hollis-Palmo, corr. 1990.

9 ♕xc3 ♕h4!?

The drawback to this idea of Korchnoi's seems to be that his queen becomes cut off from the queenside.

10 b3 0-0 11 ♗b2 f6 12 d5!

A nice thematic line-opening sacrifice.

12...exd5 13 ♖d1!

(see next diagram)

13...d4

Both 13...c6 14 cxd5 cxd5 15 ♕c7 and 13...dxc4?! 14 ♖d4 ♕g5 15 ♕xc4+ ♔h8 16 ♕xc7 ± illustrate the strength of White's concept.

14 ♖xd4 ♕h5 15 ♗e2 ♕g6 16

♖g4 ± ♕b1+ 17 ♗d1 ♘c6 18 0-0 ♕f5 19 ♖g3 ♕e5?!

19...♘e5!?.

20 ♕d2 ♕e8 21 ♗c2 ♘e5

At first glance the knight on e5 looks strong, but White can always evict it with f4 when he chooses.

22 h4! d6 23 ♕e2 f5? 24 f4 ♘g4 25 ♗xf5

Winning, but 25 ♗xg7 ♔xg7 26 ♗xf5 ♖xf5 27 ♕xg4+ ♔f6 28 ♕g7+ ♔e6 29 e4 ♖f7! (29...♗xe4? 30 ♖e3) 30 ♕g4+ ♔e7 31 ♖e1 is also strong.

25...♖xf5 26 ♕xg4 ♖f7 27 ♗xg7 ♕d7 28 ♕xd7 ♖xd7 29 ♗c3+ ♔f8 30 f5! ♖e8 31 f6 ♗e4 32 ♖f4 ♗g6 33 ♔f2 ♔f7?

33...♖e4.

34 h5! 1-0

Game 78

Hübner-de Firmian
Manila IZ 1990

1 d4 ♘f6 2 c4 e6 3 ♘c3 ♗b4 4 e3 b6 5 ♘e2 ♘e4

Anastasian has essayed 5...0-0 here, with a view to playing ...d5 and

...♗a6. After 6 a3 ♗xc3+ 7 ♘xc3 d5 his practice has seen:

⇨ 8 cxd5 exd5 9 ♗e2 c6 10 b4 ♗a6 11 b5 cxb5 12 ♘xb5 ♘c6 13 ♗d2 ♘e4 14 0-0 ♘xd2 15 ♕xd2 ♘a5 16 ♕b4 ♕d7 17 ♖fc1 ♖fc8 18 ♗f1 g6 19 g3 ♔g7 20 a4 ♖c6 21 ♖xc6 ♘xc6 22 ♕a3 ♘e7 23 a5 ♗xb5 24 ♗xb5 ♕xb5 25 ♕xe7 bxa5 26 ♕a3 a4 27 ♕xa4 ♕xa4 28 ♖xa4 a5 = Karpman-Anastasian, Podolsk 1989.

⇨ 8 ♗d3 ♗a6 9 cxd5 ♗xd3 10 ♕xd3 exd5 11 0-0 ♖e8 12 b4 ♘bd7 13 ♗b2 a6 14 ♖ad1 ♖e6 15 ♖fe1 ♕e7 16 ♘e2 ♘h5 17 ♕f5 ♘df6 18 ♘c3 c6 19 ♕f3 b5. With the thought of getting a knight to c4, Black is well placed here, but was later outplayed in Sadler-Anastasian, Cappelle la Grande 1991.

6 ♗d2

The rapid chess game Speelman-de Firmian, played at the Brussels Swift (rapid) tournament in 1992, took an unusual turn here: 6 a3!? ♕h4 7 ♘g3 ♗xc3+ 8 bxc3 ♗b7 9 ♗d3 f5 10 0-0-0 0-0 11 ♖e1 ♘c6 12 f3 ♘d6 13 ♖b1 ♗a6 14 ♕e2 ♘a5 15 c5 ♗xd3 16 ♕xd3 bxc5 17 dxc5 ♕c4! 18 ♕d4 ♘c6 19 ♕xc4 ♘xc4 20 ♖b7 ♖fc8 21 ♖d1 ♖ab8 22 ♖xb8 ♖xb8 23 ♖xd7 ♖b1 24 ♘e2 ♘6e5 25 ♖d8+ ♔f7 26 ♔f2 ♔e7 27 ♖d4 ♘b2 28 ♗xb2 ♖xb2 29 h3 ♖a2 with chances for both sides.

6...♘xd2 7 ♕xd2 ♗a6

The other plan is 7...♗b7 8 a3 ♗e7:

⇨ 9 ♘f4!? ♗g5!? 10 ♗d3 0-0 (it is far too dangerous to take the pawn on g2: 10...♗xf4 11 exf4 ♗xg2? 12 ♖g1 ♗b7 13 0-0-0 g6 14 f5! ±) 11 0-0 ♗xf4 (11...d5 12 cxd5 ♗xf4 13

exf4 exd5 = is more accurate) 12 exf4 d5 13 c5! bxc5 14 dxc5 d4 15 ♘e4! f5 (winning a pawn but White's subsequent lead in development is enough to win it back, and more) 16 ♘g5 ♕d5 (16...h6?! 17 ♘f3 ♗xf3 18 gxf3 ±) 17 ♘f3! ♕xc5 18 ♖fe1 ♗xf3 19 gxf3 ♖e8 20 ♖ac1 ♕b6 21 ♗xf5 ± ♘d7 22 ♗e4 ♖ab8 23 b4 ♘f6 24 ♗c6 ♖e7 25 ♖e5 ♖be8 26 ♖b5? (26 f5! ±) 26...♕a6 27 ♖a5 ♕b6 28 ♖b5 ♕a6 ½-½ Rodriguez-I.Sokolov, Barcelona 1992.

⇨ 9 0-0-0?! ♘c6! 10 ♔b1 ♘a5 11 ♘f4 ♗a6 12 c5 ♗xf1 13 ♖hxf1 0-0 14 b4!? (not many players would play this!) 14...♘c4 15 ♕a2 d5 16 cxd6 ♘xd6 17 d5 e5 18 ♘d3 e4 19 ♘e5 ♗f6 20 ♘c6 ♕d7 21 ♖c1 ♕f5 22 ♕e2 ♖fe8 23 ♖fd1 a6 24 ♔a2 b5 25 f4 exf3 26 gxf3 ♕h5 27 ♖c2 g6 28 ♖d3 ♗g7 29 e4 f5 30 e5 ♗xe5! 31 ♘xe5 f4 32 ♘g4 ♖xe2 33 ♘xe2 ♕g5 34 ♖xc7 h5 35 h4 ♕d8?? (making a mess of it; 35...♕xh4! 36 ♘h6+ ♔h8 37 ♘f7+ ♘xf7 38 ♖xf7 ♖e8 39 ♘c3 ♕f2+ 40 ♔b3 ♕f1! 41 ♔c2 ♖e3! 42 ♖xe3 fxe3 43 d6 e2 44 d7 e1♘+! was right) 36 ♖d7! ♕f8 37 ♘h6+ ♔xh6 38 ♖xd6 ♕g7 39 ♘d4 ♖e8 40 ♖d2 ♔h8 41 ♖xa6 ♕e5 42 d6 ♖d8 43 ♘b3 ♕c3 44 d7 ♔g7 45 ♖ad6 ♕xf3 1-0 Suba-Luce, London 1990.

8 a3 ♗xc3 9 ♘xc3 d5 10 b4

A convoluted plan to avoid the exchange of bishops.

10...dxc4 11 b5 ♗b7 12 e4 a6 13 ♗xc4 0-0 14 0-0 axb5 15 ♗xb5 ♕e7 16 a4 ♖d8 17 ♕e3 ♘c6 18 ♖fd1 ♘b4 19 ♕d2 h6 20 ♖ad1 ♗a6 21 ♕e2

White's centre gives him the edge.

21...♗b7 22 h3 ♔f8 23 ♕f1 ♔g8 24 ♕e2 ♔f8 25 ♖b2 ♘c6 26 ♕c4 ♘a5 27 ♕a2 ♔g8 28 ♖bd2 ♔h8 29 ♕c2 ♗a6 30 ♗xa6 ♖xa6 31 d5 ♖aa8 32 ♘b5 exd5 33 exd5 ♖d7 34 d6 cxd6 35 ♘xd6 ♖c7?

A mistake; 35...♕e6 was quite adequate.

36 ♘xf7+! ♔g8

The only move; 36...♕xf7? 37 ♖d8+.

37 ♘xh6+ gxh6 38 ♕g6+ ♔f8 39 ♖d3 ♕e8 40 ♖f3+ 1-0

Game 79

I.Sokolov-D.Johansen
Manila OL 1992

1 d4 e6 2 c4 ♘f6 3 ♘c3 ♗b4 4 e3 b6 5 ♘e2 ♘e4 6 f3 ♘xc3 7 bxc3 ♗e7 8 e4 ♘c6 9 ♘g3 ♗a6 10 ♗d3 ♘a5 11 ♕e2 d6!

This is stronger than 11...0-0, as the black king should keep his options open.

12 0-0 ♕d7 13 ♖b1 h5

A standard method of embarrassing a knight on g3.

14 ♖e1 h4 15 ♘f1 c5 16 ♗e3 ♖c8 17 ♘d2 e5 18 f4 ♗f6 19 dxe5 dxe5 20 ♘f3 ♕e6 21 fxe5 ♗e7 22 ♖f1 ♗xc4 23 ♗g5 ♗xd3 24 ♕xd3 ♘c6 25 ♗xe7 ♕xe7 26 ♖bd1 0-0

Finally! This is really the best moment.

27 ♕d7 ♕xd7 28 ♖xd7 h3

This pawn is lost anyway, so it might as well cause some damage.

29 gxh3 ♖ce8 30 ♔g2 ♘xe5 31 ♖xa7 ♘c4 32 ♖f2

This position looks OK for White but is in fact quite awkward. For instance the obvious 32 ♖e1 is met by 32...♖a8 33 ♖xa8 ♖xa8 34 ♖e2 ♖a3 when 35 ♖c2? fails to the knight fork on e3.

32...♖xe4 33 ♘g5 ♖e5!

34 ♘xf7?! ♘e3+! 35 ♔g3 ♖f5 36 ♖e2 ♘f1+ 37 ♔g2 ♖8xf7 38 ♖xf7 ♔xf7 39 ♔g1 ♔f6 40 ♔g2

Although the knight on f1 is trapped, White is unable to attack it a second time and he gradually runs out of moves.

40...b5 41 ♔g1 c4 42 ♔g2 ♔g5 43 ♔g1 ♔h4 44 ♔g2 ♖f6 45 a3 g6 0-1

Game 80

Petursson-Nijboer
Wijk aan Zee 1990

1 d4 ♘f6 2 c4 e6 3 ♘c3 ♗b4 4 e3 b6 5 ♘e2 ♗b7 6 a3 ♗e7

The alternative is 6...♗xc3+ 7 ♘xc3 0-0 when 8 ♗d3 is worth considering, whilst practice has seen:
⇨ 8 d5 c6 9 e4 cxd5 10 exd5 exd5 11 cxd5 ♕e7+ 12 ♗e3 ♕e5 13 ♗c4 ♖c8 14 ♗a2 ♗a6 15 ♕d4 d6 16 ♕xe5 dxe5 17 f3 ♘bd7 18 0-0-0 ♗c4 (18...e4!?) was very slightly better for White in Benjamin-Adianto, Pan Pacific 1991.
⇨ 8 ♗d2!? c5 9 dxc5 bxc5 10 ♕c2 ♕e7 11 f3 d5 12 ♗d3 ♘c6 13 ♘e2 ♖fd8 14 0-0 ♘e5 15 ♗a5 ♖d7 16 ♖ad1 dxc4 17 ♗xc4 ♘d5 18 ♗xd5 exd5 with good play for Black; Suba-Adianto, Manila OL 1992.
    7 ♘g3!?
    This is supposed to be inferior because 7...h5 is possible, embarrassing the white knight. I wonder why Nijboer didn't play it? White's other tries:
    1) 7 d5 is considered normal: 7...0-0 (7...b5?! 8 dxe6 fxe6 9 cxb5!? 0-0 10 ♘f4 g5 11 ♘d3 d5 12 h4 gxh4 13 ♖xh4 must be better for White; Nikitin-Koriabkin, Moscow 1991) and now:
    1a) 8 g3 b5 9 b3 bxc4 10 bxc4 ♘a6 11 ♗g2 ♘c5 12 0-0 ♖b8 13 a4 ♖e8 14 ♕c2 c6 15 ♖d1 ♕c7 16 ♘d4

♘a6? 17 d6! ♕xd6 (17...♗xd6 18 ♘db5 is also good for White) 18 ♘xc6 ♘b4? (better to give the exchange) 19 ♘xb4 ♕xb4 20 ♖b1 ♕xc4 21 ♖xb7 ♖xb7 22 ♗xb7 d5 23 ♕d3 ♕xd3 24 ♖xd3 winning easily; Ravi-Cullip, British Ch 1989.
    1b) 8 ♘g3 and again play diverges:
    ⇨ 8...d6 (the normal move) 9 e4 (9 ♗e2 ♘bd7 10 0-0 and now 10...♖e8 11 f4!? c6 12 dxe6!? fxe6 13 ♗f3 ♕c7 14 b3 ♖ad8! 15 ♗b2 d5! = Hort-Stoica, Porz v Bucharest 1991, or 10...a6 11 e4 ♖e8 12 b4 c6 {Black's line-up of pawns on the sixth rank gives a strange impression} 13 ♗b2 ♗f8 14 ♕b3 ♖c8 15 dxc6 ♖xc6 16 ♖fd1 ♖c7 17 a4 ♕a8 18 f3 ± Astolfi-Gavrikov, Nîmes 1991) 9...♘bd7 10 ♗e2 ♖e8 11 0-0 a6 12 ♗f4 ♖c8 13 ♕d2 ♘f8 14 ♖ad1 ♕d7 15 ♗e3 ♕d8 16 b4 c6 (again, but this time Black has overlooked something!) 17 e5! cxd5 (17...dxe5 18 d6 ±, or 17...♘6d7 18 exd6 ♗xd6 19 dxc6 ♖xc6 20 b5) 18 exf6 ♗xf6 19 ♘a4 dxc4 20 ♘xb6 d5 21 ♘xc8 with an overwhelming material advantage; Levitt-Emms, British Ch 1992.
    ⇨ 8...♗d6!? (an unusual square for this bishop) 9 f4 exd5 10 cxd5 ♖e8 11 ♗e2 c6 12 e4 ♗f8 13 d6 c5 14 e5 ♗xg2 15 ♖g1 ♗b7 16 ♗e3 ♘c6 17 ♕d2 ♖c8 18 exf6 ♕xf6 19 ♘ge4 ♕h4+ 20 ♗f2 ♕d8 21 ♘g5 ♘d4 22 ♗xd4 cxd4 23 ♕xd4 g6 (White must be better, although in practice it is quite tricky) 24 f5 ♗g7 25 ♕d3 ♖c5 26 fxg6! hxg6 27 ♘xf7? (probably 27 h4 would have been a more sensible way to proceed) 27...♕h4+ 28

🕮g3 ♗xc3+ 29 bxc3 ♗e4 30 ♕e3
♔xf7 ∓ 31 0-0-0 ♗f5 32 ♕f3 ♕a4
33 ♔d2 ♕c2+ 34 ♔e1 🕮ce5 35 🕮g2
🕮xe2+ 36 🕮xe2 🕮xe2+ 37 ♕xe2
♕xe2+ 38 ♔xe2 ♗g4+ 39 ♔d2
♗xd1 40 ♔xd1 ♔e6 41 ♔e2 ♔xd6
42 ♔f3 ♔e5 43 ♔g4 ♔f6 44 c4 g5
0-1 Chernin-Balashov, Lvov 1990.

2) 7 b4!? (a novel plan to gain
space on the queenside immediately)
7...a5 8 b5 d6 9 🕮g3 h5!? 10 ♗e2 h4
11 ♗f3! ♕c8?! (11...♗xf3 12 ♕xf3
hxg3 13 ♕xa8 🕮xh2 fails to the surprising 14 0-0! ♔d7 15 fxg3 🕮g4
16 🕮xf7!, but 11...d5 was a better
choice) 12 🕮ge4 🕮xe4 13 🕮xe4
🕮d7 14 h3? (14 🕮c3! ±) 14...f5 15
🕮c3 🕮f6 16 0-0 d5! 17 ♗b2 ♕d7 18
🕮c1 0-0 19 c5! bxc5 20 dxc5 c6 21
🕮a4 ♕e8 22 b6 g5? 23 ♗e2 ♕g6 24
♗e5! 🕮d7 25 ♗c7 ± e5? 26 f3 ♕e6
27 e4! fxe4 28 fxe4 🕮xf1+ 29 ♗xf1
🕮f6 30 exd5 🕮xd5 31 ♗c4 ♔g7 32
♗xd5 cxd5 33 ♕g4 ♕xg4 34 hxg4
♗c6 35 b7? (throwing away the win;
35 ♗e5 was the right move)
35...♗xb7 36 c6 ♗a6 37 🕮b6 🕮e8
38 ♗xe5+ ♔f7 39 🕮c3 d4 40 ♗xd4
♗d6 41 ♗f2 🕮e7 42 🕮f3+ ♔e6 43
🕮f5 🕮c7! = 44 🕮a4! ♗xa3 45 🕮xa5
🕮xc6 46 ♗e3 ♗e7 47 ♗xg5 ♗xg5
48 🕮xg5 ♔f6 49 🕮h5 ♔g6 50 🕮c5
♗e2 51 🕮e4 🕮e6 52 🕮f2 ♗xg4 53
🕮xh4 ♗f5 54 🕮f4 🕮e2 55 g4 ♗xg4
½-½ Speelman-Kengis, London
1991.

**7...d5 8 cxd5 🕮xd5 9 ♗b5+ c6
10 ♗c4 0-0 11 e4 🕮xc3 12 bxc3 c5
13 0-0 🕮c6 14 ♗e3 🕮c8 15 ♗a2
cxd4 16 cxd4 🕮a5 17 ♕d3 ♕d6 18
d5!**

Breaking through in the centre.
18...g6

**19 e5! ♕xe5 20 dxe6 fxe6 21
♕d4 🕮c5 22 ♕d7 ♕d6 23 ♗xe6+
♔g7 24 ♗d4+ ♔h6 1-0**

Game 81

Ivanchuk-Timman
Hilversum m(2) 1991

**1 d4 🕮f6 2 c4 e6 3 🕮c3 ♗b4 4 e3 b6
5 🕮e2 ♗a6 6 🕮g3 ♗xc3+ 7 bxc3 d5
8 ♗a3**

An interesting try is 8 ♕f3. After
8...0-0 9 cxd5 ♕xd5 10 e4 ♕a5 we
have:
➪ 11 ♗e2 ♗xe2 12 🕮xe2 🕮bd7 (12
🕮xe2 c5 13 0-0 cxd4 14 cxd4 🕮bd7
15 a4 🕮fc8 16 ♕d3 ♕b4 17 f3 ♕c4
18 ♕xc4 🕮xc4 19 ♗f4 🕮ac8 = Brun-
ner-Huss, Leukerbad 1992) 13 0-0
c5 14 🕮g3 cxd4 15 cxd4 🕮ac8 16
e5?! (too committal; if there is no
mate then White is positionally
worse) 16...🕮d5 17 ♕g4 ♔h8 18
🕮h5 🕮g8 19 ♕f3 f5 20 exf6 🕮7xf6
21 🕮xf6 🕮xf6 22 ♗f4 ♕f5 23
🕮fe1 🕮d5 24 ♗g3 ♕xf3 25 gxf3
🕮ge8 ∓ Sadler-Brunner, Altensteig
1992.

⇨ 11 ♗xa6 ♕xa6 12 ♗g5!? ♘bd7 13 ♕e2! ♕xe2+?! 14 ♔xe2 ± c5 (this ending shouldn't be too bad for Black) 15 a4 ♖fc8 16 ♖hc1 ♔f8 17 f3 ♘e8 18 ♗f4 cxd4 19 cxd4 ♔e7 20 ♘f1 ♔d8?! (20...♖xc1 21 ♗xc1 was better, with only a small edge to White) 21 ♖cb1! ♖c4 22 ♔d3 ♖ac8 23 a5 ♖c2 24 ♗d2 ♘d6 25 axb6 axb6 26 ♘e3 and White gradually increased his advantage in Knaak-Wahls, Baden-Baden 1992.

8...♗xc4 9 ♗xc4 dxc4 10 ♕a4+

If White wishes to avoid the following ending then he can try 10 e4!? ♕d7 11 0-0 ♕b5 12 ♕c2 ♘c6 13 ♖fe1 0-0-0 14 ♖eb1 ♕a5 15 ♗b4 ♕g5 16 ♕e2 h5 17 ♘f1 h4 18 f3 ♘h5 19 ♕xc4 ♘f4 20 ♖b2 which was not too clear in Vaiser-Rechlis, Tel Aviv 1992; White has the centre but Black does have good kingside counterplay.

10...♕d7 11 ♕xc4 ♕c6 12 ♕xc6+ ♘xc6 13 c4 0-0-0 14 ♖c1

⇨ 14 ♔e2 ♖d7 (14...♔b7 15 f3 ♖d7 16 ♖hd1 ♖hd8 17 ♖ac1 a6 18 ♘f1 h5 19 ♘d2 ♘g8 20 ♘e4 = Thorsteins-Kotronias, Reykjavik 1992) 15 ♖hd1 ♖hd8 16 ♗b2 ♘a5 17 ♖ac1 ♘e8 18 ♗a1 c5 19 dxc5 ♖xd1 20 ♖xd1 ♖xd1 21 ♔xd1 bxc5 22 ♘e4 ♘xc4 23 ♘xc5 ½-½ Züger-Huss, Leukerbad 1992.

14...♔b7 15 ♔e2

Ivanchuk suggests 15 f3 ±.

**15...h5!? 16 f3?! h4 17 ♘f1 ♖h5!
18 ♗b2 ♘a5?**

18...♖a5 is unclear.

19 e4 ± b5 20 ♘e3 bxc4 21 d5 exd5 22 ♗xf6 gxf6 23 ♘xd5

One small inaccuracy and Black's position is a complete wreck!

23...c6 24 ♘xf6 ♖b5 25 ♖c2 ♖d6 26 ♘g4 f5 27 ♘f2 ♖g6 28 ♖g1 f4 29 ♘h3 ♖f6 30 ♖d1 ♔c7 31 ♔d2 ♖c5 32 ♖dc1 ♖f8 33 ♔e1 ♔b6 34 ♘f2 ♖g5 35 ♔f1 ♔b5 36 ♘d1 ♖fg8 37 h3 ♔b4 38 ♖b1+ ♔a4?

An error, but it was only a matter of time before Black's weak pawns began to drop off anyway.

39 ♘b2+ ♔a3 40 ♘xc4+ ♘xc4 41 ♖b3+ ♔a4 42 ♖xc4+ ♔a5 43 ♖c2 ♖8g6 44 ♖b7 1-0

Game 82

Lautier-Wahls
Dortmund 1989

1 d4 ♘f6 2 c4 e6 3 ♘c3 ♗b4 4 e3 b6 5 ♘e2 ♗a6 6 ♘g3

⇨ 6 ♕a4 c5 7 a3 ♗xc3+ 8 ♘xc3 0-0 9 d5! ♕e7 10 f3 exd5 11 cxd5 ♗xf1 12 ♔xf1 d6 13 ♔f2 ♘bd7 14 ♖f1?! (14 e4) 14...a6 15 e4 b5 16 ♕c2 ♘e5 (Black has a perfectly reasonable 'Benoni-style' position) 17 ♔g1 c4 18 ♗e3 ♘fd7 19 ♗d4 ♖ac8 20 ♘d1! ± ♘c5 21 ♘e3 ♘b3 22 ♘f5 ♕c7 23 ♕c3!? (intending to answer 23...♘xa1 with 24 f4 and an attack on g7) 23...g6 24 ♘h6+ ♔g7 25 ♗e3 ♕a5 (trying to avoid the complications) 26 ♕xa5 ♘xa5 27 f4 ♘d7 28 f5 ♘b7 29 ♖ae1 f6 30 fxg6 hxg6 31 ♘g4 ♖h8 32 h3 ♖cf8 33 ♖e2 ½-½ Speelman-Timman, Linares 1991.

6...0-0

⇨ 6...h5!? 7 h4 g6 8 e4 ♘h7 9 e5 ♗e7 10 ♗d3 ♘c6 11 ♗e3 ♘b4?! 12 ♗e2 ♗xh4 13 ♕a4 ♗e7 14 a3 ± ♗b7 15 axb4 ♗xg2 16 ♖h2 ♗c6 17 b5 ♗b7 18 ♘xh5!? (White must have the advantage after a simple move like 18 ♘ge4) 18...gxh5 19 ♖xh5 f5 20 0-0-0 a6 21 ♕c2 axb5 22 d5 ♖a1+ 23 ♘b1 ♗c5 24 dxe6 ♗xe3+ 25 fxe3 ♗e4 26 ♗d3 ♗f3 27 ♗xf5 ♗xd1 28 exd7+ ♔e7 29 ♕xd1 ♕g8 30 ♖xh7+ ♖xh7 31 ♗xh7 ♕xc4+ 32 ♗c2 ♔d8 33 b3 ♕c3 34 ♕d4 ♕xd4 35 exd4 ♔xd7 36 ♔b2 ♖a8 37 ♘c3 (two pieces and a pawn are more than a match for a rook) 37...c6 38 ♗f5+ ♔c7 39 ♘e4 b4 40 ♔c2 ♖f8 41 ♘f6 ♖h8 42 ♗h7 ♖a8 43 ♔d3 ♖a1 44 ♔c4 ♖c1+ 45 ♔xb4 c5+ 46 dxc5 ♖xc5 47 e6 ♔d8 48 ♗g8 ♖f5 49 ♘d7 ♔c7 50 ♗f7 ♖f4+ 51 ♔b5 ♖f5+ 52 ♔c4 b5+ 53 ♔b4 ♔d6 54 ♘b6 ♖e5 55 ♘c8+ ♔c7 56 e7 1-0 Knaak-Inkiov, Stara Zagora Z 1990.

7 e4 ♘c6 8 e5!?

A recent idea; 8 ♗d3 is habitual: 8...e5 9 d5 ♗xc3+ 10 bxc3 ♘a5 11 ♕e2 ♘e8 12 ♗a3 d6 13 0-0 ♘f6 14 f4 ♘d7 15 f5 f6 16 ♘h5 ♘c5 17 ♗xc5 bxc5 18 g4 ♖b8 19 h4 and White's kingside pawn charge outweighs his weaknesses; Sadler-K.Arkell, London 1991.

8...♘e8 9 ♕a4!? ♗b7 10 ♗d3 ♘xd4!?

An amazing move: Black gives up a piece to break out.

11 ♕xb4 c5 12 ♕a4 ♗xg2

(see next diagram)

13 ♗e4 ♗xe4 14 ♘cxe4 ♘f3+ 15 ♔f1 ♘xe5 16 f4 ♘g6 17 ♕d1 d5 18 cxd5 exd5

Black has three pawns for the piece and the white king is a little exposed—this makes for interesting play.

19 ♘g5 ♘f6 20 f5 ♘e5 21 ♗f4

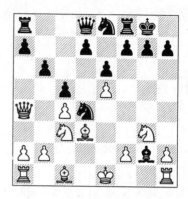

♖e8 22 ♘f3 ♘c4 23 b3 ♘e3+ 24 ♗xe3 ♖xe3 25 ♔g2 d4 26 ♖e1 ♘g4 27 ♘f1 ♖xe1 28 ♕xe1 ♕d5 29 h3 ♘f6 30 ♕e5 ♕c6 31 ♖e1 h6 32 ♘1d2 ♖d8 33 ♔f2 ♔h8 34 ♕e7 ♖d7 35 ♕f8+ ♔h7 36 ♘e5 ♕c7 37 ♘xd7 ♕h2+ 38 ♔f1 ♕xh3+ 39 ♔e2 ♕g4+ 40 ♔f2 ♕h4+ 41 ♔e2 ♕g4+ 42 ♔f2 ♕h4+ 43 ♔e2 ½-½

Game 83

Rajković-Martin
Gosa v Wood Green 1991

1 d4 ♘f6 2 c4 e6 3 ♘c3 ♗b4 4 e3 b6 5 ♘e2 ♗a6 6 a3 ♗e7

⇨ 6...♗xc3+ 7 ♘xc3 d5 8 b3 0-0 (8...♘c6 is likely to transpose, Goormachtigh-Mikhalchishin, Sas van Gent 1990 continuing: 9 ♗e2 dxc4 10 bxc4 ♕d7 11 a4 0-0 12 0-0 ♖fd8 13 ♗b2 ♘a5 14 ♘b5 c6 15 ♘a3 ♕e7 unclear) 9 a4 (9 ♗e2 ♘c6 10 a4 ♕d7 11 0-0 dxc4 12 ♗a3 ♖fd8 13 b4 ♗b7 14 b5 ♘a5 15 ♖b1 e5 16 ♗b4 exd4 17 ♖xa5 d3 18 ♗b4 dxe2 19 ♕xe2 c5 with advantage; Lesiège-Brunner, Manila OL 1992)

9...♘c6 10 ♗a3 ♖e8 11 ♗e2 e5!? 12 dxe5 ♘xe5 13 ♘xd5 ♘xd5 14 cxd5? (exposing himself to a violent attack; 14 ♕xd5 ±) 14...♗xe2 15 ♔xe2 ♕g5 16 ♔f1 ♖ad8 17 ♕d2 ♘g4 18 ♖d1 ♕f5 (Black is already winning since he threatens both ...♖xd5 and ...♘xe3+) 19 e4 ♖xe4 20 f3 ♘e3+ 21 ♔g1 ♖xd5 22 ♕xd5 ♘xd5 23 fxe4 ♕xe4 ∓ Petursson-Seul, Clichy 1991.

7 ♘f4 d5 8 cxd5

⇨ 8 ♕f3 is an aggressive option: 8...c6 9 b3 0-0 10 ♗b2 ♗d6 11 ♗d3 ♖e8 12 0-0 ♘bd7 13 cxd5 ♗xd3 14 ♘xd3 exd5 15 ♕d1 ♘e4 16 ♘e2 ♖c8 17 ♘ef4 ♕h4 18 ♖c1 ♕h6 19 g3 g5! 20 ♘g2 ♕h3 21 f3 ♘xg3! (Black has a deadly attack) 22 hxg3 ♗xg3 23 ♖f2 ♗h2+ 24 ♔f1 ♖xe3 25 ♖e2 ♖xf3+ 26 ♘f2 ♗f4 27 ♖e7 ♕h1+ 28 ♔e2 ♕xg2 29 ♕g1 ♕xg1 30 ♖xg1 ♖xb3 was crushing in Sadler-Wells, Dublin 1991.

8...♗xf1 9 ♔xf1 exd5

⇨ 9...♘xd5 10 ♘cxd5 exd5 11 ♕h5 c6 12 ♘e6 g6 13 ♕e5 ♗f6 14 ♘xd8+ ♗xe5 15 ♘xc6 ♘xc6 16 dxe5 ♘xe5 17 ♗d2 ♔e7 18 ♗c3 f6 (this is a well-known ending that is considered slightly better for White, but Adams seems to draw easily enough) 19 ♔e2 ♔e6 20 ♖hd1 ♖hd8 21 ♖d4 f5 22 ♖ad1 ♖d7 23 h3 h5 24 f3 ♖ad8 25 h4 ♘c6 26 ♖a4 a5 27 g4

fxg4 28 fxg4 d4! 29 ♗xd4 b5 30 ♖c1 ½-½ Rechlis-Adams, Manila IZ 1990; on 30...bxa4 31 ♖xc6+ White will have just enough compensation for the exchange.

10 b4?! 0-0 11 ♕b3 ♘c6! 12 a4 ♕d7 13 ♗a3 ♖fe8 14 h3 ♖e6! 15 ♖c1 ♖ae8 16 ♔g1

White's position looks solid enough. However his king is a trifle uncomfortable.

16...♘xd4!

A thunderbolt!

17 exd4 ♖e1+ 18 ♔h2 ♘g4+! 19 hxg4 ♕d6+ 20 ♔h3 ♕h6+ 21 ♔g3 ♖8e3+ 22 fxe3 ♕xe3+ 23 ♔h4 ♕f2+ 24 ♔h3?

Instead 24 g3 g5+ 25 ♔xg5 ♕e3+ 26 ♔h5 ♕g7 27 g5 held out chances for survival.

24...g5! 25 g3 ♖e6 0-1

7

The system with ...b6 and ...d5 has come into the limelight recently following Timman's championing of it in two games of his successful Candidates Semi-final against Yusupov. It is a particularly useful opening to have in one's repertoire as it can arise from a wide variety of move-orders, for instance: 1 d4 d5 2 ♘f3 ♘f6 3 c4 e6 4 ♘c3 ♗b4 5 e3 0-0 6 ♗d3 b6 7 0-0 ♗b7 8 a3 ♗d6 or even 1 d4 ♘f6 2 ♘f3 e6 3 c4 b6 4 e3 ♗b7 5 ♘c3 d5 6 cxd5 exd5 7 ♗b5+ c6 8 ♗d3 ♗b4 9 0-0 0-0.

Normally, after 7 0-0 ♗b7 8 a3, Black will answer with 8...♗d6 and White will most likely play either an immediate 9 b4 or first exchange on d5. In the first case it seems that Black's chances are not in any way worse and once he has successfully played ...e5 he can face the future with confidence, game 84 being a fine example.

However, in the last few years, Speelman has been playing 9 b3!? with impressive results (game 85). This system will no doubt start to attract a lot of followers.

In game 86, on 9 cxd5 exd5 10 b4 a6 White tries 11 ♕b3 with the plan of exchanging dark-squared bishops by a4, b5 and ♗a3. I have always found this position quite difficult to play for Black, but Timman seems to have no such problems.

The other option for White, 11 b5, is essayed in game 87, but again Black's opening can be considered a success, although he later goes astray.

Polugaevsky likes to trick Black into this position using unusual move-orders, but in game 88 he meets with the interesting novelty, 10...♘e4!?, plays carelessly, and nearly pays a heavy price.

Game 89 covers White's most aggressive plan on the kingside, 9 ♘e5 and 10 f4 *à la* Pillsbury. Naturally, Black must be careful lest he finds himself mated, but all in all his chances are not worse.

Finally, should White play a3 too early Black can try ...♗a6, as in game 90.

Game 84

Hübner-Khalifman
Bundesliga 1991

1 d4 ♘f6 2 c4 e6 3 ♘c3 ♗b4 4 e3 0-0 5 ♗d3 d5 6 ♘f3 b6 7 0-0 ♗b7 8 a3 ♗d6

This is the natural and most aggressive square for the bishop, I consider the alternatives to be worse: ⇨ 8...♗xc3 9 bxc3 ♘bd7 10 cxd5 exd5 11 a4 c5 12 ♘d2 ♖e8 13 ♖e1 ♕c7 14 f3 ♖ad8 15 ♘f1 ♘f8 16 ♖a2 ♕c8 17 ♘g3 ♗a6 18 ♗b1 ♘g6 19 ♖f2 cxd4 20 cxd4 (the schema that has arisen is a common one in the Nimzo-Indian, and is known to favour White, who can prepare the e4 push) 20...♕c3 21 ♘f5 ♗c4 22 ♗c2 ♘e7 23 ♗d2 ♕b2 24 g4 ♘xf5 25 gxf5 ♖c8 26 ♗c1 ♕c3 27 e4 (White plays very well, despite this being a thirty-minute game) 27...dxe4 28 fxe4 ♖cd8 29 ♖d2 ♕h3 30 ♖g2 ♕c3 31 ♗g5 ♔h8 32 ♖d2 h6 33 ♖e3 ♕b4

34 ♖h3 ♘h7 35 ♗xd8 ♖xd8 36 ♖g3
♗a6 37 e5 f6 38 e6 ♗b7 39 h4 ♖c8
40 d5 ♕c5+ 41 ♔g2 ♕d6 42 ♗e4
♔g8 43 ♖c2 ♖d8 44 ♕g4 ♕e7 45
♖gc3 ♗xd5 46 ♗xd5 ♖xd5 47 ♖c7
♖d2+ 48 ♔f1 1-0 Ivanchuk-Kam-
sky, Tilburg (active) 1992.
⇨ 8...♗e7 9 b4 c5?! (9...dxc4 10
dxc4 c5) 10 cxd5! cxd4 11 ♘xd4
♘xd5 12 ♗b2 ♘xc3 13 ♗xc3 ♗f6?!
14 ♕c2 h6 15 ♗e4 ♕d7! 16 ♖ad1
♖c8 17 ♘b5! ♗xe4 18 ♕xe4 ♕c6
19 ♕xc6 ♘xc6 20 ♗xf6 gxf6 21
♖c1 a6 22 ♘d6 ♖c7 23 g4! (fixing
Black's f-pawn; the rook and knight
endgame that has arisen is very difficult, perhaps even lost, for Black)
23...♖d8 24 ♘e4 ♔g7 25 ♖c3 ♖cc8
26 ♖fc1 ♘e7 27 ♔g2 ♖xc3 28 ♖xc3
♘d5? 29 ♖c6 ♖d7 30 ♘d6 ± ♔g6
31 ♘c8 ♖b7 32 ♔f3 a5 33 b5 e5 34
h4 a4 35 h5+ ♔g7 36 ♘d6 ♖b8 37
♔e4 ♘e7 38 ♖c7 ♔f8 39 ♘f5
♘xf5 40 ♔xf5 ♔g7 41 ♖a7 ♖c8 42
♖xa4 winning without any undue
problems; Lautier-Mirallès, France
1991.
  9 b4
⇨ 9 ♕e2 c5 10 dxc5 bxc5 11 e4!? (a
sharp alternative to 11 ♖d1) 11...d4
12 ♘b5 ♗e7! (12...e5 13 b4!) 13 e5
♘e8 14 b4? (14 a4 ♘c6) 14...a6 15
♘d6 ♘xd6 16 exd6 ♕xd6 17 bxc5
♕xc5 18 ♖b1 ♗xf3 19 ♕xf3 ♘d7
20 ♗f4 ♗d6 21 ♖b7 ♖ad8 22 ♕h3
f5! 23 ♗g5 ♕c6 24 ♖fb1 ♖b8 25
♖xb8 ♖xb8 26 ♖xb8+ ♗xb8 27
♗f1 ♘c5 28 ♗d2 ♘e4 29 ♗e1 ♕d6
30 f3 d3! ∓ 31 fxe4 ♗a7+ 32 ♗f2 d2
33 ♗xa7 d1♕ 34 exf5 ♕f4 35 ♗f2
♕xc4 0-1 Djurić-Khalifman, Ljubljana Vidmar mem 1991.
  9...dxc4 10 ♗xc4 ♘bd7 11 ♗b2

11...a5
⇨ 11...♕e7?! (this is known to be an
inaccuracy; first 11...a5 12 b5 avoids
what follows) 12 ♘b5! a6 13 ♘xd6
cxd6 14 b5 axb5 15 ♗xb5 ♘e4 16
♘d2? (16 ♕e2 was much better;
White had no doubt overlooked the
coming combination) 16...♘xd2 17
♕xd2 ♗xg2! 18 ♔xg2 (18 ♗xd7
♗f3 19 e4 ♕h4 20 ♖fc1 ♕g4+ 21
♔f1 ♕g2+ 22 ♔e1 ♕g1#) 18...♕g5+
19 ♔h1 ♕xb5 ∓ 20 d5 e5 21 ♖ab1
♕a4 22 ♗c3 ♕c4 23 ♗b4 ♘c5 24
f3 f5 25 ♖g1 ♖f6 26 ♖bc1 ♕h4 27
♕e2 ♕h5 28 ♖g2 ♖g6 29 ♖cg1 ♖c8
30 ♕f1 (30 ♖xg6 hxg6 31 ♕g2
♔f7 ∓) 30...♖xg2 31 ♕xg2 ♕f7 32
♖d1 ♘d3! 33 ♕d2 (33 ♗xd6 ♕xd5
34 ♗b4 ♘f2+ ∓) 33...e4 34 ♗xd6
♕xd5 35 ♗g3? (35 fxe4! fxe4 36
♗g3) 35...exf3! 36 ♔g1 ♖d8 37 ♕c2
h6 38 ♕c7 ♕a2! 0-1 Torre-
Korchnoi, Manila IZ 1990.
  **12 b5 e5 13 ♖e1 e4 14 ♘d2 ♕e7
15 f4**
  The famous game Portisch-
Petrosian, Lone Pine 1978, went 15
♗e2 ♖ad8 16 f3 and culminated in a
fine win for Black. Hübner's idea
leaves his central pawns a bit rickety.

15...exf3 16 gxf3?!

White should have played 16 ♘xf3 ♘e4 17 ♘d5 ♕d8! with equality.

16...♖ad8 17 ♕e2 ♖fe8 18 ♕f2 ♘f8 19 ♘de4! ♘g6 20 ♘xd6 cxd6! 21 ♗f1 ♘h5 22 e4 ♘hf4 23 ♕g3 d5!

Now Black is slightly better.

24 exd5

White has to agree to the isolation of his d-pawn as 24 e5 f6! 25 ♗c1 ♕c7! is unpleasant.

24...♕d7 25 ♖xe8+ ♖xe8 26 ♖e1 ♖xe1 27 ♕xe1 ♘xd5 28 ♘e4 ♕e7 29 ♕g3 ♘df4 30 ♗c1 ♗xe4 31 ♗xf4 ♗d5 32 ♗c1 h6 33 ♗d3 ♕f6 34 ♗e3 ♗xf3 35 ♗xg6 fxg6 36 h4?

In time-trouble White misses a problem-like draw: 36 ♕f4! g5 37 ♕xf6 gxf6 38 d5 ♗xd5 39 a4! when the bishop will mop up the queenside pawns leaving technical equality. With the queens on the board the exposure of the white king is decisive.

36...♗d5 ∓ 37 ♕f4 ♕e7 38 ♕e5 ♕d7 39 ♔f2 ♕xb5 40 ♔g3 ♕d7 41 ♕b8+ ♔h7 42 ♕xb6 ♕f5 0-1

Game 85

Speelman-Chandler
Hastings 1991

1 d4 ♘f6 2 c4 e6 3 ♘c3 ♗b4 4 e3 0-0 5 ♘f3 b6 6 ♗d3 ♗b7 7 0-0 d5 8 a3 ♗d6 9 b3!?

This is something of a pet line of Speelman's, and he has been very successful with it, too.

9...♘bd7 10 ♘b5 ♗e7 11 ♗b2 c5
⇨ In his annotations Speelman queries this move and instead recommends 11...a6!? 12 ♘c3 ♗d6, and it wasn't long before this was tried against him: 13 ♖e1 c5!? 14 cxd5 exd5 15 e4! dxe4 (15...cxd4 16 ♘xd5 ♘xd5 17 exd5 ♗xd5? 18 ♗xh7+!) 16 ♘xe4 ♘xe4 17 ♗xe4 ♗xe4 18 ♖xe4 ♘f6 19 ♖e2! ♖c8 20 dxc5 ♖xc5! 21 ♖d2 ♖d5! 22 ♖xd5 ♘xd5 23 g3 ± ♘c7 24 ♕c2 ♘e6 25 ♖d1 ♕a8 26 ♕f5 ♗e7 27 ♖d7 ♖e8 28 h4 ♘f8 29 ♕g4 ♘e6 30 ♕f5 ♕c8? (he should certainly repeat moves here; although White has a very menacing position the players were unable to find a truly convincing continuation in the *post mortem*) 31 ♘g5! ♘xg5 32 ♖xe7 ♘f3+ 33 ♔h1 1-0 Speelman-Greenfeld, Tilburg 1992.

12 ♖e1 ♘e4 13 ♕c2
⇨ Speelman deviated at this point in his game with Polugaevsky, Hastings 1993, possibly fearing an improvement: 13 cxd5!? exd5 14 dxc5 ♘dxc5!? 15 ♗f1 a6 16 ♘bd4 ♗f6 17 b4 ♘e6 18 ♕b3 ♖c8 19 ♖ac1 ♕d7 20 ♘xe6?! (20 ♘e2 ±) 20...fxe6 21 ♗xf6 gxf6! ∓ 22 ♕b2 e5 23 ♘d2 ♘d6 24 g3 ♖xc1 25 ♖xc1 ♖c8 26

♗g2 ♔g7 27 h4 ♖c7 28 ♕a1 ♘c4 29 ♘xc4 ♖xc4 30 ♖d1! ♕f5? (30...♕c8 31 ♕b2 ♖c2 was correct) 31 ♖d2 (not 31 ♗xd5?? ♖c2 32 f4 ♗xd5 33 ♖xd5 ♕h3 ∓) 31...♕c8 32 ♕f1! ♕e6?! 33 ♕d1 ♕c8 34 ♔h2 e4 35 ♗h3! (White is well on top now) 35...♕e8 36 ♕g4+ ♔g6 37 ♕e6 b5 38 ♕b6 ♕f7 39 ♗e6 ♕c7 40 ♕a7 ♔g6 41 ♗xd5 ♗xd5 42 ♕xc7 ♖xc7 43 ♖xd5 ♖c3 44 h5+ ♔h6 45 ♖d6 ♖xa3 46 ♖xf6+ ♔xh5 47 ♖f4 a5 48 ♖xe4 axb4 49 ♖xb4 ♖a5 50 ♔h3 ♔g6 51 g4! h5 52 gxh5+ ♔xh5 53 f4 ♔g6 54 ♔g4 ♔f6 55 e4 ♔e6 56 e5 ♔d5 57 ♔f5 ♔c5 58 ♖b1 b4 59 e6 b3 60 e7 1-0.

13...f5?!

This is too loosening.

14 ♖ad1 a6 15 ♘c3 ♗d6 16 dxc5! ♘dxc5 17 cxd5 exd5 18 b4 ♘e6 19 ♕b3! ♘xc3 20 ♗xc3 ♖c8 21 ♘d4!? ♘xd4 22 ♗xd4 ♕c7 23 g3 ♗e5?!

But 23...b5 24 ♕b2 is also somewhat in White's favour.

24 ♗xa6! ♗xa6 25 ♕xd5+ ♗f7 26 ♗xe5 ♕c2 27 ♕e6 ♕e4 28 ♖d7 ♗c4 29 ♖c1! 1-0

Game 86

Yusupov-Timman
Linares Ct (9) 1992

1 d4 ♘f6 2 c4 e6 3 ♘c3 ♗b4 4 e3 0-0 5 ♗d3 d5 6 ♘f3 b6 7 0-0 ♗b7 8 cxd5 exd5 9 a3 ♗d6 10 b4 a6 11 ♕b3 ♘bd7 12 a4 ♕e7 13 ♗a3

Alternatively 13 ♖b1 and:

⇨ 13...♖fe8 14 b5 a5 15 ♖a1 ♘f8 16 ♗a3 ♖ad8 17 ♗xd6 ♖xd6 18 ♖ac1 ♘e4 19 ♘e2 ♘g6 20 ♘g3 ♕d7 21 ♖c2 c5 22 bxc6 ♗xc6 23 ♗b5 ♗xb5 24 axb5 ♖f6 25 ♖fc1 ♖xf3? 26 ♖c7! ♕g4 27 ♕xd5 ♘xg3 28 gxf3 ♘e2+ 29 ♔h1 ♕e6 30 ♕xe6 fxe6 31 ♖1c2 picking up a knight; Muir-Rechlis, Novi Sad OL 1990.

⇨ 13...c6 14 ♗f5 g6 15 ♗h3 b5 16 axb5 axb5 17 ♘g5 ♘b6 (aiming for c4) 18 e4?! dxe4 19 ♖e1 ♕c7 20 ♘cxe4 ♘xe4 21 ♖xe4 ♘d5 22 ♗d2 ♗xh2+ with a clear plus; Pavlović-Khuzman, Vrnjačka Banja 1991.

13...♖fd8

⇨ 13...♖fb8?! 14 ♗f5 ♘f8 15 ♖fc1 g6 16 ♗h3 c6 17 g3 ♗c8 18 ♗g2 ♗b7 19 ♖e1 ♘e6 20 e4?! dxe4 21 ♘xe4 ♘xe4 22 ♖xe4 c5 ½-½ Polugaevsky-Lautier, France 1992.

14 ♖fe1 ♘f8 15 b5 ♗xa3 16 bxa6 ♗xa6 17 ♗xa6 ♖xa6 18 ♖xa3 c5 19 ♖a2 ♘e4! 20 ♖c1 c4 21 ♕b5 ♘xc3 22 ♖xc3 ♕b7 23 ♘d2 ♖da8 24 ♖ca3 ♕d7 25 ♕b4

White starts to go astray. 25 ♕xd7 ♘xd7 26 ♘b1 f5 27 ♘c3 would have maintained the balance.

25...♘g6 26 g3? h5 27 ♘b1 h4 28 ♘c3 ♕g4 29 ♕b2 hxg3 30 fxg3 ♘e7 31 ♕f2

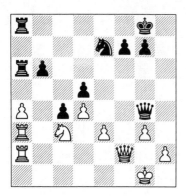

31...b5! ∓ 32 ♘xb5 ♖xa4 33 ♖xa4 ♖xa4 34 ♘c3 ♖xa2 35 ♕xa2 ♕e6 36 ♕e2?! ♘f5 37 ♔f2 ♘d6 38 ♕c2 f5 39 ♘e2 ♘e4+ 40 ♔g2 ♘f6 41 ♘f4 ♕e4+?

After building a winning advantage, Black falls at the final hurdle; 41...♘g4! 42 ♘xe6 ♘xe3+ 43 ♔f3 ♘xc2 44 ♔f4 c3 wins.

42 ♕xe4 dxe4 43 ♔f2! ♘g4+ 44 ♔e2 ♘xh2 45 ♘g6 c3 46 ♘e7+ ♔f7 47 ♘xf5 ♘f1 48 ♔d1 ♔f6 49 g4 g6 ½-½

Game 87

Yusupov-Timman
Linares Ct (5) 1992

1 d4 ♘f6 2 c4 e6 3 ♘c3 ♗b4 4 e3 0-0 5 ♗d3 d5 6 ♘f3 b6 7 0-0 ♗b7 8 cxd5 exd5 9 a3 ♗d6 10 b4 a6 11 ♕b3 ♕e7 12 b5 axb5 13 ♘xb5 ♘bd7 14 ♗b2

A new move in this position. Previously 14 a4 (14 ♖b1 c5 15 ♗c2 ♗c6 16 ♘xd6 ♕xd6 17 ♕b2 ♕e6 18 ♕a1 ♗a4 19 ♗xa4 ♖xa4 20 dxc5 ½-½ Portisch-Chandler, Moscow

1990) had been seen most frequently:

⇨ 14...c5 15 ♘xd6 ♕xd6 16 ♗a3 ♗a6 17 ♖fd1 ♗xd3 18 ♕xd3 ♕c6 19 ♘e5 ♕xa4 20 ♘xd7 ♕xd7 21 dxc5 bxc5 22 ♗xc5 ♖xa1 23 ♖xa1 with a slight advantage to White, although he later blundered and lost; Semkov-Nikčević, Rome 1990.

⇨ 14...♗a6 15 ♘xd6 ♗xd3 16 ♕xd3 ♕xd6 17 ♖d1 ♖fe8 18 ♗b2 ♖a7 19 ♕c2 c5 is more or less balanced; Lukacs-Lengyel, Hungary 1991.

14...c5 15 ♘xd6 ♕xd6 16 ♗f5 c4! = 17 ♕c2 g6 18 ♗xd7 ♘xd7 19 ♘e5 ♖fe8 20 ♗c3 ♗c6 21 ♕b2 ♗a4?

Equality can be maintained with 21...f6.

22 e4! f6 23 ♘xd7 ♕xd7 24 e5!

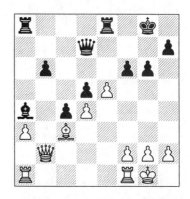

24...♕e6 25 exf6 ♕xf6 26 ♖fe1 ♖xe1+ 27 ♖xe1 ♖e8 28 ♖e5 ♖xe5 29 dxe5 ♕e6?!

29...♕f4! offered better chances.

30 ♗d4 ♗b3 31 h3 h5 32 ♕d2 ♗a4 33 ♕g5

White's advantage is substantial, in spite of the opposite-colour bishops.

33...♔f7 34 g4 hxg4 35 hxg4 ♔e8 36 ♔g2 ♔d7 37 ♔g3 ♗d1 38 f3 ♔c7 39 ♕f6! ± ♕xf6 40 exf6 ♔d7 41 ♗xb6 c3 42 ♗d4 c2 43 ♗b2 ♔e6 44 g5 ♗e2 45 ♔f2 ♗b5 46 ♔e3 ♗e8 47 ♔d3 ♗a4 48 ♔c3 ♔d6 49 ♗c1 ♔e6 50 ♔b4 1-0

Game 88

Polugaevsky-A.Sokolov
France 1992

1 d4 ♘f6 2 c4 e6 3 ♘f3 b6 4 e3 ♗b7 5 ♘c3 ♗b4 6 ♗d3 0-0 7 0-0 d5 8 a3 ♗d6 9 cxd5 exd5 10 b4 ♘e4!?

A suggestion by Yudovich.

⇨ 10...c6 11 ♗b2 ♖e8 12 ♖e1 ♘bd7 13 ♕b3 a5 14 ♖ad1 axb4 15 axb4 ♗f8 16 ♗f5 g6 17 ♗h3 ♕e7 18 ♗a3 ♗a6 19 ♘d2 ♗c4 20 ♕b2 b5 21 f3 ♘b6 22 e4 ♕a7 23 ♘db1 ♘h5 24 g3 dxe4 25 fxe4 ♗g7 26 ♕f2 ♗b3 27 ♖d3 ♘c4 28 ♗c1 ♖ad8 29 g4 ♘f6 30 ♗g5 ♘d7 31 ♗xd8 ♖xd8 (I'm not sure that Black has enough for the exchange, but his pieces soon manage to surround the white king) 32 d5 ♕xf2+ 33 ♔xf2 ♘de5 34 ♖g3 cxd5 35 exd5 ♗f8 36 ♘xb5 ♗c2 37 ♗f1 ♗xb4 38 ♖c1 ♗c5+ 39 ♔e1 ♖e8 40 ♖xc2 ♘f3+ 41 ♔d1 ♖e1# (0-1) Muir-Milošević, Bern 1990.

11 ♕b3 ♖e8 12 ♗b2 ♖e6 13 ♖ad1 ♖h6 14 ♘e5?

White fails to take Black's attack seriously.

14...♘xc3 15 ♗xc3 ♗xe5 16 dxe5 ♕h4 17 h3 d4!

This should win.

18 ♗c4

Desperation.

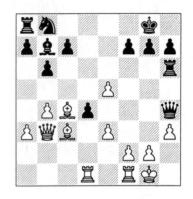

18...dxc3?

18...♗xg2 wins immediately.

19 ♗xf7+ ♔h8 20 ♗d5 c6 21 ♗f3 ♕e7 22 ♗g4 c5 23 b5 a6 24 a4

Black had become terribly short of time by this stage.

24...axb5 25 axb5 ♖g6 26 ♕xc3 ♖xg4 27 hxg4 ♘d7 28 f4 ♘f8 29 g5 ♗e4 30 ♕c4 ♕b7 31 ♖d2 ♗f5 32 ♖d6 ♘g6 33 ♖fd1 ♘f8 34 ♖d8 ♖xd8 35 ♖xd8 ♕e7 36 ♖b8 g6 37 ♕d5 ♔g7 38 ♖xb6 ♗e6 39 ♖b7 ♘d7 40 ♕d6 1-0

Game 89

Sadler-Polugaevsky
Hastings 1993

1 d4 ♘f6 2 c4 e6 3 ♘c3 ♗b4 4 e3 0-0 5 ♗d3 d5 6 ♘f3 b6 7 0-0 ♗b7 8 cxd5 exd5 9 ♘e5

It is pointless playing first 9 a3 ♗d6, and then 10 ♘e5, as White finds himself effectively a tempo down on one of the main lines. Sher-Palac, Bled 1992 bears this out: 10...c5 11 f4 ♘c6 12 ♕f3 cxd4 13 ♘xc6 ♗xc6 14 exd4 ♖e8 15 ♗e3

♘e4 16 ♗xe4 dxe4 17 ♕f2 ♕d7 18
f5 f6 and Black was fine.

9...♘bd7

Black has a wide choice here:

1) 9...♗e7 is perhaps a little passive, Pinter-Renet, Haifa 1989 continuing: 10 f4 c5 11 ♕f3 ♘c6 12
♕h3 ♘xe5 13 fxe5 ♘e4 14 ♗xe4
dxe4 15 d5 ♖e8 with unclear play.

2) 9...♗d6. White may now pur-
sue the bishop further, or initiate
kingside play:

⇨ 10 ♘b5!? ♗e7 11 b3 c5 12 ♗b2
♘bd7 13 ♖c1 a6 14 ♘c3 cxd4 15
exd4 ♖e8 16 f4 b5 17 ♗f5 ♘f8 18
♘e2 ♘e4 19 ♘g3 ♘xg3 20 hxg3
♗d6 21 ♕f3 ♕b6 22 ♖f2 ♖e7 23
♖e1 ♖ae8 24 ♖e3 f6 25 ♘g4 ♕a5
26 ♗c3 ♖xe3? 27 ♘xf6+ ♔f7 28
♗xa5 ♔xf6 (28...♖xf3 29 ♘xe8
♖xf2 30 ♘d6+) 29 ♕g4 ♔f7 30
♗d2 with advantage to White; Gure-
vich-Bareev, Moscow 1990.

⇨ 10 f4 c5 11 ♕f3 (the theoretical
move in this position) 11...♘c6 12
♕h3 (12 ♘e2 ♘e4 13 ♖d1 ♘b4 14
♗b1 f6 15 ♘d3 a5 16 g4 ♖e8 17 ♘f2
♕e7 18 a3 ♘a6 19 dxc5 ♘axc5 20
♘d4 ♘xf2 21 ♔xf2 ♘e4+ is better
for Black; Brionne-Arnason, St
Martin 1992) 12...g6 13 ♗d2 (13
♔h1!?) 13...cxd4 14 ♘xc6 ♗xc6 15
exd4 ♘e4 16 ♗xe4 dxe4 17 f5 ♗c5
18 dxc5! (prior to this 18 ♗e3?! ∓
had been played) 18...♕xd2 19 ♖ad1
♕g5 (if 19...♕xb2? 20 f6 and ♕h6 is
decisive) 20 ♖d6 ♖ac8 21 b4! bxc5
22 b5? (better the immediate 22
♘d5! ♗xd5 23 ♖xd5, threatening f6
deflecting the black queen from h6,
and taking on c5) 22...♗a8 23 ♘d5
♗xd5 24 ♖xd5 h5 25 ♕c3 e3
(25...♖fd8! ∓) 26 h4 ♕xh4 27 ♕xe3

♖fe8 28 ♕d2 ♖cd8 29 fxg6 fxg6 30
♕c2 ♔g7 31 ♕c3+ ♔h6 32 g3
♕e4?? 1-0 (33 ♕d2+) Vaiser-Arna-
son, Helsinki 1991.

3) 9...c5 10 ♘e2 c4 11 ♗c2 b5 12
b3 ♗d6 13 ♖b1 ♕c7 14 bxc4 bxc4
15 ♘c3 a6 16 f4 ♘c6 17 ♘g4 ♘xg4
18 ♘xd5 ♕a5 19 e4 ♗c8 20 h3
♘xd4 21 hxg4 ♗c5 22 ♗e3 ♘xc2
23 ♕xc2 ♗e6 24 ♗xc5 ♕xc5+ 25
♕f2 ♕xf2+ 26 ♔xf2 ♗xd5 27 exd5
♖fd8 28 ♖fd1 and it looks as though
White, if anybody, has a slight edge
in this endgame, but, in fact, he
went on to lose; Vaiser-Rashkovsky,
Moscow Tal mem 1992.

10 f4

White can also play on the queenside: 10 ♕a4 ♗d6 11 ♘xd7 ♘xd7
12 b4 a6 13 ♕b3 ♕h4 14 g3 ♕h5 15
♘e2 ♘f6 16 ♘f4 ♕g4 17 f3 ♕d7 18
♗d2 c5 19 bxc5 bxc5 20 dxc5 ♗xc5
but Black has fair chances; Hraček-
Dautov, Nîmes 1991.

10...c5 11 ♗d2

In the following game the players
reached the same position, but having played an extra move each: 12
♘e2!? (bringing an extra attacking
unit over to the kingside) 12...cxd4
13 exd4 a6 14 ♘g3 ± ♖e8 15 ♗e3
♗f8 16 h4 b5 17 h5 ♖c8 18 ♕f3 ♖c7
19 ♖ad1 ♘e4! 20 h6 g6 21 f5 ♘xe5
22 dxe5 ♕h4! 23 ♗xe4 dxe4 24 ♕f4
♕xf4 25 ♗xf4 e3 26 ♗xe3 ♖xe5 27
♗f4 ♖c2 28 ♖f2 ♖xf2 29 ♔xf2 ♖d5
30 ♖e1 ♖d4 31 ♗e3 ♖d7 ∓ 32 f6
(else Black will play ...f6 and ...♔f7)
32...♖d6 33 ♗g5 ♖d5 34 ♗e3 ♖d6
35 ♗g5 ♖d5 36 ♗e3 ♗d6 37 ♖c1
♔f8? (37...♗e5) 38 ♘e4! ♔e8 39
♘xd6+? (missing his chance; 39 g4
followed by ♘g5, eyeing the h-pawn,

would have turned the tables) ♖xd6
40 ♗g5 ♔d7 41 ♖c2 ♔e6 42 g4 ♖d4
43 ♖e2+ ♗e4 44 ♗e3 ♖c4 ½-½
Yusupov-Timman, Linares 1991.

11...♘e4 12 ♘xe4 dxe4 13 ♗c4
♗xd2 14 ♕xd2 ♘xe5 15 fxe5 ♗d5
16 ♗a6!?

This improvement was found in
the *post mortem* to Sadler-Speelman,
Hastings 1993, played a couple of
days before. That game continued:
16 b3 cxd4 17 exd4 ♖c8 18 ♖ac1
♕d7 19 ♕e3 h6 20 ♖fe1 ♖fd8 21
♗xd5 ♖xc1! 22 ♗xf7+ ♔xf7 23 e6+
♕xe6 24 ♖xc1 ½-½.

16...♕e7 17 dxc5 ♕xe5?!

Black should try 17...♖fd8!?.

18 ♖fd1 ♗c6 19 ♖ac1 ♖ab8 20
♕d6 ♕e8 21 b4 bxc5 22 bxc5 ♖b2
23 ♗c4 ♕c8 24 ♕e5! ♖b8 25 h3
♕b7 26 ♖d6 ♖bc8 27 ♖f1 ♔h8 28
h4 f6 29 ♕d4 ♕c7 30 ♗a6 ♖b8 31
♖c1 h6 32 ♗c4 ♖fe8 33 ♗d5 ♗xd5
34 ♕xd5 ♖b5 35 a4 ♖a5 36 ♕d4
♖c8 37 c6 ♖a6 38 ♖d7 ♕g3

39 ♕xe4?!

In time-trouble White misses a
simple win: 39 c7! ♖xa4 40 ♖d8+
♔h7 41 ♖xc8 ♖xd4 42 ♖h8+ ♔xh8

43 c8♕+ ♔h7 44 exd4.

39...f5!

39...♖xa4 40 ♕f3!.

**40 ♕f4 ♕xf4 41 exf4 ♖axc6 42
♖xc6 ♖xc6 43 ♖xa7 ♖c4 44 g3 ♖c3
45 ♔f2 ♖c2+ 46 ♔e3 ♖c3+ 47 ♔d4
♖xg3 48 ♔e5 ♖h3 49 a5 ♖xh4 50 a6
♖h1 51 ♖b7 ♖a1 52 a7 ♔h7 53
♔xf5 ♖a5+ 54 ♔g4 ½-½**

Game 90

Speelman-Ehlvest
Linares 1991

**1 d4 ♘f6 2 c4 e6 3 ♘c3 ♗b4 4 e3
0-0 5 ♗d3 d5 6 ♘f3 b6 7 a3**

Black can also develop the light-
squared bishop more actively after 7
0-0, i.e. 7...♗a6 8 cxd5 ♗xd3 9
♕xd3 exd5 10 ♘e5 ♖e8 11 ♖e1 c5
12 a3 c4 13 ♕f5 ♗xc3 14 bxc3 ♖e6
15 e4 g6 16 ♕f3 dxe4 17 ♖xe4 ♕d5
18 ♖e3 ♘c6 19 ♘xc6 ♕xf3 20 gxf3
♖xc6 21 ♗d2 ♘d5 when Black was
already doing rather well in Ra-
donjić-Anastasian, Pula 1990.

**7...♗xc3+ 8 bxc3 ♗a6 9 cxd5
♗xd3 10 ♕xd3 ♕xd5! =**

11 0-0

⇨ 11 c4 ♕b7 12 ♗b2 ♘bd7 13 ♖d1 ♖fd8 14 0-0 ♖ac8 15 ♖fe1 ♕e4 16 ♕c3 c5 17 d5 exd5 18 ♖xd5 ♘f8 19 ♖e5 ♕d3 20 ♖e7 ♕xc3 21 ♗xc3 ♘6d7 22 ♖d1 ♘e5! 23 ♖xd8 ♘xf3+ 24 gxf3 ♖xd8 25 ♖xa7 ♖d1+ 26 ♔g2 f6 (White has won a pawn, but in return his bishop is awkwardly placed) 27 ♖b7 ♖d3 28 ♗b2 ♖b3 29 ♗c1 ♘g6 30 ♖b8+ ♔f7 31 ♖b7+ ♔g8 32 ♖b8+ ♔f7 33 ♖b7+ ♔e6 34 a4 ♖b1 35 ♗a3 ♘h4+ 36 ♔h3 ♘xf3 37 ♔g2 ♘h4+ 38 ♔h3 ♘f3 39 ♔g2 ♘e1+ 40 ♔h3 ♘d3 41 ♔h4 ♖g1 0-1 Granda-Tal, Buenos Aires 1991.

11...c5 12 ♖e1 ♕e4!

Continuing the fight for e4 that Black started on move 1.

13 ♕e2 ♖c8 14 ♗b2 ♘bd7 15 ♖ac1 h6 16 ♘d2 ♕b7 17 e4 cxd4 18 cxd4 ♖xc1 19 ♖xc1 ♖c8 20 ♖xc8+ ♕xc8 21 ♕d3 ♕c6 22 f3 ♘e8 23 ♕c4 ♕xc4 24 ♘xc4 f5 25 ♔f2 = fxe4? 26 fxe4 b5 27 ♘a5 ♘d6 28 ♔f3! a6?! 29 ♗c3 ♘b6 30 ♗b4 ♘bc4? 31 e5!! ♘f5

Not 31...♘xa5? 32 exd6 ♘c6 33 d7 winning.

32 ♘xc4 bxc4 33 ♔e4 h5 34 d5 ♔f7 35 d6 ♔e8 36 ♗d2 ♔d7 37 g3? ♔c6 38 ♗f4 ♔d7 39 h3 ♔c6 40 a4 ♔d7 41 g4 hxg4 42 hxg4 ♘h4 43 ♗g3 ♘g6 44 ♔d4 ♔c6 45 ♔xc4 ♘h8 46 ♔d4 ♘f7 47 ♗h4 ♘h6 48 ♗g5 ♘xg4 49 ♗e3 ♘h2 50 ♔e4 ♘g4 51 a5 ♔d7?

51...g6 still held the draw.

52 ♗f4 ♘f2+ 53 ♔e3 ♘d1+ 54 ♔d4 ♔c6 55 ♗e3! g5! 56 ♗xg5 ♘b2 57 ♗e3! ♔a4 58 ♔c4 ♘b2+ 59 ♔c3 ♘d1+ 60 ♔d4 1-0

8

At the precise moment when the black bishop is deprived of its retreat to e7, White attempts to gain the bishop pair without compromising his pawn structure. Attention has frequently been focused upon this system as a means of avoiding Hübner's variation.

In games 91 to 93 we look at 5...b6, a strange line that has only recently become popular. Black defends his c-pawn and prepares to retreat his bishop to a5, maintaining the pin. Attempts to win the bishop with b4 have failed since Black can control b4 with ...♘a6 and ...♕e7 if need be.

Psakhis is the outstanding expert on this line for Black, and a number of his fine efforts are contained in the notes to game 91. However, in the main game he is well beaten when faced with Rechlis' 10 f3!?, and once again in game 92—I was amazed at how well the young Lautier played whilst I watched this game in Paris.

Black reacts badly to White's novel 8 ♘g3 in the next game and gets completely wiped out.

In the variation 5...d5 6 a3 ♗xc3+ 7 ♘xc3 cxd4 8 exd4 dxc4 9 ♗xc4, an old favourite of Botvinnik, analysed in game 94, White gains the bishop pair but also an IQP. 12 ♕f3 looks to me like White's strongest choice, and Kasparov demonstrates exactly how to play it afterwards.

In the rest of this chapter we consider 5...cxd4 6 exd4 d5 7 c5. Strangely, after gaining space on the queenside with c5, White then directs his attention to the kingside, and can build up a very dangerous attack; witness game 95. In this same line Black seems, nevertheless, to be fine if he plays 16...♗c6!

One of the most original innovations in recent years, 9...♕d7!?, occurred in game 96. Despite the successful outcome, Black's idea has found few imitators. Perhaps the black position is just too difficult too play correctly?

Game 91

Rechlis-Psakhis
Tel Aviv 1992

1 d4 ♘f6 2 c4 e6 3 ♘c3 ♗b4 4 e3 c5 5 ♘e2 b6 6 a3 ♗a5

Naturally, this line can also come from variations considered in chapter 6.

7 ♖b1

After 7 ♗d2 0-0 we consider:

⇨ 8 ♘f4 ♗xc3 9 ♗xc3 ♘e4 10 ♕c2 ♘xc3 11 ♕xc3 d6 12 ♗d3 ♘d7 13 ♕c2 ♘f6 14 g4?! (rather double-edged; there is probably too much play in the centre for this to be really justified) 14...h6 15 0-0-0 cxd4 16 exd4 ♘xg4 17 ♕d2 ♕h4 18 ♖df1 ♗b7 19 f3 ♘f6 20 ♖hg1 ♔h8 21 ♔b1 e5 22 ♕g2 ♖g8 23 ♘e2 exd4 24 ♘g3 ♗c8 25 ♕d2 ♗h3 26 ♖f2 ♖ae8 ∓ Reinemer-Adamski, Giessen 1992.

⇨ 8 d5 d6 9 ♘g3 exd5 10 cxd5 ♗b7 11 e4 ♖e8 12 ♗b5 ♘bd7 13 0-0!? ♗xc3 14 ♗xc3 ♘xe4 15 ♗xg7?! (15 ♘f5! g6 16 ♘h6+ ♔f8 17 ♕f3 was unclear) 15...♔xg7 16 ♕g4+ ♔h8

17 ♕xd7 ♕xd7 18 ♗xd7 ♘xg3 19 fxg3 ♖e7 20 ♗g4? (20 ♗a4!? is better, but Black has the advantage due to White's weak d-pawn) 20...♗xd5 21 ♖ad1 ♗c4 22 ♖f4 d5 23 ♗f3 ♖ae8! (and not 23...♖d8?? 24 ♖xc4) 0-1 Granda Zuniga-Psakhis, Aruba 1992. No doubt White resigned because he had just realized that he could not recapture the d-pawn: 24 ♗xd5? loses to 24...♖e1+ 25 ♖xe1 ♖xe1+ 26 ♔f2 ♖f1+ followed by ...♖xf4 and ...♗xd5.

7...♘a6

An alternative is 7...♕e7:

⇨ 8 ♕a4!? ♘a6 9 dxc5 ♘xc5 10 ♕c2 ♗xc3+ 11 ♘xc3 ♗b7 12 b4 ♘ce4 13 ♘xe4 ♗xe4 14 ♗d3 ♗xd3 15 ♕xd3 0-0 16 ♗b2 ♖fc8 17 0-0 ♘e8 18 ♖bc1 d6 19 f4 ♖c7 20 e4 ± because of the space advantage and the strong bishop on b2; Serebrianik-Cvetković, Vrnjačka Banja 1991.

⇨ 8 ♗d2 ♘c6 9 d5! ♘e5! 10 ♘g3 ♗xc3 11 ♗xc3 d6 12 ♗e2 ± exd5 13 cxd5 h5 14 h4 0-0 15 e4 ♘fg4 16 f3 f5!? (Black feels obliged to sharpen the struggle as otherwise the weakness on h5 will cause problems) 17 fxg4 fxe4 18 ♕d2?! (18 ♘xh5!?) 18...♘d3+ 19 ♗xd3 exd3+ 20 ♔d1 ♗xg4+ 21 ♔c1 c4 was most unclear in Züger-Medančić, Lugano 1989.

8 ♗d2 0-0 9 ♘g3 ♗b7 10 f3!?

The normal continuation is 10 ♗d3 (10 d5?! ♗xc3! 11 ♗xc3 exd5 12 cxd5 ♘xd5! ∓) 10...cxd4 11 exd4 ♗xc3 12 bxc3 d5:

⇨ 13 0-0 dxc4 14 ♗xc4 ♘b8 15 ♖e1 ♕d6 16 a4 ♘bd7 17 ♗d3 ♖ac8 18 a5 ♖fe8 with a balanced position; Knaak-Psakhis, Baden-Baden 1992.

⇨ 13 cxd5 ♕xd5! 14 ♕e2 ♘b8 15 f3 ♕a2! 16 ♘e4 (rather than lose a pawn after 16 0-0 ♕xa3) 16...♘xe4 17 fxe4 ♗a6! 18 0-0 ♗xd3 19 ♕xd3 ♕xa3 20 ♕g3 f6! (Black defuses any potential White attack with a series of precise moves) 21 ♗f4 e5! 22 dxe5 ♕c5+! 23 ♔h1 ♘c6 ∓ 24 e6 ♘e5 25 h3? ♖fe8 26 ♗xe5 ♕xe5 27 ♕xe5 fxe5 28 c4 ♖xe6 ∓ Nenashev-Psakhis, Moscow Alekhine mem 1992.

10...cxd4 11 exd4 ♗xc3 12 bxc3!? d6 13 ♗d3 ♘b8

The black knight is awkwardly placed on a6 and must move, but it takes time.

14 0-0 ♘bd7 15 f4 ♕c7 16 f5

This pawn will play a large role in the coming attack, as it hinders Black's defence.

16...e5 17 ♘h5 ♖ac8 18 d5!? ♖fe8?

Black should play 18...♕c5+ 19 ♔h1 e4 ∞.

19 ♗e3! ♕d8 20 ♗g5! ♔h8 21 ♕e1 ♕c7 22 ♘xf6 gxf6 23 ♗e3 ± ♖g8 24 ♕h4 ♖g7 25 ♖f3 ♖cg8 26 ♔h1

26...♕d8

26...♖xg2?? would fail to the queen sac: 27 ♕xh7+! ♚xh7 28 ♖h3+ ♚g7 29 ♗h6+.

27 ♖h3 ♘f8? **28 ♗h6 ♖g4 29 ♕h5 ♘d7 30 ♕xf7 ♖8g7 31 ♗xg7+ ♖xg7**

The rest of the game is a formality.

32 ♕h5 ♘c5 33 ♗c2 ♕g8 34 ♕h4 ♖g5 35 ♖e1 ♕g7 36 ♖ee3 ♖xg2 37 ♖eg3! ± ♖xg3 38 ♖xg3 ♕f8 39 ♖g6 b5 40 ♖xf6 ♕e7 41 ♕h6 1-0

Game 92

Lautier-Psakhis
Paris 1989

1 d4 ♘f6 2 c4 e6 3 ♘c3 ♗b4 4 e3 b6 5 ♘e2 c5 6 a3 ♗a5 7 ♖b1 ♘a6 8 ♗d2 0-0 9 d5

⇨ 9 dxc5!? bxc5 10 ♘f4 ♗b7 11 ♗d3 d5 12 cxd5 exd5 13 0-0 ♗c7 14 ♘ce2 ♕d6 15 ♘g3 g6 16 b4! undermines the black centre, and secures an edge; Dziuban-Serper, USSR 1991.

9...♗b7

⇨ 9...exd5 10 cxd5!? d6 11 f3 ♖b8 12 ♘f4 ♗xc3 13 ♗xc3 ♖e8 14 ♚f2! (White is happy to play this as he intends to throw his kingside pawns forward, and for this reason the rook is useful on h1) 14...♘c7 15 e4 a5 16 ♗e2 ♖a8 17 a4 ♗d7 18 g4 b5 19 h4 b4 20 ♗d2 ♗c8 21 g5 ♘d7 22 ♕c2 ♗a6 23 ♗xa6 ♘xa6 24 ♘g2 ♖c8 25 b3 c4 26 bxc4 ♘b6 27 ♘e3 ♘c5 28 h5 ♕d7 29 ♘f5 ♘xc4 30 ♕xc4 ♘xe4+ 31 ♕xe4 ♖xe4 32 fxe4 ♖c2 33 ♖hc1! ♖xd2+ 34 ♚e3 (threatening both 35 ♚xd2 and 35 ♖c8+!) 34...♖xd5 35 ♘e7+ ♚f8 36 ♘xd5 ♕g4 37 ♚d4 f6 38 g6 hxg6 39 hxg6 ♕xg6 40 ♖c7 1-0 Maximenko-V.Gurevich, Simferopol 1991.

10 ♘f4

⇨ 10 e4?! exd5 11 exd5 ♘g4!? (without the other pieces to help, this knight move looks like a blow into thin air, but in fact, the white position is badly coordinated and seems unable to fend it off)

12 ♘g3 (12 f3 didn't fare much better in Jelen-Grosar, Ljubljana Iskra 1992: 12...♘e5 13 ♘f4 ♕f6 14

♔f2 ♗xc3 15 bxc3 ♘c7 16 g4 ♗a6
17 ♘h5 ♕h4+ 18 ♔g2 f5 19 ♗f4
fxg4 20 ♗xe5 gxf3+ 21 ♔g1 f2+ 22
♔g2 ♕e4+ 0-1) 12...♕h4! 13 ♗e2
♖ae8 14 ♘ce4 ♘xh2!? 15 ♘d6 f5!
16 ♘xb7? (16 ♘xe8 ♖xe8 17 b4 ∞)
16...f4! 17 ♘f1 f3! 18 ♖xh2 ♕xh2!
19 ♘xh2 fxg2 20 ♗xa5 g1♕+ 0-1
Gual-Garbarino, Spain 1991.

**10...♗xc3 11 ♗xc3 ♘e4 12 ♕c2
♘xc3 13 ♕xc3 ♘c7 14 ♖d1 exd5 15
cxd5 d6 16 ♗e2 ♖e8 17 0-0 ♕g5 18
♗f3 ♕e5 19 ♕d2 ♖ad8 20 ♖fe1
♗c8 21 g3 ♗f5 22 ♗g2 ♗e4?**

It is probably better not to waste
time provoking the advance of the
white centre that White was clearly
intending anyway.

**23 f3 ♗f5 24 e4 ♗d7 25 ♘e2 f5
26 ♘c3 ♗b5 27 ♘xb5 ♗xb5 28
♗h3! fxe4 29 ♖xe4 ♕h5 30 ♗g4
♕g6 31 ♗e6+**

Now e6 becomes the focal point
of the play, cutting across the black
position.

31...♔h8

**32 ♖de1 ♖f8 33 ♔g2 ♕f6 34 f4
♗e8 35 g4 ♗d7 36 f5**

Further solidifying e6; White

plays with a maturity that belies his
years.

**36...♕h4 37 ♕f4 ♗b5 38 ♖1e3
♖de8 39 ♕xd6 ♕f6 40 ♕e5 ♖d8 41
♔g3 g5 42 ♕xf6+ ♖xf6 43 h4 h6 44
♖e1 ♔g7 45 ♖h1 ♗e8 46 ♖e2
gxh4+ 47 ♔f4 ♗f7 48 ♔e5 b5 49
♖xh4 c4 50 g5 hxg5 51 ♖h7+ 1-0**

Since 51...♔xh7 52 ♔xf6 ♗e8 53
♖h2+ forces mate.

Game 93

Nenashev-Kayumov
Tashkent 1992

**1 d4 ♘f6 2 c4 e6 3 ♘c3 ♗b4 4 e3 c5
5 ♘e2 b6 6 a3 ♗a5 7 ♖b1 ♘a6 8
♘g3!?**

⇨ 8 ♕a4 is another unusual idea:
8...♕e7 (8...♗b7!) 9 dxc5 ♘xc5 10
♕d1 ♗xc3+ 11 ♘xc3 ♗b7 12 f3
♘h5 13 b4 ♕h4+ 14 ♔e2 (this looks
awkward at first glance, but in fact
White repels the invaders with gain
of tempo and straightens out his development) 14...♘a6 15 ♕d4 ♘g3+?!
(15...♕e7 was better, but ± anyway)
16 hxg3 ♕xh1 17 ♕xg7 0-0-0 18
♘b5 ♖hg8 19 ♕e5 d6 20 ♘xd6+
♖xd6 21 ♕xd6 recouping his invest-
ment with interest; Garcia Palermo-
Leskovar, Ibercaja 1992.

**8...0-0 9 ♗d3 d5 10 cxd5 cxd4 11
exd4 ♗xc3+!? 12 bxc3 exd5 13 0-0
♘b8?!**

This plan is too slow.

**14 ♖e1 ♗a6 15 ♗g5 ♗xd3 16
♕xd3 h6 17 ♗xf6 ♕xf6 18 ♖e5
♖d8 19 ♘h5 ♕c6?**

Even after the superior 19...♕g6
20 ♕xg6 fxg6 21 ♘f4 White has an

evident advantage.

20 ⅏be1 ⊘d7 21 ⅏e6! ♕c7 22 ⅏e7 ♕d6 23 ⅏1e6!

The rooks take turns to occupy this square that appears 'unoccupiable'.

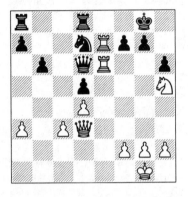

23...♕xa3 24 h4! ⊘f8 25 ♕g3 ⊘xe6 26 ⅏xe6 ♕f8 27 ⅏xh6 f5

White's attack is crushing, for example: 27...g6 28 ⊘f6+ ⌾g7 29 ⅏h7+ ⌾xf6 30 ♕e5#.

28 ⊘f6+ ⌾f7 29 ♕g6+ ⌾e7 30 ⊘xd5+

30...⅏xd5 31 ♕e6+ ⌾d8 32 ♕xd5+ ⌾c7 33 ⅏c6+ 1-0

Game 94

Kasparov-Psakhis
La Manga match (6) 1990

1 d4 ⊘f6 2 c4 e6 3 ⊘c3 ♗b4 4 e3 c5 5 ⊘e2 d5 6 a3 ♗xc3+ 7 ⊘xc3 cxd4 8 exd4 dxc4 9 ♗xc4 ⊘c6 10 ♗e3 0-0 11 0-0 b6 12 ♕f3!

To my mind, the most dangerous of White's various alternatives.

⇨ 12 ♕d3 ♗b7 13 ⅏ad1 h6 14 ♗f4!? ⊘e7 15 ♗a2 ⊘g6 16 ♗e5? ⊘xe5 17 dxe5 ♕xd3 18 ⅏xd3 ♗a6! 19 ⅏g3 ⊘h5 20 ⅏f3 ♗xf1 21 ⌾xf1 g5 ∓ Knaak-Razuvaev, Palma 1989.

⇨ 12 ⅏c1 ♗b7 13 ♗a2 ⅏c8 14 d5 ⊘xd5 15 ⊘xd5 exd5 16 ♗xd5 ♕d7 17 ♗f3 ♕e7 18 ⅏e1 ⊘e5 19 ♗xb7 ♕xb7 20 ⅏xc8 ⅏xc8 21 ♗d4 ⊘g6 is fairly equal; Chernin-Miles, Rome 1990.

⇨ 12 ⅏e1 ♗b7 13 ♗a2 ♕d7 14 d5! ± exd5 15 ⊘xd5 ⊘xd5 16 ♕xd5 ⅏ad8 17 ♕xd7 ⅏xd7 18 ⅏ad1 ⅏xd1 19 ⅏xd1 ⅏d8 20 ⅏xd8+ ⊘xd8 21 f3. The two bishops are very effective in this type of position; eventually White created two weaknesses on a7 and h7, and won, in Knaak-Lautier, Novi Sad OL 1990.

12...♗b7 13 ♗d3

⇨ 13 ♕h3 ⊘e7 14 ♗d3 ⊘g6 15 f4 ⊘d5 16 f5 exf5 17 ⊘xd5 ♗xd5 18 ♗xf5 ♕h4 bringing White thoughts of an attack to an abrupt halt, with equality; Vaiser-Mednis, Palma 1989.

13...⅏c8 14 ⅏ad1

⇨ 14 ♕h3 ⊘e7 15 ♗g5 ⊘g6 16 ⅏ad1 h6!? 17 ♗xg6 hxg5 18 ♗b1 g6 19 ⅏fe1 ⌾g7 20 ♕g3 g4 21 ♕e5 ⅏h8 22 ♕f4 ⅏c7 23 ♗d3 ⅏d7 24

♗b5 ♖d6 25 ♗e2 ♖h5 (putting the h-file to good use) 26 ♕e3 ♕d7 27 ♗f1 a6 28 ♖d3 a5 29 ♖d2 ♕c6 30 ♖ed1 ♖d8 31 ♕g3 ♖dh8 32 d5? (White was in a bad way in any case, but this precipitates events) 32...exd5 33 ♘b5? ♘e4 0-1 Garcia Palermo-Oll, Rome 1990.

14...♖c7 15 ♕h3 ♘e7 16 ♗g5! ♘g6 17 ♕g3!? ♖d7 18 d5!

18...exd5

Although Black appears to be controlling the d5 square five times, this is the only way to capture: 18...♗xd5 19 ♗b5 ♖c7 20 ♘xd5 exd5 21 ♗xf6 gxf6 22 ♕b3 ±.

19 ♗f5 ♖e7 20 h4! ♕c7! 21 ♕xc7 ♖xc7 22 ♖fe1!

White can recapture on d5 when he wants, but prefers not to part with his queen's bishop.

22...♖e7?!

Better was 22...h6.

23 ♘b5! ♖fe8 24 ♖xe7 ♘xe7 25 ♗h3 ♗c8 26 ♗xc8 ♖xc8 27 ♘xa7 ♖c2 28 b4 ♔f8 29 ♗e3

Now it is clear why Kasparov was so reluctant to exchange his bishop for the knight on f6, even though he

could have doubled Black's kingside pawns.

29...♘f5 30 ♗xb6 ♘g4 31 ♗c5+ ♔e8 32 ♘b5 ♖a2 33 ♘c3 ♖xa3 34 ♘xd5 f6 35 b5 ♖b3 36 b6 1-0

Game 95

Lautier-Yudasin
Manila IZ 1990

1 d4 ♘f6 2 c4 e6 3 ♘c3 ♗b4 4 e3 c5 5 ♘e2 cxd4 6 exd4 d5 7 c5 ♘e4

Good equalizing chances but little more are offered by 7...e5!?:

⇨ 8 dxe5 ♘e4 9 a3 ♗xc3+ 10 ♘xc3 ♘xc3 11 bxc3 ♕a5 12 ♕b3 0-0 13 ♗e2 ♘d7 14 ♗e3 ♘xe5 15 0-0 ♘c4 16 ♗d4 ♕c7 17 ♖fe1 ♗d7 18 ♗xc4 dxc4 19 ♕xc4 ♖fe8 with the opposite-colour bishops virtually assuring the draw; Vaiser-Psakhis, Nîmes 1991.

⇨ 8 a3 ♗xc3+ 9 ♘xc3 exd4 10 ♕xd4 0-0 11 ♗b5! ♗d7 12 0-0 ♗xb5 13 ♘xb5 ♘c6 14 ♕d3 ♘e4 15 ♗e3! a6 (15...♘e5!) 16 ♘c3! ♘xc3 17 bxc3 ± Knaak-Browne, Palma 1989.

8 ♗d2 ♘xd2

⇨ 8...♘c6 9 ♘xe4 dxe4 10 ♗xb4 ♘xb4 11 ♘c3 f5 12 ♗b5+ ♗d7 13 0-0 ♗xb5 14 ♘xb5 0-0 15 f3 e3 16 f4 ♕f6 17 ♕a4 a6 18 ♘c7 e2 19 ♖f2 ♕xd4 20 ♘xe6? (20 ♘xa8 ♖d8! 21 ♖e1 ♕xc5 22 ♕b3 ♘d3 =) 20...♕e3?? (overlooking 20...♕d2! 21 ♕b3 e1♕+ 22 ♖xe1 ♕xe1+ 23 ♖f1 ♕d2 24 ♖d1 ♕c2 winning) 21 ♖e1 ♕xe6 22 ♕xb4 ♕xa2 23 ♖fxe2 ♕d5 24 ♖e5 ♕c6 25 ♖e7 ± ♖ab8 26 ♖1e6 ♕c8 27 ♕d4 ♖f7 28 ♕e5

♕f8 29 ♖e8 1-0 Bareev-Aseev, Leningrad 1990.

9 ♕xd2 a5

⇨ 9...b6 10 a3 ♗xc3 11 ♘xc3 bxc5 12 ♗b5+ ♗d7 13 dxc5 a5 14 0-0 a4 15 ♗d3?! 0-0 16 f4 ♕a5! 17 f5! ♕xc5+! 18 ♔h1 exf5! 19 ♗xf5?! d4! was unclear in Georgadze-Golod, Forli 1992.

10 a3 ♗xc3 11 ♘xc3 a4 12 ♗d3 b6

After 12...♗d7 13 0-0 ♘c6 White does best not to allow the capture on d4:

⇨ 14 ♖ae1?! ♘xd4 15 ♘xd5 ♗c6 16 ♘b6 ♖a5 17 ♖d1 ♖xc5 18 ♗e4 ♕xb6 19 ♕xd4 0-0 20 ♖c1 ♖b5 21 ♕xa4 ♗xe4 22 ♕xe4 ♖xb2 23 ♖b1 and White's technique was good enough to secure the draw in Ivanchuk-Seirawan, Tilburg 1992.

⇨ 14 ♗c2 ♘e7 15 ♖fe1 b6 16 ♕d1!? (the threat to a4 forces Black's next) 16...bxc5 17 dxc5 ♕a5 18 ♘xd5!? (the point of White's play, opening up the black king) 18...exd5 19 ♕xd5 ♗e6 20 ♕g5 ♘g6 21 ♖e4 0-0 22 ♖xa4 ♕b5 23 ♖xa8 ♖xa8 24 ♗xg6 hxg6 25 ♖d1 f6 26 ♕e3 ♗b3 27 ♖c1 ♖e8 28 ♕c3 ♗d5 29 b4 ♖e5 30 h4 ♖e4 31 ♖d1 ♗c6 32 ♖d4 ♕e2 33 ♖xe4 ♕xe4 34 f3. I suppose this should be fairly equal as White's queenside pawns are securely blockaded; however in Rechlis-Portisch, Manila IZ 1990 Black tried too hard to win, and went on to lose.

13 cxb6 ♕xb6 14 ♗c2!? ♗d7 15 0-0 0-0 16 ♖fe1 g6?!

Causing a dangerous weakening of the kingside. Two superior choices:

⇨ 16...♗c6! 17 ♖e3 ♘d7 18 ♖g3 ♖fc8 19 ♖d1 ♘f8 (the aim of Black's move-order is to be able to get in this important defensive move) 20 h4 ♕c7 21 h5 h6 22 ♖e1 ♔h8 23 ♕d1 ♕d7 24 ♘e2 ♗b5 25 ♘c3 ♗c6 26 ♘e2 ♗b5 27 ♘c3 ½-½ Speelman-Khalifman, Reykjavik 1991.

⇨ 16...♖c8 17 ♖ad1 ♕d8 18 ♖e3 ♕f8 (the queen, however, is not ideally suited to defensive duties) 19 h4 ♖c4 20 ♗d3 ♖c7 21 ♗b1 ♖b7 22 h5 ♘c6 23 ♘xa4 ♘xd4 24 ♕xd4 ♖xa4 25 b4 ♖c7 26 ♖g3 ♖a8 27 ♗d3 ♗a4 28 ♖e1 ♗c2 29 ♖c1 ♖ac8 30 ♕e5 ♖c6 31 b5 and White managed to push his queenside pawns through, in Knaak-Lerner, Lugano 1989.

17 ♖e3! ± ♖c8

White was threatening ♖h3 and ♕h6. Instead 17...♕xb2? is met by 18 ♖b1 ♕xa3 19 ♘xd5 ♕d6 20 ♘f6+ ♔g7 21 ♖f3 e5 22 ♘h5+! gxh5 23 ♕g5+ ♔h8 24 ♖f6! ♕e7 25 ♕h6 e4 26 ♗xe4 ±.

18 ♖d1 ♗c6 19 ♖f3! ♘d7?!

Hoping to get to f8, but White's next move puts paid to that idea; better is 19...♖a7! 20 h4.

20 ♕f4 ♖f8 21 ♖h3

The storm clouds are gathering over Black's kingside.

21...♕xb2 22 ♗b1! ♖ab8?

22...♖fb8 23 ♖xh7! ♔xh7 24 ♕xf7+ ♔h8 25 ♗xg6 ♘f8 26 ♕f6+! ♔g8 27 ♗f7+ ♔h7 28 g4!! ±.

23 ♕h4 h5 24 ♕g5 ♔g7 25 ♖g3 ♖h8 26 ♗xg6 ± f6 27 ♕h4! ♖h6 28 ♗xh5+ ♔h8 29 ♕g4 ♖h7 30 ♗g6 f5 31 ♕f4 1-0

Game 96

Levitt-M.Gurevich
Tel Aviv 1989

1 d4 ♘f6 2 c4 e6 3 ♘c3 ♗b4 4 e3 c5 5 ♘e2 cxd4 6 exd4 d5

⇨ 6...0-0 has not been too popular recently: 7 a3 (7 d5 is more critical) 7...♗e7 8 ♘f4 d6 9 ♗e2 ♖e8 10 0-0 ♗f8 11 ♗e3 g6 12 ♖c1 a6 13 c5 (13 b4 ±) 13...♗g7 14 ♘a4 ♘c6 15 ♘b6 ♖b8 16 b4 d5 17 ♕b3 g5 18 ♘h3 h6 19 ♖cd1! e5 20 dxe5 ♘xe5 21 ♘xc8 ♕xc8 22 ♖fe1 ♖e7 23 ♗f1?! (23 f4! would have been more testing) 23...♕c7! 24 ♗d4 ♖be8 25 ♗xe5 ♖xe5 26 ♖xe5 ♕xe5 27 f3 g4 28 ♘f2 g3! 29 hxg3 ♕xg3 30 ♕d3 h5?! 31 ♕f5 ♖e6 32 ♘h1 ½-½ Georgadze-Kasparov, Debrecen 1992.

7 c5 ♘e4 8 ♗d2 ♘xd2 9 ♕xd2 ♕d7!?

Gurevich's interesting move; vacating d8 clears a route to f6 for the bishop. The still unanswered question is: does the bishop pair compensate for the loss of time?

⇨ Another idea along similar lines is 9...♕f6!?: 10 a3 ♗a5 11 g3 ♕f3!

(forcing White to waste time bringing his king to safety) 12 ♖g1 ♘c6 13 b4 ♗c7! 14 ♗g2 ♕f6 15 f4 0-0 = 16 ♖f1 ♘e7 17 ♖c1 ♗d7 18 ♖f2 ♕h6 19 ♔f1 ♔h8 20 ♔g1 (finally; however Black may have been able to put the time gained to better use, by trying to blockade the queenside, for instance) 20...f5 21 b5 a6 22 b6 ♗d8 23 ♔h1 ♘c6 24 ♘g1 g5 25 ♘f3 gxf4 26 gxf4 ♗e7 27 ♘e2 ♖g8 28 ♖g1 ♖g4 29 ♗f1 ♖ag8 30 ♖fg2 ♗f6 31 ♕e3 ♖8g6 32 ♕f2 ♕g7 33 ♖xg4 ♖xg4 34 ♖xg4 ♕xg4 35 ♕g3 ♔g7 36 ♔g2 ♔f8 37 ♕xg4 fxg4 38 ♘e5 ♘xe5 39 fxe5 and White's advanced pawn chain gives him the nod; Knaak-van der Wiel, Palma 1989.

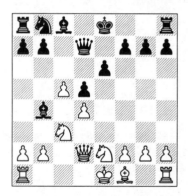

10 a3 ♗a5 11 g3 ♗d8 12 b4

After 12 ♗g2 there can follow:

⇨ 12...b6 13 0-0 0-0 14 f4 ♘c6 15 b4 bxc5 16 dxc5 ♖b8 17 ♖ab1 ♔h8 18 ♖fd1 ♗f6 19 b5 ♘a5 20 ♘e4 ♗d8 21 ♕b4 ♕c7 22 ♘d6 ♗e7 23 ♘d4 ♘c4! 24 ♘xc4 ♗xc5 25 ♕a5 ♗xd4+ 26 ♖xd4 ♕c5 27 ♕c3 dxc4 ∓ Lautier-Garcia, Terrassa 1991.

⇨ 12...a5 (aiming to stop b4) 13 b3

b6 14 0-0 0-0 15 b4 ♗a6 16 ♖fb1
♗xe2 17 ♘xe2 ♕a7 18 ♘c3 ♗f6 19
♘xd5! (Black has failed to develop
his queenside and pays the penalty)
19...exd5 20 ♗xd5 axb4 21 cxb6
♕a5 22 ♗xa8 ♕xa8 23 ♖xb4 ♘c6
24 b7 ♕a7 25 ♖c1 ♘xd4 26 ♕e3
♕b8 27 a4 ♕d6 28 ♖bb1 ♗e5 29
♖c8 ♘c6 30 ♖xc6 1-0 Knaak-Skembris, Dortmund 1990.

12...0-0 13 ♗g2 b6 14 0-0 ♗e7 15
♖ab1 a5 16 ♖fc1! axb4 17 axb4
♖d8 18 h4

Better is 18 b5! ∞.

18...♕e8! 19 ♔h2 bxc5 20 dxc5
♘a6 21 ♘f4 ♖b8 22 ♘d3 ♘c7 23
♗f1 ♗f6 24 f4

24...♗b7

Black has managed to blockade
White's queenside pawns securely;
can White stop Black's central
pawns?

25 ♘e5 d4 26 ♘d1 ♗xe5 27 fxe5
♕c6 28 ♗g2 ♕xg2+ 29 ♕xg2 ♗xg2
30 ♔xg2 ♖d5

Winning the e-pawn while maintaining the blockade of the b- and c-pawns.

31 ♖b3

31 ♘b2! ♖xb4 (or 31...♖xe5 32
♘c4) 32 ♘d3 was a better defence.

31...♖xe5 32 ♘b2 ♔f8 33 ♘a4
♔e8! ∓ 34 ♘b6 ♘b5 35 ♖a1 ♖d8 36
♔f3? d3 37 ♔f2 ♖e2+ 38 ♔f1 ♖h2
39 ♔g1 ♖c2 40 ♖d1 ♘c3 0-1

9

Hübner's variation was so successful in the 1970s that players switched to 3 ♘f3 in droves. Then, more recently, White players were prepared to play the Nimzo-Indian but avoided playing 6 ♘f3, either by playing the knight to e2 on moves 5 or 6, or by playing an early a3. This trend continues, and is justified, since Hübner's variation still scores well for Black.

In the first game (game 97) White plays 8 e4, blocking the centre. Black makes the mistake of castling kingside too early and gets wiped out by a wonderful sacrificial attack.

Game 98 demonstrates how enduring Black's positional pluses can be if he succeeds in reaching the endgame.

In the subsequent games White plays 9 ♕c2, keeping the centre more fluid. In particular he may try to use the e4 and d5 squares for his pieces. In game 99 Black manages to gain the advantage but soon finds himself involved in a real hand-to-hand fight. In game 100 Black tries to cut across White's plan by playing 9...h6, denying White's knight access to g5. The middlegame is interesting in that it is Black who opens up the position, and very successfully too!

Game 97

V.Raičević-I.Raičević
Yugoslav Ch 1991

1 d4 e6 2 c4 ♘f6 3 ♘c3 ♗b4 4 e3 ♗xc3+ 5 bxc3 c5 6 ♘f3 ♘c6 7 ♗d3 d6 8 e4 e5 9 d5

White may instead refuse to advance immediately; 9 h3 h6 10 ♗e3 b6 and now:
⇨ 11 d5 ♘e7 12 g3 ½-½ Balashov-Yudasin, Moscow 1991.
⇨ 11 0-0 ♕c7! (Black should always think twice before castling kingside in this variation) 12 ♕d2 ♗d7 13 d5 ♘e7 14 ♔h2 0-0-0 15 ♘g1 g5 16 g3 ♘h7 17 f4 exf4 18 gxf4 ♘g6 19 ♘f3 gxf4 20 ♗xf4 ♘xf4 21 ♕xf4 ♘g5! 22 h4 f6 23 ♕g3 ♘f7 24 ♖g1 ♖df8 25 ♖af1 ♕d8 26 ♗e2 ♕e7 27 ♕f4 ♘g5! 28 ♗d3 ♘h3 and Black wins; Kristiansen-L.B.Hansen, Tåstrup 1990.
⇨ 11 ♕e2 ♕c7! 12 d5 ♘e7 13 ♘h4 g5 14 ♕f3 ♘fg8 15 ♘f5 ♘xf5 16 exf5 ♘f6 17 g4 ♕e7 18 ♕g3 ♗a6 19 h4 0-0-0 20 0-0-0 e4 21 ♗e2 ♘d7 22 hxg5 hxg5 23 ♕g2 ♖hg8 24 ♖h6 ♖de8 25 ♖dh1 ∞ Ibragimov-Serper, USSR 1991.

9...♘e7 10 ♖b1!?

1) The main continuation here is 10 ♘h4. After 10...h6 11 f4:
⇨ I remember reading, some twenty years ago, in Gligorić's book on the (first) Fischer-Spassky match, that 11...exf4? 12 ♗xf4 g5 13 e5 ♘g4 14 e6 was winning for White. In the game Lukacs-Somlai, Borsodtavho 1991, Black put this to the test. However, after 14...♘f6 15 0-0 fxe6 16 ♗e5 dxe5 17 ♖xf6 gxh4 18 ♕h5+ ♔d7 19 ♖xe6 ♖g8 20 ♕xe5 1-0, it would seem that Gligorić was right!
⇨ 11...♘g6 12 ♘xg6 fxg6 13 0-0 0-0 14 ♖b1 (14 fxe5 dxe5 15 ♕e1 ½-½ Karpman-Ulybin, Minsk 1990,

doesn't tell us a great deal) 14...b6 15 ♖b2 ♕e7 16 h3 ♗d7 17 f5 (17 ♕e1 ♘h5! 18 f5 ♘f4) 17...gxf5 18 exf5 e4 19 ♗e2!? (an attempted improvement on 19 ♖e2 ♘e5 20 ♕e1 ♗xf5 21 ♗f4 of Spassky-Hort, Tilburg 1979) 19...♖ae8 20 g4 ♘h7 21 ♕e1 ♘g5 22 ♕g3 e3 23 ♗d3 ♕f6!? (intending to sacrifice the exchange to open up the white position) 24 ♗xe3 ♖xe3! 25 ♕xe3 ♖e8 26 ♕c1 (26 ♕g3? ♕xc3 27 ♖b3 ♕d4+) 26...♘xh3+ 27 ♔h1 ♕h4 28 ♖h2 ♕xg4 29 ♕d2? (29 f6) 29...♘g5 30 ♖g2 ♕h3+ 31 ♖h2 ♕e3 and now, instead of 32 ♕xe3? ♖xe3 33 ♖e2 ♖xd3 34 ♖e7 ♗a4! winning (Webb-Povah, corr. 1990), White should play 32 ♖e2.

2) 10 h3 (Spassky's old move, but it has little merit) 10...h6 11 ♗e3 ♕a5 12 ♕b3 ♕c7 13 ♘d2 ♘h5 14 g3 g5 (a common move in this system; Black inhibits the f4 break) 15 0-0-0 ♘g6 16 ♗e2 ♘f6 17 ♖df1 ♕e7 18 ♕b1 ♔d8 19 ♘f3 ♔c7 20 h4 g4 21 ♘e1 ♘h5 22 ♕c2 ♕e8 23 ♗d3 ♗d7 24 ♕d2 ♕f8 25 ♘c2 ♕g7 26 ♔b2 ♖af8 27 ♘a3 a6 28 ♔a1 b6 29 ♖b1 ♖b8 30 ♖b3 ♘e7 31 ♖hb1 ♕g6 32 ♕b2 ♘c8 33 ♘c2 ♕g7 34 ♕a3 a5 35 ♕c1 f5! (just as White was about to play ♘a3-b5, following extensive preparation) 36 exf5 ♗xf5 37 ♗xf5 ♘xf5 38 ♗d2 ♖f8 39 ♘a3 ♖b7 40 ♖3b2 ♖f6 41 ♕d1 ♔d8 42 ♕a4 ♘fe7 43 ♗e3 ♖f3 44 ♘c2 ♖f6 45 ♘e1 ♕e4 46 ♖d1 ♖c7 47 ♕b5 ♘f5 48 ♗c1 ♔e7! (having closed the kingside, Black decides that it is the safest place for his king) 49 ♕a4 ♔f7 50 ♘d3 ♘g7 51 ♘e1 ♔g8 52 ♗e3 ♖cf7 53 ♕c6 ♖f8 54 ♕a4 ♘f5

55 ♗c1 ♖6f7 56 ♘d3 ♔g7 57 ♘e1 ♖f6 58 ♕d7+? (58 ♘d3 ∓) 58...♘fe7 59 ♘d3 ♕xc4 60 ♘xe5 dxe5 61 d6 ♖8f7 62 dxe7 ♘xe7 ∓ 63 ♕d2 ♖e6 64 ♕e1 e4 65 ♖bd2 ♘c6 66 ♖e2 ♖f3 67 ♖d7+ ♔f8 68 ♗e3 ♔e8 69 ♖b7 ♘e5 70 ♖b2 ♘d3 71 ♕d2 ♖ff6 72 ♖b1 ♖d6 73 ♕c2 a4 74 a3 ♔d8 75 h5 ♔c8 76 ♖a7 b5 77 ♖g7 b4 78 ♖d1 b3 79 ♕e2 ♘e5 80 ♕e1 ♖xd1+ 81 ♕xd1 ♖d6 82 ♖g8+ ♔c7 83 ♖g7+ ♔c6 84 ♕c1 0-1 Kamsky-Karpov, Linares 1991. It is unusual to have so many pieces still on the board at move 84.

10...♘g6!?

An alternative is 10...h6.

11 g3 0-0 12 h4 ♗g4 13 ♖xb7 ♘xe4?

It was necessary to chase the rook off the seventh rank by playing 13...♕c8 first, e.g. 14 ♖b3 ♘xe4 15 h5 ♘h8 16 ♗xe4 f5 17 ♗d3 e4 18 ♗e2 exf3 with unclear complications. Now White sets off the fireworks!

14 ♗xe4 f5 15 h5!! fxe4 16 hxg6! hxg6

16...♗xf3 17 ♖xh7 ♕f6 18 ♕d2 ♕xg6 19 ♖bxg7+ wins quickly.

17 ♘xe5! ♗h5

Of course, if 17...♗xd1 then 18 ♘xg6 and 19 ♖h8 is mate.

18 ♖xh5 gxh5 19 ♘g6 ♖f7 20 ♖xf7 ♔xf7 21 ♕xh5 ♕f6 22 ♘e7+!

The final point: 22...♔xe7? 23 ♗g5.

22...g6 23 ♕h7+ ♕g7 24 ♕xg7+ ♔xg7 25 ♘c6 ♖h8 26 ♗f4 ♖h1+ 27 ♔e2 ♖a1 28 ♗xd6 ♖xa2+ 29 ♔e3 a5 30 ♗xc5 1-0

Game 98

Balashov-Vaganian
Odessa 1989

1 d4 ♘f6 2 c4 e6 3 ♘c3 ♗b4 4 e3 c5 5 ♗d3 ♘c6 6 ♘f3 ♗xc3+ 7 bxc3 d6 8 0-0 e5 9 ♘d2 0-0 10 d5

1) 10 ♖e1 was introduced by Beliavsky:

⇨ 10...h6 11 d5 ♘e7 12 ♕c2 (12 e4 would transpose into the main game) 12...♘e8 13 e4 f5 14 exf5 ♗xf5 15 ♘e4 ♕d7 16 ♖b1! b6 17 ♖b2 ♘f6 18 ♘g3 ♗xd3 19 ♕xd3 ♘h7 20 ♖be2 ♖f7 21 f4! ± exf4 22 ♗xf4 ♖af8 23 ♖e6 ♘c8 (a bad square for a knight, but d6 must be defended) 24 ♗d2 ♕d8 25 ♘e4 ♕h4 26 h3 ♘f6 27 ♘xd6? (too greedy; 27 ♘xf6+ ♖xf6 28 ♖xf6 ♕xf6 is still a little better for White. If nothing else, this move must be condemned because it relieves Black of his problem piece) 27...♘xd6 28 ♖xd6 ♘h5 29 ♖de6 ♕f2+ 30 ♔h2 ♖f3! 31 ♖6e3 ♘f4 32 ♕f1 ♕xf1?! (good enough, but 32...♕g3+ is mate in three) 0-1 Neverov-Gagarin, Smolensk 1991.

⇨ Black played more actively in the stem game for 10 ♖e1: 10...cxd4 11 cxd4 exd4 12 exd4 ♗g4! (or 12...♘xd4!?) 13 f3 ♗h5 14 ♘e4 ♘xe4 15 ♗xe4 ♖c8 16 ♕d3 ♗g6 17 ♗a3?! (17 ♗d2! =) 17...♖e8 18 ♖ab1 ♘a5 19 ♖ec1 b6 20 ♗b4! ♘c6 21 ♗d2 ♕f6 22 ♗c3 ♕g5 23 ♖e1 h6 24 ♖b5 (Beliavsky-Adorjan, Thessaloniki OL 1988) when 24...♕f4! 25 g3 (25 ♗xg6 ♖xe1+ 26 ♗xe1 fxg6 ∓) 25...♗xe4 26 fxe4 ♕g4 would have been better for Black.

2) 10 ♘e4 b6?! (10...exd4 11 cxd4 ♗f5) 11 f4 exd4 12 cxd4 ♖e8 13 ♕f3 ♗b7 14 d5 ♘b4 15 ♗b1 ♘xe4 16 ♗xe4 ♕e7 17 ♗b1 ♕f6 18 ♕f2? (18 ♗d2! avoids losing two pawns) 18...♕c3 19 ♖d1 ♕xc4 20 ♗b2 ♘xd5 21 ♗d3 ♕b4 22 a3 ♕b3 23 ♖ab1 ♕a4 24 ♗c2 and now, instead of the ridiculous 24...♕c4?! 25 ♗d3 ♕a2? when 26 ♕c2 ♘f6 27 ♗c4 ♗e4 28 ♕xe4 ♖xe4 29 ♗xa2 ♖xe3 30 ♖xd6 won at a canter in Djurhuus-Chekhov, Gausdal 1991, 24...♕a5! or 24...♕d7 must be assessed ∓.

10...♘e7 11 e4

Or 11 ♕c2 g6 12 f4 ♘g4 13 ♘f3 exf4 14 exf4 ♘f5 15 ♖e1 ♘h4! (very interesting; it is considered best to play for a kingside blockade here with 15...h5!, ...♘g7, ...♗f5, etc, but Black has something else in mind) 16 ♘g5 h6 17 ♘e4 ♗f5 18 ♗d2 (thus far following Keene-Browne, Surakarta/Denpasar 1982 which continued: 18...♘f6 19 ♘g3 ♗xd3 ±) 18...♘xg2!! 19 ♔xg2 ♕h4 20 ♖h1 (20 h3? ♗xe4+ 21 ♗xe4 ♕f2+ and mate, or 20 ♗e3 ♕xh2+ 21 ♔f1 ♕h3+ ∓) 20...♗xe4+ 21 ♗xe4 f5!

22 🖵af1 (any move of the bishop allows mate) 22...fxe4 ∓ 23 ♕xe4 🖵ae8 24 ♕d3 (naturally 24 ♕xg6+? ♔h8 25 ♕d3 🖵g8 would mate quickly) 24...♔g7 25 h3 ♘f6 26 🖵b1 b6 27 🖵be1 ♘h5 28 🖵xe8 🖵xe8 29 🖵f1 🖵e4! 30 🖵f3 🖵xf4 31 ♗xf4 ♘xf4+ 32 🖵xf4 ♕xf4 ∓ Ziewitz-Stilling, corr. 1990.

11...h6 12 🖵e1 ♘h7!

In these closed positions, ...f5 commonly solves Black's problems.

13 ♘f1 f5 = 14 exf5 ♗xf5 15 ♘g3 ♗xd3 16 ♕xd3 ♕d7 17 a4 🖵f7 18 a5 🖵af8 19 f3 ♘f5 20 ♘xf5 🖵xf5 21 🖵b1 🖵8f7 22 🖵b2? ♕d8! ∓ 23 🖵xb7

23...🖵xf3 24 gxf3 🖵xb7 25 f4!? ♕h4! 26 ♕g3 ♕xg3+ 27 hxg3 e4! 28 f5!

Not 28 🖵xe4?! 🖵b1 29 🖵e1 ♘f6 30 ♔f1 ♘g4 ∓.

28...🖵b1 29 ♔f1 ♔f7 30 g4?!

30 ♗f4!.

30...♘f6 31 ♗f4 🖵xe1+ 32 ♔xe1 ♘xg4 33 ♗xd6 a6 34 ♗xc5?

It is hard to believe that White could be lost here, but it soon transpires that his pieces are dominated by the knight which arrives on c4.

34...♘e5 35 ♗d4 ♘xc4 36 ♔f2 g6! 37 fxg6+ ♔xg6 38 ♗b6 ♔f6! 39 ♗c7 h5 40 ♔g3 ♔f5 41 ♔f2 h4 0-1

Game 99 C ML

Yusupov-Ivanchuk
Brussels Ct 1991

1 d4 ♘f6 2 c4 e6 3 ♘c3 ♗b4 4 e3 c5 5 ♗d3 ♘c6 6 ♘f3 ♗xc3+ 7 bxc3 d6 8 0-0 e5 9 ♕c2

This seems to be flavour of the month at the moment.

9...0-0 10 ♘g5

⇨ 10 dxc5? (too simplistic) 10...dxc5 11 ♘g5 h6 12 ♘e4 b6 13 ♘xf6+ ♕xf6 14 ♗e4 ♗b7 15 ♗d5 ♘a5 16 e4 🖵ad8 17 ♗e3 ♗a6 (17...🖵xd5 18 cxd5 ♘c4 is also good for Black) 18 ♕a4 ♕e7 19 f4 ♕e8! (winning the c-pawn) 20 ♕a3 ♗xc4 21 ♗xc5 bxc5 22 ♕xa5 ♗xf1 ∓ Trofimov-Nikolenko, Moscow Tal mem 1992.

⇨ 10 ♗b2? (the bishop is misplaced here) 10...🖵e8 11 ♘d2 ♕e7 12 e4 cxd4 13 cxd4 exd4 14 🖵ae1 ♘g4 15 a3? ♕e5! 16 ♘f3 ♕h5 17 h3 ♘ge5 18 ♘xd4 ♘xd4 19 ♗xd4 ♘f3+ 20 gxf3 ♗xh3 0-1 Yndesdal-Thorhallsson, Gausdal 1991.

10...h6 11 ♘e4

⇨ 11 ♘h7!? ♘xh7 12 ♗xh7+ ♔h8 worked out well for White in Rogers-Frias, London 1992: 13 ♗e4 ♕c7 14 f4 exd4 15 cxd4 cxd4 16 f5! f6 17 exd4 🖵e8 (if 17...♘xd4 18 ♕d3 ♘c6 19 ♗a3 🖵d8 20 🖵ad1 wins the d-pawn) 18 ♗a3 b6 19 ♕d3 ♗b7 20 ♗d5 ♘a5 21 ♗e6 ♗c8 22 ♗d5 ♗b7 23 ♗e6 ♗c8 24 d5!? ♘xc4 25 ♗c1 ♘e5 26 ♕h3 ♗xe6 27 dxe6 ♖ac8 28 ♗f4 ♕c5+ 29 ♔h1 ♔h7 30 ♕h5 ♕b5! 31 a4 ♕b4 32 h3 ♖e7 33 ♖ad1 ♕xa4 34 ♖xd6 ♕e8 and now 35 ♕xe8 ♖cxe8 36 ♗xe5 fxe5 37 ♖e1 would have led to a promising endgame advantage for White.

11...b6 12 ♘xf6+ ♕xf6 13 ♗e4

The reasoning behind White's play is that Black's only significant weakness is d5. Therefore White exchanges the f6 knight and then tries to put his bishop on d5, where it may well become very strong.

13...♗b7 14 dxc5 dxc5 15 ♗d5 ♘a5 16 e4 ♕g6 17 f4 ♗xd5?

Better is 17...exf4 18 ♗xf4 ♖ad8 ∓.

18 cxd5 exf4 19 ♗xf4 ♖ae8 20 ♖ae1 ♘c4 21 ♕e2 ♘e5 22 ♗g3 ♕d6 23 ♕h5 ♕e7 24 ♖f5 ♘d3 25 ♖e3 c4 26 d6 ♕e6 27 ♖d5 ♖d8 28 h3 ♖d7 29 ♔h2 a6 30 a4 ♖e8!? 31 ♖d4 f5 32 ♖exd3!?

After 32 e5 ♖f8 the threat of ...f4 is annoying.

32...cxd3 33 exf5 ♕e2 34 ♕g6 ♖e4! 35 ♗f4! ♖f7

35...♖xf4! 36 ♖xf4 d2 would have been more testing.

36 ♗e5!?

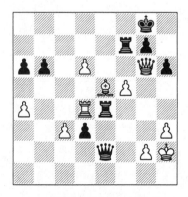

36...♖xd4 37 cxd4 d2 38 d7 ♕xe5+! 39 dxe5 d1♕ 40 e6 ♕d6+ 41 ♕g3 ♖xd7 42 exd7 ♕xd7 43 f6 ± b5 44 axb5 axb5 45 fxg7 ♕xg7 46 ♕b3+ ½-½

Game 100

Volke-Yudasin
Podolsk 1991

1 d4 ♘f6 2 c4 e6 3 ♘c3 ♗b4 4 e3 c5 5 ♗d3

If White plays 5 ♘f3 instead, then Black can consider a sort of 'accelerated' Hübner: 5...♗xc3+ 6 bxc3 d6 7 ♗e2 ♕e7!? 8 0-0 e5 9 ♘e1 e4 10 f3 ♗f5 11 fxe4 ♗xe4 12 ♘d3 ♘bd7 13 ♘f2 0-0 14 a4 ♗g6 15 ♕b3 ♖ab8 16 ♖a2 ♘e4 17 ♘h3 f5 18 ♗d3 ♘df6 19 ♘f4 ♖bc8 20 g3 ♗f7 21 ♔g2 ♖c7 22 ♗b2 ♖fc8 23 d5 (after provoking d5 Black can now proceed on the kingside) 23...g5 24 ♘h3 ♗g6 25 ♗c1 ♘g4 26 ♗e2 h5 27 ♔h1 ♕e5 28 a5 ♖h7 29 ♘g1 h4 30 ♘f3 ♕e7 31 gxh4 gxh4 32 ♗d1 h3 33 ♖a2 ♖g7 34 ♘e1 ♕h4 35 ♘d3 ♔h7 36 ♕b2 ♖cg8 37 ♘f4 ♗h5 38 ♘d3 ♕g5 0-1 Speelman-Agdestein, Hastings 1991.

5...♘c6 6 ♘f3 ♗xc3+ 7 bxc3 d6 8 0-0

⇨ 8 ♘d2 e5 9 ♘b3 ♕e7 10 0-0 e4 11 ♗e2 0-0 12 a4 ♗f5 13 ♖a2 h6 14 ♔h1 ♗g6 15 ♗a3 b6 16 ♗c1 ♕c7 17 ♗d2 a5 18 ♘a1 ∞ Ionescu-Mokry, Haifa 1989.

8...e5 9 ♕c2

⇨ 9 d5 ♘e7 10 ♕c2 0-0 11 ♘e1 h6!? 12 g3 ♗h3 13 ♘g2 ♘d7 14 f4 f5 15 ♗d2?! e4 16 ♗e2 ♘f6 17 ♖fb1 b6 ∓

Nikolaev-Kiselev, Podolsk 1991.
⇨ 9 ♘g5 0-0 10 f4 exf4 11 ♖xf4 h6
12 ♘h3 ♕e7 13 ♖b1 ♘d8 14 ♖b2
♘e6 15 ♖f1 ♘h7 16 ♕h5 ♘eg5 17
♘f4 f5 18 ♘d5 ♕d8 19 ♖bf2 ♘f6 20
♘xf6+ ♕xf6 21 h4 ♕f7 22 ♕e2
♘h7 23 g4 ♕e7 24 gxf5 ♕xh4 25
e4. White has constructed a very impressive centre, and went on to win
in Burlov-Gavrilov, Moscow 1990.

9...h6!?

At least this avoids ♘g5.

**10 d5 ♘e7 11 ♘d2 0-0 12 h3
♗d7**

⇨ 12...♘e8 13 f4 f5 14 e4 exf4 15
exf5 ♗xf5 16 ♖xf4 ♕d7 17 ♗b2?
(17 g4 ±) 17...g5 18 ♖f2 ♘g7 =
Volke-Kiselev, Podolsk 1991.

13 f4 exf4 14 exf4 ♘h8 15 ♘f3?!

15 f5 b5! is unclear; White had
probably under-estimated Black's
plan.

**15...b5! 16 cxb5 a6! 17 bxa6?!
♘exd5 ∓ 18 ♗d2 ♕c7! 19 ♖fe1 c4!**

Black's counter-attack proceeds
like clockwork.

**20 ♗f5?! ♗xf5 21 ♕xf5 ♖xa6 22
g4? ♕a7+ 23 ♔g2 ♖xa2! 24 ♖xa2
♕xa2**

25 ♔g3

Unfortunately for White, 25 g5
fails to 25...g6 26 ♕b1 ♘xf4+.

**25...♖b8 26 ♖c1 g6 27 ♕c2 ♖b2
28 ♕d1 ♘e4+ 0-1**

10

Again, White avoids all the potential disadvantages of the doubled pawn complex, but can also forget all about getting the bishop pair as Black's king's bishop has a ready-made retreat to e7 or f8.

After 5...d5, 6 cxd5 exd5 7 g3 is a popular line, White continuing his development whilst the central situation is relatively tranquil. Games 101 and 102 illustrate Black's latest aggressive strategy involving a very early ...♗f5.

The rest of this chapter covers 6 a3 ♗e7. In game 103 two marginal lines, 7 ♘g3 and 7 ♘f4 are considered, neither of which pose Black too many problems.

The main continuation, 7 cxd5, obliges Black to choose how to recapture on d5.

In game 104, against Agdestein, following the older 7...♘xd5 8 ♕c2 ♘d7 9 e4, Gurevich gains a large opening advantage and then converts it in an interesting endgame; but in his subsequent game against Polugaevsky he finds himself in trouble even more quickly when faced with the strong innovation 11...♗f6. Gurevich has also been toying with 9 g3 although, as yet, the positions he has obtained are far from remarkable.

On 7...exd5, White's sharp plan of 8 h3 and 9 g4 had enjoyed some success until it was completely defused by Kharitonov (notes to game 105). The ...♘e8 and ...f5 plan is worth remembering as it can crop up in associated lines. The main game

covers 8 g3, which is not particularly troublesome for Black providing he remembers to play ...a5, ...c6 and (against f3) ...c5! in good time.

Game 101

Bönsch-Hübner
Munich 1990

1 d4 ♘f6 2 c4 e6 3 ♘c3 ♗b4 4 e3 0-0 5 ♘e2 d5

⇨ 5...b6 (rarely played) 6 a3 ♗xc3+ 7 ♘xc3 d5 8 ♗d3 ♗a6 9 cxd5 ♗xd3 10 ♕xd3 exd5 11 0-0 ♖e8 12 f3 ♘bd7 13 ♗d2 c5 = Meister-Anastasian, Armenia 1991.

⇨ 5...c6?! (a novel idea that does not work out too well) 6 a3 ♗a5 7 b4 ♗c7 8 e4 d5 9 e5 ♘fd7 10 ♘f4 ± Grotnes-Schmittdiel, Gausdal 1992.

⇨ 5...♖e8 6 a3 ♗f8 7 d5 (7 g3 d5 8 cxd5 exd5 9 ♗g2 a5 10 0-0 c6 11 ♗d2 ♘a6 12 ♖c1 ♘c7 13 f3 ♘e6 14 ♗e1 c5 15 ♗f2 b6 16 ♕d2 ♗a6 {Black has developed his pieces in a very logical way} 17 ♖fd1 ♗c4 18 ♘f4 cxd4 19 exd4 ♘xf4 20 ♕xf4 b5 21 ♖e1 ♖xe1+ 22 ♗xe1 ♗d6 23 ♕d2 ♕d7 ½-½ Bischoff-Khalifman, Hamburg 1991) 7...d6 8 ♘g3 c6!? 9 ♗e2 exd5 10 cxd5 cxd5 11 ♘h5 ♘xh5 12 ♗xh5 d4 (gaining time) 13 ♕xd4 ♘c6 14 ♕d1 ♗e6 15 ♗f3 g6 16 0-0 ♗g7 17 ♘d5 ♘e5 18 ♗e2 ♖c8 19 e4 ♘c4 20 ♖b1 ♕h4 21 ♘f4 ½-½ Chernin-Khalifman, Wijk aan Zee 1991. Black's activity counterbalances his weaknesses.

6 cxd5 exd5 7 g3 c6 8 ♗g2 ♘a6 9 0-0 ♗f5!?

Quite often White will advance

his kingside pawns in this variation, so there is a risk that this piece will become a target. However Hübner obviously judges that this need not be a problem.

10 f3 ♖e8 11 g4 ♗g6 12 ♘f4 ♘d7 13 ♖f2 ♘b6

The knight's presence on b6 dissuades another White plan, a3 and b4, because c4 will become weak, as well as reinforcing d5.

14 ♗f1?!

Hübner recommends 14 a3 ♗f8 15 e4 ♘c7 16 b3 with equality.

14...♘c7 15 ♘xg6?!

Another imprecision; 15 a3 is preferable.

15...hxg6 16 ♕d3?! ♕h4 17 a3?! ♗d6 18 b3 ♘e6 19 ♖aa2 ♖ad8 20 a4? ♘d7 21 ♘e2 ♘df8 22 ♖c2 ♘h7 ∓

23 ♘f4 ♘xf4 24 exf4 ♘f8 25 f5 gxf5 26 ♕xf5 ♘e6

The ideal square for the knight; White's d4 pawn is a real cause for concern.

27 ♗e3 ♖e7 28 ♖ce2 ♖de8 29 ♕d3 ♕f6 30 ♕f5 ♘xd4 31 ♗xd4 ♕xd4 32 ♖xe7 ♖xe7 33 ♕d3 0-1

Game 102

Rivas-Polugaevsky
Logroño 1991

1 d4 ♘f6 2 c4 e6 3 ♘c3 ♗b4 4 e3 0-0 5 ♘e2 d5 6 cxd5

⇨ 6 ♕b3!? (I've never seen this before!) 6...c5 7 g3 ♘c6 8 cxd5 ♘a5!? 9 ♕a4 ♕xd5 (heading straight into wild complications) 10 ♕xb4 ♕xh1 11 ♕xa5 ♘g4 12 ♗d2 ♘xh2 13 0-0-0 ♘xf1 14 ♘f4 e5 15 dxe5 ♗g4 16 ♖e1 ♕g1 17 ♘e4 ♗f5 18 ♘d6 ♗g4 19 ♕b5 c4 20 e6 ♗xe6 21 ♕h5 ♕xf2 22 ♖e2 ♘xg3 23 ♖xf2 ♘xh5 24 ♘xh5 and White's pieces managed to hold on against Black's pawns in Grotnes-Kishnev, Copenhagen 1991.

6...exd5 7 g3 c6 8 ♗g2 ♗f5!? 9 ♕b3?!

⇨ 9 f3 is more normal: 9...c5 10 a3 cxd4 11 axb4?! (11 ♘xd4 ± is preferable) 11...dxc3 12 ♘xc3 ♘c6 13 b5 ♘b4 14 0-0 ♕b6 15 ♕d4 ♕xd4 16 exd4 ♗d3 17 ♖d1 ♗c2 18 ♖f1 ♗d3 19 ♖d1 ♗c2 20 ♖f1 ½-½ Yrjölä-Wians, Novi Sad OL 1990.

9...♘a6 10 a3 ♗xc3+ 11 ♘xc3 ♕d7 ∓ 12 ♗d2 ♖fe8 13 f3 c5 14 0-0 h5!

Stopping any thoughts White may have had of expanding on the kingside.

15 ♖fe1 ♖ac8 16 ♖ac1 ♖c6! 17 ♕d1 ♗h3 18 ♗h1 h4 19 ♖e2 ♗f5 20 ♗e1 hxg3 21 hxg3 ♖ce6

Clamping down hard on e4 and envisaging pushing the queenside pawns.

22 ♗f2

Better than 22 dxc5?! ♘xc5 23 ♘xd5 ♕xd5 24 ♕xd5 ♘xd5 25 ♖xc5 ♘xe3 ∓.

22...c4 ∓ 23 ♖e1 b5 24 ♘e2 g5 25 g4 ♗g6 26 ♕d2 b4! 27 axb4 ♖b6 28 b5 ♖xb5 29 ♘c3 ♖b6 30 ♖a1 ♘b4 31 ♘a4 ♘c2 32 ♘xb6 axb6 33 ♗g2 ♘xe1 34 ♕xe1 ♕e6 35 ♖a6?! ♗d3 36 ♕b4? c3! ∓ 37 ♖a1 c2

More incisive is 37...♘xg4!.

38 ♕d2 ♗g6 39 ♖c1

While White is trying to capture the c-pawn, which is like a thorn in his side, Black prepares a breakthrough on the kingside.

39...♕d6 40 ♗f1 ♕e6 41 ♗e2 ♔g7! 42 ♔f1 ♖h8 43 ♗d3 ♘xg4!

44 ♗xg6 ♘xf2 45 ♗xc2 ♕h3+ 46 ♔e2 ♕g2! 0-1

Game 103

Chernin-Kir.Georgiev
Dortmund 1991

1 d4 ♘f6 2 c4 e6 3 ♘c3 ♗b4 4 e3 0-0 5 ♘e2 d5 6 a3 ♗e7 7 ♘f4

The knight may instead choose a different square: 7 ♘g3 c5 (or 7...c6 8 ♗d3 b6 9 0-0 ♗b7 10 ♕e2 ♘bd7 11 ♖d1 ♕c7 12 ♗d2 ♖ad8 13 ♖ac1 ♕b8 14 cxd5 ♘xd5 15 ♗b1 ♖fe8 16 e4 ♘f4 17 ♕g4 ♘g6 18 ♘h5 ♘f6 19 ♘xf6+ ♗xf6 20 ♗e3 e5 21 d5 ♘e7 22 ♗a2 ♖d6 23 ♕h5 ♖f8 24 ♖c2 ♖dd8 25 ♖cd2 cxd5 26 exd5 g6 27 ♕h3 ♘f5 with equal chances for both sides; Nenashev-Tiviakov, Moscow Alekhine mem 1992) 8 dxc5 ♗xc5 9 b4 ♗e7 10 ♗b2 a5! 11 b5 dxc4 12 ♗xc4 ♘bd7 13 0-0 and now:

⇒ 13...♘b6 14 ♗d3 e5 15 ♕e2 ♗g4 16 f3 ♗e6 17 ♖fd1 ♕e8 18 ♘ce4 ♘fd7! ∓ 19 ♘f2 f5?! (loosening; 19...f6!) 20 ♖ac1 ♖c8 21 ♖xc8 ♕xc8 22 e4 f4 23 ♘f5 ♗c5 24 ♔h1 ♕e8?! 25 g3! fxg3 26 hxg3 ♘a4 27 ♗a1! ♖xa3 28 ♘g4 (Black has won a pawn, but storm clouds are gathering around his king) 28...♗b4! 29 ♔g2 ♗c3 30 ♕c2 ♗xa1 31 ♕xa4 ♗xf5 32 exf5 ♗d4 33 ♕xa5 ♘c5 34 ♗b1 ± ♔h8 35 ♕b4 b6 36 ♕c4? (missing a chance to put the h-file to good use: 36 ♖h1! ♘d7 37 f6 g6 38 ♕d6 ♕f7 39 ♗xg6! ±) 36...♘d7 37 ♗e4 ♘f6 38 ♘xf6 gxf6 39 ♕c6 ♕e7 40 ♖d2 ♕b4 41 ♖e2 ♗c5 42 ♕d7 ♕d4 43 ♕xd4 ½-½ Chernin-Granda Zuniga, Pamplona 1991.

⇒ 13...b6 (this must be good as well; Black intends to fianchetto his queen's bishop and use the c5 square) 14 ♕e2 ♗b7 15 ♖fd1 ♕c7 16 ♖ac1 ♘c5 17 ♗d3 ♕b8?! (17...♖fd8 is perfectly satisfactory) 18 ♗b1 ♖d8 19 ♕c2 ♖xd1+ 20 ♖xd1 ♕f8? 21 ♘a4! (winning a pawn because of the ♗xf6 threat)

21...♖d8 22 ♘xb6 ± Nenashev-Sturua, Moscow Alekhine mem 1992.

7...c6

The most solid, but there is also:

⇨ 7...dxc4 8 ♗xc4 c5 (I think that this is a good equalizing line) 9 dxc5?! (9 d5 e5 =) 9...♕xd1+ 10 ♔xd1!? ♗xc5 11 b4 ♗e7 12 ♗b2 ♘c6 13 ♔e2 ♗d7 14 ♘d3 ♖fd8 15 ♗b3 b5 16 ♖hc1 a5 17 ♘xb5 axb4 18 axb4 ♘xb4 19 ♖xa8 ♖xa8 20 ♘xb4 ♗xb4 21 ♘d4 is completely equal; Goormachtigh-Motwani, Sas van Gent 1992.

⇨ 7...b6!? 8 cxd5 exd5 9 ♗d3 ♖e8 10 0-0 c5 11 ♘h5 ♗b7 12 ♗b5 ♖f8 13 ♕f3 cxd4 14 exd4 ♘c6 15 ♗e3 ♘a5 16 ♖fe1 ♘xh5 17 ♕xh5 ♖c8 18 ♗f4 ♘c4 19 ♗xc4 ♖xc4 20 ♖ad1 ♕d7 21 ♖e3 with some prospects of a kingside attack; Nenashev-Kiselev, USSR 1991.

8 b3

⇨ 8 ♗d3 ♘bd7 9 cxd5 exd5 10 0-0 ♖e8 11 f3 ♘b6 12 ♔h1 c5 13 a4 cxd4 14 exd4 a5 15 b3 ♗d7 16 ♗d2 ♗c6 17 ♗c2 ♘bd7 18 g4 h6 19 ♘ce2 ♕b6 20 ♗e1 ♗d6 21 ♗g3 ♕c7 22 ♕d2 ♗e7 23 ♘d3!? (White seems to have the edge, he intends to exchange dark-squared bishops and play ♘g3-f5, but Black has his own ideas) 23...♘e4!? (opening up the diagonal to the white king) 24 fxe4 dxe4 25 d5 exd3 26 ♕xd3 ♖xe2 (and on 27 ♕xe2? ♗xd5+ 28 ♔g1 ♗xg3 Black wins) 27 ♕h7+ ♔f8 28 ♖xf7+! ♔xf7 29 ♖f1+ ♘f6 30 ♗g6+ ♔e7 31 ♕xg7+ ♔d8 32 ♕xf6+ ♔e7 33 ♕xe7+ ♖xe7 34 dxc6 ♗xg3 35 ♖f8+ ♔c7 36 ♖xa8 ♗e1 37 cxb7 winning; Kharlov-Kharitonov, Moscow Tal mem

1992. Had White seen all this at move 23 or was he lucky?

8...♘bd7 9 ♗d3 dxc4 10 bxc4 e5 11 ♘fe2 exd4 12 exd4 ♖e8 13 0-0 ♘f8 14 h3 ♗d6

The position is balanced.

15 ♕c2 ♗c7 16 ♖d1 ♘g6 17 ♖b1!

Note that White defers a decision on his queen's bishop; it is not yet clear where it might be best employed.

17...♕d6?! 18 ♘g3 ♕xd4?

A tactical error.

19 ♗xg6 ♗xg3 20 ♘e4! ±

20...♖xe4 21 ♗xe4 ♕xf2+ 22 ♕xf2 ♗xf2+ 23 ♔xf2 ♘xe4+ 24 ♔f3 f5 25 ♖d8+ ♔f7 26 ♗e3 b6 27 ♖bd1 c5 28 ♔f4! ♘f6 29 ♗c1 ♔g6 30 ♗b2 ♘h5+ 31 ♔e3 ♔g5 32 ♔f2 g6 33 ♖f8 ♗b7 34 ♖xa8 ♗xa8 35 ♖d7 a5 36 g3?! f4 37 gxf4+ ♔xf4 38 ♖d6 ♘g3 39 ♖f6+ ♘f5 40 ♖xb6 ♔e4 41 ♖a6 ♗b7 42 ♖xa5 ♘e3 43 ♖xc5? ♘d1+ 44 ♔g3 ♘xb2 45 ♖b5 ♘xc4 46 ♖xb7 ♘xa3 47 ♔g4 h6 48 ♖e7+ ♔d5 49 ♔f4! ♘c4 50 ♖e8! ♘b2! 51 ♖d8+ ♔e6 52 ♖d4 ♔f6 53 ♔e4! h5 54 ♔e3! ♔e5 55 h4 g5 56 hxg5 h4 57 ♖xh4 1-0

Game 104

M.Gurevich-Agdestein
Manila IZ 1990

**1 d4 ♘f6 2 c4 e6 3 ♘c3 ♗b4 4 e3
0-0 5 ♘e2 d5 6 a3 ♗e7 7 cxd5
♘xd5 8 ♕c2**

⇨ 8 g3 b6 9 ♗g2 ♗b7 10 0-0?! (10
e4) 10...♘xc3 11 ♘xc3 ♗xg2 12
♔xg2 c5 13 d5 exd5 14 ♘xd5 ♘d7
15 ♗d2 ♘f6 16 ♘xe7+ ♕xe7 17 f3
♖fd8 18 ♕c2 ♖d6 19 e4 ♖ad8 20
♗c3 ♖d3 (the position is strikingly
similar to Ravi-Suba in chapter 11)
21 ♖ad1 c4 22 ♖xd3 cxd3 23 ♕d2
♘e8 24 ♖d1 ♘c7 25 ♕e3 ♘d5 ∓
Cruz Lopez-Dautov, Nîmes 1991.

8...♘d7 9 e4

Mikhail Gurevich has been ex-
perimenting with 9 g3!? here. After
9...♘xc3 10 bxc3 c5 11 ♗g2:

⇨ 11...♕c7 12 a4!? ♖b8 13 a5 b5 14
axb6 axb6 15 0-0 b5 16 ♖b1 ♖b6! 17
♖d1 ♗b7 18 e4 cxd4 19 ♘xd4 ♗a6
20 ♗f4!? e5 21 ♘f5 ♘f6! 22 ♗g5 h6
23 ♗xf6 ♗xf6 24 ♘e3 ♗b7 25 ♗h3
♖d8 26 ♖xd8+ ♕xd8 27 ♗f1 ♕a8
28 ♗d3 ♗g5 29 c4?! ♗xe3 30 fxe3
♖d6 31 cxb5 ♕d8 32 ♗e2 ♖d2 33
♖d1 ♖xd1+ 34 ♕xd1 ♕xd1+ 35
♗xd1 (although White has an extra
pawn, his twin e-pawns are useless)
35...♔f8 36 ♔f2 ♔e7 37 ♔f3 f5 38
♗c2 ♔d6 39 g4 fxg4+ 40 ♔xg4 g6
41 ♔f3 ♔c5 (coming round to mop
up the b-pawn) 42 ♗b3 ♗c8!
(42...♔xb5? 43 ♗f7 g5 44 ♔g4 ♔c5
45 ♔h5 ♔d6 46 ♔xh6 ♔e7 47 ♗d5
±) 43 ♗f7 g5 44 ♗g6? (White has to
be careful he does not lose after this)
44...♗d7! 45 ♗f5 ♗xb5 46 ♗c8 h5

47 ♗f5 ♗e8 48 ♔g3 ♔d6 49 h4! =
g4 50 ♗h7 ♗f7 51 ♗f5 ♔e7 52 ♔f2
♔f6 53 ♗d7 ♗g6 54 ♗c6 ♔e7 55
♗d5 ♔d6 56 ♔g3 ♗e8 57 ♗g8 ♔c5
58 ♗h7 ♔c4 59 ♗f5 ♔d3 60 ♔f2
♗f7 61 ♗h7 ♔d2 62 ♗f5 ½-½
M.Gurevich-Petursson, Wijk aan
Zee 1990.

⇨ 11...♖b8! 12 e4 e5 13 0-0 b5 14
♖d1 ♕c7 15 dxe5 ♘xe5 16 ♘f4
♗g4 17 ♖e1 c4 18 ♘d5 ♕d7 19 ♗f4
♘d3! 20 ♗xb8 ♘xe1 21 ♖xe1 ♖xb8
22 ♕c1 ♖d8 23 e5 ♗e6 24 ♖d1
♗xd5 25 ♗xd5 was roughly equal
in M.Gurevich-Motwani, Ostend
1991.

⇨ 11...♖b8! 12 e4 e5 13 0-0 b5 14
♖d1 ♕c7 15 dxe5 ♘xe5 16 ♘f4
♗g4 17 ♖e1 c4 18 ♘d5 ♕d7 19 ♗f4
♘d3! 20 ♗xb8 ♘xe1 21 ♖xe1 ♖xb8
22 ♕c1 ♖d8 23 e5 ♗e6 24 ♖d1
♗xd5 25 ♗xd5 was roughly equal
in M.Gurevich-Motwani, Ostend
1991.

9...♘xc3 10 ♘xc3 c5

10...e5 11 dxe5 ♘xe5 12 ♗e2 ±.

11 d5 ♘e5?!

Probably a mistake. Better is
11...♗f6!? (Black would rather have
an isolated e-pawn than lose control
of d5) 12 dxe6 fxe6 13 ♗e3 ♗d4 14
♗xd4 cxd4 15 ♘b5 ♘e5! 16 ♖d1
♗d7 17 ♖xd4 ♕b6?! (17...♕f6! 18
♕d2 ♗xb5 19 ♗xb5 a6 20 ♗d7
♕g6 would be very awkward to
meet) 18 ♖d6 ♖ac8 19 ♕d2 ♕c5 20
♘c3 ♖xf2! = 21 ♕xf2 ♕xd6 22 ♗e2
b6 23 0-0 ♕c5 24 ♕xc5 ♖xc5 25
♔f2 ♔f7 26 ♔e3+ ♔e7 27 g3 a5 28
♖d1 g5 29 ♖h1 h6 30 h4 ♘f7! =
M.Gurevich-Polugaevsky, Reggio
Emilia 1991.

**12 ♗e2 exd5 13 ♘xd5 ♗d6 14
♗e3 b6 15 0-0-0**

Instead 15 0-0 can be met by
15...♕h4!?.

15...♘g4 16 f4 f6

Better than 16...♘xe3?! 17 ♘xe3
♕c7 (the queen sacrifice 17...♗xf4?
18 ♖xd8 ♗xe3+ fails to 19 ♖d2) 18
e5 ♗e7 19 ♘d5 ♕b7 20 ♗f3 ±.

17 ♗g1 ♔h8 18 h3 ♘h6 19 ♗e3 ♗b7 20 ♖d2 ♕e8 21 ♖hd1 ♖d8 22 g4

White has a large plus—more space, control of the d-file and use of the d5 square.

22...♘f7 23 ♘c3! ♕e7 24 ♗c4 ♗b8 25 ♗d5 ♘d6 26 ♗xb7 ♘xb7 27 ♖xd8 ♖xd8 28 ♖xd8+ ♕xd8 29 ♕d2! ♔g8

29...♕e8 30 ♕d5 ±.

30 ♕xd8+ ♘xd8

At first sight it appears strange that White should exchange all his pieces so happily but experience tells him that his advantage is easiest to exploit in the endgame.

31 ♔d2 ♔f7 32 ♔d3 ♘e6 33 ♘d5 g5?! 34 f5 ♘d8 35 ♔c4 ♘b7 36 ♘c3 ♗e5 37 ♔d5 ♔e7 38 ♘d1 h6 39 b3 ♘d6 40 ♘f2 ♔d7 41 ♘d3 ♗a1 42 a4 ♘f7 43 ♗f2 ♘d8 44 ♗g3 ♘c6 45 e5 fxe5 46 ♗xe5 ♗d4 47 ♗xd4 ♘xd4

47...cxd4 48 b4 a6 49 f6 ±.

48 b4 ♘e2 49 bxc5 ♘c3+ 50 ♔c4 ♘e4

If 50...♘xa4 51 ♔b4 corners the knight and forces 51...♘xc5 52 ♘xc5

bxc5+ 53 ♔xc5 with a winning king and pawn ending.

51 ♔d4 1-0

Game 105

Bronstein-Bareev
Rome 1990

1 d4 e6 2 c4 ♘f6 3 ♘c3 ♗b4 4 e3 0-0 5 ♘e2 d5 6 a3 ♗e7 7 cxd5 exd5 8 g3

The most logical move, but there are others:

⇨ 8 h3 c6 9 g4 ♘e8! (easily the best plan) 10 ♘g3 ♘d6 11 ♗d3 f5! 12 ♕c2 (if 12 gxf5 ♘xf5 13 ♘xf5 ♗xf5 14 ♗xf5 ♖xf5 15 ♕g4 ♕f8 ∓) 12...g6 13 ♖g1?! ♗h4! 14 ♗d2 (14 gxf5 ♗xg3! 15 fxg6 ♗h4! 16 gxh7+ ♔h8 17 e4 ♖xf2 18 ♖g8+ ♔xh7 ∓) 14...♗xg3 15 ♖xg3 ♘e4 16 ♘xe4 fxe4 17 ♗f1 ♖f7! ∓ (the backward f-pawn is weak) 18 ♗g2 ♕h4 19 ♗b4 ♘d7 20 ♗f1 a5 and Black went on to win in Nikitin-Kharitonov, Moscow 1991.

⇨ 8 b4 c6 9 ♘g3 ♖e8 10 ♗d3 b5?! (10...♘bd7 =) 11 0-0 (11 ♗d2!) 11...a5 12 ♖b1 axb4 13 axb4 ♘a6 14 ♘a2 ♘c5? (rather misguided; a simple move like 14...♗d6 would have been better) 15 dxc5 ♖xa2 16 ♕b3 ♖a4 17 ♗b2 ♗e6 18 ♕c3 ♗f8 19 ♗c2 ♖a8 20 f3 ♕c7 21 ♕d3 ♗e7 22 ♘h5 ♕d8 23 ♘xg7! winning; Gavrikov-Stajčić, Vienna 1990.

8...a5

⇨ 8...♖e8 9 ♗g2 c6 10 0-0 a5 11 f3 c5 12 g4 h6 13 ♕e1 ♘c6 14 ♕f2 ♖b8! 15 ♘g3 b5 (while White is building up on the kingside Black can't afford to remain idle) 16 ♘ce2 b4 17 h3?! bxa3 18 bxa3 ♖b3 ∓ 19 ♖d1 a4! 20 ♖a2 ♗d6 21 ♖c2 ♛b6 22 ♘f1? (22 ♘c3!?) 22...cxd4 23 ♘xd4 ♘xd4 24 ♖xd4 ♗xa3 25 ♖xa4 ♗xc1 26 ♖xc1 ♖b2? (26...♗a6 ∓) 27 ♛e1 ♗a6 28 ♖d4 ♖b3 29 ♖c3 ♗xf1 30 ♗xf1 ♛a5! 31 ♖dd3 d4 32 ♖c1 ♛a3 33 ♖xb3 ♛xb3 34 ♖b1 ♛xe3+? 35 ♛xe3 dxe3 36 ♗c4 g5 37 ♔f1 ♖c8 38 ♗b4! ♘d7 39 ♔e2 ♘e5 40 ♗d3 = ♖c1 41 ♔xe3 ♖e1+ 42 ♗e2 ♖h1 43 ♔e4 ♘g6. Of course, the ending should be drawn, but the black knight is just that little bit more useful than the white bishop. Black actually managed to win in Wessman-Lalić, Novi Sad OL 1990.

⇨ 8...♘bd7!? 9 ♗g2 ♘b6 10 0-0 ♖e8 11 b3 ♗f5 12 f3 c5 13 g4 ♗g6 14 ♘f4 cxd4 15 exd4 ♖c8 16 ♘xg6 hxg6 17 ♛d3 ♗d6 18 h3 ♗b8 19 ♗d2 ♛d6 20 f4 ♖cd8 21 ♖f2 a6 22 g5 ♘e4! (Black must play actively here) 23 ♘xe4 dxe4 24 ♗xe4 ♘d5 25 ♖af1 ♗a7 ∞ 26 ♔g2 ♘e7 27 ♗b4 ♛e6 28 f5 gxf5 29 ♗xf5 ♛d5+ 30 ♖f3 ♘c6 31 ♗h7+ ♔h8 32 ♛f5 ♖e2+ 33 ♔g3 ♛xd4 34 h4? (allowing mate but White was losing anyway) 34...♗b8+ 35 ♔h3 ♖h2+ 0-1 Vera-Chandler, Novi Sad OL 1990.

9 ♗g2 ♘a6 10 0-0 c6
⇨ 10...♖e8!? (this was suggested by Bareev in his annotations to the main game, the idea being to answer 11 f3 with 11...c5, saving a move) 11 ♘f4! (this is the problem, however, against which I could find no satisfactory reply when I looked at this position a couple of years ago. After 11...c6 12 f3, 12...c5? is clearly not

good as the d-pawn is *en prise*; how then to proceed? In this game Black finds his best chance) 11...c6 12 f3 ♘c7 13 e4 c5! 14 e5 ♘d7 15 ♘fxd5 ♘xd5 16 ♘xd5 cxd4 17 ♘xe7+ ♛xe7 18 f4 ♘c5! 19 ♗d2 ♗f5 20 b4 ♘e4 21 bxa5 ♘c3! 22 ♛b3 ♖xa5 23 ♗xc3 dxc3 24 ♛xc3 ♖ea8 25 ♖f3 ♗e4 26 ♖e3 ♗xg2 27 ♔xg2 b5! 28 ♖c1 g6 29 ♛c5 ♛xc5 30 ♖xc5 ♖xa3 31 ♖xa3 ♖xa3 32 ♖xb5 ♖a2+ 33 ♔h3 h5 34 ♖b7 ♖e2 35 ♔h4!? (in an apparently lifeless position the game suddenly flares up anew) 35...♖xh2+ 36 ♔g5 h4! 37 e6! (37 gxh4 ♔g7 38 e6?? ♖g2#) 37...hxg3! 38 e7 (not 38 ♖b8+? ♔g7 39 e7 g2 40 ♖g8+ ♔xg8 41 e8♛+ ♔g7 42 ♛e3 ♖h1 ∓) 38...♖h5+ 39 ♔g4 (39 ♔f6?? ♖f5#) 39...f5+ 40 ♔xg3 ♔f7 41 ♖b6 ½-½ Guliev-Prandstetter, Ceske Budejovice 1992. The final sequence is worth committing to memory.

11 f3 c5

This is almost invariably the reply to f3; on the one hand it is dangerous for White to let White play e4 unmolested, and on the other, Black can afford to play the IQP position now that White has weakened e3.

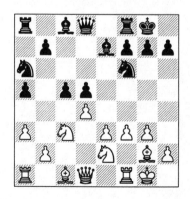

12 g4 h6! 13 ♗d2 ♖e8 14 ♗e1
♘c7 15 ♗f2 b6 16 ♖e1 ♘e6 17 ♕d2
♗d6 18 ♖ad1 ♗b7 19 ♘b5?!

Better is 19 ♗g3 ±.

19...♗b8 20 a4 ♗c6 21 ♘ec3
cxd4! = 22 ♘xd4 ♘xd4 23 exd4
♗d6 24 ♗h4 ♕c7 25 ♗f1 ♗f4 26
♕g2 ♖xe1 27 ♖xe1 ♕d6 28 ♗b5
♖e8 29 ♖xe8+ ♘xe8 30 ♗g3 ♗e3+
31 ♗f2 ♗c1 32 ♗g3 ♗e3+ 33 ♗f2
♗f4 34 ♗g3 ♗xb5 35 ♘xb5 ♗e3+
36 ♗f2 ♕b4! 37 ♗xe3 ♕e1+ 38
♕f1 ♕xe3+ 39 ♔g2 g5 40 ♕f2 ♕d3
41 h4 gxh4 42 ♕xh4 ♕c2+ 43 ♔h3
♕xa4 44 ♘c3 ♕xd4 45 ♕xh6 ♕f6
46 ♕xf6 ♘xf6 47 g5??

Overlooking a nasty tactic; 47
♔g3 would have kept the game
level.

47...d4! 48 ♘b5 d3 49 ♔g3

If 49 gxf6 d2 50 ♘c3 b5 51 ♔g3
b4 52 ♘d1 a4 the a-pawn cannot be
stopped.

49...d2 0-1

11

In this chapter we examine developments in the systems where White plays 5 ♗d3 and then a later ♘e2 (instead of ♘f3), avoiding doubled pawns.

The line 5...d5 6 cxd5 exd5 7 ♘e2 is a favourite of Mikhail Gurevich. Play is similar to that in chapter 10, with White trying to utilize his kingside pawn majority. In game 106, following 7...♖e8, White introduces a new possibility, the queen sortie e1-h4. The idea is to add extra weight to his kingside build-up; Black responds in an appropriate manner.

Game 107 considers the move 7...c5 when, after 8 a3 cxd4 9 exd4 Black can either retreat his bishop or take on c3. This last move obtained a bad reputation due to a brilliant Kasparov victory over Tal, but remains viable.

The rest of the chapter dwells on the line 6 ♘e2 c5. It was this variation that sparked much of the Nimzo-Indian revival some years ago, avoiding, as it does, Hübner's variation (from the move-order 4 e3 c5 5 ♗d3 ♘c6 6 ♘e2 d5 etc.).

In game 108, against the slightly unusual 7 a3, Suba does well with his innovation 8...♗a5!?. Games 109 to 111 cover the main variation 7 cxd5 cxd4 8 exd4 ♘xd5.

A common plan for Black here is the re-routing of the king's bishop to g7 to put pressure on d4. Game 109 is a perfect illustration of Black's possibilities once he gets a grip on d5.

In game 110 White's 10 ♕c2 meets with a new reply, but he quickly manages to convert to a favourable ending.

One of the problems with the IQP positions that commonly arise here is the placing of White's king's knight on e2 (instead of f3) where it exerts a less direct effect on the centre.

Often, the upshot of this is that Black can force through an equalizing ...e5 as in Knaak-Chernin and Malishauskas-Serper (game 111). Indeed I doubt that 10 ♗c2 will remain White's most popular move here as it seems from this last game that Black can force play into a dull ending should he so desire.

Game 106

M.Gurevich-Polugaevsky
Reggio Emilia 1992

1 d4 ♘f6 2 c4 e6 3 ♘c3 ♗b4 4 e3 0-0 5 ♗d3 d5 6 cxd5

⇨ 6 a3 dxc4 (6...♗xc3+ is dealt with in chapter 16) 7 ♗xh7+ ♔xh7 8 axb4 ♘c6 (8...e5 9 ♘f3 exd4 10 ♘xd4 ♘d7 11 b5 ♘b6 12 0-0 a6 13 bxa6 c5 14 axb7 ♗xb7 15 ♖xa8 ♕xa8 16 ♘f5 g6 17 ♕g4 ♖d8 18 e4 ♘f6 19 ♕g5 ♘h7 1-0 Gulko-Benko, Aruba 1992) 9 b5 ♘b4 10 ♖a4! (a very awkward move to meet; after 10...♘d3+? 11 ♔f1 Black loses his c-pawn) 10...a5 11 ♘f3 ♗d7 12 e4 ♘d3+ 13 ♔f1 ♘xc1 14 ♕xc1 c6 15 b6 ♔g8 16 ♖xc4 ♕xb6 17 ♖c5 a4 18 h4 a3 19 bxa3 ♕a6+ 20 ♔g1 ♕xa3 21 ♔h2 b6 22 ♖g5 ♕xc1 23 ♖xc1 ± Jelen-I.Farago, Sas van Gent 1992.

6...exd5 7 ♘e2 ♖e8 8 0-0 ♗d6 9 f3

⇨ 9 ♘f4 c6 10 f3 a5 11 ♔h1 ♗xf4 12 exf4 b6 13 f5 ♗a6 14 ♗xa6 ♘xa6 15 ♗g5 ♕d6 16 ♕d2 ♘d7 17 ♖ae1 b5 18 ♖e3 ♘f8 19 ♖fe1 ♖xe3 20 ♕xe3 f6 21 ♗f4 ♕d7 with equal chances; Galliamova-Polugaevsky, Tumba-Aruba 1992.

9...c5 10 ♕e1!? ♘c6 11 ♕h4 ♗e7

The bishop is forced to move to a less active square as 12 ♘xd5 was threatened.

12 ♕f2 a6 13 g4

⇨ 13 a3 b5 14 ♔h1 b4 15 axb4 ♘xb4 16 ♗b1 a5 17 ♖d1 ♗d7 18 ♗d2 ♕b8 19 ♗e1 = Alexandrov-Kiselev, Wisla 1992.

13...b5 14 ♘g3 b4 15 ♘ce2 a5 16 g5 ♘d7 17 f4 ♗a6 18 ♗xa6 ♖xa6 19 h4

As White cannot play e4 he has therefore embarked on a general kingside advance. Meanwhile, Black has been looking for counterplay on the opposite wing, where he enjoys a pawn majority.

19...♘f8 20 f5?! ♗d6
20...f6!?.

21 ♗d2 ♕b6! 22 ♔g2 cxd4 23 exd4 ♗xg3 24 ♘xg3! ♕xd4 25 ♕xd4 ♘xd4

Although Black has won a pawn, White will be able to win it back easily enough.

26 ♖ad1 ♘c6 27 ♗f4 d4 28 ♖fe1 ♖d8 29 ♖d2 ♘d7 30 ♖c1 f6 31 ♖c4 ♘de5 32 ♗xe5 ♘xe5 33 ♖cxd4 ♖xd4 34 ♖xd4 ♖c6 35 ♘e4 ♖c2+ 36 ♔g3!?

Rather simpler was 36 ♖d2 ♖xd2+ 37 ♘xd2 ♘d3 38 ♘c4 =; was White trying to win?

36...♖xb2 37 ♖d8+ ♔f7 38 ♖a8 ♖xa2 39 ♖a7+ ♔f8 40 ♘c5 ♖a3+ 41 ♔f2 ♖a2+ 42 ♔g3 ½-½

Game 107

Fedorowicz-van der Sterren
Wijk aan Zee 1990

1 d4 ♘f6 2 c4 e6 3 ♘c3 ♗b4 4 e3 0-0 5 ♗d3 d5 6 cxd5 exd5 7 ♘e2 c5 8 a3

⇨ 8 0-0 ♘c6 9 f3!? ♖e8 10 ♖f2 h5!? 11 a3 ♗xc3 12 bxc3 ♕d6 13 ♘g3 h4 14 ♘f5 ♗xf5 15 ♗xf5 ♖e7 16 ♖e2 ♖ae8 17 ♗d3 ♘d7?! (17...h3! ∞) 18 ♖b1! ♘f8 19 h3! ± ♕f6 20 a4 b6 21 ♗b5! ♘g6 22 a5! ± cxd4 23 cxd4 ♘xa5!? 24 ♗xe8 ♖xe8 25 ♖a1 ♖e7 26 ♖ea2 ♘c4 27 ♕d3 a5 28 e4 ♘f4 29 ♗xf4 ♕xf4 30 ♖b1?! f5! 31 e5 ♖e6! 32 ♖c2 (although White has won the exchange for a pawn, the position is not really suited to rooks as they lack fully open files on which to operate, the c4 knight blocking the c-file) 32...♔h7! 33 ♖b5?! ♖g6 34 ♖f2 a4 35 ♖c2 a3 36 ♔h1 ♘e3! 37

♖f2 ♖c6? (Black has managed to obtain some really serious counterplay, and now 37...♘xg2! 38 ♖xg2 ♖xg2 39 ♔xg2 a2 would have drawn) 38 ♖b1 ♘c4 39 ♖e2 ♘b2? 40 ♕xa3 ♖c1+ 41 ♖e1 ♖c2 (expecting 42 ♖xb2 ♕d2 43 ♖xc2 ♕xe1+ with a draw) 42 ♕xb2! ♖xb2 43 ♖xb2 ♕xd4 44 e6! 1-0 Spraggett-Rivas, Manila OL 1992.

8...cxd4 9 exd4 ♗d6

⇨ 9...♗xc3+ 10 bxc3 b6! (improving over the 10...♘e7 of his game against Kasparov) 11 0-0 ♗a6 12 ♗c2 ♘bd7 13 ♖e1 ♖e8 14 ♗f4!? ♖c8 15 ♘g3 ♖xc3 16 ♕d2 ♖c6! 17 ♘f5?! ♖ce6 18 ♖xe6 ♖xe6 19 ♗e5 ♘xe5 20 dxe5 ♖xe5! 21 ♕g5 ♖xf5 22 ♕xf5 ♕d6! 23 ♖d1 ♕xa3? (23...g6 was better, giving his king some room) 24 ♕e5 ♕c5? 25 ♗f5?? (missing the decisive 25 ♖xd5! ♘xd5 26 ♕b8+ ♕f8 27 ♗h7+ ±) 25...♗c4 ∓ 26 ♖a1 ♗b5 27 ♕b8+ ♘e8 28 ♕xa7 g6 29 ♗d7 ♗xd7 30 ♕xd7 ♘f6 31 ♕a4 ♘e4 32 ♕e8+ ♔g7 33 ♕e5+ f6 34 ♕f4?! b5 35 ♖c1 ♘c3 36 ♔h1 b4 37 ♕f3 ♕d4 38 ♕g3 ♕e5?! ½-½ Christiansen-Tal, San Francisco 1991.

10 0-0 ♘c6 11 f3 ♘h5?! 12 g4 ♕h4

This queen sally is not justified by the position; it is White who holds the advantage on the kingside.

13 ♖f2 ♘f6 14 ♗f4! ♗xf4 15 ♘xf4 ♕g5! 16 ♘g2 ♘xd4 17 h4 ♕e5 18 g5 ♘e8 19 f4 ♕d6 20 ♗xh7+

(see next diagram)

20...♔xh7 21 ♕xd4

After all the forcing moves White is well and truly in the driving seat.

21...♘c7 22 f5 ♗d7 23 f6 g6 24 h5! ♕g3 25 hxg6+ fxg6 26 ♕f4

The correct decision—the endgame is simple for White with his protected passed f-pawn.

26...♕xf4 27 ♘xf4 d4 28 ♖d1 ♗f5 29 ♖xd4 ♖ae8 30 ♖fd2 ♔g8 31 ♖e2 ♖xe2 32 ♘cxe2 ♘e6 33 ♘xe6 ♗xe6 34 ♖e4 ♗f7 35 ♘c3 ♖d8 36 ♔f2 b6 37 ♔e3 ♖c8 38 ♖e5 ♖c4 39 ♘e4 ♖c2 40 ♘d6 ♖xb2 41 ♖e7 ♗a2 42 ♖xa7 ♖b3+ 43 ♔d4 ♖f3 44 ♖g7+ ♔f8 45 ♖b7 1-0

In view of 45...♔g8 46 ♖xb6 ♖xa3 47 ♖b8+ ♔h7 48 f7 ±.

Game 108

Ravi-Suba
Kuala Lumpur 1992

1 d4 ♘f6 2 c4 e6 3 ♘c3 ♗b4 4 e3 0-0 5 ♗d3 c5 6 ♘e2 d5 7 a3 dxc4 8 ♗xc4 ♗a5!? 9 0-0 ♕e7 10 d5

⇨ 10 ♕c2 ♗d7 11 ♗d3 cxd4 12 exd4 h6 13 ♗f4 ♖c8 14 ♖ad1 ♗c6 15 b4 ♗b6 16 b5 ♗d7 17 ♕b3 ♗e8 18 ♘e4 ♘d5 19 ♗d6 ♕d8 20 ♘f4 ♘c3 21 ♖c1 ♗xd4 (winning a pawn, although White's active pieces offer compensation) 22 &b4 ⟒xe4 23 &xe4 Xxc1 24 Xxc1 ⟒d7 25 ⟒e2 &b6 26 ₩g3 Xc8 27 Xd1 &c7 28 ₩e3 a5 29 &c3 Xb8 30 g3 ₩g5 31 ₩xg5 hxg5 32 &d4 &b6 33 Xc1 &xd4 34 ⟒xd4 ⟒f6 35 &g2 Xd8 ∓ Sadler-Suba, London 1991.

10...&xc3! 11 ⟒xc3 exd5 12 ⟒xd5 ⟒xd5 13 &xd5 &e6 14 &xe6 ₩xe6 = 15 ₩c2 ⟒d7 16 &d2 ⟒f6 17 f3 Xfd8 18 e4 c4

Played to gain the use of the d3 square.

19 &c3 ⟒h5?! 20 f4 Xd3 21 Xae1 Xad8 22 ₩f2

White's centre, supported by all his pieces, appears very mobile.

22...⟒f6 23 f5 ₩c6 24 ₩h4 Xe8 25 Xf4 b5 26 &h1 h6 27 e5?

White's attempted attack will fall short because of back-rank problems.

27...⟒d5 28 Xg4 ⟒xc3 29 f6 g6 30 bxc3

30 ₩xh6 fails to ₩xf6!.

30...&h7 31 ₩f2 Xxe5! 0-1

This seems a little premature, but 32 Xxe5 ₩xf6! 33 &g1! ₩xe5 34

₩xf7+ ₩g7 35 Xf4! h5 is clearly better for Black.

Game 109

Dzindzichashvili-A.Sokolov
Manila IZ 1990

1 d4 ⟒f6 2 c4 e6 3 ⟒c3 &b4 4 e3 0-0 5 &d3 c5 6 ⟒e2 d5 7 cxd5 cxd4 8 exd4 ⟒xd5 9 0-0 ⟒c6 10 a3 &e7
⇨ 10...&d6 11 ⟒xd5 exd5 12 &f4 &g4 13 f3 &h5 14 &xd6 ₩xd6 15 ₩d2 &g6 16 &b5 ⟒e7 17 Xfe1 ⟒c8 18 ⟒f4 ⟒b6 19 b3 Xac8 20 ⟒xg6 hxg6 21 a4 a6 22 &f1 ⟒d7 = Lempert-Serper, Moscow 1991.
⇨ 10...⟒xc3 11 bxc3 &d6 12 ⟒g3 (designed to meet 12...e5 with 13 ₩h5! g6 14 ₩h6 exd4 15 ⟒h5 &e5 16 &g5 with an attack) 12...&xg3? 13 hxg3 e5 14 d5! ⟒e7 15 c4 &f5 16 Xe1 f6 17 a4 &xd3 18 ₩xd3 ₩d7 19 &a3 Xfd8 20 a5! ± Xac8 21 Xed1 ⟒f5 22 Xab1 h5 23 c5 ⟒d4 24 d6 ₩f7 25 a6 b5?! 26 cxb6! Xc3 27 ₩e4 Xxa3 28 b7 ₩f8 29 ₩d5+ &h7 30 Xxd4! exd4 31 ₩xh5+ &g8 32 ₩d5+ ₩f7 33 b8₩ ₩xd5 34 ₩xd8+ &h7 35 ₩c8? (35 d7 ±) 35...₩xd6 36 ₩f5+? (better is 36 Xb5! with a mating attack, but both players were in time-trouble) 36...&g8 37 ₩c8+ &h7 38 ₩f5+? ½-½ Skalik-Serper, Gdynia 1991.

11 &c2
⇨ 11 ₩c2 g6 12 Xd1 &f6 13 &e4 ⟒ce7 14 ₩b3 b6 15 ⟒xd5 ⟒xd5 16 &h6 Xe8 17 ₩f3 &b7 18 Xac1 &g5 19 &xg5 ₩xg5 20 ₩g3 ₩xg3 21 hxg3 = Hort-Ribli, Bundesliga 1992.

11...Xe8 12 ₩d3 g6 13 ₩f3 &f6

14 ♖d1 ♗g7 = 15 ♗e4 ♘xc3 16
bxc3 ♗d7 17 ♕g3 ♖c8 18 ♗g5 ♕c7
19 ♕h4 ♘a5

The c4 square beckons.

20 ♗f6 ♗xf6 21 ♕xf6 ♕d8 22
♕f3 ♗a4 23 ♖e1 ♖e7! 24 h4 ♖ec7
25 h5

As White is in a bad way on the
queenside, he looks for counterplay
on the other side of the board.

25...♕g5 26 hxg6 hxg6 27 ♕h3
♗b5 28 ♗d3 ♗xd3 29 ♕xd3 ♘c4 ∓

30 a4 ♘d6 31 ♖eb1 ♔g7 32 ♕e3
♕xe3 33 fxe3 b6 34 a5 bxa5 35
♖xa5 ♘c4 36 ♖a6 ♘xe3 37 ♖ba1
♘d5 38 ♖xa7 ♘xc3 39 ♖xc7 ♘xe2+
40 ♔f2 ♖xc7 41 ♔xe2 ♖c2+ 42 ♔f3
♖d2 43 ♖a4 ♗f6 44 ♖b4 ♔g5 45
♖a4 f5 46 ♖b4 ♗f6 47 g4 ♖d3+?

A bad error; Black can create two
connected passed pawns versus one
by means of 47...♔g5! 48 gxf5 exf5
49 ♔e3 ♖d1.

48 ♔e2 ♖a3 49 ♖b6 ♖a5 50 gxf5
♔xf5 51 ♖b8 ♖a2+ 52 ♔e3 ♖a3+
53 ♔f2 g5 54 ♖f8+ ♔g4 55 ♖f6 ♖a6
56 ♔e3 ♔g3 57 ♔e4 g4 58 ♔e5
♖a5+ 59 ♔e4 ♖a6 60 ♔e5 ♖a5+
½-½

Game 110

Speelman-Salov
Linares 1992

1 d4 ♘f6 2 c4 e6 3 ♘c3 ♗b4 4 e3 c5
5 ♗d3 ♘c6

⇨ 5...d5 6 ♘e2 cxd4 7 exd4 dxc4 8
♗xc4 ♘bd7!? is a curiosity; Pla-
chetka-Robatsch, Austria 1992, continued 9 a3 ♗e7 10 0-0 ♘b6 11 ♗a2
♗d7 12 ♘f4 ♗c6! 13 ♖e1 ♘bd5
14 ♘cxd5 ♘xd5 15 ♕g4 0-0?
(15...♘xf4!) 16 ♘h5! g6 17 ♗h6
♖e8 18 ♖xe6! (White's attack proceeds like clockwork) 18...♕c8 19
♗xd5 ♗xd5 20 ♖xe7! winning.

6 ♘e2 cxd4 7 exd4 d5 8 cxd5
♘xd5 9 0-0 0-0 10 ♕c2 ♘f6!?

⇨ 10...h6 11 ♖d1 (11 a3 ♗d6!? 12
♘e4 ♗c7 13 ♖d1 ♕h4 14 g3 ♕h5
15 ♘4c3 ♘xc3 16 ♘xc3 e5 {if
Black can play this advance successfully, he should be equal} 17 ♗e2
♗f5 18 ♕b3 ♗g4! {Black initiates
an interesting tactical mêlée} 19
♗xg4 ♕xg4 20 ♕xb7 ♘xd4 21
♕xc7 ♖ac8 22 ♕b7 ♖xc3 23 ♖xd4
½-½ Speelman-M.Gurevich, Munich 1992; 23...♖xc1+ 24 ♖xc1 ♕xd4
is a dead draw) 11...♗d6 12 ♗e4
♘ce7 13 ♕b3 b6 14 ♗xd5 exd5 15
♗f4 ♗g4 16 f3 ♗e6 17 ♖ac1 a6 18
♘a4 ♖b8 19 ♕d3 ♖a8 20 ♗xd6
♕xd6 21 ♕a3 ♖fd8 22 ♕xd6 ♖xd6
23 ♖c7 with a clear edge for White;
Lerner-Makarov, Helsinki 1992.

11 a3 ♗e7 12 ♖d1 h6 13 ♗f4!
♖e8 14 ♗c4! ± ♗f8 15 h3 ♘d5 16
♗g3 ♗d6 17 ♖ac1 ♘ce7 18 ♗a2
♘xc3 19 ♕xc3 ♗xg3 20 ♘xg3 ♘d5
21 ♕f3! b6 22 ♗xd5 ♕xd5 23

♕xd5 exd5 24 ♖c7 g6 25 ♖dc1

White should play 25 ♘f1! here, as after Black's next move it becomes impossible.

25...♗a6! 26 b3 ♖ac8 27 ♖xc8 ♖xc8 28 ♖xc8+ ♗xc8 29 ♘e2 ♔f8 30 ♘c3 ♗d7 31 ♔h2 ♗c6 32 h4

Although the bishop is tied down to the d-pawn, with care this ending should be drawn.

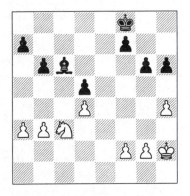

32...♔e7 33 g4 g5 34 ♔g3 f6 35 f4 ♔f7 36 ♘d1 ♗d7 37 ♘e3 ♔g7 38 b4 ♗e6 39 ♘d1 ♗d7 40 ♘c3 ♗c6 41 ♘d1 ♗d7 42 ♘e3 ♗e6 43 hxg5 hxg5 44 f5 ♗f7 45 ♘d1 ♔f8 46 ♘c3 ♔e7 47 ♔f2 ♔d7 48 ♔e3

48 ♘b5 ♗e8 49 ♘xa7 ♔c7 =.

48...♔c6 49 ♔d3 ♗e8 50 ♔c2 ♔d6 51 ♔b3 ♗d7 52 b5 ♗e8 53 ♔b4 ♗d7 54 a4 ♗e8 55 a5 ♗d7 56 ♘a4 ♔c7 ½-½

Game 111

Zlotnik-A.Sokolov
Moscow 1991

1 d4 ♘f6 2 c4 e6 3 ♘c3 ♗b4 4 e3

0-0 5 ♗d3 c5 6 ♘e2 d5 7 cxd5 cxd4 8 exd4 ♘xd5 9 0-0

⇨ 9 a3 ♗d6! (9...♗e7 10 0-0 ♘c6 11 ♗c2 ♘f6 12 ♗g5 b6 13 ♕d3 g6 14 ♖ad1 ♗b7 15 ♗b3 ♖c8 16 ♗a2 ♕d6 17 ♗f4 ♕d7 18 d5 exd5 19 ♘xd5 ♘xd5 20 ♗xd5 ♗f6 21 ♘c3 ♗g7 = Jelen-Kiselev, Ljubljana Iskra 1992) 10 ♗c2 ♘xc3 11 ♕d3 g6 12 bxc3 e5 = 13 ♕f3 exd4 14 cxd4 ♘c6 15 0-0 ♕h4 16 h3 ♘xd4 17 ♘xd4 ♕xd4 18 ♗h6 (forcing a draw) 18...♖e8 19 ♖ad1 ♕e5 20 ♖xd6 ♕xd6 21 ♗b3 ♕e7 22 ♗g5 ♕f8 23 ♗h6 ½-½ Knaak-Chernin, Dortmund 1991.

9...♘c6 10 ♗e4

The most common move at this juncture is 10 ♗c2:

1) 10...♗d6! 11 ♘e4 and now:

⇨ 11...♘ce7 12 ♘2c3 ♗c7 13 ♖e1 ♗b6 14 ♘g5 ♘f6 15 ♘f3 h6 16 ♗f4 ♘c6 17 ♗e5 ♘g4 18 ♕d3 f5! (playable, as Black has good control of e5) 19 ♖ad1 ♘gxe5 20 dxe5 ♕xd3 (the ending is better for Black, he has the two bishops and e5 needs defending) 21 ♗xd3 a6 22 h4 ♔f7 23 a3 ♖d8 24 h5 ♗c7 25 ♘a4 ♖b8 26 b4 ♔e7 27 g3 ♗d7 28 ♘h4 ♗e8 29 ♘g6+ ♗xg6 30 hxg6 ♘xe5 winning a pawn and the game; Sadler-Schlosser, Altensteig 1992.

⇨ 11...♗e7 12 a3 e5! (12...b6 is more combative) 13 dxe5 ♘xe5 14 ♘f4 ♘xf4 15 ♗xf4 ♘g6 (15...♕xd1 16 ♖fxd1 ♘c4 17 ♗d6 ♘xd6 18 ♘xd6 ♖d8 ½-½ Sadler-Winants, France 1992) 16 ♗e3 (16 ♗g3? ♕xd1 17 ♖axd1 f5 ∓) 16...♗e6 17 ♕h5 ♕d5! 18 ♕xd5 (18 ♘g5 h6 19 ♗e4 ♕b5! 20 a4 ♕a5 21 ♗d2 ♕xd2 22 ♘xe6 ♘f4! 23 ♘xf4 ♕xf4 =) 18...♗xd5 19 ♖fd1 ♗c6 20 ♘c3

&f6 21 &d4 &xd4 22 Xxd4 Xfd8 23
Xad1 Xxd4 24 Xxd4 ♔f8 25 f3 ♔e8
26 ♔f2 Xd8 27 Xxd8+ ♔xd8 28
♘e4 ½-½ Malishauskas-Serper,
Beskidy 1991.

2) 10...Xe8 11 a3 &f8 12 ♕d3 g6
13 Xd1 ♘xc3 14 bxc3 b6 15 ♘g3
&b7 16 ♘e4 ♘a5 17 ♘g5 &e7 18
♕g3 ♕d5 19 &e4 ♕b3 20 ♕f3 Xf8
21 Xe1 Xab8 22 &f4 &xe4 23 ♘xe4
Xb7 24 &h6 Xc8 25 ♘f6+ ♔h8 26
d5! (a long combination based on the
insecure position of the black king)
26...Xxc3 (if 26...exd5, then 27
Xxe7! kills the defender of the kingside dark squares) 27 ♕f4 Xc4 28
♕e5 ♕c3 29 ♕xc3 Xxc3 30 dxe6
fxe6 (obviously 30...&xf6? 31 exf7
Xc8 32 Xe8+) 31 Xxe6 Xc6 32 Xae1
Xxe6 33 Xxe6 b5 34 ♘d5 1-0
Sadler-Howell, Hastings 1991.

10...Xe8!?

An interesting idea, daring White
to open the e-file. Instead 10...♘f6
11 &f3 is normal:

⇨ 11...h6 12 &f4 &xc3 13 bxc3
♘d5 14 &c1 ♘a5 15 ♕d3 b6 16
&xd5 exd5 17 ♘f4 Xe8 18 ♕f3 &b7
19 ♘h5 ♕d6 20 &f4 ♕g6 21 Xfe1
♘c4 22 h3 Xe6 and with a strong
knight on c4, it is Black, if anyone,
who has the advantage; Lempert-
Makarov, Moscow 1991.

⇨ 11...&d7 12 a3 &e7 13 &f4 Xc8
14 b4 ♘e8 15 ♕d2 &d6 16 Xfd1
&xf4 17 ♘xf4 ♘f6 18 Xac1 b6 19
g3 h6 20 ♕e3 ♘e7 21 d5 exd5 22
♘cxd5 ♘exd5 23 ♘xd5 Xxc1 24

Xxc1 Xe8 25 ♕f4 ♘xd5 26 &xd5
&e6 27 &xe6 Xxe6 is completely
equal; Lempert-Sokolov, Moscow
1991.

**11 ♕b3 &f8 12 Xd1 ♘a5 13 ♕c2
g6 14 ♘f4 ♘f6 15 &f3 &d7 16 a3
&c6 17 &e2 Xc8 18 b4 &e4 19 ♕b2
♘c4 20 ♕b3 &d5 21 ♘fxd5 ♘xd5
22 ♘a4**

Too ambitious; 22 ♘xd5 exd5 23
&f3 =.

**22...♘d6 23 &f3 ♘f5 24 &b2
&g7 25 ♘c5 b6 26 ♘e4 ♘d6?!**

Better is 26...♕d7 ∓.

**27 ♘d2 ♘f5 28 ♘c4? ♘h4 29
&e2**

The alternative 29 &e4 f5 30 &d3
♘xg2! amounts to the same thing.

29...♘xg2!

30 ♔xg2 ♘f4+ 31 ♔f3

31 ♔f1 is met by 31...♕d5 ∓.

**31...♕h4 32 &f1 ♕xh2 33 ♘d6
♘h3 34 ♘xc8 ♕xf2+ 35 ♔g4 ♘g1
36 d5 h5+ 37 ♔g5 &h6+ 0-1**

12

Most of this chapter deals with the position after 7 0-0 dxc4 8 ♗xc4 when 8...cxd4 9 exd4 b6 and 8...♘bd7 are two prime possibilities, leading to positions of a similar genre.

To begin with, however, we tie up a few loose ends in the sub-games of game 112. First, if White wishes to refute 6...b6, he must try 7 d5; all the same, Black seems to be fine after the accurate 8...h6. Another little-played system is 6...c5 7 0-0 b6, but an examination of the game Salov-Hjartarson suggests that this is not so bad either.

Judging by the ease with which Black assumes the ascendancy in Yusupov-Timman, the system with 7...♘bd7, popular in the 1960s, may start catching on again.

In game 113 Black revives an old idea of Bronstein's (7...dxc4 8 ♗xc4 ♗d7!?) with success.

The normal move after 8...cxd4 9 exd4 is 9...b6, which was a great favourite of Karpov's. In the positions with an isolated pawn or hanging pawns that arise, Black must play with circumspection. White has been making a big score recently, often with relatively unsophisticated attacking plans. For instance, in game 114, despite playing normal-looking moves against Gurevich's slightly unusual move-order, Black is quickly on the receiving end of a winning combination.

Game 115 is a marvellous example of Ivanchuk's 'power-chess', whilst Dolmatov's pawn sacrifice in game 116 is interesting, but probably only good enough for a draw.

The move 8...♘bd7, which is dealt with in games 117 to 123, is similar to the previous line but perhaps a bit more flexible.

The line with 9 ♘e2, considered in game 117, does not offer White a great deal; although he avoids compromising his pawn structure the position becomes fairly symmetrical and tends to drawishness. That said, it is probably wise to avoid ECO's recommendation here, as Speelman's 11 e4!, found over the board, is awkward for Black.

The move 9 ♕b3, covered in game 118, has attracted some interest this last few years but Black should be OK.

If White plays 9 a3 then 9...♗xc3 is certainly playable, but strengthens the white centre.

9...cxd4! is best, and in game 119, Black shows what this variation is all about: first you give White hanging pawns, then you blockade them, and then you destroy them. Game 120 covers a strange variation where White avoids the weakened centre, but at a cost in time.

9 ♕e2 is White's most dangerous move, whereupon the 9...a6!? of game 121 is a useful method of avoiding the ultra-sharp variations and, as we shall see from the notes, White must show a good deal of care to avoid conceding the important central light squares.

Objectively speaking I suspect that the line 9 ♕e2 b6 10 d5!?, examined in game 122, is a little better for White; however, practically speaking, it is Black who has all the chances. Game 123 deals with the move 10 ♖d1 and features an amazing finale.

Game 112

Yusupov-Timman
Linares Ct (3) 1992

1 d4 ♘f6 2 c4 e6 3 ♘c3 &b4 4 e3 0-0 5 &d3 c5 6 ♘f3 d5

⇨ 6...b6!? (a flexible move; White's only attempt at refutation is to push in the centre) 7 d5 exd5 8 cxd5 h6! (better than 8...&b7 9 e4 c4 10 &c2 d6 11 0-0 ♖e8 12 ♖e1 ♘bd7 13 &g5 a6 14 a3 &c5 15 ♘a4 ♕c7 16 ♘xc5 ♕xc5 17 ♕d4 b5 18 ♕xc5 ♘xc5 19 ♘d2 ♘fd7 20 b4 cxb3 21 ♘xb3 ♘xb3 22 &xb3 ♘c5 23 &c2 ♖ac8 although even here Black has reasonable chances; Balashov-Aseev, Odessa 1989) 9 0-0 (9 e4 ♖e8 10 0-0 &xc3 11 bxc3 ♘xe4 12 ♖e1 ♘f6 13 ♖xe8+ ♘xe8 14 &f4 d6 15 ♕d2 &g4 16 &xh6 &xf3 17 gxf3 gxh6 18 ♕xh6 ♕f6 19 &h7+ ♔h8 20 &g6+ ♔g8 21 &h7+ ½-½ Timman-Gelfand, Moscow Alekhine mem 1992) 9...&xc3 10 bxc3 ♘xd5 11 e4 ♘c7 12 e5 &a6 13 c4 f5! 14 exf6 (14 ♕c2 &b7! 15 &xf5 &xf3 16 gxf3 ♘c6 ∓) 14...♕xf6 15 ♖b1 ♘c6 16 &b2 ♕f7 17 ♘e5! ♘xe5 18 &xe5 ♘e6?! (although White's bishops are strong, Black seems to be better after 18...d5!) 19 ♕g4 ♘f4 20 &xf4 ♕xf4 21 ♕g6 &b7 22 ♕h7+ ♔f7 23 ♕g6+ (White is not obliged to take the perpetual; 23 ♖bd1! should be

slightly better for him) 23...♔g8 24 ♕h7+ ♔f7 25 ♕g6+ ½-½ Knaak-Chernin, Palma 1989.

7 0-0

7...♘bd7

⇨ 7...b6 8 cxd5 exd5 9 a3 &xc3 10 bxc3 &a6 11 &xa6 ♘xa6 12 ♕d3 ♕c8 13 &b2!? c4 14 ♕c2 ♖e8 15 ♖fe1! ♕b7 16 ♘d2 ♖e6 17 ♖e2 ♖ae8 (the fight revolves around control of e4; if White can push e3-e4 with impunity then he should gain the advantage) 18 ♖ae1 ♘e4 19 ♘f1 f5 20 f3 ♘d6 21 a4 b5! 22 axb5 ♘c7 23 &a3 ♘dxb5 24 &b4 ♘a6 25 &a5 g6 26 ♖b1?! (26 ♕a4! ♕c6 27 ♕a2 ±) 26...♘b8! 27 ♕a4 a6 = 28 ♖be1 ♘c6 29 e4 ♘xa5 30 ♕xa5 dxe4 31 fxe4 fxe4?! (Black starts going astray; 31...♖xe4! 32 ♖xe4 ♖xe4 33 ♖xe4 ♕xe4! 34 ♕xa6 ♘xc3 35 ♕xc4+ ♘d5 = was very satisfactory) 32 ♘e3! ♘d6 33 ♖f1 ♕b5 34 ♕a2 ♕b3 35 ♕a1 ♘b5 36 ♘d5 e3 37 ♕e1 ♖d8? (now Black collapses) 38 ♖xe3 ♖xe3 39 ♕xe3 ♖xd5 40 ♕e8+ 1-0 Salov-Hjartarson, Reykjavik 1991.

8 cxd5 exd5 9 a3 &xc3

If instead 9...♗a5, then 10 b4! cxb4 11 ♘b5! is a strong pawn sacrifice that Gligorić discovered during his match with Tal, but did not have the chance to use until some time after.

10 bxc3 ♖e8 11 a4?

11 ♘d2.

11...c4 12 ♗c2 ♘e4 ∓ 13 ♗xe4 dxe4 14 ♘d2 b6 15 f3

15 ♘xc4 is impossible: 15...♗a6 16 ♘d6 ♗xf1 17 ♘xe8 ♗xg2 ∓.

15...♗b7 16 fxe4 ♗xe4 17 ♘xe4 ♖xe4 18 ♖a2 ♘f6 19 ♖af2 ♕d6 20 ♖f5 ♖ae8 21 h3 h6 22 a5 ♕e6 23 ♕f3 ♖e7 24 ♕g3? ♘d5 ∓ 25 ♕b8+ ♔h7 26 axb6 axb6 27 ♗d2

White has such a terrible position, it's incredible that he manages to draw.

27...f6 28 ♕a8 ♘xe3 29 d5 ♕d6 30 ♗xe3 ♖xe3 31 ♕a1 ♕g3??

31...♖xh3 32 gxh3 ♕g3+ 33 ♔h1 ♖e2 was one way to finish the game.

32 ♕b1! ∓ ♖e1 33 ♕xb6 ♖7e2 34 ♖5f2 f5?

34...♖xf1+ 35 ♔xf1 ♖xf2+ 36 ♕xf2 ♕d3+ 37 ♔g1 ♕xd5 ∓.

35 d6! ♖xf1+ 36 ♔xf1 ♖e5 37

♕d4 ♕h2 38 ♖e2 ♖xe2 39 ♔xe2 ♕xg2+ 40 ♔d1 ♕h1+ 41 ♔c2 ♕g2+ 42 ♕d2 ♕e4+

The proximity of White's d-pawn to the queening square obliges Black to take the perpetual.

43 ♔c1 ♕h1+ 44 ♔c2 ♕e4+ 45 ♔c1 ♕h1+ ½-½

Game 113

Knaak-Yusupov
Hamburg 1991

1 d4 ♘f6 2 c4 e6 3 ♘c3 ♗b4 4 e3 0-0 5 ♗d3 d5 6 ♘f3 c5 7 0-0 dxc4 8 ♗xc4 ♗d7!?

Yusupov makes an interesting choice, playing this variation against Knaak, who had written the relevant section in *ECO*.

9 a3

⇨ 9 e4?! (an entirely new move here, but White never really gets enough for the pawn) 9...cxd4 10 e5 dxc3 11 exf6 ♕xf6 12 ♗g5 ♕g6 13 bxc3 ♗c5 14 ♗d3 ♕h5 15 ♗e4 ♗c6 16 ♖e1 h6 17 ♗f4 ♗xe4 18 ♖xe4 ♘c6 ∓ Djurić-Bischoff, Biel 1991.

9...♗a5 10 ♕e2 ♗c6 11 ♖d1 ♘bd7 12 d5 exd5 13 ♘xd5 ♘b6 14 ♘f4

14 ♘xb6 ♕xb6 15 ♘e5 ♗a4 16 ♖d3 ♕c7 17 ♘g4 is given as ± but Yusupov had analyzed further and realized that 17...♘xg4 18 ♕xg4 ♖ad8 is unclear.

14...♕c7 15 ♗a2 ♖ae8 ∓ 16 ♗d2 ♗xd2 17 ♖xd2 ♘e4 18 ♖c2 ♕e7 19 ♖ac1 ♗a4 20 b3 ♗c6 21 ♘d2! ♘d7 22 ♗b1 ♕g5 23 ♘f1 ♖e7 24 ♕d1 ♖fe8 25 f3 ♘ef6 26 ♘h3 ♕h6

I do not like Black's plan of
...♕g5-h6, as the queen is offside.

**27 ♖d2 ♘e5 28 ♘f2 ♗b5 29 f4
♘g6 30 ♗d3 ♗xd3 31 ♖xd3 b6 32
♖d8 ♘h4 33 ♘g4 ♕g6 34 ♘xf6+
♕xf6 35 ♕d7 ♔f8 36 ♖xe8+ ♖xe8
37 ♖d1 g6 38 ♕xa7**

38...♕c6

Thus Black regains his pawn, but
the resulting ending is only level.

**39 ♖d2 ♖a8 40 ♕d7 ♕xd7 41
♖xd7 ♖xa3 42 ♘d2 = ♔e8 43 ♖d5
♘f5 44 g4 ♘e7 45 ♖d3 f5! 46 g5?!
b5 47 ♖d6 ♖a2 48 e4? ♖c2 ∓ 49 e5
♘c8 50 ♖d3 c4 51 bxc4 bxc4 52
♖d4 c3 53 ♘b3 ♘b6 54 ♖b4 ♘d5
55 ♖b8+ ♔e7 56 ♖b7+ ♔d8 57 e6
♔c8 58 ♖b5? ♘xf4 59 ♘d4 ♖d2 60
♖c5+ ♔d8 61 ♘f3 ♖b2 62 ♘d4
♖b1+ 0-1**

Game 114

M.Gurevich-L.B.Hansen
Tåstrup 1992

**1 d4 e6 2 c4 ♗b4+ 3 ♘c3 c5 4 e3
cxd4 5 exd4 ♘f6 6 ♗d3 d5 7 ♘f3**

**0-0 8 0-0 dxc4 9 ♗xc4 b6 10 ♗g5
♗b7 11 ♘e5**

⇨ 11 ♕d3 ♗xc3 12 bxc3 ♘bd7 13
♖fd1 ♖c8 14 ♗b3 ♕c7 15 ♖ac1
♘e4 16 ♗h4 ♕f4 17 c4 ♘df6 18
♕e3 ♕xe3 19 fxe3 ♖c7 20 ♘e5
♖fc8 21 ♖c2 ♘e8 22 a4 ♘8d6 must
be at least equal for Black; Rozen-
talis-Bilunov, Podolsk 1989.

11...♗e7!?

⇨ 11...♘bd7!? (a risky innovation
as Black allows his kingside to be
compromised; perhaps 11...♗xc3 12
bxc3 ♕c7 13 ♗d3 ♘bd7 14 ♖e1?
{14 ♘xd7} 14...♘xe5 15 dxe5 ♕c6
16 ♗f1 ♘e4 17 ♗h4 ♕xc3 18 ♗d3
♘c5 ∓ Velimirović-Østenstad, Novi
Sad OL 1990 is better) 12 ♘xd7
♕xd7 13 ♗xf6 gxf6 14 d5! (White
cannot permit Black to play ...♕c6)
14...♗xc3 15 bxc3 ♗xd5 16 ♕g4+
♔h8 17 ♕d4 ♖ac8? (17...♕d8 18
♗xd5 exd5 19 ♖fe1 ♖c8 is not clear)
18 ♕xf6+?! (first 18 ♗a6! ♖c5 and
then 19 ♕xf6+ ♔g8 20 ♖ad1! would
have given White a powerful attack)
18...♔g8 19 ♗d3 (of course, it's also
possible to take the draw: 19 ♕g5+
♔h8 20 ♕f6+ ½-½ Ulybin-Sorokin,
Cheliabinsk 1991) 19...♕d8 20 ♕h6
f5 21 c4 ♗xg2 22 ♕xe6+ ♔g7 23
♕e5+ ♖f6! (Black manages to hold
the balance with several precise defensive moves) 24 ♖fd1 ♖c5! 25
♕c3 ♗c6 26 ♗e4 ♕c7! 27 ♗xc6
♕xc6 28 ♖ac1 b5 29 cxb5 ♖xc3 30
bxc6 ♖fxc6 31 ♖xc3 ♖xc3 32 ♖d7+
♔g6 33 ♖xa7 h5 34 ♖a4 h4 35 ♖xh4
♖a3 = 36 ♔g2 ♖xa2 (even without
his f-pawn Black could draw this) 37
♔g3 ♖a1 38 f3 ♔g5 39 ♖b4 f4+! 40
♔h3 ♖a2 41 ♖b5+ ♔g6 ½-½ Yusu-
pov-Ivanchuk, Brussels (6) 1991.

12 ♖e1

⇨ 12 ♕e2 (certainly not 12 ♘xf7?
♔xf7 13 ♗xe6+ ♔xe6 14 ♕b3+
♔f5 15 h4 ♔g6 16 ♖fe1 h6 17 ♕c2+
♔f7 18 ♗xf6 ♔xf6 19 h5 ♔f7 20
♕b3+ ♔e8 21 d5 ♖f6 22 ♖e3 ♔f8
23 ♖ae1 ♖f7 24 ♕c2 ♔g8 25 ♕g6
♘a6 26 d6 ♗f8 0-1 Horber-Tolnai,
Bern 1992) 12...♘bd7 13 ♖ad1 ♖c8
14 ♖fe1 ♗d5? (an unthematic move
that loses; better is 14...♘d5 15
♗xd5 ♗xd5 16 ♗xe7 ♕xe7 17
♘xd5 ±) 15 ♗a6 ♖a8 16 ♘xd5
♘xd5 17 ♘c6 ♕e8 18 ♘xe7+♘xe7
19 d5 ♘xd5 20 ♗b7 ± ♕b8 21 ♗xa8
♕xa8 22 ♕g4 ♔h8 23 ♖d3 1-0
Knaak-Marinelli, Lugano 1989.

12...♘c6?!

This natural move allows a tactical stroke.

13 ♗a6! ♕c8

13...♗xa6 14 ♘xc6 ♕d6 15
♘xe7+ ♕xe7 16 ♘d5 ±.

14 ♗xb7

⇨ 14 ♕f3?! (this is not so strong, but
White manages to retain a small advantage all the same) 14...♘a5 15
♗xb7 ♕xb7 16 ♕xb7 ♘xb7 17
♘c6 ♗d8 18 ♖ac1 ♘a5 19 ♘xd8

♖axd8 20 ♘e4 ♖xd4 21 ♘xf6+
gxf6 22 ♗xf6 ♖f4 23 ♗g5 ♖c4 24
♖xc4 ♘xc4 25 b3 ♘a5 26 ♖c1 f6 27
♗e3 ± Petran-A.Petrosian, Budapest
1991.

**14...♕xb7 15 ♕f3 ♖ac8 16 ♖ac1
♘d5!? 17 ♘xd5 ♗xg5 18 ♘xc6!
exd5 19 ♕xd5 ♗xc1 20 ♘e7+ ♕xe7
21 ♖xe7 ♗xb2 22 g3 ± a5 23 ♖d7
♖b8 24 ♕b3 ♗c1 25 ♖d6 b5 26
♕c3 ♗g5 27 ♕xa5 ♗f6 28 d5 b4 29
♕a4 h6 30 ♖d7 ♖fe8 31 d6 ♖e6 32
♕a7 ♖b5 33 ♕a8+ ♔h7 34 ♕f3?!**

34 ♖xf7 ♖xd6 35 ♕e4+ ♔g8 36
♕e8+ would have been rather more
efficient.

**34...♖b6 35 ♕d3+ ♔g8 36 ♖a7
♖b8 37 d7 ♖d8 38 ♖c7 ♔f8 39 ♕b5
♔e7 40 ♕xb4+ ♖d6 41 ♕e4+ ♖e6
42 ♕b4+ ♖d6 43 a4 ♗d4? 44 ♖c4
1-0**

Game 115

Ivanchuk-Karpov
Linares 1991

**1 d4 ♘f6 2 c4 e6 3 ♘c3 ♗b4 4 e3
0-0 5 ♗d3 d5 6 ♘f3 c5 7 0-0 cxd4**

The game Yusupov-Rozentalis,
Groningen 1992, took an unusual
turn: 7...dxc4 8 ♗xc4 b6 9 ♗d2!?
cxd4 10 ♘xd4 ♗b7 11 ♕e2 ♘c6 12
♘xc6 ♗xc6 13 ♖fd1 ♕e7 14 a3 ♗c5
15 ♗e1 ♖fd8 16 f3 ♖xd1 17 ♖xd1
♖d8 18 ♗f2 h6 19 ♖xd8+ ♕xd8 20
♕d3 ♕xd3 21 ♗xd3 ♔f8 22 e4
½-½.

**8 exd4 dxc4 9 ♗xc4 b6 10 ♗g5
♗b7**

⇨ 10...h6!? 11 ♗xf6!? (this eases
Black's position; why not 11 ♗h4

instead?) 11...♕xf6 12 ♘e5 ♗b7 13 ♕g4 ♗xc3 14 bxc3 ♖c8 15 f4 (15 ♖fe1) 15...♘c6 16 ♘d7?! ♕f5 17 ♕xf5 exf5 18 ♗d3 ♖c7 (White's c- and d-pawns offer good targets) 19 ♘e5 ♘xe5 20 fxe5 g6 21 ♖ac1 ♖ac8 22 c4 ♗d5 winning a pawn; Velimirović-Ilinčić, Vrnjačka Banja 1992.

11 ♖c1

11... ♘c6

Or 11...♘bd7 12 ♕e2 and now:
➪ 12...♖c8 13 ♘e5 ♗xc3? (inferior; 13...♕c7 is best) 14 ♖xc3 ♗d5? (14...♕e8 is a better bet) 15 ♗xd5 ♖xc3 (15...exd5 16 ♘c6 isn't a great deal of help either) 16 ♘xf7! 1-0 Zsinka-Kohlweyer, Frankfurt 1990. After 16...♖xf7, 17 ♕xe6 wins.
➪ 12...♗xc3 13 ♖xc3 ♕b8 14 ♖e3!? (14 ♖a3 ♘g4 15 g3 ♘gf6 16 ♘e5 ♘xe5 ½-½ Gomez-Garcia, Spanish Ch 1991; 14 ♗h4 followed by ♗g3 looks more logical to me) 14...♘g4 15 ♘e5 ♘xe3?! (after 15...♘dxe5 16 ♖xe5 ♘xe5 17 fxe5 it remains to be proved whether White has enough compensation for the exchange) 16 ♘xd7 ♕d6 17 ♘f6+!

gxf6 18 ♗xf6 ♖fc8 19 fxe3 ♗e4 20 ♗e5 ♕e7 21 ♖f6 ♖c6 22 ♕g4+ ♗g6 23 ♕g5 ♔f8 24 ♕h6+ ♔e8 25 ♗b5 ♕d7 26 ♗xc6 ♕xc6 27 h4 ♕c2 28 ♖f2 ♕d1+ 29 ♔f1 ♕h5 30 ♕f4 ♖c8 31 d5 exd5 32 ♗f6 ♔f8 33 g4 1-0 Gual-Campos Moreno, Barcelona 1989.

12 a3

➪ 12 ♖e1 ♗e7 13 a3 ♖c8 14 ♗a2 ♘d5 15 ♗d2! (normally it is not in White's interest to exchange pieces in this type of position) 15...♘xc3 16 ♗xc3 ♗f6 17 d5 exd5 18 ♗xd5 (opening up the position like this gives White an initiative, but as Black's position is solid, he should be able to hold) 18...♗xc3 19 ♖xc3 ♘a5? (19...♖c7) 20 ♖xc8 ♕xc8 21 ♘e5 ♗xd5 22 ♕xd5 ♕b7 23 ♕d6 ♖e8 24 ♖e3 f6? (obvious, but bad; 24...h6 would have been the best method of avoiding back-rank problems, e.g. 25 b4 f6 26 ♘g4 ♖xe3 27 ♘xe3 ♘c6 =)

25 ♘g6! ♖a8 (25...♔f7 26 ♘h8+! ♖xh8 27 ♕e6+ and 25...♕f7 26 ♖xe8+ ♕xe8 27 ♕d5+ both lead to mate) 26 ♘e7+ ♔h8 27 ♕e6 1-0

Speelman-Levitt, London 1992. 28
♘g6+ is the threat, and 27...h6 28
♖h3 ♖d8 29 ♖xh6+! gxh6 30 ♕xf6+
leads to mate in two.

**12...♗e7 13 ♕d3 ♘d5 14 ♗xd5
exd5 15 ♗xe7 ♘xe7 16 ♖fe1 ♖c8
17 h4 h6 18 h5 ♖c7!**

Good defence, preparing ...♘c8-
d6.

19 ♘b5?! ♖xc1 20 ♖xc1 ♗a6?!
Better is 20...a6.
21 a4 ♗xb5?
21...♕b8 22 ♘e5 ♖c8 is better; as
played, Karpov is unable to oppose
rooks on the c-file.
**22 ♕xb5 ♘f5 23 g3! ♘e7 24 ♘e5
♕d6 25 ♕a6 ♘f5?!**
25...♕b4 offered more counterplay.
**26 ♕d3 ♘e7 27 ♕f3 ± a5 28 ♔g2
f6 29 ♘d3 ♖c8 30 ♖e1 ♖c4 31
♘f4?!**
31 ♕e3 ♔f7 32 ♘f4 was strong.
**31...♖xd4 32 ♘g6 ♘xg6 33 hxg6
♔f8 34 ♕f5 ♖c4 35 g4?! 1-0**
On time, but White is still sub-
stantially better, for example 35...d4
36 ♖e6 ♖d8 37 ♕b5! ♖b4 38 ♕c6
followed by ♕b7.

Game 116

Dolmatov-Speelman
Hastings 1990

**1 e4 c6 2 d4 d5 3 exd5 cxd5 4 c4
♘f6 5 ♘c3 e6 6 ♘f3 ♗b4 7 ♗d3
dxc4 8 ♗xc4 0-0 9 0-0 ♘bd7**

A reasonable alternative is 9...a6,
hoping to play ...b5 and ...♗b7.
White then has a number of options,
but only the last of these is promising:

⇨ 10 a3 ♗xc3 11 bxc3 b5 12 ♗d3
♗b7 13 a4 ♕d5 14 axb5 axb5 15
♖xa8 ♗xa8 16 ♕e2 ♖c8 17 ♗d2
♘e4 18 ♗xe4 ♕xe4 19 ♕xe4 ♗xe4
20 ♘e5 ♘c6 21 ♘xc6 ♗xc6 ½-½
Goldin-Kharitonov, Moscow 1989.

⇨ 10 ♗g5 ♗e7 11 ♕e2 b5 12 ♗d3
♗b7 13 ♖ad1 ♘bd7 14 ♘e5 ♘d5 15
♗e3 ♖c8 16 ♖c1 ♘xc3 17 bxc3
♘xe5 18 dxe5 ♗a3 19 ♖cd1 ♕c7 20
♗d4 ♗d5 21 ♗xh7+?! (White was
getting outplayed, so he hits out)
21...♔xh7 22 ♕h5+ ♔g8 23 ♖d3
♖fd8 24 ♖h3 ♔f8 25 ♕h8+ ♔e7 26
♕xg7 ♖g8 27 ♕f6+ ♔e8 28 ♖g3
♖xg3 29 fxg3 ♕e7 30 ♕h8+ ♕f8 31
♕f6 ♖c4 ∓ Zsinka-Arkhipov, Hungary 1991.

⇨ 10 ♗d3!? b5 11 a4 bxa4 12 ♖xa4
a5 13 ♗g5 ♗a6 14 ♘e5 h6 15 ♗h4
♗e7 16 ♖e1 ♗xd3 17 ♕xd3 ♘d5 18
♗xe7 ♘xe7 19 ♕b5 ♖a6 20 ♘c4
♕xd4 21 ♖d1 ♕a7 22 ♖xa5 ♘ec6
23 ♖xa6 ♕xa6 24 ♕c5 ♕b7 25 ♘e4
♕b4 26 g3 ♕xc5 27 ♘xc5 = Hüb-
ner-Assmann, Lugano 1989.

⇨ 10 ♕d3?! b5 11 ♗b3 ♘bd7 12
♗g5 ♘c5! 13 ♕d1 ♘xb3 14 ♕xb3
♗e7 15 ♖ad1 ♗b7 16 ♘e5 h6 17

♗h4 ♖c8 18 ♖fe1 ♘d5 19 ♗xe7
♘xe7 20 ♘e4 ♗xe4 21 ♖xe4 ♕d5
22 ♕xd5 ♘xd5 23 ♘d7 ♖fd8 24
♘c5 ♘c3! 25 bxc3 ♖xc5 26 ♖e3 b4
27 cxb4 ♖xd4 28 ♖f1 ♖xb4 ∓
Maurer-Wirthensohn, Lenk 1992.
⇨ 10 a4, containing Black's queenside expansion, should keep a small
advantage.

**10 ♗g5 ♗xc3 11 bxc3 ♕c7 12
♗d3!?**

With correct play this pawn sacrifice should lead to a draw.

**12...♕xc3! 13 ♖c1 ♕a5 14 ♘e5
♘xe5**

⇨ 14...♕d5!? (this is probably best
if Black wants to try to win) 15 ♖e1
♔h8 16 ♖e3 ♕xd4? (16...b5! ∞) 17
♖c4 ♕d5 18 ♖h4?! (18 ♘xd7!
♘xd7 19 ♕h5 h6 20 ♖h4 ♘f6 21
♕xh6+! wins) 18...♘xe5 19 ♗xf6
♘g6 20 ♖e5? (better is 20 ♖eh3! ±)
20...♕xe5! 21 ♗xe5 ♘xh4 22 ♗d6
♖d8 23 ♗e7 ♖d4 24 ♗xh4 e5! 25
♕e2? ♖xh4 26 ♕xe5 ♗e6 27 g3 ♖a4
28 h4 ♔g8 29 h5 h6 30 ♗c2 ♖c4 0-1
Ivanović-Mirković, Yugoslav Ch
1991.

**15 ♖c5 ♕a3 16 dxe5! ♕xc5 17
♗xf6**

17...♖e8?!

Black can draw with 17...gxf6 18
♕g4+ ♔h8 19 ♕h4 f5 20 ♕f6+ ♔g8
21 ♖e1 ♕c7! 22 ♖e3 ♖d8 =.

**18 ♗xh7+!! ♔xh7 19 ♕h5+ ♔g8
20 ♕g5 ♕f8 21 ♖d1! ± b6 22 ♖d4
♗a6 23 ♖g4 ♗e2 24 ♗xg7 ♗xg4 25
♗xf8+ ♔xf8 26 ♕xg4 ♖ac8 27 h4
♔e7 28 ♕g5+ ♔d7 29 ♕f4 a5 30
♕xf7+ ♔c6 31 ♕f3+ ♔c5 32 ♕e3+
♔c6 33 ♕f3+ ♔c5 34 ♕a3+**

White makes hard work of this
ending; in fact while watching the
end of this game I had the nagging
feeling that Black was going to 'pull
off a result'.

**34...♔c4 35 ♕b3+ ♔c5 36 a4!
♖b8 37 ♕c3+ ♔d5 38 f4 ♔e4 39
♕f3+?! ♔d4 40 ♕c6 ♔e3 41
♕c1+?! ♔e2 42 h5 ♖ec8 43 ♕f1+
♔d2 44 ♕b5 ♔e3 45 g3 ♔d4 46
♔g2 ♔c3 47 h6?! ♖h8 48 ♕d7 b5
49 axb5 a4 50 b6 a3 51 ♕a4 ♔b2 52
♕b4+ ♔a2 53 h7 ♖bc8 54 b7 ♖c2+
55 ♔f3 ♖b2 56 ♕c5 ♖b3+ 57 ♔g4
♔b2 58 ♕c8 ♖xh7 59 b8♕ ♖g7+ 60
♔h5 ♖gxg3 61 ♕d6 ♖h3+ 62 ♔g6
♖bg3+ 63 ♔f7 ♖h7+ 64 ♔xe6
♖h6+ 65 ♔f5 ♖xd6 66 exd6 a2 67
d7 a1♕ 68 ♕b7+ 1-0**

Game 117

Speelman-Kosten
English Ch 1991

1 d4 ♘f6 2 c4 e6 3 ♘c3 ♗b4 4 e3
0-0 5 ♗d3 d5 6 ♘f3 c5 7 0-0 dxc4 8
♗xc4 ♘bd7 9 ♘e2 ♘b6?!

During the game I was undecided
as to whether to follow *ECO's* recommendation 9...♘b6, or to play

Karpov's 10...♕e7. In retrospect 9...cxd4 10 ♘exd4 is superior, with the following possibilities:

⇨ 10...♕e7!? 11 a3 ♗d6 12 ♘b5 ♗b8 13 ♗d2 a6 14 ♗b4 ♘c5 (this pin is not too dangerous) 15 ♘c3 ♗d7 16 ♕d4 ♖c8 17 a4 ♗a7 18 ♕h4 ♗c6 19 ♘e5 ♗e8 20 ♗e2 ♕c7 21 ♘c4 ♖d8?! (missing 21...♘d5! 22 ♘xd5 exd5 23 ♘d2 ♘xa4 ∓) 22 a5 ± ♘b3 23 ♖ad1 ♗c5 24 ♗xc5 ♘xc5 25 ♕g3?! (25 ♘b6!) 25...♕xg3 26 hxg3 ♗c6 = 27 f3 ♘b3! 28 e4 ♔f8 29 ♔f2 ♔e7 30 ♔e3 ♘h5 31 ♔f2 ♘f6 32 ♖xd8 ♖xd8 33 ♗d1? ♘d2 ∓ 34 ♘d5+ exd5 35 ♘xd2 dxe4 36 ♘b1 exf3 37 ♗xf3 ♗xf3 38 gxf3 ♖d5 39 ♘c1 ♖b5 40 ♖c2 ♔d7 41 ♘c3 ♖xa5 42 ♖d2+ ♔e7 43 g4 ♖c5 44 ♔e3 h6 45 ♔d4 ♖c6 46 ♖g2 ♖d6+ 47 ♔e5 ♘d7+ 48 ♔f4 ♘c5 49 ♖e2+ ♔d7 50 ♔g3 ♖d3 51 ♖e5 ♘e6 52 ♘e4 ♔c6 53 ♖f5 f6 54 ♘xf6 ♘d4! 55 ♘h5 ♘xf5+ 56 gxf5 ♖d7 57 ♔f4 ♖e7 0-1 Beliavsky-Karpov, Reggio Emilia 1989/90.

⇨ 10...♕c7 11 ♗e2! ♖d8 12 ♗d2 ♗f8! 13 ♖c1 ♕b6 14 ♕c2 ♘c5 15 ♘e5 ♘ce4 16 ♗e1 ♕c5 17 ♘c4?! ♗d7! 18 ♗f3?! ♕d5! (another unusual self-pin) 19 ♘d2 ♖ac8 20 ♕b1 ♖xc1 21 ♕xc1 e5 22 ♘xe4 ♘xe4 23 ♘e2 ♕d3? (better is 23...♗c6! ∓, based on the pretty point 24 ♘c3 ♘xc3 25 ♗xd5? ♘e2+) 24 ♗a5! = ♖c8 25 ♕d1 ♘c5 26 ♕xd3 ♘xd3 27 ♗c3 ♗c6 28 ♗xc6 ♖xc6 29 ♖d1 ♖d6! (and not 29...♘xb2? 30 ♗xb2 ♖c2 31 ♗c3! ♖xe2 32 ♗d2 trapping the rook) 30 ♘g3 b5 31 a3 f6 32 ♘e4 ♖d7 33 ♔f1 ♘c5 34 ♖xd7 ♘xd7 35 ♗a5?! ♔f7 36 ♔e2 ♗e7?! 37 ♘c3 a6 38 ♘d5 ♗d6 39 ♗b4 ♔e6 40 e4

♗xb4 41 ♘xb4 ♘c5 42 ♔e3 ♔d6 43 ♘d3 ♘b3! ∓ 44 f4! a5 45 fxe5 fxe5 46 ♘e1 a4 47 ♘f3 ♘c5 48 ♘g5 h6 49 ♘f7+ ♔e6 ½-½ Speelman-Beliavsky, Reykjavik 1991.

10 ♗d3 cxd4 11 e4!

Better than 11 ♘exd4 ♖e8 12 ♕b3 ♗f8 =.

11...♖e8 12 e5 ♘fd7 13 ♘exd4 ♘f8 14 ♗e4 ♘d5 15 ♕b3 ♗c5 16 ♖d1 h6 17 h3 b6 18 ♗e3 ♕e7

18...♗b7? fails to 19 ♘xe6! fxe6 20 ♗xc5 ±.

19 ♖ac1

Or 19 ♗xd5 exd5 20 ♕xd5 ♗b7 when Black will have no trouble capturing the e-pawn.

19...♘xe3 20 fxe3?!

Up to this stage I had been under considerable pressure, but I think that 20 ♕xe3 is better, as the text allows a freeing exchange 'sacrifice'.

20...♗a6

Forced anyway, since 20...♗b7? 21 ♗xb7 ♕xb7 22 ♖xc5 wins.

21 ♗xa8 ♖xa8 22 ♘c6?! ♕c7 23 ♘fd4 ♗b7 24 ♕c3 a5 25 ♘xa5

If White didn't have this, he would lose a piece.

25...♖xa5 26 b4 ♖xa2 27 ♖c2 ♖xc2 28 ♕xc2 ♕xe5 29 bxc5 bxc5 ∓ 30 ♘b5 ♕xe3+ 31 ♕f2 ♕b3

After the exchange of queens Black will lose the c-pawn, with a draw.

32 ♖f1 f6?!

32...f5 would avoid what follows.

33 ♘d6 c4??

A time-trouble blunder that deserves to lose.

34 ♕a7 ♗d5 35 ♕f7+

My opponent felt that 35 ♖xf6! was winning but had insufficient time to analyse it.

35...♔h7 36 ♘e8 ♕e3+ 37 ♖f2

Not 37 ♔h2 ♕e5+ 38 g3?? ♕e2+ mating.

37...♕e1+ 38 ♖f1

White risks being worse if he tries 38 ♔h2 ♕e5+ 39 g3 f5 40 ♕xf8 ♕a1.

38...♕e3+ 39 ♖f2 ♕e1+ 40 ♖f1 ♕e3+ ½-½

Game 118

Kir.Georgiev-Ribli
Novi Sad OL 1990

1 d4 ♘f6 2 c4 e6 3 ♘c3 ♗b4 4 e3 0-0 5 ♗d3 c5 6 ♘f3 d5 7 0-0 dxc4 8 ♗xc4 ♘bd7 9 ♕b3 a6

⇨ 9...b6 10 d5 e5?! (10...♗xc3 11 dxe6 ♗a5! 12 exd7 ♕xd7 =) 11 ♖d1 ♗xc3 12 ♕xc3 e4 13 ♘g5 h6 14 ♘e6! fxe6 15 dxe6 ± ♔h8 16 exd7 ♗xd7 17 b3 ♕e7 18 ♗b2 with some advantage for White; G.Georgadze-Magay, Manila OL 1992.

10 a4 ♕e7

The most accurate; 10...♖b8 11

♖d1 ♕c7 12 ♗d2 b6 13 ♖ac1 ♗b7 14 ♗e2 ♗xc3 15 ♗xc3 ♘e4 16 ♗e1 ♗d5 17 ♕a3 ♕b7 18 ♘e5 ♘ef6 19 ♘xd7 ♘xd7 20 f3 cxd4 21 e4 ♗c6 22 ♖xd4 ± Portisch-Sax, Moscow 1990.

11 ♖d1 ♖d8

Or 11...♗a5 and now:

⇨ 12 ♕c2 h6 13 b3 cxd4 14 exd4 ♘b6 15 ♘e5 ♖d8 16 ♖d3 ♘bd5 17 ♘a2 ♘e4 18 ♖h3 ♘df6 19 ♗b2 ♕c7 20 ♕e2 ♗b6 21 ♖d1 ♗d7 22 ♖f3 ♗e8 23 ♖f4 ♘g5 24 ♖xf6! (initiating a dangerous attack) 24...gxf6 25 ♘g4 ♘h7 26 ♘xh6+ ♔h8 27 ♕g4 ♗c6 28 d5 ♗xd5 29 ♗xd5 ♖xd5 30 ♖xd5 exd5 31 ♘b4 ♖f8 32 h4 ♕e7 33 ♘d3 ♕e4 34 ♕g3 d4 35 ♗a3 ♕g6 36 ♗xf8 ♘xf8 37 ♕xg6 fxg6 38 ♘f7+ ♔g7 39 ♘d6 ♘d7 40 ♘xb7 ♘e5 41 a5 ♗a7 42 ♘xe5 fxe5 43 b4 d3 44 ♔f1 d2 45 ♔e2 ♗xf2 46 ♘c5 ♔f7 47 ♘xa6 ♖xh4 48 ♘c5 ♗d8 49 ♘d7 1-0 Spraggett-Suba, Roses 1992.

⇨ 12 dxc5?! ♘xc5 13 ♕a3 ♗d8 14 b4 ♘cd7 15 e4 b5! 16 axb5 ♘b6 17 ♗e2 axb5 18 ♕b2 ♘a4 19 ♘xa4 bxa4 20 ♗e3 ♘xe4 ∓ 21 ♘d2 ♗b7 22 ♗b5 ♕f6 23 ♗d4 ♕g5 24 ♘xe4 ♗xe4 25 ♗f1 ♗e7 and White managed to draw after a hard struggle in Semkov-Suba, Sitges 1992.

12 ♗d2 ♘b6?!

Better is 12...♗a5.

13 ♗e2 cxd4 14 exd4 ± h6 15 a5! ♘bd5 16 ♘e5 ♗d7!? 17 ♗f3 ♗d6!

17...♗c6? is a mistake: 18 ♘xd5 ♘xd5 19 ♗xd5 ♗xd2 20 ♗xc6 winning.

18 ♘xd5 exd5

18...♘xd5! 19 ♗xd5 exd5 20 ♕xd5 ♗g4 =.

19 ♘xd7!

Not 19 ♗xd5? ♗xe5 20 dxe5 ♘xd5 21 ♕xd5 ♗g4 picking up the exchange.

19...♕xd7 20 ♖ac1 ♖ac8 21 g3 ± ♘e4 22 ♗e3 ♕b5!? 23 ♕xb5 axb5 24 ♗e2 ♗b4 25 ♗xb5 ♗xa5 26 ♗d3 ♗b6 27 h4 ♘d6 28 b3 ♖a8 29 ♖a1 ♖dc8 30 ♔f1 ♔f8 31 ♔e2 ♔e7 32 ♖a4! ♖xa4 33 bxa4 ♖a8 34 ♖b1 ♗c7 35 ♗c2 ♖d8 36 g4 ♔e6 37 ♖c1?! ♗b6 38 ♖b1 ♗a5 39 ♗f4 ♖c8 40 ♗d3 b6 41 ♖c1 ♖xc1 42 ♗xc1 ♗c3 43 ♗e3 ♘c4?!

43...♔d7-c6 with the idea of ...b5 would be somewhat simpler. Once the pawns are all on one wing the knight comes into its own.

44 ♗xc4 dxc4 45 d5+! ♔xd5 46 ♗xb6 ♗d4! 47 ♗d8!?

The king and pawn ending after 47 ♗xd4 ♔xd4 48 ♔d2 c3+ 49 ♔c2 ♔c4 50 a5 ♔b5 51 ♔xc3 ♔xa5 52 ♔c4 ♔b6 53 ♔d5 ♔c7 is drawn.

47...c3! 48 ♔d3 ♗xf2 49 ♔xc3

49...♔e4

49...♔d6! 50 ♔d3 ♔d7 51 ♔e2 ♗g3 52 ♔f3 ♗e1 53 ♔e2 =.

50 ♔c4 ♗e1 51 ♗e7! ♔e5?

The final mistake; 51...f5! 52 gxf5 ♔xf5 53 h5 g5! 54 hxg6 ♔xg6 55 ♗b4 ♗g3 56 a5 h5 57 a6 ♗b8 58 ♗d6 ♗a7 59 ♔c5 ♗b8 60 ♔d5 h4 61 ♔c6 h3 62 ♗g1 ♗a7! =.

52 ♗b4 ± ♗xb4 53 ♔xb4 h5 54 gxh5 ♔d6 55 ♔c4 ♔c6 56 ♔d4 ♔b6 57 ♔e5 1-0

Game 119

Göhring-Ribli
Bundesliga 1989

1 d4 ♘f6 2 c4 e6 3 ♘c3 ♗b4 4 e3 0-0 5 ♘f3 c5 6 ♗d3 d5 7 0-0 dxc4 8 ♗xc4 ♘bd7 9 a3 cxd4!

⇨ 9...♗xc3 10 bxc3 b6 11 ♖e1 ♗b7 12 ♗d3 ♗e4 (12...♘e4 is also slightly better for White) 13 ♗f1 ♕c7 14 ♘d2 ♗g6 15 ♗b2 e5 16 e4 ♖ad8 (16...cxd4 17 cxd4 exd4 18 ♗xd4 ♘c5 is unclear) 17 d5 ♘e8 18 c4 ♘d6 19 a4 (although d6 is a good blockading square for Black's knight, White's bishop on b2 will become very strong if he can play f4 at some stage, opening the a1-h8 diagonal. The immediate 19 f4 exf4 20 e5 ♘f5 21 ♕f3 ♘e3 is unclear) 19...♖de8 20 ♖a3 f5 (Black decides not to hang around) 21 exf5 ♘xf5 22 ♗d3 ♕d6 23 ♕g4 (23 ♘e4!? ♕e7 24 ♘g3) 23...h6 24 ♕g5 ♗xd3 25 ♖xd3 ♘f5 26 ♘e4 ♕e7 27 ♕xe7 ♖xe7 28 ♖f3?! ♘d4 29 ♖xf8+ ♔xf8 30 f3 ♘f6 (with equality) 31 ♔f2 ♔e8 32 ♘d6+ ♔d7 33 ♘b5 a6 34 ♘c3 ♘e8 35 ♘e4 ♘d6 36 ♘xd6 ♔xd6 37 ♖b1 ♖b7 38 ♖a1 ♘b3 39 ♖e1 ♘d4 ½-½ Korchnoi-Hübner, Manila IZ 1990.

10 exd4 ♗xc3 11 bxc3 ♕c7 12 ♕d3

⇨ 12 ♕e2 b6 (12...♘b6 13 ♗d3 ♘bd5 14 c4 ♘f4 =) 13 ♗d2 ♗b7 14 ♗d3 ♖fe8 (14...♘d5 15 ♕e4 ♘5f6 16 ♕e2 ♘d5 17 ♕e4 ½-½ Zudov-Tal, Leningrad 1991) 15 ♖fe1 ♘d5 16 ♘e5 ♘xe5 17 dxe5 ♘e7 18 ♕h5 ♘g6 19 ♖e3 ♖ed8 20 ♖h3!? (can this really be sound?) 20...♕c6 21 ♕xh7+ ♔f8 22 f3 ♖xd3 23 ♗g5 ♕c5+ 24 ♔h1 ♔e8 25 ♕xg7 ♕xa3 26 ♖g1 ♕f8 27 ♕f6 ♖ad8 28 ♖h7 ♖8d5 29 ♖h6 (threatening ♖xg6) 29...♖xe5 30 ♖xg6 ♖f5 31 ♖g8! ♖xf6 32 ♖xf8+ ♔xf8 33 ♗xf6 ♖d5 34 ♖a1 e5 (the way the game ends makes me think that Black was in time-trouble) 35 h3 a5 36 ♖b1 b5 37 c4 ♖d6 38 ♗xe5 ♖e6 39 ♖xb5 a4 40 ♖xb7 ♖xe5 41 ♖a7 ♖e1+ 42 ♔h2 1-0 Brunner-Ćirić, Suhr 1992.

12...b6!?

⇨ I prefer 12...e5! 13 dxe5 ♘xe5 14 ♘xe5 ♕xe5 15 f4!? (more combative than 15 ♕g3 ♕xg3 16 hxg3 ♗e6! ∓, or 15 ♕d4 ♕xd4 16 cxd4 ♗e6! 17 ♗xe6 fxe6 ∓) 15...♕a5 16 ♕d4 ♖e8 17 ♗a2 ♖e4 18 ♕d2 ♗e6 19 ♗xe6 ♖xe6 20 ♖b1 ♖d8 21 ♖b5 ♖xd2 22 ♖xa5 ♖c2 23 ♖xa7 h5 24 ♔h1 ♖ee2 25 ♖g1 ♘e4 (Black polishes his opponent off with a nice combination) 26 h3 ♘g3+ 27 ♔h2 ♘f1+ 0-1 Boguslavsky-Kholmov, Voskresensk 1992. 28 ♖xf1 ♖xg2+ gives mate, and otherwise the bishop is lost.

13 ♖e1

⇨ 13 ♗a2 ♗b7 14 ♗g5 ♘e4 (14...b5! 15 ♖fe1 ♗d5 16 ♗b1 ♖fc8 17 ♗d2 ♕c4 with good play for Black thanks to his light-squared grip; Neverov-

Krzywicki, Katowice 1992) 15 c4 ♘xg5 16 ♘xg5 ♘f6 17 ♕g3 ♕xg3 18 hxg3 ♖fd8 19 ♖fd1 ♖d7 20 ♖d2 ♖ad8 21 ♖ad1 h6 22 ♘h3 ♘e4 23 ♖d3 e5! (hanging pawns lose their dynamism when one of them is forced to advance) 24 d5 ♘d6 25 ♖e3 e4 26 ♘f4 ♗a6 27 ♖c1 ♖c8 28 ♖ec3 ♖dc7 29 ♘e2 ♗xc4 ∓ Karpman-Levin, Belgrade 1992.

13...♗b7 14 ♗a2 ♖ac8 15 ♗d2

15 ♗b2?! ♗d5 ∓.

15...♗d5 16 ♗b1

Naturally White must try to avoid the exchange of light-squared bishops, but c4 and d5 are already in the hands of Black.

16...♖fd8 17 ♘e5 ♘f8 18 ♕h3 ♘e8!

Played to repel White's active knight.

19 ♗d3 f6 20 ♘g4 ♘d6 21 ♕g3 ♘g6 22 ♘e3 ♗e4 23 ♗f1 ♕f7 24 f3 ♗b7 25 a4 e5 26 a5 b5 27 a6 ♗c6 28 ♕f2 e4 29 f4 ♘e7 30 ♖ab1 ♘d5 31 ♘xd5 ♕xd5

It is instructive to see how Ribli has gained complete light-square control.

32 ♗e3 ♖c7 33 ♖b4 ♖dc8 34 ♕d2 ♗d7 35 ♖c1 ♖c6 0-1

White's a-pawn is lost, and he has no active play.

Game 120

Semkov-Kosten
Metz 1992

1 d4 ♘f6 2 c4 e6 3 ♘c3 ♗b4 4 e3 0-0 5 ♗d3 d5 6 ♘f3 c5 7 0-0 dxc4 8 ♗xc4 ♘bd7 9 a3 cxd4! 10 ♘b5!?

White may instead try 10 axb4 dxc3 11 bxc3 ♕c7 12 ♕e2 (12 ♕b3 might be preferable) 12...♘b6 13 ♗d3 e5 14 e4 ♗e6:

⇨ 15 ♗e3 ♘fd7 16 ♖fc1 (16 c4! ♗xc4 17 ♖fc1 is unclear) 16...♖fc8 17 ♘d2 ♕d6 18 ♗b5 a6 19 ♗xd7 ♘xd7 20 f3 b5 21 ♖a3 ♖c6 ∓ 22 ♘b3 ♗xb3 23 ♖xb3 ♕c7 24 ♖a3 h6 25 ♕a2 ♘f8 26 c4!? soon fizzled out to equality, though Black managed to win a long endgame, in Villeneuve-Kosten, Torcy 1991.

⇨ 15 ♖a5 ♘fd7 16 ♘g5 ♗c4 17 f4 a6 18 fxe5 ♗xd3 19 ♕xd3 ♘c4 20 e6 fxe6 21 ♖xf8+ ♖xf8 22 e5 g6 23 ♕h3 ♕b6+ 24 ♖c5 h5 25 ♘e4 ♘xc5 26 bxc5 ♕b1 27 ♕xe6+ ♔h8 28 h3 ♕xc1+ 29 ♔h2 ♕f4+ 30 ♘g3 h4 0-1 Tsemekhman-Anapolsky, Duisburg 1992.

10...♗e7 11 ♘bxd4 e5 12 ♘f5 ♘b6 13 ♘xe7+ ♕xe7 14 ♗e2 ♖d8

I feel that Black's lead in development and space advantage more than compensate for the two bishops.

15 ♗d2 ♗g4 16 ♖c1 h6

After the game my opponent told

me that this is an improvement over a Russian game that he had seen.

17 ♕e1

White is forced to squirm around.

17...♘bd5 18 ♖c4 ♕e6 19 ♕c1 ♘e7!?

I thought that the coming combination was winning for me.

20 ♗b4 e4 21 ♗xe7

21 ♘d4? ♖xd4 22 ♗xg4 ♕xc4 is good for Black.

21...♕xe7 22 ♖c7

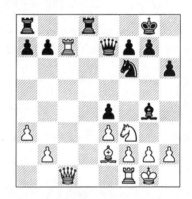

22...exf3!! 23 ♖xe7 fxe2 24 ♖e1 ♖d1 25 f3!

25 ♕c3 ♘d5 ∓.

25...♖xc1 26 ♖xc1 ♗d7 27 ♔f2 ♗b5

27...♗c6 ∓.

28 ♖xb7 a6?

28...♗a6! 29 ♖b4 ♖d8 30 ♖d4 ♖xd4 31 exd4 ♘d5 is probably winning; the rook is tied to the back rank to stop tricks like ...♘e3xg2, and the black king can advance.

29 a4! ♗xa4 30 ♔xe2 ♗b5+ 31 ♔f2 ♖d8 32 ♖c2 g5 33 e4 ♘h5 34 g3 ♘f6 35 e5 ♘e8 36 ♖b6 ♔g7 37 f4 ♖d5 38 ♔e3 ♖d7??

38...♖d3+ is equal, but pressing

for a win in time-trouble, I allow the exchange of rooks.

39 ♖d2 ♖xd2 40 ♔xd2 gxf4 41 gxf4 ♘c7 42 ♖d6 ♘e8 43 ♖b6 ♘c7 44 f5 ± ♘d5 45 ♖d6 ♘b4 46 ♔e3 ♘c6 47 ♔e4 ♘a5 48 ♖d8 ♘b3 49 ♖c8 a5 50 ♖c7 ♗e8 51 h4 a4 52 ♔d5 ♘d2 53 ♖c3 ♗d7 54 ♖d3 ♘b3 55 ♖g3+ ♔f8 56 e6 ♗b5 57 ♔d6 fxe6 58 fxe6 ♘d4 59 ♔d5 ♘e2 60 ♖e3 ♗a6 61 ♔d6 ♘d4 62 ♖e4 ♘b5+ 63 ♔d7 ♗c8+ 64 ♔xc8 ♘d6+ 65 ♔d8 1-0

Game 121

Ivanchuk-Speelman
Reykjavik 1991

1 e4 c6 2 d4 d5 3 exd5 cxd5 4 c4 ♘f6 5 ♘c3 e6 6 ♘f3 ♗b4 7 ♗d3 dxc4 8 ♗xc4 0-0 9 0-0 ♘bd7 10 ♕e2

From a pure Nimzo-Indian move-order (4 e3 0-0 5 ♗d3 d5 6 ♘f3 c5 7 0-0 dxc4 8 ♗xc4 ♘bd7 9 ♕e2), 9...a6 10 a4 ♘b6 11 ♗d3 cxd4 12 exd4 ♘bd5 transposes directly to the main game, whilst alternatively:
⇨ 10 a3 ♗a5!? 11 ♗a2 cxd4 12 exd4 ♗xc3! (Kasparov's recipe; now that the bishop is on a2 there is less pressure on b5) 13 bxc3 b5 14 a4 ♗b7 15 ♗b1 ♕c7 16 ♗d2 ♗d5 17 ♗d3 ♗c4 18 ♘e1 ♘b6 19 ♘c2? (losing a pawn, but White was worse anyway) 19...♗xd3 20 ♕xd3 ♘xa4 21 ♘b4 ♕b7 22 ♖a2 ♖fc8 23 ♖b1 ♘e4 0-1 Lesiège-Kosten, Hyères 1992.
⇨ 10 ♖d1 b5 11 ♗d3 ♗b7 12 ♗d2 cxd4 13 exd4 ♘b6 14 ♗g5 ♗e7 15 a3 ♘fd5 16 ♘e4?! ♗xg5 17 ♘fxg5

♘f4 18 ♕g4? ♘xd3 19 ♖xd3 ♗xe4 0-1 Iashvili-Dorfman, Oviedo (Active) 1992.

10...a6 11 a4 ♘b6 12 ♗d3 ♘bd5 13 ♘xd5 exd5 14 ♗g5 ♕d6! 15 ♘e5 ♘e4 16 ♗f4 ♕e7! 17 f3 ♘d6 18 ♕f2 ♗f5! 19 ♗xf5 ♘xf5 20 ♘d3 ♗d6!

20...♖ac8 21 g4! ♘h4 22 ♗g3 ♘g6 23 h4 would allow White a certain kingside initiative.

21 ♖fe1 ♕d8 22 ♗xd6 ♕xd6! 23 a5?! ♖ac8! ∓ 24 ♖ad1! ♖c7 25 ♘c5 ♘xd4 26 ♘xa6 ♕xa6

26...♘xf3+ 27 ♕xf3 bxa6 28 ♕xd5 ♕b4! ∓.

27 ♕d4 ♕xa5 ½-½

Game 122

Korchnoi-Sax
Skellefteå 1989

1 d4 ♘f6 2 c4 e6 3 ♘c3 ♗b4 4 e3 0-0 5 ♗d3 d5 6 ♘f3 c5 7 0-0 dxc4 8 ♗xc4 ♘bd7 9 ♕e2

⇨ 9 ♗d3 is an important option: 9...b6 10 a3 (10 ♘e4?! cxd4 11 exd4 ♗b7 12 ♘g3 ♗d6 13 ♕e2 ♖c8 14 ♘e5 ♘xe5 ∓ 15 dxe5 ♗xe5 16 ♗xh7+ ♔xh7 17 ♕xe5 ♕d5 18 ♕xd5 ♘xd5 and the c-file and d5 square grant Black some advantage; F.Portisch-Siklosi, Hungary 1992) 10...cxd4 11 exd4 ♗xc3 12 bxc3 ♕c7 13 ♗d2 ♗b7 14 ♖e1 ♖fe8 (I consider Farago's 14...♖ad8! 15 ♘e5 ♘xe5 16 ♖xe5 ♖d5! to be Black's best line) 15 ♘e5 ♖ad8!? 16 f4 ♘f8! 17 ♕c2! (17 ♕e2 ♘d5 18 ♖ac1 f6) 17...♘d5 18 f5 exf5 19 ♗xf5 f6?! (Black will pay later for the weakening of e6; better is 19...♘g6! =) 20 ♘f3 ♘e7 21 ♗e4 ♗xe4 22 ♖xe4 ♘c6 23 c4 (23 ♖ae1?! ♖xe4 24 ♕xe4 ♘a5 ∓) 23...♖xe4 24 ♕xe4 ♘b8 25 d5 ♖c8 26 ♖c1 ♕c5+ 27 ♘d4! (27 ♕e3 ♕xe3+ 28 ♗xe3 ♘bd7 =) 27...♕xa3 28 ♘f5 ♖d8 (28...♔h8 29 ♘xg7 ♔xg7 30 ♕g4+ ♔h8 31 ♕xc8 ±) 29 ♖e1! (while Black's pieces are languishing on the back rank, White prepares an attack) 29...♘bd7 30 ♕e7 ♕c5+ 31 ♖e3 ± ♕xe7 32 ♖xe7 ♘e5 33 ♖xg7+ ♔h8 34 ♖c7 (34 ♗h6?! ♘fd7! 35 ♖e7 ♔g8 36 ♗g7 ♘f7 ∓) 34...♘fd7 35 ♗c3 a5 36 ♘d6 ♔g8 37 ♘e4 ♖f8 38 h3! a4 39 ♖a7 a3 40 ♘d6 f5 41 ♖xa3 f4 42 ♗d4 h6 43 ♖a7 f3 44 g3 h5 45 ♔f1 ♖d8 46 ♗xe5 ♘xe5 47 ♖e7 ♘d3 (47...♘g6 48 ♖e6 ♘f8 49 ♖f6 ♔g7 50 ♘e4 ♖e8 51 ♖f4 ♘g6 52 ♘d6 ±) 48 ♖e3 ♘b2 49 ♖b3 ♘d1 50 ♖xb6 f2 51 ♖b1 ♘c3 52 ♖b3 ♘d1 53 ♖d3 1-0 Gulko-Lobron, Manila IZ 1990.

9...b6 10 d5 ♗xc3 11 dxe6 ♘e5 12 exf7+ ♔h8 13 bxc3 ♗g4 14 e4 ♕e7

⇨ 14...♘h5 15 ♗d5 ♕f6!? (the example 15...♕c8?! 16 ♔h1 ♗xf3 17 gxf3 ♕h3 18 ♖g1 ♘xf3 19 ♖g2 ♖ad8 20 c4 ♘h4 21 ♖g1 ♘f3 22 ♖g2 ♘h4 23 ♖g1 ½-½ Muir-Greenfeld, Haifa 1989, was quoted as an interesting method of securing the draw, but what, I wonder, had Black planned against 23 ♖g3! ♘xg3+ 24 fxg3 ♘g6 25 ♗b2 when White has a serious advantage?) 16 ♗g5 ♘xf3+! (not 16...♕xg5 17 ♘xg5 ♗xe2 18 f4 ♘g6 19 ♖fe1 ♗d3 20 ♗xa8 ±) 17 gxf3 ♕xg5 18 fxg4 ♘f4 (now Black sets in motion an interesting attack

on the dark squares and it's not clear how White can defend) 19 ♕f3 ♖ad8 20 c4 (perhaps 20 ♖fe1!?) 20...♕e5 21 ♔h1 ♖d6 22 ♕g3 ♖h6 23 g5 ♖h3 24 ♕g4 g6! 25 ♖g1 ♔g7 26 ♖ae1 h5! 27 gxh6+ ♖xh6 ∓ 28 ♕f5 ♖xh2+! 29 ♔xh2 ♖h8+ 30 ♔g3 gxf5 31 ♔f3+ ♘g6 32 ♖xg6+ ♔xg6 33 ♖g1+ ♔f6 34 ♖g8 ♔e7 35 ♔g2 ♕h2+ 36 ♔f1 ♕h1+ 37 ♖g1 ♕h3+ 38 ♔e1 ♕c3+ 0-1 Lesiège-Pogorelov, Cannes 1992.

15 ♖e1 b5 16 ♗xb5 ♘h5 17 ♗c4!?

⇨ 17 ♗g5 ♕e6 18 ♕e3 ♗xf3 19 gxf3 ♕xf7 20 ♗e2 ♘g6 21 f4 is interesting, but not 17 ♗e8? which has been known to be a mistake since Knaak-Farago, Sochi 1980. A correspondence game Lujambio-Lopepe, 1989, continued 17...♖axe8! 18 fxe8♕ ♕xe8 19 ♕e3 ♗xf3 20 gxf3 ♘xf3+ 21 ♔f1 ♘xh2+ 22 ♔g2 ♘f3 23 ♖d1 ♕g6+ 24 ♔f1 ♕g1+ 25 ♔e2 ♘g3+! 0-1 because of 26 fxg3 ♕g2+ 27 ♕f2 ♘g1+ 28 ♔d3 ♕xf2.

17...♕f6 18 ♗d5

18 ♗g5! ♗xf3 19 ♗xf6 ♗xe2 20 ♗d5 gxf6 21 ♗xa8 ♗d3 22 ♗d5 ♘f4 23 ♖e3 Knaak-Lukacs, Berlin 1982, might be best.

18...h6 19 ♕e3 ♘xf3+ 20 gxf3 ♗xf3 21 ♔f1 ♖ad8!

21...♖xf7 22 ♗xf7 (22 ♗xa8? ♕g6!) 22...♕xf7 23 ♗a3 ♖e8 24 ♖ad1 ♖xd1 25 ♖xd1 ♕xa2 26 ♗xc5 ♕c4+ 27 ♔g1 ♖xe4 28 ♖d4! ♖g4+ is only equal.

22 e5?

White should play 22 ♗e6!.

22...♕a6+ 23 c4 ♗xd5 24 e6 ♕xc4+ 25 ♖e2 ♕g4! 26 ♗b2 ♘f4 ∓ 27 e7

27...♗c4 28 exf8♕+ ♖xf8 29 f3
♗xe2+ 30 ♔e1 ♕h4+ 31 ♔d2
♕d8+ 32 ♔c2 ♗d3+ 33 ♔c1 ♖xf7
34 ♗e5 ♕a5 35 a4 ♕b4 0-1

Game 123

Høi-Ernst
Copenhagen 1991

1 d4 ♘f6 2 c4 e6 3 ♘c3 ♗b4 4 e3
0-0 5 ♗d3 d5 6 ♘f3 c5 7 0-0 dxc4 8
♗xc4 ♘bd7 9 ♕e2 b6 10 ♖d1
⇨ 10 a3 cxd4 11 axb4 dxc3 12 bxc3
♕c7 13 ♗b2 ♗b7 14 ♗a6 ♗xa6 15
♖xa6 ♖fc8 16 ♖d1 h6 17 h3 ♕b7 18
b5 ♘c5 19 ♖aa1 a6 ± Beliavsky-
Karpov, Linares 1989.
⇨ 10 ♗d2 ♗b7 is seen occasionally:
11 ♖fd1 cxd4 12 ♘xd4 ♕e7 13
♖ac1 ♖ac8 14 a3 ♗d6 15 ♗a2 ♖fd8
16 f3 a6 17 e4 ♘e5 18 ♗e3 ♘fd7 19
f4 ♘c6 20 ♘f3 b5 21 b4 ♗c7 22 e5
♘cb8 23 ♘g5 ♗a8 (Black has allowed White to make significant
progress) 24 ♕c2 g6 25 ♕f2 h6 26
♘ge4 ♔g7 27 h3 ♘c6 28 ♘d6 ♗xd6
29 exd6 ♕f8 30 ♗b1 ♘f6 31 ♗c5
♖d7 32 a4 bxa4 33 ♘xa4 ♖b8 34

♘b6 ♖xb6 35 ♗xb6 ♖xd6 36 ♗c5
♖xd1+ 37 ♖xd1 ♕b8 38 ♗d6 ♕b5
39 ♕b2 a5 40 ♗d3 ♕d5 41 ♗e2
♘d4 42 ♗f1 ♘f3+ (the game becomes very exciting) 43 gxf3 ♕xd1
44 ♗e7 ♕xf3 45 ♗xf6+ ♔h7 46
bxa5 ♕xf4 47 ♕f2 ♕c7 48 ♗e5!
♕xe5 49 ♕xf7+ ♔h8 50 ♕f8+ ♔h7
51 ♕xa8 ♕e3+ 52 ♔h1 ♕e1 53
♕b7+ ♔h8 54 ♕b5 h5 55 a6 ♕a1 56
♔h2 e5 57 ♗g2 ♕d4 58 ♕b8+ ♔h7
59 ♕c7+ ♔h6 60 a7 1-0 Costa-
Brunner, Suhr 1992.

10...cxd4 11 exd4 ♗b7
⇨ 11...♗xc3 12 bxc3 ♕c7 13 ♗a3
♖e8 14 ♘e5 ♗b7 15 ♗d3 ♘f8 16 c4
♘g6 17 ♘xg6 hxg6 18 ♗b2 ♖ac8 19
f3 ♕f4! 20 ♕d2 ♕xd2 21 ♖xd2 ♗a6
(this type of ending is quite good for
Black as in the absence of queens,
the hanging pawns aren't so dynamic, and are therefore more of a
target) 22 ♖c1 ♘d7 23 ♔f2 ♘b8 24
d5 (it is probably wise to play this
before Black plays ...♘c6-a5 with
strong pressure on c4) 24...exd5 25
cxd5 ♖xc1 26 ♗xc1 ♖d8 27 ♗xa6
♘xa6 28 ♔e3 ♘c7 29 d6 (29 ♔e4
looks better to me as now the pawn
gets lured forward to its doom)
29...♘b5 30 d7 f6 31 a4 ♘c7 32 ♗a3
♔f7 33 ♗b4 ♘a6 34 ♗a3 ♘b8 35 a5
♖xd7 36 axb6 axb6 37 ♖c2 ♖a7 38
♗d6 ♘d7 ∓ Torre-Lobron, Manila
IZ 1990.

12 ♗g5
⇨ 12 ♘e5!? ♖c8 13 ♗g5 ♗xc3 14
bxc3 ♕c7 15 ♘xd7 ♘xd7 16 ♗b5
♗d5 17 ♕g4 f5 18 ♕h3 h6 19 c4!
♗xg2! 20 ♕xg2 hxg5 21 ♕xg5 ±
Skembris-Beliavsky, Haifa 1989.

12...♗xc3 13 bxc3 ♕c7 14 ♗d3
♕xc3

⇨ 14...h6 15 ♗d2 ♖fe8 16 ♖e1 ♖ac8 17 ♖ac1 ♕d6 18 a4 ♖ed8 19 ♗a6 ♕d5 20 ♗xb7 ♕xb7 21 ♕b5 ♘e4 22 c4 ♘xd2 23 ♘xd2 ♘c5! (no doubt overlooked by White) 24 dxc5 ♖xd2 25 cxb6 ♕xb6 26 c5 ♕xb5 27 axb5 ♖b2 28 b6 axb6 29 cxb6 ♖b8 30 ♖b1 ♖8xb6 31 ♖xb2 ♖xb2 32 h4! with a technical draw; Hübner-Suba, Manila OL 1992.

15 ♖ac1

⇨ 15 ♘e5 ♕a5 16 ♕e3 ♖fe8! (16...♕d5 17 ♕h3 h6 {17...g6!?} 18 ♗c4 ♕d6?! 19 ♗f4 ♕e7 20 ♖d3 ♘xe5 21 dxe5 ♘e4 22 ♗xh6!) 17 a4!? ♕d5 18 f3 ♘xe5! 19 ♕xe5 ♕xe5 20 dxe5 ♘d5 ∓ Brilla Banfalvi-Bang, corr. 1990.

15...♕a5 16 ♘e5 ♕d5 17 f4 ♖ac8 18 ♗c4 ♕d6 19 f5 ♘xe5 20 ♕xe5 ♕c6 21 d5 ♕c5+ 22 ♗e3 ♕b4 23 ♗d2 ♕c5+ 24 ♗e3 ♕a3 25 ♖c3 ♕a5 26 ♗d4 ♖xc4! 27 ♕xf6! ♖xd4

Obviously 27...gxf6?? allows immediate mate.

28 ♕xd4 ♕xd5 29 ♕xd5 ♗xd5 30 a4 g6 31 f6

After 31 fxe6 the game would be fairly equal, but White goes for more.

31...h6 32 ♖dc1 g5 33 ♖c8 ♖xc8 34 ♖xc8+ ♔h7 35 ♖c7 ♔g6 36

♖xa7 ♔xf6 37 ♖a6 ♗b3 38 ♔f2 ♔e5 39 ♔e3 f5 40 ♔d2 f4 41 ♔c3 ♗d5 42 ♖xb6 ♗xg2 43 a5 f3 44 ♖b2 ♔e4 45 a6 ♔e3 46 ♖f2 ♔xf2 47 a7

White has no doubt made the mistake, as one does, of assuming that he will draw easily with a queen more.

47...♔g1 48 a8♕

48...f2

An amazing position has arisen. Black is certainly not losing, but can he be winning? A queen for a bishop down!

49 ♕a7 e5 50 ♕e3 e4 51 ♔d4 ♗f3 52 h3 ♗h1 53 ♔e5 ♗g2 54 ♔f5 ♗f3 55 ♔g6 ♔g2 56 ♕d2 ♔g3 57 ♕c1 ♔xh3 58 ♔xh6 g4 59 ♔g5 ♔g2 60 ♕b2 e3 0-1

13

The heyday of the main line was in the 1950s, and a lot of the theory was established then. Nowadays it's not too common a sight.

In game 124 we examine 8 cxd5, which is an interesting method of avoiding the highly analysed variations. Also, after White's principal move 8 a3 most players will take on c3, but there are alternatives—in particular the trappy possibility 8...♗a5. Theoretically it does not have a good reputation, but over the board it can be very dangerous.

The system with 9...♕c7, considered in game 125, might be starting to catch on, as Black has been scoring well.

Another reliable move is 9...b6, and we consider this in game 126.

After 9...dxc4 10 ♗xc4 ♕c7 we reach the mainline proper. On move 11 White has a plethora of alternatives, and it is quite unclear which of these is best. Yusupov seems to think it's 11 ♗d3 and he certainly does well with it; witness game 127.

And finally, in game 128, we look at the other popular move, 11 ♗a2, and the alternatives.

Game 124

Lempert-Ionov
Moscow 1991

1 d4 ♘f6 2 c4 e6 3 ♘c3 ♗b4 4 e3 0-0 5 ♗d3 d5 6 ♘f3 c5 7 0-0 ♘c6 8 cxd5

Unusual. 8 a3 is almost invariably played, whereupon 8...♗xc3 takes up the rest of this chapter. Some rarer eighth move alternatives:

1) 8...dxc4 9 ♗xc4 cxd4 10 exd4 and:

➪ 10...♗e7 11 ♖e1 a6 12 ♗a2 b5?! (this is known to be a mistake; perhaps 12...♗d7 is more circumspect) 13 d5! (in the game Sinkovics-Blatny, Biel 1991 the players reached the identical position with a move less, continuing: 12 ♗g5?! ♗b7 13 ♖c1 ♖c8 14 ♗xf6? {a miscalculation} 14...♗xf6 15 ♘e4 ♗xd4! 16 ♖xc6 ♗xc6 17 ♘xd4 ♗xe4 18 ♖xe4 e5 0-1, due to 19 ♖xe5 ♕xd4) 13...♘xd5 14 ♘xd5 exd5 15 ♕xd5 ♗b7 16 ♕h5 ♕d6 17 ♗g5 ♖ad8 18 h4?! (18 ♖ac1 ♗xg5 19 ♘xg5 and 18 ♗xe7 ♘xe7 19 ♘g5 ♕g6 20 ♕xh7+ are both to White's advantage) 18...h6 19 ♗e3 ♕f6! 20 b4 ♗d6 21 ♖ad1 ♗c7 22 ♗c5 ♖xd1 23 ♖xd1 ♖d8 24 ♖e1 ♗c8 25 ♘g5? (25 ♗d5) 25...hxg5 26 hxg5 g6 27 ♕h6 ♕g7 28 ♕h4 ♗f5 29 g4 ♘e5 30 ♔g2 ♗xg4 31 ♖xe5 ♕xe5 32 ♕xg4 ♕h2+ 33 ♔f3 ♕h1+ 0-1 Razuvaev-Haba, Bundesliga 1991.

➪ 10...♗xc3 11 bxc3 h6?! (this is an unnecessary weakening of the king's protection; 11...♕a5 is normal) 12 ♕d3 b6 13 ♗f4 ♗b7 14 ♖fe1 ♘h5 15 ♗d2 ♕f6 16 ♗a2 ♘e7 17 ♘e5 ♘f4 18 ♕g3 (it seems that White has blundered his g-pawn, but in fact the coming complications end in his favour) 18...♘xg2 19 ♘xf7! ♘f5 20 ♘xh6+! ♕xh6 21 ♖xe6 ♘xg3 22 ♖xh6+ ♖f7 23 fxg3 gxh6 24 ♖f1 ♖af8 25 ♗xh6 ♔h7 26 ♗xf8 ♖xf1+

1-0 Clement-Carlier, Benidorm 1989.

2) 8...cxd4 9 cxd5!? (9 exd4 is simpler) 9...exd5 10 axb4 dxc3 11 b5 ♘b4 12 ♗e2 ♘e4 13 ♕b3 cxb2 14 ♗xb2 a5 15 bxa6 ♘xa6 16 ♕d1 ♗g4 17 h3 ♗h5 18 ♖a4 f6 19 ♕d4 ♖c8 20 ♖d1 ♘ac5 21 ♖b4 Speelman-Ljubojević, Linares 1991. The two bishops and better pawn structure give White some compensation for the pawn.

3) 8...♗a5 and now:

⇨ 9 cxd5 exd5 10 dxc5 ♗xc3 11 bxc3 ♕a5 12 ♕c2 (the main line) and now, in the game S.Hansen-Hector, Copenhagen 1991, Black tried 12...♗g4!? 13 ♘d4 ♕xc5 14 a4 ♖fc8 15 ♘xc6 ♖xc6 16 ♗d2 ♗h5 17 ♖fb1 ♖c7 18 ♖b4 ♗g6 19 ♖ab1 b6 20 f3 ♖e8 21 ♖b5 ♕c4! (an exclamation mark for humour) 22 e4 ♕c6 23 e5 ♘d7 24 f4 ♗e4 25 a5 bxa5 26 ♖xa5 ♘c5 27 ♗xe4 ♘xe4 =.

⇨ 9 h3 (novel) 9...♕e7!? (9...dxc4 10 ♗xc4 cxd4 11 exd4 ♗b6 is perfectly adequate) 10 ♕e2 ♖d8 11 ♖d1 cxd4 12 exd4 dxc4 13 ♗xc4 ♗b6 14 ♗g5 ♗xd4!? (rather risky; Black starts grabbing pawns but pays a heavy price) 15 ♘e4 h6 16 ♗h4 g5 17 ♗g3 ♘xe4 18 ♕xe4 ♗xb2 19 ♖xd8+ ♕xd8 20 ♖b1 ♗g7 21 h4! gxh4 22 ♗xh4 ♕d7 23 ♗g3 ♕e7 24 ♘e5 ♕c5 25 ♘xf7 ♘d4 26 ♘e5 ♘c6 27 ♘xc6 ♕xc6 28 ♕g6 ♕d7 29 ♗e5 ♕f7 30 ♕g3 ♔h8 31 ♖d1 ♔h7 32 ♖d8 h5 33 ♗d3+ 1-0 Høi-Hector, Tåstrup 1990.

8...exd5 9 ♘e5

⇨ 9 dxc5 is a strange idea: 9...♗g4 10 ♘a4 ♕e7 11 ♗e2 ♗xc5 12 ♘xc5 ♕xc5 13 b3 ♘e4 14 ♗b2 ♖ad8 15 ♖c1 ♕a5 16 a3 ♗xf3 17 ♗xf3?! (17

gxf3!?) 17...♘d2 18 b4 ♘xf3+ 19 ♕xf3 ♕b6 20 ♖fd1 d4 21 exd4 ♘xd4 22 ♕e3 ♘e6 23 ♕xb6 axb6 and Black was OK in Djurhuus-Sowray, Gausdal 1991.

9...♕d6!

⇨ 9...♕c7 can't be bad either. G.Georgadze-Abramović, Belgrade 1992 continued 10 ♘xc6 ♕xc6 11 a3 ♗xc3 12 bxc3 ♗g4 13 f3 ♗h5 14 a4 ♗g6 15 ♗b5 ♕c7 16 ♗a3 a6 17 ♗d3 ♖fe8 18 ♗xg6 hxg6 19 ♖e1 c4 20 ♕c2 ♕c6 21 a5 ♖ab8 22 ♗c5 ♘d7 23 ♗b4 f5 24 h3 ♖e6 25 g4 ♖be8 with a balanced position.

10 ♘xc6 bxc6 11 f3 c4 12 ♗c2 c5 13 ♕e1 ♗d7 14 ♕h4 ♖fe8 15 ♗d2 ♗a5 16 ♖ad1 ♖ab8 17 ♗c1 h6 18 ♔h1 ♗d8 19 ♕f2 ♗c7 20 g4 cxd4! 21 exd4 ♘h7 22 ♕g2! ♗c6! 23 ♘e2 ♘f8?

Better is 23...♕d7 24 ♘f4 ♖bd8 25 ♘h5.

24 ♘g3 ♕d7 25 ♘h5

The immediate threat is ♗xh6. White's kingside build-up is beginning to look dangerous.

25...♗d8 26 f4 ♘e6? 27 g5 hxg5 28 fxg5 g6 29 ♘f6+ ♗xf6 30 gxf6 ± ♘f8 31 ♗f5 ♕d6 32 ♗g5 ♘h7?

Black's position was starting to look a bit ropey anyway, but this loses on the spot.

33 &xg6 fxg6 34 f7+ ♔g7 35 &f4! ♕e6 36 &e5+ ♔h6 37 fxe8♕ &xe8 38 &de1 ♕d7 39 &e3 g5 40 &h3+ 1-0

Game 125

Portisch-Beliavsky
Amsterdam 1990

1 d4 ♘f6 2 c4 e6 3 ♘c3 &b4 4 e3 c5 5 &d3 ♘c6 6 ♘f3 d5 7 0-0 0-0 8 a3 &xc3 9 bxc3 ♕c7 10 cxd5

The most appropriate move. Others:

⇨ 10 ♕c2 (not particularly good) 10...&d7 11 cxd5 exd5 12 c4 dxc4 13 ♕xc4 ♘a5 14 ♕xc5 ♕xc5 15 dxc5 ♘b3 16 &b1 ♘xc5 = Meulders-Renet, Lyons Z 1990.

⇨ 10 ♕e2 dxc4 11 &xc4 e5 12 dxe5 ♘xe5 13 ♘xe5 ♕xe5 14 f4? (badly weakening e4) 14...♕e7 15 &d3 &e8 16 &e1 &g4 17 ♕c2 &ad8 18 h3 ♕d7! 19 &xh7+ ♘xh7 20 hxg4 ♕xg4 21 c4 ♕g3 22 ♕f2 ♕xf2+ 23 ♔xf2 &e4 ∓ Martinovsky-Dizdar, Groningen 1991.

⇨ 10 a4?! dxc4! 11 &xc4 b6 = was the actual move-order of the game Hübner-Lobron, which is dealt with later.

10...exd5 11 ♘h4

⇨ 11 &b2 &g4 12 ♕e1 &xf3 (12...&h5 followed by ....&g6 is sounder) 13 gxf3 ♕d7 14 ♔h1 ♕h3 15 ♕d1 cxd4 16 cxd4 ♕h4 17 ♕e2 ♘e7 18 &g1 ♘g6 19 &g3 ♘h5 20 &g4 ♕e7 21 &ag1 with a double-

edged position; Karpman-Magerramov, Podolsk 1989.

⇨ 11 a4 c4!? 12 &c2 &g4 13 ♕e1 &xf3 14 gxf3 ♕d7 15 ♕e2 &fe8 16 ♔h1 ♕h3 17 &g1 ♘h5 18 e4 &e6 19 &e3 ♘e7 20 &ab1 b6 21 &g5 &h6 22 &g4 ♘f6 23 &g2 &h5 24 e5 ♘e8 25 f4 f5 26 &d1 &h4 27 ♕f1 &h6 28 ♕g1 ∞ ½-½ Azmaiparashvili-Vaganian, Manila OL 1992.

⇨ 11 dxc5?! &g4 12 a4 ♘e5 13 &e2 ♘xf3+ 14 &xf3 &xf3 15 ♕xf3 &fe8 16 &b1 ♘e4 17 &b4 &ad8 18 h3 ♘xc5 was fine for Black in Fauland-Renet, Leukerbad 1992.

⇨ 11 h3 c4 12 &c2 ♘e7 13 ♘h2!? (planning f3 and later e4 or g4; 13 ♘e5 &f5 14 f3 &xc2 15 ♕xc2 ♘c6 16 ♘g4 ♘h5 17 e4 f5 18 exf5 ♘g3 19 &e1 ♘xf5 20 &g5 h6 21 &f6 ♕d7 22 ♘e5 ♘xe5 23 &xe5 {the bishop looks very imposing on e5} 23...&ae8 24 ♕f2 &e6 25 g4 ♘d6 26 &e3 ♘e4 27 ♕g2 ± Rodriguez-Dizdar, Barcelona 1991) 13...&f5 14 f3 &g6 15 &e1 &fe8 16 ♘f1 ♘c8 17 a4 ♘d6 18 &a3 &e6 19 ♕d2 &ae8 (again applying the required clamp on e4) 20 g4 &xc2 21 ♕xc2 h5 22 ♔g2 g6 23 ♕f2 hxg4 24 hxg4 ♘h7 25 ♘g3 ♕d7 26 a5 ♘g5 27 ♕f4 ♘de4!? 28 fxe4 &xe4 29 ♕xg5 &xg4+ 30 ♕xg4 ♕xg4+ (Black has won the white queen, but at a great cost in material) 31 ♘g3 ♔g7 32 &d6 &h8 33 &h1 &xh1 34 &xh1 ♕e6 35 &f4 f6 36 &b1 ♕a6 37 ♔f2 g5 38 &d6 ♔g6 (and certainly not 38...♕xd6?? 39 ♘f5+) 39 &b4 ♕e6 40 &h1 ♕g4 41 &h8 ♕d1 42 &g8+ ♔h7 43 &f8 ♔g6 44 &e7 ♕c2+ 45 ♔g1 ♕xc3 46 &xf6+ ♔h7 47 &f7+ ♔g6 48 &f6+ ♔h7 49 &f7+ ♔g6 50

♖f6+ ½-½ Lobron-Dizdar, Bundesliga 1991. White's king is too exposed for him to consider playing on.

11...♕a5!?

One of several possibilities:

1) 11...♖e8 12 f3 ♗d7 13 ♖a2 ♘e7 14 g3 ♕a5 15 ♗d2 ♗a4 16 ♕b1 c4 17 ♗c2 ♗xc2 18 ♕xc2 ♘g6 19 ♘f5 ♖e6 20 ♖b1 ♕c7 21 a4 ♖ae8 22 ♖ab2 b6 23 a5 ♘e7 24 axb6 axb6 25 ♘xe7+ ♖8xe7 26 ♖b5 with only a slight advantage for White; Portisch-Tatai, Cannes 1992.

2) 11...♘e7 and now:

2a) 12 a4 ♖e8 13 ♗a3 c4 14 ♗c2 ♘g6 15 ♘f5 ♘e4 16 ♗xe4 (16 ♕h5!? ♘xc3 17 ♘g3! b5 and now, in Knaak-Tischbierek, Berlin 1989, 18 f4 would have been strong) 16...♖xe4 17 ♘g3 ♖e8 18 ♕h5 ♕c6 19 a5 ♗e6 (thus far following a game of Korchnoi's, which went instead 19...♘f8 =) 20 f4 f5! 21 ♘xf5 ♗xf5 22 ♕xf5 ♖xe3 23 ♕g5 h6 24 ♕g4 ♘f8 25 ♖ae1 ♖xe1 26 ♖xe1 ♖e8 27 ♗xf8 ½-½ Sadler-King, London 1992.

2b) 12 g3 with a further division:
⇨ 12...♗h3 is the usual move. Tirabassi-Taksrud, corr. 1991 then continued 13 ♖e1 ♘g6 14 ♘g2 c4 15 ♗c2 ♘e4 16 ♗b2 ♕d7 (only this is new) 17 f3 ♘g5 18 ♗c1 ♗xg2 19 ♔xg2 ♕h3+ 20 ♔h1 f5! 21 ♖f1 ♖f6? (21...♖ae8) 22 ♕e2+ ♖e8 23 e4! ♘e6!? 24 ♕g2 ♕xg2+ 25 ♔xg2 fxe4 26 fxe4 ♘c7 27 e5 ±.
⇨ 12...♘g6 13 ♘g2 ♘e4 14 c4?! cxd4 15 cxd5 ♘c3 16 ♕h5 ♕d7 17 ♗b2 ♕h3 18 ♕xh3 ♗xh3 19 exd4 ♘xd5 ∓ Howell-King, British Ch 1989.

12 ♗b2 ♖e8 13 ♕c1?!
Better is 13 ♖e1.

13...♗d7 14 ♘f5?! ♕c7 15 ♘g3 ♘a5 16 ♕d1 ♖ad8 17 ♖e1 ♘e4 ∓ 18 ♘f1 ♗f5 19 f3 ♘d6

Keeping an eye on both c4 and e4.

20 ♗xf5 ♘xf5 21 ♕d3 ♘d6 22 ♖ab1 cxd4 23 cxd4 ♕c4 24 ♕d2 ♕a4! 25 ♗c1 ♖c8 26 ♕b4 ♕xb4 27 axb4 ♘ac4 28 ♘g3 ♘b5 29 ♔f2 ♘cd6 30 ♖b2 ♘xd4!

Winning a pawn.

31 ♖d1 ♘4b5 32 ♘e2 ♘c4 33 ♖b3 ♘b6 34 ♖d2 f6 35 ♗b2 ♔f7 36 ♗a1 ♖ed8 37 ♘d4 ♘xd4 38 ♗xd4 ♘c4 39 ♖d1 a6 40 g4?! ♖d7 41 h4?! ♔e6 42 ♔g3 ♘d6 43 ♖bd3 ♖c4 44 ♗c3 h5 45 gxh5 ♘f5+ 46 ♔f2 ♖dc7 47 ♗e1 ♖xh4 48 ♖xd5 ♖h2+ 49 ♔g1

49...♖g2+! 50 ♔xg2 ♘xe3+ 51 ♔g3 ♘xd5

And the rest, as they say, is a matter of technique.

52 ♖d4 ♖c1 53 ♖e4+ ♔f7 54 ♔f2 ♖c2+ 55 ♔g3 ♘e7 56 ♔h3 ♘c6 57 ♗g3 ♖d2 58 ♔g4 ♘d4 59 ♖e1 ♖d3 60 ♖c1 ♘c6 61 b5 axb5 62 ♖c5 b4 63 ♖b5 b3 64 f4 b6 65 ♖xb6 ♘a5 66

♗h4 ♘c4 67 ♖b7+ ♔e6 68 f5+ ♔e5
69 h6 ♘e3+ 70 ♔f3 ♘d5+ 71 ♔e2
♘f4+ 72 ♔f2 gxh6 73 ♖b5+ ♘d5
74 ♔e2 ♔e4 75 ♖b8 ♘f4+ 76 ♔f1
♖d1+ 77 ♔f2 b2 0-1

Game 126

Yusupov-Lobron
Munich 1992

1 d4 ♘f6 2 c4 e6 3 ♘c3 ♗b4 4 e3
0-0 5 ♗d3 d5 6 ♘f3 c5 7 0-0 ♘c6 8
a3 ♗xc3 9 bxc3 b6
⇨ 9...♖e8!? (an unusual move at
this stage) 10 cxd5?! (this justifies
Black's previous move; 10 ♘e5
♘xe5 11 dxe5 ♘d7 12 f4 dxc4 13
♗xc4 ♘b6 14 ♗b3 ♗d7 15 a4 ♗c6
16 a5 was clearly better for White,
Borishenko-Korchnoi, Czula 1965)
10...exd5 11 c4? cxd4 12 exd4 ♗g4
13 ♗b2 ♕d7 14 h3 ♗h5 15 ♖c1 (and
not 15 g4? ♘xg4!) 15...♖ad8 16
cxd5 ♘xd5 17 ♖c5 h6! 18 ♕c2 (18
♘e5 ♖xe5!) 18...♗xf3 19 ♗f5 ♕e7
20 gxf3 ♘f4 21 ♔h1 ♕h4 22 ♔h2
♖e2 23 ♕c1 ♖xf2+ 0-1 Sauberli-
Komarov, Bad Ragaz 1991.
10 cxd5 exd5 11 ♘e5 ♗b7 12
♗b2!? c4 13 ♘xc6 ♗xc6 14 ♗c2
♖e8 15 a4 a5 16 ♕e2 ♕e7 17 ♖fe1
g6 18 f3 ± ♘h5 19 e4 dxe4 20 fxe4
♘f6! 21 e5 ♕e6 22 ♗c1 ♘d7 23
♗h6 f6
Black has allowed the white centre to progress in order that he may
exchange it like this.
24 ♖ad1 fxe5 25 ♕d2 ♕d5 26
♗e4 ♕d6 27 dxe5! ♕xd2 28 ♖xd2
♘xe5 29 ♖de2 ♔f7 30 ♖f1+ ♔g8 31
♗xc6 ♘xc6 32 ♖ef2 ♘e5 33 h3

♖ab8 34 ♖f6

Black is almost completely paralysed because of the possible threat
of mate on f8.

34...♖ec8 35 ♔h2 ♖e8 36 ♔g1
♖ec8 37 ♔h1 ♖e8 38 ♔h2 ♖ec8 39
♔g1 ♖e8 40 ♔h2 ♖ec8 41 ♖6f4 ♖e8
42 h4 ♖ec8 43 ♔h3 ♖e8 44 ♖f6
♖ed8 45 g3 ♖e8 46 g4 b5!

Otherwise White can calmly continue with his plan of pawn-h5xg6.

47 axb5 a4 48 b6 a3 49 ♖a1 ♘d7
50 ♖d6 ♖e7 51 ♖xa3 ♖xb6 52 ♖a8+
♔f7 53 ♖xb6?

53 ♖d4 ±.

53...♘xb6 54 ♖h8 ♔e6 55 h5
gxh5 56 gxh5 ♘d5 57 ♖c8 ♘xc3 58
♖xc4 ½-½

Game 127 C M L

Yusupov-Ivanchuk
Brussels Ct (2) 1991

1 d4 ♘f6 2 c4 e6 3 ♘c3 ♗b4 4 e3 c5
5 ♗d3 ♘c6 6 ♘f3 d5 7 0-0 0-0 8 a3
♗xc3 9 bxc3 dxc4 10 ♗xc4 ♕c7 11
♗d3 e5 12 ♕c2 ♖e8

Black has a wide choice of moves here, and it is not clear which is the best:

⇨ 12...♗g4 13 ♘xe5 ♘xe5 14 dxe5 ♕xe5 15 f3 ♗d7 16 ♖e1?! ♖fd8?! (missing 16...♗a4! ∓) 17 a4 ♖ac8 18 e4 c4 19 ♗f1 ♘d5 20 ♗d2 ♘b6 21 ♗e3 ♘xa4 22 ♗xa7?! (22 ♗d4 followed by the advance of the e-and f-pawns offered more chances) b6 23 ♕f2 ♕xc3 24 ♗xb6 ♘xb6 25 ♕xb6 ♕b3 ∓ Murdzia-Aleksandrov, Sas van Gent 1992.

⇨ 12...♖d8 13 ♖e1 ♗g4 14 ♘xe5 ♘xe5 15 dxe5 ♕xe5 16 f3 ♗e6 17 ♗f1 ♘d5!? 18 ♗b2? (the bishop has no future here; 18 ♗d2) 18...c4 19 e4 ♘f4 20 ♖ad1 ♕b5 21 ♖d4 ♘d3 22 ♗xd3? (22 ♖e2 seems more sensible; now the d-pawn becomes strong) 22...cxd3 23 ♕d2 ♖ac8 24 ♖c1 h6 25 h4 ♗c4 26 ♕f2 ♗b3! 27 ♖b4 ♕c6 28 ♖xb3? (falling in with Black's plans; White could struggle on with 28 ♕d2) 28...d2 29 ♖d1 ♕a4 30 ♖xd2 ♕xb3 31 g3 ♖xd2 32 ♕xd2 ♕b6+ 33 ♕f2 ♖d8 0-1 Tsev-remes-Tolnai, Komotini 1992.

13 dxe5 ♘xe5 14 ♘xe5 ♕xe5 15 f3 ♗d7 16 a4

⇨ 16 ♖e1?! ♖ad8?! (again 16...♗a4! ∓) 17 a4 ♗c6 18 e4 ♘d5 19 ♗d2 ♘b4? (a rather unsuccessful tactic, 19...♘b6 is perfectly satisfactory) 20 cxb4 ♕d4+ 21 ♗e3 ♕xd3 22 ♕xd3 ♖xd3 23 b5 ♗d7 24 ♖ad1 ♖xd1 25 ♖xd1 ♗e6 26 ♗xc5 ± Norri-A.Shneider, Helsinki 1992.

16...♖ac8

⇨ 16...♖ad8 is also a good move: 17 e4 ♗c6 (or 17...♘h5!? 18 ♖e1 ♘f4 19 ♗f1 ♗c6 20 ♗e3 ½-½ Brunner-Luther, Altensteig 1992) 18 ♗c4

♖d7 19 a5 ½-½ Lukacs-Almasi, Budapest 1991.

17 ♖e1 ♖ed8!

⇨ 17...h6!? 18 e4 ♘d5 19 ♗d2 ♘f4 20 ♗f1 c4 21 ♗e3 ♕c7 22 ♕d2 ♘e6 23 ♗xc4! (winning a pawn) 23...♕xc4 24 ♕xd7 ♘c5 25 ♕b5 ♘d3 26 ♖ed1 ♕xb5 27 axb5 ♖xc3 28 ♗xa7 ♖a8 29 ♗d4 ♖xa1 30 ♖xa1 ♖b3 31 b6 ♔h7 32 h4 ♘b4 33 ♖d1 h5 34 ♔f2 ♘d3+ 35 ♔g3 ♔g6 36 ♖d2 ♘b4 37 ♗g1 ♖d3 38 ♖b2 ♘c6 39 ♖b5 f6 40 ♔h3 ♔h6 41 ♗h2 ♔g6 42 ♗c7 ♘e7 43 ♔g3 ♘c8 44 ♔f4 ♖d2 45 g4 hxg4 46 fxg4 ♘e7 47 ♔e3 ♖g2 48 ♔f3 ♖d2 49 h5+ ♔f7 50 ♖a5 ♘c6 51 ♖d5 ♖b2 52 ♖d7+ ♔g8 53 ♔f4 ♖f2+ 54 ♔g3 ♖b2 55 e5! (it has not been easy to make progress, but finally White is ready for action) 55...fxe5 (55...♘xe5 56 ♗xe5 fxe5 57 ♖xb7 is hopeless) 56 g5 g6 57 h6 ♖b3+ 58 ♔f2 e4 59 ♗d8 ♖f3+ 60 ♔e2 ♘e5 (now White brings the game to its conclusion with a small combination) 61 h7+ ♔h8 62 ♗f6+ ♖xf6 63 ♖d8+ 1-0 Yusupov-Ljubo-jević, Belgrade 1991.

18 e4 ♘d5 19 ♗d2 ♘b6 20 a5 c4!

Taking the game into an opposite-colour bishop position, which offsets the doubled pawns to some extent.

21 axb6 cxd3 22 ♕xd3 ♗e6 23 ♕e3 axb6 24 ♖eb1! ♕c5 25 ♕xc5 bxc5?

Natural but bad; 25...♖xc5 26 ♗e1 ♖c6 27 ♖b4 was only very slightly better for White.

26 ♗e1! ♖d7 27 ♖b5 h6 28 ♖ab1 ♗c4 29 ♖xb7 ♖xb7 30 ♖xb7 ♖a8 31 ♖d7 ♖a2 32 h4 ♖e2 33 ♗d2 ♔f8 34 ♗f4 ♖c2 35 ♖d8+ ♔e7 36 ♖g8 ♔f6 37 ♗d6 ♖xc3 38 ♗xc5 ♖c1+ 39 ♔h2 g6 40 ♗e3 ♖c2 41 ♗xh6 ♗f1 42 ♗g5+ ♔e6 43 ♖e8+ ♔d7 44 ♖d8+ ♔c7 45 ♖f8 ♖xg2+ 46 ♔h1 ♔d6 47 ♖xf7 ♖g3 48 ♖f6+ ♔e5 49 ♖f8 ♔d4 50 ♖d8+ ♔c4? 51 e5 ♗h3 52 ♖f8 ♗f5 53 ♖xf5! gxf5 54 e6 ♖xf3 55 e7 ♖f1+ 56 ♔g2 ♖e1 57 h5 1-0

The h-pawn cannot be stopped.

Game 128

Gulko-Grünfeld
Philadelphia 1991

1 d4 ♘f6 2 c4 e6 3 ♘c3 ♗b4 4 e3 0-0 5 ♗d3 c5 6 ♘f3 d5 7 0-0 ♘c6 8 a3 ♗xc3 9 bxc3 dxc4 10 ♗xc4 ♕c7 11 ♗a2

Possibly White's most popular choice, moving the king's bishop out of harm's way, while maintaining the pressure on the a2-g8 diagonal. Others:

⇨ 11 ♗e2 e5 12 ♕c2 ♗g4?! (or 12...♖d8 13 ♗b2 ♗g4 14 dxe5 ♘xe5 15 c4 ♘xf3+ 16 gxf3 ♗h3 17

♖fd1 ♕c6 18 ♕c3 ♘e8 19 ♔h1 f6 was unclear, Ibragimov-Aleksandrov, USSR 1991) 13 d5 ♘e7 14 e4 ± c4 15 ♘e1 ♗xe2 16 ♕xe2 ♘d7 17 a4 ♘c8 18 ♗a3 ♘d6 19 ♗xd6 (White must capture this knight now, because otherwise Black will play ...♘c5) 19...♕xd6 20 ♘c2 f5 21 exf5 ♕xd5 22 ♖fd1 ♕f7 23 ♘e3 ♖ac8 24 ♖d5 ♖fe8 25 ♖b5 ♘f6 26 ♕f3 e4 27 ♕f4 ♖cd8 28 g4 ♘d5 29 ♘xd5 ♖xd5 30 ♖xd5 ♕xd5 31 ♖e1 ♕c6?! (31...♕d3 would have given White more problems; as played Black allows White's kingside pawns to become a significant factor) 32 g5 ♕d5 33 h4 ♖e5 34 ♕g4 ♖xf5 35 ♖xe4 ♕c5 36 ♕e2 h6 37 g6 ♕c6 38 ♕xc4+ ♕xc4 39 ♖xc4 (it is not just the extra pawn but also the restriction of the black king by the pawn on g6 that is decisive here) 39...♔f8 40 ♖c7 ♖f4 41 h5 ♖f5 42 ♖xb7 ♖xh5 43 ♖f7+ ♔g8 44 f4 ♖a5 45 c4 ♖xa4 46 ♖c7 ♔f8 47 f5 a5 48 c5 ♖c4 49 c6 a4 50 ♖f7+ ♔e8 51 ♖xg7 ♖xc6 52 ♖a7 ♔f8 53 ♖xa4 ♖c5 54 ♖f4 ♔g7 55 f6+ ♔f8 56 ♖g4 1-0 Knaak-Schmittdiel, Dortmund 1991.

⇨ 11 a4?! b6 12 ♗a3?! (the bishop is not particularly useful here) 12...♖d8 13 ♕e2 ♗b7 14 h3 ♖ac8 15 ♗a2?! ♘a5 ∓ 16 ♘e5 ♗d5! 17 ♗b2? (allowing Black to transpose into a very advantageous ending) 17...cxd4 18 cxd4 ♕c2 19 ♖fe1 ♕xe2 20 ♖xe2 ♗xa2 21 ♖xa2 (White has got into a bit of a mess, but his position is fairly solid) 21...♘d5 22 ♖a1 f6 23 ♘f3 ♖c4 24 g3 ♔f7 25 ♔f1 ♖d7 26 ♘d2 ♖c6 27 ♗a3? ♘c4 28 ♘xc4 ♖xc4 29 a5?

(giving Black a passed pawn, and putting White's pawn on the same colour square as his bishop; 29 ♗b2 and, if possible, 30 e4, was a better try) 29...b5 30 ♗c5 a6 ∓ 31 ♖b2 e5 32 ♔e1 f5 33 g4 f4! 34 ♖b3 ♔e6 (completely undermining the white bishop) 35 ♗b6 fxe3 36 fxe3 e4 37 ♖a2 ♖f7 38 ♖f2 ♖c1+ 39 ♔d2 ♖xf2+ 40 ♔xc1 ♖f3 0-1 Hübner-Lobron, Munich 1992.

⇨ 11 ♗b5 ♗d7 12 a4 ♘e7 13 ♗xd7 (13 ♗d3) 13...♘xd7 14 e4 ♖fd8 15 ♗g5 ♘f8 16 ♕b3 f6 17 ♗c1 ♘c6 18 ♖d1 ♘a5 19 ♕a2 cxd4 20 cxd4 ♕c4 21 ♗d2 ♕xa2 22 ♖xa2 ♘c6 23 ♗e3 b6 24 ♖c2 ♖ac8 25 ♖dc1 ♘e7 with equality; Balashov-Kharitonov, Moscow 1990.

⇨ 11 ♕e2?! e5 12 ♗b5!? (12 d5 e4 13 dxc6 ♗g4! 14 cxb7 ♕xb7 15 ♕b2 ♕xb2 16 ♗xb2 exf3 ∓) 12...e4 13 ♗xc6 bxc6 14 ♘e5 ♘d5 15 ♕c4!? (an intriguing position; at first glance it seems that White must lose something) 15...f6 16 ♘d3 exd3 17 e4 ♕a5 18 exd5 ♗a6 19 ♕a2 c4 20 dxc6 ♕xc3 21 ♗e3 ♕a5 22 ♖fc1 ♕d5 23 ♖c3! ♖ac8 24 ♖xd3 ♖xc6 25 ♖c3 ♖e8 26 ♖ac1 ♖ce6 with only the tiniest of advantages for Black; Husari-Tischbierek, Novi Sad OL 1990.

11...♖d8

⇨ 11...e5 is the more common option: 12 h3 e4 13 ♘h2 b6 (13...♘e7 14 ♗b2 ♗e6 15 c4 cxd4 16 ♗xd4 ♘d7 17 ♕c2 ♕c6 18 ♖ab1 b6 19 ♖b5 ♖ac8 20 ♕b2 f6 21 ♖c1 ♘f5 22 ♘f1 ♘d6 23 ♖b3 ♘c5 24 ♗xc5 ♕xc5 25 ♘d2 f5 is better for Black; Pinter-Fauland, Haifa 1989) 14 c4 ♖d8 15 ♗b2 cxd4 16 exd4 ♘e5 17 d5

♘d3 18 ♗d4 (here it would be a mistake to concede his dark-squared bishop by 18 ♗xf6) 18...♕f4 19 ♕e2 ± ♖e8 20 ♖ad1? ♗xh3! 21 ♗e3 (White loses after 21 gxh3? ♕g5+ 22 ♔h1 ♘f4) 21...♗g4 22 ♘xg4 ♕xg4 23 ♕xg4 ♘xg4 24 ♗d4 ♘ge5 25 f3 exf3 26 gxf3 ♘f4 27 ♖d2 ♘ed3 28 ♔h2 ♖ad8 29 ♖g1 ♘e5 30 ♔g3 ♘eg6 31 ♖gd1 ♘e2+ 32 ♔f2 ♘xd4 33 ♖xd4 ♘e5 with a solid extra pawn; Knaak-Schmittdiel, Dortmund 1990.

12 ♕c2!? ♘a5 13 ♕e2 ♘d5! 14 ♗d2 b6 15 ♖ac1 ♗b7 16 ♘e5 ♘f6! 17 f3?!

Better is 17 ♖fd1.

17...♕e7 18 ♖fd1 ♖ac8 19 ♗e1 cxd4 20 exd4 ♘d5!?

Returning again to this square to threaten ...♕xa3, which was not possible immediately, of course, because of 21 ♘xf7! ♔xf7 22 ♕xe6+ and mate.

21 c4

21...♘f4

This is probably no worse than 21...♕xa3 22 cxd5! (22 ♘xf7? ♘f4 23 ♕d2 ♘h3+! −+) 22...♖xc1 23

♖xc1 ♕xc1 24 dxe6! (noticed by John Nunn; 24 ♘xf7 ♗xd5 25 ♗xd5 ♖xd5 26 ♕xe6 ♔f8 27 ♘d6 only leads to a small advantage) 24...fxe6 25 ♗xe6+ ♔f8 26 ♘d7+ ♔e7 (26...♖xd7? 27 ♗xd7 g6 28 ♕e8+ ♔g7 29 ♕e7+ leads to mate) 27 ♗f5+ ♔d6 28 ♘e5!! (*Typesetter's note*: noticed by Tony Kosten)

28...♖f8 29 ♘d3, with 30 ♕e5+ and 31 ♘b4+ to come, and White wins.

22 ♕e3 ♘h5 23 ♗b4 ♕e8 24 ♗xa5 bxa5 25 ♖b1 ♖c7 26 ♕d2 a4 27 ♕a5 ♖e7?

Missing the threat.

28 ♘xf7 ♖xf7 29 ♕xh5 g6 30 ♕e5 ♕e7 31 c5 ♗c8 32 ♖b8 ♖f5 33 ♗xe6+ 1-0

14

The 4 f3 variation, which was first played by the Hungarian GMs Portisch and Forintos, has been transformed in the last few years from an insignificant side-variation into one of the most important systems against the Nimzo-Indian, largely through the efforts of young ex-Soviet players such as Shirov, whose exciting style seems perfectly adapted to the ultra-sharp positions that often arise.

The most obvious reply to 4 f3 is 4...d5 and after the almost invariable 5 a3 Black is faced with a choice: exchange on c3 or retreat?

Firstly, we cover the retreats 5...♗e7 and also 5...♗d6.

Personally, I feel that White holds most of the trumps here and that perhaps players of the black pieces should pass on to the second half of this chapter!

In game 129 we take a quick look at the alternatives to 5 a3 and 5...♗e7, and also the variation 5...♗e7 6 e4 dxc4!?. Despite the ease with which Ljubojević obtained a draw in his game against Kasparov, there have been few takers for his new sixth move. Following 6...dxe4 7 fxe4 e5 8 d5 Black can try 8...0-0, 8...a5 or Christiansen's 8...c6. Although White has a semi-open f-file in this variation, strangely it is on the queenside where his advantage lies and not on the kingside. He should prepare the advance of his queenside majority as soon as possible, as games 129 and 130 demonstrate.

The line with 8...♗c5 and 9...♘g4 is superficially attractive for Black; he attacks f2 very early with two pieces and forces the white king to 'go walkabout'. However, it soon turns out that, while the white king is quite safe behind his strong centre, the black minor pieces are themselves the targets. In game 132 we look at what is probably Black's best move, 11...b5, whilst in game 131 we consider the alternatives. A series of sensational White wins has turned Black's attention to other, less painful variations.

6...c5 has become very fashionable of late. In game 133 we examine 7 dxc5 ♗xc5, which is an extremely wild variation although it appears that Black can hold the balance with 8...♗xg1!; also Oll's 7...d4 deserves to be seen more often.

As for 7 cxd5 exd5 8 e5, it seems that Black has difficulty holding his own in this ultra-sharp line. White can elect to play a promising ending as in Ilinčić-Čabrilo, or the complications after 12 ♘f3!? analysed in game 135, although Gutman's 9 f4 should probably be discarded. Game 136 contains Shirov's masterpiece against Eingorn in the variation 8 dxc5 ♗xc5 9 e5. Black's one bright spot is the note Shirov-Rausis (11...♗xg1!) to this game.

The rest of this chapter covers 5...♗xc3+ 6 bxc3 c5 7 cxd5 ♘xd5. This has long been considered to be a variation of the Sämisch (i.e. 4 a3 ♗xc3+ 5 bxc3 c5 6 f3 d5 7 cxd5 ♘xd5) but since it almost invariably arises from 4 f3 nowadays, it seems only natural to include it here. In my opinion it is Black's strongest and most reliable possibility against 4 f3, and current results seem to bear this out. Obviously, Black is threatening 8...♘xc3 followed by 9...cxd4, so White's choice is limited: he can either play 8 dxc5 and get on with his development or play 8 ♕d3/8 ♕d2 keeping his centre intact.

Although the old move of Keres', 8 dxc5, strikes one as anti-positional, its justification lies in the open files and scope for White's bishop pair that it offers. Black has two ways to proceed: 8...♕a5 initiating queenside counterplay, or 8...f5, attempting to restrain White's centre. In the first of these lines, after 9 e4, Black has to decide where to place his knight. For a long time it was a straight choice between c7 and e7. Since Karpov introduced (after 9...♘e7 10 ♗e3 0-0 11 ♕b3) 11...♕c7 in the Candidates final, it has quickly become Black's main move. On top of this, Hjartarson successfully played 9...♘f6, so that now few players bother with 9...♘c7.

After 8...♕a5 9 e4 ♘e7 10 ♗e3 0-0 11 ♕b3 ♕c7! White has tried four replies. In the initial game Timman essayed 12 ♗b5 but Black soon got the upper hand, whilst 12 ♖d1 is also considered in game 137. Game 138 covers 12 ♘h3, whilst 12 a4, which could well be White's best move, is dealt with in game 139. The assessment of this variation may well depend upon the evaluation of Milov's 18 ♗b5!?, seen in the notes.

A further possibility for Black, 9...♘f6, emerged in 1991. This also appears to be completely satisfactory, as can be seen from game 140.

In game 141 we look at 8...f5, which has a good reputation, and leads to double-edged positions.

It would not be unreasonable to name the 8 ♕d3 variation after the Latvian GM Shirov.

Although it was played a good deal in the 1960s, it is Shirov who has done so much, by the brilliance of his play, to popularise it in the last few years. At first sight it seems strange to put the queen on such an exposed square before developing the other pieces, but once White does finally manage to castle, he is often in a position to start a decisive attack, thanks to his strong bishops and mobile centre.

Game 142 covers 8...cxd4 9 cxd4 ♘c6 10 e4 ♘b6 11 ♗e3 0-0 when, although Black might be OK, the crushing nature of Shirov's victories has had a very dissuasive effect. I suppose it was only inevitable that the success of 8 ♕d3 would set players thinking about its 'sister' variation 8 ♕d2 and this is mentioned in the notes to game 142. Results so far have been far from encouraging for White.

Following Timman's success against Gurevich the attention of Black players became firmly focused on the line 8...0-0 9 e4 ♘e7. At first 10 ♗e3 (game 143) was tried, but recently White (and in particular Shirov) has enjoyed spectacular success with the sharp 10 f4!? analysed in game 144.

The last word (if such a thing could ever be said about a chess opening!) concerning 8 ♕d3 now seems to be 8...b6, threatening the unpleasant 9...♗a6. Shirov suffered two bad setbacks at Biel (both in game 146), and even vowed that he would give up the variation. Perhaps Marin's 10 c4 (game 145) is best, but it appears that anyone wishing to play 8 ♕d3 will have to find something new.

Game 129

Shirov-Christiansen
Biel 1991

1 d4 ♘f6 2 c4 e6 3 ♘c3 ♗b4 4 f3 d5 5 a3

⇨ 5 ♕a4+!? ♘c6 6 a3 ♗e7 7 e3 0-0 8 ♘ge2!? (8 f4 stops Black's ...e5, but after 8...♘b8 9 c5 c6 the position is equal) 8...dxc4 9 ♕xc4 e5 10 d5 ♘a5! 11 ♕a4 c6 12 b4 ♘c4 13 dxc6 bxc6 14 ♘g3 ♗e6 15 ♘f5 ♗xf5 16 ♗xc4 ♘d5! (threatening both ...♘xc3 and ♘b6) 17 ♘e4?! (17 ♕b3) 17...♗xe4 18 fxe4 ♘b6 19 ♕b3 ♘xc4 20 ♕xc4 a5 21 ♖b1 axb4 22 axb4 ♖a4 23 ♕c3 ♕b6 24 ♗d2? (24 0-0) 24...♕b5 25 ♔f2 ♖d8 26 ♖hc1 ♖a3!! 27 ♕c2 (if 27 ♕xa3? ♖xd2+ followed by ...♕e2 with a quick mate) 27...♖ad3 28 ♖d1 c5 29 ♗e1 (29 bxc5? ♖xd2+) 29...♖xd1 30 ♖xd1 ♖xd1 31 ♕xd1 cxb4 ∓ Chabanon-Kosten, Clermont-Ferrand 1992.

5...♗e7

Instead 5...♗d6 can be met by:

1) 6 c5 (note that both 6 e4 c5 7 dxc5 ♗xc5 and 6 e4 c5 7 cxd5 exd5 8 dxc5 ♗xc5 transpose to variations of 5...♗e7 considered later) 6...♗e7 7 b4 0-0 8 ♗g5 b6 9 e3 a5 10 ♗d3 c6

11 ♘a4 ♘bd7 12 ♘e2 ♗a6 (achieving a desirable exchange) 13 0-0 ½-½ Marin-Spassov, Sitges 1992.

2) 6 ♗g5 ♗e7 7 e3 and now:

⇨ 7...♘bd7!? 8 ♗d3 c5 9 ♘ge2 0-0 10 0-0 cxd4 11 ♘xd4 ♘b6 12 cxd5 ♘fxd5 13 ♗xe7 ♕xe7 14 ♘xd5 ♘xd5 15 ♘c2 ♗d7 16 ♕d2 ♖fd8 17 ♖ac1 ♗a4 18 ♕f2 ♖d6 19 ♖fe1 ♖ad8 20 ♗f1 a6 when Black was at least equal in Yakovich-Renet, Palma 1989.

⇨ 7...0-0 8 ♗d3 c5!? 9 dxc5 ♗xc5 10 cxd5 h6!? (10...exd5 should be met not by 11 ♗xf6 ♕xf6 12 ♘xd5? ♕xb2 13 ♘c7? ♕xg2 ∓, but by 11 b4! ♗e7 12 ♘ge2 ±) 11 ♗xf6 ♕xf6 12 ♕d2! exd5 13 ♘xd5 ♕h4+! 14 g3 ♕h5 15 ♖c1! (15 ♘c7? ♕e5! ∓) 15...♗d6 (not 15...b6? 16 ♗e4 ±, but 15...♘d7!? is possible) 16 f4! ♗e6 17 ♗e4 ♘d7 18 ♕d1! ♕xd1+ 19 ♖xd1 ♖fd8 20 ♗f3 ♖ac8 21 ♘e2 ± ♗c5 22 b4 ♗f8 23 ♔f2 (White has managed to consolidate his extra pawn) 23...a5 24 ♖b1 axb4 25 axb4 ♗xd5 26 ♗xd5 ♘f6 27 ♗f3 ♖c2 28 ♖hd1 ♖dc8 29 ♖d4 ± Yakovich-Garcia Martinez, Bayamo 1990.

6 e4 dxe4

⇨ 6...dxc4!? 7 ♗xc4 c5 8 dxc5 ♕xd1+ 9 ♔xd1 (9 ♘xd1 ♗xc5 10 b4 ♗b6 11 ♗e3 ♗xe3 12 ♘xe3 ♘c6 13 ♘e2 ♗d7 14 ♔f2 ♔e7 15 h3 ♖ac8 16 ♖ac1 ½-½ although White has much more space; Arencibia-Rodriguez, Cali Z 1990) 9...♗xc5 10 ♘b5 ♗b6 = 11 e5 ♘d5 12 ♘d6+ ♔e7 13 f4 ♘c6 14 ♘f3 ♘e3+ 15 ♗xe3 ♗xe3 16 g3 ♖d8 17 b4 f6 18 ♔e2 ♗d4 19 b5!? (trying to complicate) 19...♗xa1 20 bxc6 fxe5 21 ♘xc8+ ♖axc8 22 ♖xa1 exf4 23 ♖b1

♖xc6 24 ♖xb7+ ♔f6 25 ♖b4 fxg3 26 hxg3 h5 27 ♔e3 a5 ½-½ Kasparov-Ljubojević, Linares 1990. Many a player would be tempted to continue with Black here.

    7 fxe4 e5 8 d5 c6 9 ♘f3 0-0 10 ♗d3 ♗g4 11 h3!? ♗xf3 12 ♕xf3 a5

Black gains nothing from stopping White from castling short:

⇨ 12...♗c5 13 ♗g5 ♘bd7 14 0-0-0 a6 15 ♖hf1 ♕c7 16 ♔b1 cxd5 17 exd5 b5 18 ♕g3 ♘e8 19 ♕h4 g6 20 ♗h6 bxc4 21 d6! ♗xd6 22 ♗xc4 with a winning attack; Lerner-Ivanov, New York 1990.

    13 0-0 ♘bd7 14 ♗e3 ± a4

Black deems this to be necessary to hinder White's queenside expansion, but a4 will need defending.

    15 ♔h1! ♘e8 16 ♗c2 ♘c5 17 ♖ad1 ♕a5 18 ♕f2! ♖d8 19 ♕g1?!

Played to threaten d6, which did not work immediately because of (19 d6?) 19...♖xd6! 20 ♗xc5 ♖f6 winning, but 19 ♔g1! was a more natural road to the same goal, e.g. 19...cxd5 20 exd5 ♗d6 21 ♘b5! ±.

    19...cxd5 20 ♘xd5 ♗d6 21 ♘c3!

Threatening ♖xd6 and forcing a further weakness.

    21...b6 22 ♘b5

Winning a pawn.

    22...♗e7 23 ♖xd8 ♗xd8 24 ♗xc5 bxc5 25 ♕xc5 ♕d2 26 ♕f2 ♕h6 27 ♗xa4 ♘f6 28 ♘d6?

White could secure a large advantage with 28 ♘c3 ♘h5 29 ♗d1! ♘f4 30 ♘d5 ♗g5 31 c5.

    28...♘g4 29 ♕f3 ♕xd6 30 ♕xg4 ♕d3 31 ♕f3 ♕xc4 32 ♗b3 ♕c7! 33 ♗d5

Tying Black to the defence of f7 and preparing the advance of his queenside. Although Black struggles mightily the result is never really in doubt.

    33...g6 34 ♕e3 ♔g7 35 ♖c1 ♕b8 36 b4 ♗b6 37 ♕c3 ♗d4 38 ♕c6! ♕a7! 39 a4 ♗e3 40 ♖f1 f5 41 a5 ♕d4? 42 ♕d6! ♗g5 43 a6 ♕d3 44 ♖f3 ♕d2 45 ♕xe5+ ♔h6 46 a7 fxe4 47 ♖xf8 ♕e1+ 48 ♔h2 ♗e3

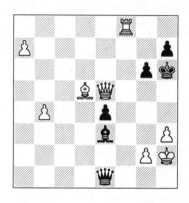

    49 ♕f4+! ♗xf4+ 50 ♖xf4 ♕c1 51 ♖f7! 1-0

Game 130

Lin Ta-Tong Yuanming
China 1990

1 d4 ♘f6 2 c4 e6 3 ♘c3 ♗b4 4 f3 d5 5 a3 ♗e7 6 e4 dxe4 7 fxe4 e5 8 d5 a5

⇨ 8...0-0 9 ♘f3 ♗g4 10 ♗e2 ♗c5 11 ♘xe5?! ♗xe2 12 ♕xe2 ♗d4 13 ♘f3 ♗xc3+ 14 bxc3 ♘xe4 15 0-0 ♖e8 16 ♕d3 ♘d7 ∞ Savchenko-Maksimović, Pula 1990.

    9 ♗d3 0-0 10 ♘f3 ♗g4 11 0-0 ♘bd7

⇨ 11...♘a6 12 ♗c2 ♘d7 13 ♖b1 ♗c5+ 14 ♔h1 ♕e7 (attempting to

deter b4 for good) 15 ♘a4 ♗d4 16
♕e1 ♗xf3 17 ♖xf3 ♘ac5 18 ♘xc5
♗xc5 19 b4 axb4 20 axb4 ♗d4 21 c5
♖a6 22 ♗b3 ♖g6 23 h3 b6 24 d6
cxd6 25 c6 ∞ Gallego-Taimanov,
Oviedo (active) 1992.

12 h3!

Better than 12 ♗c2 ♘e8 13 ♗a4
♘c5 14 ♗xe8 ♕xe8 15 ♗e3 a4 Gut-
man-Taimanov, Paris 1989.

12...♗xf3

⇨ 12...♗h5 13 ♖b1 ♘e8 14 ♗e3 c6
15 dxc6 bxc6 16 b4 axb4 17 axb4 c5
18 b5 ± Moskalenko-Novikov,
USSR 1989.

13 ♖xf3!

After 13 ♕xf3 ♘e8 White has
tried:

⇨ 14 ♔h1 ♗c5 15 ♘a4 ♗d4 16
♗e3 c5 17 dxc6 bxc6 18 c5!? ♕e7
19 ♕f2!? (an interesting temporary
pawn sacrifice, but 19 ♖ac1 was
simpler) 19...♘xc5 20 ♘xc5 ♕xc5
21 ♖ac1 ♕d6 22 ♗xd4 exd4 23 ♖c4
♖d8 (23...c5? 24 ♖fc1 ♖c8 25 b4 ±)
24 ♕c2 ♘f6 25 ♖xc6 ♕g3 26 ♖c5?
♘d7 27 ♖xa5? ♘e5 ∓ 28 ♖d1 ♖d6
29 ♖d5 ♘f3! 30 gxf3 ♕xh3+ 0-1
Chabanon-Kosten, Paris 1991.

⇨ 14 ♖b1! ♗c5+ 15 ♗e3 ♕e7 16
♘a4 ♗xe3+ 17 ♕xe3 c5 (yet another try at blocking the queenside)
18 dxc6 bxc6 19 c5 ♘c7 20 ♗c4
♘b5 21 ♖f2 ♔h8 22 ♗xb5 cxb5 23
♘b6 ♘xb6 24 cxb6 ♖fb8 25 ♖c1
♕e6 26 ♖c7 ♖xb6 27 ♖fxf7. White
has used his b-pawn as a deflection
to gain two rooks on the seventh, and
in Khenkin-Bergström, Gausdal 1991,
went on to win.

**13...♘e8 14 ♗d2 ♗c5+ 15 ♔h1
♘d6 16 ♖b1**

White prepares to push b4 and c5,

and against this simple plan Black
has little defence.

**16...♗d4 17 b4 axb4 18 axb4 f5!
19 c5! ♗xc3?!**

19...♘xe4! is better: 20 ♘xe4
fxe4 21 ♖xf8+ ♕xf8 22 ♗xe4 ±.

**20 ♗xc3 ♘xe4 21 ♗xe4 fxe4 22
♖xf8+ ♕xf8 23 c6!**

The point of White's 19th move,
winning back his pawn with a decisive advantage.

**23...bxc6 24 dxc6 ♘b6 25 ♗xe5
♕e7 26 ♕b3+ ♔h8 27 ♗d4! ♘c8
28 b5**

White's bishop dominates the
black knight and his c- and b-pawns
are on the threshold.

**28...h6 29 ♕d5 ♘d6 30 b6! cxb6
31 ♗xb6 ♘e8 32 ♕d7! ♕f6 33 c7
♕c3 34 ♖f1 ♔h7 35 ♕f5+ ♔h8 36
♕xe4 1-0**

Game 131

Shirov-Dautov
Daugavpils 1989

1 d4 ♘f6 2 c4 e6 3 ♘c3 ♗b4 4 f3 d5

5 a3 ♗e7 6 e4 dxe4 7 fxe4 e5 8 d5 ♗c5

Should Black play 8...♘g4, then 9 ♘f3 will transpose, but White can also play 9 ♗e2!:

⇨ 9...♗c5 10 ♗xg4 ♕h4+ 11 g3 ♕xg4 12 ♕xg4 ♗xg4 13 h3 ♗h5 14 g4 ♗g6 15 ♘f3 ♘d7 16 b4 ♗e7 17 0-0 b6 18 ♗g5 ♗xg5 19 ♘xg5 slightly favours White due to his space advantage; Malaniuk-Ulybin, Simferopol 1988.

⇨ 9...h5!? 10 ♘f3 ♗c5 11 ♕c2 ♗f2+ 12 ♔f1 0-0 13 ♖d1 ♗c5 14 h3 f5 15 hxg4 fxg4 16 ♔e1 gxf3 17 gxf3 h4 18 ♗e3 ♗d4 19 ♕d2 ♗xe3 20 ♕xe3 a5 21 c5 h3 (this serves as a minor distraction) 22 ♘f2 ♕h4 23 ♔d2 h2 24 ♗c4 ♖f6 25 ♘d3 ♖h6 26 ♖af1 ♘d7 27 ♖f2 ♕g3 28 ♕e2 b5 29 ♗a2 b4 30 ♖g2 ♕h4 31 ♖gxh2 rounding up the h-pawn with a considerable advantage; Moskalenko-Garcia Padron, Fuerteventura 1992.

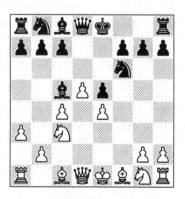

9 ♘f3

Better than 9 ♗g5 h6 10 ♗h4 ♗d4! 11 ♘ce2 ♘xe4! (not 11...♗xb2 12 ♖a2) 12 ♕xd4 (a desperado queen! Of course 12 ♗xd8?? would allow

12...♗f2 mate) 12...♕xh4+ 13 g3 exd4 14 gxh4 c5 15 dxc6 ♘xc6 16 ♖d1 ♗g4 17 ♗g2 f5 18 h3 ♗h5 19 ♗f3 ♗f7 20 ♘xd4 ♘xd4 21 ♖xd4 0-0 and after all the excitement Black is just a tiny bit better in the endgame; Kutuzović-Malaniuk, Pula 1990.

9...♘g4 10 ♘a4 ♗f2+

⇨ 10...♘d7!? is interesting, e.g. 11 b4 ♗f2+ 12 ♔e2 ♗d4 13 ♘xd4 exd4 14 ♕xd4 0-0 ± Alonso-Alvarez, Cuba 1991; or 11 ♘xc5 ♘xc5 12 ♕c2 f5 ∞.

11 ♔e2 ♗d4?!

The superior 11...b5 is considered in the next game. Otherwise:

⇨ 11...♖h4?! 12 g3 ♗e7 13 h3 ♘f6 14 ♘c3 0-0 15 ♔f2 a5 16 ♔g2 ♘bd7 17 ♗d3 ♘e8 18 ♗e3 g6 19 ♕d2 ♘g7 20 ♗c2 ♔h8 21 ♖hf1 ♖a6 22 ♖ae1 f6 23 ♘a4 c5 24 ♘c3 ♘b6 25 ♗d3 ♗d7 26 g4 ♘c8 27 ♘e2 ♗d6 28 ♘g3 and with so much more room to manoeuvre White was able to prepare a winning breakthrough in Malaniuk-Douven, Alma-Ata 1989.

⇨ 11...c5?! 12 dxc6 ♗d4 13 c7 ♕xc7 14 ♘d5 ♕d8 15 ♘xd4 exd4 16 ♕xd4 0-0 17 h3 ♘c6 18 ♕c3 ♕h4 19 g3 ♕h5 20 ♘f4 ♕e5 21 ♕xe5 ♘gxe5 22 ♔e3 Khenkin-Boudre, Paris 1991. White is a pawn up with the better position.

12 ♘xd4 exd4 13 ♕xd4 0-0 14 h3!

⇨ 14 ♔d3?! ♘c6! 15 dxc6 ♘f2+ 16 ♔c3 ♘d1+ 17 ♔d3 ♘f2+ ½-½ Malaniuk-Dautov, Sverdlovsk 1989.

14...♕h4?!

Even after the superior 14...♘f6 15 ♗g5 ♘c6 16 ♕f2! White retains a clear advantage.

15 g3! ♕h5

15...♕xg3 16 hxg4 ♗xg4+ 17
♔d2 ♕f3 18 ♖g1 ♘c6 19 ♕e3
♕d1+ 20 ♔c3 ±.

16 ♗g2

Allowing Black a discovered
check, but it is quite harmless.

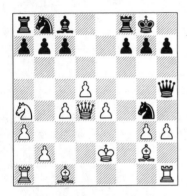

**16...♘e5+ 17 g4 ♗xg4+ 18 hxg4
♕xg4+ 19 ♔f2 ♘bd7 20 ♕d1**

A piece up, White can simply try
to exchange the attacking units.

**20...♕g6 21 ♕h5 ♘g4+ 22 ♔e2
♘de5 23 ♗f4! 1-0**

Game 132

Prudnikova-Sakhatova
USSR 1991

**1 d4 ♘f6 2 c4 e6 3 ♘c3 ♗b4 4 f3 d5
5 a3 ♗e7 6 e4 dxe4 7 fxe4 e5 8 d5
♗c5 9 ♘f3 ♗g4 10 ♘a4**

⇨ 10 b4?! ♗f2+ 11 ♔e2 c5! 12 ♘b5
a6! 13 ♕a4 axb5!! (a profound exchange sacrifice) 14 ♕xa8 ♗d4! ∓
15 ♘xd4 cxd4 16 ♕xb8 0-0 17 ♔e1
♕h4+ 18 g3 ♕f6 19 ♗f4 g5 20 c5
exf4 21 ♕d6 ♕g7 22 ♗d3 ♘e5 23
♔d2 f3 24 ♕e7 g4 25 ♗xb5 ♘g6 26

♕g5 h6 27 ♕h5 d3 28 ♗xd3 ♖e8 29
h3 ♖e5 30 hxg4 ♖xh5 31 gxh5 ♘e5
32 ♖ae1 ♕g5+ 33 ♔c2 f2 34 ♖d1
♕e3 0-1 Malaniuk-Ivanchuk, Moscow 1988.

**10...♗f2+ 11 ♔e2 b5 12 h3 bxa4
13 hxg4**

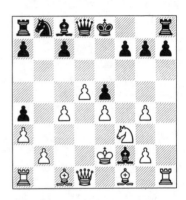

13...♗g3

⇨ 13...♗c5!? 14 ♕xa4+ c6! 15 b4
♗d4 16 ♘xd4 exd4 17 g5! ♕e7 18
♔f2! 0-0 19 ♗d2! ♕e5! 20 ♗e2!
♕xe4? (opening the diagonal to-
wards his king; 20...f5 ±) 21 ♕b3!
♕e7 22 ♕d3 f5 23 ♕xd4 ♘d7 24
♖ae1 c5 25 ♕h4 h6 26 gxh6 ♘f6
(naturally the ending after 26...♕xh4
27 ♖xh4 is hopeless for Black) 27
♗f3 ♘e4+ 28 ♖xe4 1-0 Yakovich-
Herrera, Santa Clara 1990.

**14 ♖h3 ♗f4 15 ♗xf4 exf4 16
♕d4 f6**

⇨ 16...0-0 17 ♖h4 g5? 18 ♖h6! ±
Raičević-Ruban, Pula 1989.

17 ♖h4! 0-0 18 ♔d2

⇨ Better than 18 c5 ♘d7 19 ♔d2
♘e5 20 ♗c4 (20 ♘xe5 dxe5 21
♕xe5?? ♕xh4) 20...♕e8 21 ♖ah1
h6 22 ♘xe5 fxe5 23 ♕c3 ♖b8 24 g5
± Wells-Lendwai, Graz 1991.

18...c5 19 ♕c3 ♘d7 20 ♗d3 h6 21 ♖ah1 ♖b8 22 ♗c2 ♖e8 23 ♖h5! ♘f8?

In view of what follows, 23...♖b6 would have been prudent.

24 g5! fxg5

25 ♖xh6! gxh6 26 ♖xh6 ♖b6 27 ♕h8+ ♔f7 28 ♖h7+ ♘xh7 29 ♕xh7+ ♔f8 30 ♕h8+ ♔f7 31 ♕h7+ ♔f8 32 ♕h8+ ♔f7 33 ♕h7+? ½-½

White spoils her masterpiece; 33 ♘e5+! ♖xe5 34 ♕xd8 wins.

Game 133

Shirov-Yudasin
Lvov Z 1990

1 d4 ♘f6 2 c4 e6 3 ♘c3 ♗b4 4 f3 d5 5 a3 ♗e7 6 e4 c5 7 dxc5 ♗xc5

⇨ 7...d4!? 8 ♘b5 e5 9 b4 0-0 10 ♘d6 (the knight had no retreat-square anyway) 10...♗xd6 11 cxd6 b6 12 ♗d3 ♗xd6 13 ♘e2 a5 14 ♗d2 ♘a6 15 0-0 ♗e6 16 f4 ♕c7 17 ♖c1 axb4 18 axb4 exf4 19 ♗xf4 ♕d7 20 e5 ♘g4 21 ♗e4 ♖ad8 22 b5? (conceding another square; 22 ♕d3!)

22...♘b4! 23 ♕d2? d3 24 ♘g3 ♕d4+ 25 ♔h1 ♘c2 26 ♗g5 ♘ce3 (Black's knights are swarming all over White's position) 27 ♖f4 ♕xe5 28 ♗xd8 ♖xd8 29 ♖f3 ♘xc4 30 ♕b4 d2 31 ♖d1 ♘ge3 32 ♖xe3 ♘xe3 33 ♗xh7+ ♔xh7 34 ♕h4+ ♔g6 35 ♕xd8 ♘xd1 36 ♕xd2 ♘e3 37 ♕d3+ ♗f5 0-1 Malaniuk-Oll, Odessa 1989.

8 b4 ♗xg1!

A significant improvement on 8...♗d6?! which can be met by:

⇨ 9 ♗b2 ♗e5 10 ♕d2 0-0 11 ♖d1 ♘bd7 (11...♕e7!?) 12 ♘h3 dxe4 13 f4! ♗c7 14 ♘f2 b6 15 ♘cxe4 e5 16 ♘d6! ♕e7 17 ♗e2 exf4 18 0-0! ♗xd6 19 ♗f3 ♖b8 20 ♕xd6 ♕xd6 21 ♖xd6 ♗b7 22 ♗g4! ♘xg4 23 ♘xg4 ± h5 24 ♖xd7 hxg4 25 ♖xf4+ f6 26 ♖xg4 ♖f7 27 ♖d6 and after the bizarre complications White found himself in a won ending in Malaniuk-V.Gurevich, Kherson 1989.

⇨ 9 cxd5 ♗e5 10 ♘ge2 exd5 11 f4 ♗xc3+ 12 ♘xc3 ♗g4 13 ♕d3 ♘xe4 14 ♘xe4 dxe4 15 ♕xe4+ ♕e7 16 ♗d3 ♘c6 17 0-0 ♕xe4 18 ♗xe4 0-0 19 h3 ♗e6 20 ♗b2 Moskalenko-Atalik, Budapest 1991. With two powerful bishops on an open board, White has every prospect of winning.

9 ♖xg1 ♕c7

Simultaneously hitting h2 and c4, but 9...a5!? might be even better. Then 10 b5? ♕c7! and 10 ♗b2 axb4 11 axb4 ♖xa1 12 ♕xa1 ♕b6 ∓ are no good, so practice has seen:

⇨ 10 cxd5 axb4 11 ♘b5 0-0 12 dxe6 ♕xd1+ 13 ♔xd1 ♗xe6 14 ♗b2 ♘c6 15 ♗d3 ♘d7 16 axb4 ♘xb4 17 ♖xa8 ♖xa8 18 ♗b1! ♗a2 19 ♔d2 ♗xb1

½-½   Bagirov-Krogius,   Moscow 1991.

⇨ 10 ♖b1 axb4 11 axb4 0-0?! (11...♛c7) 12 cxd5 exd5 13 ♘xd5 ♗e6 14 ♘xf6+ ♛xf6 15 ♗b2 ♛h6 16 ♛d2 ♛xh2 17 ♔f2 ♘c6 18 b5 ♘e5 19 ♗e2 ♖fd8 20 ♛e3 ♘c4 21 ♗xc4 ♗xc4 22 ♛g5 ♛h6 23 ♛xh6 gxh6 24 ♗f6 ♖d6 25 e5 is better for White as he will win Black's h6 pawn sooner or later; Yakovich-Hernandez, Bayamo 1990.

10 g3 dxc4 11 ♘b5 ♛e5 12 ♘d6+ ♔e7

For once in this variation it's the black king that takes an early step.

13 ♗f4 ♛c3+ 14 ♗d2! ♛d4 15 ♘xc4 b5! 16 ♘e3 ♗d7 17 ♖c1 ♘a6?

Better is 17...♘c6!.

18 ♔f2 ♖ac8 19 ♗c3! ♛xd1 20 ♖xd1

White is much better here, with his bishop pair and extra space.

20...♖hd8 21 ♗e2 ♘b8 22 ♘b2 ♗c6 23 ♘d3 ♘bd7 24 ♗d4! a6 25 ♘c5?! e5 26 ♗e3 ♘xc5 27 ♗xc5+ ♔e8 28 a4! ♖d2! 29 ♔e3 ♖a2 30 a5! ♖d8

31 ♗b6?

An incomprehensible move, luring both black rooks onto his second rank; instead 31 ♖gd1! ♖xd1 32 ♖xd1 ♖a3+ 33 ♔f2 ♖a2+ 34 ♔e1 ♔d7 35 ♗b3 is good for White.

31...♖dd2 32 ♗d3 ♔d7 33 ♖c5 ♗xe4! 34 ♗xe4 ½-½

Since 34...♖e2+ 35 ♔d3 ♖ad2+ 36 ♔c3 ♘xe4+ 37 fxe4 ♖c2+ is a draw by perpetual check.

Game 134

Ilinčić-Čabrilo
Cetinje 1992

1 d4 ♘f6 2 c4 e6 3 ♘c3 ♗b4 4 f3 d5 5 a3 ♗e7 6 e4 c5 7 e5 ♘fd7 8 cxd5 exd5 9 ♘xd5

⇨ 9 f4!? ♘c6 10 ♘f3 cxd4 11 ♘xd4 0-0 12 ♗e3 ♘c5 13 ♗e2 ♘e6! 14 ♛d2 f6! 15 ♗f3? (15 0-0 fxe5 16 fxe5 ♘exd4 17 ♗xd4 ♖xf1+ 18 ♖xf1 ♗e6 =) 15...fxe5 16 ♘xe6 ♗xe6 17 ♗xd5 ♗xd5 18 ♛xd5+ ♛xd5 19 ♘xd5 exf4 20 ♘xf4? ♗h4+ 21 g3 ♖ae8 (Black has amassed a significant lead in development which he puts to good use) 22 ♔d2 ♗f6 ∓ 23 ♗c5 ♖f7 24 ♖ae1 ♘e5 25 ♖e4 ♖c7 26 ♗d4 ♘f3+ 27 ♔e3 ♖xe4+ 28 ♔xe4 ♘xd4 29 ♘d5 (perhaps White was relying on this move to save his piece) 29...♖c4 30 ♘xf6+ gxf6 31 ♔d5 ♖a4 32 ♖f1 ♘c6 33 ♖xf6 ♖d4+ 34 ♔c5 ♖d2 35 b4 ♘e5 36 ♖h6 ♘g4 37 ♖d6 b6+ 38 ♔c6 ♘e5+ 39 ♔c7 ♖xd6 40 ♔xd6 ♘c4+ 0-1 Gutman-Aseev, Wiesbaden 1991.

9...cxd4 10 ♘xe7 ♛xe7 11 f4 f6

12 ♕xd4 fxe5 13 ♕e3 ♘c6 14 ♘f3 0-0 15 ♗d2! ♔h8

⇨ 15...a5 16 fxe5 ♘dxe5 17 ♘xe5 ♘xe5 18 0-0-0 ♗f5 19 ♗c4+! ♔h8 20 ♗c3 ± ♖ac8 21 ♕xe5 ♕g5+?! 22 ♖d2 ♖xc4 23 ♖f1 h6 24 ♕xa5 ♔h7 25 ♕e5? (25 ♕d5 ± was preferable) 25...♗e4! (threatening both ...♖xf1# and ...♕xe5, as the bishop on c3 is pinned and only offers illusory defence of e5) 26 ♕xe4+ ♖xe4 27 ♖xf8 ♖e2 ∓ Malaniuk-Eingorn, Moscow 1988.

⇨ 15...♖xf4!? (a reasonable exchange sacrifice as the white king is stuck in the centre) 16 ♕b3+ ♔h8 17 ♗xf4 exf4+ 18 ♗e2 ♘f6 ∞ 19 ♕c4 ♘g4 20 0-0 ♘e3 21 ♕xf4 ♘xf1 22 ♖xf1 ♗g4 is equal, although White later blundered and lost in Malaniuk-Dziuban, Alma-Ata 1989.

16 fxe5 ♘dxe5 17 ♘xe5 ♕xe5 18 ♕xe5 ♘xe5 19 ♗b4! ♖e8 20 0-0-0 ♗g4 21 ♖e1 ♘c6 22 ♖xe8+ ♖xe8 23 ♗c3 ♗e2 24 ♗xe2 ♖xe2 25 ♖e1 ♖xe1+ 26 ♗xe1 ♔g8 27 ♔d2 ♔f7 28 ♔e3 ♔e6 29 ♗c3 g6 30 ♔e4 h5

This type of endgame, with bishop against knight and a slightly

better king, offers good winning chances.

31 ♗e1 ♘e5 32 ♗f2 ♘c4 33 ♗xa7 ♘xb2 34 ♔d4 ♔d6 35 ♗b8+ ♔e6 36 ♔c5 ♔d7 37 ♔d5 ♘d3 38 ♗g3! ♘b2 39 ♗e1 ♘d3 40 ♗d2 ♘b2 41 h3! ♘d3 42 a4 b6 43 ♗e3 ♘b2 44 ♗xb6 ♘xa4 45 ♗d4 ±

Dominating the knight.

45...h4 46 ♔e5 ♔e7 47 ♔f4 ♔e6 48 ♔g5 ♔d5 49 ♗f2 ♘b2 50 ♗xh4 ♘d1 51 ♔xg6 ♘e3 52 g4 ♔e4 53 ♗g5 ♘c4 54 ♗f6 ♘e3 55 ♔g5 ♔f3 56 ♗d4 1-0

Game 135

Beliavsky-Spassky
Linares 1990

1 d4 ♘f6 2 c4 e6 3 ♘c3 ♗b4 4 f3 d5 5 a3 ♗e7 6 e4 c5 7 cxd5 exd5 8 e5 ♘fd7 9 ♘xd5 cxd4 10 ♘xe7 ♕xe7 11 f4 f6 12 ♘f3!? fxe5 13 ♗c4 ♘c6

⇨ 13...♘b6?! 14 ♗b3 ♗g4 15 fxe5 ♘c6 16 0-0 0-0-0 17 ♗g5 ♗xf3 18 ♕d2 ♕xe5 19 ♖xf3 ♘d5 20 ♗xd8 ♖xd8 21 ♗xd5 ♕xd5 22 ♖c1 ♔b8 23 ♕f4+ gives White some chances of exploiting his material advantage; Ivanchuk-Dimitrov, Adelaide 1988.

⇨ 13...d3!? (might be best) 14 b4! (in order, in some lines, to stop the annoying check on c5; 14 fxe5 ♘xe5 15 ♘xe5 ♕xe5+ 16 ♔d2 ♖f8! = Arencibia-Schneider, Cuba 1989) 14...e4 15 0-0 ♘c6 16 ♖e1! ♘f6 17 ♗xd3 ♗g4 18 ♗xe4 ♘xe4 19 ♕d5 ♖d8 20 ♕xe4 ♗xf3 21 gxf3 ♕xe4 22 fxe4 ♘d4 23 ♖f1 0-0! (so far this is all analysis by Shirov, who assesses the position as ±) 24 ♗e3?!

½-½ Zsu.Polgar-Adorjan, Debrecen 1990. 24...♘c2 25 ♗c5 ♘xa1 26 ♗xf8 ♖xf8 27 ♖xa1 ♖xf4 is equal, but 24 ♖a2 seems better.

14 0-0 e4 15 ♗d5!

⇨ 15 ♘g5? ♘f6 16 b4 h6 17 ♘xe4 ♘xe4 18 ♕h5+ ♔f8 19 ♖e1 ♘f6! 20 ♖xe7 ♘xh5 21 ♖f7+ ♔e8 22 ♗b2 ♗d7 23 ♖d1 ♖c8 24 ♗a2 a6 25 h3 ♘g3 26 ♖xg7 ♘f5 27 ♖e1+ ♘ce7 28 ♗xd4 ♘xg7 29 ♗f6 ♗e6 30 ♗xg7 ♗xa2 31 ♗xh8 ♔f7 and Black's extra piece told in Murshed-Klinger, Novi Sad OL 1990.

15...♘f6

Obviously 15...exf3? is met by 16 ♗xc6 and if 16...bxc6? 17 ♖e1.

16 ♗xc6+ bxc6 17 ♘xd4 0-0 18 ♗e3 ♗a6

Maybe 18...♗d7!?, but White is better; the black pawn structure is very ragged.

19 ♖e1 c5 20 ♕b3+ ♔h8 21 ♘c6 ♕e8 22 ♘e5 ♖b8 23 ♕c2 ♘d5 24 ♕xe4

Aiming for a direct attack.

24...♘xe3 25 ♖xe3 ♖xb2 26 ♖h3 h6 27 ♘g6+ ♔g8 28 ♘e7+ ♔h8 29 ♖e1 ♖f6 30 ♖g3 ♕d8 31 ♘g6+ ♔g8 32 h4 ♖d2?

Either 32...♕d4+ 33 ♕xd4 cxd4 34 f5!? ♖b8, or 32...♖b8 33 ♘e7+ ♔h8 34 ♘c6 ♗b7! would have been preferable.

33 ♕e8+ ♔h7 34 ♘f8+! ♔g8 34...♖xf8 35 ♕g6+.

35 ♘d7+ ♕xe8 36 ♖xe8+ ♔f7 37 ♘xf6 ± gxf6 38 ♖a8 ♔e6 39 ♖xa7 ♗d3 40 ♖g8 c4 41 ♖c7 ♖a2 42 ♖c5 ♖xa3 43 ♖gc8 h5 44 ♖xh5 c3 45 ♖hc5 c2 46 h5 ♗e4 47 h6 ♔f7 48 ♖8c7+ ♔g6 49 h7 ♖a8 50 g4 f5 51 gxf5+ ♗xf5 52 h8♘+ ♔f6 53 ♖5c6+ 1-0

Game 136 CML

Shirov-Eingorn
Stockholm ~~1990~~ 1989

1 d4 e6 2 c4 ♗b4+ 3 ♘c3 ♘f6 4 f3 d5 5 a3 ♗e7 6 e4 c5 7 cxd5 exd5 8 dxc5 ♗xc5 9 e5 ♘fd7 10 ♕xd5 0-0!? 11 f4 ♕b6

More promising is 11...♗xg1! 12 ♖xg1 ♕b6 (12...♕h4+? 13 g3 ♕xh2 14 ♕g2! {with a clear plus for White} ♕xg2 15 ♖xg2! ♘c5 16 ♗e3 ♘b3 17 ♖d1 ♗h3 18 ♖c2 ♗xf1 19 ♔xf1 ♘c6 20 ♘b5! ♖ad8 21 ♘d6 a6 22 ♖c3 ♘ca5 23 ♗b6 ♖d7 24 ♖d5 1-0 Khenkin-Barle, Voskresensk 1990 – one of the misplaced knights is lost) 13 ♖h1 and now:

⇨ 13...♘c5?! 14 b4 ♘e6 15 ♘a4 ♕c7 16 ♗e3+ ♘c6 17 ♕d6 (forcing off the queens) 17...♕xd6 18 exd6 ♖e8 19 ♔f2 ♗d7 20 ♘c5 ♘xc5 21 bxc5 ♘b8 22 ♖b1 b6 23 ♗b5! bxc5 24 ♗xc5 ♗xb5 25 ♖xb5 ♘d7 26 ♗b4 (Black is quite lost) 26...g6 27 ♖c1 ♖e6 28 ♖c7 a5 29 ♖xa5 ♖xa5

30 ♗xa5 ♖xd6 31 ♗b4 ♖d5 32 a4
1-0 Gelfand-Spassky, Linares 1990.
⇨ 13...♘c6! 14 ♗c4? (14 ♕b5 ♘d4!
15 ♕xb6 ♘xb6 16 ♗d3 ♖d8 is less
clear) 14...♘dxe5! (if Black didn't
have this he would be clearly worse)
15 fxe5 ♗e6 16 ♕b5 ♗xc4 17 ♕xc4
♘xe5 18 ♕b5 ♕d4 (White's king is
caught in the middle) 19 ♗d2 ♘d3+
20 ♔d1 ♖fd8 21 ♔c2 ♘f2 22 ♕e2
♘xh1 23 ♖xh1 ♖ac8 24 ♖f1 ♕a4+
25 ♔c1 ♕b3 ½-½ Shirov-Rausis,
Daugavpils 1990. Black can consider advancing his queenside
pawns, but White should have sufficient resources.

12 ♘f3 ♗f2+ 13 ♔e2

Again, White's king is awkwardly placed, but it is not easy for
Black to get at it.

**13...♘c5! 14 b4 ♖d8 15 bxc5
♗xc5 16 ♕e4!? ♕b3! 17 ♗d2
♖xd2+!**

Winning back his sacrificed
material, but afterwards it is White's
turn and he proceeds to win the game
with a sharp attack.

18 ♔xd2 ♕b2+ 19 ♔d3 ♕xa1

20 e6!! fxe6 21 ♘g5 g6 22 ♕e5!

♗e7 23 ♘xe6 ♔f7?

23...♗f8! 24 ♘xf8 ♘c6 25 ♕f6
♕a3! 26 ♔d2! ±.

24 ♕g7+! ♔e8

White wins after 24...♔xe6 25
♔c2! ♕xa3 26 ♗b5! ♘c6 27 ♗c4+
♔d7 28 ♖d1+.

25 ♘c7+ ♔d8 26 ♕h8+! ♔d7

26...♔xc7 27 ♘d5+ wins the
queen on a1.

27 ♘xa8 ♕xa3 28 ♔c2 1-0

Game 137

Timman-Karpov
Kuala Lumpur Ct (3) 1990

1 d4 ♘f6 2 c4 e6 3 ♘c3 ♗b4 4 f3 d5
5 a3 ♗xc3+ 6 bxc3 c5 7 cxd5 ♘xd5
8 dxc5 ♕a5 9 e4 ♘e7 10 ♗e3 0-0 11
♕b3 ♕c7!

Karpov's strong innovation.
Black intends ...♘e7-c6-a5 and
...♘b8-d7, aiming at the squares c5
and c4.

12 ♗b5

Or 12 ♖d1 (12 ♘h3 and 12 a4 are
dealt with in the next two main

games) with various playable alternatives:

⇨ 12...♘d7! 13 ♗b5?! (giving up the c-pawn without a fight. 13 ♕c4 is more testing, but even then after 13...♘ec6!? 14 ♘h3 b6 15 cxb6 axb6 Black has a fine position; he threatens ...♗a6 and ...♖xa3) 13...♘xc5 14 ♕c4 b6 15 ♗xc5?! (even after 15 ♘e2 a6! 16 ♗a4 e5 and ...♗e6 White is clearly worse) 15...bxc5 16 ♘e2 ♘g6 17 0-0 ♘e5 18 ♕a2 ♖b8 ∓ 19 c4 ♗b7 20 ♕c2 ♖fd8 21 ♕c3 h6 22 ♘g3 ♘g6 23 ♘e2 ♘e5 24 ♘f4 a6 25 ♗a4 ♗c6 26 ♗c2 ♗e8 27 ♘h5 f6 28 ♘f4 ♗f7 29 ♗a4 ♖xd1 30 ♖xd1 ♖d8 31 ♖xd8+ ♕xd8 32 ♔f2 ♕b8 with a small edge to Black since White's bishop has little future; Lin Ta-Petursson, Manila IZ 1990.

⇨ 12...♘ec6 13 f4 ♘a5 14 ♕b4 ♘a6 15 ♗xa6 bxa6 16 ♘f3 ♖b8 17 ♕a4 ♗b7 18 ♘e5 ♖fd8 19 0-0 f6 20 ♘c4 ♘xc4 21 ♕xc4 ♕c6 22 f5! (the only way to defend the e-pawn) 22...♔f7 23 ♗f4 ♖bc8 24 ♖fe1 g6 25 ♕xe6+ ♕xe6 26 fxe6+ ♔xe6 27 ♗d6 is better for White, but the opposite-colour bishops make a draw the likely outcome; Bykhovsky-Abramović, New York 1990.

⇨ 12...♘bc6 13 f4 e5!? (the prelude to an unusual sacrifice) 14 f5 ♗xf5?! (this looks quite dangerous, but it's hard to believe that it's sound) 15 exf5 ♘xf5 16 ♗c1 ♖ad8 17 ♗e2 ♕e7 18 ♕c4 e4 19 ♖xd8 ♖xd8 20 ♘h3 ♘a5 21 ♕b5 ♕h4+ 22 ♘f2! (unfortunately for Black, White can solve his development problems simply like this, winning a piece immediately afterwards with a double

attack) 22...e3 23 0-0 exf2+ 24 ♖xf2 1-0 Yakovich-Kharitonov, Podolsk 1989.

12...♘ec6 13 ♖d1

⇨ 13 f4 (more adventurous) 13...♘a5 14 ♕b4 ♘a6 (I would prefer to play the immediate 14...e5!? here, for instance: 15 f5 ♘a6 16 ♗xa6 bxa6 17 ♖d1 ♖b8 with some initiative) 15 ♗xa6 bxa6 16 ♖d1 e5 17 ♘f3 ♖b8 18 ♕a4 exf4 19 ♗f2 ♗e6 20 0-0 ♖fc8 21 ♖d5 (offering the exchange to connect his queenside pawns, but Black is not interested) 21...♘b7 22 ♖e5 ♕a5 23 ♕b4 ♕c7 24 ♕a4 ♕a5 ½-½ Lin Ta-Smyslov, Manila IZ 1990.

13...♘a5

⇨ 13...e5 (despite Karpov's success in the main game, he nevertheless decided to play slightly differently when the players met again, at Linares the next year) 14 ♕a2 ♘a5 15 ♕d5 ♗d7 16 ♗xd7 ♖d8 17 ♕d6 ♕xd6 18 ♖xd6 ♘xd7?! (obvious, but bad; 18...♖xd7 19 ♔f2 ♘c4 is equal) 19 ♔f2 ♘c4 20 ♖d5 ♘f6 21 ♖xd8+ ♖xd8 22 ♘e2 ♖c8 23 ♖b1 ♖c7 24 ♗g5 ♔f8 25 ♖b4 ♘a5 26 ♖b5 ♘c4 27 ♖b4 ♘a5 28 ♗e3 ♘d7 29 ♘c1 b6? 30 cxb6 axb6 31 ♘a2 with a sound extra pawn, although Black managed to draw in Timman-Karpov, Linares 1991.

14 ♕b4

The queen can find herself exposed here; perhaps 14 ♕a2 is better as in the previous note.

14...e5 15 ♘e2 ♗e6 16 c4?!

There was no point to this pawn offer; maybe 16 ♘c1 ∞.

16...a6 17 ♗a4 ♘xc4 18 ♗f2 ♘c6 19 ♕c3 ♕a5

White's weaknesses will be more easily exploited in the endgame.

20 ♗xc6 bxc6 21 ♕xa5 ♘xa5 22 0-0 ♖ab8 23 ♘c3 ♖b3 24 ♘a4 ♖xa3 25 ♘b6 ♘c4 26 h3 h5 27 ♖c1 ♘b2 28 ♖b1 ♘d3 29 ♖fd1 f5! 30 exf5 ♖xf5 31 ♖d2 ♘xf2+ 32 ♔xf2 e4 33 ♖e1 e3+ 34 ♖xe3 ♖xe3 35 ♔xe3 ♖xc5

With two passed pawns, and the better minor piece, this must be assessed as clearly better for Black.

36 ♘d7 ♖b5 37 f4 a5 38 ♘e5 ♗d5 39 ♖c2 ♖b6 40 g4 a4?!

Time pressure; 40...♖b3+ 41 ♔d4 hxg4 42 hxg4 ♖b4+ is clearly winning.

41 ♖c3 h4?!

41...♖b3+ is still good. Now White manages to hold on.

42 ♘g6 ♖b3 43 ♔d2 ♖b2+ 44 ♔d3 ♔f7 45 ♘e5+ ♔e8 46 f5 ♗g2 47 ♔d4 ♖b5 48 ♘g6 ♖b4+ 49 ♔e5 ♖b3 50 ♖c2 ♗xh3 51 ♖xc6 ♗g2 52 ♖e6+ ♔d7 53 ♘xh4 ♗c6 54 ♖g6 ♖e3+ 55 ♔d4 ♖e7 56 ♔c5 ♖e5+ 57 ♔b4 ♖e4+ 58 ♔c5 ♖e5+ 59 ♔b4 ♖e7 60 ♔c5 ♗b7 61 ♔b4 ♗c6 ½-½

Game 138

Dreev-Anand
Madras Ct (1) 1991

1 d4 ♘f6 2 c4 e6 3 ♘c3 ♗b4 4 f3 d5 5 a3 ♗xc3+ 6 bxc3 c5 7 cxd5 ♘xd5 8 dxc5 ♕a5 9 e4 ♘e7 10 ♗e3 0-0 11 ♕b3 ♕c7 12 ♘h3 e5

Although this move, threatening to take on h3, would appear obvious, 12...♘ec6 has also been seen occasionally: 13 ♘f4 (agreed drawn here in Dreev-Sax, Manila IZ 1990!) 13...♘a5 14 ♕a4 ♗d7 15 ♗b5 ♘bc6 16 0-0 a6 17 ♗xc6 ♗xc6 18 ♕b4 ♗b5 19 ♖fe1 ♘c4 ½-½ Arencibia-Lalić, Seville 1990; instead 13 ♖b1 e5 14 ♘f2 transposes to the next note.

13 ♘f2 ♘ec6 14 ♘d3

White's idea is to play the knight to d5 via b4.

Previously 14 ♖b1 had been tried: 14...♘a5 15 ♕a4 ♗e6 (15...♗d7 is worse: 16 ♗b5 ♗e6 17 0-0 a6 18 ♗e2 ♘d7 19 ♕b4 ♖ac8 20 c6! bxc6 21 ♗xa6 ♖b8 22 ♕e7 ± Arencibia-Franco, Havana 1990) 16 ♗e2 ♘d7 17 ♖b5 b6 18 0-0 with three possibilities:

➭ 18...♖fc8 (I like this best) 19 ♖fb1 ♘b7 20 ♘d3 ♕c6 21 ♕c2 ♘bxc5 22 ♘xc5 ♘xc5 23 ♗xc5 a6! (in order to capture on c5 with his queen) 24 ♖xb6 ♕xc5+ 25 ♔f1 ♕xa3 26 ♕c1 ♕xc1+ 27 ♖xc1 a5 with the very slightest of advantages for Black; Marin-Lautier, Manila IZ 1990.

➭ 18...♖fb8 19 ♖fb1 h6 20 g3 bxc5? (20...♘b7! 21 ♘d3 bxc5 22 f4 ♘b6 23 ♕c2 ♗d7 24 ♘xe5 ♗xb5 25

♖xb5 is unclear; after the move played Black gets mated surprisingly quickly) 21 ♖xb8+ ♖xb8 22 ♖xb8+ ♘xb8 (obviously forced, but it allows the white queen to penetrate) 23 ♕e8+ ♔h7 24 f4 ♘c4?! 25 f5! ♘xe3? 26 fxe6 ♕b6 27 exf7 ♕b1+ 28 ♗d1 ♘xd1 29 ♕g8+ ♔g6 30 f8♘+ 1-0 Arencibia-Lobron, Manila IZ 1990.

⇨ 18...♘b7 19 cxb6 axb6 20 ♕b4 ♘d6 21 ♗xb6 ♕c6 22 ♗e3 ♖fc8 23 ♖a5 ♖xa5 24 ♕xa5 ♖a8 25 ♕b4 ½-½ Yakovich-A.Sokolov, Moscow 1990.

14...♗e6! 15 ♕b5 ♘d7 16 ♗e2

White is unable to execute his plan as yet: 16 ♘b4?! a6 17 ♕a4 ♘a5 18 ♘d5 ♗xd5 19 exd5 ♘xc5 20 ♕b4 ♖ac8! is good for Black. Anand's analysis continues 21 d6? ♕xd6 22 ♕xa5 ♘b3 ∓.

16...♘a5 17 0-0 ♖ac8 18 ♖fd1 ♗b3?

An inaccuracy; instead 18...♗c4 19 ♕b4 ♘b8 is equal.

19 ♖d2

19 ♘b4 was now possible, e.g. 19...♗xd1 20 ♖xd1 ♘c6 21 ♘d5 ♕b8 22 ♖b1 with plenty of compensation for the exchange.

19...♗c4 20 ♕b4 ♘b8!

A lovely redevelopment of the knight.

21 ♖b1 ♘a6 22 ♕b2 ♗xd3 23 ♗xd3 ♘xc5

Black gives a model example of playing with the 'knight pair'.

24 ♗f1 b6 25 c4 ♘e6 26 ♖bd1 ♘xc4 27 ♗xc4 ♕xc4 28 ♕xe5 ♕b3 29 ♖d3 ♕a2! 30 ♕d5?! ♕e2 31 ♕d6??

Time-trouble rears its ugly head.

31...♖cd8 32 ♕xd8 ♘xd8 33 ♗f2 ♕a2 34 ♖xd8 ♕xa3 35 ♗g3 h6 36 ♖8d7 ♖c8 0-1

Game 139

Gelfand-de Firmian
Moscow GMA 1990

1 d4 ♘f6 2 c4 e6 3 ♘c3 ♗b4 4 f3 d5 5 a3 ♗xc3+ 6 bxc3 c5 7 cxd5 ♘xd5 8 dxc5 ♕a5 9 e4 ♘e7 10 ♗e3 0-0 11 ♕b3 ♕c7

⇨ 11...e5 is doubtful: 12 ♗c4 ♕c7 13 ♘e2! (13 a4 would transpose to the main game, whilst 13 ♗d5 ♘a6 14 ♕c4 ♗d7 15 ♖b1 ♖ab8 16 ♘e2 ½-½ was Gelfand-Brunner, Dortmund 1990) 13...♘ec6 14 ♗d5 ♘a5 15 ♕b2 ♘a6 16 c4! ('cementing' the bishop on d5) ♗d7 17 0-0 ♘xc5 18 f4 ♘ab3? 19 ♖ab1 exf4? 20 ♘xf4 ♖ae8 21 ♖f3! ♕e5 22 ♕xe5 ♖xe5 23 ♘d3 1-0 Beliavsky-Hjartarson, Moscow GMA 1990. After 23...♘xd3 24 ♖xb3 ♘e1 25 ♖f1 ♘c2 26 ♗xa7 Black's knight is stranded.

12 a4

This move gives White the possibility of defending the c5 pawn with ♕a3.

12...e5

Instead 12...♘d7!? is one possibility: 13 ♕a3 f5! 14 ♘h3 fxe4 15 fxe4 ♘g6 16 ♘f2 ♘de5 17 ♗e2 ♘f4 18 ♗xf4 ♖xf4 19 0-0 ♗d7 20 ♖ad1! = Golod-Makarychev, USSR 1990.

However, the main, and possibly best line here is 12...♘ec6 13 f4 ♘a5 14 ♕a3 and now:

1) 14...b6!? (compare with the next line) 15 ♘f3 ♗a6 (Black intends to capture on a6 with the knight instead of the rook) 16 ♘d2 ♗xf1 17 ♖xf1 ♘d7 18 cxb6 axb6 19 ♔f2 ♖fc8 20 ♖fc1 ♘c5 21 ♔e2? ♘cb3! (winning the exchange because of 22 ♘xb3 ♕c4+ 23 ♔f2 ♘xb3) 22 ♕b4 ♘xa1 23 ♖xa1 ♘c4 24 ♘xc4 ♕xc4+ 25 ♕xc4 ♖xc4 26 ♗xb6 ♖cxa4 27 ♖xa4 ♖xa4 28 ♔f3 and in Soffer-Law, Biel 1992, White managed to hold on for a draw, attained some 47 moves later.

2) 14...♘d7 15 ♘f3 b6! (another string to Black's bow; this pawn sacrifice is a necessary part of Black's plan to eliminate the c5 pawn which exerts such a cramping effect on his game. He receives a sufficient return for the pawn in the form of the pressure down the a- and c-files) 16 cxb6 axb6 17 ♘d2. It now seems that the bishop should go to a6:

2a) 17...♗b7 leaves White in possession of two very potent bishops after either of the following moves:
➪ 18 ♗e2 ♖fc8 19 0-0 ♕xc3 20 ♗b5?! (20 ♖fb1 ±) 20...♕xa3 21 ♖xa3 ♗c6 22 ♖b1? (22 ♖d3! with the idea of ♖d6 is better, because

Black's b-pawn is weak and White's bishop is strong) 22...h6 23 ♖d3 ♗xb5 24 axb5 ♖a7 25 ♖a1 ♖ac7 26 ♔f2 ♘c5 27 ♖da3 ♘c4 28 ♗xc5 ♘xd2 29 ♗xb6 ♖c2 30 ♔g1 ♘xe4 31 ♗e3 ♖b2 32 ♖a4 ♘c3 33 ♖a8 ♖xa8 34 ♖xa8+ ♔h7 35 b6 ♖b1+ 36 ♔f2 ♘d1+ 37 ♔e2 ♘xe3 38 ♔xe3 ♖xb6 Azmaiparashvili-A.Sokolov, Moscow GMA 1990. Black has a pawn more, although the game should be drawn.

➪ 18 ♗b5 ♘f6 19 0-0 ♘xe4 20 ♘xe4 ♗xe4 21 ♕b4 ♗d5? (a tactical error; 21...♕b7 is better, Aagaard-Wedberg, Copenhagen 1991 continuing 22 ♖f2 ♖fc8 23 ♖c1 ♖ab8 24 ♗f1 ♗d5 25 c4 ♗xc4 ½-½. However, 23 ♗f1 looks more dangerous, followed by 24 ♖b2. If White can swap his c-pawn for Black's b-pawn, then his a-pawn supported by his two bishops will become very dangerous) 22 c4! ♘xc4? (this just loses a piece, but if instead 22...♗b7, then 23 c5 bxc5 24 ♗xc5 is clearly to White's advantage; his bishops are very powerful) 23 ♖fc1 ♖fc8 24 ♖a3! ♕b7 25 ♗xc4 ♗xg2 26 ♗xb6 ♕e4 27 ♖g3 ♗f1 28 ♕b2 g6 29 ♗xf1 1-0 Lin Ta-Li Wenliang, China 1990.

2b) 17...♗a6! and now:
➪ 18 ♗xa6 (it seems that White can avoid this exchange—see the next line) 18...♖xa6 19 0-0 ♖fa8 20 ♕b4 ♘b7 21 ♖a2 ♕c6 22 ♖fa1 ♘dc5 (this completes the rounding up of the a-pawn) 23 c4 h6 24 e5 ♖xa4 25 ♖xa4 ♖xa4 26 ♖xa4 ♘xa4 27 ♗d4 ♕d7 28 ♘f3 ♘bc5 29 h3 ♘d3 30 ♕d2 ♘ac5?! drew eventually in Khalifman-van der Wiel, Wijk aan

Zee 1991, but 30...♘dc5 = is somewhat simpler.

⇨ 18 ♗b5!? ♗xb5 (18...♘c4 19 ♗xc4 ♗xc4 20 ♕b4 ♗a6?! 21 c4! ♘c5! 22 0-0 ♖fd8 23 a5 is unpleasant; Milov-Nielsen, Buenos Aires 1992) 19 axb5 ♘c4 20 ♕xa8 ♘xe3 21 ♕c6 ♕xf4 22 g3! ♘g2+ 23 ♔d1 ♕g4+ 24 ♔c1 might be favourable for White; Milov-Grünfeld, Israel 1993.

13 ♗c4 ♘ec6 14 ♕a3 ♘a5 15 ♗d5 ♘a6 16 ♖b1

After 16 c4!? ♗e6 17 ♖c1 ♖ac8 18 ♘e2 ♘xc5 19 0-0 b6 Black's mighty knight on c5 and pressure down the c-file is balanced by the bishop on d5; Malaniuk-Kir.Georgiev, Moscow 1990.

16...♗e6 17 ♗xe6 fxe6 18 ♕a2 ♘xc5 19 ♗xc5 ♕xc5 20 ♕xe6+ ♔h8 21 ♘e2 ♕e3! 22 ♕xe5 ♖ad8!!

Only a vegetarian could find such a beautiful move!

23 ♕xa5 ½-½!

One possibility is 23...♖d2 24 ♕b5 ♖fd8 25 ♕c4 a6 26 a5 h6 27 ♖f1 ♖8d3 28 ♕c8+ ♔h7 29 ♕f5+ with a draw. Instead 28 ♖f2?? fails to 28...♖xe2+ 29 ♖xe2 ♕g1#.

Game 140

Moskalenko-Lukacs
Budapest 1991

1 d4 ♘f6 2 c4 e6 3 ♘c3 ♗b4 4 f3 d5 5 a3 ♗xc3+ 6 bxc3 c5 7 cxd5 ♘xd5 8 dxc5 ♕a5 9 e4 ♘f6 10 ♗e3 0-0 11 ♕b3 ♘fd7!

An idea of the Icelandic GM Olafsson. Essentially play will be very similar to that of the previous games. Should Black play ...♕c7, ...♘bc6 and ...♘a5, there could be a direct transposition.

12 a4

This may be White's strongest. In the original game in this line, White played otherwise:

1) 12 ♖d1 (not 12 ♘e2? because of the reply 12...♘xc5. Now, however, 12...♘xc5 would be an error allowing White to iron out his pawn structure with 13 ♕b4 ±) 12...♕c7 and now White must take care:

⇨ 13 ♕c4 ♘a6 14 c6 ♘e5 (14...bxc6 might be even better. Dreev-Goldin, New York open 1991 continued 15 f4 ♘b6 16 ♕d4 c5 17 ♕d6 ♕b7 18 ♔f2 ♕xe4 19 ♗d3 ♕a4 20 ♘f3 ½-½ although the final position is unclear, to say the least) 15 ♕a4 ♘xc6 16 ♗xa6 bxa6 17 ♗c5 ♖e8 18 ♘e2 e5 19 0-0 ♗e6 20 ♕xa6 ♘a5 21 ♗d6 ♗c4! (a fine riposte) 22 ♗xc7 ♗xa6 23 ♔f2 ♘b7 24 ♖d5 f6 25 ♖b1 ♖ac8 26 ♗a5 ♖e7 27 ♗b4 ♖ec7 28 a4 ♗c4 29 ♖d2 a5 30 ♗a3 ♗xe2 31 ♔xe2 ♖xc3 32 ♖xb7 ♖xa3 with a draw the likely result; Maximenko-Draško, Vrnjačka Banja 1991.

⇨ 13 ♘e2?! (faced, in this game,

with a new move, White falters)
13...♘xc5 14 ♕c4 b6 15 ♕d4 ♗a6
16 ♘g3 ♗xf1 17 ♖xf1 ♘c6 18 ♕d6
♕b7 19 ♗xc5 ♖fd8 20 ♕f4 ♖xd1+
21 ♔xd1 bxc5 (Black is well on top
at this stage) 22 ♔e1 ♕b2 23 ♘e2
♕xa3 winning a pawn, but White
struggled on and finally managed to
achieve a draw in Gutman-Hjartar-
son, Bundesliga 1991.

2) 12 ♕b4 ♕c7 13 ♖d1 ♘c6 14
♕a4 ♘ce5 15 ♕d4 ♘c6 16 ♕a4
♘ce5 17 ♕d4 ♘c6 ½-½ Timman-
Karpov, Tilburg 1991.

12...♕c7 13 ♕a3 ♘c6

⇨ 13...♘a6 didn't work out too well
in Moskalenko-Lawson, St Martin
1991: 14 ♗xa6 bxa6 15 ♘e2 ♘e5 16
0-0 ♘c4 17 ♕c1 e5 18 f4 ♗b7 19
fxe5 ♘xe3 20 ♕xe3 ♖ac8 21 ♖ab1
♗a8 22 e6 fxe6 23 ♖xf8+ (exchanging the rooks to defend his c-pawn)
23...♖xf8 24 ♖f1 ♕c6 25 ♖xf8+
♔xf8 26 ♘d4 ♕xe4 27 ♘xe6+ ♔e7
28 ♕xe4 ♗xe4 29 ♘d4 and White
won without too many problems.

⇨ 13...f5!? led to obscure play after
14 ♘h3 ♘c6 15 ♗c4?! ♘de5 16
♗e2 fxe4 17 fxe4 ♘g6 18 g3 ♘ce5
19 ♘f4 ♘xf4 20 ♗xf4 ♖xf4!? 21
gxf4 ♘g6 in Andrienko-Aleksan-
drov, Jurmala 1991. Black won on
move 79.

14 ♘h3 ♘a5 15 ♗b5

⇨ 15 ♗e2 b6! 16 cxb6 axb6 17 ♔f2
♗a6 (the same recipe as Khalifman-
van der Wiel) 18 ♖hd1 ♗xe2 19
♔xe2 ♘c4 ½-½ Sakaev-Blatny,
Brno 1992.

⇨ 15 ♖d1 e5 16 ♘f2 ♘f6 17 ♗e2
♗e6 18 0-0 ♖ac8 19 ♕b4 ♘b3 20
♘d3 ♘d7 (putting the utmost pressure on c5) 21 f4 ♘dxc5 22 f5 ♘a6

23 ♕a3 ♗c4 24 ♕b2? (evidently
missing Black's powerful next
move, after which White's position
falls apart) 24...♖ac5! 25 ♘xc5
♘xc5! 26 ♗xc4 ♘xa4 27 ♗xf7+
♕xf7 28 ♕a1 ♘xc3 ∓ Gutman-
Fahnenschmidt, Bundesliga 1992.

15...♘e5 16 ♗f4?

Losing a pawn; 16 ♕b4 ♘ec6 17
♕a3 ♘e5 is equal.

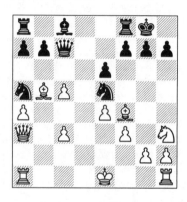

16...♘xf3+! 17 gxf3 e5 18 ♗e3! ∓
♗xh3 19 ♖g1 ♔h8 20 0-0-0 a6 21
♗e2 ♗e6 22 ♕b4 ♖ac8 23 ♔b2

The white king is safe here and
might even prove an asset in an
endgame.

23...♘b3 24 ♗c4 ♗xc4 25 ♕xc4
♘a5

25...♘xc5 26 ♕xc5 ♕xc5 27
♗xc5 ♖xc5 28 ♖d7 is nearly equal
owing to the activity of the white
pieces, but is worth a try.

26 ♕b4 ♖fd8 27 ♖d5 ♘c6 ½-½

Game 141

Beliavsky-Portisch
Amsterdam 1990

1 d4 ♘f6 2 c4 e6 3 ♘c3 ♗b4 4 f3 d5
5 a3 ♗xc3+ 6 bxc3 c5 7 cxd5 ♘xd5
8 dxc5 f5 9 ♘h3

White has a large range of alternatives:

1) 9 ♕c2 0-0 10 e4 fxe4 11 fxe4
transposes to line '2b' below, while
avoiding the 10...e3 of line '2a', and
so may be a nuance. It is interesting
that the Timman-Karpov game mentioned below started just this way.
Should Black try to take advantage
of White's omission of e4 by playing
(9 ♕c2) 9...f4, then 10 ♗xf4! ♘xf4
11 ♕a4+ ♘c6 12 ♕xf4 e5 13 ♕c4 ±.
Strangely, in the game Sakaev-Brodsky, USSR 1991, White preferred 10
g3?! 0-0 11 c4 ♘e3 12 ♗xe3 fxe3 13
♕c3 ♕g5 14 f4 ♕xc5 15 ♗g2 ♘c6
16 ♘f3 h6 17 ♖b1 b6 18 ♖b5 ♕d6
19 c5 bxc5 20 ♖xc5 ♘e7 21 ♕xe3
♘d5 22 ♕d4 ♕a6 23 ♔f2 ♗b7 24
♖b1 when he was a pawn to the good
anyway.

2) 9 e4 fxe4 10 ♕c2 and now:

2a) 10...e3 11 ♗d3 ♘d7 12 c4
♘f4 13 ♗xe3 ♘xc5?! (13...♕a5+ 14
♔f2 ♘xd3 = is better) 14 ♗xh7
♕h4+ 15 ♔f1 ♕xh7 16 ♕xh7 ♖xh7
17 ♗xc5 b6 18 ♗e3 ♘d3 19 ♘h3
♖h4! (Black has to find a lot of good
moves to keep his game alive; if
19...♗a6?, then 20 ♘g5 ♖h6 21 ♘e4
±) 20 ♘f2 ♘xf2 21 ♔xf2 ♖xc4 22
♖ac1 ♗a6 23 ♖xc4 ♗xc4 24 ♗d4
with an edge to White; Yakovich-
Naumkin, Moscow 1990.

2b) 10...0-0 11 fxe4 when Black
has tried:

⇨ 11...♕h4+ 12 g3 ♕f6 13 ♗g2
♕xc3+ 14 ♕xc3 ♘xc3 15 ♗f4 ♗d7
16 ♘e2 ♘a4 17 ♗d6 ♖c8 18 e5 ♗c6
19 ♗h3! (stronger than the formerly

played 19 ♗xc6 bxc6 =) 19...♗d7
(19...♗xh1 20 ♗xe6+ ♔h8 21 ♗xc8
♘a6 22 ♗f5 ♘6c5 23 ♖c1 b6 24
♖c4-h4 ±) 20 ♗g2 ♗c6 21 ♗h3
♗d7 22 ♖c1 ♘a6 23 c6! ♖xc6 24
♖xc6 bxc6 25 0-0 ♘6c5?? (as
Spassky once said: "knights are at
their weakest when they are defending each other". After something
sensible like 25...h6, White's bishops are strong, but a pawn is a
pawn!) 26 ♖f4 1-0 Khenkin-Karpman, Minsk 1990.

⇨ 11...♘f4 is more solid: 12 ♘f3
♕c7 13 ♗e3 ♘d7 14 ♗c4 ♘xc5 15
0-0 ♗d7 16 ♖ae1!? (Timman avoids
16 e5 which was thought to give
White the advantage, on account of
16...♗a4 17 ♕b1 unclear) 16...b6 17
♗d4 ♗a4 18 ♕d2 ♘b3 19 ♗xb3
♗xb3 20 ♘e5 ♘g6 21 ♕g5 ♕e7! 22
♕g3 ♘xe5 ½-½ Timman-Karpov,
Reykjavik 1991.

3) 9 c4 ♕h4+ 10 g3 ♕xc4 with
another subdivision:

⇨ 11 ♗b2!? ♘e3 12 ♕c1 ♕xc1+ 13
♖xc1 0-0 14 ♗h3 (the bishop does
nothing here, of course; White just
wants to avoid its exchange)
14...♗d7 15 ♔d2 ♘d5 16 f4 (fixing
e5 for White's pieces, but conceding
e4) 16...♘a6 17 ♘f3 ♖ac8 18 ♗d4
♖fd8 19 e4 ♘f6 20 exf5 exf5 21 ♔e3
♘g4+ 22 ♗xg4 fxg4 23 ♘e5 ♘c7
24 ♖hd1 ½-½ Georgadze-Balashov,
Odessa 1989.

⇨ 11 e4 ♕c3+ 12 ♗d2 ♕e5 13 ♗g2
(13 ♗d3) 13...fxe4 14 fxe4 ♘c3 15
♕c1 ♘xe4 16 ♗f4 ♕d4 17 ♗e3
♕d3 18 ♘e2 0-0 19 ♘f4 ♕c3+ 20
♕xc3 ♘xc3 21 ♔d2 ♘b5 22 ♖hb1
a6 23 a4 = Moskalenko-Karpman,
Simferopol 1990.

4) 9 e3, though sensible, is rarely played. Following 9...♕a5 10 ♕d4 0-0 11 ♗d2 ♘c6 12 ♕c4 ♕c7 13 ♖b1 ♘a5 14 ♕d3 ♖d8 15 c4 ♘f6 16 ♕c3 b6 17 cxb6 axb6 18 ♘e2 e5 19 c5 bxc5 20 ♖b5 ♘d5 21 ♕xc5 ♕xc5 22 ♖xc5 ♘b3 23 ♖c2 White was struggling in the game Quinteros–Sunye-Neto, Buenos Aires 1990, although he later won.

9...0-0

⇨ 9...♕a5 10 ♘f4 ♗d7 11 ♕b3 ♘c6 12 ♘d3 0-0 13 ♗d2 ♕c7 14 c4 ♘f6 15 e3 e5 16 ♗e2 e4 17 ♘f4 exf3 18 ♗xf3 ♘e5 19 0-0 ♕xc5 20 ♗b4 ♘xb4 21 axb4 ♕c8 22 c5+ ♔h8 23 ♖ac1 a6 24 ♖fd1 ♗c6 25 ♘e6 ♗a4 26 ♕xa4 ♕xe6 27 ♖c3 ♘e4 secures equality since on this square the knight is the equal of the bishop; Milov-Sakaev, Sochi 1990.

10 c4 ♕h4+

The other choice is 10...♘f6:

⇨ Here Nigel Davies tried 11 ♗f4 against Schneider at Gausdal 1990, but after 11...♕a5+ 12 ♕d2 ♕xd2+ (12...♕a4 13 ♕b4 ♘c6 14 ♕b5 ♖d8 15 ♖b1 ♘a6 16 ♕xc6 bxc6 17 ♖d1 ♖xd1+ 18 ♔xd1 ♘xc5 19 e3 ♗a6 20 ♘f2 ♘fd7, Eliet-Pogorelov, Cannes 1992, has less point) 13 ♔xd2?! ♘a6 14 ♔c2 ♗d7 15 ♘f2 ♘xc5 16 e3 ♖fc8 17 ♖b1 ♗a4+ 18 ♔c3 b5 19 ♗e2 ♘fd7 20 ♘d1 ♘b6 21 ♘b2 ♗b3 his king became too exposed and he soon lost.

⇨ 11 ♕xd8 ♖xd8 12 ♘f2 ♘c6 13 e3 e5 14 ♗b2 ♗e6 15 ♘d3 ♘d7 16 ♖c1 e4 17 fxe4 fxe4 18 ♘f4 ♗f7 19 ♗e2 ♘xc5 20 0-0 ♖d2 21 ♗c3 ♖a2 22 ♖a1 ♖c2 23 ♖fc1 ♖xe2 24 ♘xe2 ♘b3 25 ♘g3 ♗xc4 26 ♘xe4 ♖d8?! (in the light of what follows,

26...♘xa1! and then ...♖d8 would be better) 27 ♖cb1 ♘xa1 28 ♖xb7! ♖d1+ 29 ♔f2 ♖f1+ 30 ♔g3 ♘c2 31 ♖xg7+ ♔f8 32 ♖c7 ♗d5 33 ♘g5 ♔e8 34 e4 ♔d8 35 ♖xh7 ♗b3 36 h4 and the h-pawn managed to advance all the way to the queening square in Yurtaev-Utemov, Podolsk 1990.

11 ♘f2 ♕f6!?

Black introduces a sharp new alternative to 11...♘f6.

12 ♗d2 ♘c3 13 ♕c1 ♘a4 14 ♗g5 ♕f7 15 ♘d3 ♘d7 16 ♕e3

This seems a rather excessive length to go to, to defend c5.

16...e5! 17 c6!

Instead 17 ♘xe5 ♘xe5 18 ♕xe5 ♗e6 gives Black an edge.

17...bxc6 18 ♘xe5 ♘xe5 19 ♕xe5 ♖e8 20 ♕a5 ♘b6 21 e3 h6

Black could keep some initiative with 21...f4 22 e4 h6 23 ♗h4 ♘xc4!.

22 ♗f4 ♗e6 23 ♔f2 ♗xc4 24 h4 ♖ad8 25 ♖c1 ♗xf1 26 ♖hxf1 ♘d5 27 ♖xc6 ♕h5?

Better is 27...♕e7 28 ♔g1 ♕h4 29 ♕xa7 ♘xf4 =.

28 ♖h1 ♖d7 29 ♕a4 ♖ed8 30 ♕c4 ♔h7 31 ♗e5

Taking up a powerful post. Black will soon regret not having taken this piece.

31...♘b6 32 ♕c1 ♖d2+ 33 ♔g3 ♕f7 34 h5 ♕e7 35 ♗f4 ♖2d7 36 ♕c2 ♕f7 37 e4! fxe4 38 ♕xe4+ ♔h8 39 ♗e5 ♔g8 40 ♖g6 1-0

Game 142

Shirov-Renet
Corrèze match (3) 1991

1 d4 ♘f6 2 c4 e6 3 ♘c3 ♗b4 4 f3 d5 5 a3 ♗xc3+ 6 bxc3 c5 7 cxd5 ♘xd5 8 ♕d3

Or 8 ♕d2:

⇨ 8...f5!? (previously Black prefaced this thrust with 8...cxd4 9 cxd4) 9 ♘h3 0-0 10 e3 ♘c6 11 ♗c4 ♘a5 (11...♕h4+ 12 ♘f2 cxd4 13 cxd4 f4 14 exf4 ♕xf4 15 ♗xd5 ♕xd2+ 16 ♗xd2 exd5 17 ♗c3 with equality; Pein-Kosashvili, Tel Aviv 1992) 12 ♗a2 ♗d7? (Black can secure equality with 12...cxd4 13 cxd4 and only then 13...♗d7) 13 c4 ♘f6 14 ♗b2?! (14 d5) 14...cxd4 15 exd4 ♖c8 16 ♖c1 b5! 17 cxb5 ♖xc1+ 18 ♕xc1 ♕b6 19 ♕c5 ♖c8 20 ♕xb6 axb6 21 ♔d2 ♘c4+ 22 ♗xc4 ♖xc4 23 ♘f4 g5 24 ♘d3 ♗xb5 25 ♖e1 ♖c6 26 ♘b4 ♖d6 27 g4!? (the ending is level but White starts over-pressing and finds himself worse) 27...fxg4 28 fxg4 ♔f7 29 h3 ♔g6 30 ♘d3 ♗xd3 31 ♔xd3 h6 32 a4 ♔f7 33 ♖f1 ♔g6 34 ♖c1 ♘d5 35 ♔e4 ♖d8 (Black has the superior minor piece, but White should have good chances of holding) 36 ♖c6 ♔f6 37 ♔d3?? ♘b4+ 38 ♔e4 ♘xc6 39 d5+ ♔f7

40 dxc6 ♖c8 0-1 Shirov-Beliavsky, Biel 1992.

⇨ 8...cxd4 9 cxd4 ♘c6!? 10 e4 ♘b6 11 ♗b5 0-0 12 ♘e2 ♗d7 13 0-0 ♘e5! 14 ♖b1 ♘ec4 15 ♕d3 ♗xb5 16 ♖xb5 ♕d7 17 ♖b4 ♘e5! 18 ♕e3 ♘c6 19 ♖b1 ♖ac8 20 ♖d1 ♘c4 21 ♕d3 ♘6a5 22 ♘c3 b6 23 a4 ♖fd8 24 ♗g5 f6 25 ♗h4 ♘e5! (dance of the knights!) 26 ♕e2 ♘g6 27 ♗e1 ♖c4! 28 d5 e5 looks equal; Pein-Farago, Amantea 1992.

8...cxd4 9 cxd4 ♘c6 10 e4 ♘b6 11 ♗e3 0-0 12 ♗e2

I think that this is the most accurate move here, aiming to complete kingside development.

⇨ 12 ♖d1 ♗d7 (or 12...f5 13 ♘h3 fxe4 14 ♕xe4 ♘d5 15 ♘g5 ♘f6 16 ♕d3 ♕a5+ 17 ♗d2? {17 ♖d2 must be better} 17...♕d5 18 ♘e4!? ♘xe4 19 fxe4 ♕xd4 20 ♕xd4 ♘xd4 21 ♗c3 ♘c2+ 22 ♔d2 ♖f2+ 23 ♔c1 ♘e3 24 ♖d8+ ♖f8 25 ♖xf8+ ♔xf8 26 ♗e2 e5 27 ♔d2 and after his original pawn sacrifice White had succeeded in gaining the upper hand, Chabanon-Mirallès, French Ch 1991, although drawn in 51 moves) 13 ♘h3 ♘a5 14 ♕c3? (this turns out to do little to deter the knight coming to c4) 14...♘ac4! 15 ♗xc4 ♖c8 16 0-0 ♖xc4 17 ♕a1 ♕e7 18 ♗g5 f6 19 ♗d2 ♖fc8 20 ♗b4 ♕f7 21 ♘f4 ♗b5 ½-½ Bagirov-Piket, Palma 1989.

12...♕h4+!?

Part of Renet's match preparation, but it's not clear that forcing g3 achieves a great deal. Others:

1) In his next game with Black in the same match, Renet tried Ivanchuk's idea 12...♗d7 13 ♘h3 ♘a5:

⇨ In the inaugural game in this line, Shirov-Ivanchuk, USSR 1989, the more passive 14 ♗d2 occurred, when 14...♘bc4 15 ♗b4 ♖e8 16 0-0 ♗b5! 17 ♕c3 ♖c8 18 ♖fc1 ♘d6!? 19 ♗xa5 ♖xc3 20 ♗xd8 ♖c1+ 21 ♖xc1 ♖xd8 22 ♘f4 was level, although Black later blundered and lost.

⇨ 14 ♗g5! f6 15 ♗d2 ♘bc4 16 ♗b4 ♖e8 17 ♘f4 ♖c8 18 0-0 ♗b5 19 d5!? ♕b6+ 20 ♔h1! (curiously, this is a new move, the entire game up to this point having been played before: 20 ♖f2?! e5 21 ♘h5 ♘d6 22 ♕d1 ♗e2 23 ♕xe2 ♘b3! {coming to d4} 24 ♖b1 ♘d4 25 ♕d3 ♖c2! 26 ♖ff1 ♖ec8 27 ♔h1 ♖8c7 and Black has a dominating position; Khenkin-Ulybin, Voskresensk 1990) 20...♘d6 21 ♕d1 ♗xe2 22 ♕xe2 ♘b3 23 ♖ad1 ♘d4 24 ♕f2 e5 25 ♘h5 ♖ed8 26 ♕g3 ♘e8 27 f4 (undermining the strong black knight) 27...♘e2 (Black falls apart) 28 ♕g4 ♘xf4 29 ♘xf4 exf4 30 ♗e7 ♘d6? 31 ♗xf6 1-0 Shirov-Renet, Corrèze (5) 1991.

2) 12...f5 and now:

2a) 13 ♘h3?! fxe4 14 fxe4 e5 15 d5 ♗xh3 16 gxh3?! ♕h4+ 17 ♔d2 ♘a5 18 ♖ac1 ♖ac8 19 ♗g4 ♖f2+! 20 ♔d1 ♘ac4 (threatening ...♘b2+) 21 ♖b1 ♘xe3+ 22 ♕xe3 ♘c4 23 ♕c3 ♖d2+ 24 ♕xd2 ♘xd2 25 ♖xb7 ♖f8 26 ♔xd2 ♕f2+ 27 ♔c3 ♕e3+ 28 ♔b2 ♖f2+ 0-1 Matveeva-Bojković, Belgrade Jugometal wom 1992.

2b) 13 ♖d1 ♔h8 (in the game Shirov-Ulybin, Santiago 1990, following 13...♗d7 14 ♘h3 fxe4 Shirov tried 15 fxe4, which had been thought to be a mistake because of 15...e5; however this is obviously not the case as after 16 d5 ♗xh3 17 dxc6! ♕h4+! 18 g3 ♕e7 19 ♖g1 bxc6 20 ♕d6 he retained a slight edge, although the game was later drawn) 14 ♘h3 fxe4 15 ♕xe4 ♘d5 16 ♘g5 ♘f6! (a significant improvement on the game Taimanov-Hamann from 1966 where 16...g6 was played) 17 ♕d3 ♕a5+ 18 ♖d2 and here:

⇨ 18...♘e7! is best, avoiding the immediate weakening of g6: 19 0-0 ♘ed5 20 ♖b2 ♘xe3! 21 ♕xe3 h6 22 ♘e4 ♘d5 23 ♕b3 b6! 24 ♘d6 ♗d7 25 ♗c4 ♗a4 26 ♕d3 ♘f4 27 ♕e4 ♕c3? (better is 27...♖ad8 28 ♕e5 ♕c3! 29 ♖b4 ♕xa3 30 ♖fb1 ♗c2 ∓) 28 ♘f7+! ♔g8 29 ♖b4 ♕d2 30 ♖f2 ½-½ Savchenko-Gipslis, Gausdal 1992.

⇨ 18...h6?! 19 ♘e4 ♘e7 20 ♗f4! ♘ed5 21 ♗d6! (typically, Shirov displays a great deal of energy in the final phase of the game) 21...♖f7 22 0-0 ♗d7 23 ♖c2 ♗c6 (Black has a firm hold on d5, but e5 and e6 are weak) 24 ♗e5 ♘af8? 25 ♘c5! ♖e8 26 f4 ♕d8 27 ♕h3 ♕e7 28 ♗d3 b6 (this loses the exchange, but if 28...♕ff8 29 ♗g6 forces the defender of e6 to move) 29 ♘b3?! (29 ♘e4) 29...♗a4 30 ♗g6 ± ♖ff8 31 ♗xe8 ♖xe8 32 ♖a2 ♖c8 33 ♖c1 ♕e8 34 ♖aa1 ♗c6 35 ♘d2 ♘h5 36 ♖f1 ♗b7 37 ♘e4 ♔g8? 38 ♘d6 1-0 Shirov-Unzicker, Daugavpils 1990.

13 g3 ♕e7 14 f4 f5 15 ♘f3 fxe4?!

15...♔h8 16 0-0 ♗d7 17 ♖ae1 ♗e8 is better.

16 ♕xe4 ♘d5 17 ♗c4! ♔h8 18 0-0 ♘f6 19 ♕d3 ♗d7 20 ♖ae1!

Targeting e6.

20...♕d6 21 ♗d2 ♖ae8 22 f5! ± ♘d5

If 22...exf5 23 ♗f4 traps the black queen in mid-board, but White forces resignation anyway with a delightful combination.

23 fxe6 ♗xe6 24 ♘g5 ♗g8

25 ♖xe8 ♖xe8 26 ♕xh7+! ♗xh7 27 ♘f7+ ♔g8 28 ♘xd6 1-0

Game 143

Arencibia-Adla
Havana Capablanca mem 1992

1 d4 ♘f6 2 c4 e6 3 ♘c3 ♗b4 4 f3 d5 5 a3 ♗xc3+ 6 bxc3 c5 7 cxd5 ♘xd5 8 ♕d3 0-0 9 e4 ♘e7!?

By retreating the knight to e7 Black leaves the path to a5 open for his queen, whence he can quickly build up pressure against White's centre.

10 ♗e3

1) 10 a4 is another possibility: 10...♘bc6 11 ♗a3 cxd4 12 cxd4 and now:

⇨ 12...♕xd4!? 13 ♕xd4 ♘xd4 14 ♗xe7? (expecting to trap the errant knight on a1, but it is not to be; the line 14 0-0-0! ♘dc6 15 ♗b5 e5 16 ♗xc6 ♘xc6 17 ♗xf8 ♔xf8 seems White's best bet, with unclear play) 14...♘c2+ 15 ♔d2 ♘xa1 16 ♗xf8 ♔xf8 17 ♗c4 ♗d7 18 ♘e2 ♖c8 19 ♗xe6 ♖c2+! 20 ♔d3 fxe6 21 ♖xa1 ♖b2 and Black has a winning position; Agrest-Pieniazek, Poland 1992.

⇨ 12...♕c7 13 ♕c3 f5 14 ♗d3 fxe4 15 ♗xe4 (by recapturing on e4 with a piece White establishes a strong square there, and can exert pressure along the e-file) 15...♖d8 16 ♘e2 ♘d5 17 ♕d3 ♘f6 18 0-0 ♗d7 19 ♖ac1 ♗e8 20 ♘e3 ♘xe4?? (it is a mistake to open the f-file now; 20...♕d7 was just slightly better for White) 21 fxe4 ♗h5? 22 ♘f4 ♗f7 23 d5! exd5 24 exd5 ♕e5 25 ♕f2! ♗xd5 26 ♖c5 ♘e7 27 ♗b2! ♕f5 28 ♕g3 1-0 Yakovich-Serper, USSR Ch 1991.

2) 10 dxc5?! ♕a5 11 ♗f4 ♘bc6 12 ♗d6 e5 13 ♕d2 ♖d8 14 ♗c4 b6 15 ♖d1 ♗a6 16 ♗xa6 ♕xa6 17 ♕c1 bxc5 18 ♘e2 ♕a5 = Shirov-Gavrikov, Biel 1991.

3) 10 ♘h3 and:

⇨ 10...cxd4 11 cxd4 ♘bc6 (11...b6 12 ♕e3 ♗a6 13 ♗xa6 ♘xa6 14 ♗b2 ♖c8 15 0-0 ♕d7 16 ♖f2! ♖fd8 17 ♘f4 ♘c7 18 ♘h5 ♘e8 19 d5 ± Khenkin-Balashov, Cappelle la Grande 1992) 12 ♗b2 ♕a5+ 13 ♗c3 ♕c7 14 ♗e2 ♖d8 15 ♕e3 ♕b6 16 ♔f2 ♗d7 17 ♖ab1 ♕c7 18 ♖hc1 ♗e8 19 ♘f4 ♘g6 20 ♘h5 ♕e7 21 g3 f6 22 d5 exd5 23 exd5 ♕xe3+ 24 ♔xe3 ♘ce7 25 ♖xb7 ♘xd5+ 26 ♔f2 ♘ge7 27 ♗c4 ♗xh5 28 ♖xe7 ♘h8 29 ♗xd5 ♖xd5 when White has some initiative, but Black should draw; Chabanon-Dautov, Lippstadt 1991.

⇨ 10...♘bc6 11 dxc5 (much better than 11 ♗e3? ♕a5 12 ♔f2 ♖d8 13 ♗e2?! cxd4 14 cxd4 ♘xd4! 15 ♗xd4 ♕a4! 16 ♕c4 ♕xc4 17 ♗xc4 ♖xd4 ∓ Shirov-Budnikov, USSR Ch 1991, although the game was drawn in the end) 11...♕a5 12 ♖b1 e5 13 ♖b5 ♕a6 14 ♘f2 ♖d8 15 ♕b1 ♕a4 16 ♕b3 ♕xb3 17 ♖xb3 ♘a5 18 ♖b5 ♘ec6 19 f4 ♗e6 20 ♗e2 ♖d7 21 f5 ♗b3 22 f6 a6 23 ♖b6 ♖ad8 24 ♖f1 ♗e6 25 fxg7 ♘c4 26 ♗xc4 ♗xc4 27 ♗g5 with sharp play and some advantage to White; Sakaev-Lutz, Dortmund 1992.

10...♕a5

This seems to be more accurate than 10...♘bc6?!, when White has a pleasant choice:

⇨ 11 dxc5!? is certainly worth considering, as Black's pieces are no longer well placed to attack the c5 pawn; Malaniuk-Ortega, Amantea 1991 continued: 11...♕a5 12 ♕c2 ♘e5 13 ♘e2 ♘c4!? 14 ♗f2 b6 15 ♘d4!? ♗a6 16 a4! ♕xc5 (White was threatening to snare the black queen with 17 ♘b3, and 16...bxc5 17 ♘b3 ♕b6 18 ♘xc5 was not worth contemplating) 17 ♘xe6 ♘e3 18 ♕d2 ♘xf1 19 ♗xc5 ♘xd2 20 ♗xe7 ♖fc8 21 ♔xd2 fxe6 22 a5! and although White is only a pawn up in an opposite-colour bishop ending, the presence of rooks (and Malaniuk's technique!) makes it winning.

⇨ 11 ♗e2 ♕a5 12 ♔f2 ♖d8 13 ♕c4 cxd4 14 cxd4 ♕h5?! (not a good square for the queen, but 14...♗d7 15 ♘h3 e5? 16 ♘g5 ♗e8 17 d5 ♘d4 18 ♗xd4 exd4 19 ♖hd1 ♖ac8 20 ♕b4 was also good for White in Savchenko-Reeh, Gausdal 1992) 15

h4! ± f5 16 ♖d1 ♕f7 17 ♘h3 h6 18 ♘f4! fxe4 19 fxe4 ♗d7 (I cannot see any immediate refutation of 19...g5!?) 20 ♔g3 ♘c8 21 d5 exd5 22 ♕xd5 ♕xd5 23 ♘xd5 ♘8e7 24 ♘c7 ♖ac8 25 ♗c4+ ♔h7 26 ♘e6 ♗xe6 27 ♗xe6 ♖xd1 28 ♖xd1 ♖d8 29 ♖xd8 ♘xd8 30 ♗d7. This endgame should probably be winning for White, with two strong bishops. However, a series of time-trouble mistakes left him fighting for a draw in Marin-Lobron, Manila OL 1992.

11 ♔f2

⇨ When first faced with this variation, White reacted with 11 ♕d2 ♖d8 12 ♗d3 ♘bc6 13 ♘e2 b6 14 ♖a2 ♗a6 15 0-0? (White is just a little worse after 15 ♗xa6 ♕xa6 16 0-0; Wiedenkeller-Schneider, Swedish Ch 1991, ran on: 16...♖ac8 17 ♖d1 cxd4 18 cxd4 ♘a5 19 ♕d3 ♕c4 20 ♕xc4 ♘xc4 21 ♔f2 ♘xe3 22 ♔xe3 ♖c4 23 ♖aa1 ♘c6 24 ♖dc1 ♘a5 25 ♖xc4 ♘xc4+ 26 ♔d3 b5 27 ♖b1 a6 and 0-1 on move 74) 15...cxd4 16 ♘xd4 (a sad necessity, as Black wins after 16 cxd4? ♗xd3 17 ♕xd3 ♘b4) 16...e5 17 ♘xc6 ♘xc6 18 c4 ♗xc4 19 ♕xa5 ♘xa5 20 ♗xc4 ♘xc4 ∓ Gurevich-Timman, Amsterdam 1991.

⇨ 11 ♗d2 ♕c7 12 ♕e3 ♖d8 13 ♗d3 ♘bc6 14 ♘e2 ♕d7 15 ♗b5 (the only way to defend e4) 15...a6 16 ♗xc6 ♘xc6 17 ♔f2 b5 18 ♖hd1 ♘a5 19 ♗e1 ♘c4 20 ♕g5 ♘b2 = Khenkin-Holmsgaard, Gausdal 1991.

11...b6 12 dxc5

Starting wild complications.

12...♗a6 13 ♕d6 ♗xf1 14 ♕xe7 ♘c6 15 ♕d6 ♗b5 16 cxb6 ♕xc3 17 ♘h3 axb6 18 ♗xb6 ♖fd8!

19 ♗xd8 ♖xd8 20 ♕c7 h5!

Coming to cut off a possible escape route for the king via g3.

21 ♖a2 h4 22 ♕f4 ♗c4 23 ♖ha1

Obviously 23 ♖aa1?? loses to 23...♖d2+.

23...♗xa2 24 ♖xa2 ♖d1 25 ♖e2 ♘e5 26 ♕xh4 ♘g6 27 ♕g5 ♕xa3 28 ♖c2 ♕a7+ 29 ♔e2 ♕d7 30 ♘f2 ♖b1 31 ♖d2 ♕b5+!

A fitting end to an exciting game.

32 ♕xb5 ♘f4+ 33 ♔e3 ♘xg2+
½-½

In view of 34 ♔d3 ♖xb5 =.

Game 144

Shirov-Chandler
Hastings 1991

1 d4 ♘f6 2 c4 e6 3 ♘c3 ♗b4 4 f3 d5 5 a3 ♗xc3+ 6 bxc3 c5 7 cxd5 ♘xd5 8 ♕d3 0-0 9 e4 ♘e7 10 f4!?

When it transpired that 10 ♗e3 wasn't particularly effective White cast around for alternatives. 10 f4 is a risky idea of Khenkin's that Shirov has taken up with great success. White advances in the centre despite

having only developed his queen.

10...b6

⇨ 10...♕c7 11 ♘f3 b6 12 ♕e3 ♗a6 13 ♗xa6 ♘xa6 14 0-0 ♖ae8 15 ♗b2 ♕b7 16 ♖ae1 f5 17 ♕d3 ♘c7 18 c4 ± (White's centre begins to roll) 18...cxd4?! 19 ♕xd4 ♖f7 20 ♘g5 ♘c6 21 ♕d3 ♖ff8 22 exf5 ♖xf5 23 ♘xe6 1-0 Shirov-Olafsson, Reykjavik 1992.

⇨ 10...♕a5 11 ♗d2 ♕a4 12 ♕b1 ♗d7? 13 ♘f3 ♗c6 14 ♗d3 ± ♘d7 15 0-0 h6? 16 f5!! cxd4 (because the bishop on c6 has no squares, 16...exf5? is impossible: 17 d5 fxe4 18 dxc6 exf3 19 cxd7 and White wins) 17 cxd4 ♔h8 18 ♗b4 ♖ae8 19 fxe6 fxe6 20 ♕b2 ♖f4 21 ♖fe1 ♘g6 22 ♗d6 ♖f6 23 e5 ♖f5 24 ♗xf5 exf5 25 e6 ♘f6 26 ♘e5! ♔h7! 27 ♘xg6 ♔xg6 28 ♖ac1 ♘e4 29 ♗e5 ♖xe6 30 ♗xg7! ♕a5 31 ♗e5 ♕d5 32 ♖f1 h5 33 ♗f4 ♗b5 34 h3 ♗c4 35 ♕b4 b5 (Black's grip on the light squares offers some compensation for the exchange, but he should be lost. However, the game gets turned on its head in White's time-trouble) 36 ♕f8?? ♖xe5 37 dxe5 ♕d4+ 38 ♔h2?? (38 ♔h1 ♘g3+ 39 ♔h2 ♕xf4 40 ♕f6+ ♔h7 41 ♕e7+ is equal) 38...♕xe5 39 g3 ♕b2+ 39 ♔g1 ♕xc1+ 0-1 Shirov-Kir.Georgiev, Manila OL 1992.

⇨ 10...f5 11 ♘f3 ♘bc6 12 dxc5 ♕a5 13 exf5 ♖xf5 14 ♘g5 h6 15 ♘e4 e5 16 g4 (with only two pieces in play White goes over to the attack!) 16...♖f8 17 f5 ♔h8 18 ♗g2 b6 19 f6! ♘g8 20 0-0 gxf6 21 ♕d6 ♗b7 22 ♗xh6! ♘xh6 23 ♖xf6 ♘f7 24 ♖h6+ ♘xh6 25 ♕xh6+ ♔g8 26 ♕g6+ ♔h8 27 ♘g5 ♕xc5+ 28 ♔h1 ♕e7

29 ♕h6+ ♔g8 30 ♗d5+ ♖f7 31 ♕h7+ 1-0 Khenkin-Schneider, Gausdal 1991.

11 ♕e3

Another queen move!

11...♗a6

⇨ 11...♗b7 might be more effective: 12 ♘f3 ♕c8 13 ♗d2 f5 14 ♗d3 fxe4 (exchanging the light-squared bishops is a desirable objective for Black) 15 ♗xe4 ♗xe4 16 ♕xe4 ♕c6 17 ♕e2 ♘d7 18 0-0 ♘d5 19 ♘g5 ♖ae8 20 ♖ae1 cxd4 21 cxd4 h6 22 ♘xe6 (forcing a draw) 22...♘c7 23 d5 ♕xd5 24 ♘xc7 ♖xe2 25 ♘xd5 ♖xd2 = Shirov-Lutz, Biel 1992.

12 ♗xa6 ♘xa6 13 ♘f3 cxd4 14 cxd4 ♘c7 15 a4!? f5 16 ♗a3 fxe4 17 ♕xe4 ♕d5 18 ♕c2?! ♕a5+ 19 ♕d2?!

19 ♔f2 ♘cd5 would have been unclear.

19...♕xa4 20 0-0 ♕e8?!

Better is 20...♕d7 21 ♘e5 ♕e8 ∓.

21 ♖ae1 h6

22 d5! ♘exd5!

22...♘cxd5? walks into the crushing 23 ♖xe6 ♕f7 24 ♖fe1 ♖fe8 25 ♗xe7 ♘xe7 26 ♕a2 ♔f8 27 ♘e5.

23 ♗xf8 ♕xf8 24 ♘d4 ♕d6 25 ♖c1 ♖f8 26 ♘c6 a5 27 ♘e5 ♖d8 28 ♖c6 ♕b4 29 ♕c1 ♕d4+?

In time-trouble, Black slips up.

30 ♔h1 ♘xf4? 31 ♘f3 ♕d3 32 ♖xc7 ♘e2 33 ♕a1 1-0

Game 145

Marin-Petursson
Manila OL 1992

1 d4 ♘f6 2 c4 e6 3 ♘c3 ♗b4 4 f3 d5 5 a3 ♗xc3+ 6 bxc3 c5 7 cxd5 ♘xd5 8 ♕d3 b6! 9 e4 ♗a6 10 c4

The only way to avoid the exchange of bishops on f1. Other moves are considered in the next game.

10...♘c7

Black may instead try 10...♘e7 11 d5 exd5 12 exd5 0-0 13 ♗b2 ♘d7 (13...♘c8!? intending ...♘d6) 14 ♘h3 ♖e8 15 0-0-0 ♘g6 16 ♕c3 ♕f6 17 ♕xf6 ♘xf6 18 ♗xf6 gxf6 19 ♔d2 ♖ad8 20 ♘f2 f5 21 a4 ♔g7 (the ending is not very pleasant for Black as he is quite passive) 22 ♗d3 ♘f4 23 ♖c1 ♔f6 24 g3 ♘xd5 (deciding to sacrifice a piece for some activity) 25 cxd5 ♖xd5 26 ♔c2 c4 27 ♗f1 ♖a5 28 ♖a1 ♖e3?! 29 ♘d1 ♖xf3 30 ♗e2 ♖b3 31 ♘c3 ± Marin-Motwani, Manila OL 1992.

However, I think that 10...♘f6 is Black's best move here; Shirov analyses:

⇨ 11 e5?! ♘fd7 12 ♕e4 cxd4! 13 ♕xa8 ♘c5 14 ♖b1 ♕c7 15 f4 ♗b7 16 ♕xa7 ♘bd7 17 ♘f3 0-0 18 ♘xd4 ♖a8 ∓.

⇨ 11 d5 exd5 12 exd5 0-0 ∓. For instance 13 ♘h3 ♖e8+ 14 ♔f2 (14

♗e2? allows 14...♘xd5, or even 14...♘c6!? 15 ♗g5 ♕xd5!) 14...♘bd7 (or 14...♘g4+!?) 15 ♗b2 ♘e5 16 ♕c3?! b5!? 17 cxb5 ♘xd5 18 ♕xc5 ♖c8 19 ♕xa7 ♖c2+ and Black is better.

⇨ 11 dxc5 ♘bd7!.

11 d5 exd5 12 exd5 0-0 13 ♘h3 ♖e8+ 14 ♔f2 ♘d7 15 ♘g5 ♘f6 16 ♕c2

Black was threatening ...♘cxd5.

16...h6 17 h4 ♕d6 18 ♗b2 ♕f4!

Black would like to force the annoying knight on g5 to move.

19 ♗xf6 ♕xf6 20 ♕h7+ ♔f8 21 ♖d1! hxg5 22 d6 g6 23 dxc7 g4 24 ♕h6+ ♕g7

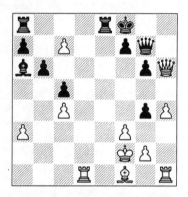

25 ♕d2

Here Marin gives 25 ♕f4!: after 25...♕e5 26 ♕xg4 ♗c8 27 ♕g5 ♕xg5 28 hxg5 ♗e6 29 ♗d3 ♔e7 30 ♖h7 White has some advantage.

25...♕e5 26 fxg4 ♗c8 27 ♗e2 ♕xe2+!

A nice simplifying combination.

28 ♕xe2 ♖xe2+ 29 ♔xe2 ♗xg4+ 30 ♔e3 ♗xd1 31 ♖xd1 ♔e7 32 ♖d8! ♖xd8 33 cxd8♕+ ♔xd8 34 g4 ♔e7 35 a4 ♔f6 36 ♔e4 ♔e6 37 ♔f4

♔f6 38 ♔e4 ♔e6 39 ♔f4 ♔f6 40 ♔e4 ½-½

Game 146 C/ML

Shirov-Karpov
Biel 1992

1 d4 ♘f6 2 c4 e6 3 ♘c3 ♗b4 4 f3 d5 5 a3 ♗xc3+ 6 bxc3 c5 7 cxd5 ♘xd5 8 ♕d3 b6!

This move is suddenly all the rage, but it is not a new move at all. Rather, in the search for an antidote to 8 ♕d3, 8...b6 has been 'rediscovered'. See, for example, the game reference from 1964 in the note to White's 10th move.

9 e4

⇨ 9 dxc5 bxc5 10 e4 ♗a6 11 ♕d2 ♗xf1 12 ♔xf1 ♘b6 13 ♕xd8+ ♔xd8 ∓ 14 ♘e2 ♘8d7 15 a4 ♖b8 16 ♘g3 ♘c4 17 ♔e2 ♔e7 18 a5 ♖b3 19 ♔d3 ♘de5+ 20 ♔c2 ♖b5?! (20...♖hb8 21 ♖a2 f6!) 21 f4! ♘g4 22 ♖e1 ♖d8 is equal, though Black went on to win in Shirov-Arnason, Reykjavik 1992.

9...♗a6 10 ♕d2

⇨ 10 ♕c2 ♗xf1 11 ♔xf1 ♘e7 12 ♘e2 0-0 13 ♗e3 (13 ♔f2 ♘bc6 14 ♖d1 cxd4 15 cxd4 ♖c8 = Keller-Unzicker, Lenzerheide 1964) 13...cxd4 14 cxd4 ♘bc6 15 ♔f2 ♖c8 (rather similar to the aforementioned game) 16 ♕a2 ♕d7 17 ♖hd1 ♘a5 (this position looks fairly level) 18 d5? exd5 19 ♘f4 ♕a4 20 ♘xd5!? ♖c2+ 21 ♕xc2 ♕xc2+ 22 ♖d2 ♕b3 23 ♘xe7+ ♔h8 ∓ Kilpi-Aseev, Helsinki 1992. White has insufficient compensation for his queen.

10...♗xf1 11 ♔xf1 ♘e7 12 ♘e2 ♘bc6!?

⇨ 12...0-0 13 a4 ♘bc6 14 dxc5?! ♕c7! 15 ♕d6 ♕b7 16 ♔f2 ♖ad8 17 ♕g3 ♘g6?! (after 17...f5! 18 cxb6 fxe4 19 ♕c7 ♕xb6 20 ♕xb6 axb6 21 ♖b1! Black has an edge) 18 ♗e3 f5 19 exf5 exf5 20 ♖ad1! bxc5 21 ♗xc5 ♖fe8 22 ♖xd8 ♖xd8 23 ♕g5! ♖d5 24 ♗d4 ♘xd4 25 cxd4 ♕b6? 26 ♖c1 ± h6 27 ♖c8+ ♔f7 28 ♕c1 ♘e7 29 ♕c4 ♕e6 30 ♖b8 ♖d6! 31 ♕b5 ♕d7 32 ♖b7 ♕xb5 33 axb5 ♖b6 34 ♖xb6 axb6 35 ♘c3 with a decisive advantage; Shirov-Hübner, Manila OL 1992.

13 dxc5 ♕c7!

An improvement over the 13...♕c8 of Shirov-Kir.Georgiev, Biel 1992, which continued: 14 ♕e3 0-0! 15 cxb6 ♖d8! 16 ♔f2 axb6 17 ♖b1 ♘e5 18 ♕xb6 ♕c4?! (18...♘c4! 19 ♕b5 ♘g6 intending ...♘e5-d3 ∓) 19 ♗e3 ♘d3+ 20 ♔g3 f5?! 21 ♗g5! ♖d7 22 ♘d4? (White misses his chance: 22 ♗xe7 ♖xe7 23 ♕d6! ±. Now Black gets the opportunity to embark on a spectacular king-hunt) 22...f4+!! 23 ♔h4 ♘g6+ 24 ♔h5 ♘f8 25 ♕c6

25...♕a2!! 26 ♖hg1 e5! (offering the rook again) 27 ♕xa8 ♕f7+ 28 ♔h4 h6! ∓ 29 g4 hxg5+ 30 ♔h3 exd4 31 cxd4 ♘f2+ 32 ♔g2 ♕a2 (Black has garnered two pieces for his rook, and his attack persists) 33 ♕b8 ♘d3+ 34 ♔h1 ♕e2! 35 ♖gf1 ♖xd4 36 ♕b3+ ♔h7 37 ♕b5 ♖d6! 38 h4 ♘g6! 39 ♕xg5 ♘xh4 40 ♕xh4+ ♖h6 41 ♕xh6+ ♔xh6 0-1.

14 ♕f4

White soon gets into trouble after this, so perhaps 14 ♕d6 =.

14...e5 15 ♕g4 0-0 16 ♔f2 ♘a5! 17 cxb6 ♕xb6+! ∓ 18 ♗e3 ♕c6! 19 ♖hd1 ♘c4 20 ♗g5

Otherwise what can he do with his king?

20...f6 21 ♗c1 ♕b6+! 22 ♔g3 f5

23 exf5 ♘xf5+

White is lost.

24 ♔h3 ♘ce3 25 ♗xe3 ♘xe3 26 ♕e4 ♕e6+ 27 ♔g3 ♘xd1 28 ♖xd1 ♖ad8 29 ♖e1 ♕f5 30 ♕xf5 ♖xf5

The ending is relatively trivial.

31 ♔f2 ♖d2 32 ♖b1 ♖a2 33 ♖b5 ♖xa3 34 c4 ♖f6 35 ♖xe5 ♖c6 36 c5 ♖a5 37 ♖e7 ♖cxc5 38 ♘f4 ♖e5 39 ♖c7 ♖a4 0-1

15 Black's other possibility of attacking the white centre is 4...c5, although after 5 d5 and a subsequent e4 it becomes, if anything, even more imposing. This is a difficult line to handle for both players. It is interesting that Shirov, who knows as much about it as anyone, awarded 4...c5 a ?! in some recent annotations of his, and I must say I agree with him—I have managed to lose every time I have played this as Black!

The examples in game 147 cover lines with ...d6 and ...♘h5; unfortunately, after 9 g4! Black is almost obliged to play an endgame in which White's additional space should guarantee him the edge. In game 148 we deal with ...d6 and ...0-0, but Shirov's accurate 8th move should spell the end for Black's passive system.

A rather more enterprising continuation, 5...b5, is examined in game 149. I feel that this move gives Black reasonable over-the-board chances, although any slip-ups such as in Khenkin-Kotronias are liable to be severely punished. At the time of writing, Khenkin's 11 ♔f2 appears to be the last word for White.

A sort of delayed ...b5 is considered in game 150, but Black seems worse.

Apart from 5...b5, Black's most active move is 5...♘h5, threatening ...♕h4+. White can meet this with either 6 g3 (games 151 and 152) with reasonable chances for both players, or with the completely random double pawn sacrifice 6 ♘h3!? (game 153). For better or for worse Black

should accept this sacrifice; Adams gets into terrible trouble against Shirov when he does not (6...d6, note to game 153).

Finally we look at 4...♘c6!?, which is a rare and unusual alternative that might not be so bad. The examples in game 154 should be compared with the Pein-Dorfman game in chapter 16.

Game 147

Beliavsky-Kir.Georgiev
Reggio Emilia 1990

1 d4 ♘f6 2 c4 e6 3 ♘c3 ♗b4 4 f3 c5 5 d5

⇨ 5 a3 is very rarely tried: 5...♗a5!? (5...♗xc3+ is a Sämisch) 6 d5 b5!? 7 e4 0-0 8 ♗d2 bxc4 9 ♗xc4 ♗a6 10 b3 exd5 11 exd5 d6 12 ♘ge2 ♗xc4 13 bxc4 ♘bd7 14 0-0 ♘e5! ∓ 15 ♕a4 ♕e8! 16 ♕b3 (unfortunately, 16 ♕xa5 loses to 16...♘xc4, when the bishop on d2 is hanging) 16...♖b8 17 ♕a2 ♕d7?! (17...♘d3 18 ♖ab1 ♗xc3! 19 ♘xc3 ♕e5!) 18 f4 ♘eg4 19 ♕c2 ♖fe8 20 ♖f3 h5? 21 h3 ♘h6 22 f5 ♖e5?! 23 ♖af1 ♖be8 24 ♗f4 ♕e7? (Black has completely lost the thread of the game) 25 ♗xe5 ± ♕xe5 26 ♕c1 ♗xc3 27 ♘xc3 ♕d4+ 28 ♔h2 ♕xc4 29 ♕g5 h4 30 ♕f4 ♕xf4+ 31 ♖xf4 winning; Zsu.Polgar-Vojska, Novi Sad OL 1990.

5...♗xc3+

⇨ 5...d6 6 e4 0-0 (6...b5?! 7 dxe6 ♗xe6 8 ♗f4 ♕a5 9 ♔f2 ♗xc3 10 bxc3 0-0 11 cxb5 ♕xc3 12 ♘e2 ♕b2 13 ♗xd6 ♖c8 14 a4 ♘e8 15 ♗f4

♘d7 16 ♕c1 ♕f6 17 ♗g5 ♕e5 18
♗f4 ♕f6 19 ♕c3 ± Dreev-Yudasin,
Manila IZ 1990) 7 ♘e2 ♘h5 8 g4
♕h4+ 9 ♔d2 ♘f6 10 ♕e1 ♕xe1+
leads to very similar play: 11 ♔xe1
♘bd7! 12 ♘g3 b5!? 13 g5 ♘e8 14
cxb5 exd5 15 exd5 ♘b6 16 ♔f2
♗xc3 17 bxc3 ♘xd5 18 ♗d2 a6?!
(18...♗e6!? 19 a4 ♘b6 20 a5 ∞) 19
a4 axb5 20 ♗xb5 ♘dc7 21 c4 f6 22
♖he1 ♖a7 23 ♘e4 ♗b7 24 gxf6
♗xe4 25 ♖xe4 ♘xf6 26 ♖e2 (with
the bishop pair on an open board,
White should be nearly winning)
26...d5 27 ♔g2 d4 28 ♖e5 ♘xb5 29
cxb5 c4 30 a5? (a mistake; 30 ♗b4
♖b8 31 a5 ±) 30...c3 31 ♗e1 ♖b8 32
a6 c2 33 ♗d2 ♔f7 34 ♔f2 ♘d7 35
♖d5 ♔e6 36 ♖xd4 ♖xb5 37 ♖c4
♖b1 38 ♖a2 ♖b6 ½-½ Beliavsky-
Korchnoi, Amsterdam 1990.

**6 bxc3 d6 7 e4 ♕e7 8 ♘e2 ♘h5 9
g4! ♕h4+ 10 ♔d2 ♘f6 11 ♕e1!
♕xe1+ 12 ♔xe1 h6 13 ♘g3 ♘bd7**
⇨ 13...b6 14 ♗f4! e5 15 ♗e3 g6 16
h4 (it is noticeable that White avoids
moving his a-pawn, and just tries to
break through on the kingside)
16...♘a6 17 ♗e2 ♘c7 18 ♔d2 ♔f8
19 ♖ag1 ♘ce8 20 g5 hxg5 21 hxg5
♖xh1 22 ♖xh1 ♘d7 23 ♖h8+ ♔e7
24 ♘h1! ± ♗b7 25 ♖h7 and White
eventually won Black's g-pawn in
Azmaiparashvili-Arnason, Moscow
1990.

14 ♗e2 b6 15 a4?!
⇨ 15 h4 ♗a6 16 ♗f4! ♘e5 17 ♗xe5
dxe5 18 a4 ±.

**15...♗a6 16 a5 ♔e7 17 f4 g6 18
♔f2 h5 19 g5 ♘e8 20 ♖d1 e5 21 f5
♘c7 22 f6+ ♔d8 23 ♖d2?**
White's space advantage is impressive, but he has no pawn breaks

and has to be careful with his c-
pawn; better is 23 ♘f1, when
23...b5! ± keeps White's advantage
to a minimum.

**23...bxa5! 24 ♖xa5 ♘b6 25
♖da2 ♗xc4 26 ♗xc4 ♘xc4 27 ♖a7
♔d7 28 ♖7a4 ♖hb8 29 ♘e2 ♔c8 ∓**

**30 ♔e1 ♘b6 31 ♖xa8 ♖xa8 32
♖xa8+ ♘cxa8 33 ♗e3?**
Black has the strong outpost c4
for his knight and the white bishop is
useless.

**33...♘c4 34 ♗f2? ♘ab6 35 ♘g3
♘a4 36 ♘e2 ♘ab2 37 ♘c1 ♔b7 38
♔e2 ♔a6 39 ♘d3 ♔b5? 40 ♘e1?
♘a4 41 ♘f3 ♘xc3+ 42 ♔d3 ♘b2+
0-1**

Game 148

Shirov-Korchnoi
Biel 1992

**1 d4 ♘f6 2 c4 e6 3 ♘c3 ♗b4 4 f3 c5
5 d5 d6 6 e4 ♗xc3+ 7 bxc3 0-0 8
♘e2!**
⇨ 8 ♘h3?! (a funny idea) 8...♕a5 9
♗d2 exd5 10 cxd5 ♗xh3 11 gxh3

♘h5 12 ♖g1 (hoping for play along the g-file) 12...♘d7 13 ♖g5 g6 14 ♕c2 ♘g7 15 0-0-0 f6 16 ♖g2 f5 17 exf5 ♖xf5 18 ♗d3 ♖xf3 19 ♗xg6! (White must strike now, for if Black gets the chance to play ...♘e5 it's all over) 19...hxg6 20 ♕xg6 ♖xc3+! 21 ♔b1 ♕b4+ 22 ♔a1 ♕d4 23 ♕e6+ (White is forced to take the perpetual since 23 ♕xg7+ ♕xg7 22 ♖xg7+ ♔xg7 23 ♗xc3+ is good for Black) 23...♔h7 24 ♕h6+ ♔g8 25 ♕e6+ ½-½ Dokhoian-A.Petrosian, Erevan 1989.

8...♖e8 9 ♘g3 ♕a5 10 ♗d2 ♗d7 11 ♗e2 ♗a4 12 ♕c1 ♘bd7 13 0-0 a6 14 ♗f4!

⇨ 14 ♖f2 ♕c7 15 ♕f1 b5 16 dxe6 fxe6 17 cxb5 axb5 18 ♗xb5 ♗xb5 19 ♕xb5 c4 ∞ Novikov-A.Petrosian, Polanica Zdroj 1989.

14...♕c7 15 ♕d2 ♘e5

Black does not want to play 15...e5? as 16 ♗g5 h6 17 ♗xh6! gxh6 18 ♕xh6 is winning.

16 ♗g5 ♘ed7 17 ♗d1 ♖xd1 18 ♖axd1 b5 19 dxe6 ♖xe6 20 ♘f5 ♘e8 21 ♗e7! ±

21...♘b6 22 ♗xd6 ♘xd6 23

♘xd6 g6 24 ♖fe1 f6 25 f4! ♖d8 26 e5?

Trying to strengthen d6, but the e-pawn becomes a weakness; 26 ♘xb5 was much simpler.

26...fxe5 27 fxe5?! ♘xc4 28 ♕d5 ♕d7 29 a4!

Temporarily diverting the black knight.

29...♘b2 30 ♖d2 ♘xa4 31 ♖f1! ♘b6 32 ♕xc5 ♖b8 33 ♖df2?

33 ♕e3! ±.

33...♖e7 34 ♘e4? ♕c7 35 ♘f6+ ♔g7 36 ♕e3 ♕xe5 37 ♘h5+ ♔g8

Neither 37...gxh5? 38 ♖f7+ nor 37...♕xh5? 38 ♕xe7+ were possible.

38 ♕xb6 gxh5 39 ♕xa6 ♕e3 40 ♕a2+ ♔h8 41 ♔h1 ♖g8 42 ♕b2 ♕e5 43 h3 ♖c7 44 ♖f8 ♖xf8 45 ♖xf8+ ♔g7 46 ♖f3 ♕e1+ 47 ♔h2 ♕e5+ 48 ♖g3+ ♔h8 49 ♕d2 ♖c8 50 ♕d4 ♕xd4 51 cxd4 b4 52 d5 ♖d8 53 ♖b3 ½-½

Game 149

Khenkin-Epishin
Minsk 1990

1 d4 ♘f6 2 c4 e6 3 ♘c3 ♗b4 4 f3 c5 5 d5 b5 6 e4 bxc4 7 ♗xc4 ♘xd5!
⇨ 7...d6 8 ♘e2 0-0 9 0-0 e5 10 ♕d3 ♗xc3 11 ♕xc3 ♘bd7 12 ♗e3 ♘b6 13 ♗d3 ♗d7 14 ♖ac1 ♖b8 15 ♕d2 ♖e8 16 ♘g3 a6 17 b3 ♗b5 18 ♘f5 ♗xd3 19 ♕xd3 ♕c7 20 ♕xa6 ♖a8 21 ♕e2 ♖a3 22 ♖c2 ♖ea8 with some counterplay; Meister-Neverov, Kuibyshev 1990.

8 ♗xd5

In this variation Black obtains the bishop pair and some activity, whilst

White has the d5 square and pressure along the d-file; not 8 exd5?! ♕h4+.

8...exd5 9 ♕xd5 ♘c6 10 ♘e2

⇨ 10 ♗g5!? ♕b6 11 ♘e2 ♗xc3+?! 12 bxc3 ♗a6 13 ♖d1 0-0 14 ♔f2 ♖fe8 15 ♗f4! ♘a5 16 ♖he1 ♗b5 17 ♘g3 ± ♗c4?! 18 ♕xd7 ♗xa2? (Black did not enjoy the best of positions, but this just loses a piece) 19 ♗c7 ♕b2+ 20 ♖e2 ♕xc3 (if 20...♕a3 21 ♗xa5 ♕xa5 22 ♖a1 pins and wins) 21 ♖xa2 ♘b3 22 ♘e2 ♕b4 23 ♖xa7 h6 24 ♗e5 1-0 Georgadze-Chernin, Lvov Z 1990.

10...♗a6

⇨ 10...0-0?! 11 0-0 ♖b8?! 12 ♗f4 ♖b6 13 ♗d6 ♘e7? (losing the exchange) 14 ♕e5 ♘g6 15 ♕g3 ± ♗a6 (making a virtue out of necessity; 15...♖e8 is met by 16 ♗c7) 16 ♗xf8 ♘xf8 17 ♖fd1 ♗a5!? 18 ♖ab1 ♖h6 19 ♕f2 ♗c7 20 g3 ♘e6 21 ♘d5 ♗e5 22 f4 ♗d6 23 ♘e3 ♗f8 24 ♘g4 ♖h5 25 ♕f3 ♗b7 26 ♘c3 (picking up a second exchange with 26 ♘f6+ can't have been bad) 26...f5! 27 ♘e5 ♕e8 28 ♖xd7 fxe4 29 ♕g4 ♗a8 30 ♖xa7?! ♖h6 31 ♕d1?! c4 32 ♘d7?! ♘xf4 33 gxf4 ♗c6!? 34 ♘d5? (the final mistake; 34 ♘xf8 e3 35 ♕d4! ±) 34...♕g6+ 35 ♔h1 e3 0-1 Gelfand-Short, Linares 1990.

11 ♗e3

Other possibilities:

1) 11 ♔f2 (this seems the best move; obviously White would prefer to castle, but 11 0-0? ♗xc3 12 ♘xc3 ♗xf1 wins the exchange) 11...0-0 12 ♖d1 and now:

⇨ 12...♗xc3?! 13 bxc3! (13 ♘xc3 ♘b4 14 ♕xd7?! ♘d3+ wins the exchange) 13...♗xe2 14 ♔xe2 ♕b8! 15 h3! ♔h8 16 ♔f2 f5 17 exf5 ♘e5

18 ♗f4 ♖xf5 19 ♖ab1 ♕e8 20 ♕e4 g6 21 ♔g3 ♖b8? (allowing a neat combination) 22 ♖xb8 ♕xb8 23 ♖xd7! ♖xf4 24 ♖b7! ♖xf3+ 25 gxf3 1-0 Khenkin-Kotronias, Chalkidiki 1992.

⇨ 12...♗a5 13 ♕h5 (13 ♕g5 f5 14 ♕xd8 ♖axd8 15 exf5 ♘b4 16 ♔g1 d5 ½-½ Moskalenko-Atlas, Podolsk 1990) 13...♘b4 14 ♘f4 ♘c2 15 ♖b1 ♖b8 16 ♘cd5 ♘d4 17 b4 f5 18 ♗b2 ♗c7 19 ♘xc7 ♕xc7 20 ♘d5 ♕e5 21 ♗c1 (unfortunately for White, 21 bxc5?! allows 21...♖xb2+ 22 ♖xb2 ♘xf3 which is most unpleasant) 21...♕e6 22 ♗f4 d6 23 bxc5 ♖xb1 24 ♖xb1 dxc5 25 ♖b8 tending to equality; Crouch-Conquest, Cappelle la Grande 1991.

2) 11 ♘g3!? 0-0 12 ♔f2 ♖b8 13 ♖d1 ♘d4 (the drawback to White's strategy; the d4 square is no longer controlled by a knight) 14 ♗f4 ♖b6 15 a3 ♗xc3 16 bxc3 ♖b2+ 17 ♖d2 ♖xd2+ 18 ♗xd2 ♘e6 19 ♖b1 ♕a5 20 ♘f5 ♕xa3 ∞ Gutman-Kurz, Bundesliga 1992.

11...♕b6

⇨ 11...♖b8! 12 ♗xc5? (after this White is obliged to part with her queen; 12 ♖d1 was a better choice) 12...♖b5 13 ♗xb4 ♖xd5 14 ♘xd5 ♘xb4 15 ♘xb4 ♕a5 16 a3 0-0 (16...d5! 17 ♘c3 dxe4 18 0-0-0! ∞) 17 ♘c3 ♗c4 18 0-0-0 ♗e6 19 ♘bd5 ♕c5 20 ♖d2 ♖c8 21 ♖hd1 ♔f8 22 h3 a5 23 ♖d4 ♖b8 ½-½ Prudnikova-Zaitseva, USSR 1991. White's position is very solid.

12 0-0-0?

Sending his king the wrong way; 12 ♔f2 gives White an edge.

12...0-0 13 a3 ♖ab8!

Starting a well-calculated attack.

14 axb4 ♘xb4 15 ♗xc5

What else? If 15 ♕xc5 then both 15...♘d3+ 16 ♖xd3 ♕xb2+ and 15...♘a2+ were strong.

15...♕h6+ 16 ♕d2 ♘d3+ 17 ♔b1 ♖xb2+! 18 ♕xb2 ♘xb2 19 ♖d6!

19 ♔xb2 ♖b8+ 20 ♔c2 ♗xe2 21 ♘xe2 ♕c6 22 ♖d5 ♖b5 gives Black a clear plus.

19...♗d3+! 20 ♔xb2 ♖b8+ 21 ♔a1

White has a temporary material advantage, but he will have to return some of it to avoid getting mated.

21...♕d2 22 ♗a3 ♖b3 23 ♗c1 ♕c2 24 ♖xd3

24...♖b6!!

24...♕xd3 25 ♗b2 ∓.

25 ♖d4

25 ♗a3 ♖a6 26 ♘b1 ♕xd3 27 ♘ec3 ♖xa3+ 28 ♘xa3 ♕xc3+ wins for Black.

25...♖a6+ 26 ♖a4 ♖xa4+ 27 ♘xa4 ♕xa4+ 28 ♔b1 ♕b5+ 29 ♗b2 ♕d3+ 30 ♔c1 ♕xe2 31 ♖d1 ♕xg2 32 ♖xd7 h6 33 ♖d2 ♕xf3 34 e5 a5 0-1

Shirov-Savon
USSR Ch 1991

1 d4 ♘f6 2 c4 e6 3 ♘c3 ♗b4 4 f3 c5 5 d5 0-0 6 e4 d6 7 ♘e2

⇨ 7 ♗d3 b5 8 ♘e2 exd5 9 cxd5 a6 10 0-0 ♘bd7 11 ♔h1 ♖e8 12 g4!? (very ambitious) 12...♘e5 13 ♘g3 c4 14 ♗e2 ♗c5 15 g5 ♘fd7 16 f4 b4 17 ♘a4 ♘d3! 18 ♗xd3 cxd3 19 ♕xd3 a5 20 ♘xc5 ♘xc5 21 ♕d4 ♕e7 22 e5 dxe5 23 fxe5 ♗b7 (23...♗d7 would give good play on the light squares) 24 ♔g1 ♘d7? (too passive; 24...♖ad8!? 25 ♘f5 ♕xe5 26 ♕xc5 ♗a6!? was worth serious consideration) 25 ♗f4 ♘f8 26 ♘f5 ♕d7 27 ♘d6 ♕g4+ 28 ♔h1 ♘e6 29 ♕d2 ♘xf4 30 ♘xb7 ♘g6 31 e6 fxe6 32 d6 ♖eb8 33 ♘c5 ♖d8 34 d7 ♘e5 35 ♖f4 ♕h3 36 ♖af1 ♘g6 37 ♖4f3 ♕g4 38 ♕d6 ♘h4 39 ♖3f2 ♕c4 40 ♕xe6+ ♕xe6 41 ♘xe6 1-0 G.Flear-Kosten, British Ch 1989.

7...b5

After 7...♖e8 White has two options, which, however, lead to similar types of positions:

⇨ 8 ♘g3 ♗xc3+ 9 bxc3 ♕a5 10 ♗d2 ♗d7 11 ♗e2 ♗a4 12 ♕c1 ♘bd7 13 0-0 a6 14 ♗f4 ♕c7 15 ♖b1 ♘f8 16 h4 (as the knight on f8 is clearly coming to g6, White prepares to kick it away) 16...b5 17 ♕d2 ♘g6 18 ♗g5 ♘d7 19 h5 ♘gf8 20 h6 g6 21 f4 ♖ab8 22 e5 exd5 23 cxd5 dxe5 24 d6 ♕c6 25 ♗e7 c4 26 f5 ♖xe7 27 dxe7 ♕c5+ 28 ♖f2 ♕xe7 29 ♘e4 ♘c5 30 ♕e3 ♗c2 31 fxg6 hxg6 32 ♘f6+ ♔h8 33 ♖bf1 ♘d3 34 ♗xd3

♗xd3 35 ♖e1 e4 36 ♕d4 ♖d8??
(36...♘e6 37 ♕e5 ♕c7 had to
be tried) 37 ♘d5+ was winning for
White in Wells-King, London 1991.
⇨ 8 a3 ♗a5 9 ♘g3 ♗xc3+ 10 bxc3
♕a5 11 ♗d2 ♗d7 12 ♗e2 ♗a4 13
♕b1 ♘bd7 14 ♖a2 ± ♖ab8 15 0-0 a6
16 ♖b2 ♕c7 17 ♖e1 ♘f8 18 ♗d3
♘g6 19 f4 e5 20 f5 ♘f4 21 ♗f1 ♔h8
22 ♕c1 b5 23 ♗xf4 exf4 24 ♕xf4
♖e5?! 25 ♖eb1 h6 26 cxb5 axb5 27
c4 b4 28 axb4?! (unnecessarily giving Black chances; 28 ♗d3 b3 29
♖d1 ±) 28...cxb4 29 ♕e3? b3! 30
♖a1? (Black's position has improved immeasurably over the past
few moves) 30...♖b4! 31 ♗d3 ♘d7
32 ♘e2 ♘c5 33 ♘c3 ♘xd3 34 ♕xd3
♖xc4! ∓ ½-½ Timman-Korchnoi,
Rotterdam 1990.

8 ♘f4!

Another important Shirov innovation; luring Black's e-pawn forward deprives him of central
counterplay. Instead after 8 dxe6
♗xe6 9 ♘f4 bxc4 10 e5 there can
follow:
⇨ 10...dxe5 11 ♕xd8 ♖xd8 12
♘xe6 fxe6 13 ♗xc4 ♘d5 14 ♗g5
♖e8 15 0-0-0! ♘xc3 16 bxc3 ♗xc3
17 ♖d6 (White will win his pawns
back with a profit) 17...♔f7 18 ♔c2
h6 19 ♔xc3 hxg5 20 ♖e1 a5 21 ♖xe5
♖a7 22 ♖dxe6 ♖xe6 23 ♖xe6 ♔f8
24 ♖g6 ± Marin-Inkiov, Stara
Zagora Z 1990.
⇨ 10...♘e8 11 ♘xe6 fxe6 12 exd6
♘xd6 13 ♗e2 ♕h4+ 14 g3 ♕d4
(Black's pawn structure is very
ragged, but he does have an extra
pawn and the d4 square) 15 ♗d2
♘c6 16 a3 ♗a5 17 ♕a4 ♗xc3 18
bxc3! (White wants to regain control

of d4) 18...♕d5 19 ♗f4 ♘e5 20 0-0
♖ad8 21 ♗xe5 ♕xe5 22 ♗xc4 ♕xc3
23 ♗xe6+ with equality; Yakovich-
Kiselev, Belgorod 1991.

**8...e5 9 ♘fe2 bxc4 10 ♘g3 ♗a6
11 ♗g5 h6 12 ♗e3 ♗c8?**

Clearly Black considers it more
important to guard f5 than to defend
c4, which will be lost in the long run
anyway. Nevertheless this does represent a waste of time; better is
12...♘bd7 13 ♘f5 ♘e8 14 g4! ∞.

13 ♗xc4 ♘bd7 14 0-0

14 ♖c1 ±.

**14...♘b6 15 ♗e2 ♗xc3 16 bxc3
♗d7 17 a4 ♖b8 18 a5 ♘a8 19 ♕d2
♕e7 20 f4 exf4 21 ♖xf4 ♘c7 22
♖af1 ♘ce8 23 ♕d3! ♖b3 24 ♗c1!
♕e5 25 ♕d1 ♖b7 26 ♕c2 ♘h7 27
a6?**

The immediate 27 ♗g4! ♗xg4 28
♖xg4 would have been very strong.

**27...♖b6 28 ♗g4?! ♗b5! 29 ♖f5
♕e7 30 ♗e2 ♗d7 31 ♖5f4 ♘ef6 32
♗b2 c4 33 ♗xc4? ♘g4 34 ♗c1
♕h4**

35 ♖xg4 ♕xg4 36 ♗e3 ♗b5 37
♗xb5 ♖xb5 38 ♘f5?
38 ♗xa7 ♖a8 39 ♕d3!.

38...♘f6?

38...♘g5! 39 ♘xd6 ♖a5 40 c4 ♖xa6 41 c5 ♖xd6! 42 cxd6 ♕xe4 =.

39 ♖f4

Winning the queen.

39...♕h5 40 ♖h4 ♕xh4 41 ♘xh4 ♖e8 42 ♗xa7 ♖xe4 43 ♘f3 ♖a5 44 ♗d4 1-0

Game 151

Soffer-Romanishin
Bad Lauterberg 1991

1 d4 ♘f6 2 c4 e6 3 ♘c3 ♗b4 4 f3 c5 5 d5 ♘h5 6 g3 f5 7 e4

⇨ 7 ♗d2 d6 8 ♕c2 0-0 9 0-0-0 (this whole idea involving queenside castling looks disreputable to me) 9...♘d7 10 e3 ♘e5?! (10...e5) 11 ♗e2 ♘f6 12 ♘h3 exd5 13 cxd5 ♘e8! 14 ♘f2 ♘c7 15 f4 ♘g6! 16 ♔b1 ♖b8 17 ♖c1?! b5 18 ♗f3 ♗xc3 19 ♕xc3 b4 20 ♕c2 ♘b5 ∓ 21 ♔a1 ♕a5 22 ♖d2 ♗a6 23 ♗d1 ♕b6?! (23...♖fe8! 24 ♖e1 ♘c3 25 bxc3 bxc3 26 ♖d3 ♖b2 is winning) 24 ♗e2 ♕a5 25 ♕b3 ♘e7 26 ♖c2 ♔h8 27 h3 ♖b6 28 ♗c4 (attempting to keep the potential energy of Black's queenside build-up in check) 28...♖fb8 29 ♗d2 ♘c7 30 g4 ♗xc4 31 ♕xc4 ♕a6 32 b3 ♕c8 33 gxf5 ♘xf5 34 ♕d3 a5 35 ♖g1 a4 36 bxa4 (else Black will take on b3 and open the a-file himself) 36...♕d7 37 ♘d1 h6 38 ♘b2 b3 39 ♖cc1 bxa2 40 ♗c3 ♖b3 41 ♖g2 ♘e8 42 ♖cg1? c4! 43 ♕d2 ♕a7 44 e4 ♘e3 45 ♖xg7 ♘xg7 46 ♗xg7+ (if 46 ♖xg7 instead, then 46...♕xg7 47 ♗xg7+ ♔xg7 is winning, for instance: 48 ♘xc4 ♘xc4 49

♕d4+ ♔g8 50 ♕xc4 ♖a3! and ...♖b1) 46...♕xg7 47 ♖xg7 c3 0-1 Beliavsky-Ehlvest, Reggio Emilia 1990.

7...0-0

⇨ 7...♗xc3+ 8 bxc3 f4 (8...♕f6?! 9 f4! ♘xg3 10 hxg3 ♕xc3+ 11 ♗d2 ♕xg3+ 12 ♔e2 fxe4 13 ♕b3! ♕xb3 14 axb3 exd5 15 cxd5 d6 16 ♗h3 0-0 17 ♗xc8 ♖xc8 18 ♘h3 ♘d7 19 ♗c3 ± Moskalenko-Holzhäuer, St Martin 1991) 9 dxe6 fxg3 10 ♕d5 g2 (obviously expecting 11 ♗xg2 when he can defend h5 with gain of tempo by 11...♕h4+, but Black was in for a surprise) 11 ♕xh5+! g6 12 ♕e5 ♕h4+ 13 ♔e2 gxh1♕ (it is not often that Black has an extra queen by move thirteen and is completely lost!) 14 ♕xh8+ ♔e7 15 ♕g7+ ♔xe6 16 ♗h3+ ♔d6 17 ♕f8+ ♔c7 18 ♗f4+ ♕xf4 19 ♕xf4+ d6 20 ♖d1 ♘c6 21 ♕xd6+ ♔b6 22 ♕g3 h5 23 ♗xc8 ♖xc8 24 ♘h3 h4 25 ♕f2 1-0 Ivanchuk-Csom, Erevan 1989. To add to his woes Black loses his second queen.

8 e5 ♗xc3+ 9 bxc3 f4 10 ♘e2 d6

Black can hardly afford to open up the h-file by 10...fxg3?.

11 ♘xf4 ♘xf4 12 ♗xf4 dxe5 13 ♗xe5 ♘d7 14 ♗d6 ♖e8 15 ♗f4?!

White should opt for 15 dxe6! ♖xe6+ 16 ♔f2 16 ♕b6!? ∞.

15...♕f6 16 ♔f2 ♕xc3 17 ♖c1 ♕f6 18 dxe6?!

White's last chance for equality was 18 ♗h3 e5 19 ♗xd7 =.

18...♘f8! 19 ♗g2 ♗xe6 20 ♗e3 ♖ad8

Black has finished his development.

21 ♕b3 ♘d7 22 ♖hd1 ♘e5 23

♗xc5 ♖xd1 24 ♖xd1 ♗xc4 25 ♕a4 b5 26 ♕xa7

26...♗e2! ∓ 27 ♖d4

27 ♔xe2? is obviously out of the question due to 27...♘c6+.

27...♗xf3 28 ♖f4 ♘d3+ 29 ♔xf3 ♘e1+ 30 ♔g4 ♕e6+ 31 ♖f5 ♘xg2 32 ♗d4 h5+ 33 ♔h3 ♕xf5+ 34 ♔xg2 ♖e2+ 35 ♗f2 ♕d5+ 36 ♔g1 ♖xa2 37 ♕b8+ ♔h7 0-1

Game 152

Sakaev-Lerner
USSR Ch 1991

1 d4 ♘f6 2 c4 e6 3 ♘c3 ♗b4 4 f3 c5 5 d5 ♘h5 6 g3 f5

⇨ 6...d6 7 e4 exd5 8 cxd5 0-0 9 ♗g2 f5 10 ♗d2 fxe4 11 ♘xe4 ♗f5 12 ♗xb4?! cxb4 13 ♘h3 ♕b6 (stopping White from castling) 14 ♘ef2 ♖e8+ 15 ♔f1 ♗d7 16 f4 ♗b5+ 17 ♔g1 ♗e2 18 ♕c2 ♗g4 19 ♘g5 ♘f6 20 ♘ge4 ♘bd7 21 h3 ♖ac8 22 ♕d3 ♗h5 23 g4 ♗g6 24 ♘xf6+ ♘xf6 25 f5 ♗f7 with very good play for Black, who is threatening to round

up the d-pawn; G.Flear-K.Arkell, British Ch 1989.

7 e4 d6

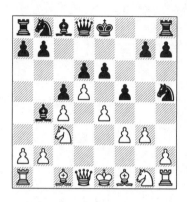

8 dxe6

⇨ 8 exf5!? is possibly an improvement: 8...♗xc3+ 9 bxc3 exf5 10 ♘h3! 0-0 11 ♗e2 ♖e8 12 0-0 ♘d7 13 ♕c2 (13 a4 ½-½ Shirov-Balashov, Lvov Z 1990) 13...♘f8 (13...♘e5 14 ♘g5 h6 15 f4! ±) 14 ♗d3 g6 15 ♗g5 ♕c7 16 ♖ae1 ♗d7 17 ♕d2 ♗a4 18 g4 (driving Black back) 18...♘g7 19 ♗h6 ♖xe1 20 ♖xe1 ♖e8 21 ♖xe8 ♗xe8 22 ♕g5 fxg4 23 fxg4 (Black is being squeezed) 23...♕f7 24 ♕d8 ♕d7 25 ♕f6! ♕xg4+ 26 ♔f2 ♕d7 27 ♘g5 b6 28 ♔e1 ♕b7 29 ♗f1 (White needs an extra attacking unit) 29...a6 30 ♗h3 b5 31 ♗c8! ♕a7 32 ♘e6 ♘fxe6 33 ♗xe6+ 1-0 Ilinčić-Levin, Belgrade 1992.

8...fxe4 9 f4 ♘f6 10 f5 ♘c6?!

It is important to break up the pawn chain with 10...g6.

11 a3?

11 ♘e2! ♘e5 12 ♕a4+ ♔e7 13 ♗g2 ♘d3+ 14 ♔f1 is much better for White.

11...♗xc3+ 12 bxc3 0-0 13 ♘h3

♛a5 14 ♗b2?

14 ♗d2 is not good because of 14...e3, but 14 ♕d2 is the right move.

14...♘d4

15 g4 ♘f3+ 16 ♔e2 ♕a6 17 g5 ♗xe6! 18 gxf6 ♗xc4+ 19 ♔e3 ♖xf6

A good operation for Black who has destroyed his opponent's powerful centre.

20 ♘f4? ♖xf5 21 ♘d5 ♖f7 22 ♗h3 ♖e8 23 ♖c1 ♕c6 0-1

Since ...d5-d4 is coming.

Game 153

Arencibia-Yudasin
Novi Sad OL 1990

1 d4 ♘f6 2 c4 e6 3 ♘c3 ♗b4 4 f3 c5 5 d5 ♘h5 6 ♘h3 ♕h4+

⇨ 6...d6!? 7 g4! ♘f6 8 ♗g2 ♗xc3+ 9 bxc3 e5 10 ♘f2 (or 10 0-0 ♕a5 11 ♕b3 0-0 12 ♘f2 ♘bd7 13 ♗g5 ♔h8 14 e3 ♘g8 15 ♘e4 ♕c7 16 f4 f6 17 ♗h4 ♘h6 18 h3 exf4 19 exf4 ♘b6 20 a4 ♗d7 21 f5 with an overwhelming position; Gallego-Izeta, Madrid

1992) 10...♘bd7 11 0-0 h6 12 e3! ♕a5?! 13 ♕d3 ♘b6 14 f4! ♕a4 15 g5 hxg5 16 fxg5 ♘g8 17 ♘e4 ♕d7 (naturally the c-pawn is immune to capture: 17...♘xc4?? 18 ♕xc4 ♕xc4 19 ♘xd6+) 18 ♗d2 ♕e7 19 ♖f2 ♗g4 20 ♖af1 ♘h5 21 ♘g3? (21 a4! was the most accurate: 21...0-0-0 22 a5 ♘a8 23 a6! b6 24 ♘g3 ♗g6 25 ♘f5 ±) 21...♗g6 22 ♗e4 (exchanging Black's best defensive piece) 22...♕xg5 23 ♗xg6 ♕xg6? (23...fxg6 was the only chance) 24 ♕xg6 fxg6 25 ♖f8+ ♔d7 26 ♖xa8 ♘xa8 27 ♖f8 ♘b6 28 e4! ± (Black's kingside is completely paralysed) 28...♔e7 29 ♖b8 ♔f6 30 ♖f8+ ♔e7 31 ♖b8 ♔f6 32 h4! ♖xh4 33 ♖f8+ ♔e7 34 ♖xg8 (the rest of the game is a formality) 34...♘xc4 35 ♗c1 ♖h7 36 ♖b8 ♘a5 37 ♗g5+ ♔d7 38 ♔g2 ♔c7 39 ♖e8 ♘c4 40 ♖e6 a5 41 ♖xg6 b5 42 ♘f5 b4 43 cxb4 axb4 44 ♗e7 ♖h8 45 ♗xd6+ ♘xd6 46 ♖xg7+ 1-0 Shirov-Adams, Biel 1991.

7 ♘f2 ♕xc4 8 ♗d2?!

The critical continuation is 8 e4! ♗xc3+ 9 bxc3 ♕xc3+ 10 ♗d2 and:

1) 10...♕e5 11 ♖c1 b6 12 g4 ♘f6 13 f4 ♕c7 14 g5 ♘g8 15 ♗c3 ♔f8 16 d6 ♕d8 (Black's two developed pieces have been forced to return to their starting squares) 17 ♕d2 h6 18 ♕b2 ♖h7 19 g6 fxg6 20 ♖g1 ♘f6 21 ♖xg6 ♕e8 22 ♖g1 ♕f7 23 ♗d3 ♗a6 24 ♗b1 ♘e8 25 e5 ♕xf4?! (taking the chance to relieve the pressure by returning some material, but 25...♖h8 was better) 26 ♗xh7 ♕e3+ 27 ♔d1 ♕f3+ 28 ♔e1 ♕e3+ 29 ♔d1 ♕f3+ 30 ♔c2! ♕xf2+ 31 ♔b1 ♕xb2+ 32 ♔xb2 g5 33 h4 ♘g7 34 hxg5 with a considerable

advantage; Ulybin-Kholmov, Voskresensk 1990.

2) 10...♕d4 11 ♕c1 and now Black may give up a piece immediately, or (more sensibly) reserve this option:

⇨ 11...♕f6?! 12 g4 exd5 13 gxh5 0-0 14 ♖g1 ♖e8 15 ♗g5 ♕d4 16 ♗e3 ♕b4+ 17 ♗d2 ♕b6 18 ♖g5 dxe4 19 fxe4 d5 20 ♕c3 f6 21 h6 g6 22 ♖xd5 ♘d7 23 ♗c4 with a great position, and a piece more for White; Sakaev-Bladikis, Duisburg 1992.

⇨ 11...exd5!? 12 ♗c3 ♕a4 13 ♕g5 d4! (13...d6 14 ♕xh5 d4 15 ♗d2 ♗e6 16 ♗e2 ♘c6 17 0-0 0-0-0 18 ♖fc1 c4 19 f4 f6 20 ♗d1 ♕a3 21 ♗g4 1-0 Marin-Vehi, Roses 1992) 14 ♗d2 0-0 15 ♕xh5 c4 16 ♗e2 ♘c6 17 0-0 Flear-Franklin, London 1989; now 17...d6! 18 f4 f5 was best.

8...♗xc3! 9 ♗xc3 ♕xd5 10 ♕a4 ♘c6 11 ♖d1

11...♘d4!

A nice trick that allows Black to sort himself out to some extent.

12 e3 ♕c6 13 ♕c4 b5?! 14 ♕d3 b4 15 ♗xd4 cxd4 16 ♕xd4 ♕b6! 17 ♕e5?

Better is 17 ♕xb6 ∓.

17...♘f6 18 ♖d6 ♕b8 19 ♕c5 0-0

White controls more space, but Black's extra pawn should count.

20 ♗d3 a5 21 0-0 ♗b7 22 ♘e4 ♗xe4 23 fxe4 ♕a7! 24 ♕d4 ♖fd8! 25 e5 ♘d5! 26 ♗e4 ♘xe3 27 ♗xa8?

Probably played in the hope of imprisoning Black's knight at the end, but this just facilitates Black's task.

27...♕xd4 28 ♖xd4 ♘xf1 29 ♗e4 ♘e3 30 h3 g6 31 g4 ♖c8 32 ♔f2 ♘c4 33 ♖xd7 ♘xb2 34 ♖a7 ♘c4 35 ♔f3 ♘xe5+ 0-1

Game 154

Shirov-Speelman
Hastings 1991

1 d4 ♘f6 2 c4 e6 3 ♘c3 ♗b4 4 f3 ♘c6 5 e4 b6!?

⇨ 5...e5 6 a3 ♗xc3+ 7 bxc3 d6 transposes to a Sämisch position, e.g. 8 ♗e3 0-0 9 ♘e2 ♘a5 10 ♘g3 ♘d7! (the start of a very interesting manoeuvre designed to force White to play d5) 11 ♗d3 ♘b6 12 ♕e2 ♗e6! 13 d5 ♗c8 14 0-0 ♘d7 15 ♖ab1 b6 16 ♕f2 ♗a6 17 ♘f5 ♔h8 18 ♕g3 ♖g8 19 ♖b4!? c5 20 ♖a4 (there is no way back for this rook) 20...♕f8 21 ♕h3 ♗c8 22 f4 ♘b7 23 ♖f3 ♘f6 24 fxe5 dxe5 25 ♕h4 ♘d6 26 ♘h6 ♘fe8 27 ♘xg8 ♔xg8 28 g4 ♗d7 29 ♗c2 h6 30 g5 hxg5 31 ♗xg5 f6 32 ♗e3 ♔f7 33 ♖g3 ♔e7 34 ♔g2? ♔d8 35 ♕h7 ♔c7 36 h4 a5 37 h5 ♖b8 38 h6 g5 39 ♕g6 ♕f7 40 ♕xf7 ♘xf7 41 h7 ♘ed6 Pein-Dorfman, Cannes 1992. Now

the manoeuvre 41...♘g7! intending
...♘h5-f4 would have been very favourable to Black.

⇨ 5...d5 6 cxd5 exd5 7 e5 ♘g8 8 a3
♗a5 9 f4!? (9 ♗b5 ♗d7 10 ♘e2
♗xc3+ 11 bxc3 ♘xe5 12 ♕b3 with
unclear complications in Khenkin-
Dokhoian, Werfen 1990) 9...♘ge7
10 ♗e3 0-0 11 ♘f3 ♗g4 12 ♗e2
♘f5 13 ♗f2 ♗xf3 14 ♗xf3 ♘h4 15
b4 ♘xf3+ 16 ♕xf3 ♗b6 17 ♖d1
♘e7 18 f5 is very promising indeed
for White; Marin-Barle, Manila OL
1992.

⇨ 5...d6 6 ♘e2 e5 7 d5 ♗xc3+ 8
♘xc3 ♘e7 9 ♗e3 0-0 10 ♕d2 a5 11
g4 ♘d7 12 ♘e2 ♘c5 13 ♘g3 ♘g6
14 ♗e2 ♗d7 15 h4! ♗xh4 16 ♖h2
♘g6 17 0-0-0 ♖e8 18 ♖dh1 ♘f8 19
♘h5 f6 20 ♘xg7 ♖e7 21 ♘f5 ♗xf5
22 gxf5 ♕d7 23 ♗h6 ♕a4 24 ♔b1
♔f7 25 ♖g1 ♕b4 26 f4! ♔e8 and 1-0
Malaniuk-Rashkovsky, Espergærde
Politiken Cup 1992. 26...♕xd2?
loses to 27 ♗h5+, but even after
26...♔e8 Black saw that 27 ♕xb4
axb4 28 ♖g8 ♖f7 29 ♗h5 would be
crushing.

6 ♗g5

⇨ 6 ♘e2 0-0 7 a3 ♗e7 8 ♘g3 d6 9
♗e3 ♘d7 10 d5 ♘ce5 11 ♗e2 ♘g6
12 f4 e5 13 f5 ♘f4 14 ♗f3 ♘c5 15
b4 ♘cd3+ 16 ♔d2 ♗d7 17 ♘f1 c6
18 dxc6 ♗xc6 19 g3 b5 20 gxf4
♘b2 21 ♕b3 ♘xc4+ 22 ♔e2 a5 23
bxa5 exf4 24 ♗xf4 with a whole
piece more; Shabalov-Kolev, Manila OL 1992.

**6...h6 7 ♗h4 e5 8 ♘e2 ♕e7 9 d5
g5 10 ♗f2 ♘b8 11 a3 ♗c5**

It is no minor achievement to exchange the dark-squared bishops.

12 ♗xc5 bxc5 13 d6!

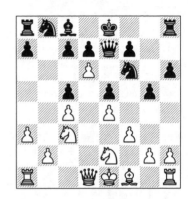

Obtaining play along the d-file; if
Black had had the chance to play
...d6 himself, White would have had
no advantage.

**13...♕xd6 14 ♕xd6 cxd6 15
♘b5 ♔d8 16 ♘xd6 ♖h7 17 b4 ♘a6
18 b5 ♘c7 19 h4 g4 20 f4 ♘ce8 21
♘xe8 ♔xe8 22 fxe5 ♘xe4 23 g3
♗b7 24 ♗g2 ♖b8 25 ♖d1 f5 26 exf6
♖f7 27 0-0 ♖xf6 28 ♖fe1 ♔d8 29
♘f4 ♘d6 30 ♘h5 ♖g6 31 ♘f4 ♖f6
32 ♗xb7 ♖xb7 33 ♖d5 ♘xc4 34
♘e6+ ♖xe6!**

The simplest way to defuse the
pressure.

**35 ♖xe6 ♖xb5 36 ♖xh6 ♖b3 37
♖h8+ ♔c7 38 ♖h7 ♔c6 39 ♖dxd7
♖xg3+ 40 ♔f2 ♖f3+ 41 ♔e2 ♖e3+
42 ♔f2 ½-½**

16

The Sämisch variation hasn't been played so much recently, and when it has, Black hasn't fared too badly. In particular, the main line discussed in the final two games of this chapter has held up remarkably well despite several new attempts at refutation by White.

First, though, we look at a sort of delayed Sämisch that was a favourite of Botvinnik's, 4 e3 0-0 5 ♗d3 d5 6 a3 ♗xc3+ 7 bxc3. Game 155 considers the seventh move alternatives to the 7...dxc4, which is itself covered in game 156.

After 4 a3 ♗xc3+ 5 bxc3 0-0 6 f3 d5 7 cxd5 Black should play 7...exd5 (game 157), although White is a little better strategically, since 7...♘xd5, whilst apparently very similar to the position considered in the second half of chapter 14, allows White a strong tactical possibility (8 e4!) due to the absence of a pawn on c5.

In game 158, Black's plan of pushing his e-pawn to e4 before White can play e4 himself is very laudable, but later, when White plays f3, he will have use of the half-open f-file. I.Sokolov manages to put this file to good use.

The variation 5...c5 6 e3 ♘c6 7 ♗d3 0-0 is traditionally Black's most solid choice. He will follow up with ...b6 and ...♗a6 pressurizing the weak white c4 pawn. In game 159 Karpov surprises Yusupov with a new continuation and forces a pleasant ending, whilst in game 160 White's novelty falls flat.

Game 155

Suba-Sax
Manila OL 1992

1 d4 ♘f6 2 c4 e6 3 ♘c3 ♗b4 4 e3 0-0 5 ♗d3 d5 6 a3 ♗xc3+ 7 bxc3 c5
⇨ 7...c6 8 ♘f3 b6 9 0-0 ♗a6 10 cxd5 ♗xd3 11 ♕xd3 cxd5 12 c4 ♘c6 13 cxd5 ♕xd5 14 ♗b2 e5 15 ♕e2 e4 16 ♘e5 ♖ac8 17 ♖fc1 ♘a5 18 h3 h6 = Smyslov-Serper, Tilburg (active) 1992.
⇨ 7...e5!? 8 ♘e2 (8 dxe5?! dxc4 9 exf6 ♕xd3 10 ♕xd3 cxd3 11 fxg7 ♖d8 12 ♘f3 ♘c6 13 c4 ♘a5 14 ♘d2 ♗e6 ½-½ Rechlis-Sax, Manila IZ 1990; probably 8 cxd5! is best) 8...e4 9 ♗b1 (9 ♗c2 dxc4 10 ♘g3 ♖e8 11 0-0 ♗g4 12 ♕e1 c5 13 ♖b1 ♕c7 14 a4 ♘c6 15 ♖b5 a6?! 16 ♖xc5! ∞ Suba-Chandler, London 1990) 9...dxc4 10 ♘g3 ♖e8 11 f3 exf3 12 ♕xf3 ♗g4 13 ♕f2 c5 14 0-0 cxd4 15 cxd4 ♘c6 16 ♗b2 ♕a5 17 e4 c3 18 ♗c1 ♕b6 19 ♗e3 ♕b2?! (attempting to exchange queens, but it turns out that it involves Black in the sacrifice of his queen instead. On the other hand it is not easy to find a fully satisfactory move for Black here) 20 ♗c2 ♗e6 21 ♖fb1 ♘g4 22 ♕e2 ♘xe3 23 ♖xb2 cxb2 24 ♖b1 ♘xd4 25 ♕xe3 ♘xc2 26 ♕c3 ♖ac8 27 ♕xb2 b6 28 ♘h5 f6 29 ♖f1 ♗e3 30 ♘xg7 ♘xf1 31 ♘xe8 ♖xe8 32 ♔xf1 ± Petursson-Westerinen, Östersund Z 1992.
8 cxd5 exd5 9 ♘e2 b6
⇨ 9...♗g4 would transpose to the game Sadler-Abramović, Oberwart 1990: 10 0-0 ♗h5 11 ♖b1 ♕c7 12 f3 ♗g6 13 ♘f4 ♘c6 14 g4 ♖ad8 15

♖b2 ♖fe8 16 h4!? (rather than calmly prepare the e4 break, White decides to throw everything up the kingside) 16...♗xd3 17 ♕xd3 ♘e7 18 g5 ♘d7 19 h5 ♘f8 20 e4?! ♘e6 21 ♘xe6 fxe6 22 ♖g2 e5 (the thematic central reaction) 23 g6 h6 24 f4 exd4 25 f5 dxe4 26 ♕c4+ ♘d5 27 ♗xh6 b5! 28 ♕xb5 gxh6 29 f6 (this looks very dangerous) 29...♘xf6 30 ♖xf6 ♕e5 31 ♖f7 dxc3 32 ♕b3 ♕d5 33 ♕xc3 ♕d1+ (the flip side of White's play: his king is wide open) 34 ♔h2 ♕xh5+ 35 ♕h3 ♕e5+ 36 ♔h1 ♖d1+ 37 ♖g1 ♖xg1+ 38 ♔xg1 ♕g5+ 39 ♔h1 e3 40 ♕d7 ♕h5+ 0-1.

10 0-0 ♗a6 11 ♗xa6 ♘xa6 12 ♕d3

⇨ 12 f3 ♖e8 13 ♕d3 ♕c8 14 ♖a2 (14 ♘g3) 14...♘c7 15 g4 ♕a6 16 ♕xa6 ♘xa6 (after the exchange of queens, the ending should be quite reasonable for Black) 17 ♘f4 ♘c7 18 a4 ♘e6 19 ♘d3 ♖ec8 20 ♗d2 ♘e8 21 ♗e1! (looking for a more fruitful square) 21...♘d6 22 ♗g3 ♘c4 23 ♖e1 ♖f8 24 ♔g2 ♖ac8 25 h4 h6 26 ♖ae2 ♖fd8 27 ♖d1 ♖e8 28 ♖de1 ♖e7 29 f4 ♘f8 30 f5 ♘d7 31 g5 ♖ce8 32 ♔f3 ♖e4 33 ♘f2 ♖4e7 34 ♗f4 cxd4 35 cxd4 ♘b8?! (35...h5) 36 gxh6 ♘c6 37 hxg7 ♔xg7 38 f6+ (winning) 38...♔xf6 39 ♗g5+ ♔e6 40 ♗xe7 1-0 Spraggett-Oll, Terrassa 1990.

12...♘c7 13 dxc5

A departure from the standard plan in such positions, f3 and the preparation of e4.

13...bxc5 14 c4 ♖b8 15 ♖a2!

Another fine new move from the Suba 'laboratory'.

15...♕e7 16 cxd5 ♘cxd5 17 ♖c2

♖fc8 18 ♘g3 ♕c7 19 e4 ♘f4 20 ♕f3 ♘g6 21 ♗b2 ♖b6 22 ♘f5 ± ♕b7! 23 ♗xf6 ♖xf6 24 ♖d1 ♕c7 25 ♕g4 ♖e6 26 f3 ♖d8! 27 ♖dc1

Reminding Black of the frailty of his c-pawn.

27...♖c6 28 h4 h5?

A faulty combination; 28...f6 29 h5 ♘e5 30 ♕g3 ♖d3! ∞ was better, but not 30...♘d3?! 31 ♕xc7 ♖xc7 32 ♖d1 ♖cd7 33 ♘e3! ♘f4 34 ♖xd7 ♖xd7 35 ♖xc5 ♖d3 36 ♘f5 ±.

29 ♕xh5 ♘f4

30 ♕g5??

Presumably overlooking the threat. Instead 30 ♕g4 ♖g6 31 ♘e7+! ♕xe7 32 ♕xf4 wins easily.

30...♘h3+! 31 gxh3 ♖g6 32 ♖xc5 ♖xg5+ 33 hxg5 ♕f4

White would have reasonable chances were his king not so completely exposed.

34 ♖c8 ♖xc8 35 ♖xc8+ ♔h7 36 ♔f2 ♕d2+ 37 ♔f1 ♕d1+ 38 ♔f2 ♕d2+ 39 ♔f1 ♕xg5 40 ♖c7 ♕f4 41 ♖xf7 ♕xf3+ 42 ♔g1 0-1

Following 42...♕d1+ 43 ♔f2 ♕c2+, Black will pick up the rook on f7 with a check on a2 or b3.

Game 156

Speelman-Karpov
Linares 1991

1 d4 ♘f6 2 c4 e6 3 ♘c3 ♗b4 4 e3
0-0 5 ♗d3 d5 6 a3 ♗xc3+ 7 bxc3
dxc4 8 ♗xc4 c5 9 ♘e2

9...♘c6

⇨ 9...♕c7 10 ♗d3 e5 11 0-0 (11
e4!? cxd4 12 cxd4 exd4 13 0-0 ♘c6
14 h3! ♖e8 15 ♘g3 ♘e5 16 ♗f4
♗d7 17 ♗xe5! ♕xe5 18 f4 was unclear in Lein-Hjartarson, Reykjavik
1990) 11...♘c6 12 ♗b2 e4 13 ♗b1!?
♘a5 14 ♗a2 c4 15 ♘f4 b6 16 a4 ♖e8
17 ♖e1 (17 ♗a3!) 17...♗b7 18 ♗a3
♘d5 ∓ 19 ♗b4 ♘xf4 20 exf4 ♘b3?!
21 ♗xb3 cxb3 22 ♕xb3 ♕xf4 23 c4
= ♖ac8 24 a5! (always a useful idea:
White exchanges his isolated a-
pawn, and creates a weakness on b6)
24...♗a6 25 ♖ac1 h6 26 axb6 axb6
27 ♕a2! ♗b7 28 ♗d2 (intending to
put pressure on b6 from e3)
28...♕d6?! 29 ♗e3 ♖a8?! 30 ♕b3
♖e6 31 d5 ♖g6 32 c5?! (32 ♖b1 ±)

32...♕d7 33 c6 ♕h3? (33...♖xg2+!
34 ♔xg2 ♕g4+ 35 ♔f1 ♗a6+ 36
♖c4 ♕h3+ 37 ♔e2 ♕h5+ 38 f3
exf3+ 39 ♔f2 ♕xh2+ 40 ♔xf3
♕h3+ forces a draw) 34 ♗g5??
(flashy, but completely unsound;
simply 34 g3 is good for White)

34...♕xb3 35 cxb7 ♖b8 36 ♖c8+
♔h7 37 ♖xb8 ♖xg5 38 ♖e8 ♕f3??
(38...♖xg2+ 39 ♔xg2 ♕f3+ draws,
but 38...♕h3! 39 g3 ♖h5 wins!) 39
g3 ± ♖f5 40 ♖f1 1-0 (time) Sadler-
Chandler, London 1991.

**10 0-0 e5 11 ♖b1?! ♕c7 12 ♗a2
♖d8 13 ♕c2 b6! 14 ♘g3?! exd4?!**

Missing 14...♗a6!: 15 ♖e1 cxd4
∓ or 15 ♖d1?? cxd4 16 cxd4 ♘xd4!
∓.

**15 cxd4 cxd4 16 exd4 ♗e6 17
♗xe6 fxe6 18 ♗g5 ♖ac8 19 ♗xf6
gxf6 20 ♖bc1 ♖xd4 21 ♖fe1**

The looseness of Black's kingside
offers compensation for White's
pawn.

**21...♕f7 22 ♕c3! ♖dd8 23 ♘e4
e5 24 ♕g3+ ♔h8 25 ♕h4 ♘d4?**

Black should play 25...♕e7! 26
♕xf6+ ♕xf6 27 ♘xf6 ♔g7! 28 ♘e4
♘d4 =.

26 ♖xc8 ♖xc8 27 ♘xf6 ♕g6?! 28 ♘g4! ♘e2+ 29 ♔h1 ♘f4 30 h3 ♖e8 31 ♖d1! ♕g7 32 ♖d8

32...♖g8 33 ♖xg8+

The exchange of rooks simplifies White's task.

33...♕xg8 34 ♕f6+ ♕g7 35 ♕d8+ ♕g8 36 ♕e7 ♘g6 37 ♕xa7 ♕e6 38 ♕b8+ ♔g7 39 ♕c7+ ♔h8 40 ♘h6 ♕f6 41 ♕c8+ ♔g7 42 ♘f5+ ♔f7 43 ♕d7+ ♔f8 44 g3 h5 45 h4 ♔g8 46 ♔g2 ♘f8 47 ♕d5+ ♔h7 48 ♕b7+ ♔g8 49 ♘e7+ ♔h8 50 ♘d5 ♕d6 51 ♕f7! ♘g6 52 ♘f6 1-0

Game 157

Khenkin-Kuzmin
Leningrad 1991

1 d4 ♘f6 2 c4 e6 3 ♘c3 ♗b4 4 f3 d5 5 a3 ♗xc3+ 6 bxc3 0-0

⇨ 6...c6 7 e3 0-0 8 ♘h3 b6 9 cxd5 cxd5 10 a4 ♕c7 11 ♗d2 ♗a6 12 ♗xa6 ♘xa6 13 ♕e2 ♘b8 14 0-0 ♘bd7 15 e4 e5 16 ♘f2 ♖fe8 17 ♖fe1 ♖ac8 18 a5 bxa5 19 ♕b5 dxe4 20 fxe4 exd4 21 cxd4 ♕c4 22 ♕xc4

½-½ Bareev-Rozentalis, Leningrad 1990.

⇨ 6...♘h5!? 7 ♘h3 c5 8 ♘f2 ♘c6 9 e3 0-0 10 ♗e2 ♘f6 11 0-0 ♖e8 12 ♖a2! b6 13 cxd5! exd5 14 ♗b5 ♖e6 15 e4! led to a significant plus for White in Ilinčić-Jevtić, Yugoslav Ch 1992.

⇨ 6...♘bd7 7 cxd5 exd5 8 e3 ♘h5 9 ♘h3 ♘b6 10 ♘f2 0-0 11 e4 f5 12 exf5 ♕e8+ 13 ♗e2 ♘a4 14 ♕b3 ♖xf5 15 ♖a2 ♘f4 16 ♗xf4 ♖xf4 17 0-0 ♘b6 18 ♗d3 ♗f5 ½-½ Sakaev-Kuzmin, St. Petersburg 1992.

7 cxd5 exd5

⇨ 7...♘xd5?! 8 e4! ♘xc3?! (8...♘b6 ±) 9 ♕b3 ♘xe4!? (9...♕xd4?! 10 ♗b2 ♕e3+ 11 ♗e2 ♘d5 12 ♕xe3 ♘xe3 13 ♔f2 ♘d5 14 exd5 exd5 15 ♖c1! ± Moskalenko-Levin, USSR 1989; the pawns are insufficient compensation for a piece) 10 fxe4 ♕xd4 11 ♕b1 e5 12 ♘f3 ♕d6 13 ♗e3 b6 14 ♗c4 ♗e6 15 ♕b3 ♗xc4 16 ♕xc4 ♘c6! 17 0-0 (17 ♖d1? ♕xa3 18 ♕xc6 ♕xe3+) 17...♘a5 18 ♕c3 f6 (Black's position is fairly solid, but a piece is generally worth more than three pawns in the middlegame) 19 ♖ad1 ♕e7 20 ♘h4! ± g6 21 ♗h6 ♖f7 22 ♕g3 ♔h8 23 ♖d3 ♖g8 24 ♖df3 ♘c6 25 ♕f2 f5+ 26 exf5 ♘d4 27 ♖f4? (a nice idea, very much in the style of the Chinese IM, but Black is not forced to capture the rook. Simply 27 ♖h3! ♘xf5 {27...gxf5 28 ♗e3 ±} 28 ♘xf5 gxf5 29 ♗c1 with the idea of 30 ♗b2 is crushing) 27...♕d6! (not 27...exf4 28 ♕xd4+ ♕f6 29 ♕xf6+ ♖xf6 30 ♗xf4 ♖e8 31 fxg6 hxg6 32 ♗e5 ±) 28 ♖xd4? (28 ♖g4) 28...♕xd4 29 ♗e3 ♕d5 30 ♕c2 gxf5 31 ♘xf5 c5

32 g3 ♖d8 33 ♗g5 ♕d3 34 ♕xd3??
(a bad decision—White cannot afford to play the ending as the value of Black's rook and two pawns increases with respect to White's minor pieces; better is 34 ♕b2! ♖e8 35 g4) 34...♖xd3 35 g4 h5! ∓ (Black's resourcefulness pays off) 36 ♖e1 hxg4 37 ♖xe5 ♖xa3 38 ♘h6 ♖d7 39 ♘xg4 ♖a2 40 ♗f6+ ♔g8 41 ♖e1 b5 42 ♗g5 ♖d4 43 ♘f6+ ♔f7 44 h4 ♔g6 45 ♘e4 ♖c2 46 ♘g3 b4 47 ♖e6+ ♔f7 48 ♖e7+ ♔f8 49 ♖e2 ♖xe2 50 ♘xe2 b3! 0-1 Lin Ta-Agdestein, Manila IZ 1990.

8 e3 ♗f5

⇨ 8...b6 (exchanging the light-squared bishops is a sensible idea) 9 ♗d3 ♗a6 10 ♘e2 (only this is new; formerly 10 ♗xa6 ♘xa6 11 ♕d3 ♕c8 had been played) 10...♕c8 11 e4 ♗xd3 12 ♕xd3 ♕a6 13 ♕e3 dxe4 14 fxe4 ♘bd7 15 0-0 ♖ae8 16 e5 ♘d5 17 ♕f3 ♕c4 (taking a firm grip on the light squares) 18 ♘g3 f6 19 ♗h6 gxh6 20 ♕g4+ ♔h8 21 ♕xd7 ♖d8 (21...fxe5? 22 ♘h5 ♖xf1+ 23 ♖xf1 ♖g8 24 ♖f8! ±) 22 ♕e6 ♖de8 23 ♕d7 ♖d8 24 ♕e6 ♖de8 25 ♕d7 ½-½ Beliavsky-Ljubojević, Linares 1990.

9 ♘e2 ♖e8!?

The introduction to a typical piece sacrifice on g4. Others:
⇨ 9...a5 (also with the aim of sacrificing on g4, but Black never gets anywhere near enough compensation) 10 g4 ♘xg4 11 fxg4 ♕h4+ 12 ♔d2 ♗e4 13 ♖g1 ♕xh2 14 ♕e1 ♖a6 15 ♕g3 ♕h6 16 ♕xc7! ♖d6 17 g5 ♕h2 18 ♖g3 ♖fd8 19 a4 ♘a6 20 ♕e7 ♖6d7 21 ♕e5 ♘c7 22 ♗h3 ♖e8 23 ♕f4 ♘e6 24 ♕f1 ♖c7 25

♕g1 exchanging queens and winning; I.Sokolov-Djurić, Ljubljana Vidmar mem 1991.
⇨ 9...c5 is more usual: 10 g4 ♗g6 11 ♘f4 ♘c6!? 12 ♗g2 ♖c8 13 0-0 ♘a5 14 ♖a2 h6 15 ♘xg6 fxg6 16 ♖e1 ♖c6 17 ♖f2 cxd4 18 cxd4 ♕b6 19 ♖b2 ♕c7 20 e4 ♔h8 21 e5 ♘g8 22 f4 with the better chances; Malaniuk-Ivanchuk, Lvov 1988.

10 g4 ♗xg4!? 11 fxg4 ♘xg4 12 ♖a2! ♘c6 13 ♕d3! ♘a5 14 e4!!

Excellent defence; now 14...♖xe4 15 ♗g2 ♖e6 16 ♕g3 would free White's position whereupon he would be able to make his extra piece count.

14...c5?! 15 ♗g2! ♘b3 16 0-0?

16 e5 would have clarified matters somewhat.

16...cxd4 17 cxd4 ♘xc1 18 ♘xc1 ♕h4! 19 h3 dxe4 20 ♗xe4 ♘f6! 21 ♗xb7 ♖ad8 22 ♘b3 ♕h6?! 23 ♗g2 ♖e3 24 ♕c4 ♕g5 25 ♘c5 ♖xh3 26 ♘e4 ♕e3+ 27 ♖af2 ♖h6! 28 ♘xf6+ ♖xf6 29 d5 h5 30 ♕e2 ♕c5 31 ♔h1 ♖xf2 32 ♕xf2 ♕xf2 33 ♖xf2 ♔f8 34 ♖c2

This ending should probably be

drawn, but now the clock starts taking an active role in the game.
34...♖d7?! 35 ♖c5 ♔e7 36 ♗h3 ♖b7 37 ♗c8?! ♖b3 38 a4 ♔d6 39 ♖a5 ♖c3?! 40 ♗h3??
40 ♗b7 ±.
40...♖xh3+ 41 ♔g2 ♖e3 42 ♖xa7 ♖e5 43 ♖xf7 g5 44 a5 ♖xd5 45 a6 ♖a5 46 a7 ♔e6 47 ♖g7 ♔f6 48 ♖h7 h4 49 ♔h3 ♖a3+ 50 ♔h2?

Throwing away the draw, the point being that after 50 ♔g2! ♔g6 51 ♖b7 ♔h5 52 ♔f2!, 52...h3 is no longer check and so White can play 53 ♖b3 =.
50...♔g6 51 ♖b7 ♔h5 52 ♔g2 h3+ 0-1

Game 158

I.Sokolov-van der Wiel
Wijk aan Zee 1991

1 d4 e6 2 c4 ♘f6 3 ♘c3 ♗b4 4 e3 c5 5 ♗d3 ♘c6 6 a3 ♗xc3+ 7 bxc3
⇨ The point of White's move-order is to transpose into a favourable version of the Sämisch variation. For instance, were Black now to try to play Hübner's variation, then White could put his king's knight not on f3 but on e2. For example 7...d6 8 ♘e2 e5 9 0-0 0-0 10 ♘g3 when a perpetual on the queen featured in the game Zsu.Polgar-Krasenkov, Lillafüred 1989: 10...♖e8 11 d5 ♘e7 (11...e4 12 dxc6 exd3 13 cxb7 ♗xb7 14 ♕xd3 ♕d7 is unclear) 12 f4 exf4 13 exf4 ♕a5 14 f5 b5 (Black cannot just lie still and be crushed by White's prospective kingside attack) 15 ♗g5 ♕xc3 16 ♘e2 ♕e5 17 ♗f4 ♕b2 18

♖b1 ♕xa3 19 ♖a1 ♕b2 20 ♖b1 ♕a3 21 ♖a1 ♕b2 22 ♖b1 ½-½.

7...e5 8 ♘e2 e4 9 ♗b1 0-0 10 ♘g3 ♕a5?! 11 ♗d2 ♖e8 12 0-0 d6 13 f3 exf3 14 ♕xf3 cxd4 15 exd4 ♘xd4 16 ♕d3 ♘c6

17 ♖xf6!
Ripping open Black's kingside.
17...gxf6 18 ♕xh7+ ♔f8 19 ♘e4 ♖e6 20 ♗c2 ♘e5 21 ♖f1 ♔e7 22 ♔h1
22 h3! ±.
22...♕a6! 23 ♗b3 ♕xa3 24 ♘xf6! ♖xf6 25 ♗g5 ♗e6! 26 ♗xf6+ ♔d7 27 ♗xe5 dxe5 28 ♗c2 ♔c7
The black king tries to make good its escape to the queenside.
29 ♕e4? ♕xc3 30 ♖b1 ♖b8 31 h3 f5? 32 ♕h4 ♕xc2 33 ♕e7+ ♔d7 34 ♕xe5+ ♔c8 35 ♕h8+ ♔c7 36 ♕e5+ ♔c8 ½-½

Game 159

Yusupov-Karpov
Linares 1993

1 d4 ♘f6 2 c4 e6 3 ♘c3 ♗b4 4 e3 c5 5 ♗d3 ♘c6 6 a3 ♗xc3+ 7 bxc3 0-0

8 ♘e2 b6 9 e4 ♘e8 10 0-0 ♗a6 11 f4 f5 12 ♘g3 g6

Lending support to f5. 12...♘d6 is discussed in the next game.

13 ♗e3

Following 13 dxc5 Black managed to get the upper hand in the game Agrest-Mochalov, Azov 1991: 13...♘a5 14 ♗e3 ♘xc4 15 ♗xc4 ♗xc4 16 ♖e1 fxe4 17 ♘xe4 ♗d5 (the bishop is very strong on the a8-h1 diagonal) 18 ♕d3 bxc5 19 ♘xc5 ♘d6 20 ♗d4 ♖c8 21 ♕e2 ♘f5 22 ♗f2 ♖f7 with an edge.

13...cxd4!

⇨ 13...d6 is not so dynamic, but no doubt playable. Aleksandrov-Tunik, Smolensk 1991, continued 14 d5 ♘e7 15 dxe6 ♘g7 16 exf5 gxf5 17 ♖e1 ♕e8 18 ♗f2 ♖f6 19 ♖a2 ♖d8 20 ♖d2 ♗b7 21 ♗f1 d5 (Black does not want to dissolve White's forward c-pawn, but the pressure on d6 was becoming too much) 22 cxd5 ♖xd5 23 ♖e5 ♖xd2 24 ♕xd2 ♗c8 25 ♕d6 ♘g6 26 ♖e1 ♗xe6 (finally winning back his e-pawn) 27 ♗d3 ♕d7 28 ♕xd7 ♗xd7 ∓.

⇨ 13...♘d6 14 exf5!? ♘xc4!? (this caused quite a surprise; Karpov grabs a hot exchange) 15 ♗xc4 (15 ♕e2? loses a pawn: 15...♘xe3 16 ♕xe3 cxd4 17 cxd4 ♗xd3 18 ♕xd3 exf5 ∓ Döring-Komarov, Dortmund 1992) 15...♗xc4 16 fxg6 ♗xf1 17 ♕h5 ♕e7 18 ♖xf1 hxg6 19 ♕xg6+ ♕g7 20 ♕d3 cxd4 21 cxd4 ♕h7! 22 ♕b5?! (22 f5 ♘e7 23 ♖f3 is correct) 22...a6! ∓ 23 ♕b3 ♘e7 24 ♖f3 ♖ac8 25 ♕xb6 ♖c6?! (25...♘d5 ∓) 26 ♕a5 ♘d5 27 ♘f1 ♕f5 28 ♕e1 ♖b8 29 ♕h4 ♔f7 30 h3 ♖c3 31 ♔h2 ♖g8 32 ♘g3 ♕f6 33 ♕h5+ ♕g6 34 ♕e5 ♕g7! 35 ♕d6 ♔e8 36 f5 ♕e7 (Karpov misses 36...♖xe3! in time-trouble, e.g. 37 f6 ♕xg3+! 38 ♖xg3 ♖exg3 39 f7+ ♔xf7 40 ♕xd7+ ♔f6 with unstoppable mate) 37 ♕b8+ ♕d8 38 ♕e5 ♕c7? 39 ♕xc7? ♖xc7 40 fxe6 dxe6 41 ♘e4 ♖c2 42 ♗d2 a5 43 ♖b3 ♔d7 44 ♖b5 ♖a8 45 a4 ♔c6 46 h4 ♖c4 47 ♖c5+ ♖xc5 48 dxc5 ♘b4 49 h5 ♔d5 50 ♘f6+ ♔e5 51 ♗c3+ ♔f4 52 g4 ♖d8 53 h6 ♔g5 54 h7 ♔g6 55 ♔g3 ♘c6 56 ♔f4 ♔g7 57 g5 ♖d3 58 ♗e5 ♖d1 59 g6?? (another blunder when down on the clock; 59 ♗d6 =) 59...♖f1+ 60 ♔g5 ♘xe5 61 ♘h5+ 0-1 Yusupov-Karpov, London Ct (3) 1989.

14 cxd4 d5!

Apparently Karpov had been saving up this innovation for many years.

15 cxd5

White already has difficulties. 15 exd5?! exd5 16 cxd5 ♗xd3 17 ♕xd3 ♕xd5 gives Black a clear positional advantage—the d5 square is a strongpoint and White's bishop is hemmed in by its own pawns.

15...♗xd3 16 ♕xd3 fxe4 17 ♕xe4

♕xd5 18 ♕xd5 exd5 19 ♖ac1 ♖c8
20 f5

Forced—White must find some
room for his bishop.

**20...♘d6 21 fxg6 hxg6 22 ♖xf8+
♔xf8 23 h4 ♘c4 24 ♗g5 ♘xd4 25
h5?** gxh5 **26 ♖f1+ ♔e8 27 ♘xh5
♘xa3 28 ♘g7+ ♔d7 29 ♖f7+ ♔c6
30 ♖xa7 ♘ac2**

The black knights are well placed
to escort the b-pawn home, whilst
the white knight on g7 is temporarily
out of play.

**31 ♗f6 b5 32 g4 b4 33 ♖a2 b3 34
♖b2 ♔c5 35 ♘f5 ♖g8**

Taking play into a winning rook
and pawn endgame.

**36 ♘xd4 ♖xg4+ 37 ♔f2 ♘xd4 38
♗xd4+ ♔xd4 39 ♖xb3 ♖e4!**

Cutting off the white king.

40 ♖h3 ♖e8 0-1

Game 160

Piket-Salov
Dortmund 1992

**1 d4 ♘f6 2 c4 e6 3 ♘c3 ♗b4 4 a3
♗xc3+ 5 bxc3 c5**

⇨ Black can also try to make do
without playing this move, for instance: 5...0-0 6 e3 b6 7 ♗d3 ♗a6 8
e4 ♘e8 9 ♘f3 ♘c6 10 0-0 ♘a5 11 e5
f5 12 ♗g5 ♕c8 13 ♘d2 d5 14 exd6
♘xd6 15 ♕e2 ♕d7 16 ♗f4 ♖ae8 17
♖ab1 ♕c6 18 ♖b4 ♗b7 (I doubt
whether Black should raise the seige
of c4) 19 ♘f3 ♘f7 20 h4 ♕d7 21
♖d1 c5 22 ♖bb1 ♗xf3?! (Black embarks on a dangerous adventure; he
opens the position for the white bishops) 23 ♕xf3 cxd4 24 cxd4 ♕xd4 25

♗xf5 ♕c5 26 ♖b5 ♕c6 27 ♗e4
♕xc4 28 ♗d3 ♕a4 29 ♕h5 h6 30
♖b4 ♕xa3 31 ♕g6 ♘h8 32 ♕h7+
♔f7 33 ♗d6 1-0 Vaganian-Chu-
chelov, Porz Citroën Cup 1992.
♖f4+ will be a killer.

6 e3 ♘c6 7 ♗d3

⇨ 7 ♘e2 (I don't see any great advantage in deferring the development of the king's bishop here)
7...0-0 8 ♘g3 d6 9 e4 b6! (Black
doesn't bother with the prophylactic
9...♘e8, as he realizes that 10 ♗g5 is
not a problem) 10 ♗g5?! (perhaps
10 d5 ♘a5 =) 10...h6 11 h4 ♖e8
(now ...hxg5 really is a threat) 12
♗e3 ♗a6 13 ♗d3 ♖c8 14 ♕e2 cxd4
15 cxd4 ♘a5 16 ♖c1 ♖e7 17 ♘f1
(the knight is needed on d2 to defend
c4) 17...♖ec7 18 ♘d2 d5 19 exd5
exd5 20 c5 ♗xd3 21 ♕xd3 ♘g4 22
0-0 ♘xe3 23 fxe3 ♕xh4 ∓ 24 ♖f5
♕d8 25 e4 ♖d7 26 e5 ♖c6 27 ♘f3
♘c4 28 ♖f1 ♖b7?! 29 ♕h5 (White,
who has been positionally outplayed, starts limbering up for a
big heave-ho on the kingside)
29...bxc5? (he should certainly have
considered a defensive move here!)
30 ♘g5! g6 (if 30...hxg5? 31 ♕h7+
♔f8 32 ♕h8+ ♔e7 33 ♖xf7+ wins)
31 e6! f5 32 ♘f7 ♖xf7 33 exf7+
♔xf7 34 ♖xh6 ♕g5 35 ♖h3 ♕g4 36
dxc5 ♖xc5 37 ♕b3 (Black would not
be doing too badly were it not for the
lack of cover for his king) 37...♘d6
38 ♕b8 ♖c2 39 ♖h7+ ♔e6 40
♖e1+ ♖e2 41 ♕g8+ 1-0 Zsu.Polgar-
Granda Zuniga, Aruba 1992.

7...0-0 8 ♘e2 b6 9 e4 ♘e8 10 0-0

The hyper-aggressive 10 e5 ♗a6
11 h4 d6! 12 ♗g5 ♕c7 13 f4 (13
♕c2 h6 14 exd6 ∞) 13...♘a5 14 ♘g3

♗xc4 rebounded in C.Holland-Chernin, London 1989, as Black is already better.

10...♗a6 11 f4 f5 12 ♘g3

An important innovation was seen in the correspondence game Hollis-Hovde, 1991: 12 exf5 exf5 13 dxc5 bxc5 14 ♘g3 g6 15 ♗e3 d6 (15...♕a5 is also playable, as the attempted refutation 16 ♗xf5 fails: 16...gxf5 17 ♕xd7 ♕c7 18 ♕d5+ ♔h8 19 ♕xc5 ♕d6 20 ♖fd1 ♕xc5 21 ♗xc5 ♖f7 22 ♖d5 ♘g7 23 ♗f2 ♖c8 24 ♖ad1 ♔g8 25 c5 ♗c4 26 ♖d7 ♗e6 27 ♖7d6 ♖e7 28 ♖e1 ♔f7 ∓ Markotić-Masserey, Geneva 1991) 16 ♗xf5 gxf5 17 ♕d5+ ♖f7 18 ♕xc6 ♗b7! (rather than recapturing on c4 Black goes over to the attack, in which his bishop is the prime mover) 19 ♕a4 h5! 20 ♖ab1 ♘g7 21 ♖f2 h4 22 ♖fb2?! hxg3 23 ♖xb7 ♖xb7 24 ♖xb7 ♕e8! 25 ♕xe8+ ♖xe8 26 ♗d2 ♖e2 with a winning ending.

12...♘d6

Putting immediate pressure on the c-pawn.

⇨ 12...fxe4!? (unusual) 13 ♘xe4 cxd4 14 cxd4 ♘f6! (14...♘xd4 15 ♘g5 ♘f6 16 ♗b2 ∞) 15 d5 exd5 16

cxd5 ♗xd3 17 ♕xd3 ♘xe4 18 ♕xe4 ♕f6! (Black has managed to equalise) 19 ♗b2 ♕xb2 20 dxc6 dxc6 21 ♕xc6 ♕d4+ 22 ♔h1 ♖ad8 23 ♖ae1 ½-½ Yusupov-Beliavsky, Groningen 1992.

13 ♖e1?! ♗xc4 14 ♗xc4 ♘xc4 15 exf5 cxd4

If 15...exf5 then 16 ♕d3.

16 ♕d3! ♘6a5 17 cxd4 ♕f6! 18 fxe6 dxe6 19 ♖a2! ♖ad8 20 ♖ae2

White must counterattack; it is pointless getting tied down to the defence of d4.

20...♕xd4+ 21 ♕xd4 ♖xd4 22 ♖xe6 ♖d7 23 f5 ♘b3 24 a4? ♘c5! 25 ♖e7 ♖f7 26 ♖e8+ ♖f8 27 ♖8e7 ♖fd8! 28 ♘h5 ♖xe7 29 ♖xe7 ♖d7 30 ♖e1 ♔f7 31 ♗g5?! ♘xa4 32 f6 g6 33 ♘g7 ♘c5 34 h4 ♘d6 35 h5 ♘de4! ∓

Black's queenside pawns guarantee the win.

36 hxg6+ hxg6 37 ♗e3 ♘xf6 38 ♗xc5 ♔xg7 39 ♗a3 ♘g4 40 ♗b2+ ♔f7 41 ♗c3 ♖d3 42 ♖c1 ♘e3 43 ♗e1 ♔e6 44 ♔f2 ♘g4+ 45 ♔e2 ♖e3+ 46 ♔d2 ♖a3 47 ♖c6+ ♔f5 48 ♔e2 ♖a2+ 49 ♗d2 ♘e5 50 ♖c8 b5 51 ♖c5 ♔e4 52 ♔d1 ♘c4 53 ♗c1 a6 54 ♖g5 ♘e5 55 g3 ♖h2 0-1

17 In actual fact, in this chapter we are only looking at the continuations that do not effect an immediate transposition into lines considered in other chapters. The most important line is 4...b6 5 ♗g5 (naturally, 5 e3, 5 ♕b3 and 5 ♕c2 are considered elsewhere) which was popularized by the World Champion, Garry Kasparov.

Essentially, the main variation in this line is 4 ♘f3 b6 5 ♗g5 h6 6 ♗h4 ♗b7. It is interesting to observe that Black seems to have decided his best continuation is to play ...♗xc3+, ...d6, ...♘bd7, ...♕e7 and then ...e5, deciding on his subsequent plan according to White's set-up. Games 161 to 165 all represent variations on this theme.

Game 161 looks at Kasparov's 6 ♘d2!?, whilst game 162 shows White breaking through on the queenside. Game 163 is a really beautiful game from Hulak which demonstrates Black's tactical possibilities.

It is interesting that, sooner or later, White must sacrifice his forward c-pawn. Black players should take note and be especially vigilant regarding c5. In game 165 the move c5 was the start of a winning combination; Beliavsky's 13 ♕a4+ is worth remembering.

The last game, 166, covers the older variation where Black plays ...g5 and ...♘e4xg3.

Funnily enough, it appears that White's strongest line here is to capture away from the centre, contrary to expectations.

Game 161

Kasparov-Psakhis
La Manga match (2) 1990

1 d4 ♘f6 2 c4 e6 3 ♘f3 b6 4 ♘c3 ♗b4 5 ♗g5 ♗b7 6 ♘d2!?
⇨ 6 ♕c2 h6 7 ♗h4 0-0 (7...♗xc3+ 8 ♕xc3 d6 9 ♘d2 ♕e7 10 c5 0-0 11 e3 bxc5 12 dxc5 e5 13 ♕b4 ♗d5 14 cxd6 cxd6 15 e4 a5 16 ♕b6 ♘bd7 17 ♕e3 ♗e6 18 ♗b5 ♘c5 19 0-0 ♖fb8 20 a4 ♗d7 21 ♗xd7 ♘cxd7 22 ♘c4 ♕e6 23 ♖ac1 ♘xe4! 24 ♕xe4 d5 gave Black at least equality in Georgadze-Lerner, Odessa 1989) 8 e3 d6 9 ♗d3 ♘bd7 10 0-0-0 ♗xc3 11 bxc3 (11 ♕xc3 is quite playable, but White has a different set-up in mind) 11...♕e7 12 ♖hg1 c5 13 ♘d2 b5! (White has been teeing up for g4-g5 so Black must act quickly) 14 g4?! g5! 15 ♗g3 ♖fc8 16 h4 cxd4 17 exd4 ♘b6 18 hxg5 hxg5 19 cxb5?! a6 20 bxa6 ♗xa6 21 ♗xa6 ♖xa6 ∓ (completing the opening-up of White's queenside) 22 ♖h1 ♘bd5 23 ♘b1 ♘b4! 24 ♕b3 ♘xa2+ 25 ♔c2 ♘d5 26 ♔d2 ♘axc3 27 ♘xc3 ♘xc3 28 ♖c1 ♕a7! 29 ♖xc3 ♖a2+ 30 ♔e3 ♖xc3+ 31 ♕xc3 ♖a3 32 ♖c1 e5 0-1 G.Flear-Kosten, France 1989.

6...♗xc3 7 bxc3 h6! 8 ♗h4 g5 9 ♗g3 d6 10 e3 ♕e7! 11 h4 ♖g8 12 hxg5 hxg5 13 ♗e2 ♘c6! 14 ♕c2 0-0-0 15 0-0-0 ♖h8 16 e4 ♔b8 17 ♘b3 ♘d7! 18 ♗d3 ♕f6 19 ♖xh8 ♕xh8! 20 c5

Thematic, but not quite correct in this position. Instead 20 f3 is equal.
20...dxc5 21 ♗b5 ♕f8! 22 d5?!
White should prefer 22 dxc5 ∞.

22...♘ce5! 23 d6 f6

Certainly not 23...cxd6?? 24 ♗xd7 ♖xd7 25 ♗xe5 ±, but 23...c6! gives Black a clear advantage.

24 dxc7+ ♔xc7 25 ♕e2? ♕e7 26 ♘d2 ♘f8 27 ♘c4 ♖xd1+ 28 ♕xd1 ♘fg6 29 ♕h5

Threatening to take on g6, of course.

29...♗xe4 30 ♕e2 ♗d5 31 ♘xe5 ♘xe5 32 ♗xe5+ fxe5 33 ♕xe5+ ♔b7 34 f3 ∓ a6 35 ♗d3 b5 36 ♔b2 c4 37 ♗c2 b4

The advance of Black's queenside pawns doesn't seem to amount to very much.

38 ♗e4! bxc3+ 39 ♔c2! ♕d7 40 ♔xc3 ♕b5 41 ♕xe6! ♕a5+ 42 ♔d4 ♕d2+ 43 ♔c5 ½-½

Game 162

Epishin-Shneider
Leningrad 1990

1 d4 ♘f6 2 c4 e6 3 ♘f3 b6 4 ♘c3 ♗b7 5 ♗g5 h6 6 ♗h4 ♗b4 7 e3 ♗xc3+ 8 bxc3 d6 9 ♘d2 ♘bd7 10 f3
⇨ 10 ♖b1!? e5 11 f3 ♕e7 12 ♗f2

0-0 13 ♗e2 ♖ae8 14 0-0 ♘h5?! (preparing f5 with 14...♘h7 was better) 15 ♖e1 ♕g5?! 16 ♕a4! ± exd4 17 h4! (an important interpolation; 17 cxd4? ♖xe3!) 17...♕d8 18 cxd4 a5 19 ♘f1 ♔h8 20 ♗d3 f5 21 ♖ed1 ♖e6 22 c5!? dxc5 23 ♗b5 c6 24 ♗c4 ♖d6 25 dxc5 ♘xc5 26 ♕c2 ♖xd1 27 ♖xd1 ♕e7 28 a4 ♗c8 29 ♗e1! ♘a6 30 ♖d4 ♘b4 31 ♕d1 f4? (relieving White of any potential problems with e3) 32 e4 ♘f6 33 ♗f2 ♗d7 34 ♖d6 b5 35 ♗b3 bxa4 36 ♗xa4 ♖c8 37 ♗c5 ♕e8 38 ♕d4 ± ♘a6 39 ♖xf6?! (unnecessary; 39 ♗b6 c5 40 ♗xd7 cxd4 41 ♗xe8 ±) 39...gxf6 40 ♕xf6+ ♔h7 41 ♗d6? (going the wrong way; 41 ♗d4 ♕g8 42 ♕xf4 ±) 41...♘b4 42 ♗xf4 ♕f8 43 ♕d4 ♗e6 44 ♗e3 ♕g7 45 ♕d6?! ♖g8 46 g3 ♗c4 47 g4 ♕f8 48 ♕g3 ♕b8 49 ♗f4?! ♕d8 50 ♗e5 ♕b6+ 51 ♔g2 ♘d3 52 ♗c3 ♖f8 53 ♕d6 ♕f2+ 0-1 Malaniuk-Chandler, Moscow 1990.

10...♕e7
⇨ 10...e5 11 e4 0-0 12 ♗d3 ♕e8 13 g4!? (very sharp) 13...c6 14 ♕e2 d5 15 0-0 ♕e6 16 exd5 cxd5 17 ♗f5 ♕c6 18 dxe5 ♖fe8 19 ♗g3 dxc4 20 ♖ae1 ♘c5 21 ♕f2 g6 22 ♗e4 ½-½ Gelfand-Eingorn, Odessa 1989. The final position is completely wild.

11 e4 e5 12 ♗e2 g5 13 ♗f2 ♘h5 14 g3 0-0-0 15 0-0 ♘g7 16 ♖e1 c5 17 a4 a5

Better this than allowing White to play a5, although b6 will become a sensitive point.

18 ♖b1 ♖hf8 19 ♘f1! f5 20 ♘e3 fxe4 21 ♘d5

The reason White has been reluctant to play d5 is that he wanted the square for a piece.

21...♕f7 22 ♘xb6+ ♘xb6 23 ♖xb6 g4?

Better is 23...♘f5! 24 dxc5 dxc5 25 ♕c1 exf3 26 ♗f1 e4 27 ♗h3+ ♖d7 28 ♕b1! although White is then clearly better.

24 f4 h5 25 dxc5 dxc5 26 ♕b3 ♕c7?! 27 ♖b1 ♖f7 28 ♕a3 ♗a8 29 ♖1b5 ♔d7 30 ♖xc5!

30...♕xb6 31 ♖d5+ ♗xd5 32 ♗xb6 ♖b8 33 cxd5 ♖xb6 34 ♗b5+ ♔d8 35 fxe5 ♖bb7 1-0

Game 163

Khalifman-Hulak
Bled/Rogaška Slatina 1991

1 d4 ♘f6 2 c4 e6 3 ♘f3 b6 4 ♘c3 ♗b4 5 ♗g5 ♗b7 6 e3 ♗xc3+ 7 bxc3 d6 8 ♘d2 ♘bd7 9 f3 h6 10 ♗h4 ♕e7 11 ♗e2 e5 12 e4 ♘f8 13 ♘f1 ♘g6 14 ♗f2 ♘f4 15 ♘e3 0-0

⇨ 15...♘6h5 16 ♗f1! g6 17 d5? (it is better to keep the position fluid with 17 g3 ♘e6 18 ♗g2 ±) 17...♗c8! 18 c5!? bxc5! 19 ♕a4+ ♗d7 20 ♕a5 (this is only a minor inconvenience

for Black) 20...♕d8 21 ♘c4 0-0 22 ♗e3 ♔h7 23 ♖b1 ♖b8 24 ♖b3 ♘g7 (24...f5! 25 g3 fxe4 26 fxe4 ♘h3 ∓) 25 g3 ♘fh5 26 g4 ♘f4 27 h4 h5?! 28 g5 f6 29 ♗xf4 exf4 30 gxf6 ♕xf6 31 ♔d2 ♖xb3 32 axb3 c6 33 ♕c7 cxd5 34 exd5 ♖d8 35 ♗d3 ♗e8! 36 ♖e1 ♗f7? (Black should not allow the rook on to his second rank; 36...♖d7 ∓) 37 ♖e7 ♖f8 38 ♘xd6 ♗xd5 39 ♗e4 ♗g8 40 ♗d3 ♔h6?? (40...♗d5) 41 ♘e4 ♕xh4 42 ♖xg7 ♖d8 43 ♖xg6+! ♔xg6 44 ♘d6+ 1-0 Benjamin-Arnason, Novi Sad OL 1990.

16 ♗f1?!

Underestimating the danger; 16 0-0 maintains equality.

16...♖fe8 17 g3

17...♗xe4! 18 fxe4

18 gxf4 is no better: 18...exf4 19 fxe4 fxe3 20 ♗g3 ♘xe4 ∓.

18...exd4! 19 ♕xd4 c5 20 ♕d2 ♘xe4 21 ♕c2 ♕f6! 22 ♗g1

22 gxf4 is met by 22...♘xf2 ∓.

22...♘xc3 23 gxf4 d5 24 ♗g2 ♖ad8 25 cxd5 ♘xd5 26 0-0-0 ♘xe3 27 ♗xe3 ♕a1+ 28 ♕b1 ♕c3+ 29 ♕c2 ♕xe3+ 30 ♔b1 ♖xd1+ 31 ♖xd1 ♕xf4 ∓ 32 ♗c6 ♕b4+ 33 ♔a1

♖e1 34 ♖xe1 ♕xe1+ 35 ♔b2 g6 36
♗b5 ♕b4+ 37 ♕b3 ♕xb3+

Swapping the queens is the simplest option; with two extra pawns on each wing, this ending should be a formality.

38 ♔xb3 f5 39 ♔c3 ♔f7 40 ♔d3
g5 41 a4 ♔f6 42 ♗e8 g4 43 ♔e3
♔g5 44 ♗b5 h5 45 ♗f1 h4 46 h3 g3
47 ♔f3 ♔f6 48 ♔f4 c4 49 ♔e3 c3 50
♔d3 ♔e5 51 ♔xc3 ♔e4 52 ♔d2
♔f3 0-1

Game 164

Kamsky-Hjartarson
Manila OL 1992

1 d4 ♘f6 2 ♘f3 e6 3 c4 b6 4 ♘c3
♗b4 5 ♗g5 ♗b7 6 e3 h6 7 ♗h4
♗xc3+ 8 bxc3 d6 9 ♘d2 ♘bd7 10
f3 ♕e7 11 ♕a4 0-0 12 ♗d3 e5 13 e4
♕e8 14 0-0 ♘h5 15 ♖fe1

⇨ 15 ♖ae1 ♘f4 16 ♗c2 a6?! 17
♗g3! ♘e6 18 ♗f2 ♕e7 19 ♗e3
♘f6?! 20 ♕a3! ♖fe8 21 ♖b1 ♗c8 22
c5! bxc5 23 dxe5 dxe5 24 ♘c4 (in return for the pawn sacrificed White has the c4 square and good play for his bishops) 24...♘f4! 25 ♗xc5 ♕e6
26 ♗b3 ♘e2+! 27 ♔h1 ♘xc3 28
♖bc1 ♘b5 29 ♕a5 ♕c6! 30 ♗f2
♕b7 31 a3 ♘d4 32 ♗a2 ♘c6 33
♕c5 ♗d7 34 ♖b1 ♕c8 35 ♗g3?! (allowing Black back into the game; 35
♖fd1! ±) 35...♘h5! 36 ♗xe5 ♘xe5
37 ♘xe5 ♗e6 38 ♗xe6 ♕xe6 39
♘g4! ♘f6 40 ♘xf6+ ♕xf6 41 ♕xc7
± ♖ac8 42 ♕b7 ♖c2 43 ♖fc1?! ♕c3!
44 ♖d1 ♕c4 45 ♕d7 ♖f8 46 h3 ♖a2
47 ♖d4 ♕c2 48 ♖g1 ♖b8 49 e5 ♖b1
50 ♕g4 ♖xg1+ 51 ♔xg1 ♕c5! 52

♔h2 ♕xe5+ 53 ♕f4 ♕xf4+ 54 ♖xf4
½-½ Psakhis-Grünfeld, Tel Aviv
1990. The endgame is a technical draw, although Black could have made White suffer a bit, had he felt like it.

15...♘f4 16 ♗c2! c5! 17 ♖ad1!?
♘e6?!

Provoking White into closing the position, but it wastes time.

18 d5 ♘g5?! 19 ♘f1 ♕e7 20
♔h1 ♖fd8 21 ♘e3 ♘f8 22 ♘f5 ♕f6
23 ♕a3 ♘g6 24 ♗g3 ♗c8 25 ♕c1
♘h7 26 ♕d2 ♘e7 27 ♘e3 ♗d7 28
♖f1 ♘g6 29 ♘f5 ♖e8 30 ♖b1 ♖ab8
31 ♗f2 ♘e7 32 g4 ♘g6 33 ♗g3!
♘hf8 34 h4

White uses his strong knight on f5 as the focal point around which he builds his offensive.

34...♘f4 35 ♖f2 ♘8g6 36 ♖h2
♗xf5 37 exf5 ♘f8 38 ♖g1?!

Simpler is 38 g5! ♕e7 39 ♖g1 with a clear advantage for White.

38...g5 39 fxg6 fxg6

40 g5 ±

White has slowly but surely built up a powerful attack.

40...hxg5 41 hxg5 ♕g7 42 ♖h6!

♘h5 43 ♗e4 b5 44 ♕c2 ♘xg3+ 45 ♖xg3 ♗b6! 46 ♗xg6 ♖eb8 47 ♕f5! bxc4 48 ♖g1 ♖b2 49 ♗h7+?! ♔h8 50 ♕h3?

White should play 50 ♗g6 intending ♗h5 ±.

50...♘xh7 51 g6 ♖2b7

Saving the queen, as after 52 ♖xh7+ ♕xh7 53 gxh7 ♖xh7 Black wins it back.

52 ♕h5?! ♖f8 53 ♖g2 ♖xf3! 54 ♔g1 ♖b1+ 55 ♔h2 ♖b7 56 ♔g1 ♖b1+ 57 ♔h2 ♖b7 58 ♔g1 ♖b1+ ½-½

Game 165

Beliavsky-Gulko
Reggio Emilia 1991

1 d4 ♘f6 2 c4 e6 3 ♘f3 b6 4 ♘c3 ♗b4 5 ♗g5 ♗b7 6 e3 h6 7 ♗h4 ♗xc3+ 8 bxc3 d6 9 ♘d2 g5 10 ♗g3 ♕e7

⇨ 10...♘bd7 11 h4 ♔e7 12 ♕e2! ♕g8 13 e4 ♕g6 14 h5 ♕h7 15 f3 ♖he8 16 ♕e3! ♔f8 17 e5 ± dxe5 18 dxe5 ♘g8 19 ♗d3 ♕g7 20 0-0 ♘c5 21 ♗c2 ♘e7 22 ♗h2! ♖ad8 23 g4 with a big plus; Ravi-Brynell, Manila OL 1992.

11 h4

⇨ 11 a4 ♘c6!? 12 ♘b3 h5 13 f3 h4 14 ♗f2 a5 15 ♗e2 0-0-0 16 ♕b1 g4 17 e4 ♖dg8 18 ♕c2 h3 (Black's kingside counterplay has arrived very fast) 19 g3 gxf3 20 ♗xf3 ♘g4 21 0-0 ♗g5 22 ♕d2 ♕g6 23 ♕f4 e5 24 ♕xg4+ ♕xg4 25 ♗xg4+ ♖xg4 26 d5 ♘e7 Dokhoian-Lerner, Lvov Z 1990. Black has a large advantage, as sooner or later his light-squared bishop will wreak havoc with White's queenside pawns.

11...♖g8 12 hxg5 hxg5

13 ♕a4+!?

⇨ 13 ♗e2 ♘c6 14 ♕a4 0-0-0 15 ♗f3 ♕d7 16 ♖h6 ♘a5 17 ♕b5 a6 18 ♕xd7+ ♘xd7 19 ♔e2 ♖g7 20 ♖ah1 ♖dg8 21 ♖h7 ♗xf3+ 22 gxf3 with equality; Rashkovsky-Zhidkov, Kiev 1989.

⇨ 13 ♖h2 c5 14 ♗e2 ♘bd7 15 ♗f3 0-0-0 16 ♗xb7+ ♔xb7 17 ♕f3+ ♔c7 18 a4 a5 19 0-0-0 g4 20 ♕f4 e5 21 ♕f5 ♕e6 22 ♕xe6 fxe6 23 ♖h6 ♖df8 24 ♔c2 exd4 25 cxd4 ♔c6? (walking into an unpleasant tactic) 26 d5+! exd5 27 cxd5+ ♔c7 28 ♘c4 ♘e4 29 ♖xd6! ± ♘xg3 30 ♖c6+ ♔b7 31 fxg3 ♖f2+ 32 ♖d2 ♖f6 33 ♘d6+ ♔b8 34 e4 (White has two big passed pawns marching through the centre) 34...♘e5 35 ♖xb6+ ♔c7 36 ♘e8+ ♔xb6 37 ♘xf6 ♖f8 38 ♖f2 ♔c7 39 ♖f5 ♘c4 40 ♘xg4 ♖g8 41 ♖f7+ ♔c8 42 ♖f4?? (falling for a one-mover) 42...♖xg4 43 ♖xg4 ♘e3+ 44 ♔d3 ♘xg4 45 ♔c4 ♘f6 46 ♔xc5 ♘xe4+ 47 ♔b6 ♔d7 48 ♔xa5 ♘c3 49 ♔b4 ♘xd5+ 50 ♔c5 ♔e6

½-½ Cifuentes-Dorfman, Polanica Zdroj 1992.

⇨ 13 ♖b1 ♘c6 14 ♕a4 0-0-0 15 ♖b5 ♘d7 16 ♗e2 ♖h8 17 ♖xh8 ♖xh8 18 ♗f3 f5 19 ♖b2 ♘db8 20 c5 ♖h1+ 21 ♔e2 d5! (closing the h1-a8 diagonal and threatening ...♗a6+) 22 cxb6 axb6 23 ♔d3 ♗a6+ 24 ♔c2 f4! 25 exf4 ♕h7+ 26 f5 ♕xf5+ 27 ♔b3 b5 0-1 Dannevig-Lerner, Gausdal 1992. 28 ♕a3 allows mate in seven moves starting with 28...♘xd4+ 29 cxd4 ♕d3+ 30 ♔b4 ♘c6+ etc.

13...♕d7!?

⇨ 13...♘c6?! 14 c5! ♔f8 15 ♗b5 ♘a5 16 c6 ♗c8 17 e4 e5 18 d5 ± Campos-Vehi, Barcelona 1991. The pawn chain is too strong.

14 ♕d1 ♕e7 15 ♖h6!? ♘bd7 16 ♕a4 a5?

Black should play 16...♔f8! followed by ...♔g7.

17 c5! ±

17...dxc5 18 ♗xc7 ♘d5 19 ♘e4! ♘xc7 20 ♘f6+ ♔f8 21 ♕xd7 ♕xd7 22 ♘xd7+ ♔e7 23 ♘xb6

A pawn up with a solid position should be sufficient advantage to win.

23...♖ab8 24 dxc5?! ♘d5 25 ♖c1 ♘xb6 26 cxb6 ♗a8! 27 ♖b1 ♖gc8 28 ♔d2 ♖c6 29 f3 ♖cxb6 30 ♖xb6 ♖xb6 31 ♔c2 ♖b8 32 ♗c4 ♗c6 33 ♖h5 ♔f6 34 ♖h1 ♗a4+ 35 ♗b3 ♗c6 36 ♖d1 g4! 37 ♖d4 gxf3 38 gxf3 ♖h8 39 ♔d3 ♔e7 40 f4 f5 41 ♗a4 ♗e4+ 42 ♔c4 ♖h3 43 ♖d7+ ♔f6 44 ♔d4 ♖h2 45 ♖a7 ♖xa2 46 ♗e8 ♖d2+ 47 ♔c4 e5 48 fxe5+ ♔xe5 49 ♖xa5+ ♗d5+ 50 ♔c5 ♖c2 51 ♖a3 ♔e4 52 ♗b5 ♖a2! 53 ♖xa2 ♗xa2 54 ♗d7 ♗b1! ½-½

Game 166

Salov-van der Wiel
Amsterdam 1991

1 d4 ♘f6 2 ♘f3 e6 3 c4 b6 4 ♘c3 ♗b4 5 ♗g5 ♗b7

⇨ 5...h6 6 ♗h4 g5 7 ♗g3 ♘e4 8 ♕c2 ♗b7 9 ♗e5!? ♗xc3+ 10 bxc3 f6 11 ♘d2 fxe5 12 ♘xe4 exd4 13 cxd4 ♕e7 14 e3 ♘c6 15 ♗e2 0-0-0 16 0-0 ♕h7! (forcing the play into a promising ending) 17 ♗d3 ♘b4 18 ♘d6+ cxd6 19 ♗xh7 ♘xc2 20 ♗xc2 ♗a6 21 ♖fc1 ♗xc4 22 ♗b3 d5 23 ♗xc4 dxc4 24 ♖xc4+ ♔b7 25 ♖c2 ♖c8 ∓ Barbero-Farago, Hungary 1991.

6 e3 h6 7 ♗h4 g5 8 ♗g3 ♘e4 9 ♕c2 ♗xc3+

⇨ 9...d6 10 ♗d3 ♗xc3+ 11 bxc3 f5 12 d5 ♘d7 13 ♘d4 ♘dc5 14 dxe6 ♖f8 15 ♗e2! (White plans to hold on to his extra e6 pawn) 15...♕f6 16 ♗h5+ ♔e7 17 ♗f7 ♖xf7! (forced; 17...♘xg3?! 18 hxg3 ♗e4?? would allow the amusing 19 ♕xe4! fxe4 20 ♘c6#) 18 exf7 ♕xf7 19 0-0 ♘xg3

20 fxg3 ♗e4 21 ♕f2 ♖f8 (Black certainly has a reasonable position for the exchange) 22 g4 ♕xc4 23 gxf5 ♖f6 24 ♕g3 ♗d3 25 h4! ♘e4 26 ♕g4 c5 27 hxg5 hxg5 28 ♘e6 ♗xf1 29 ♖xf1 ♕d3 30 ♕h3 ♕xc3 31 ♕h7+ ♖f7 32 ♕g8 ♕xe3+ 33 ♔h2 ♕g3+ 34 ♔h1 ♕h4+ 35 ♔g1 ♖xf5! (hoping to force a draw) 36 ♖xf5 ♕e1+ 37 ♖f1 ♕e3+ 38 ♔h2 ♕g3+ 39 ♔g1 ♕e3+ 40 ♔h2 ♕g3+ 41 ♔g1? (41 ♔h1 was a little better for White) 41...♕e3+ 42 ♔h2 ½-½ Kamsky-Salov, Moscow Alekhine mem 1992.

10 bxc3 ♘xg3 11 fxg3

Unnatural, but probably best; White can put the f-file to good use.

⇨ 11 hxg3 d6 12 ♗d3 ♘d7 13 ♗e4 ♗xe4 14 ♕xe4 ♘f6 15 ♕c6+ ♔e7 16 ♘d2 ♕d7 17 ♕xd7+ ♘xd7 18 ♔e2 c5 19 ♖h3 g4 20 ♖h4 h5 21 f4 gxf3+ 22 gxf3 = P.Short-Adams, Dublin 1991.

11...g4 12 ♘h4 ♕g5 13 ♕d2 d6!? 14 ♗d3 ♘d7 15 0-0 h5 16 ♖f4 ♖h6! 17 ♖af1 ♖f6 18 ♕f2 ♔e7 19 e4 ♖h8 20 c5! bxc5 21 ♗b5! c6 22 ♗d3!

Intending 23 ♘f5+! exf5 24 e5!.

22...♗c8! 23 ♔h1 ♖hh6! 24 e5! dxe5 25 dxe5 ♕xe5 26 ♘f5+!

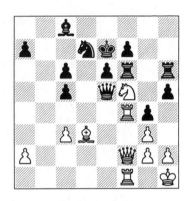

26...♖xf5! 27 ♖xf5 exf5 28 ♖e1 ♔f6! 29 ♖xe5 ♘xe5 30 ♕xc5 ♗e6! 31 ♕f8! ♖h7 32 ♗b1

If the a-pawns were not on the board Black would be fine.

32...♘d7 33 ♕d8+ ♔g6 34 h4 gxh3 35 gxh3 ♘f6 36 ♔h2 ♔g7 37 ♕a5 ♔g6 38 ♕xa7 ♖h8 39 ♕b6 ♖a8

After 39...♘d7! ± White would have more work to do.

40 ♕b2 ♖d8 41 ♕e2! ♔g7 42 a4 ♖b8 43 ♗d3 ♖a8 44 ♗c2 ♖b8 45 ♗d3 ♖a8 46 ♕c2 ♔g6 47 c4 c5 48 ♕a2 ♖d8 49 ♕e2 ♖d4 50 a5 ♗c8 51 ♕f3 ♘e4 52 g4 hxg4 53 hxg4 fxg4 54 ♗xe4+ f5 55 ♕xg4+ ♔f6 56 ♕h4+ ♔e5 57 ♕h8+ ♔xe4 58 ♕xc8 f4 59 ♕e6+ ♔f3 60 a6 1-0

18

The 4 g3 system surged in popularity after the 1985 and 1986 World Championship matches between Kasparov and Karpov. Indeed, Kasparov used it as one of his main weapons for some time after. Since this time the best defensive plans for Black have been worked out, but 4 g3 has remained an important possibility, not least because the positions can arise from such a wide variety of openings: the English Opening, the Réti, the Catalan, etc.

The most common move-order is 1 d4 ♘f6 2 c4 e6 3 ♘c3 ♗b4 4 ♘f3 and now if Black wishes to avoid the positions after 4...b6 5 ♗g5 he will play 4...c5. Now, a lot of players are loathe to allow Hübner's variation, which could occur after 5 e3 ♘c6 6 ♗d3 ♗xc3+ and the only reasonable alternative is 5 g3. This explains the relative importance of the variation 4 g3 c5 5 ♘f3 which we will consider first. Of course, by using this move-order White does deprive Black of certain possibilities—although since systems with ...c5 are generally considered to be Black's best, this is of little obvious objective benefit.

So, following 4 g3 c5 5 ♘f3 cxd4 6 ♘xd4 0-0 7 ♗g2 d5, White has a choice to make: 8 cxd5, 8 0-0 or 8 ♕b3. We will examine them in this order.

In game 167, after 8 cxd5 ♘xd5 9 ♗d2, Salov plays 9...♘xc3, keeping his dark-squared bishop, and introduces the move 11...♘d7!?. Personally, I feel that 9...♗xc3 is simpler, avoiding any loss of time. Black's

possibilities are amply demonstrated in game 168.

The pawn sacrifice 8 0-0 dxc4 has fallen out of favour recently, probably because Black can get at least equality very easily with Smagin's 11...♗xc3! 12 ♘xc3 ♘xc3 13 bxc3 ♘c5!; Romanishin's innovation in the notes to game 169 does little to change this assessment. Black can also try for more with 11...♗d7 but as Gipslis-Romanishin shows, he must be careful.

On the other hand, 8 ♕b3 generated a great deal of interest with the discovery that, after 8...♗xc3+, 9 ♕xc3 was possible. At first Black took the opportunity to push 9...e5 10 ♘b3 d4 with unclear play (game 170). Mihai Suba seems to have been in the vanguard of developments in this line, producing some wonderful games in the process.

In game 171 Johansen tries 10 ♘c2!? instead, but it does not seem to work too well.

In my opinion, Black's simplest and best move after 10 ♘b3 is 10...♘c6 (game 172) and results seem to have borne this out.

The variations where Black attempts to take the maximum profit from the pin of c3 (4...c5 5 ♘f3 cxd4 6 ♘xd4 ♘e4 — see game 173) have also undergone recent testing and have proved to be satisfactory.

Black also has the possibility of playing an early ...d5, when the positions that arise bear a great similarity to those from the Catalan. Essentially White must choose between taking on d5, dissolving the central tension (game 174), and allowing

Black to take on c4 (game 175) — I get the distinct impression from this game that it is Black who has all the chances if White sacrifices the c4 pawn.

Finally, in game 176, we examine some other variations, in particular 4...c5 5 ♘f3 ♘c6 when Suba's innovation on move 12 reaps instant rewards.

Game 167

Kasparov-Salov
Linares 1990

1 ♘f3 ♘f6 2 c4 e6 3 ♘c3 ♗b4 4 d4 c5 5 g3 cxd4 6 ♘xd4 0-0 7 ♗g2 d5 8 cxd5 ♘xd5 9 ♗d2 ♘xc3 10 bxc3 ♗e7 11 ♖b1

Threatening 12 ♖xb7.
⇨ 11 0-0 is pretty insipid. The game Fish-Tolnai, Budapest 1992 continued 11...e5 12 ♘c2!? ♘c6 13 ♘e3 ♗e6 14 c4 ♖c8 15 ♘d5 ♗c5 16 ♖b1 ♕d7 17 e3 b6 18 ♗c3 ♗f5 19 ♖b2 ♕e6 20 ♖d2. Both sides' pieces are well placed.
11...♘d7!?
An innovation that is based on the line 12 ♗xb7 ♗xb7 13 ♖xb7 ♕c8! 14 ♖b1 ♘b6, with good compensation for the pawn. 11...a6 is standard, but recently Black has also tried:
⇨ 11...♕d7!? (I believe this first occurred in the game Karasev-Agrest, USSR 1990, with the continuation: 12 ♗f4 ♗f6 13 ♘b5 a6! 14 ♘c7 ♗xc3+ 15 ♔f1 ♖a7 ∓) 12 0-0 ♘a6 (12...e5 13 ♘f3 ♘c6 is good) 13 ♗e3 ♖d8 14 ♕c2 e5 15 ♘b5 ♗c5 16 ♖fd1 ♕e7 17 ♖xd8+ ♕xd8 18 ♖d1

♕e7 19 ♕e4 ♖b8 20 ♘xa7 ♗d7 21 ♖d5 ♗xe3 22 ♕xe3 and, although a pawn up, White experiences difficulties extracting his knight from a7; van Wely-Bertholee, Amsterdam 1990.
⇨ 11...e5 (this is supposed to be inferior, but Black has a pawn sacrifice in mind) 12 ♘c2 (12 ♖xb7 is critical) 12...♘c6 13 0-0 ♗e6!? 14 ♖xb7 ♘a5 15 ♖b5 ♖b8 16 ♖xb8 ♕xb8 with some compensation; Grigore-Prakash, Oakham 1992.
12 0-0! ♘b6
⇨ 12...♘c5 13 ♗f4 f6 14 ♗e3 e5 15 ♘b3 ♘a4 16 ♕c2 ♕c7 17 c4 ♗e6 18 c5 ♖ab8 19 ♖fc1 f5 20 ♘d2 f4 ½-½ Graf-J.Fries Nielsen, Bundesliga 1990.
13 ♗f4 ♘d5 14 ♕b3

14...♘xf4
Kasparov is often happy to allow this rearrangement of his pawns.
15 gxf4 ♕c7?!
Better is 15...♗d6 16 e3 e5 17 fxe5 ♗xe5 18 f4 ♗f6 ∞.
16 e3 a6 17 ♖fd1
White has completed his development, and his scruffy pawn structure

is more than offset by the pressure he exerts, particularly on b7.

⇨ 17 ♕b6?! ♕xb6 18 ♖xb6 ♖a7 19 a4 ♖d8 20 ♖fb1 ♖d7 21 ♖6b3 g6 22 ♔f1 ♖c7 23 ♔e1 ♗f6 24 ♔d2 ♔g7 is fairly level; Bedos-Illescas Cordoba, France 1991.

17...♖a7 18 c4?!

White can secure a small advantage with 18 ♘f3! ♗f6 19 c4 b5! 20 ♖bc1 bxc4 21 ♕xc4 ±.

18...♗c5?! 19 ♘f3! a5!

19...b6 20 ♘e5 ±.

20 ♘g5! h6! 21 ♘e4 a4 22 ♕b5!? ♖a5 23 ♕b2 b6 24 ♕e5 ♕xe5?! 25 fxe5 ♗a6 26 ♗f1 ♗b7?! 27 ♘xc5 ♖xc5 28 f4!

28 ♖xb6 allows 28...♗f3 29 ♖db1 ♖xe5 =.

28...♗a6 29 ♖d4 ♖fc8 30 ♖b4 a3 31 ♗e2 ± g5 32 ♔f2

In order to make headway White is obliged to make use of his king.

32...♔g7 33 ♔e1 ♖8c6 34 ♖d6?

A slip; 34 ♔d2 gxf4 35 exf4 f6 36 ♖a4 ±.

34...♖c7 35 ♖d4 gxf4 36 exf4 f6 37 exf6+ ♔xf6 38 ♔d2 ♖7c6 39 ♖e4 ♔f5 40 ♔e3 ♔f6 41 h3 e5 42 ♗f3! ♖d6! 43 h4 ♗c8 44 fxe5+ ♖xe5 45 ♖xe5 ♔xe5 46 ♖b5+ ♔f6 47 ♗d5 ♗d7! 48 ♖b3 b5 49 ♖xa3 ♗e6! = 50 ♖d3 ♗xd5 51 cxd5 ♔e5 52 h5 ♖xd5 53 ♖xd5+ ♔xd5 54 ♔f4 ♔c4 ½-½

Game 168

Ricardi-Gulko
Manila OL 1992

1 d4 ♘f6 2 c4 e6 3 ♘c3 ♗b4 4 ♘f3 c5 5 g3 cxd4 6 ♘xd4 0-0 7 ♗g2 d5 8 cxd5 ♘xd5 9 ♗d2 ♗xc3

⇨ 9...♘b6!? (a new idea that seems to work out well for Black) 10 ♘c2 ♗e7 11 ♘e3 ♘c6 12 0-0 ♘d4 13 ♖c1 e5 14 ♖e1 ♖b8 15 ♘cd5 ♘xd5 16 ♘xd5 ♗e6 17 e4 ♗g5! (by exchanging the dark-squared bishops Black hopes to secure the d4 square for his knight) 18 ♗xg5 ♕xg5 19 f4 (White for his part, attempts to undermine d4, but Black will obtain the e5 square in return) ♕d8 20 fxe5 ♘c6 21 ♕d2 ♘xe5 22 ♔h1 ♔h8 23 ♕d4 f6 24 ♖c3 b6 25 ♖ec1 ♖f7 26 ♕b4 ♖c8 27 ♘f4 ♖xc3 28 ♕xc3 ♗g4 29 h3 ♗d7 30 ♕b3 ♕e8 31 ♘d5 ♗c6 32 ♔h2 h5 33 ♖c3 ♖d7 34 ♕b4 ♕b8 35 ♕d4 ♕d6 36 ♕f2 ♖d8 37 ♕c2 ♖d7 38 a3 ♗b7 39 ♕a4 ♗c6 40 ♕a6 ♗b7 41 ♕f1 ½-½ Lautier-Ulybin, Tilburg 1992.

10 bxc3 e5 11 ♘b5

This knight has two other reasonable squares:

1) 11 ♘b3 ♘c6 12 c4 ♘b6 13 c5!? ♘c4 14 ♕c2 ♘xd2 15 ♖d1 ♗e6 16 ♖xd2 ♗xb3 17 axb3 ♘d4 18 ♕c3 ♕c7 19 0-0 ♖ac8 led to equality in Campos-Grosar, Manila OL 1992.

2) 11 ♘c2 ♘c6 and now:

⇨ 12 ♘b4!? ♘ce7 13 0-0 ♗e6 14 ♗g5 ♕c7 15 ♕a4 h6 16 ♗xe7 ♘xe7 17 ♕b5 ♖ab8 18 ♘d3 ♖fc8 19 ♕xe5 ♕xe5 20 ♘xe5 ♖xc3 ∓ van Wely-Dautov, Krumbach 1991. Black's queenside pawn majority is the most important factor here.

⇨ 12 ♖b1 ♘b6 13 ♘e3 ♗e6 14 c4 ♘xc4 15 ♘xc4 ♗xc4 16 0-0 (16 ♖xb7 is met by the awkward 16...♘d4) 16...♘d4 17 ♖e1 ♗xa2 18 ♖xb7 ♗d5 19 ♗xd5 ♕xd5 ∓ Khariton-Lecuyer, Paris 1991.

⇨ 12 c4 (probably best) 12...♘de7 13 ♘e3 ♗e6 14 0-0 ♖c8 15 ♗c3 f6 16 ♘d5 ♘f5 (maybe Black had a better possibility in 16...♕e8!? 17 ♕b3 b6 18 ♖fd1 ♕h5 with counterplay on the kingside) 17 ♕d3 ♕e8 18 ♖fb1 b6 19 e3 ♕h5 20 a4 (the a-pawn is a static weakness but a dynamic strength, attacking Black's solid queenside) 20...♘h6!? 21 a5 bxa5 22 ♖b7 ♖f7 23 ♖xf7 ♘xf7 24 ♗xa5 ♗h3 25 ♕d1! ♕xd1+ 26 ♖xd1 ♗xg2 27 ♔xg2 ♔f8 28 ♗c7 ♔e8 29 c5 ♘e7 (29...e4 ∓) 30 ♘xe7 ♔xe7 31 ♗a5 ♔e6 32 ♗b4 = Lautier-Gurevich, Barcelona 1992.

11...♘c6!?

This seems more logical than the previously played 11...a6 12 ♗c1 ±.

12 c4

This is a standard idea: on the one hand White would like to play c5 cramping Black on the queenside, and on the other he can hardly afford to let Black establish a piece on c4.

⇨ 12 0-0?! ♗e6 (12...♘b6! ∓ is more accurate—c4 is weak) 13 ♗c1 a6 14 c4 ♘b6 15 ♕xd8 ♖axd8 16 ♘c7! ♘xc4! (16...♗xc4?! 17 ♗a3) 17 ♖b1 ♘d4? (Black gets involved in a totally unnecessary combination that loses a piece; 17...♗c8 18 ♘xa6 ♘d4 is simple and good) 18 ♘xe6 fxe6 19 ♗g5 ♘xe2+ 20 ♔h1 ♘d2? 21 ♖bd1 ♘xf1 22 ♗xd8 winning, as the knight on f1 is trapped; Chabanon-Boudre, Torcy 1991.

12...♘b6

Also fine is 12...♘de7.

13 c5 ♘c4 14 ♕c2 a6! 15 ♕xc4 ♗e6

Gaining a free tempo.

16 ♕c2

After 16 ♕a4 axb5 17 ♕xb5 ♘d4 18 ♕b2 ♗c4 19 e3 ♗d5 Black has good compensation for the pawn.

16...axb5 17 0-0 ♘d4

Utilizing the half-open a-file with 17...♗d5! 18 ♗xd5 ♕xd5 19 ♗e3 ♖a3! was even better.

18 ♕e4 ♖xa2 19 ♖xa2 ♗xa2 20 ♕xe5 ♗c4 21 ♗e3! ♘xe2+ 22 ♔h1 b4 23 ♕e4

White has no time for 23 ♗xb7? ♘xg3+!.

23...♕d3 24 ♕xb7?!

Equality could be maintained with 24 ♖b1! ♕xe4 25 ♗xe4 ♘c3 26 ♖xb4 ♘xe4 27 ♖xc4 f5 =.

24...b3 25 ♕b4

Unfortunately for White, 25 c6? ♗d5 26 ♖e1 ♕e4!! 27 ♗xe4 ♗xe4+ leads to mate.

25...♕c3! 26 ♕b6

26...♘xg3+! 27 hxg3 ♗xf1 28 ♗xf1 b2 ∓ 29 ♔g2 ♕c2 30 ♗d3

White's bishops are curiously unable to stop the b-pawn.

30...♕xd3 31 ♕xb2 ♕d5+ 32 ♔h2 h6 33 ♕b6 ♖a8 34 ♕b2 ♕e4 35 ♕c3 ♖a4 36 ♕b2 ♖b4 37 ♕e2 ♖b1 38 f3 ♕e5 39 ♕d3 0-1

Game 169

Gipslis-Romanishin
Groningen 1990

**1 d4 ♘f6 2 ♘f3 e6 3 c4 ♗b4+ 4 ♘c3
c5 5 g3 cxd4 6 ♘xd4 0-0 7 ♗g2 d5 8
0-0 dxc4 9 ♕a4**

⇨ 9 ♘c2 ♗xc3 10 bxc3 ♕a5!? 11
♘e3 ♘c6 12 ♘xc4 ♕xc3 13 ♕a4
♗d7 (not bad, but 13...♕xa1 14 ♗b2
b5! might also favour Black) 14 ♗b2
♘d4! 15 ♗xc3 ♘xe2+ 16 ♔h1
♗xa4 17 ♗e5 ♖ac8 18 ♘d6 ♖c5
with a pawn more; Dannevig-Mot-
wani, Gausdal 1992.

⇨ 9 ♗g5?! h6 10 ♗xf6 ♕xf6 11
♘db5 ♘c6 12 ♕a4 ♕e5! 13 ♖ad1 a6
14 e3 ♗d7! (relieving the pin on the
a6 pawn) 15 ♖xd7 axb5 16 ♕xb5
(giving up a piece, but otherwise
there was little hope) 16...♗xc3 17
♖xb7 ♕xb5 18 ♖xb5 ♘a7 19 ♖c5
♗b4 20 ♖xc4 ♖ab8 21 ♖d1 ♘c8 22
a3 ♗e7 23 b4 ♘b6 24 ♖c7 ♖fd8 25
♖xd8+ ♗xd8 ∓ Speelman-Timman,
London Ct 1989.

9...♘a6

⇨ 9...♕a5?! 10 ♕xa5 ♗xa5 11
♘db5 ♘c6 12 ♖d1! ♖b8 13 ♗e3 a6
14 ♘d6 ♗xc3 15 bxc3 ♘d5 16
♗xd5 exd5 17 ♖xd5 ± b5 18 a4
♗e6 19 ♖c5 ♘a5 20 axb5! ♘b3 21
♖xa6 ♘xc5 22 ♗xc5 ♖fd8 23 b6 f6
24 f3 ♗d5 25 e4 ♗c6 26 ♔f2 with a
dominating position for the exchange; Orlov-Annageldiev, Belgorod 1989.

10 ♘db5

⇨ 10 ♖d1 ♗d7 11 ♕c2 ♕c8!? 12
♗g5 ♗e7 13 ♖ac1 ♘c5 14 ♗xf6
♗xf6 15 ♘cb5 ♗xd4! 16 ♘xd4 ♗a4

17 b3 cxb3 18 ♕b2 bxa2 winning;
Renet-von Gleich, Lugano 1989.

10...♘d5 11 ♖d1 ♗d7

Black's most promising continuation is 11...♗xc3! 12 ♘xc3 ♘xc3
13 bxc3 ♘c5 14 ♕c2 ♕c7 and now:

1) 15 ♖d4?! e5 16 ♖xc4 ♗e6 ∓ 17
♖h4!? f5 and here:

⇨ 18 ♗e3 ♖ad8 19 g4 (attempting to
justify the rook's position on h4)
19...b6 20 ♖f1 ♕e7 21 ♖h5 g6 22
♗g5 ♕f7 23 ♖h4 ♖d6 24 gxf5 gxf5
25 ♖d1 ♖xd1+ 26 ♕xd1 ♗xa2 27 c4
♘e6 28 ♗d5 ♕g6 29 ♕d2 ♖f7 30
♔h1 ♕xg5 31 ♕xg5+ ♘xg5 32 ♖h5
h6 33 h4 ♔g7 34 hxg5 ♖c7 35
gxh6+ ♔g6 36 ♖h4 ♖h7 with a winning position for Black; Enkhbat-
Grosar, Manila OL 1992.

⇨ 18 a4 h6 19 ♖b4 b6 20 ♗e3 ♖ac8
21 a5 f4!? is unclear; Orlov-Zagre-
belny, Belgorod 1989.

2) 15 ♗a3!? ♖b8 16 ♖d4 b6 17
♖xc4 ♗b7 18 ♗xb7 ♖xb7 19 ♖d1
♖bb8 20 ♖cd4 ♖bc8 21 ♗xc5 ♕xc5
22 ♕a4 ♕xc3 23 ♕xa7 ♕b2 24
♖4d2 ♕b5 (a rather sterile equality
has resulted) 25 ♕a3 h6 26 ♖b2
♕c4 27 ♕d3 ♕a4 28 a3 ♖c5 29 ♕b3
♕a8 30 ♕xb6 ½-½ Romanishin-
Portisch, Reggio Emilia 1991.

**12 ♘xd5 exd5 13 ♖xd5 ♕e8! 14
♗e3 ♖c8 15 ♖ad1 ♗c6 16 ♖f5!**

Much better than 16 a3? ♗c5! 17
♖xc5 ♘xc5 18 ♗xc5 ♗xb5 19
♕xa7 ♕xe2 ∓ which has occurred a
couple of times. For instance Lapin-
ski-Gipslis, Daugavpils 1990, continued 20 ♖f1 ♖fd8 21 ♗b6 ♖d1 22
♕xb7 ♖cd8? (22...♖e8 is somewhat
simpler) 23 ♗e3?? (23 ♗xd8 c3 24
♕xb5 ♕xb5 25 ♖xd1 cxb2 26 ♖b1
was worth a try) 23...c3 0-1.

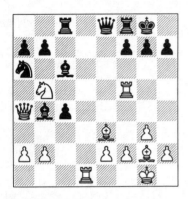

16...♗xg2

Taking the exchange by 16...g6 17 ♗xc6 bxc6 18 ♕xa6 gxf5 19 ♘xa7 ♖c7 20 a3 ♗e7 21 ♕xc4 is worse.

17 ♔xg2 ♗c5 18 ♗xc5 ♕e4+?! 19 f3! ♘xc5 20 fxe4 ♘xa4 21 ♖d7 ♘xb2 22 ♘c3! ♘a4

Surely a miscalculation; 22...g6! 23 ♖b5 ♘a4 24 ♘xa4 c3 25 ♘xc3 ♖xc3 leaves White only slightly better.

23 ♘xa4 c3 24 ♖c5! c2 25 ♖dc7 1-0

Game 170

Ward-Suba
British Ch 1990

1 c4 ♘f6 2 ♘c3 c5 3 ♘f3 e6 4 d4 cxd4 5 ♘xd4 ♗b4 6 g3 0-0 7 ♗g2 d5 8 ♕b3 ♗xc3+

Almost always played, but there are a couple of interesting alternatives:

⇨ 8...♗c5?!? 9 ♘f3? (missing 9 ♗e3! ♘a6 10 cxd5 ♘g4 11 ♘c2! ±) 9...d4 10 ♘a4 ♗e7 11 0-0 ♘c6 12 ♗f4 ♘d7 13 ♖ad1 e5 14 ♗c1 ♕c7 15 e3 ♘a5 16 ♕c2 dxe3 17 ♗xe3 ♕xc4 ∓ Pedersen-Law, Gausdal 1991.

⇨ 8...♘a6!? 9 cxd5 ♘xd5 10 0-0 ♘xc3! 11 bxc3 ♗e7 12 ♖d1 ♘c5 13 ♕c2 ♗d7 14 ♗f4 (14 a4 ♕e8 15 ♘b5! ♗xb5 {if 15...a6 then 16 ♘c7 ♗xa4 17 ♖xa4 ♕xa4 18 ♕xa4 ♘xa4 19 ♘xa8 ♖xa8 20 ♖d7} 16 axb5 ♕xb5 17 ♗e3 ♖fd8 18 ♖db1 ♕d7 19 ♗xc5 ♗xc5 20 ♖xb7 ♕d6 21 ♗e4 g6 = Lautier-Kholmov, Sochi 1989) 14...♖c8 15 ♘b5 a6 16 ♘d6 ♗a4 17 ♘xc8 ♕xc8 18 ♕d2 ♖d8 19 ♕e1 ♗xd1 20 ♖xd1 ♖xd1 21 ♕xd1 ∓ Gross-Bolbochan, Los Angeles 1991.

9 ♕xc3

⇨ Recently 9 bxc3 has rarely been played. Here is one example: 9...e5?! (9...♘c6!) 10 ♘b5 ♗e6!? 11 ♗a3 dxc4 12 ♕a4 ♗d5 13 0-0-0 ♗xg2 14 ♖xd8 ♖xd8 15 ♖d1 with advantageous to White; Adianto-Lyrberg, Gausdal 1992.

9...e5 10 ♘b3 d4 11 ♕a5 ♕e8!?

An improvement over the older 11...♕e7:

⇨ 12 ♕c5 ♕e6?! (12...♕xc5) 13 f4! ♘bd7 14 ♕b4 d3 15 0-0 (after 15 exd3? exf4+ the white king is caught in the centre) 15...dxe2 16 ♖e1 ♕g4 17 ♕c3 e4 18 h3 ♕e6 19 ♘d4 ♕e7 20 b4! ± h5 21 ♖xe2 ♘b6 22 a4 ♕c7 23 ♖c2 a6 24 a5 ♘bd7 25 ♗b2 with a significant advantage to White; van Wely-Hulak, Amsterdam 1989.

⇨ 12 0-0 ♘c6 13 ♕c5 ♕e6 (or 13...♕c7! 14 f4 ♘d7! 15 ♕d5 Piket-Beliavsky, Amsterdam 1989, and now 15...♘f6 =) 14 f4 ♘d7 15 ♕d5 ♘b6 16 ♕xe6 ♗xe6 17 fxe5 (17 c5!)

c1 ♗d5 44 ♕d2 ♗e4 45
7 46 ♕d8 ♕f6 47 ♕d2 ♕c6
+ ♔h7 49 ♕e5 ♔g8 50
f7 51 ♕a7+ ♔e6 52 ♕g7
♔h4 ♔c4 54 ♕f7+ ♔d4 55
c4 56 ♕a2+ ♔d4 57 ♕a7+

Game 173

Serper
k 1990

6 2 c4 e6 3 ♘c3 ♗b4 4 ♘f3
cxd4 6 ♘xd4 ♘e4 7 ♕d3

ething of a Serper speciality.
7...♕a5 8 ♘b3 (8 ♘db5? a6
axb5 10 ♗d2 bxc4 11 ♕xc4
a3 d5 13 ♕a2 ♕c7 14 ♗g2
♘e4 ♗xd2+ 16 ♘xd2 e5 17
6 ∓ Scholseth-Fossan, Gjøvik
...♘xc3 gives White a choice:

d2 is probably the most prom-
9...♘e4 10 ♕xe4 ♗xd2+ 11
0-0 12 ♗g2 ♘c6 13 ♕c2!? d5
0 d4 15 ♕d3 e5 16 f4 g6 17
♕c7 18 fxe5 ♗f5 19 ♕d2

♕xe5 20 ♗xc6 bxc6 21 ♕xd4 ♕e2
22 ♖ae1 ♕d3 23 ♖e3 ♕xd4 24
♘xd4 ♗h3 25 ♖fe1 ± Wells-Kins-
man, British Ch 1989.
⇨ 9 ♘xa5 ♘e4+ 10 ♗d2 ♘xd2+ 11
♕xd2 ♘xd2 12 ♔xd2 ♘c6 13 ♘xc6
dxc6 14 ♔c3 (14 ♗g2 ♔e7 15 ♖hd1
e5 16 ♔c3 ♗e6 17 ♖d2 ♖hd8 18
♖ad1 ♖xd2 19 ♖xd2 ♖d8 ½-½
Anastasian-Sturua, Podolsk 1989)
14...e5 15 ♗g2 ♗e6 16 ♖hd1 ♖d8
(16...♔e7 17 a4 ♖hd8 18 a5 ♖ac8 19
♖xd8 ½-½ Ioseliani-Brunner, Biel
1990) 17 ♖xd8+ ♔xd8 18 ♖d1+
♔c7. Black should not lose this
position, although he did in Laketić-
Popov, Yugoslav Ch 1991.

8 bxc3 ♘c5 9 ♕e3

Possibly not the best:
⇨ 9 ♕f3!? d6 10 ♗g2 ♘bd7 11 0-0
♘e5! 12 ♕f4 ♘xc4?! (12...♗d7 13
♘b3 ♖c8 14 ♕d4 f6! 15 ♕xd6 b6!
16 ♕d4 ♘a4 ∞ Kramnik-Serper,
Gdynia 1991) 13 ♘b3 ♘b6 14 ♘xc5
dxc5 15 ♕e5! (regaining the pawn)
15...0-0 16 ♕xc5 ♖e8 17 ♗a3 ♖b8
(Black suffers from development
problems) 18 ♖ad1 ♗d7 19 ♕h5
♘c4 20 ♗c1 ♖c8 21 ♖d4 e5 22 ♖h4
♗f5 (losing material, but 22...h6? 23
♗xh6 was even worse) 23 ♖xc4
♕xc4 24 ♕xf5 was winning for
White in Kumaran-Ruban, Hastings
1991/92.
⇨ 9 ♕d2 b6 10 ♘b5 0-0 11 ♘d6
♗b7! 12 ♘xb7 ♘xb7 13 ♗a3
(White has the two bishops, but
Black's position is very solid)
13...♖e8 14 ♗g2 ♘c6 15 ♖d1 ♕f6
16 0-0 ♖ed8 17 ♕c2 ♖ac8 18 ♕a4
♘ba5 19 ♗b4 (White can hardly
hope to hold on to the c-pawn anyway) 19...♘xc4 20 ♗xc6 dxc6 21

17...♘xc4 18 ♘c5 ♗g4 19 ♘xb7
♘4xe5 20 ♖f2 ♖ab8 21 ♗f4 ♖xb7
22 ♗xe5 ♖b5 23 ♗d6 ♖c8 24 ♖c1
♖d8 25 ♖xc8 ♗xc8 26 b3 and White
has the tiniest of advantages; Olafs-
son-Tisdall, Östersund Z 1992.

12 0-0

White has other, possibly superior, moves:
⇨ 12 f4! ♘c6 13 ♕c5 exf4 14 ♗xf4
♗g4 15 0-0 ♖d8 (the e-pawn is
slightly poisoned: 15...♗xe2? 16
♖ae1 d3 17 ♗d6 ♘e4 18 ♗xe4
♕xe4 19 ♗xf8 ±) 16 ♖ae1 ♘e4 17
♕b5 ♘d6?! (17...♗c8!) 18 ♕g5 f5?
19 ♗xd6! ♖xd6 20 h3! ♖g6 (Black
decides to sacrifice a piece rather
than play 20...♗xe2 21 ♗d5+ ♔h8
22 ♘c1 d3 23 ♘xd3) 21 ♕f4 ♗h5
22 g4 (risky; 22 ♔h2! ±) 22...♗xg4
(22...fxg4? 23 ♗d5+) 23 hxg4 ♖xg4
24 ♕d6 ♕e3+ 25 ♖f2 ♖f6 26 ♕d5+
♔h8 27 ♔f1 ♘e7! 28 ♕d8+? (another slip-up; 28 ♕f3! ♖fg6 29 ♖d1
♖g3 30 ♕xb7 should win) 28...♘g8
29 ♖d1 ♖xg2! 30 ♔xg2 (30 ♖xg2
♖h6) 30...♖g6+ 31 ♔f1 ♕h3+ 32
♔e1 ♖g1+ 33 ♔d2 ♕e3+ 34 ♔c2
♖xd1 35 ♔xd1 ♕xf2 ∓ 36 ♘xd4
♕f1+ 37 ♔c2 ♕f4 38 ♕d5 ♕e4+ 39
♕xe4 fxe4 (Black's passed g- and h-
pawns offer good winning chances)
40 ♘b5 ♘f6 41 ♘xa7 g5 42 ♔d2 g4
43 ♔e1 g3 44 ♘b5 ♘g4 45 ♔f1
♘e3+ 46 ♔g1 h5 47 ♘d6 h4 48 c5!
♔g7 49 ♘xb7! ♔f6 50 ♘d6? (50 c6!
holds the balance) 50...♔e5 51 b3 h3
52 ♘c4+ ♔xc4 53 bxc4 ♔f4 54 c6
♔e3 55 c7 h2+ 0-1 Orlov-Karpman,
Minsk 1990.
⇨ 12 ♗g5 ♘c6 13 ♕c7!? (this looks
better than 13 ♕d2 ♘d7 14 f4? f6 15
♗h4 ♘b6 16 ♕c1 exf4 17 gxf4 ♗g4

19 ♖e1 ♖d8 ∓ Crouch-Suba, Halifax
1990) 13...♕e6 14 ♗xf6 gxf6 15
♖c1 ♘b4 16 ♕a5 ♘a6 17 c5 ♘b8 18
0-0 ♘c6 19 ♕c7 (White's queen
seems surprisingly comfortable on
c7) 19...a5 20 f4 ♕d7 21 ♕d6 ♕xd6
22 cxd6 ♖d8 23 fxe5 fxe5 24 ♗xc6
bxc6 25 ♖xc6 ♗e6 26 ♘c5 ♗d5 27
♖b6 ♖ac8 28 ♖c1 e4 29 a3 ♔g7 30
b4 axb4 31 axb4 ♖a8 32 d7 ± Wells-
Suba, Hastings 1991.

12...♘c6 13 ♕a4!?

⇨ 13 ♕c5 ♗d7 14 ♗g5 ♕e6 15 f4
b6 16 f5 ♕e8 17 ♕g3 ♕d6 ♕b8 18 ♕a3
♕d8 19 ♘d2 h6 20 ♗h4 ♖c8 21
♖ac1 ♕e7 22 c5 bxc5 23 ♘e4 d3 24
♕xd3 ♘d4 25 ♕e3 ♕h7 26 ♖f2 ♖g8
27 ♕a3 ♗c6 28 ♗xf6 gxf6 29 ♕xc5
♕xc5 30 ♘xf6+ ♔g7 31 ♘h5+ ♔h8
32 ♖xc5 when, following the complications, White has a winning advantage; Galliamova-Hsu Li Yang,
Oakham 1992.

**13...h6 14 ♘c5 a5 15 a3 e4 16 b4
♕e7 17 ♘b3 ♖d8 18 ♗b2 e3! 19 f4
♗h3!!**

A beautiful sacrifice of the bishop
to unpin the a-pawn.

20 ♗xh3 axb4 21 ♕b5 bxa3 22

♗c1 ♘e4 23 ♗g4 d3 24 exd3 ♖xd3 25 c5 ♘f2! 26 ♖xf2

If instead 26 ♗f3 then 26...e2!. With the text White returns some material, but Black's initiative persists.

26...exf2+ 27 ♔xf2 ♕e4 28 ♖a2 ♕d5 29 ♖d2 ♖xd2+ 30 ♗xd2 a2 31 ♗f3 ♕xf3+! 32 ♔xf3 a1♕ 33 ♕xb7

Obviously, 33 ♘xa1 ♘d4+ is the point of the combination.

33...♕h1+ 34 ♔e3 ♖b8 0-1

Game 171

Johansen-Suba
Kuala Lumpur 1992

1 d4 ♘f6 2 ♘f3 e6 3 c4 c5 4 ♘c3 cxd4 5 ♘xd4 ♗b4 6 g3 0-0 7 ♕b3 ♗xc3+ 8 ♕xc3 d5 9 ♗g2

Suba points out that 9 cxd5 ♕xd5 10 ♘f3 ♖d8! 11 ♗e3 ♘c6 12 ♗g2 e5 13 0-0 e4 14 ♘d2 ♗f5 is to Black's advantage.

9...e5 10 ♘c2!? d4 11 ♕d3 ♘c6 12 0-0 h6 13 b4?!

This leaves the c4 square weak, but 13 f4?! e4! 14 ♗xe4 ♘xe4 15 ♕xe4 ♖e8 16 ♕d3 ♗g4 is also better for Black.

13...♗e6 14 c5 ♗d5 ∓

The exchange of light-squared bishops is very desirable for Black.

15 e4 dxe3 16 ♗xe3 ♗xg2 17 ♕xd8 ♖fxd8 18 ♔xg2 ♘d5 19 ♗d2 ♘c7 20 ♖fd1 ♖d3 21 ♗e1 e4!? 22 a4! ♘e6 23 ♘e3 a5 24 b5 ♘cd4 25 c6 bxc6 26 bxc6 ♘xc6 27 ♖ac1 ♘e5

27...♘cd4 28 ♘c4 ♘b3 maintains Black's edge.

28 ♗c3 ♖xd1 29 ♖xd1 ♘d3 30

♖b1 h5!? 31 ♖b5

Winning the a-pawn, so Black looks for play on the other wing.

31...h4 32 ♖xa5 ♖c8 33 ♗d2 ♘d4 34 ♘f5! h3+ 35 ♔xh3 ♘xf2+

36 ♔h4??

No doubt this can be put down to the clock; 36 ♔g2 was forced.

36...♘f3+ 37 ♔h5 g6+ 0-1

Since 38 ♔h6 ♘g4 is checkmate.

Game 172

Beliavsky-Portisch
Reykjavik 1991

1 d4 ♘f6 2 c4 e6 3 ♘c3 ♗b4 4 ♘f3 c5 5 g3 cxd4 6 ♘xd4 0-0 7 ♗g2 d5 8 ♕b3 ♗xc3+ 9 ♕xc3 e5 10 ♘b3 ♘c6!

More logical than 10...dxc4 11 ♘a5 ♘d5 12 ♕d2 ♘c6 13 ♘xc4 ♗e6 14 0-0 b5 15 ♘a3 a6 16 ♘c2 ♖c8 17 e4 ± Thorsteins-Browne, Reykjavik 1990.

11 cxd5?!

This seems too accommodating. White may consider 11 ♗g5!? or:

⇨ 11 0-0 d4! (this is stronger now that White is deprived of the annoying ♕a5 manoeuvre; 11...dxc4?! is playable, if less logical: 12 ♕xc4 ♗e6 13 ♕b5 ♕b6 14 ♕xb6 axb6 15 ♗e3 ♖a6 16 ♘c1 ♘d5 17 ♗xd5 ♗xd5 ½-½ van Wely-Winants, Wijk aan Zee 1990) 12 ♕c2 h6 13 e3 a5! (fighting for the d4 square) 14 ♗d2 ♕b6 15 ♖ae1 ♖d8 16 exd4 a4 17 ♘c1 ♘xd4 18 ♕c3 ♕c7 19 ♘d3 ♗g4 20 f3 ♗xf3! 21 ♗xf3 ♘xf3+ 22 ♖xf3 e4 23 ♖fe3 ♕d6 24 ♘f2 ♕xd2 25 ♘xe4 ♘xe4 26 ♖xe4 ♕xc3 27 bxc3 ♖d2 with enough advantage to win; Kumaran-Gulko, Vienna 1991.

11...♘xd5 12 ♕d2

White has also tried 12 ♕c5 ♗e6, but without any great success:

⇨ 13 0-0 ♖c8 14 ♕b5 a6! 15 ♕xb7 ♘cb4 16 ♗xd5 (the only way to extract the queen from b7, but it's a high price to pay, as the kingside light squares will be a constant worry) 16...♖b8 17 ♕a7 ♕xd5 18 ♕c5 ♕e4 19 ♕e3 ♕a8 20 ♕f3 e4 21 ♕f4 ♘c2 22 ♖b1 e3 23 f3 ♖b4 24 ♕g5 h6 25 ♕a5 ♗xb3 26 axb3 ♖xb3 27 ♖d1 ♕c6 28 ♕f5 ♕c4 (White is bound hand and foot) 29 ♖d3 ♖xd3 30 ♕xd3 ♕xd3 31 exd3 ♖e8 0-1 van Wely-Stefansson, Arnhem 1989.

⇨ 13 ♗d2 ♘de7 (13...a5 14 ♕b5 ♕c7 15 ♕b6 ♗d5 16 f3 ♖a6 17 ♕e3 ♘e6 18 ♖d1 ♕e7 19 ♗c3 ♗xb3 20 axb3 ♘c5 21 0-0 ♖xb3 22 ♖d5 ♕e6 23 ♖b5 ♖bd4 24 ♗xd4 ♘xd4 25 ♖xe5 ♕d6 26 f4 ± Gaprindashvili-Bojković, Belgrade Jugometal 1992) 14 ♗c3 b6 15 ♕a3 ♕e8 16 ♖d1 ♖d8 17 ♖xd8 ♕xd8 18 0-0 ♕b8 19 ♖d1 ♕d8 20 ♖xd8+ ♕xd8 (with control of the d-file Black has

all the
♘e4 h6
the initi
♘c2 26 .
♗d2 ♘a
♘a2 the
on this
on to w
tisch, Reg

12...♕
♘d4

Black
posed pos

15 ♘x
♕f4 ♗g6
♕a6 20 ♗

Black e
bours.

21 h4 ♕
♖ab8 24 ♕

25 ♖a1 ♕
♗d5 exf2+ 28
♔h8 30 ♖a2
♕a3 ♖xf1+?
♕xh5 35 ♖a8
37 ♕xa8+

White defen

37...♗g8 38
♔h7 40 ♕a8

g6 43 ♕
♔h3 ♔g
48 ♕b2
♕b8+ ♔
♔d5 53
♕a7+ ♔
½-½

Glek-S
Podols

1 d4 ♘
c5 5 g3
♗xc3+ ♕

Som
Instead
9 ♕xe4
0-0 12
d4 15 ♘
0-0 ♗e
1991) 8

⇨ 9
ising:
♘xd2
14 0-0
♘b3

♕a6 c5 22 ♕xc4 cxb4 23 ♕xb4 g6 24 ♕a4 ♕e7 25 ♖xd8+ ♖xd8 26 ♖d1 ♖xd1+ 27 ♕xd1 ♕c5 with an insignificant positional superiority; van Wely-Serper, Tunja 1989.

9...b6 10 ♗g2 ♗b7 11 ♗xb7 ♘xb7 12 ♕f3 ♘c6! 13 ♘xc6 dxc6 14 0-0!?

Better than 14 ♕xc6+?! ♕d7 15 ♕xd7+ ♔xd7 16 ♗a3 ♖hc8 17 0-0-0+ ♔e8 18 ♖d4 ♖c7 19 ♔c2 ♖ac8 20 c5 (opting for an inferior rook ending since if White allows ....♘a5xc4, the knight on c4 will dominate his bishop) 20...♘xc5 21 ♗xc5 ♖xc5 22 ♖d3 ♖c4 23 ♖hd1 ♖8c7 and Black managed to make his edge count in Blagojević-Serper, Pula 1990.

14...♘a5 15 ♗f4 0-0?!

15...♕f6! 16 ♕e3 0-0 ∓.

16 ♗e5!

16...♕g5

White is using tactics to defend his c4 weakness, for 16...♘xc4?! is met by 17 ♗xg7!, and if 17...♘d2 then 18 ♕f4!.

17 ♗d6 ♖fd8 18 c5 ♖d7 19 ♖ad1 ♖ad8 20 ♖d4 ± bxc5 21 h4! ♕g6 22

♗xc5 e5! 23 ♖a4 ♘b7 24 ♗xa7 ♖a8 25 ♖g4 ♕e6 26 ♗e3 ♖xa2

Re-establishing material equality.

27 ♖b4 h6 28 ♔g2 f5 29 ♖fb1 e4 30 ♕f4 ♘d6 31 ♖d1 ♘c4 32 ♖xd7 ♘xe3+ 33 ♕xe3 ♕xd7 34 ♕c5?! ♔h7 35 ♕c4 ♖c2 36 ♖b6 ♕d5! = 37 ♕xc6 ♕xc6 38 ♖xc6 ♖xe2 39 ♔f1 ♖c2 40 h5 ♖c1+ 41 ♔g2 ♖c2 42 ♔f1 ½-½

Game 174

Kapetanović-Serper
Vienna 1991

1 ♘f3 d5 2 d4 ♘f6 3 c4 e6 4 ♘c3 ♗b4 5 cxd5 exd5 6 g3 0-0 7 ♗g2 c6 8 0-0 ♘bd7

Black may instead try 8...♖e8:

⇨ 9 a3 ♗xc3 10 bxc3 ♘e4 11 ♕c2 ♘d6 12 ♗f4 ♕e7 13 ♗xd6 (rather than allowing the knight to settle on c4) 13...♕xd6 14 c4 dxc4 15 ♕xc4 ♘d7 16 ♖fe1 ♘b6 17 ♕d3 h6 18 a4 ♘d5 19 a5 ± van Wely-Rozentalis, Berlin 1991.

⇨ 9 ♘e5 ♘bd7 10 ♘d3 ♗xc3 11 bxc3 ♘e4 12 ♕c2 ♕a5 13 ♘b4 ♘df6 14 f3 ♘d6 15 ♗g5 ♗f5 16 ♘d3 ♘d7 17 ♗f4 ♘b5 18 ♖fc1 ♕a3 19 e4 dxe4 20 fxe4 ♗xe4! (envisaging an exchange sacrifice that offers good chances) 21 ♗xe4 ♖xe4 22 ♘e5 ♘f6 23 ♗g5 ♖xe5 24 dxe5 ♕c5+ 25 ♔h1 ♕xe5 26 ♗xf6 ♕xf6 27 c4?! ♘d4 ∓ Galliamova-Lutz, Dortmund 1992.

9 a3

⇨ 9 ♗f4 ♖e8 10 ♕c2 ♘f8 11 ♖ad1 ♘g6 12 ♗c1 ♕e7 13 ♖fe1 ♘e4 14 ♕b3 ♗f5 15 ♘d2 ♘g5!? 16 ♘f3

♘xf3+ 17 ♗xf3 ♗xc3! (this is a necessary part of Black's plan to control e4) 18 ♕xc3 ♕d7 19 ♗h1 ♖e7 20 f3 ♖ae8 21 e3 h5 22 b3 a6 23 ♖e2 ♘f8 24 ♗a3 ♖e6 25 ♗xf8 ♖xf8 26 ♖de1 ♖d8 27 ♗g2 ♖g6 28 ♖d2 h4! 29 g4? (provoking a winning sacrifice; better is 29 ♔f2) 29...♗xg4! 30 fxg4 ♕xg4 31 ♔f1 h3? (31...♖dd6 32 ♖c1 h3 33 ♗h1 ♖df6+ 34 ♔e1 ♕g1+ is more efficient) 32 ♗h1 ♖dd6 33 ♖f2 ♖df6 34 ♖f4 ♕g1+ 35 ♔e2 ♕xh2+ 36 ♔d1 ♖xf4 37 exf4 ♖g1 38 ♕f3 ♖xe1+ 39 ♔xe1 ♕g1+ 40 ♔e2 ♕xd4 41 ♕xh3 ♕xf4 42 ♕c8+ ♔h7 43 ♗f3 d4 44 ♕e8? d3+ 45 ♔f2 g6 46 ♕d7 d2 47 ♔e2 d1♕+! 48 ♕xd1 ♕h2+ 49 ♔f1 ♕xa2 50 ♗g4 ♕a5 51 ♗c8 ♕c7 52 ♕g4 a5 53 ♗d7 ♕d6 54 ♗c8 b5 55 ♕d7 ♕xd7 56 ♗xd7 a4 57 bxa4 bxa4 58 ♗xc6 a3 59 ♗d5 f5 60 ♔e2 g5 61 ♔d3 ♔g6 62 ♔c3 ♔f6 63 ♔b3 ♔e5 64 ♗c6 g4 65 ♔xa3 ♔d4 66 ♔b2 g3 67 ♔c2 ♔e3 68 ♔d1 ♔f2 0-1 Epishin-Romanishin, Terrassa 1991.

9...♗d6 10 b4 a6 11 ♘e1 b5?!

Planning ...♘b6-c4, masking the c6 weakness, so White turns to attack the problem from another angle.

12 e4! dxe4 13 ♕c2 ♗b7 14 ♘xe4 ♘xe4 15 ♗xe4 ♘f6 16 ♗g2 a5 17 ♖b1 axb4 18 axb4 ♕b6 19 ♘d3?!

Offering a pawn to force the positionally-favourable exchange of dark-squared bishops, but it is not necessary.

19...♕xd4 20 ♗e3 ♕g4 21 ♗c5 ♖ad8! 22 ♖fe1! ♕g6 23 ♖bc1 h5!

The game starts to become very exciting.

24 ♕a2! ♘d5 25 ♘e5 ♕f6 26 ♕a7! ♗xe5!

Starting a long, forcing tactical sequence.

27 ♗xf8 ♗d4 28 ♗c5 ♕xf2+ 29 ♔h1 ♘e3! 30 ♖g1 ♗xc5 31 ♕xc5 ♖d2 32 ♖ce1!

Parrying ...♘xg2, as ♖e8+ forces mate.

32...♖e2 33 ♖xe2 ♕xe2 34 ♕e7! ♕f2! 35 ♕xb7 ♘xg2 36 ♕xc6 ♘e3 37 ♕e8+ ♔h7 38 ♕e4+ f5 39 ♕f4 ♕d2 40 h3 ♕d5+ 41 ♔h2 ♕d2+ 42 ♔h1 ♕d5+ 43 ♔h2 ½-½

Game 175

Gulko-Yusupov
Linares 1990

1 ♘f3 d5 2 d4 ♘f6 3 c4 e6 4 g3 ♗b4+ 5 ♘c3 dxc4 6 ♗g2 0-0
⇨ 6...♗d7!? 7 ♘e5 ♗c6 8 ♘xc6 ♘xc6 9 0-0 ♕d7 10 ♕a4 ♘d5 11 ♘xd5 exd5 12 e4 ♗e7 13 exd5 ♘b4 14 ♕xd7+ ♔xd7 15 ♗d2 ♘d3 16 b3 ♗f6 17 ♗c3 b5 18 bxc4 bxc4 19 ♖fd1 ♖ab8 20 ♗e4 ♖he8 21 ♗xd3

cxd3 22 ♖xd3 ♖e2 23 ♗d2 ♖b2 24 ♗e3 ♖xa2 25 ♖xa2 ♖xa2 26 ♗f4 ± Sunye Neto-Sisniega, Bogota 1991.

7 0-0 ♘c6

⇨ 7...♗d7!? 8 ♘e5 ♗c6 9 e4 ♗xc3 10 ♘xc6 ♘xc6 11 bxc3 e5 12 d5 ♘a5 13 f4 ♘d7 14 ♗h3 b6 15 ♗xd7 ♕xd7 16 fxe5 ♖fe8 17 ♗f4 ♖ad8 18 ♕h5 ♘b7 19 ♕h4 ♖c8 20 ♖f3 ♘c5 21 ♖af1 ∞ Gausel-Agdestein, Östersund Z 1992.

⇨ 7...♘bd7 8 ♕c2 ♖b8 9 e4 h6 10 ♗f4 b5 11 a4 a6 12 axb5 axb5 13 d5 ♗xc3 14 bxc3 exd5 15 ♘d4 (aiming to secure the c6 square for the knight) 15...♘xe4! (Black makes a fine exchange sacrifice, although 15...♖b6 16 exd5 ♘b8 was possible, if rather passive) 16 ♘c6 ♕f6 17 ♘xb8 ♖xb8 18 ♗xe4 dxe4 19 ♕xe4 ♘d7 20 ♗xc7 ♘c5 21 ♕f4 ♗c6 (in return for the exchange Black has a pawn and two very good minor pieces) 22 ♕d6 ♕f3 23 ♕f4 ♕b7 24 ♗d6 ♗h3 25 f3 ♘d3 26 ♕e3 ♖d8 27 ♖a7 ♕d5 28 ♗c7 ♖a8 29 ♖fa1 ♖xa7 30 ♕xa7 ♕xf3 31 ♕a8+ ♕xa8 32 ♖xa8+ (White has managed to fend off the attack) 32...♔h7 33 ♖a2 ♔g6 34 ♗d6 ♗f5 35 ♗f8 g6 36 ♖a5 h5 37 ♖xb5+ ♔e4 38 ♗g7 ♔f3 39 ♗h6 ♔e2 40 ♖a5 ♗e6 41 ♖a2+ ♔f3 ½-½ Psakhis-Illescas Cordoba, Palma 1989. White's king is trapped and he can make no progress.

8 ♖e1

⇨ 8 a3!? ♗a5!? 9 ♗g5 h6 10 ♗xf6 ♕xf6 11 ♕a4 ♗b6 12 e3 ♘a5?! 13 ♘e5 ♕e7 14 ♘e4! (not 14 ♘xc4? ♗d7 ∓) 14...♖d8 15 ♘xc4 ♗d7 16 ♕c2 ♘xc4 17 ♕xc4 ♗c6 = 18 ♕c3 ♖d7 19 ♖ac1 ♖e8 20 ♘c5 ♗xg2 21 ♔xg2 ♗xc5 22 ♕xc5+ e5?! 23 dxe5

♕xc5 24 ♖xc5 b6 25 ♖c6 ♖xe5 26 ♖fc1 with an edge for White, Illescas Cordoba-Yusupov, Linares 1990.

8...♘d5

⇨ 8...♖b8 9 e4 b5 10 e5 ♘d5 11 ♘g5 h6 (White must search for kingside play) 12 ♘ge4 ♗e7 13 a3 f5 14 exf6 ♗xf6 15 ♘xf6+ ♖xf6 16 ♕h5 ♘xc3 17 bxc3 ♘e7 18 ♕c5 ♘d5 19 ♕xa7 ♗b7 (Black has returned the pawn to improve his pieces) 20 ♗d2 ♕f8 21 ♖f1 ♗c6 22 ♕c5 ♕xc5 23 dxc5 ♖d8 = Wesseln-Enders, Bundesliga 1991.

9 ♕c2 ♗e7! 10 ♘e4?! ♘db4! 11 ♕xc4 ♕d5! ∓

An unusual fork.

12 ♕xd5 exd5 13 ♘c3 ♘c2 14 ♗f4 ♗e6 15 ♘b5 ♗d8! 16 ♘xc7 ♗xc7 17 ♗xc7 ♖ac8 18 ♗f4 ♗g4! 19 e3 ♖fd8 20 h3 ♗xf3 21 ♗xf3

White's kingside is very solid, but Black can use the open c-file for his rooks.

21...♘6b4 22 ♗g4 ♖c6

Imprecise; 22...♘xe1 23 ♖xe1 ♖c2 ∓.

23 ♖ed1 ♘xa1 24 ♖xa1 ♘d3 25 ♗f5 ♘xf4 26 gxf4 g6 27 ♗g4 ♔f8?

28 ♔f1 b6 29 a4! ♖c2 30 ♖b1 ♔e7
31 ♔e1 ♔d6 32 ♗d1 ♖c7 33 ♔d2
♖dc8 34 ♗b3 b5??

Giving up a pawn for nothing.

35 axb5 ♖b8 36 ♗a4 ♖c4 37 ♗c2
♖bc8 38 ♗d3 ♖a4 39 h4 ♖a2 40
♗e2 ♔e6 = 41 ♗d3 ♖c7 42 ♗e2
♔d7 43 ♗f1 ♖a5 44 ♗d3 ♔c8? 45
♔e2 ♔b7 46 h5 ♖a2 47 ♔f3 ♖d7 48
♔g3 ½-½

Game 176

Parker-Suba
Dublin 1991

1 d4 ♘f6 2 c4 e6 3 ♘c3 ♗b4 4 ♘f3
c5 5 g3 ♘c6

After 5...b6 6 ♗g2 ♗b7 7 0-0
cxd4 8 ♕xd4 there can follow:
⇨ 8...0-0 9 ♗g5 h6 10 ♗f4 ♘c6 11
♕d3 ♘a5! 12 ♘d2 (perhaps White
should not be so ready to exchange
the light-squared bishops) 12...♗xg2
13 ♔xg2 d5 14 cxd5 ♗xc3! 15 ♕xc3
♘xd5 16 ♕f3 ♕f6 ∓ 17 b4 ♘c6 18
♘e4 ♕g6 19 ♔h1 e5 20 ♗e3 ♘cxb4
with a solid extra pawn; Lesiège-Va-
ganian, Toronto 1990.
⇨ 8...♘c6 9 ♕d3 0-0 (9...♖c8 10
♗f4 ♘a5 11 ♖ac1 ♖xc4 12 ♘b5 d5
13 a3 ♗e7 14 ♘c7+ ♔f8 15 ♘e5
♖xc1 16 ♖xc1 ♘d7 17 b4 ♘xe5 18
♗xe5 ♘c6 19 ♖xc6! ♗xc6 20 ♕c3
winning; van Wely-Steingrimsson,
Kecskemet 1991) 10 ♗f4!? (10 b3
♖c8 11 ♗f4 d5 12 cxd5 ♗xc3 13
♕xc3 ♘xd5 14 ♕d2 ♘xf4 15 ♕xf4
♕e7 16 ♖fd1 ♖fd8 17 ♘e5 ½-½ van
Wely-Rodriguez, Amsterdam 1989)
10...♖c8 11 ♗d6 (White tries hard to
exploit the hole on d6 but it doesn't

seem to amount to much) 11...♗xd6
12 ♕xd6 ♕e7 13 ♖fd1 ♕xd6 14
♖xd6 ♘e7 15 b3 ♘f5 16 ♖d3 d5 17
♘e5 ♗a6 18 e4 dxc4 19 ♘xc4 ♗xc4
20 bxc4 ♘e7 21 e5 ♘g4 22 f4 ♘f5
(the black knights seem quite comfortable here) 23 ♘b5 ♘ge3 24
♘xa7 ♖xc4 = van Wely-Komarov,
Dortmund 1992.

6 ♗g2 ♘e4 7 ♕d3
⇨ 7 ♗d2 ♘xd2 8 ♕xd2 cxd4 9
♘xd4 ♘e5 10 ♘c2 ♗e7 11 b3 0-0
12 0-0 a6 13 ♖ad1 ♕c7 14 ♘e4 d6
15 f4 ♘g6 16 ♘f2 ♗d7 17 e4 ♖fd8
18 ♘g4? (the unguarded situation of
the knight allows Black a central
counter) 18...d5 19 f5 exf5 20 exf5
dxc4 21 ♕c3 (21 fxg6 ♗xg4 picks
up the exchange) 21...♗c5+ 22 ♔h1
♘e7 23 bxc4 ♗xf5 24 ♘ce3 ♗e6 ∓
Unzicker-Yudasin, Moscow 1991.

7...cxd4
⇨ 7...♕a5 8 d5 exd5 (8...♘e7 9
♕xe4 ♗xc3+ 10 ♗d2 ♗xd2+ 11
♘xd2 0-0 12 ♕c2 exd5 13 cxd5 d6
14 0-0 ♗f5 15 e4 ♗g6 16 f4 f6 17
♕c3 ♕xc3 ½-½ Pedersen-Grønn,
Gausdal 1991) 9 cxd5 ♘xc3 10 bxc3
♗xc3+ 11 ♗d2 ♗xd2+ 12 ♘xd2
♘d4 13 e3 ♘b5 14 d6 0-0 15 0-0
♕a6 16 ♖fd1 ♘c7 17 ♘c4 (Black
will experience great difficulties developing his queenside) 17...♘e6 18
a4 ♘d8 19 a5 ♘c6 20 ♕c3 ♖b8 21
♗f1 ♖e8 22 ♘b6 winning the queen;
Gaprindashvili-Sturua, Tbilisi 1991.

8 ♘xd4 ♘xc3 9 bxc3 ♘e5 10
♕c2 ♗e7!

Suba's games are always interesting from a theoretical point of view.
10...♗e7 is a significant improvement over 10...♗c5?! 11 ♕a4 0-0 12
♘b3 ♗e7 13 c5! ±.

11 ♖b1

White submits to his fate; after swapping the c4 pawn for the b7 pawn the black knight will settle on c4, and c3 will be weak. 11 ♕a4!? should be tried.

11...♘xc4 12 ♗xb7 ♗xb7 13 ♖xb7 ♕c8 14 ♖b3 0-0 15 0-0 ♕a6 16 e4 ♖ac8 ∓ 17 ♕e2 ♗c5 18 ♘f3 ♕a4 19 ♗f4 d6 20 ♘g5 e5 21 ♗c1 ♕d7 22 ♘f3 ♗b6 23 ♖d1 ♕g4 24 ♔g2 f5!

With the black pieces so well placed it is inevitable that he should be able to attack on either side at will.

(see next diagram)

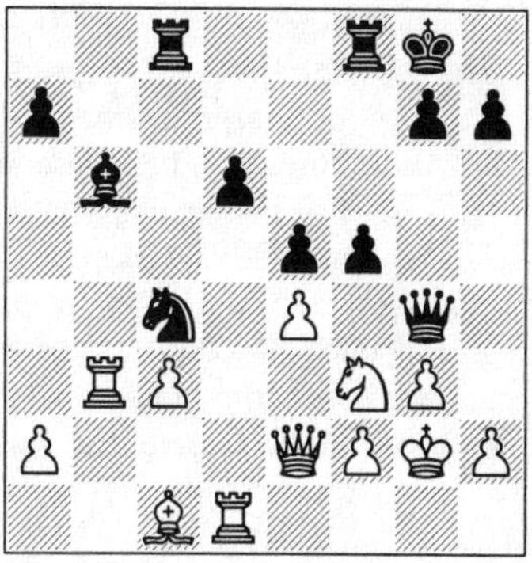

25 exf5 ♕xf5 26 ♖f1 d5 27 ♖b5

♕d7 28 ♖b3 ♖f5 29 ♗e3 ♗xe3 30 fxe3 ♕c6 31 g4 ♖f6 32 ♖b4 ♖cf8 33 ♖bb1 d4 34 cxd4 exd4 35 exd4 ♖e6 36 ♕d3 ♘e3+ 37 ♔g1 ♖xf3 38 ♖b8+ ♔f7 39 d5 ♕xd5 0-1

19

During the 1920s 4 ♕b3 was considered to be the main line in the Nimzo-Indian Defence. For instance, it featured heavily in the 1929 Alekhine-Bogoljubow match, but then went into severe decline. However, following the sudden surge in popularity of the 4 ♕c2 variation, I have for some time been expecting the 4 ♕b3 system likewise to 'take-off'. There is, after all, a great deal of similarity between them; indeed, certain move-orders may transpose, for instance: 4 ♕b3 c5 5 dxc5 ♘a6 6 a3 ♗xc3+ 7 ♕xc3 ♘xc5 is a topical variation arising from 4 ♕c2 (4...c5 5 dxc5 ♘a6 6 a3 etc.) dealt with in chapter 3.

Despite this, and despite Seirawan's successful use of 4 ♕b3 to beat Timman in their 1990 Hilversum match, 4 ♕b3 has remained resolutely on the sidelines.

Notice that I have decided to include the 4 ♘f3 b6 5 ♕b3 variation in this chapter as well, rather than with the other 4 ♘f3 material, because of the obvious resemblance, although the move-order 4 ♕b3 c5 5 ♘f3 b6 is unlikely to occur as such.

In game 177, following 4 ♘f3 b6 5 ♕b3 c5 (the most popular variation, although it arises almost invariably from the move-order 1 d4 ♘f6 2 c4 e6 3 ♘f3 b6 4 ♘c3 ♗b4 5 ♕b3 c5) there followed 6 a3 ♗xc3+ and after White's eighth move slip he was in some difficulty.

Despite this 6...♗a5 is certainly the move *à la mode*, and was the battleground for the aforementioned

Seirawan-Timman match, where several impressive games were produced, Timman becoming a victim of Seirawan's incisive play.

Game 178 contains these and follows the emergence of 7 ♗g5 h6 8 ♗h4 as the critical continuation. It soon became clear that Black had to take radical steps to break the annoying pin and the theory was quickly refined in game 179.

Instead of 6 a3 White can also play 6 ♗f4 or 6 ♗g5, and these are covered in game 180, but the results are not exactly wonderful as yet.

Black does have alternatives to 5...c5: 5...♕e7, which should be met by the strong 6 ♗f4!, and 5...a5; these are explored in game 181.

The final two games in this chapter deal with 4 ♕b3 proper.

Of course, after this Black's choice is somewhat limited by his bishop being *en prise*. 4...♘c6, which is discussed in game 182, whilst solid, does little to hinder White's construction of a pawn centre.

Black's optimum choice is 4...c5 when 5 dxc5 is normal; 5 ♘f3 is considered a little lame, and in game 183 Speelman manages to make Black's set-up look very aggressive indeed.

Game 177

M.Gurevich-Kasparov
Linares 1991

1 d4 ♘f6 2 ♘f3 e6 3 c4 b6 4 ♘c3
♗b4 5 ♕b3 c5 6 a3 ♗xc3+ 7 ♕xc3
0-0

Alternatively 7...♗b7 8 dxc5 bxc5 9 ♗g5 0-0 10 e3, and now:

⇨ 10...♕e7 11 ♗e2 d6 12 0-0 ♘bd7 13 b4 ♖ac8 14 b5 h6 15 ♗f4 g5! (striking quickly on the kingside) 16 ♗g3 ♘e4 17 ♕c2 f5 18 ♘d2 e5 19 f3 ♘xg3 20 hxg3 ♖f6 21 ♗d3 ♖cf8 22 g4 e4! (Black is understandably reluctant to concede control of e4) 23 fxe4 fxg4 24 ♖xf6 ♖xf6 25 ♖f1 ♘e5 ∓ Zlatilov-Rajković, Ptuj 1991.

⇨ 10...d6 11 ♗xf6 ♕xf6 12 ♕xf6 gxf6 13 0-0-0 ♖d8 14 ♗e2 ♔f8 15 ♖d2 a5 16 ♖hd1 ♔e7 17 b3 ♘c6 18 a4 f5 19 g3 ♖ab8 20 ♔b2 ♗a8 Simonenko-Anastasian, USSR 1991. This ending, which is reminiscent of certain endings arising in chapter 2, is fine for Black.

8 g3?

An error that is mercilessly exploited by the World Champion.

⇨ 8 dxc5 bxc5 9 ♗g5 ♘c6 10 e3 h6 11 ♗h4 g5 12 ♗g3 ♘e4 13 ♕c2 f5 14 0-0-0 ♕f6 15 ♗d3 ♘xg3 16 hxg3 (Black can easily defend his h6 pawn) 16...♗b7 17 ♗e2 ♖ad8 18 ♘e1 ♔g7 19 ♘d3 d6 20 ♗f3 ♖f7 21 ♖d2 ♘e5 22 ♘xe5 ♕xe5 ½-½ Seirawan-Arnason, Manila OL 1992.

8...cxd4! 9 ♕xd4 ♘c6 10 ♕h4 ♗b7 11 ♗g2 ♖c8

Black has completed his development and sets his sights on the c4 pawn.

12 ♗d2 ♘a5! 13 ♗xa5 bxa5 14 b4?!

But if 14 0-0, then 14...a4! fixes White's queenside structure.

14...♕c7 15 c5? d6 16 ♖c1 axb4 17 axb4 dxc5 18 ♖xc5 ♕b6 19 ♖xc8 ♖xc8 20 0-0 ♗a6

20...♖c2! is more accurate.

21 ♘e5 ♗xe2 22 ♖e1 ♗b5 23 ♕f4 h6 24 h4 ♗e8 25 g4?

White seeks chances on the kingside, but this creates a weakness as well.

25...♖d8 26 g5 ♖d4 27 ♕f3 hxg5 28 hxg5 ♘d5! 29 ♖c1 ♕b8! ∓ 30 ♕g3 ♘f4 31 ♕e3 ♕d8 32 ♘f3 ♖xb4 33 ♗f1 ♘d5! 34 ♕xa7 ♖g4+ 35 ♔h1 ♘f4 36 ♕b7 ♔h7 37 ♕e4+ f5 38 gxf6+ ♔g6 39 ♕b7 ♕xf6 40 ♖e1 ♘d5 41 ♗g2 ♘f4 42 ♗f1 ♘d3! 0-1

Game 178

Seirawan-Timman
Hilversum match (3) 1990

1 d4 ♘f6 2 c4 e6 3 ♘f3 b6 4 ♘c3 ♗b4 5 ♕b3 c5 6 a3 ♗a5 7 ♗g5

⇨ 7 e3 (not as critical as 7 ♗g5) 7...0-0 8 ♗e2 ♘e4! 9 d5! ♗xc3+! 10 bxc3 ♗a6 11 ♗b2 ♕e7 12 ♖d1 ♖e8 13 ♗d3 ♘d6!? (this looks like an ideal blockading square for the knight, but Black will be unable to develop his queenside pieces with his d-pawn on d7; 13...f5 ∓ might be preferable) 14 ♕c2 e5! 15 ♘d2 (15 ♗xh7+ ♔h8 16 ♗e4 f5 17 ♗xf5 e4 ∓) 15...e4 16 ♗e2 ♘f5? (16...f5! 17 0-0 g6! 18 ♗c1! ♘f7 19 ♔h1 d6 is a better way to complete development) 17 0-0 d6? 18 ♘xe4! ♕xe4 19 ♗d3 ♘xe3 20 fxe3 ♕xe3+ 21 ♖f2! (in return for the pawn sacrificed White has obtained a substantial lead in development) 21...g6 22 ♗c1 ♕e7 23 ♖df1! ♘d7 24 ♖xf7 ♕xf7 25 ♖xf7 ♔xf7 26 ♗f4! ♘e5 27 ♗xe5 (revealing the point of White's play: 27...♖xe5 is impossible because of 28 ♕a4 ♗b7 29 ♕d7+ winning the all-important d-pawn) 27...dxe5 28 ♗e4! ♗xc4? 29 ♕a4 b5 30 ♕a5 a6 31 d6 ♖ad8 32 ♕c7+ ♔g8 33 d7?! (33 h4 ♗e6 34 ♗c6! ♖f8 35 ♕e7 ♗c4 36 h5 gxh5 37 ♗e4 ♗f7 38 d7 wins) 33...♖f8 34 h4 ♗e6 35 ♕xe5 ♔f7! 36 ♗c6 c4 37 ♕d6?! (another slip; 37 g4!) 37...h5 38 ♔h2? (38 ♔f2) 38...♖g8! 39 ♔g3 g5! 40 hxg5 ♖xg5+ 41 ♔h2?! ♖f5 42 a4 bxa4 43 ♗xa4 a5 44 ♕d4 ♔e7 45 ♕e4 ♖g8 46 ♗c6 ♔d6 47 ♕d4+ ♔xc6 48 d8♘+ ♖xd8 49 ♕xd8 ♖c5 50 ♔g3 ♖f5 51 ♔h4 ♖c5 52 ♕e7 ♗d7 53 ♔g3 ♖d5 54 ♔f4 ♔b5 55 ♕e4 ♗c6 56 ♕b1+ ♔c5 57 ♕a2 ♔b5 58 ♕b2+ ♔c5 59 g3 ♖d3 60 ♕a3+ ♔b6 61 ♕b2+ ♔c5 62 ♕f2+ ½-½ Seirawan-Timman, Hilversum (1) 1990.

7...h6

⇨ 7...0-0 8 e3 ♗b7 9 dxc5 ♗xc3+ 10 ♕xc3 bxc5 11 ♗d3 d6 12 ♗xf6 ♕xf6 13 ♕xf6 gxf6 14 ♘d2 ♖d8 15 f4 ♘c6 16 0-0-0 ♔f8 17 g4 h6 18 ♖hg1 = Smyslov-Eismont, Moscow Alekhine mem 1992.

⇨ 7...♘c6 8 0-0-0 (8 e3 h6 9 ♗xf6 ♕xf6 10 ♖d1 0-0 11 ♗e2 ♗a6 12 0-0 ♗xc3 13 ♕xc3 cxd4 14 ♘xd4 ♘xd4 15 ♖xd4 d5 16 ♕d2 ♗xc4 17 ♗xc4 dxc4 18 ♖xc4 ♖fd8 ½-½ Pieterse-Hoeksema, Dutch Ch 1991) 8...♗xc3 9 d5! (White manages to resist the temptation to play the 'obvious' 9 ♕xc3) 9...exd5? (9...♗e5! 10 dxc6 ♗c7 =) 10 cxd5 ♗e5 11 dxc6 ♕e7 12 cxd7+! ♗xd7 13 e3! ♖d8

14 ♖xd7! ♖xd7 (14...♔xd7 is no better: 15 ♕a4+ ♔e6 16 ♗c4+ ♔f5 17 ♕c2+ ±) 15 ♗b5 ♗d6 (15...0-0 loses immediately to 16 ♗xd7 ♕xd7 17 ♘xe5) 16 ♖d1 0-0 17 ♗xd7 ♕xd7 18 ♗f4! c4 19 ♕c2 ♘e8 20 ♘g5! f5 21 ♕xc4+ ♔h8 22 ♗xd6 ♘xd6 23 ♕d5 ♖d8 24 ♘e6! (and not 24 ♕xd6?? ♕c8+ 25 ♔b1 ♖xd6 26 ♖xd6 ♔g8! ∓) 24...♕c8+ 25 ♔b1 ♖d7 26 ♕xd6! 1-0 Seirawan-Timman, Hilversum (5) 1990.

8 ♗h4

This is White's most ambitious possibility. Others:

⇨ 8 ♗d2?! is insipid: 8...0-0 9 e3 cxd4 10 exd4 ♗a6! 11 ♕c2 ♗xc3 12

♗xc3 d5 ∓ Seirawan-van der Wiel, Rotterdam 1989.

⇨ 8 ♗xf6 ♕xf6 9 d5!? (9 e3 fared rather well in Smyslov-Brennink-meijer, Groningen 1989: 9...0-0 10 ♗e2 ♗a6 11 0-0 ♗xc3 12 ♕xc3 ♖c8 13 ♖fc1! d5 14 dxc5 ♕xc3 15 ♖xc3 ♖xc5 16 b4 ♖c7 17 ♖ac1 ♘d7 18 b5 ♗b7 19 cxd5 ♖xc3 20 ♖xc3 ♗xd5 21 ♖c7 ♘c5 22 ♘e5 with an edge in the endgame, which Smyslov, with his legendary technique, converted) 9...0-0 10 e3 d6 11 ♗d3 exd5 12 cxd5 a6 13 0-0 b5 14 ♘e4 ♕e7 15 ♕d1 ♗b7 16 ♗c2 ♘d7 17 ♖b1 ♘e5 ∞ 18 ♘g3 g6 19 e4 Kamsky-de Firmian, New York 1991. The position has evolved into a sort of Benoni, with chances for both players.

8...♘c6? 9 0-0-0! ♗xc3 10 ♕xc3 cxd4 11 ♘xd4 ♘e4 12 ♕h3!

The only way to defend the bishop.

12...♕c7 13 ♘b5 ♕e5 14 ♕e3 f5 15 f4 ♕b8 16 g4! 0-0 17 ♗g2 d5 18 gxf5 exf5 19 ♗xe4!

19...fxe4

19...dxe4 allows a decisive penetration along the g-file: 20 ♖hg1

♗e6 21 ♖g6 ±.

20 cxd5 ♗a6 21 ♘c3 ♘a5 22 d6 ♘c4 23 ♕d4 1-0

Game 179

Psakhis-Grünfeld
Israel 1991

1 d4 ♘f6 2 c4 e6 3 ♘f3 b6 4 ♘c3 ♗b4 5 ♕b3 c5 6 a3 ♗a5 7 ♗g5 h6 8 ♗h4 g5!?

⇨ 8...♗b7 9 0-0-0 ♗xf3 10 gxf3 ♘c6 11 e3?! (11 ♘b5! ♘xd4 12 ♘xd4 cxd4 13 ♖xd4 ♖c8 14 ♔b1 ±) 11...♗xc3 12 ♕xc3 cxd4 13 exd4 ♖c8 14 d5 ♘a5 15 ♔b1 exd5 16 ♖xd5 ♖c6 17 ♗h3 with strong threats to d7 which Black felt obliged to answer with 17...♖e6, giving up the exchange in Fayard-Emms, Cappelle la Grande 1991.

9 ♗g3 ♘e4!

Black has at least one alternative that is worth considering:

1) 9...♘c6 10 0-0-0 ♗xc3 11 ♕xc3 ♘e4 12 ♕c2 ♘xg3 13 hxg3 cxd4 14 ♘xd4 ♘xd4 15 ♖xd4 ♗b7 16 e3 ♕f6 17 ♔b1 ♖c8 18 ♕d2 ♖c7 19 f3 ♔d8 20 ♗e2 ♔c8 21 g4 d5 22 cxd5 ♗xd5 23 e4 ♗b7 24 ♖d1 ± Gheorghiu-Leuba, Switzerland 1991.

2) 9...g4!? 10 ♘d2 cxd4 and now:
⇨ 11 ♘cb1 ♘e4! 12 ♕d3 ♘xg3 13 ♕xd4 (White must go in for the complications since 13 hxg3 ♗xd2+ 14 ♘xd2 ♘c6 slightly favours Black) 13...♗xd2+ 14 ♘xd2 ♘xh1 15 ♕xh8+ ♔e7 16 ♕xh6 ♗b7 17 ♕g5+ ♔e8 18 ♕g8+ ♔e7 19 ♕g5+ ♔e8 20 ♕g8+ ♔e7 ½-½ Dreev-

Kiselev, USSR Ch 1991.
⇨ 11 ♘b5!? might be an improvement: 11...♗xd2+ 12 ♔xd2 ♘e4+ 13 ♔e1 d6 14 ♕d3 ♘xg3 15 ♕xd4 ♘xh1 16 ♕xh8+ ♔e7 17 ♕xh6 ♘d7 18 ♖d1 ♗a6 19 ♕f4 ♗xb5 20 ♕xd6+ ♔e8 21 cxb5 g3?! (although Black has a nominal extra piece, it is unlikely to be able to escape from h1; still, it is a mistake to permit White to round it up so easily) 22 hxg3 ♖c8 23 ♕d4 e5 24 ♕g4 ♕c7 25 ♕h3 ♘xf2 26 ♔xf2 ♕c5+ 27 ♔e1 ♘f6 28 ♕f5 ♔e7 29 g4! (starting the final attack without even bothering to develop his bishop, which remains steadfastly on f1 the entire game) 29...♖c7 30 g5 ♘h5 31 g4 ♘g7 32 ♕f6+ ♔f8 33 ♖d8+ 1-0 Malaniuk-Lendwai, Kecskemet 1991.

10 e3 ♘c6 11 ♗d3 ♘xg3 12 hxg3 g4 13 d5!

13...gxf3
Probably 13...exd5 14 cxd5 gxf3 15 dxc6 fxg2 16 ♖g1 ♕f6 is best, with likely equality.
14 dxc6 fxg2 15 ♖g1 ♕f6 16 ♗e4! d5?

Trying to accelerate his development, but it would be better to hang on to his pawns:
⇨ 16...♗xc3+ 17 ♕xc3 ♕xc3+ 18 bxc3 d6! 19 0-0-0 (the question is: after White recaptures on g2, is his extra, tripled, pawn on c6 of any value?) 19...♗a6 20 ♖xd6 ♖d8 21 ♖xd8+ ♔xd8 22 ♖d1+ ♔c8 23 ♗xg2 ♖d8 24 ♖h1 ♗xc4 25 ♖xh6 ♔c7! 26 ♖h7?! (26 ♖f6 ±) 26...♖f8 27 ♗e4 ♔d6 28 g4 ♗b5 29 c7 ½-½ Yrjölä-Lerner, Helsinki Open 1992.
17 cxd5 exd5 18 ♗xd5 ♗e6 19 ♗xe6! ♕xe6 20 ♕xe6+ fxe6 21 0-0-0 ♗xc3 22 bxc3 ♖d8 23 ♖xg2 ♖xd1+ 24 ♔xd1 ♔e7 25 ♖h2
Training his sights on the Achilles' heel of Black's position, the h6 pawn.
25...♔d6 26 ♔e2 ♔xc6 27 g4! ♖g8 28 ♖h4 ♖g6 29 f4 e5?
Precipitating the end.
30 f5 ♖d6 31 ♔f3 ♔d5 32 c4+! ♔xc4 33 g5+ 1-0

Game 180

M.Gurevich-Shneider
Moscow Alekhine mem 1992

1 d4 ♘f6 2 c4 e6 3 ♘f3 b6 4 ♘c3 ♗b4 5 ♕b3 c5 6 ♗f4
⇨ 6 ♗g5!? h6 7 ♗h4 ♘c6 8 0-0-0 ♗a6 9 d5 ♘a5 10 ♕c2 g5 11 ♗g3 ♗xc4 12 ♘e5 ♗xc3 13 ♘xc4 ♘xc4 14 ♕xc3 b5 15 b3 ♘b6 16 ♗e5 ♘fxd5 17 ♕f3 f6 18 ♗d6 (threatening mate in one) 18...♔f7 19 e4 ♘b4 20 ♗xb5 a6 21 ♗e2 ♘c8 22 ♗xc5 ♕c7 23 ♕h5+ ♔g7 24 ♔b1 and having recovered his two pawns, White

has a winning position; Lev-Kogan, Israeli Ch 1992.

6...♗b7

⇨ 6...♘c6! 7 e3 cxd4 8 ♘xd4 ♘xd4 9 exd4 ♕e7 10 ♗d3 ♗b7 11 0-0 0-0 12 ♗g5 ♗xc3 13 bxc3 h6 14 ♗h4 g5 15 ♗g3 ♗e4 16 ♗e2 ♗g6 17 ♕b4 ♕xb4 18 cxb4 ♘e4 19 ♖fc1 ♖fc8 was fairly level in Dreev-Hraček, Arnhem 1989.

⇨ 6...♘e4 7 e3 ♗b7 8 ♗d3 0-0 9 0-0 ♗xc3 10 bxc3 f5 11 d5 g5 12 ♗xe4 fxe4 13 ♗xg5 ♕e8 14 ♘d2 exd5 15 cxd5 ♖f5 16 ♗f4 ♗xd5 17 ♕c2 ♖f6 18 ♖ad1 ♕g6 is somewhat unclear, although the white king enjoys the better protection; Dreev-Arkhipov, Moscow Alekhine mem 1992.

7 e3

Instead 7 dxc5! bxc5 8 0-0-0 looks stronger.

7...0-0 8 ♗d6 ♗xc3+ 9 bxc3

Obviously 9 ♕xc3?? ♘e4 would not do at all.

9...♖e8 10 ♗d3 ♘e4 11 ♗xe4 ♗xe4 12 0-0 ♘c6 13 ♘d2 ♘a5 14 ♕a4 ♗c6 15 ♕d1 ♘b7 16 ♗g3 d5 17 cxd5 ♕xd5 18 ♘f3 cxd4 19 cxd4 ♘a5 20 ♖e1 f5!?

This weakens e5, but puts paid to White's hope of playing e4.

21 ♕e2 ♖ac8 22 ♖ec1 ♗b7 23 ♕b2 ♘c4 24 ♕b3 g5 25 ♘e1 g4!

Getting a strong grip on the h1-a8 diagonal.

26 f3 gxf3 27 ♘xf3 b5 28 ♗f4 ♖e7 29 ♖c2 ♖g7 30 ♖f1 a6 31 a4 ♗c6 32 axb5 axb5 33 h3

Unfortunately for White, he cannot contest the a-file as 33 ♖a2? is met by 33...♘xe3!.

33...♖a8 34 ♕b4 ♖a4 35 ♕c3 ♖a3 36 ♕e1 ♖a8 37 ♔h2 ♕e4 38

♕e2 ♖a3 39 ♘g5 ♕d5 40 ♖a2 ♖xa2 41 ♕xa2

41...♘xe3!

The same tactic, and now even more effective.

42 ♕xd5 ♘xf1+ 43 ♔g1 ♗xd5 44 ♔xf1 h6 45 ♘f3 ♗xf3 46 gxf3 b4 47 ♔e2 b3 48 ♔d2 b2 49 ♔c2 ♖g2+ 50 ♔b1 ♖f2 51 ♗xh6 ♖xf3 52 ♔xb2 ♖xh3 0-1

Game 181

Mikhalchishin-Deleyn
Sas van Gent 1990

1 d4 ♘f6 2 c4 e6 3 ♘f3 ♗b4+ 4 ♘c3 b6 5 ♕b3 ♕e7!?

The other method of protecting b4 is 5...a5, when there may follow:

1) 6 g3 ♗b7 7 ♗g2 0-0 8 0-0 ♗xc3 9 ♕xc3 d6 10 b3 and now:

⇨ 10...♕c8!? 11 ♗b2 ♗e4 12 ♗h3 ♕e8 13 ♘d2 ♘bd7 14 ♘xe4 ♘xe4 15 ♕c2 f5 16 ♗g2 ♕g6 17 ♖ad1 ♘df6 18 e3 ♘g4! 19 ♕e2 ♕h5 20 h3 ♘g5! 21 ♗xa8? (21 hxg4? also loses: 21...fxg4 22 ♖fe1 ♘f3+ 23

♗xf3 gxf3 24 ♕f1 ♖f6-h6 with mate, but White could try 21 h4, or even 21 f3!) 21...♕xh3 22 f4 ♕xg3+ 23 ♕g2 ♘h3+ 24 ♔h1 ♘gf2+ 0-1 Lorscheid-Lamoureux, Torcy 1991.

⇨ 10...♘bd7 11 ♗b2 ♘e4 12 ♕e3! (this is a more active square than c2) 12...♕b8? (strange; 12...♘ef6!) 13 d5! exd5 14 cxd5 ♗xd5 15 ♘g5? (15 ♘h4! ♖e8 16 ♗xg7! ♔xg7 17 ♘f5+ ♔h8 18 ♕d4+ wins) 15...♘ef6 16 ♘xh7 ♔xh7 17 ♗xd5 ♘xd5 18 ♕d3+ f5! 19 ♕xd5 ♘c5 = 20 ♖ac1 ♕e8 21 ♕f3 ♕f7 22 ♖fd1 ♖ae8 23 ♖d4 ♖e4 24 ♖xe4 ♘xe4 25 ♕d3 ½-½ Dreev-Kiselev, Podolsk 1992.

2) 6 ♗g5 ♗b7 7 e3 h6 8 ♗h4 g5 9 ♗g3 ♘e4 10 ♗d3 d6 11 ♗xe4 ♗xe4 12 0-0-0 ♗xc3 13 ♕xc3 ♘d7 14 ♘e1 ♗b7 15 c5! (breaking up the dark squares) 15...♘f6 16 f3 ♘d5 17 ♕a3 dxc5 18 dxc5 ♕e7 19 e4 ♘b4 20 cxb6 e5 21 ♔b1 cxb6 22 ♘d3 f6 23 ♘xb4 axb4 24 ♕b3 (Black's main problem is that he cannot castle) 24...♗c6 25 ♖c1 ♗d7 26 ♖c7 ♕d6 27 ♕c2 ♕e6 28 b3 0-0 29 ♕d2 ♖f7 30 ♖d1 ♗e8 31 ♖xf7 ♕xf7 32 ♕xb4 b5 and Black retains certain drawing chances; Miles-Budnikov, Beijing 1991.

6 ♗f4!

This is the best reply, aiming at the c7 square. Less testing is 6 a3 ♗xc3+ 7 ♕xc3 ♗b7 8 g3 d6 9 ♗g2 0-0 10 0-0 ♘bd7 11 b4 when Black may try:

⇨ 11...♘e4 12 ♕c2 f5 13 ♗b2 ♘df6 14 a4 a5 (necessary, to block the pawns' charge forward) 15 b5 ♖ae8 16 ♘e1 c6 17 bxc6 ♗xc6 18 f3 ♘g5 19 ♘d3 ♘f7 20 ♖fe1 (preparing e4) 20...♖b8 21 e4 fxe4 22 fxe4 ♖fc8

23 d5! (the white pieces are well placed to support this central push) 23...♗b7 24 ♕b3 ♘d7 25 e5! ± dxe5 26 ♘xe5 ♘fxe5 27 ♗xe5 ♕c5+ 28 ♔h1 ♘xe5 29 ♖xe5 exd5 30 cxd5 ♔h8 31 ♖ae1 h6 32 h4 ♖d8 33 ♕d3 ♖bc8 34 ♕g6 ♖g8 35 ♗e4 1-0 Smyslov-Chandler, Hastings 1988.

⇨ 11...a5!? 12 ♗b2 axb4 13 axb4 ♖fc8 14 ♖fd1 c5 15 ♕b3 ♗e4 16 ♗h3 d5! (simplifying the central pawn situation) 17 bxc5 bxc5 18 ♗a3 ♕e8 19 dxc5 ♘xc5 20 ♕e3 ♘b7 21 ♘d2 ♗g6 22 ♔g2 ♘a5 23 ♖dc1 ♖d8 24 cxd5 ♘xd5 25 ♗xd5 ♖xd5 26 ♗b2 f6 27 ♗c3 ♖c8 28 ♗xa5 ½-½ M.Gurevich-Karpov, Reggio Emilia 1991.

6...♘c6

⇨ 6...♗xc3+ 7 ♕xc3 d6 8 e3 (8 ♘d2 ♗b7 9 f3 ±) 8...♗b7 9 0-0-0 ♘bd7 10 h3 0-0 11 ♕c2 ♗e4 12 ♕e2 ♖fd8 13 ♗g5 ♖ac8 14 ♘d2 ♗b7 15 e4 e5 16 d5 c6 17 ♔b1 ♖c7 18 ♕f3 ♖dc8 19 ♗e2 ♗a6 20 ♕a3 ♗b7 21 f3 a6 22 dxc6 ♖xc6 23 ♘f1! a5 24 ♘e3 ♕e6 25 ♘d5 ± gave White more room in Lev-Harvstad, Gausdal 1991.

7 a3 ♗xc3+ 8 ♕xc3 h6

I am not too keen on this.

9 d5! ♘a5 10 b4 ♘b7

The upshot of Black's eighth move.

11 dxe6 dxe6 12 e4 c5 13 ♗d3 0-0 14 0-0 ♖e8 15 e5 ♘h7 16 ♘d2 ♘f8 17 ♘e4

Targeting the f6 and d6 squares.

17...♘g6 18 ♗g3 ♗d7 19 b5!

Curbing the activity of Black's bishop. White can afford to close the queenside as he can decide the game by playing on the kingside alone.

19...a6 20 a4 a5? 21 h4! ♘f8

22 ♘f6+! gxf6 23 exf6 ♕d8 24 ♗e4 e5 25 ♗xe5!

Of course, White is not too interested in the knight on b7.

25...♘g6 26 f4! ♖a7

26...♕c8 27 h5 ♘xe5 28 fxe5 ±.

27 ♕g3 ± ♗g4

27...♔h8 28 ♗xg6 ♖g8 29 f5 ♗xf5 30 ♖xf5 ♖xg6 fails to 31 ♕xg6! fxg6 32 f7+.

28 ♕xg4 ♖xe5 29 fxe5 ♕d4+ 30 ♔h1 h5 31 ♕f3 ♘xe5 32 ♕f5 ♘g6 33 ♖ad1 ♘d6? 34 ♖xd4 ♘xf5 35 ♖d8+ 1-0

Game 182

Piket-Foisor
Corfu 1991

1 d4 ♘f6 2 c4 e6 3 ♘c3 ♗b4 4 ♕b3 ♘c6 5 ♘f3 a5

⇨ 5...d5 (transforming the position into a sort of Queen's Gambit Declined) 6 ♗g5 h6 7 ♗xf6 ♕xf6 8 e3 dxc4 9 ♗xc4 0-0 10 0-0 ♗d6 11 ♗b5 ♗d7 12 ♖fd1 a6 13 ♗e2 ♖ab8

14 ♖ac1 ♖fc8 15 ♘e4 ♕e7 16 ♘c5 ♗e8 17 ♕c3 e5! 18 dxe5 ♘xe5 19 ♘d4 ♗xc5 20 ♕xc5 ♕f6 21 f4 ♘c6 22 ♗f3 b6 23 ♕c3 ♘xd4 24 ♕xd4 ♕e7 25 e4 ♖d8 26 ♕c3 c5 27 e5 ♕e6 28 a3 ♗a4 29 ♖xd8+ ♖xd8 30 b4 ♕f5! ∓ 31 bxc5 bxc5 32 ♕a5 ♖d4 33 ♕xa6 ♕xf4 34 ♖e1 ♗d7 35 ♗e4 ♗f5? (35...g5! ∓) 36 ♗xf5 ♕xf5 37 e6 ½-½ Akopian-Serper, Manila OL 1992.

6 a3

6 ♗d2.

6...a4 7 ♕c2 ♗xc3+ 8 bxc3 d6 9 e4!? h6 10 ♗d3 e5?! 11 h3

Missing 11 c5!.

11...♕e7 12 ♗e3 ♗d7 13 ♘d2 ♘a5 14 ♖b1 ♗c6 15 g4 ♘b3!?

Offering a pawn to force White to close the centre.

16 d5

Not 16 ♘xb3? axb3 17 ♕xb3 exd4 when the e-pawn drops.

16...♗d7 17 ♘xb3 axb3 18 ♕xb3 b6 19 ♔d2 ♘h7 20 c5!? dxc5 21 f4 f6 22 ♖hf1 ♘f8 23 fxe5 fxe5 24 ♖f2 ♗a4 25 ♕b2 ♘d7 26 ♖bf1 ♖f8?

Black can hold the balance with 26...♘f6 27 c4 ♗d7 =.

27 ♖xf8+ ♘xf8 28 g5! 0-0-0 29 gxh6 gxh6 30 ♗b5 ♗xb5 31 ♕xb5 ♕d6? 32 ♔c2 ♘d7 33 ♕c6 ♖g8 34 ♖f7 ♖g2+ 35 ♔d3 c4+ 36 ♔xc4 ♕xc6+ 37 dxc6 1-0

Game 183

Christiansen-Speelman
Munich 1992

1 d4 ♘f6 2 c4 e6 3 ♘c3 ♗b4 4 ♕b3 c5 5 dxc5

After 5 ♘f3:

⇨ 5...♘e4! is thought to be Black's most accurate move: 6 ♘d2 ♗xc3 7 bxc3 ♘xd2 8 ♗xd2 ♘c6 (8...♕c7) 9 dxc5 0-0 10 g3 ♕e7 11 ♗g2 ♕xc5 12 0-0 b6 13 ♗e3 ♕h5 with fair chances; Nemet-Vezzosi, Reggio Emilia C 1991.

⇨ 5...♘c6 6 e3 0-0 (6...b6 7 a3 cxd4 8 exd4 ♗xc3+ 9 ♕xc3 ♗b7 10 ♗d3 ♘e7 11 ♗g5 ♖c8 12 0-0 ♘e4 13 ♗xe4 ♗xe4 14 ♘d2 ♗b7 15 ♖fe1 0-0 16 b3 ♖e8 17 ♕h3 d5 18 ♕g4 ♕c7 19 ♖ac1 dxc4 20 bxc4 ♘g6 = Petran-Csom, Budapest 1991) 7 a3! ♗a5!? 8 ♗d3 d5 9 0-0 cxd4 10 exd4 dxc4 11 ♕xc4 ♘d5 12 ♗e4?! (12 ♗c2 ♘xc3 13 bxc3 ±) 12...♘xc3 13 bxc3 ♘e7! 14 ♗c2 ♕d5 15 ♕d3 ♕f5 16 ♕e2 ♕h5 17 c4 ♗c7 18 ♖e1 ♘f5 19 h3 = b6 20 ♕f1 ♘h4 21 ♘xh4 ♕xh4 (Black has successfully managed to swap a pair of knights with his strange queen manoeuvres) 22 ♖e4 ♕d8 23 ♕d3 f5! (this is normally a good move in such positions if White cannot exploit e5) 24 ♖e1 ♕d6 25 g3 ♕c6 26 d5 exd5 27 cxd5 ♕f6 28 ♖b1 ♗d6 29 ♗b2 ♕h6 30 ♗e5! ♗d7 31 ♗xd6 ♕xd6 32 ♖bd1?! ♖ae8 33 ♖e3? ♖xe3 34 ♕xe3 f4 ∓ 35 gxf4 ♖xf4 36 ♖e1 ♖f7 (White finds himself with four weak pawn islands) 37 ♕e4?! ♗f5 38 ♕c4 ♕g6+ 39 ♔h1 h6 40 ♗xf5 ♕xf5 41 ♖e8+ ♔h7 42 ♕e4 ♕xe4+ 43 ♖xe4 ♖xf2 44 ♖d4 ♖f7 45 ♔g2 ♔g6 46 ♔g3 ♔f6 47 ♔f4 g5+ 48 ♔e4 ♖e7+ 49 ♔d3 ♔e5 50 a4 ♖d7 51 ♔c4 ♖c7+ 52 ♔d3 ♖c1 0-1 Pieterse-van der Wiel, Dutch Ch 1991.

5...♘c6

⇨ 5...♘a6 6 ♘f3 (6 a3 ♗xc3+ transposes to 4 ♕c2 c5 in chapter 3) 6...0-0 7 ♗g5 ♕a5 8 ♗xf6 gxf6 9 ♘d2 ♘xc5 10 ♕c2 ♗xc3 11 bxc3 b6 12 ♖d1 ♗b7 13 ♘b3 ♗e4 14 ♕d2 ♘xb3 15 axb3 ♕e5 16 f3 ♗c6 17 e3 ♔h8 18 ♗e2 ♖g8 19 0-0 ♖g6 20 e4 ♖ag8 21 ♖f2 ♕c5 22 ♕d4 ♕h5 23 b4 e5 24 ♕d3 ♖h6 25 g4 (Black's kingside pressure finally forces a concession) 25...♕g5 26 b5 ♗a8 27 ♕d2 ♕h4 28 ♖g2 ♖hg6 29 ♕e1 ♕g5 30 ♖xd7 ♕e3+ 31 ♔f1 h5 32 ♕d2 ♕xd2 33 ♖xd2 hxg4 34 ♖xg4 ♖xg4 35 fxg4 ♗xe4 36 ♖d7 ± Piket-Korchnoi, Pederij Doeksen 1991.

6 ♘f3

Akopian's preference has been 6 ♗g5 h6 (6...♗xc5 7 ♘f3 b6 8 e4 ♗e7!? 9 ♗e2 ♗b7 10 e5 ♘g4 11 ♗f4! led to a small advantage for White in Akopian-Shneider, USSR Ch 1991) 7 ♗xf6 ♕xf6 8 ♘f3, with the following possibilities:

⇨ 8...♗xc3+! 9 ♕xc3 ♕xc3+ 10 bxc3 b6! = 11 cxb6 axb6 12 e3 ♖a4! 13 ♗d3 ♗a6 14 ♔d2 ♔e7 15 ♖hb1 ♖b8 16 ♘d4 ♘xd4 17 cxd4 ♗xc4 ½-½ Akopian-Yudasin, Dos Hermanas 1992.

⇨ 8...0-0 9 e3 ♗xc5 10 ♗e2 b6 11 0-0 ♕e7 12 ♘e4 ± f5 13 ♘xc5 bxc5 14 ♖ad1 ♖b8 15 ♕a3 ♗b7 16 ♖d2 ♖bd8 17 ♖fd1 d6 18 g3 ♗a8 19 ♘e1 g5 20 ♗f1 f4 21 exf4 gxf4 22 ♗g2 ♘d4 23 ♗xa8 ♖xa8 24 ♖xd4 (White feels obliged to capture this knight before Black can play ...e5) 24...cxd4 25 ♖xd4 ♖ad8 26 ♖d2 ♕h7 27 ♕d3 d5 28 c5 e5 29 ♕a6 ♖fe8 30 ♘f3 e4 31 ♘d4 e3 32 fxe3 fxe3 33 ♖d1 ♖d7 34 ♕c6 ♔h8 35

♖f1 ♖dd8 36 ♖f6 ♕b1+ (Black's position is too loose to consider playing to win) 37 ♖f1 ♕h7 38 ♖f6 ♕b1+ 39 ♖f1 ½-½ Akopian-Greenfeld, Beer-sheva 1992.

⇨ 8...♗xc5 9 e3 b6 10 ♗e2 ♗b7 11 ♘e4 ♗b4+ 12 ♕xb4 ♘xb4 13 ♘xf6+ gxf6 14 ♔d2 ♔e7 15 ♖hc1 ♖ac8 16 a3 ♘c6 17 b4 ♘e5 18 ♘xe5 fxe5 = Akopian-Tiviakov, Mamaia 1991.

6...♘e4

An important alternative is 6...0-0 7 ♗g5:

1) 7...h6 8 ♗xf6 ♕xf6 9 e3 is the most normal:

⇨ 9...♕g6!? 10 g3 a5 11 ♖c1 a4 12 ♕d1 a3 13 b3 ♕f6 14 ♘d4 ♘xd4 15 ♕xd4 ♕f3 16 ♖g1 ♕h5 17 h4 ♗xc5 18 ♗e2 ♕f5 19 ♕f4 ♕g6 20 g4 ♗b4 21 ♔d2 (Black's queen wanderings do not seem to have achieved too much other than advancing White's development) 21...♖e8 22 ♗d3 e5 23 ♕e4 ♕f6 24 ♔e2 ♗xc3 25 g5 hxg5 26 hxg5 ♕e6 27 ♖xc3 ± Bilunov-Ruban, Podolsk 1989.

⇨ 9...♗xc5 10 ♗e2 b6 11 0-0 ♕d8 12 ♖fd1 ♗e7 13 ♖d2 a6 14 ♖ad1 ♕c7 15 ♘e4 ♖d8 16 ♘d6 ♘a5 (coming to b7 in order to eliminate the powerful d6 knight) 17 ♕c3 ♘b7 18 ♘xc8 ♖axc8 19 ♖c2 ♘c5 20 ♘d4 ♘e4 21 ♕d3 ♘c5 22 ♕a3 a5 23 ♗f3 ♕b8 24 ♘b5 ♗f8 25 ♕c3 ♘a6 26 ♕b3 ♘c5 27 ♕c3 ♘a6 28 ♕b3 ♘c5 ½-½ Piket-C.Hansen, Wijk aan Zee 1991.

2) 7...♕a5!? 8 ♗xf6 gxf6 9 ♖c1 ♗xc5 (the bishop pair compensates, to some extent, for the doubled pawns) 10 e3 b6 11 ♗e2 ♗b7 12 0-0 ♗e7 13 ♖fd1 ♘e5 14 ♘e1 ♗c6 15

a3 ♖ad8 16 ♕a2 ♘g6 17 ♖d4 ♕e5 18 ♖cd1 f5 19 ♗f3 a6 20 ♕b3 ♕a5 21 ♕c2 ♗f6 22 ♖4d3 ♕e5 23 ♖d6 ♗e7 24 ♖6d2 f4?! (Black will pay later for the loss of control of the e4 square; 24...♕g7 =) 25 exf4 ♘xf4 26 g3 ♘g6 27 ♗xc6 dxc6 28 ♘f3 ♕c7 29 h4! ♖xd2 30 ♖xd2 ♘e5 31 ♕e4 ♗f6?! 32 ♘g5! ♗xg5 33 hxg5 ♘g6 34 ♕f3 ♖d8 35 ♖xd8+ ♕xd8 36 ♘e4! (eyeing the f6 square) 36...♕d4 37 ♘f6+ ♔g7 38 ♕h5 ♔f8 39 ♕xh7 ± Piket-Wirthensohn, Hamburg 1991.

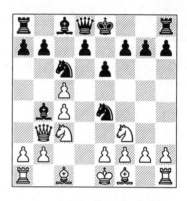

7 ♗d2 ♘xd2 8 ♘xd2 0-0 9 e3 ♗xc5 10 ♗e2

⇨ 10 ♘de4 b6 11 ♗e2 ♗e7 12 ♖d1 a6!? 13 0-0 ♕c7 14 ♖d2 f5 15 ♘g3 ♘e5 16 f4 ♘f7 17 e4 fxe4 18 ♘cxe4 ♗b7 19 ♔h1 ♖ac8 20 f5 ♘d6 21 ♘xd6 ½-½ Piket-Kir.Georgiev, Corfu 1991.

10...b6 11 ♖d1 f5 12 ♘f3 ♕f6 13 0-0 g5 14 ♘e1

White should play 14 ♘b5! g4 15 ♘e1.

14...♖f7 15 ♘b5 ♗b7 16 ♘d6 ♗xd6 17 ♖xd6 ♖c8 18 ♕d1! ♘e5 19 b3?

Better is 19 ♕d4.

19...f4! 20 exf4 gxf4 21 f3 ♖g7 ∓

Black's set-up looks very aggressive.

22 ♖f2 ♖f8 23 ♕d4 ♕g5 24 ♘d3?

Carelessly cutting off his rook's escape route.

24...♘c6! 25 ♕b2 ♕e7

(see next diagram)

26 ♖xc6

This loss of the exchange is inevitable, as 26 ♕a3? fails to 26...♘d4 ∓.

26...♗xc6 27 b4 ♕f6 28 ♗d1 d6 29 ♖d2 e5 30 c5 e4 31 ♗b3+ ♔h8 32 ♕xf6 ♖xf6 33 ♘e5! e3 34 ♖xd6 ♖xd6 35 cxd6 e2 36 ♘d3 ♗b5! 37 ♘e1 ♖d7 38 a4 ♗a6 39 b5 ♗b7 40 ♔f2 ♖xd6 41 ♔xe2 ♗d5! 42 ♗xd5 ♖xd5

The ending is relatively straightforward, and Speelman makes no mistake.

43 ♘c2 ♔g7 44 g4 h5 45 h4 ♖e5+ 46 ♔f2 ♖c5 47 ♘d4 ♖c4 48 ♘c6 a5 49 g5 ♖xa4 50 ♔e2 ♖c4 51 ♘e5 ♖d4 0-1

20

Although the Leningrad has remained steadfastly unfashionable, the strong Russian GM Bareev has consistently employed it in recent years, and has scored well, particularly at the annual Hastings tournament. Despite this, the variation does not have a particularly good reputation and Black's resources are considered more than adequate.

The pawn-grab line examined in game 184 deserves to be played more often, as from Black's point of view it offers very good winning chances, White's compensation being rather obscure. Perhaps 8 ♗b5 will start coming back into fashion. The sub-game Neverov-Obukhov features a similar variation, but this time with ...h6 and ♗h4 thrown in. This makes a good deal of difference as the bishop is less exposed on h4. However it is still playable for Black, if not for the faint-hearted.

The pawn sacrifice line 6...b5!?, examined in game 185, has few followers, but it is still far from clear that White can get an advantage.

Black's most important idea of recent years is to play ...♕e7 before playing ...e5. The principal reason is to stop White adopting set-ups based on f3 or f4, both of which are answered by ...exd5. Essentially, it makes little difference whether Black interpolates ...h6 or not, though he might be able to delay this move to take advantage of the bishop's exposure on g5 as in Hort-Smagin, game 186.

White's most natural choice is 8/9 ♗d3 when it seems that Black might prefer the flexible ...♘bd7 to closing the position with the ...e5 of game 188 (a compendium of Bangiev's best games!).

It is noticeable that Bareev prefers 9 ♘f3, which, incidentally, stops Smagin's plan of ...♕e5.

At the moment Black has found no answer to Bareev's 12 ♘e4! in game 187, and therefore he should prefer closing the game by ...e5.

Should Black play an earlier ...e5 White must choose between 9 ♗d3, 9 f3 and 9 ♕c2 although play is equal in each case. Despite the exchange of queens in game 189, Bareev still manages to conduct a superb attacking game.

Game 184

Bareev-Dautov
Moscow 1990

1 d4 ♘f6 2 c4 e6 3 ♘c3 ♗b4 4 ♗g5 c5 5 d5 d6 6 e3 exd5

⇨ 6...h6 7 ♗h4 ♗xc3+ 8 bxc3 exd5 9 cxd5 ♘bd7 10 ♗d3 ♕a5 11 ♘e2 ♘xd5 12 0-0 ♘xc3 13 ♘xc3 ♕xc3 14 ♖c1 ♕a5 15 ♕g4 0-0!? (this looks risky, but 15...g5 16 ♕e4+ ♔f8 17 ♗g3 is not without its dangers) 16 ♕e4! g6 17 ♕f4 ♔g7 18 ♕xd6 ♕xa2! 19 ♗c4 ♕b2 20 f4! b5! 21 ♖b1 ♕c3 22 ♖fc1 ♕xe3+? (22...♕a3! 23 ♖a1 ♕b2 =) 23 ♗f2 ♕e8 24 ♖xb5 ♘b6 25 ♖xc5! ♘xc4 26 ♗d4+ ♔h7 27 ♖5xc4 ♗e6 28 ♖c7 a5?? (28...♖c8 was forced) 29 ♖e7 1-0 Neverov-Obukhov, Smolensk 1991.

7 cxd5 ♘bd7 8 ♗d3
⇨ 8 ♗b5 h6 (8...0-0 9 ♗xd7 ♗xd7
10 ♘e2 h6 11 ♗h4 ♗b5 12 ♗xf6?!
♛xf6 13 ♖c1 ♛g5 14 0-0 ♗xc3 15
♖xc3 ♗xe2 16 ♛xe2 ♛xd5 ∓ Red-
mond-Arkell, Dublin 1991) 9 ♗h4
a6 10 ♗xd7+ ♗xd7 11 ♘e2 0-0 12
0-0 ♖e8 13 ♛c2 ♛e7 14 ♖fe1 b5 15
a3 ♗a5 16 ♘c1? (allowing Black to
equalize) 16...♗xc3 17 bxc3 ♛e4 18
♛xe4 ♘xe4 19 ♘e2 ♘d2 20 ♗g3
♘c4 = Taborov-Arkhipov, Belgorod
1989.
　8...♛a5 9 ♘e2 ♘xd5 10 0-0
♗xc3 11 bxc3 c4
　Clearing the fifth rank allows tactical possibilities against the loose
bishop on g5.

12 ♗c2
Other moves are suspect:
　1) 12 ♗e4?! ♘5f6 13 ♗xf6 ♘xf6
14 ♗f3 ♛c5 15 ♖b1 ♖b8 16 ♘d4 d5
17 ♖b5 ♛d6 18 ♛b1 0-0 ∓ Meur-
rens-L.Hansen, Lyngby 1989.
　2) 12 ♗f5?! gives Black a pleasant choice:
　⇨ 12...♘7b6! 13 ♗xc8 (13 ♘d4
♘xc3 14 ♛g4 h5 15 ♛f3 ♛d5 16
♛xd5 ♘bxd5 ∓ Ionescu-Eingorn,

Sochi 1986) 13...♖xc8 14 ♛d4 0-0
15 e4 ♘xc3 16 ♘xc3 ♛xg5 17
♛xd6 ♛a5 18 ♛g3 ♖fd8 19 ♘d1
♖d4 with an extra pawn and the better position; Reuben-S.Arkell, Kuala
Lumpur 1992.
　⇨ 12...0-0!? 13 ♛d2 ♘xc3 14 ♘g3
♘b6 15 ♗f6 ♗xf5 (certainly not
15...gxf6 16 e4 ±) 16 ♗xc3 ♛c5 17
♗xg7?! (17 ♗b4!? ♛c8) 17...♔xg7
18 ♛xd6 ♖fc8 19 ♘h5+ ♔g8 20
♛f6 ♔f8 21 ♛h8+ ♔e7 22 ♛f6+
♔f8 23 ♛h8+ ♔e7 24 ♛f6+ ♔d7
(Black decides, after all, that his king
is safe in the centre) 25 ♛xf7+ ♔c6
26 ♖fd1 ♖f8 27 ♛g7 ♘d5 ∓ 28 ♖d4
♖ae8 29 ♖ad1 ♖g8 30 ♛f7 ♖ef8!
(obliging White to re-establish
material equality, but the resulting
ending is quite lost for him as
Black's advanced c-pawn soon
queens) 31 ♛xd5+ ♛xd5 32 ♖xd5
♖xg2+! 33 ♔xg2 ♗e4+ 34 ♔f1
♗xd5 ∓ 35 ♖d4 c3 36 ♘g3 ♔c5 37
♔e1 b5 38 a3 a5 39 ♘e2 b4 40
axb4+ axb4 41 e4 ♗c4 42 ♖d7
♗xe2 43 ♔xe2 b3 44 ♖b7 c2 0-1
Yuneev-Dautov, Daugavpils 1989.
　12...0-0 13 ♘d4?!
⇨ 13 ♗h4 ♘e5! (an improvement
on 13...♘xc3 14 ♘xc3 ♛xc3 15 ♖c1
♛a5 16 ♛xd6 ♛e5 17 ♗g3 = Raj-
ković-Stoica, Sofia 1986) 14 ♛d2
♘g6 15 ♗g3 ♖d8 16 e4 ♘f6 17 f4 ∓
Rechlis-Levitt, Tel Aviv 1989.
⇨ 13 ♘g3 is probably best, e.g.
13...♘7f6 (13...♘e5!) 14 e4 ♘xc3
15 ♛d2 ∞ ♘g4 16 h3 f6 17 ♗f4
♘e5 18 a4 ♖d8 19 ♖a3 winning a
piece; Nielsen-Danielsen, Copenhagen 1991.
　13...♘xc3! 14 ♛h5 ♘f6 15 ♛h4
Threatening ♗xf6 and ♛xh7#,

but Black has surprising resources.

15...♘ce4! 16 ♗xe4 ♘xe4 17 ♗e7 ♖e8! 18 ♕xe4 ♕e5

A nice trick that recovers the piece with advantage.

19 ♕c2 ♕xe7 20 ♕xc4 ♗e6 21 ♕d3 ♗d5 22 ♖fe1 ♖ac8 23 ♖ad1 ♗c4 24 ♕a3 d5 25 ♕b2 b5?!

Black should play 25...b6!.

26 a3 g6 27 ♖d2

White makes the most of his position; in particular the knight on d4 is strong.

27...♕c5 28 ♕b4 ♕b6 29 ♖b2 ♖b8 30 ♖eb1 ♖ec8 31 h3 a5 32 ♕d2 ♕a6 33 ♘f3 b4?

Creating a passed a-pawn, but in return giving White a b-pawn.

34 axb4 a4 35 ♘d4 a3 36 b5! ♕d6 37 ♖b4 a2 38 ♖a1 ♖a8 39 ♕b2 ♖cb8 40 ♘c6! ♖b6?

40...♖e8! would have been a little better for Black, but after this mistake Black even falls into an inferior position.

41 ♘e5 h5? 42 ♘xc4 dxc4 43 ♖xc4 ♕f6 ± ½-½

Evidently White did not care to play for a win himself with 44 ♖xa2.

Game 185

Bareev-Gelfand
Moscow 1990

1 d4 ♘f6 2 c4 e6 3 ♘c3 ♗b4 4 ♗g5 h6 5 ♗h4 c5 6 d5 b5 7 dxe6

White's most solid move may be 7 e3. After 7...♗b7 8 dxe6 fxe6 9 cxb5 0-0:

⇨ 10 a3 ♗a5 11 ♘f3 ♕e8 12 ♗e2 d5 13 ♗g3 ♘e4 14 ♕c2 ♘d7 15 0-0 ♘xg3 16 hxg3 ♖c8 (a typical position for this line: Black has a big centre and the f-file, whilst White has a solid extra pawn) 17 ♖ad1 ♕f7 18 ♕a4 ♗b6 19 ♕g4 ♘f6 20 ♕h4 c4 21 ♘e5 ♕e8 ∞ Peng-Koen, Manila OL wom 1992.

⇨ 10 ♘f3 ♕a5 11 ♗xf6 ♖xf6 12 ♕c1!? a6 13 bxa6 ♗xa6! 14 a3 ♗xf1 15 ♔xf1 ♗xc3 16 ♕xc3 ♕b5+ 17 ♔g1 ♘c6 18 h4 ♖a4 19 ♖h3 ∞ Giulian-Read, corr. 1990.

7...fxe6 8 e4?!

⇨ 8 cxb5 is more usual: 8...0-0 9 e3 ♕a5 10 ♗xf6 ♖xf6 11 ♕c1 a6 12 bxa6 ♘xa6 13 ♗e2 ♘c7 14 ♗f3 ♘d5 15 ♘e2 ♗xc3+ 16 ♘xc3 ♗a6 17 ♕d2 ♖xf3! (working up strong light-squared threats) 18 gxf3 ♘b4 19 ♖g1 ♘d3+ 20 ♔d1 ♖b8 21 ♖b1 ♖b6 22 ♘e4 ♕xa2 23 ♕c2 d5 24 ♘c3 ♘xb2+ 25 ♔c1 ♘d3+ ½-½ Graf-Adorjan, Bundesliga 1989.

8...0-0 9 e5

Instead 9 ♗d3 bxc4 10 ♗c2 d5 11 e5 is unclear.

9...♕a5! 10 ♘e2 ♘e4 11 ♕c2 ♗b7 12 f3 ♘xc3 13 bxc3 ♗a3

Although White's development is deficient, at least he has forced

Black's king's bishop out of the game for a while.

14 cxb5 a6! 15 bxa6 ♗xa6 16 ♗e7

16...♖f7?!

Driving the bishop where it wanted to go; better is 16...♖f5! ∓.

17 ♗d6

Seeking to improve his one active piece.

17...♘c6 18 ♖d1 ♗b5 19 ♖d2 c4 20 ♕e4! ♗xd6 21 exd6 ♖af8 22 ♕e3 ♖f5 23 ♘g3 ♖d5 ½-½

Game 186

Hort-Smagin
Berlin 1990

1 d4 ♘f6 2 c4 e6 3 ♘c3 ♗b4 4 ♗g5 c5 5 d5 ♗xc3+ 6 bxc3 d6 7 e3 ♕e7 8 ♗d3 ♘bd7

Or first 8...h6 9 ♗h4 ♘bd7 and:
⇨ 10 ♘f3 e5 11 ♘d2 g5 12 ♗g3 ♔d8 (a standard idea; the king is often safest on c7) 13 ♗f5 (13 0-0 ♔c7 14 ♗f5 ♘b6 15 ♗xc8 ♖axc8 16 f4 ♘bd7 17 fxe5 ♘xe5 18 ♖f5

♘fd7 19 ♕h5 f6 20 ♖af1 ½-½ Comas-Dzhandzhgava, San Sebastian 1991) 13...♔c7 14 0-0 h5 15 h3 h4 16 ♗h2 ♘h5 17 ♖b1 ♘g7 18 ♗xd7 ♗xd7 19 f4 f6 20 fxe5 fxe5 21 ♘e4 b6 22 a4 ♗f5 23 ♕c2? (walking into a pin from which there is no escape) 23...a5 24 ♖b2 ♖ab8 25 ♕b1 ♖hf8 26 ♖bf2 ♗g6 27 ♕b5 (rather radical, but what else?) 27...♖xf2 28 ♖xf2 ♗xe4 29 ♕c6+ ♔d8 30 ♗xe5 ♘e8 31 ♗h2 ♕d7 ∓ Comas-Dizdar, Barcelona 1991.
⇨ 10 dxe6?! (the problem with this move is that it further exposes the c4 pawn, and enables Black to post his bishop on the active c6 square) 10...♕xe6! 11 ♘e2 g5 12 ♗g3 ♘e5 13 0-0 (if 13 h4!? then not 13...0-0?! 14 hxg5 hxg5 15 f4 ∞ Williams-Finocchiaro, corr. 1990, but 13...♖g8) 13...♗d7 14 ♖e1 ♕e7 15 ♘d4 (if White does nothing he will be lost) 15...♘xd3 16 ♕xd3 0-0-0 17 ♘f5 ♗xf5 18 ♕xf5+ ♕e6 19 e4 ♖he8 20 ♕xe6+ ♖xe6 21 f3 ♘d7 22 ♖ab1 ♘b6 (this spells the end for White) 23 e5 dxe5 24 ♗xe5 ♖de8 25 ♗g3 ♖xe1+ 26 ♗xe1 ♘xc4 27 ♔f2 ♔c7 28 h4 gxh4 29 f4 ♔c6 30 ♖d1 f5 31 ♖d3 ♖e4 32 ♖f3 a5 33 ♔f1 a4 34 ♖h3 ♖xf4+ 35 ♔g1 ♖e4 0-1 Yuneev-Yudasin, Leningrad 1989.

9 ♘e2 exd5

⇨ 9...h6 10 ♗h4 ♘e5 11 0-0 ♘xd3 12 ♕xd3 g5 13 ♗g3 e5 14 f4 e4 15 ♕d2 ♘h5 16 ♗e1 ♘g7 17 ♖b1 ½-½ Neverov-Savon, Moscow 1990.

10 cxd5 ♕e5 11 ♗xf6 ♘xf6 12 e4 0-0 13 f3 ♘h5! 14 0-0 f5

Black cannot afford to sit there while White prepares the advance of his centre.

15 f4 ♕e8 16 ♕c2 fxe4 17 ♗xe4 ♘f6 18 ♘g3 ♘xe4 19 ♖ae1?!

Better is 19 ♕xe4 with equality.

19...♕f7! 20 ♕xe4 ♗d7 21 ♕f3 ♗b5! 22 ♖f2 ♖ae8 ∓

23 ♖d1

White has little choice but to concede the e-file.

23...♕e7 24 f5 ♕e3 25 ♕f4! ♕xc3 26 ♕xd6 ♗d3! 27 f6 c4! 28 ♕d7 gxf6 29 h3 f5 30 ♘xf5? ♖e1+ 31 ♔h2 ♕e5+ 32 ♘g3 ♖xf2 33 ♕g4+ ♗g6 0-1

Game 187

Bareev-Chandler
Hastings 1991

1 d4 ♘f6 2 c4 e6 3 ♘c3 ♗b4 4 ♗g5 h6 5 ♗h4 c5 6 d5 d6 7 e3

Much more common than the alternative 7 f3 ♗xc3+ 8 bxc3 when there may follow:

➪ 8...g5 9 ♗g3 e5 10 e4 ♘bd7 11 ♗f2 ♘f8 12 h4 g4?! (12...♖g8 does not weaken the dark squares so much) 13 h5 ♘8h7 14 a4 ♘g5 15

♗d3 gxf3 16 gxf3 ♘fh7 17 ♕e2 ♕a5 18 ♔d2 ♗d7 19 ♕e3 ♕d8 20 ♗g3 ♕e7 21 f4! exf4 22 ♕xf4 0-0 23 ♖e1 f6 24 ♕xd6 winning; Rajković-Kurajica, Star Dojran 1991.

➪ 8...♕e7! 9 e4 ♘bd7 10 dxe6 (otherwise development is difficult, for instance: 10 ♗d3? exd5 11 cxd5 g5 12 ♗g3 ♘xd5) 10...♕xe6 11 ♗d3 ♘e5 12 ♘e2 g5 13 ♗g3 ♗d7 14 0-0 0-0-0 15 ♖b1 ♕e7 16 ♕b3 ♗c6 (this set-up occurs quite often, and is very favourable for Black) 17 ♗c2 ♘h5 18 a4 ♕c7 19 ♕a2 ♖he8 20 ♖be1 ♕a5 21 ♗f2 ♗d7! 22 ♖d1 ♗e6 23 ♗b3 ♕a6 and now in Bakić-Gligorić, Yugoslav Ch 1991, White tried the desperate piece sacrifice 24 ♘d4 but lost anyway.

7...♗xc3+ 8 bxc3 ♕e7 9 ♘f3 ♘bd7

Or 9...e5 10 ♘d2 g5 11 ♗g3 and:

➪ 11...♗f5!? (a common idea that is played to provoke White into playing e4, rendering his position less flexible—the f4 break is no longer possible, for one thing) 12 h4 (12 ♗e2 ♘bd7 13 f3 0-0-0 14 e4 ♗g6 15 ♗f2 ♘h5 16 ♕a4 ♔b8 17 g3 f5 18 ♗d3 fxe4 19 ♗xe4 ♗xe4 20 fxe4 ♘hf6 21 ♖f1 ♖df8 22 0-0-0 ♖f7 23 ♗g1 ♖hf8 is good for Black; Comas-Campos, Barcelona 1991) 12...♖g8 13 hxg5 hxg5 14 ♕b3 ♕c7 15 f3 ♘bd7 16 e4 ♗g6 17 ♗f2 g4?! 18 ♕a4! a6 19 ♖b1?! (19 ♘b3) 19...0-0-0 20 ♗h4 ♖de8 21 ♖b2 ♖h8 22 ♘b3 ♘b6 23 ♕a5 ♘fd7 24 ♗d3?! f5! 25 fxg4 (25 exf5? e4 26 fxe4 ♗xf5 opens a route to the white king) 25...fxe4 26 ♗e2 e3! 27 ♖h3 ♗e4 28 ♗f1 ♖eg8 29 ♗e7 ♖xh3! 30 gxh3 ♗f3! (imprisoning the white

king) 31 ♘c1 ♚b8 32 ♖h2 e4 33
♖b2 ♚a7 34 ♗h4 ♕c8 35 ♗g3 ♕f8
36 ♕a3 ♕f6 37 ♕b3 ♖f8 38 ♕c2
♗xg4 39 ♕g2? ♕xc3+ 0-1 Bareev-
Beliavsky, Leningrad 1990.

⇨ 11...e4 12 ♕c2 ♗f5 13 ♖b1
♗c8?! (a somewhat incomprehensible loss of time) 14 h4 ♖g8 15 hxg5
hxg5 16 ♗e2 ♘bd7 17 ♖b3 ♘f8 18
♕b1 ♘g6 19 ♖h6 ♚f8 20 ♚d1 ♚g7
(Black's king is perfectly safe here,
surrounded by his own pieces) 21
♖h1 b6 22 ♚c1 ♗f5 23 ♚b2 ♖h8 24
♚a1 ♖xh1 25 ♕xh1 ♖h8 26 ♕g1
♘e5 27 ♖b1 ♗g6 28 ♖f1 ♘eg4 29
♖c1 ♘e5 30 ♖f1 ♘eg4 31 ♖c1 ♘e5
½-½ Spassky-Renet, French Ch
1991.

10 ♘d2 0-0

⇨ 10...♘e5?! (not really an innovation, but a finger-slip! I just played
my moves in the wrong order, and
was fortunate that I wasn't completely lost!) 11 ♗xf6 gxf6 (obviously 11...♕xf6? 12 ♘e4 ±) 12 f4
♘g6 13 ♚f2 f5 14 g3 ♚d8? (14...e5)
15 dxe6! fxe6 16 ♗g2 ♚c7 17 ♖b1
♘f8? 18 e4! fxe4 19 ♘xe4 ♘d7 20
♕e2 ♘b6 21 ♘xd6! ♕xd6 22 ♖hd1
♘d5 23 cxd5 ♖e8 24 ♕h5 1-0
Bareev-Kosten, Hastings 1990.

11 ♗e2 ♘e5 12 ♘e4!

This obliges Black to weaken his
king's cover, and is more logical
than the alternatives:

⇨ 12 ♗xf6?! ♕xf6 13 f4 ♘g6 14
♘e4 ♕e7 15 dxe6 f5! ∓ (White had
probably underestimated this move
in his analysis; now 16 ♘xd6?? fails
to 16...♖d8) 16 ♘g3 ♗xe6 17 ♕d3
♖ad8 18 0-0 ♘h4 19 ♖ae1 d5 20
♕c2 ♚h8 21 ♘h1 (played to eject
the knight from h4) 21...dxc4 22 g3

♗d5?! (an unnecessary sacrifice) 23
gxh4 ♕xe3+ 24 ♘f2 ♕xf4 25 ♘g4
♕d6 26 ♖xf5 ♕e6 27 ♖e5 ♕c6 28
♖e3 ♖d6 29 ♘e5 ♕e8 30 h5 ♚g8 31
♗g4 ♖df6 32 ♕d2 ♕d8 33 ♘g6 ♗f7
34 ♕xd8 ♖xd8 35 ♘e5 1-0 Bareev-
Chandler, Hastings 1990.

⇨ 12 dxe6?! ♕xe6 13 0-0 ♖e8 14
♗g3 ♗d7 15 ♕c2 ♗c6 (Black's
pieces are excellently placed) 16
♖ad1 ♖ad8 17 h3 ♘fd7! 18 f4 ♘g6?
(a mistake; better is 18...♕g6! 19
♕xg6 ♘xg6 ∓) 19 e4 ♕e7 20 ♖de1
♗xe4 21 ♘xe4 ♕xe4 22 ♗d3 ♕c6
23 ♗xg6 fxg6 24 ♕xg6 ♘f6 25
♗h4 ♖xe1 26 ♖xe1 ♖e8 27 ♗xf6
♖xe1+ 28 ♚f2 ♕d7 29 ♚xe1 ♕e6+
30 ♚d2 ♕xf6 31 ♕xf6 gxf6 32 f5
a6 33 ♚d3 ♚f7 34 ♚e4 Bareev-
Olafsson, Hastings 1990. The king
and pawn ending that has arisen is
winning for White, albeit requiring
some accuracy.

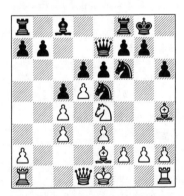

**12...g5 13 ♘xf6+ ♕xf6 14 ♗g3
♘xc4**

Temporarily picking up a pawn,
but the undefended state of the
knight on c4 permits White to win it
back in a few moves.

15 0-0 exd5 16 ♕xd5 ♗e6 17 ♕xb7 ♖ab8 18 ♕xa7 ♖b2 19 ♗xc4! ♗xc4 20 ♖fd1! ±

Suddenly it is White who has the pawn more, although there are opposite-colour bishops.

20...♗e2 21 ♖e1! ♗d3 22 ♕c7! c4! 23 ♕xd6 ♖xf2

24 e4 ♖d8 25 ♕c7 ♖b2! 26 a4! ♖e8 27 e5 ♕g6 28 ♕d6 ♗e6 29 ♕d5 h5 30 a5 h4 31 ♗f2 ♕f5 32 ♕f3?

Better is 32 ♕d4 ♖a6 33 h3 ±.

32...♖xe5 33 ♖xe5 ♕xe5 34 ♖e1 ♖b1! 35 ♖xb1 ♗xb1 36 ♕a8+ ♔h7 37 ♕b7 1-0

Black lost on time, but 37...♕f5 would have been equal.

Game 188

Bangiev-Zhugda
corr. 1990

1 d4 ♘f6 2 c4 e6 3 ♘c3 ♗b4 4 ♗g5 h6 5 ♗h4 c5 6 d5 ♗xc3+ 7 bxc3 d6 8 e3 ♕e7

The immediate 8...e5 9 ♗d3 is also common:

⇨ 9...e4 10 ♗c2 g5 (10...♕e7 11 ♘e2 ♘bd7 12 ♗a4 0-0 13 ♗xd7 ♗xd7 14 ♗xf6 ♕xf6 15 ♕b1 ½-½ Hjartarson-Sax, Tilburg 1989) 11 ♗g3 ♕e7 12 h4 ♖g8 13 hxg5 hxg5 14 ♘e2 ♔d8 15 ♗a4 ♘bd7 16 ♗xd7 ♗xd7 17 ♕b3 ♔c7 18 ♕a3 b6 19 ♔d2 ♘g4 ½-½ Hjartarson-de Firmian, Moscow 1990.

⇨ 9...♘bd7 10 ♘e2 e4 11 ♗c2 ♕e7 12 ♕b1 (12 ♗g3 ♘e5 13 ♕b1 0-0 14 ♗xe5 ♘xe4 15 ♕xe4 f5 16 ♕c2 ♘xc4 17 0-0 ♕e4 18 ♕xe4 fxe4 19 ♖fd1 ♗g4 20 ♖e1 ♗xe2 21 ♖xe2 ♖f5 22 ♖d1 b5 with Black, if anyone, having slightly the better chances; Rodin-Barsov, Moscow 1991) 12...g5 13 ♗g3 ♘f8 14 h4 ♖g8 15 hxg5 hxg5 16 ♕b5+ ♔d8 17 ♘c1 ♘g4 18 ♖b1 f5 19 ♕a5+ ♕c7 20 ♕xc7+ ♔xc7 21 ♔d2 ♗d7 22 f3 ♘xe3! 23 ♔xe3 f4+ 24 ♔d2 exf3 25 gxf3 fxg3 26 ♖h6 ♖g7 27 ♘e2 ♖f7 28 ♗e4 g2 29 ♖g1 ♖e8 30 ♖xg2 g4 31 ♖g3 ♖e5 32 ♘c1 gxf3 33 ♖xf3 ½-½ Topalov-Sax, Burgas 1992.

9 ♗d3 e5 10 ♘e2 g5

⇨ 10...♘bd7 11 ♘g3 ♘b6! (a big improvement on 11...g5? 12 ♘f5 ♕f8 13 ♗g3 ♘b6 14 f3 ± Fang-Farago, Worchester 1990) 12 ♗xf6 ♕xf6 13 0-0 0-0 14 a4 ♖e8! 15 f4 exf4 16 ♘e4 ♖xe4! 17 ♗xe4 ♘xc4 18 ♗h7+ ♔xh7 19 ♕d3+ ♕g6 20 ♕xc4 ♗h3 21 ♖a2 fxe3 (Black holds the whip hand) 22 ♕f4 ♖e8 23 ♖e2 f5! 24 ♖fe1 ♖e4 25 ♕g3 ♗g4 26 ♖xe3 f4 27 ♖xe4 (27 ♕xg4 ♖xe3!) 27...fxg3 28 hxg3 ♗f5 29 ♖4e3 c4 0-1 Fang-Yudasin, Worchester 1990.

11 ♗g3 e4 12 ♗c2 ♘bd7

⇨ 12...♔f8?! (heading in the wrong direction) 13 h4 ♔g7 14 hxg5 hxg5

15 ♖xh8 ♔xh8 16 ♔d2 ♔g7 17 ♕h1
♗g4 18 ♕h2 ♘bd7 (18...♘e8 19
♖h1 is also curtains for Black) 19
♗xd6 1-0 Bangiev-Yaniuk, Simferopol 1991.
   **13 h4 ♖g8 14 hxg5 hxg5 15 ♕b1
♔d8**
⇨ 15...b6?! 16 ♕b5!? ♗b7 17 a4 a6
18 ♕b3 a5 19 ♕b5! ♗a6 20 ♕c6
♖c8 21 ♗xd6! ♕d8 22 0-0-0!! (a
fine queen sacrifice) 22...♖xc6 23
dxc6 ♕a8!? 24 cxd7+ ♔xd7 25
♗xc5+ ♔c8 26 ♗d4 ♘g4!? 27
♘g3!? ♘xf2 28 ♘f5 ♖d8 29 ♘e7+
♔d7 30 ♘d5 ♕c6 31 ♖df1 ♗xc4?
32 ♘f6+ ♔c8 33 ♖xf2 ♖xd4 34
cxd4 ♗d3 35 ♔b2 ♕d6 36 ♗b3
♕g3 37 ♖h8+ 1-0 Bangiev-Astrak-
hantsev, corr. 1990. On 37...♔b7
there follows 38 ♗d5 ♔c7 39 ♘e4 ±.
   16 a4 a5 17 ♖a2 ♔c7 18 ♖b2!?
⇨ 18 ♖h6?! ♖a6 19 ♕b5 ♔b8 20
♖b2 ♔a7 21 ♕b3 ♘g4 ∓ occurred in
the well-known game Williams-
Karpov, Nice OL 1974.
   18...b6?!
⇨ 18...♖a6 19 ♖b5 ♖e8!? 20 ♘c1
♘g4 21 ♗d1 ♘df6 22 ♗c2 b6 ∞
Bangiev-Ionov, Budapest 1990.
   19 ♖xb6!?

Rather speculative.
   19...♘xb6 20 ♕b5 ♖a6
Black should investigate the lines
20...♕d7 21 ♕xc5+ ♔b7 22 ♕d4!?
♘g4 23 0-0 f5 24 ♖b1 ♖a6 25 c5
dxc5 26 ♕xc5 ∞ and 20...♗d7 21
♕xc5+ ♔b7 22 ♗xd6 ♕e8 23 0-0!?
♕c8 24 ♖b1! ♕xc5 25 ♗xc5 ♖a6 26
♗d4.

   21 ♕xc5+
Emphasizing the power of the g3
bishop; once Black's c5 pawn goes,
White's c4 pawn will be free to advance and his knight will have the
use of d4 and c6.
   21...♔d7 22 ♕b5+ ♔d8
Not 22...♔c7? 23 c5.
   **23 ♘d4 ♘a8 24 ♘c6+ ♖xc6 25
dxc6 ♘c7 26 ♕xa5 ♖g6 27 c5!?
dxc5 28 ♗xe4! ♖g8 29 ♗b1 ♘fd5
30 0-0 f5 31 ♗a2!**
More accurate than 31 ♖d1 f4! 32
♖xd5+ ♔e8.
   **31...♗e6 32 ♗xd5 ♗xd5 33 ♖d1
f4 34 ♖xd5+ 1-0**

Game 189

Bareev-Sax
Hastings 1990

**1 d4 ♘f6 2 c4 e6 3 ♘c3 ♗b4 4 ♗g5
h6 5 ♗h4 c5 6 d5 d6**
⇨ 6...b6!? 7 f3 ♗xc3+ 8 bxc3 d6 9
e4 e5 10 ♗d3 ♘bd7 11 ♘e2 ♘f8 12
♗f2 ♘g6 13 ♗e3 h5 14 h4 ♘g8 15
♘g3 ♘xh4 16 ♕d2 ♘g6 17 ♘xh5
♔d7! 18 0-0-0 ♕f8 19 f4 exf4 20
♗xf4 ♘f6 21 ♘xf6+ gxf6 22 ♗h6
♕e7 23 ♖hf1 ♖g8 24 ♕f2 ♘e5 25
♕xf6? ♕xf6 26 ♖xf6 ♔e7 27 ♖ff1
♖xg2? (27...♗g4 28 ♖d2 ♘xd3+ 29

♖xd3 ♗e2 ∓) 28 ♖d2 ♖g3 29 ♔c2 ♗h3 30 ♖ff2 ♖ag8 31 ♗f4 ½-½ Beliavsky-Prasad, Novi Sad OL 1990.

7 e3 ♗xc3+ 8 bxc3 e5 9 f3

Apart from this and 9 ♗d3, which was covered in the previous game, White also has:

⇨ 9 ♕c2 ♘bd7 (9...g5 10 ♗g3 ♘h5 11 ♗d3 0-0 12 ♘e2 f5 13 f3 ♕f6 14 0-0-0 ♘d7 {Black has claimed a large area on the kingside as his own} 15 ♗e1 ♘b6 16 ♘g3 ♘xg3 17 hxg3 e4! ∓ Starke-van der Sterren, Biel 1992) 10 ♘f3 ♕e7 11 ♘d2 g5 12 ♗g3 b6?! (this weakens the light squares unnecessarily) 13 ♗d3 ♔d8 14 0-0-0! ♔c7 15 f4 ♘h5 16 ♕a4! (*sic*) 16...♗b7 (16...gxf4 17 exf4 exf4 18 ♗h4! ±) 17 ♗f5 ♘xg3 18 hxg3 ♘f6 19 ♘f3! exf4 20 exf4 ♕e3+ 21 ♔b2 ♕f2+ 22 ♔b3! (the king is well protected from checks here) 22...♕xg2? 23 ♖de1 ♖ae8 24 fxg5! ♕xf3 25 gxf6 ♖xe1 26 ♕d7+ ♔b8 27 ♖xe1 b5 28 ♖e8+ ♖xe8 29 ♕xe8+ ♔c7 30 ♕d7+ ♔b6 31 ♕xb5+ ♔c7 32 ♕d7+ 1-0 Murshed-Adianto, Penang 1991.

9...g5

⇨ 9...♘bd7 10 ♗d3 0-0 11 ♘e2 ♕e7 12 0-0 ♖e8 13 f4 exf4 14 exf4 ♘f8 15 ♘g3 ♘g6 16 ♗xf6 ♕xf6 17 ♘e4 ♖xe4? (perhaps Black feared the advance of White's f-pawn to f6 but he obtains little compensation for the exchange) 18 ♗xe4 ♕xc3 19 ♗xg6 fxg6 20 ♕e2 ♗f5 21 ♖ac1 ± Bagirov-Becker, Berlin 1992.

10 ♗g3 e4 11 h4 g4!? 12 h5!

The standard reply to ...g4. White's queen's bishop will return to h4 with great effect.

12...exf3 13 gxf3 ♕e7 14 ♗h4! ♕xe3+?

Misjudging the coming ending.

15 ♕e2 ♕xe2+ 16 ♘xe2! ♘xh5

16...♘bd7 is met by 17 ♘g3 intending ♘f5.

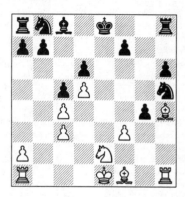

17 0-0-0!!

Ready to answer 17...gxf3 with the spectacular 18 ♖e1!! ±.

17...♘d7 18 fxg4 ♘g7 19 ♘g3 ♔f8 20 ♘e4 ♘e5 21 ♘xd6 ♗xg4 22 ♖e1 ♘f3 23 ♗e7+ ♔g8 24 ♖e3 f5? 25 ♗e2 ♘g5 26 ♗xg4 fxg4 27 ♖g1! ± ♔h7 28 ♖xg4

White has recovered the sacrificed material and his pieces have assumed powerful posts in the middle of the board.

28...♔g6 29 ♖eg3! ♘h5 30 ♖xg5+! 1-0